Theories of Personality

A Zonal Perspective

Theories of Personality
A Zonal Perspective

John M. Berecz
Andrews University

PEARSON

Boston   New York   San Francisco
Mexico City   Montreal   Toronto   London   Madrid   Munich   Paris
Hong Kong   Singapore   Tokyo   Cape Town   Sydney

Acquisitions Editor: Michelle Limoges
Editorial Assistant: Christina Manfroni
Marketing Manager: Kate Mitchell
Production Supervisor: Patty Bergin
Editorial Production Service: Pre-Press PMG
Composition Buyer: Linda Cox
Manufacturing Buyer: JoAnne Sweeney
Electronic Composition: Westwords
Interior Design: Pre-Press PMG
Photo Researcher: PoYee Oster
Cover Administrator: Elena Sidorova
Cover Designer: Jennifer Hart

For related titles and support materials, visit our online catalog at www.ablongman.com.

Between the time website information is gathered and then published, it is not unusual for some sites to have closed. Also, the transcription of URLs can result in typographical errors. The publisher would appreciate notification where these errors occur so that they may be corrected in subsequent editions.

Library of Congress Cataloging-in-Publication Data

Berecz, John M. (John Michael)
  Theories of personality: a zonal perspective / John M. Berecz.
     p. cm.
  ISBN-13: 978-0-205-43916-4
  ISBN-10: 0-205-43916-0
  1. Personality. I. Title

BF698.B37 2008
155.2--dc22

                                        2008006188

Printed in the United States of America

10 9 8 7 6 5 4 3 2 HAM 15 14 13 12

The author and his dog, Molly.

John M. Berecz received an M.A. in Counseling Psychology from American University in Washington, D.C., and a Ph.D. in Clinical Psychology from Indiana University, Bloomington. His doctoral research on smoking cessation won recognition in a nationwide competition conducted by the American Institutes for Research. Following his graduate studies, Dr. Berecz interned as a United States Public Health Fellow at Children's Hospital Medical Center in Boston. Subsequently, for over thirty years, he has pursued a professional career that has spanned both the classroom and the clinic. As a professor of Psychology at Andrews University, he has taught Theories of Personality courses at both the graduate and undergraduate levels. Additionally, he taught Abnormal Psychology, Developmental Psychology, Behavior Modification, Research Methods, and Human Sexuality. In his clinical practice he has worked with children, couples, and families.

Dr. Berecz has published five books and nearly three dozen articles in professional journals. His research and writing have covered a broad range of topics, including: addictions, stuttering, Tourette Syndrome, sexual dysfunction, as well as the role of forgiveness in psychotherapy and counseling.

He is married to Deborah Bennett Berecz, who obtained her law degree at Notre Dame and uses Collaborative Practice and mediation to ease the stress of divorce for families in transition. They have four grown sons and—at last count—five grandchildren. They make their home among the orchards and vineyards of southwestern Michigan. Dr. Berecz attenuates the stresses in his life with biking, skiing, swimming, racquetball, and spiritual meditation.

With this text, Professor Berecz, hopes to share his love of psychology and enthusiasm for Theories of Personality with new generations of student seekers.

For Deborah,

whose love surrounded and sustained me during the years I appeared mostly as a shadow silhouetted against a computer screen.

For my sons, their wives, and their children,

and

for students of personality everywhere–may you catch the excitement!

contents

When I was a kid, my father worked for a railroad based in Chicago. The downside was that Dad was gone a lot, but the upside was that we could travel free to anywhere his railroad ran a train. So, every couple summers we would climb aboard the Hiawatha Streamliner and make the journey from Chicago to the Pacific Northwest to visit my sister in Seattle.

It is difficult to convey the excitement an eight-year-old boy experiences riding the rails to places never before encountered. Leaving behind the familiar silos and red barns of Wisconsin and passing through the lake-filled meadows of Minnesota, I could only imagine what lay ahead. The prairies of North Dakota and the big skies of Montana all impressed me, but it was the mountains that indelibly etched their profiles into my brain. And it wasn't only Mount Rushmore with its presidential portraits that left me breathless; it was an entire Rocky Mountain range of snowy peaks—visible for hundreds of flat prairie miles—contrasted against a clear blue sky that I will never forget.

If that wasn't excitement enough, when we came to the Cascades in eastern Washington, we experienced a brief delay as the train crew changed out our two diesel-powered locomotives for a long, black electric-powered engine with towering trolleys that drew energy from electric cables that hung above the rails like unending ropes of black licorice. Dad explained that this electric locomotive could generate over four thousand horsepower—more than enough energy to pull our train up the steep mountain grades that lay ahead. Looking at the gleaming rails disappearing into the distant, snow-capped Cascades, I experienced something akin to the excitement of an astronaut just before lift off.

So, what does all this train talk have to do with personality? My personality journey has reminded me of those train trips to Seattle. On my first personality excursion, the engineers were a couple guys named Hall and Lindzey. Our trip began by meeting a man named Freud at a "station" known as psychoanalysis. Next, we moved on to Jung, Adler, Fromm, Horney, and Sullivan. The journey continued with stops at Allport, Eysenck, Cattell, Rogers, and a few others. And, as on my boyhood trips to Seattle, *I never looked back*. Once our Hiawatha pulled out of Union Station in Chicago, I thought only of La Crosse, Wisconsin; and once we left there, I only had eyes for Sioux Falls, South Dakota. Subsequently, I looked forward to Coeur d'Alene, Idaho and Spokane, Washington. Arriving in Seattle, I remembered only one long, linear path from Chicago to the Northwest. It was an exciting, but linear journey— steel on steel—as two-ton train wheels never deviated from the gleaming rails that stretched endlessly westward. In the end, I didn't know what Seattle had in common with Sioux Falls, and I didn't care. Coeur d'Alene and Chicago appeared as dissimilar to me at that time as Freud and Watson would in graduate school.

Too many undergraduates have a similar experience. At the end of a long and exciting journey, they "arrive in Seattle" with no way to compare or integrate the vast geography they have just traversed. The various theories—each exciting and stimulating in their own ways—appear as unrelated as Seattle and Sioux Falls. Or, if their text is heavily research oriented, they find little in common among the various research domains. Electrical activity of the brain, sensation seeking, and the human genome, appear to share little in common with learned helplessness, gender differences, or self-esteem.

A ZONAL PERSPECTIVE

But Seattle and Sioux Falls *do* share much in common. They both have school *zones*, hospital *zones*, and construction *zones*. And whether you find yourself in Chicago or Coeur d'Alene, you're likely to encounter students, teachers, and desks in a school zone; physicians, nurses, and X-ray machines in a hospital zone. This text replaces historical, categorical, and research perspectives on personality with a *zonal* approach that allows students to map both theories and research onto an interdisciplinary *grid,* enabling them to compare across theories while remaining solidly oriented in the *zone* they are studying. Instead of being confined to the linearity of historical analyses or being confused by the vast array of contemporary research, students can comprehend and make sense of an encyclopedic volume of theories and research.

Freud was fond of Greek mythological characters, famously using Oedipus, Narcissus, and others to illustrate his ideas. The current text encourages, instead, a *Janus perspective.* Janus was the Roman god who guarded doorways and watched over beginnings and endings. Janus appeared as a two-faced god, constantly *looking both ways.* Our zonal grid encourages a dual perspective—alternatively looking both up and down—from micro to macro, from parts to wholes—and back down again. The student is encouraged to *look both ways:* up and down, as well as at the *self* and the *situation.* Our grid facilitates a Janus perspective that easily shifts levels of analysis along a vertical dimension or changes focus from personal to situational variables along a horizontal dimension.

FEATURES

The "Big Four" questions (What are the parts? What makes a person go? What makes a person grow? What makes a person unique?) are asked of each theory in every chapter. Similarly, the **"Tough Twins" questions** (Is this theory testable/falsifiable? Is it useful?) challenge students to consider the rubber-meets-the-road issues of *validity* and *practical value.* These probing questions—asked again and again—nudge students to compare and synthesize theories, providing them with new appreciation for how scientists work.

Theorist at a Glance boxes present visual summaries of complex theories in a way that allows students to easily grasp the essential features of a model. This visual presentation prevents students from losing their way when reading the more detailed explanations of a particular theory.

Key Terms appear within the text in boldface, immediately followed by *italicized definitions*. This allows students to learn concepts in context. Instead of merely memorizing dictionary definitions, students grasp how theoretical terms are used within a particular zone, making learning easier and increasing retention. At the end of each chapter key terms are alphabetically listed for easy look up.

A Personal Perspective, in the form of a case study or narrative of a real-life experience captures the reader's interest at the beginning of each chapter. At the end of each chapter, Learning on the Lighter Side offers students "fun" applications of key personality concepts they have just learned. This personalized approach maximizes comprehension and retention.

Points to Remember presents a chapter summary, and Web Sites offer students opportunities to research and interact with theories in creative ways. These features are designed to maximize retention and facilitate synthesis with other theories to assist students in applying personality theories to real-life problems.

Writing style is friendly and personal, inviting the student not only to learn theoretical concepts, but to find the joy as well. Nonetheless, substance and depth are not sacrificed for a conversational tone. Theories and research receive in-depth discussion using accessible language.

ACKNOWLEDGMENTS

It's no secret that a textbook is a team project, and I've been privileged to work with a superb team of experts at Allyn & Bacon/Pearson, beginning with Karen Bowers's initial enthusiasm for this project through the present phase with Michelle Limoges's sage editorial guidance. I have appreciated the professionalism and pleasantness of the entire staff—people like Patty Bergin and Lindsay Mateiro have given the production phase a congenial quality. I'm grateful to people in art, marketing, and sales who have invested their time and energy to make this product something of which we can all be proud.

The candid feedback—positive and negative—offered by numerous reviewers has significantly improved this book, and I thank them for their time and wisdom. Gary Land read portions of the text and offered helpful suggestions. Bruce Closser read the entire manuscript, providing editorial advice. Herb Helm, Dick Proctor, Karl Bailey, and other colleagues have done more than their share of departmental work and student advising while I was immersed in this text. On several occasions I turned to Jay Brand, a cognitive psychologist with great wisdom on numerous topics. Wilfred Futcher gave me guidance regarding factor analysis.

I would like to thank the following reviewers for their suggestions: Trey Asbury, Campbell University; Laurie L. Couch, Morehead State University; David M. Fresco, Kent State University; Barry Fritz, Quinnipiac University; Dean E. Frost, Portland State University; Kevin B. Handley, Germanna Community College; Karen L. Horner, Catawba College; Tonya N. Inman, University of Houston; Randall S. Jorgensen, Syracuse University; Christine Jumpeter, University at Albany; Robin Lewis, California Polytechnic State University; William McCown, University of Louisiana at Monroe; and Andrew Mark Pomerantz, Southern Illinois University.

Numerous students have assisted me while I was writing this book. Sarah Groves and Jennifer Ramsey read portions of the text, sharing feedback from a student's perspective. Jordan Nay has been incredibly helpful, using his computer literacy to assist me with ancillaries such as Power Point and Test Bank items.

Closer to home, this project has taken an enormous bite out of what is known as "family time." My wife, Deborah, has not only encouraged me throughout, she has taken time from her own busy schedule as a family law attorney, to read pages and offer the kinds of candid feedback ("That's *great!*" or "Lose it.") to which spouses are entitled. Thanks Deb, you've been splendid.

Finally, I would like to thank my Higher Powers for the health and energy that allowed me to complete this seven-year safari. I trust that these pages will radiate the love I feel for psychology in general, and personality in particular. I hope that I have kept faith with optimism and that students will be able to glean wisdom as well as information. It's been a great trip.

John M. Berecz

Personality Student's Serenity Prayer
Grant me the determination to study dubious theories at least once;
The diligence to study deserving ones in depth,
And the wisdom to know the difference.

It's tempting to skip introductions. I've done it plenty of times—opened a box of tri-cycle parts or bookcase boards and ignored the directions, thinking "Any idiot can put this together!"—only to later discover that tricycle wheels can be put on inside-out and bookshelves have a top and bottom side. The next few pages are among the most important in the book—mapping our journey for the remaining chapters—so here at the beginning, I hope you'll take a few moments to find out where we are going and how we plan to get there.

We are about to study of one of the most fascinating areas of psychology—gripping because nothing is more *personal* than *personal*ity. We will examine our own inner workings, scrutinize our private experiences, and analyze how we are similar to—yet uniquely different from—everyone else. You may have taken courses where you've wondered, "What does this have to do with my life?" That's not likely to happen here because you will be learning about your family, your friends, and most importantly, about yourself.

You may frequently feel familiar with a topic and find yourself "knowing" from your own experiences. When, for example, we study *birth order,* you may recall what it was like to have grown up in the shadow of an older brother. Or, you may remem-ber what it was like to have *been* that older sibling, endowed with the responsibili-ties of looking after a kid sister. Such familiarity will usually prove an asset to learning, but it can also mislead, because what you perceive to be your own *self* may not be exactly what Carl Rogers meant by the term *self.* And Freud's meaning for *libido* is vastly different from what most people think of as *sex drive.* In our study of personality we will build upon this sense of familiarity, but we will move further. As we analyze, clarify, and refine how various terms are used by different personal-ity psychologists, we will fine-tune our own understanding of who we are and how we relate to others.

Three Levels of Learning

We will analyze each theory at three different levels: *description, explanation,* and *synthesis.*

(1) Description. Describing parts is the most basic level of understanding; facts are the foundation for all learning. We can't do calculus before we've learned that 2 + 2 = 4, and we can only write poetry after we've learned to read. Similarly, an understanding of personality requires that we first *describe* the *parts* of each theory. We can only begin to understand the *process* of psychoanalysis after we know how Freud constructed his model of personality with such basic *parts* as id, ego, and superego. This allows us to go to the next level.

(2) Explanation. After *describing* the parts of the digestive system (e.g., tongue, teeth, mouth, esophagus, stomach, small intestine, and colon), we are in a position to *explain* how the tongue, teeth, and mouth chew our food and mix it with saliva as the first step in the digestive *process*. Similarly, once we know the parts of a particular personality theory, we can better understand the more complex motivational and developmental processes: What makes a person *go?* What makes a person *grow?*

(3) Synthesis. This is where many textbooks leave you on your own, confining themselves to describing and explaining. You describe the parts of a personality theory, learn how they interact, and then move on to the next theory. By the end of the course, you feel as if you had read an encyclopedia—lots of interesting facts, many intriguing ideas, but no "big picture." Faced with a smorgasbord of theories and research findings, you would find it almost impossible to compare theories in order to decide which ones were most useful for your purposes without some help in *comparing* and *synthesizing* those theories. Our *zonal perspective* will enable you to compare and synthesize theories, not merely memorize terms.

A ZONAL PERSPECTIVE

Vertical Axis

In Figure i.1, the vertical axis extends from *molecular* at the bottom to *macro* at the top. Thinking vertically—from small to large or from parts to wholes—occurs quite naturally during childhood. From our earliest years we encounter different perspectives each time we climb to the top of a playground slide or compare ourselves with the new kid on the block to see if we are taller or shorter. Even when our thinking becomes more mature, we probably continue thinking of ourselves and our surroundings in terms of levels—living out our childhood years somewhere between the grass clippings on the lawn and the clouds in the sky. Even now, looking up at the sky on a clear night reminds us that we are a small part of a very large universe. Looking in the other direction with our zoology lab microscopes exposes us to an infinity of ever smaller systems-within-systems.

Scientists use different analytic "tools" at different levels of analysis. Biologists, for example, use microscopes or magnifying glasses when

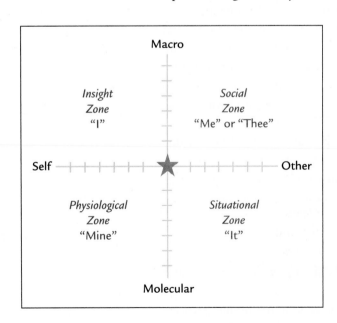

Figure i.1 ■ *Vertical axis.*

dissecting specimens or studying cells, but use binoculars or telescopes for studying birds in flight. Similarly, when studying depression, personality psychologists working in the *Physiological Zone* might utilize modern brain-imaging techniques or collect blood samples, whereas psychoanalysts working in the *Insight Zone* might analyze dream content. Researchers in the *Social Zone* might study how social support systems innoculate against depression. All might be studying depression, but at different levels—in different zones. Personality researchers utilize a variety of analytic tools ranging from molecular to macro.

A word of caution: although our vertical axis moves from molecular to macro, it is important to keep in mind that "bigger is not necessarily better." It isn't "better" to study birds in flight than to analyze the cellular structure of their wings, it's just different. Similarly, humanistic or existential theories of personality are not necessarily "better" than biochemical or behaviorist perspectives—just different. Nature appears to branch in all directions.

Horizontal Axis

In the inner world of personal experience the *horizontal axis* is one of the most basic of psychological dimensions: *self* versus *other*. At the far left we find theories of personality that see the *self* as self-aware, self-actualized, and *agentic*. This is a "take-charge" *self* that thinks, decides, acts, and functions as the "command center" of personality. Near the center of the horizontal axis, we find versions of a *self* that are less autonomous and more concerned with how *others* respond, or how *others* would behave in similar circumstances. At the far right *other* forces (*consequences* in behavioral situations, or *persons* in social situations) become dominant in shaping personality.

Personality Zones

Using a **zonal analysis** means *analyzing personality theory at the most appropriate intersection of the vertical (molecular to macro) and horizontal (self to other) axes.* Although we usually experience our surroundings as a seamless whole, the *tools and theories* we employ for investigating nature can be organized into a conceptual map (see Figure i.1). Using our grid as a map and our minds to navigate is a bit like using a Global Positioning System to assist us on our journey to visit new theoretical territories. You know that if you are exploring a tropical zone near the equator, you will expect to encounter vegetation and animals that differ drastically from those found in the "icy zones" of Antarctica or the North Pole. Similarly, in our study of personality zones, you can expect to encounter dreams in the *Insight Zone,* neurotransmitters in the *Physiological Zone,* and cultural rituals in the *Social Zone.* Using your mind as a GPS will allow you to anticipate whether you are likely to encounter parrots or penguins, snakes or seals.

We will soon discover that some theories span more than one level or range broadly across the horizontal axis. For example, sociobiology and evolutionary psychology range vertically from chromosomes to culture. At the same time, we will also learn most theories have a "center of gravity" with a majority of their constructs located in one particular zone. Let's briefly explore the four major zones in order to get an idea of where various personality theories fit.

Four Major Personality Zones

Physiological Zone (biochemical and genetic theories). In the *Physiological Zone,* personality theorists view the **person as parts,** *bits of biological or chemical compounds.* At this level of analysis the focus is not on self-awareness or on understanding how people interact with others; rather, the emphasis is on understanding physiological harmony—how one's biologically based personality parts are meshing with one another—how smoothly biochemical reactions are running. "Bottom-up" scientists prefer to analyze biochemical compounds or brain images instead of assessing interpersonal dynamics. In this zone, the study of personality is an interdisciplinary enterprise that includes the rigorous methods of neurobiology, genetics, psychoendocrinology, physiological psychology, and other "hard sciences." When studying the construct of *anxiety,* for example, physiological personality psychologists prefer to measure blood pressure, heart rate, perspiration, or cortisol levels rather than using paper-and-pencil self-reports.

There exists no genuine sense of *self* in the *Physiological Zone*; the focus is primarily on the *biology* of persons—their hormones, their neurotransmitters, and so on—as the source of personality. The closest one comes to having an awareness of *self* in this zone is realizing that *my* hormones may cause *me* to behave in certain ways, or *my* chromosomes may predispose *me* to drink excessively.

The scientific contributions of these investigators are significant, and their work is very much in the public consciousness. The average person believes that we are on the verge of discovering the "genetic basis" for just about everything from alcoholism to Parkinson's. Even your cab driver can repeat the pharmaceutical industry's mantra: "Depression is a biochemical imbalance." Thanks to the world of advertising, the "Maalox moment" (a physiological solution to stress) is almost as widely known as another biochemical fix: "This Bud's for you!"

In short, theorists working in the *Physiological Zone* use tools at the molecular end of the vertical axis, analyzing palpable substances or tracing tangible neurological pathways with high degrees of precision. They view people as "objects" composed of biochemical constituents. A "person" exists primarily as a shadow "landlord" of chemicals, chromosomes, or hormones—not as an active agent. Research in this zone is impressively precise—"hard" science—rendering it widely popular among many, although humanists and existentialists worry that it reduces persons to walking biochemical factories.

Situational Zone (conditioning/learning theories). In the *Situational Zone,* a person isn't viewed as a biochemical factory or a gene carrier, but as a *trained animal.* The level of analysis is both higher and broader than in the physiological zone, but the primary emphasis is on the *situation* rather than on the person or the person's composition. In this zone, situational *consequences* are king, and physiology or other person-based variables matter less. Conditioning is what counts.

The primary difference between a wild animal and a pet is training. We train our pets (and our children) not to defecate on the carpet. For behavioral psychologists, training explains why we do what we do. Whether it's a pigeon or a person, the same principles of conditioning apply: reinforced behaviors thrive and proliferate, while unrewarded behaviors become extinct. As B. F. Skinner, the most famous of conditioners, put it: "Behavior is shaped and maintained by its consequences" (1971, p. 18). For personality psychologists working in this zone, research involves carefully arranging circumstances and then rigorously assessing even the slightest changes in behavior. In the end, this takes the person-as-agent pretty much out of the loop: "A scientific analysis shifts the credit as well as the blame to the environment . . ." (Skinner, 1971, p. 21).

Behavioral psychologists carefully specify the situational triggers and consequences that promote or penalize specific behaviors that animals and people perform. Their scientific contribution has been great, and many of their concepts are now part of public culture. Each time we pick up a discarded beer can or pop bottle—not only for ecological consciousness, but also for the 10-cent "reinforcement"—we are testimony to the success of Skinner's revolution.

Critics point out that by focusing primarily on the *situation,* behaviorists have "gutted" people of their personalities, bypassing the importance of the "inner" life. Some skeptics predicted that this "empty organism" approach would render Skinner's radical behaviorism obsolete and that it would soon become extinct. However, the demise of behaviorism has, in Mark Twain's memorable phrase, "been greatly exaggerated," and in the laboratories of academic psychology, as well as in schools, prisons, and other applied settings, behaviorism is very much alive and well. What has taken place—instead of extinction—is cross-fertilization. Even the critics have not left behaviorism behind so much as they have *added* cognitive components. Thus behaviorism has spun off a popular variant known as **cognitive behaviorism,** *a hybrid that emphasizes the importance of cognitions and perceptions, as well as environmental consequences, in determining behavior.*

Insight Zone (psychoanalysis, object-relations, humanistic, and existential theories). In the *Insight Zone,* we begin to see the emergence of an **agentic self,** *which is a self-starting, self-steering, autonomous self.* After studying theories that view the person as a chemical plant or conditioned animal, we find that Freud created a part-animal, part-agent model of personality. Psychoanalysis is a "mixed model" in which a personal, thinking *ego (self)* is buffeted about by untamed animal instincts *(id)* arising from within one's body. Still, even with all this conflict going on, the ego remains partially *agentic*—somewhat "in charge," and capable of some rationality. The *ego* functions as a thinking, directing *agent* of the mind. Caught in a "civil war" between the animal impulses of the id and the moral restrictions of the *superego,* the ego endlessly tries to satisfy the biological urges of the organism without offending the moral police. Not an easy job!

In the *Insight Zone* constructs are broader and more comprehensive—less "objective." Therefore, the exactness and rigor with which constructs are defined is somewhat reduced, but the relevance to real-life problems appears more direct than what is found in many biochemical, behavioral, or trait theories. Psychoanalysts usually show little interest in specifying and controlling *situational* circumstances, preferring instead to help persons increase conscious awareness of why they act the way they do.

Social Zone (interpersonal and social theories). In the *Social Zone,* scope is broad and *social interactions* are seen as the most important influences shaping personality. These personality theories are located to the right of center on the *horizontal (self–other)* axis; however, at this level of analysis the *"other"* consists of other *persons or* social groups, not food pellets or circumstances. In the *Social Zone,* it is people's responses to one another that provide most of the reinforcing or punishing consequences. Personality is no longer contained within the person (as in psychoanalysis), but unfolds as the joint product of *interpersonal transactions.*

In this zone, personality emerges as a *hybrid—a fusion* that is co-created by two participants and bears some resemblance to each, much as a child displays some features of each parent. These theorists see *self* and *other* intermingling so closely that it becomes difficult to define the *self* outside the context of a relationship. As Sullivan (1964, p. 221) famously put it: "For all I know every human being has as many personalities as he has interpersonal relations. . . ." At this level, personality is seen as a *consistent interactional pattern* rather than a within-person system.

Transpersonal Zone (transpersonal/spiritual theories). In this zone we move beyond the realm of personality as a *science* to consider transpersonal and spiritual perspectives. Because these perspectives span territories beyond the individual person and involve "higher powers" that are thought to exist outside the empirical reach of laboratory methods, this zone is often neglected in the study of personality. However, since billions of people worldwide testify to the significance of God/gods in their lives, we consider it important to show respect for such transpersonal/spiritual perspectives, even if they are intrinsically unprovable. Everything of importance in the cosmos is not scientifically researchable. Great music, beauty, and art are among the significant experiences that resist scientific analysis.

PLAN OF THE BOOK

Chapters are organized in the following way:

In This Chapter You Can

Chapters begins with a brief overview of the important points to be covered. This will enable you to have a sense of direction as you proceed through the chapter.

A Personal Perspective

Here I share a personal story—mine or someone else's—to help you catch the excitement of personality psychology. If you find the study of personality boring, tedious, or irrelevant, you might seriously want to consider other fields of study, because in psychology (I believe, anyway) personality theory is "where the action is."

Introduction

Background check. Acquainting ourselves briefly with the family life, childhood, and educational experiences of the various personality theorists will help in appreciating how personal issues might tilt a theory in a particular direction. For example, Freud grew up as the apple of his mother's eye, which undoubtedly influenced the importance he placed on mother–son relationships.

Zeitgeist. Understanding the **zeitgeist,** *or the intellectual climate of the times,* provides historical context that assists us in deciding which aspects of a theory reflect the philosophies of a particular era, and which are applicable to our own lives and times. Otherwise, living during the dawn of the twenty-first century, we might be half a century or more out of synch with the milieu in which a theory was born.

Asking the "Big Four" (theory-construction) Questions

Personality theorists normally use four kinds of constructs (structural, motivational, developmental, individual-differences) to build their models, and each of our "Big Four" questions focuses on a particular kind of construct.

(1) What are the parts? *Structural constructs* are the component "parts" of a personality theory. We will want to know which "parts" a particular theorist regards as most essential. Freud's "dealership" would consider the *id, ego,* and *superego* essential "engine parts."

(2) What makes a person go? *Motivational constructs* are used by each theorist to power personality. What kind of motivational "fuel" runs the engine? Libido? Reinforcement? Self-actualization? Existential angst? In most personality theories we will find a close coupling between structure and energy—between the engine and the fuel. All personality theorists must explain how personality is fueled—what makes a person go.

(3) What makes a person grow? *Developmental constructs* help us understand how a person changes during the journey from the womb to the tomb. For behaviorists, development is a matter of experience stamping its imprint on the ***tabula rasa***— the *blank slate* of a baby's mind. Other theorists insist that all persons pass through similar *developmental stages* (e.g., oral or anal, trust versus mistrust, autonomy versus shame). Most personality theorists pay a lot of attention to how people develop, change, and yet remain consistent over time.

(4) What makes a person unique? *Individual-differences constructs* account for the *uniqueness* and *individuality* of each person. Is each of us unique primarily because of unique encounters with life, or do we come into the world temperamentally and psychologically programmed for individuality? Personality psychologists study individual differences in order to better understand how we maintain our unique identities, even while changing over time. Not surprisingly, we find profound differences among theorists. Since behaviorists see the person entering the world as a *tabula rasa,* uniqueness is seen to result from each person's unique conditioning *history.*

By contrast, humanists and existentialists see persons as actively creating meaning, so they use terms like *authenticity, choice,* and *responsibility* to describe how people shape their own unique personalities.

Facing the "Tough Twins"

After we have a clear understanding of how personality is constructed—how parts, energy, experience, and individuality combine to form a unique person—two tough questions remain: "Is it testable?" and "Is it useful?"

(1) Is it testable (falsifiable)? Among scientists the question "Is it testable?" replaces "Is it true?" Although scientists are in the business of searching out truth, *proving* truth is no simple matter. When you were a child, if you excitedly told your friend that you'd gotten a new bicycle for your birthday, it was easy enough to answer her skeptical challenge: "Prove it!" You simply took her out to the garage where your shiny new Huffy was parked and said, "See! I told you so!" That was the end of the matter; you had "proved" your assertion.

Scholars wish it were as easy to prove their theories, but alas, after centuries of wrangling about what *really* constitutes proof, they are still far from agreement. Leaving philosophers and other scholars to argue about "truth," scientists have settled for *testability* rather than *truth* as the target. One of the major ways in which personality scientists differ from other behavior analysts (such as philosophers, poets, playwrights, and journalists) is that personality psychologists seek to evaluate behavior *scientifically.* Shakespeare was surely one of the keenest analysts of human personality this world has ever produced, but he was not a *scientist.* Whereas writers and philosophers attempt to discover truth by way of the "heart," or by logical arguments, scientists use experimental methods to eliminate false hypotheses. Let's briefly look at how this process works.

To test a theory, scientists must first translate *theoretical constructs* into **operational definitions,** *or measurable operations.* Thus, *anxiety* might be defined by measurable changes in heart rate, blood pressure, or perspiration. *Hunger* could be operationally defined in terms of blood glucose levels, or by hormones present in the bloodstream. Operational definitions make it possible for researchers to test, for example, the prediction that "If a hungry child is allowed to choose between money and food, she will choose food." The outcome will depend on a number of variables such as a child's age and intelligence, and how we operationally define *"hunger."* We might expect a three-year-old to choose an ice cream cone instead of a $20 bill, whereas a ten-year-old would be less likely to do so.

With constructs operationally defined, it becomes possible to **falsify,** *to disprove a specific prediction or* **hypothesis.** In the example just cited, we might predict that a moderately hungry ten-year-old would choose a $20 bill instead of ice cream, but that an extremely hungry child would prefer food over money. Such predictions could be experimentally tested and shown to be either true or false. Such is the nature of science: instead of seeking "ultimate truth," scientists seek to eliminate competing alternative explanations by carrying out carefully designed experiments. In place of appealing to our "hearts," or convincing us by logical arguments, scientists produce data. In place of absolute "proof," scientists offer **probabilities.** A scientist might say that it is *highly probable (95 times out of 100)* that a certain result did not occur by chance; i.e., it was *probably* the result of specific variables (age, hunger, money) interacting to bring about a predicted event. The scientist sees the world as an orderly, statistically predictable place where it is possible to carefully manipulate variables in order to test predictions.

(2) Is it useful? "Does this dog hunt?" "Will this thingamajig fly?" Even a *true* theory might not be useful. For example, if we demonstrate in the laboratory that certain visualization exercises help children resist "tempting" foods, we might wonder whether such techniques might be effective *at home* with obese children. Could visualization be effectively used by alcoholics and drug addicts to lessen their reliance on drugs? These are the sort of "rubber-meets-the-road" questions that modern theories of personality must face. Laboratory-based theories must prove their worth in the real world if they are to be of enduring value. Similarly, clinically based theories of the "grand masters" such as Freud, Jung, and Erikson will maintain their influence in today's world only to the extent that they can be shown to be accurate and useful.

Summary

A brief summary of the major ideas of each chapter provides "conceptual glue" for placing the chapter in the larger array of personality theories.

Points to Remember

Concluding each chapter, *Points to Remember* is designed to make learning easier and retention more reliable.

Key Terms

Key terms are listed for easy location and to serve as a concise summary.

Web Sites

We provide two kinds of Web sites: scholarly Web sites to aid in seriously researching a topic, and "fun" Web sites to enhance learning in a more playful way.

Learning on the Lighter Side

We suggest Web sites, movies, plays, experiments, or other activities that might personalize your learning and allow you to use newly learned concepts in a practical way. Even if you have previously seen a suggested movie, when you view it again, you'll see things you never noticed before. In short, you will experience how personality theories can enrich your understanding of human functioning.

Looking Ahead

This section alerts us to what's coming next and how it relates to what we've just learned. Speaking of *looking ahead:* Chapter 1 will be brief but broad. Instead of discussing specific theories of personality, Chapter 1 will "outfit" you to study all the theories that will follow. Just as you get outfitted with boots, poles, and skis for snow skiing, the next chapter will "gear you up" with the proper intellectual equipment so you can ski the slopes of your text with efficiency and exhilaration.

Key Terms

A Zonal Approach to the Study of Personality

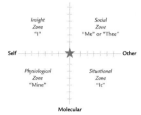

Definitions, Methods, Measurement, and Persistent Problems

IN THIS CHAPTER YOU CAN

1. Discover why *personality* is difficult to define.
2. Explore different *methods* for studying personality.
3. Learn why *validity* is so important.
4. Understand how *measurements* change at different levels of analysis.
5. Grapple with several *persistent problems* faced by personality theorists.

Our study of personality will range from the molecules that make up our cells to the stars that comprise our solar system. "Riding shotgun" with microbiologists as well as astronomers, we will ask the same questions at different levels of analysis: "Why do we behave as we do? How do these elements influence our lives? Do we matter?"

A PERSONAL PERSPECTIVE

Personality theory can sometimes sneak up on you—surprise you, catch you off guard. That's how it grabbed me, anyway. I had briefly studied **counter-transference,** *Freud's term for the unconscious emotional response of a therapist toward the client,* in graduate school, but I hadn't taken it very seriously. I didn't *really* believe in the unconscious mind—not until I met Tanya.[1]

I had completed my doctoral studies in clinical psychology at Indiana University, a place where B.F. Skinner had once been chairman of the psychology department, and rigorous research was carried out mostly in the *Physiological* and *Situational Zones.* Freud was not highly regarded at IU, so I felt like something of an alien during much of my internship

"Look, I can't promise I'll change, but I can promise I'll pretend to change."

©The New Yorker Collection 1999. Robert Mankoff from cartoonbank.com. All Rights Reserved.

---

1. Not her real name.

at Children's Hospital Medical Center in Boston, where psychoanalysis was taken seriously. Highly skeptical, I secretly sneered at the untested assumptions of Freud's psychoanalytic theory, and doubted the existence of an "unconscious" mind. One day near the end of my internship year, that suddenly changed.

One of my weekly therapy clients was a nine-year-old African American girl from the inner city whose mother had been physically abusive to her. About six weeks before the end of my internship, I told Tanya that I would be leaving in a few weeks, but that another therapist would continue seeing her. She said nothing, but a few minutes later—for no apparent reason—she hit me in the face, sending my glasses flying across the carpet. It angered me, but I stayed calm and dutifully reminded her of the "rules" of therapy: she could *say* anything she liked, but she wasn't allowed to hit me or to destroy toys.

Later that week, when I discussed this therapy session with my psychoanalytic supervisor, he seemed obsessively interested in finding out *exactly* what I had said to the mother when I returned to the waiting room with Tanya. I reluctantly admitted that I had told the mother that Tanya had hit me in the face, but had assured her that Tanya and I had "worked it out just fine." (This was a violation of confidentiality, since parents are not supposed to be privy to therapy sessions with their children.) My supervisor immediately began exclaiming: "Countertransference! Countertransference!"

At first I was resistant, claiming I hadn't *really* been angry at Tanya. However, it didn't take my supervisor long to point out that I had acted out my anger by informing Tanya's mother about what had taken place during the session. To my chagrin, I had to admit that I had probably set Tanya up for a beating by her abusive (but obsequiously-respectful-to-doctors) mother.

Commentary

I had *no conscious awareness* of how I had acted out my anger toward Tanya, but my supervisor, trained in psychoanalysis, was alert to my *countertransference* and immediately picked up on my mistake. Thus, an idea from psychoanalysis, a less-than-precise theory, refined my clinical practice in a way that could not have come from my rigorous scientific training at Indiana University. Through the subsequent years, I have continued to admire my IU professors' commitment to scientific precision; yet I have also come to value the broader perspectives provided by psychoanalytic, humanistic, and existential theories. In the study of personality, we really can have "the best of all worlds."

What Is Personality?

"What is personality?" ought to be a simple question. Your botany professor could define a "plant" as a biological entity constructed of cellulose walls and lacking locomotion or a nervous system. Truth is, petunias and palm trees are easier to comprehend than personality, because among personality psychologists there is little agreement, each defining personality in a particular way.

Even asking the question "*What* is personality?" is misleading, because it encourages us to think and talk as if personality were a *thing*. Personality is not something like a pizza that we can touch, taste, or smell. There is no *homunculus* or *little person* sitting somewhere inside your skull working the controls. Nor is personality charm or charisma, as the term is commonly used by ordinary people.

In our text, **personality** refers to *a stable core of emotions, dispositions, attitudes, and behaviors that uniquely characterize a person at a specific point in time and shape development across the lifespan.* Just as the bones of our skeletons anchor our muscles and protect vital organs, personality provides a "psychological skeleton" that anchors our moment-by-moment experiences and provides a stable framework for our hopes and aspirations.

We could think of personality as coordinating all the systems within us, including thoughts, feelings, and behaviors. Personality is the "me, myself, and I" of one's entire physiological and psychological world. Some theorists—but not all—believe that personality also includes not only "me, myself, and I," but *others* as well.

Why study personality? Personality psychologists are interested in the same kinds of practical, personal questions that attract people to the study of psychology in the first place: "How can I understand myself better?" "What makes her tick?" "Why is my boyfriend such a control freak?" "Why is Samantha repeatedly late for work?" "Why are Tom and Kim filing for divorce?" The answers to such questions are of interest to professional psychologists working in clinics, schools, factories, or prisons as well as to personality psychologists conducting research in laboratories. In this sense, *all* practicing psychologists are personality psychologists, because they attempt to understand why people behave as they do. They seek to answer the "big ticket" questions about urgent issues that confront people in daily life.

As a clinical psychologist I've spent thousands of hours listening to clients share their personal histories; and, in sorting out what is relevant and what is "filler" I've learned to pay close attention to *recurrent themes.* Just as stalactites and stalagmites are formed by slowly dripping condensation, the drip-drip-drip of daily events—and our responses to them—gradually shape our personalities. Once formed, personality channels behavior into consistent patterns that can be observed by ourselves and by others, just as visitors to Mammoth Cave can witness the results of decades of dripping moisture. Understanding how recurring behaviors shape our personalities can help us function more efficiently, get along better with others, and squeeze more flavor out of life.

Personality traits remain stable. The study of personality is useful, because what you discover about yourself or others *now* is likely to still hold true years later. Some day, if you attend your twenty-year high school reunion, you'll notice that although eye glasses, body weight, hair styles, and shoe fashions have changed, your classmates' personalities will remain surprisingly similar to what they were when you attended high school together. Sort of like watching "Twenty Years of David Letterman"; from beginning to end he's still "Letterman." Numerous long-term studies carried out over the past twenty years show that although personality traits might change during childhood, by adulthood they are quite stable (McCrae & Costa, 2005). That's why in psychology the axiom still holds: "The best predictor of future behavior is past behavior."

Constructing Your Own Theory of Personality: Constructs, Theories, Paradigms, and Zones

Our zonal perspective allows us to compare various theories of personality, select the best components from each, and utilize these in constructing our own theory of personality. Psychologists are really theory builders. Whether psychologists are clinicians, educators, or corporate consultants, they ceaselessly create theories of personality that help to clarify how individuals grow and develop, yet remain consistent over time. Even if they aren't planning a professional career in psychology, everyone functions as a "personality scientist" when trying to make sense of life. Whether you become a bartender, accountant, psychologist, realtor, tennis pro, or mortician, you will find yourself creating theories of personality to assist you in better understanding others—and yourself.

What is a construct? The "parts" of a personality theory are known as *constructs*. Put simply, a **construct** is *a mini-theory, a small component of a larger theory.* Constructs are the "bricks and mortar" used in building theories; they exist at the lowest, most concrete levels of conceptualization. Different kinds of constructs are used for different aspects of a theory. For example, Freud used the id, ego, and superego as *structural* constructs to build the "engine" for psychoanalysis, and he used libido as a *motivational* construct to energize the engine. He employed the oral, anal, and phallic stages as *developmental* constructs to describe maturational changes taking place during childhood and adolescence.

Although theoretical constructs are not palpably real—you can't touch or feel them—they serve as models of how things operate. Constructs are "as-if" entities, allowing us to view matter, for example, "as if" it were composed of atoms. In personality research, anxiety is a theoretical construct. The *anxiety construct* provides a shorthand way of describing how my heart races, my head pounds, my stomach turns somersaults, and my hands sweat when I'm worried—"as if" anxiety is inciting me to react with emotional intensity. Anxiety is not a palpable thing—not something I can touch or see—it is a *construct,* a shorthand term for describing a complex state of physiological and psychological arousal. Personality constructs assist us in describing who we are, how we developed, and what motivates us to behave the way we do—in a phrase, "what makes us tick."

What is a theory? A scientific **theory** is *a network of ideas, images, constructs, and models that relate to one another in predictable and testable ways.* Scientific theories utilize **hypotheses,** which are *tentative assumptions designed to test or explain core components of a system.* Based on hypotheses, scientists construct **models,** or *scientific metaphors, analogs, or prototypes (sometimes expressed in purely mathematical or chemical symbols).* Personality psychologists test *hypotheses* and construct *models* in order to understand better how and why people act as they do.

Theories are even more important than the microscopes or telescopes through which scientists peer, because theories function as *conceptual lenses,* bringing some elements into sharp focus while blurring others. That's the challenging part—finding the theory that creates the clearest images and utilizing the best tools for investigating that theory. For example, a speedometer provides useful information (in miles per hour) regarding how fast you are driving through the countryside, but that is not a very useful way to measure the rate at which your hair is growing. Because hair grows at approximately 10^{-8} miles per hour, a more useful measure might be *haircuts per month.*

Similarly, one size doesn't fit all when we try to understand and investigate theories of personality. This is why we have arranged our study of personality by levels

We could think of the classic theories of psychoanalysis, behaviorism, and humanism as the "stagecoaches" of personality, now replaced by modern, research-based mini-theories. Like the vehicle that delivers my mail, these contemporary theories prove to be predictable, reliable, and trustworthy. This might appear as progress, but there is a tradeoff. The new, more-precise mini-theories lack the broad scope of such classic constructs as Adler's *lifestyle,* Freud's *unconscious,* or Maslow's *hierarchy of needs.* As always, reductionistic theories appear more precise, yet smaller is not necessarily more scientific.

Still, when I'm conducting psychotherapy, the "big picture" provided by such "stagecoaches" as psychoanalysis or existentialism provides a valuable context for understanding my client(s). That's why I've included a number of these classic theories along with the more modern mini-theories. We can learn much from both. We can seek to promote scientific rigor without quashing creativity.

This is the balancing act: if we become too scientifically rigorous, we risk crushing creativity; if we are too broad and imprecise, our theories can never be proven false. In our subsequent study of personality theories we will seek scientific rigor without disparaging imagination and creativity; we will encourage *more rigor,* without allowing our thinking to undergo *rigor mortis*!

METHODS FOR STUDYING PERSONALITY

Psychologists study personality from many different perspectives. Case studies, laboratory experiments, psychological testing, and physiological assessments are but a few of the methods utilized. Let's explore a few of the more common approaches.

Case Studies (Clinical or Historical)

Clinical case studies *trace the life story of an individual in order to understand his or her personality.* Sigmund Freud, the most famous of all personality theorists, based his psychoanalytic theory almost entirely on clinical case studies. Personality theorists working in academic settings have sometimes used a similar approach—intensely studying the individual—but have defined it by various other terms (e.g., Allport, 1937—*idiographic approach;* Murray, 1938—*personology;* White, 1981—*study of lives*). When historians, biographers, journalists, or psychologists focus intensely on the psychological dimensions of a specific person, they sometimes refer to their work as *psychobiography* (e.g., McAdams and Ochberg, 1988; Winter, 1996; Berecz, 1999). Since most of the classic personality theorists (e.g., Freud, Jung, Adler, and Erikson) were practicing clinicians, it was quite natural for them to base their theories on clinical observations rather than upon carefully designed experiments.

In recent years, this has shifted dramatically with most personality psychologists actively engaging in research and relatively few providing clinical services. Laboratory experiments and psychological tests have also played a significant role in shifting personality psychology away from its reliance on clinical case studies to experimental methods. Still, case studies continue to help us understand personality from a subjective (person-centered) perspective, while experiments and tests provide us more objective (variable-centered) perspectives.

Historical case studies. If clinical case studies frequently fail to meet high standards of precision, historical case studies are even more problematic because biographers often use secondary sources, further increasing the distance between them and the people they seek to understand. Still, if historical case studies tap into a *consistent core of behaviors* that characterize a person's uniqueness across time and across situations, such analyses can prove valuable. Winter (1996), Berecz (1999), and others have studied the personalities of presidents and other political officials from a distance, by indirect means, and have demonstrated the value of such methods. In our media-permeated age, politicians become walking case studies, because their every hiccup is televised, analyzed, and dissected. Presidents Reagan and Carter, for example, are a study in personality contrasts.

Laboratory Studies

Temptation in the laboratory—Melissa's marshmallows. Contemporary personality psychologists are likely to be found carefully investigating *bits* of behavior—testing *parts* of a theory rather than some grand theory or overarching hypothesis. Consider Melissa's marshmallows:[2]

Four-year-old Melissa stares intently at the marshmallows on the table in front of her. She isn't supposed to begin eating until given a signal by the experimenter, but it is becoming harder and harder because she is doing just as the experimenter instructed her: thinking "hot" thoughts about how "sweet and chewy and soft" those marshmallows are. Now she is thinking about how "soft and sticky" they will be in her mouth, when she finally gets to eat them. "I'll just touch one to see if it as soft as I think it is," she reasons. Reaching for the marshmallow nearest her, Melissa touches it and discovers that it is as soft as she had imagined. Then, before she quite knows what is happening, the marshmallow is in Melissa's mouth, "soft and sticky," tasting "sweet and chewy and soft."

Meanwhile, at another table, Hannah isn't having nearly so much trouble waiting for the signal to begin eating, because she is following different instructions and is thinking "cool" thoughts of how "round and white . . . like the moon . . . or like a ball" these marshmallows appear.

Melissa, Hannah, and their nursery school classmates are participating in an experiment designed by Mischel and Baker (1975) to ascertain how cognitive encoding of stimuli affects eating behaviors in young children. It turns out that children like Melissa, who are given "hot" encoding instructions, have a more difficult time delaying gratification than do children like Hannah who are given "cool" cognitive sets. *Delay of gratification* is a dimension of self-control that has traditionally been considered an internal personality variable. This experiment sharpens our understanding by revealing how *delay of gratification* can be influenced by instructions, mental sets, and situational variables.

Psychological Testing

Psychometric methods: *Psychometric methods use psychological tests to assess personality.* Personality testing enjoys a long and respected tradition in psychology. If I owned a

---

2. Adapted from Mischel & Baker (1975).

BOX 1.1 ■ Contrasting Presidential Personality Styles

Ronald Reagan. President Reagan displayed an *emotional/intuitive* personality style. He was a master at reading feelings rather than numbers; he remembered stories, not statistics. Once, for example, when his cabinet members were hopelessly wrangling over how to dispose of a huge store of surplus butter, Reagan brought the meeting to a hilarious conclusion by quipping: "Four hundred and seventy-eight million pounds of butter! Does anyone know where we can find 478 million pounds of popcorn?" (Cannon, 1991, p. 130).

Like some college students (not *you,* of course!), Reagan preferred watching movies to doing his homework. On the eve of the 1983 economic summit of the world's industrialized democracies, Reagan's chief of staff, James Baker, dropped off a thick briefing book designed to bring the president up to speed for the historic event. Returning the next morning, Baker found the briefing book on the table exactly where he had deposited it the evening before—unopened. Knowing that the president hadn't even glanced at it and that in less than one hour he would be presiding over the first meeting of the economic summit, a frustrated Baker uncharacteristically chided the president, asking him why he hadn't even cracked the briefing book. "Well, Jim," Reagan calmly replied, *"The Sound of Music* was on last night" (Cannon, 1991). Nonetheless, with cue cards in hand and charm in his smile, Reagan conducted the summit without incident.

Jimmy Carter. Jimmy Carter, with his *conscientious/obsessive* personality style, would have been up half the night studying the details of the various economies represented at the summit. Not only was Carter bright, he was diligent—always prepared. Once, for example, when Jimmy was governor of Georgia, Jack Crockford, head of the Georgia Game and Fish Department, invited him to go woodcock hunting. Carter approached this recreational event with his usual hardworking seriousness: "I was supposed to be the expert," recalled Crockford, "but between Saturday and Wednesday he had read the final-word book on woodcock. He knew more about woodcock than I did . . . . He was not real good at playing . . ." (Bourne, 1997, p. 498).

Jimmy Carter, one of the brightest presidents of the second half of the twentieth century, had the personality style and intelligence of an engineer. He could have supplied you with specific details regarding the various missile systems deployed by the Department of Defense, while Reagan, the "Great Communicator," could hardly have distinguished one missile system from another. Carter's conscientious personality showed itself in his ability to work hard, focus on details, crunch numbers, and analyze data. Reagan's personality style focused on *feelings* and *impressions* instead of numbers or data. As president, Reagan negotiated an end to the Cold War, partly because his intuitive, emotionally based personality style enabled him to connect with Mikhail Gorbachev. Reagan recalled the experience in his memoirs:

> It was during the first moments of this fireside chat that I said I thought the two of us were in a unique situation. Here we were, I said, two men who had been born in obscure rural hamlets in the middle of our respective countries, each of us poor and from humble beginnings. Now we were the leaders of our countries and probably the only two men in the world who could bring about World War III. At the same time, I said, we were possibly the only two men in the world who might be able to bring peace to the world. (Reagan, 1990)

That was Ronald Reagan at his best, forming a buddy-buddy relationship with the leader of "the evil empire," softening it along the way with numerous anecdotes and one-liners. The important point is that *everyone*—friend, relative, patient, president, dictator, or religious crackpot—has a personality style that is unique, yet shares commonalities with other persons of similar style. These commonalities tend to remain consistent over time, and by mapping them, we are able to predict, with some degree of accuracy, where a person's psychological journey is likely to lead.

trucking company (I don't), and if you were seeking a job as a truck driver (you're probably not), before hiring you, I would ask you to answer a series of true–false questions on a test known as the **Minnesota Multiphasic Personality Inventory (MMPI),** *a true–false test composed of 567 questions that gives an overview of personality.* Based on your responses, I could predict whether or not you are "accident-prone." For example, if you scored high on scales 4 and 9, I might not hire you, because research shows that people with high scores on those scales tend to be rebellious toward authority and impulsive, manifest poor judgement, experience little anxiety, exhibit low frustration tolerance, and prefer action to thought. As a truck driver you would be less likely to keep accurate records of your trips, more prone to speeding and driving too many hours, and—bottom line—be more likely than other drivers to have an accident.

Physiological Methods

Sky diving for science. Seymour Epstein (1967) collaborated with Walter Fenz, a sport parachutist and psychologist, to investigate patterns of anxiety in novice (five or fewer jumps) versus experienced (100–500 jumps) sky divers. They collected *self-ratings* as well as *physiological measures* (heart rate, respiration rate, galvanic skin response) at fifteen different checkpoints along the way (e.g., the night before, the day of the jump, arriving at airport, preflight checkout, engine warm-up, takeoff, final altitude, final checkout, jump, and landing). It was an ingenious study, taking place in a natural setting, yet allowing for a level of precision in measurement that is usually possible only in the laboratory.

On both self-report and physiological measures, experienced and novice sky divers all showed elevated levels of anxiety, but with different patterns. Experienced jumpers' anxiety peaked on the morning of the jump and steadily declined thereafter, so that by the time they were actually sky diving, their anxiety was at its lowest level. By contrast, novice jumpers began with lower initial levels of anxiety that steadily increased, peaking at the "ready" signal just prior to jumping.

This study illustrates how it is possible to obtain measures of anxiety in different zones (e.g., physiological responses and self-ratings) and to compare patterns. This is a splendid example of how personality psychologists experimentally investigate theoretical constructs such as anxiety.

Sex for science. In recent years, sex researchers have utilized physiological devices to measure even slight changes in sexual arousal. In the males, a penile photoplethysmograph (dubbed the "peter meter" by some) measures changes in penile blood volume. In females, a photoplethysmograph about the size of a tampon measures vasocongestion in the genitals, a primary physiological response during sexual arousal. Utilizing such sensitive measurement devices, researchers have been able to accurately track how sexual arousal relates to personality characteristics. For example, one can show selected subjects (e.g., incarcerated rapists) movies that contain different combinations of eroticism and violence while assessing sexual arousal. Similarly, in diagnosing or treating pedophilia, it becomes possible to compare differences in sexual arousal resulting from movies depicting children versus adults.

Your body knows. With such precise physiological measurements, data emerge that might otherwise be lost. For example, in several studies on sexual arousal it was found that although there is generally a high correlation between self-ratings and physiological measures of sexual arousal, women seem less aware of their arousal levels than do men. Laan, Everaerd, van Bellen, and Hanewald

(1994) found that about half of female participants did not report arousal in their self-ratings even when physiological measures indicated arousal.

Beneath the "poker face." Similarly, Cacioppo, Petty, Losch, and Kim (1986) were able to detect subtle physiological differences when investigating the relationship between facial expressions and emotional states. Using electromyograph (EMG) recordings, they were able to detect transient emotional reactions "even in the absence of emotional expressions that are noticeable, at least under normal viewing conditions" (p. 267).

Conclusion

Finding different data in different zones. We have discussed only a small sample of the variety of methods employed by personality psychologists. As we learned earlier, most scientists do not seek ultimate "truth"; instead, they try to obtain *valid data* by utilizing instruments that are appropriate for their specific zones of analysis. When, as in the study of anxiety in skydivers, *converging data* can be obtained from different zones, it increases our confidence in the findings. Personality researchers range broadly from molecular to molar, and from self to situation. By remaining curious, and seeking to integrate data from various levels of analysis, they endeavor to form a more complete picture of human functioning.

VALIDITY AND MEASUREMENT IN DIFFERENT ZONES

Validity has different meanings at different levels of analysis, and we use different *measuring* techniques as well. It will become apparent that there is no ultimate "right way" to do things; nonetheless, at different levels of analysis some techniques are more appropriate than others. One size does *not* fit all.

How can we know if our theories are valid? We have just learned that personality psychologists utilize a wide array of techniques to investigate personality. A common theme flowing through all of these methods is a concern for **validity,** which concerns *whether a test or assessment device really measure what it claims to? and whether a personality model give a true picture of behavior.* There are several varieties of validity—some more "valid" than others. Focus Box 1.2 outlines the most important kinds of validity that concern personality psychologists.

Different measures in different zones. Theories influence the kinds of measurements we make. Although the average person thinks of microbiology as more "scientific" than social psychology, this is not necessarily so. "Truth" in the physiological zone is not more valid than truth in the social zone—it's just measured differently. But how can we be certain that we are using the appropriate measuring instruments? Short answer: There is no "right" ruler—the measuring instrument you choose depends on your questions and on your level of analysis. *Miles per hour* is a good measurement scale if you're traveling by automobile, but not if you're measuring hair growth. Scientists try to use measuring devices that are appropriate for the zones in which they are working. Focus Box 1.3 describes some common levels of measurement.

FOCUS BOX

1.2 ■ Varieties of Validity

The concept of **Validity** asks: Does a test or assessment device measure what it claims to?

Face Validity	Whether a test *appears* to measure what it is designed to. This type of validity can be misleading and is not trustworthy.
Predictive Validity	How well a test predicts future behavior. This validity is verifiable and more respected.
Convergent and Discriminant Validty	These two kinds of validity refer to how a test correlates with other tests. Convergent validity means that a test correlates with alternative measures of the same trait. Discriminant validity refers to what a test should *not* correlate with.
Construct Validity	This is Predictive, Convergent, and Discriminant validity all rolled into one. If a construct makes accurate predictions, correlates with what it's supposed to, and doesn't correlate with what it's not supposed to, it is considered a valid construct.

Putting it all together. If you feel dizzy from thinking about different kinds of validity and various kinds of measurement, take heart, it boils down to this: *at whatever level you're working, certain concepts, tools, and techniques perform better than others.* Similarly, wherever you find yourself working along the horizontal axis, some methods are better than others. It hardly makes sense to investigate *self-concept* if you're working with pigeons at the "other" end of the horizontal (self versus other) axis. This leads to a related conclusion: *the "truth" you find in one zone will differ from the "truth" you discover in another zone.* That's it. Nothing more complicated—I promise!

Applying a Zonal Perspective to Some Persistent Problems in the Study of Personality

We will conclude this chapter by illustrating how a zones-of-analysis approach might help to clarify some of the persistent problems that have plagued personality psychologists. Don't get bogged down, simply keep in mind that *everything changes at different levels of analysis and along different locations on the self-other axis.* This principle will help you throughout the remainder of this book and during your entire academic career. Nearly all fields of study involve hierarchical part–whole relationships, and most include organizational maps as well. In chemistry, for example, the periodic table serves as an organizational "grid" for classifying elements. Using your brain as a GPS makes sense whether you're studying personality or physics. Complexity theorists (e.g., Gleick, 1987) have shown that patterns exist even in such seeming random events as dripping faucets.

(1) The mind–body problem. Even without realizing it—five centuries later—we continue to suffer the effects of Rene Descartes's (1596–1650) splitting each of us into mind *and* body. Descartes created what is known in philosophy as **Cartesian dualism,** *the viewpoint that mind and body are separate entities.* Descartes famously declared, "*Cogito, ergo sum*" ("I think, therefore I am"). Descartes believed the *body* was made of matter, but the *mind* was something mysterious and intangible— separate from the body. Unlike anything else in the universe, the mind was not comprised of matter and therefore was not subject to scientific scrutiny. This split is aptly described in the following epigram:

What is mind? No matter.
What is matter? Never mind. (Edelman, 1992, p. 3)

Dualism has dogged personality theorists from earliest times. For example, Freud (Chapter 6) initially attempted to build his theory of personality based solely on biology, focusing on physiology (1895, pp. 281–397). He soon discovered, however, that he could not reconcile such a biomechanistic view of behavior with his broader clinical insights, so he created a tripartite model of the mind that he located exclusively in the *psyche.* He then connected the mind *(psyche)* to the body *(soma)* with the *instinct* construct.

A zonal approach reminds us that *mind* and *body* are terms for describing the same person at different levels of analysis. We usually study *bodily processes* in the *Physiological Zone,* while the mind—which Steven Pinker (1997, p. 24) defines as "what the brain does"—is more appropriately analyzed in the *Insight Zone.* We lessen this artificial split between body and mind by realizing that even the most eloquent thoughts of a highly trained *mind* (e.g., a commencement address by a Pulitzer prize-winning novelist) emerge from the operations of the biological brain (or "wet" mind).

Psychologists working in the *Physiological Zone* sometimes refer to themselves as "brain scientists," and they typically view "mind" as the functioning central nervous system; whereas psychologists working at higher levels of analysis frequently use "mentalistic" constructs such as "thinking, hoping, or wishing" to describe

FOCUS BOX	
1.3 ▪ Levels of Measurement	
Nominal Measurement	Uses sorting to group things together. Here something must co-occur with the measurement index. Example: Alphabetizing names.
Ordinal Measurement	Assigns values of *greater than,* or *less than,* to a scale, without inferring that each interval on the scale is equidistant. Example: "How do you feel—on a scale of 1 to 10?"
Interval Measurement	Precise assessment scale where each interval is equidistant from the next. Example: Reading the temperature on a thermometer
Ratio Measurement	Most precise measurement scale, with all intervals being equidistant and the existence of a true zero. Example: Blood pressure cuff reading zero means—no pressure!
Nonlinear Dynamical Measurement	Used in Complexity Theory or Chaos Theory, new sciences attempt to measure natural phenomenon which traditional physics cannot. These theories try to measure the systems of dripping faucets or breaking waves to discover *patterns.* Example: The Butterfly Effect

how the mind operates. Nevertheless, no matter how abstractly or philosophically we might describe the *mind,* its operations directly depend on the ceaseless functioning of a physiologically healthy brain. Mind without body is unthinkable (pun intended).

Dualism fosters reductionism. Sometimes we're tempted to think that our toenails are more real than our thoughts (even though our toenails are composed of dead cells and our thoughts are the products of living processes). When we study personality theories from a zonal perspective we more easily free ourselves from the "downward drag" of **reductionism,** which is *the attempt to discover "truth" by reducing things to simpler units— body organs to cells, musical compositions to measures and notes.* We are less likely to follow the folly of Descartes's *dualism* in believing that our minds are less "real" than our bodies—that the study of physiology is more scientifically substantial than the study of mental processes.

A zonal perspective reminds us that truth does not reside exclusively at any particular level of analysis—not even at the *biochemical* or *physiological* level! There is nothing intrinsically wrong with reductionism so long as we offset our tendency to dissect, compress, or condense with an equal-but-opposite "upward mobility" that expands, extends, and broadens.

(2) Person versus situation. Along the horizontal axis, personality psychologists have long debated whether a person's behavior is mostly due to influences in the *situation* or traits within the *person*. This debate is drawing to a close because both sides turned out to be right. In the case of momentary behaviors, the situationists are right—traits appear *not* to influence behavior very strongly. However, over longer spans of time, traits predict behavior quite well. Fleeson (2001, 2005) found that although people act quite differently on different occasions, they act similarly from one week to another.

Retirement parties and funerals. Have you ever attended a retirement party for your grandpa or a friend? If you did, you probably experienced it as similar to a birthday party in many respects—food, laughter, friends, and some kidding around. However, comparing it to a funeral, you notice drastic differences. In a funeral, some of the same sorts of tributes and testimonials are heard, but they are framed in a much more somber tone. Much is recounted about what a wonderful life the person lived, and what a difference the person made in the lives of so many others; however, the happiness of the retirement dinner is completely absent. We wouldn't *think* of sharing that joke we heard the day before. We wouldn't dare slap someone on the back and ask them what they'd been up to.

Still, even in such drastically different circumstances, enduring personality traits exert their influence. At the retirement party an extrovert might engage in lively conversation and banter with Grandpa's work associates—swapping stories, telling jokes, and blending in to become "one of the gang," while an introvert might politely greet Grandpa's colleagues without much socializing afterward. At the funeral, a shy person might sign the guest book and sit quietly throughout the proceedings, while a gregarious person might personally approach grieving relatives to express condolences and offer emotional support.

In the past, behavioral psychologists *(Situational Zone)* insisted that *situations* are responsible for eliciting, shaping, reinforcing, or punishing behavior, and they tended to de-emphasize *person* variables as unimportant. By contrast, personologists and social psychologists *(Insight* and *Social Zones)* emphasized the importance of *person variables,* dismissing situational factors as "nuisance variables" or "noise." That debate has been declared a draw, and contemporary personality psychologists (e.g., McCrae & Costa, 2003; Shoda, Mischel, & Wright, 1994) are actively investigating how persons *interact* with situations.

Spectacles and saliva. Even traditional boundaries (such as the skin) separating the person and the environment are best understood as dynamic fusion zones. For example, when your glasses are lying on a desk, they are part of the situation more than part of you. However, when you put them on and begin to read, your spectacles morph from being situational objects to becoming a part of you—even more so if they are contact lenses. Or, consider how we "drink" saliva. That's not the sort of drinking we normally think about—like drinking a soft drink or a glass of milk—because it is so much a part of our personal functioning that it happens automatically, like breathing. However, if we were to collect our saliva in a container (for experimental purposes or medical analysis) we would no longer experience this saliva as part of ourselves (it would move from left to right on our horizontal, self–other axis). Then, only a significant sum of cash could persuade us to drink it from a cup—even though we drink saliva freely, without thinking, when we experience it as part of ourselves. A zonal analysis alerts us to how intimate the connection is between ourselves and the situations we occupy. It helps us to remember that we live our lives in dynamic zones where persons and situations *interact* and *interpenetrate.*

(3) Nature versus nurture—a classic problem of causality. When the nature-nurture problem is approached from a zonal perspective, it becomes easier to see how *both* genes and environment *interact* to produce behavior. A contemporary personality psychologist puts it in these words:

> At the level of an individual, there is no nature–nurture debate . . . . It makes no sense to ask "Which is more important, genes or environment, in accounting for Sally?" At the individual level of analysis, there is simply no issue to debate. As an analogy, consider baking a cake. Each particular cake consists of flour, sugar, eggs, and water. It makes no sense to ask whether the finished cake is "caused" more by flour or more by water. Both are necessary ingredients, inextricably combined and inseparable in the finished cake. Genes and environment for one individual are like flour and water for one cake—both ingredients are necessary, but we cannot logically disentangle them to see which is more important (Larsen & Buss, 2002, p. 107).

(4) Determinism versus freedom. The question of whether we are free to choose, or our behavior is determined by circumstances, has divided scholars for centuries. Personality psychologists have differing opinions as well (e.g., behaviorists and humanists strongly disagree about how much "choice" we have in our lives). Psychologists who argue in favor of freedom (e.g., self psychologists, humanists, existentialists, etc.) usually discuss these issues in the *Insight* or *Social Zones.* In the *Physiological* and *Situational Zones* physiological and behavioral psychologists tend to view people as being pushed or pulled around by genes, reinforcers, and punishers.

B.F. Skinner believed that human behavior is constrained by the same laws of physics that a waterfall or an avalanche must follow: "We can follow the path taken by physics and biology by turning directly to the relation between behavior and the environment and neglecting supposed mediating states of mind. Physics did not advance by looking more closely at the jubilance of a falling body . . . " (Skinner, 1971, p. 25).

By contrast, Rollo May, writing from the humanistic/existential perspective (Chapter 12), suggests that freedom and determinism are coexistent and complementary: "Without determinism, and the predictability that goes with it, we have anarchy. Without freedom, and the exuberance that goes with it, we have apathy" (May, 1977, pp. 6–9).

From a zonal perspective, freedom and determinism vary as a function of level of analysis and self–other location. At lower levels, and along the situational side of the horizontal axis, our behaviors are more strongly determined by chemical, biological, and situational variables. However, at higher levels of analysis, the *agentic self (operating brain)* exerts significant starting and steering powers over our macro-behaviors.

Thus, although we have no choice in determining our given biological gender—*zero freedom!*—we do have numerous degrees of freedom in choosing how and when we visit restrooms. Babies have little choice about *when* or *where* they "go potty"—timing is determined primarily by the bladder or the bowels. However, as toddlers mature, they develop muscle control over their bowels and their bladders about the same time they develop the strength and coordination to walk. Subsequently, they experience more freedom in choosing how and where to "go potty." Still, even with such freedoms, toilet behavior is strongly determined by both gender and culture. In America, a male found urinating in a women's restroom might face arrest, and women do not find urinals to be anatomically user-friendly.

In sum, it appears that May was correct in suggesting that freedom and determinism are complementary, not opposites. The biological variables operating in the *Physiological* and *Situational Zones* provide a predictable (deterministic) base for the freedom and choices we experience in the *Insight* and *Social Zones*. Perhaps the philosophical disputes result mostly from differences in language and constructs in different zones of analysis.

(5) Stability versus change of personality over time. Researchers (e.g., Swann & Hill, 1982; Council, 1993) have pointed out that we must observe behavior on more than one occasion in order to form an accurate picture of personality functioning. Such longitudinal studies have shown personality traits to be relatively stable. McRae & Costa (2005) report that change in personality occurs mostly during childhood and adolescence. During their twenties, both men and women become slightly less emotional and thrill-seeking, and moderately more cooperative and self-disciplined—shifts that are seen as signs of "maturity." After age 30, personality traits change little. Stability rules!

Stable but unique. Stability is not the same as *uniformity*. Although longitudinal research has revealed that personality traits such as agreeableness, openness to experience, and extroversion tend to remain stable over a lifetime, these enduring traits *dynamically interact* with situational variables. Each day presents us with new situations and fresh opportunities, so although our personality traits tend to remain generally stable, new situations elicit stable but unique personal behaviors.

A person who is consistently curious, for example, will probably approach the opportunities of each day with interest and inquisitiveness. A habitually agreeable person might approach others with a Will Rogers "I never met a person I didn't like" sort of friendliness. People who are curious, affectionate, and likeable at age 30 will be pleased to know they will probably be inquisitive, warm, and winsome when they are 80.

(6) Reification. We call it **reification** when people *"thingify" or "concretize" abstract concepts such as anxiety or intelligence.* Intelligence, for example, is a theoretical construct that people tend to *reify.* Although a psychologist can measure how quickly a child performs multiplication, puts together puzzle pieces, or decodes mazes, there is no such *thing* as intelligence. There is only intelligent (quick, accurate) behaving. We are sometimes tempted to *reify* dynamic descriptors, treating theoretical constructs as if they were palpable objects. If a child responds quickly and accurately to tasks we present to her, we are inclined not only to report that she is behaving intelligently, we are also tempted to think that this behavior springs from a source somewhere inside her that we might call her *intellect*. When we see a dieting friend grit his teeth and refuse dessert, it might appear that such resolve arises from an internal source (the *will*), and we might describe such determination as *willpower*. If a person consistently behaves in a friendly manner, we are tempted to assume it arises from a source inside that we might designate a *"congeniality trait"* or a *"friendly personality."*

This tendency to reify the "parts" of personality has created the general impression that personality is a *thing*. We noted earlier that many people think of personality as if it were a *homunculus* inside the mind, pulling strings to make things happen. But if personality isn't a little person or a thing, what do we study? The next thirteen chapters clarify that question. The short answer: personality theories are about *processes,* not about *things.*

(7) Extrapolation. Scientists are in the business of **extrapolation,** that is, *extending or expanding known data or experiences into new (unknown) areas.* Scientists typically study things in controlled laboratory situations in order to limit the range of variables that might influence the outcome, and in order to be more certain that the effects they observe are indeed the result of their manipulations. In the end, however, they want to apply their findings as broadly as possible. Thus, when behavioral psychologists study learning by using pigeons or rats in a controlled laboratory environment (e.g., a "Skinner box"), their ultimate goal is not only to understand how rodents learn, but also to apply laboratory-derived "laws of learning" to understanding people working on assembly lines, or to better comprehend how school children learn. When behaviorists *extrapolate* their findings, they are thinking—literally—"outside the (Skinner) box." Aeronautical engineers do much the same thing: testing model airplanes in wind tunnels, hoping to *extrapolate* their findings to predict how real planes will respond to certain wind conditions.

From a zonal perspective, *extrapolation* usually involves moving *upward* along the vertical axis—from *molecular* levels of investigation and experimentation to *macro* levels of application. Personality psychologists are especially interested in understanding how *molecular* findings influence the cluster of *macro-behaviors and predispositions* we refer to as personality. Usually they are aware of the "leap" involved in applying research findings to practical problems, but sometimes differences are glossed over, so we must remain alert, insisting that when research findings are *extrapolated* to real life, continuing investigation is carried out at the *macro* levels of application. Airplanes crashing in real life pose a more serious problem than models failing to fly in a wind tunnel; kids failing in school is a more serious concern than rats who fail to learn a maze.

(8) Diversity. Some have questioned whether personality theories formulated by "dead white males" during the nineteenth and twentieth centuries have any relevance for us who live in today's global village at the dawn of the second millennium. We address this in three ways. First, we have included a representative number of "dead while females" (e.g., Anna Freud, Melanie Klein, Karen Horney, Margaret Mahler, and others) in our discussions. Secondly, we begin each chapter with a brief discussion of the *zeitgeist* in order to clarify the cultural/intellectual context in which the theory was formulated. Finally, in "Facing the Tough Twins" we consider to what extent the personality theories under consideration have proved useful in diverse settings and with diverse populations, and whether *current research* supports or refutes them.

Chapter Summary

The study of personality is not like learning anatomy, because personality is not a *thing* like your esophagus or intestines. Instead, personality refers to that *consistent core of enduring attitudes, emotions, and behaviors that uniquely characterizes you as an individual person—the coordinating center of all other subsystems within yourself.* Personality is studied in various ways in different zones of conceptualization, ranging from neurophysiological studies to lifestyle comparisons. Concerns about validity and measurement are always present, even though the meaning of these terms changes as we move up and down to different levels of analysis, or move back and forth horizontally to focus more or less on the person or the situation. Although problems of dualism and reductionism, nature versus nurture, determinism versus freedom, stability versus change, and reification persist at all levels of analysis, understanding which *zone* we are working in will enable us to choose appropriate "tools" for our tasks. The telephone repairperson working at the level of wires in the sky uses spiked shoes to climb poles or works while perched in a little basket on the end of a crane. The same person working on an underground cable has no use for cranes and spikes but employs a shovel or a backhoe instead.

It is not always apparent at what level of analysis one will hit pay dirt. Will the enuretic child be best served by a (*Situational Zone*) "conditioning pad" that sets off an alarm when the child begins to wet the bed, thereby teaching him to wake up before wetting? Is individual psychotherapy (*Insight Zone*) or family therapy (*Social Zone*) indicated? Some combination of the above? Or, no therapy at all? Might a regular bedtime with restricted liquids at supper do the job? It will seldom be initially clear which theoretical lens will best resolve the conceptual haze surrounding the question, "Why does Douglas wet the bed?" Answers to such questions do not typically emerge with precise outlines and clear edges.

It is in the everyday arenas of angst that personality researchers help other professional psychologists (e.g., clinicians, counselors, corporate consultants, and educators) to better understand their clients. Whether working in private settings, schools, hospitals, universities, or industry, other professionals look to personality theorists for help in figuring out why people think, feel, or behave as they do. Each time an applied psychologist encounters clients requesting help, students seeking knowledge, or corporations wishing to succeed, she must create a fresh theory of personality, distinctly designed to suit a particular person in a specific situation. Each diagnosis or treatment plan produced by a clinical psychologist, each educational plan signed by a school psychologist, and each job performance assessment package developed by an industrial-organizational psychologist draws upon a *theory (or theories) of personality.*

Frequently, personality questions are posed in less than scholarly terms: "How is this kid wired?" "If we promote her to fourth grade in September will she be able to succeed?" "If he attempts suicide another time, will he be 'successful?'" "Should we hospitalize her, or will intensive outpatient psychotherapy do the job?" But in whatever form the questions come, psychologists awash in such real-world problems yearn for help in making sense of complex situations, and frequently they turn to personality psychologists for assistance in mapping reasonable plans of action with particular people or organizations.

We are frequently able to offer assistance, but we must candidly admit that we don't always have answers.

I'm reminded of the commencement speaker who told a graduating class of physicians, "Half of what we've taught you about medicine is wrong." Then, pausing for emphasis, he added, "The problem is, we don't know which half!" Much the same is true in psychology. The knowledge-to-ignorance ratio ought to discourage arrogance. Most experimental reports conclude with the sentence "More research is needed." This is not simply protocol, it is the truth. What we *don't* know significantly outweighs what we *do* know, yet we must continue to explore.

Characteristics that will serve us well in our study of theories of personality include humility, creativity, optimism, and tolerance for ambiguity. Such qualities, combined with a zonal orientation, will equip us to confront the enigmas and conundrums of daily living with a combination of hope and humility.

There is a famous poem (quoted in Hampden-Turner, 1981, pp. 8–10) about six blind men who encountered an elephant. The first man felt its tusk and described the elephant as "like a spear." Another seized its trunk and thought he had hold of a snake, while the man who touched the elephant's leg said "It's clear to me. . . . this creature's like a tree." The man who felt the elephant's ear said, "The creature's like a fan!" Finally, the one who grabbed the tail described the creature as a rope. The poem concludes that these "men of missing sight" were all partly wrong and partly right. Surely it must be apparent that psychologists working in different zones comprehend only a portion of the "personality elephant." It behooves us to be open to the experimental findings and theoretical ideas of others in whatever zone we encounter them.

Points to Remember

1. The term *personality* refers to a *core of stable psychological features that identify and influence a particular individual over time and across various situations.* Your personality provides structure for your psychological life, much as your bones determine the basic shape of your body. Sure, you can slightly change the contours of your body by your lifestyle, but regardless of how much or how little you eat or exercise, you'll never become a kangaroo or be able to fly like an osprey.

2. Why study personality? Because personality theories provide professional psychologists working in clinical, school, and industrial settings with guidelines for practice. In a very real sense, *all* practicing psychologists are personality psychologists because they attempt to understand why people behave as they do. They ask the "big ticket" questions.

3. Personality psychologists employ a *wide variety of methods* in their attempts to understand individuals. *Historical case studies* provide a subjective "feel" for what a person is like, but they lack the precision modern scientists expect. *Psychometric* and *physiological* studies seek to replace subjectivity with scientific rigor, by employing a more focused "piecemeal" approach. By studying topics like marshmallow-eating behavior, skydiving, facial expressions, and sexual arousal,

personality psychologists try to balance precision and meaning, capturing the best of both worlds by rigorously studying personality processes in settings that simulate the natural environment.

4. Whatever their methodology, personality psychologists are always concerned with *validity: does a theory or test accurately predict or measure what it claims to?* Various varieties of validity include *face, predictive, convergent, discriminant,* and *construct validity.*

5. Researchers at different levels employ different kinds of *measures. Nominal* measurements are *names*—like numbers on baseball uniforms—that have nothing to do with order or magnitude; they are just identity tags. *Ordinal* measures *order* things from lesser to greater. The distances between small, large, and larger are not equal. *Interval* measures indicate *equal distances* between pairs of things. The inches on a yardstick are all equidistant. *Ratio* measures also have equal distances between marks, with the additional feature that "zero" really means nothing. "Zero" blood pressure means no blood is flowing.

6. Persistent problems for personality psychologists include the following:
   a. *dualism:* Descartes's view that the mind and body are separate entities
   b. *person versus situation:* the ongoing debate about whether *situation variables* or *person variables* are most important in shaping behavior
   c. *nature versus nurture:* how inherited genes/traits interact with learning to influence personality
   d. *freedom versus determinism:* the question of whether we have real choices or our behavior is determined by our circumstances
   e. *stability versus change of personality over time:* how stable traits interact with changing circumstances
   f. *reification:* the tendency to *"thingify"* or *"concretize" abstract concepts* such as anxiety or intelligence
   g. *extrapolation:* applying laboratory findings in real-life situations
   h. *diversity:* the extent to which theories formulated by "dead white males" can be broadly applied in today's global village.

   Some of these problems appear easier to understand from a zonal perspective.

Key Terms

Cartesian dualism   (12)
Clinical case studies   (7)
Construct   (4)
Countertransference   (1)
Extrapolation   (17)
Hypotheses   (4)
Minnesota Multiphasic Personality
  Inventory (MMPI)   (9)
Models   (4)

Paradigm   (5)
Personality   (3)
Personality zone   (5)
Probabilistic science   (6)
Reductionism   (13)
Reification   (16)
Theory   (4)
Validity   (11)

Web Sites

www.psych-central.com. Psych Central. An excellent Web site for general psychology with links for everything from a guide for APA style writing to graduate school information and even online psyche journals!

www.psywww.com/index.html. Psych Web. This site is ideal for students interested in psychology. It boasts job opportunities, journals, special articles, APA writing guidelines, and fun quizzes.

www.findingstone.com. Find a Therapist. You can use this site to locate the perfect therapist for you, take stress tests, read about hot current issues in psychology, or purchase E-therapy sessions, where you ask a therapist of your choice questions by e-mail.

www.psychnet-uk.com. PsychNet UK. A great site with alphabetized topics dealing with psychology. Look up anything you ever wanted to know here.

Learning on the Lighter Side

Bicentennial Man is our suggested movie for beginning our study of personality theories. In this movie, Robin Williams provides the voice for "Andrew," a robo-butler, who arrives in a packing crate and becomes part of a family. Early on, Andrew functions primarily in the *(Physiological and Situational Zones),* but as the movie progresses, he receives several electronic "upgrades" and begins to function increasingly like a human *(Insight and Social Zones).* In the end, we find ourselves emotionally experiencing Andrew's existential and theological dilemmas at the highest levels of abstraction, as he moves up the various levels from Person-as-Parts to Transpersonal-Seeker.

Looking Ahead

Maps of the mind. As we begin our journey, it is worth emphasizing that our *models* of personality are not the same as the realities they seek to delineate. Half a century ago, Alfred Korzybski (1958), the Polish American linguist and philosopher, pointed out that *maps* are *not* the same as the *territory* they depict. It is important to remember that the theories we are about to study are *maps* and *models* of personality, not the actual *territory*. Such maps and models exist in a profusion of varieties at many levels of analysis, but they all point to a central reality: the *living person*. So, although theories of personality are not real territories (they are *maps* and *models*), they are important maps, because they assist practicing psychologists in charting their pathways as they trek alongside their clients through the dregs of drug addiction, the mire of marital discord, or the deserts of depression. Theories of personality are important because they make a real difference in the lives of real people.

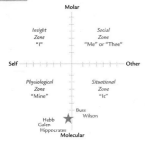

chapter 2

Ancient and Contemporary Compositional Theories of Personality

Hippocrates, Gerald M. Galen, Donald O. Hebb, Edward O. Wilson, and David M. Buss

IN THIS CHAPTER YOU CAN

1. Discover how the ancient Egyptians formulated the first compositional theories of personality, some forty *centuries* ago.

2. Learn that the Greek physicians, Hippocrates and Galen, moved the practice of medicine into the world of science by emphasizing *observation* and *experiments* in place of temple rituals.

3. Find that even wrong theories (such as *phrenology*) can stimulate scientific advances.

4. Learn how neurons work in groups known as *cell assemblies* or *neuronal groups.*

5. Wonder if sociobiologists are wrong in asserting that the primary purpose of your life is to *pass on your genes*—or, you may agree.

6. Learn how *evolutionary personality psychology* seeks to connect personality theory with our ancestral past. This proves to be *heuristically fruitful,* but *empirically difficult.*

A PERSONAL PERSPECTIVE

Suzette and Carl

Suzette

"Suzette" plops down with panache. Tucking herself into the corner of my burgundy leather couch, she spreads her arms across the back like an eagle in flight. In spite of her attempt to strike a pose of casualness, she appears small and frightened—like a little girl waiting for a dental appointment.

I glance at her intake information. Name: Susan Beckwith.[1] Age: 38. Marital status: divorced. Education: some college. Occupation: secretary/receptionist.

"You said on the phone your name was Suzette, but your chart says Susan. What would you like me to call you?"

---

1. Not her real name–adapted from a real case.

"My parents named me Susan, but I thought it was s-o-o boring. When I started high school I told everyone my name was Suzette—sounds French. (giggle) By the way, do I have to call you 'Doctor?'" (more giggling).

I survey Suzette while I weigh my response. The beginnings of wrinkles are discernible at the outside edges of her eyelids, even though her bright blue eye shadow all but obliterates them. Her voice is breathy and theatrical, and when she speaks she punctuates her conversation with giggles, much like writers use commas. Her hair is heavily streaked and the lettering on her too-small top reads:

IF I WANT YOUR OPINION

I'LL ASK FOR IT.

If one word could summarize her appearance, it would be: *incongruous*. She appears waif-like yet streetwise, childlike but flirtatious, exhibitionistic yet shy, casually indifferent while hungry for attention. She comes across like an eight-year-old playing a grownup—trying to dress like a provocative adult, but creating a caricature instead.

"What would *you* like to call me?" I reply.

"What about 'John!—No! Just kidding!" (extended giggling) "Gosh! I'm not sure what to call you, (giggles) 'Doctor' seems scary. I was always scared of doctors when I was little."

"Does 'Mister B' sound less scary?"

"I guess! Well, gee! You're the boss! . . . Right? (giggle) It's just this place seems . . . seems *spooky!*" (giggle)

"Spooky?"

"You got this big long couch and your chair looks like the kind shrinks use in movies. (giggle) And you! You've got the beard . . . the whole 'Dr. Freud' look. (giggle) I always wondered what it would be like to go to a shrink and now I'm here. (giggle) I can almost feel my head shrinking!" (extended giggling).

"So, tell me Suzette, why *are* you here? How can I be of help?"

In the weeks that follow, I always know when Suzette arrives—my secretary doesn't have to buzz me. Much as a siren alerts you to the arrival of an emergency vehicle, Suzette's laughter and repartee-on-the-run precede her down the hallway and into the waiting area. Engaging in animated banter—never serious conversation—with whomever she happens to meet, Suzette never arrives "quietly." Flirting variously with the janitor, UPS man, or security guard, she always manages to encounter someone who is happy to engage her.

The most characteristic thing about Suzette's personality style is that her intense emotions consistently cause chaos. She doesn't feel depressed, guilty, or ashamed like many of my other clients, because any negativity she might experience is immediately washed away by her emotional intensity. She appears engaged in a breathless, anxious attempt to entertain. Using her therapy sessions as a kind of Jerry Springer talk show, she regales me with vivid accounts of the previous week's escapades: fights with or among her various boyfriends, detailed accounts of affairs her friends are engaged in, gossip she picks up on her police-band scanner. Whenever I try to analyze her interactions or interpret her behaviors she becomes confused and puzzled. Simply put, Suzette seems incapable of depth. She finds herself so flooded by feelings and so overrun by emotions that thinking, planning, or logic have very little influence in her life. It's all about *feelings*. Personality psychologists refer to such emotionally intense personality styles as *hysterical* or *histrionic*.

It used to be thought (for reasons we'll explore shortly) that *hysterical* personality styles were found only in women. Today we know that this personality style is also present in men. However, because of social influences it is frequently more muted in males. Our culture expects a man to remain emotionally cool in a crisis. As one psychiatrist put it: "A man who shouts 'Oh, my God,' and bursts into tears on getting a flat tire might be towed away instead of the car" (Offit, 1995, p. 50).

Carl[2]

One morning, a few minutes before eight, Carl showed up at my office insisting that he *had* to see me *immediately*! Reluctantly he agreed to return at noon, when I promised to see him during my lunch break. Noon arrived, I grabbed a sandwich from the canteen, and Carl settled into his favorite overstuffed chair. The atmosphere in my office fairly crackled with the electricity of his excitement:

"O-o-o-o-o-h Dr. B, I . . . I . . . "

He stammered, as he tried to clear a path through his mental jumble. His pupils dilated with excitement, beads of sweat formed on his forehead, his body trembled slightly.

"Thanks for seeing me during your lunch . . . . I . . . I just *had* to see you today," he continued. "Our session yesterday was the most awesome thing that's ever happened in my life! It totally changed how I see things. It's like I walked out of here a new person! . . . I'll never be the same again!

I was curious, of course, so I swiftly glanced at my notes from our previous session, hoping to find a hint of what might have triggered Carl's epiphany. Nothing stood out. Carl continued:

"This therapy *really* is working. I feel like I've been born again—not like one of those religious types that gets worked up in a revival meeting—I feel like I'm a *totally changed* person!"

Throughout the past sessions Carl frequently colored his sessions with sensationalism—emotionally embellishing even ordinary events in order to "entertain" me. Yet now, this seemed different, as if something extraordinary had taken place–one of those illusive events that therapists sometimes call "a breakthrough." Still, I couldn't remember anything remarkable about yesterday's session. Carl slipped into silence. After a long lapse of wordlessness, I felt urged to prompt him.

"Please, go on," I said, "tell me what made such an impression on you?"

"But that's just it . . . Doc." His voice trailed off and I noticed his eyes were moist. He looked like a little boy about to burst into tears.

"That's why I *had* to come today," he murmured plaintively, *"I can't remember what we talked about!"*

What Carl had retained from yesterday's session—from *all* sessions, for that matter—was not intellectual substance, but *feelings*. For persons with histrionic personality styles, emotions override thoughts, and feelings wash away contemplation. Whether such emotions flood the individual like a tsunami—as with Suzette—or come in smaller waves as with Carl, *emotions* are paramount, and analytic thinking is minimal.

---

2. Not his real name—adapted from my clinical files.

From a *compositional* perspective, personality primarily results from one's biological makeup. We behave as we do because of our ingredients. That makes intuitive sense to us because when we were babies we shook our rattles in order to hear the little plastic pellets inside "respond" by bouncing around and making interesting sounds. As we grew older, we formed Play Doh into cigars or snakes because it was soft and pliable, and as adults we hit tennis or golf balls instead of cotton balls because they fly farther. The idea that composition determines behavior seems natural, and it began with the Egyptians some forty centuries ago.

COMPOSITIONAL THEORIES OF PERSONALITY

Compositional theories of personality in ancient Egypt—"Where is that wandering womb?"

Had Suzette been living in Egypt four thousand years ago, she would have been diagnosed as suffering from a "wandering uterus." That wouldn't have meant that she was viewed as promiscuous, only that she exhibited "jump-the-couch" emotional intensity. In ancient Egypt, physicians believed that a woman's womb was prone to "wander"—especially if she had not been sexually active. They thought that most female personality disorders were caused by shifts in the location of the uterus (or *hystera*). If a woman was deprived of sexual relations, it was believed that her uterus dried up, lost weight, and in a search for moisture rose toward the hypochondrium (a region just beneath the breastbone), blocking the flow of breath and resulting in breathlessness and anxiety.

An Egyptian document (*Kahun Papyrus*, circa 1900 B.C.E.) described a series of such symptoms that were thought to result from a displaced uterus (Veith, 1977, pp. 11–16). If the wandering womb came to rest near the abdominal cavity, it was believed to cause convulsions similar to epilepsy; if it fastened itself to the liver, the woman would lose her voice and grit her teeth; and if it attached to the heart it caused anxiety. Egyptian women who exhibited such symptoms were the *hysterical* (derived from the word *hystera*) forerunners of today's out-of-breath, flamboyant, emotionally supercharged Suzettes.

Compositional theories of personality in ancient Greece—"My bile made me do it!"

Nearly fifteen centuries after the *Kahun Papyrus* implicated the wandering uterus as the primary cause of hysterical personality, the Greek physician Hippocrates (460–377 B.C.E.) continued to endorse this notion by writing about the relationship of the wandering uterus to various other medical ailments. However, about five hundred years later, another Greek physician (Galen, ca. 129–210 C.E.) insisted that the womb did *not* wander, proposing, instead, that personality was controlled by **four humors**: *black bile, yellow bile, blood, and phlegm*. This was in keeping with the Greek belief that the cosmos was comprised of **four basic elements**: earth, air, fire, and water.

A **humor** was *a bodily fluid believed to produce a particular behavioral trait*. Galen compared the four humors to the four seasons of the year. Blood, for instance, corresponded to spring, a season Galen thought of as well tempered—neither too hot nor too cold, neither too wet nor too dry. He never clearly explained how blood, a well-tempered humor, could get along in a balanced way with three ill-tempered humors (black bile, yellow bile, and phlegm).

Although Galen described the four humors as "equal opposites," blood was, by far, the most important. Not surprisingly, bloodletting became a central technique for restoring balance in the body. If a patient suffered from an inflammatory fever, Galen recommended bloodletting to cool the inflamation. If a patient suffered from constipation or other problems that interfered with the passage of wastes, Galen believed bloodletting prevented harmful residues from accumulating. Incredibly, if a patient were bleeding to death from one part of the body, Galen recommended opening a vein in another location in order to stop the bleeding at the original site.

Four temperaments. Ultimately, Galen formulated his ideas about humors into a final theory of **four temperaments (personality styles),** *melancholic, choleric, sanguine, and phlegmatic.* Once Galen convinced his Greek pals that the womb was no longer playing hide-and-seek, personality theories became more straightforward. Depending on the particular proportions of earth, air, fire, and water that Mother Nature allocated as your share, you would end up with either a melancholic, choleric, sanguine, or phlegmatic temperament. Development didn't much matter. Those ancient Greeks weren't concerned with *how* an acorn became an oak, or a baby became an adult, nor did they worry about the motivational "why's" of behavior; all this was built into composition.

A "4 × 4" theory of personality. In Galen's final typology, *melancholics* were seen as depressed, anxious, pessimistic, and brooding; *cholerics* were restless and irritable; *sanguines* were bold, confident, and robust; while *phlegmatics* tended to be aloof, apathetic, and cold. Since the earth was the source of black bile, a predominance of which led to the melancholic personality type, and since air, fire, and water similarly led to the remaining temperaments, personality was intimately connected with the cosmos—directly deriving from the basic elements of the universe.

According to Galen's theory, if you felt bold and confident it was because you had an abundance of blood. You might be irritable and quick to fly off the handle because too much yellow bile was circulating in your body. You didn't *choose* to be audacious

TABLE 2.1

4 × 4 Compositional Theory of Personality

4 ELEMENTS	Earth	Air	Fire	Water
4 QUALITIES	Cold	Dry	Hot	Wet
4 HUMORS	Black Bile	Yellow Bile	Blood	Phlegm
4 TEMPERAMENTS/ PERSONALITY STYLES	Melancholic: Depressed Pessimistic Brooding	Choleric: Irritable Restless Explosive	Sanguine: Bold Robust Confident	Phlegmatic: Aloof Apathetic Cold

or adventuresome, you didn't *decide* to blow your stack, it was the natural outcome of your composition; your personality was biologically preordained. You couldn't choose your dominant emotions any more than you could choose your primary mode of locomotion: fish swim (because they have gills and fins), birds fly (because they are composed of feathers and very light bones), and we walk (because we have heavy bones and no wings).

Compositional theories of personality dominated medicine for forty centuries (not a bad life span as theories go!). Perhaps the simplicity of these theories accounts for their longevity: not a lot of constructs to quibble about, not much theoretical complexity, and only a few parts to keep track of (where has that womb wandered off to now?). For the Greeks, your personality was your poker hand: Mother Nature shuffled the deck and dealt the cards. You played your hand as best you could. Fish swim, birds fly, melancholics cry.

What about uniqueness? Compositional personality theorists (Egyptian, Greek, and contemporary alike) allow for some variety of expression within particular personality styles, but only within the boundaries set by composition. It's a bit like constructing a rocking chair; you could build it from a variety of different materials— wood, plastic, or metal. You might even decide to create an inflatable rocking chair made of rubber, but a rocking chair constructed of oatmeal or Jell-O would be compositionally dysfunctional.

Science trumps superstition. In light of our present understandings, we might smugly smile at some of the ancient formulations or cringe at the idea of opening a vein in one part of the body to stop the bleeding at another site. Still, looking at the work of the Greeks after twenty-five centuries, we can still be inspired today by how they employed careful observations and elementary experiments to refine their primitive ideas into better theories. It was Hippocrates' *scientific attitude* toward the practice of medicine (replacing temple rituals with experiments and observations) that gained him such respect during his lifetime and the title "Father of modern medicine" twenty-five centuries later. For instance, when writing about epilepsy, known in that era as "The Sacred Disease," Hippocrates said: "It is thus with regard to the disease called Sacred: it appears to me to be nowise more divine nor more sacred than any other diseases, but has a natural cause from which it originates like other affections" (Adams, 1939, p. 355).

Similarly, Galen was not satisfied with the anatomy and physiology taught by his teachers, so he carried out dissections of various animals to confirm or disprove existing theories. He demonstrated that he could stop the squeal of a pig with a very simple operation, thus refuting those who claimed that the voice came from the heart. Even more dramatically, Galen induced various paralyses by severing the spinal cord at different levels, thus demonstrating it to be an extension of the brain, connected to various nerves.

Summary of ancient compositional theories. We can summarize by noting that personality theories have spent nearly forty centuries in the *Physiological Zone,* and the idea that one's personality is determined by body composition is still popular. Although today we no longer believe that a wandering uterus causes supercharged emotionality, the pharmaceutical industry has largely convinced people that most emotional problems are due to a "chemical imbalance."

"Oh, yeah? Well, I think you're the one with the biochemical imbalance."

PHARMACEUTICAL THEORIES OF PERSONALITY

Zeitgeist

In American psychology, much of the twentieth century was dominated by what Hall and Lindzey (1957, p. 337) termed "buoyant environmentalism." Behaviorism was king, and compositional theories hinting of biological determinism were readily rejected. For example, although William Sheldon (1940, 1954) took more than 46,000 photos of male college students and categorized them into three body types that he believed were correlated with personality styles, he exerted almost no influence on American psychology.

Recently, however, the *zeitgeist* in American psychology has tilted toward compositional reductionism—piggybacking, perhaps, on the dramatic successes of molecular biologists in mapping the human **genome**, *the total set of genes carried by a species.* We may have stopped searching for Suzette's "wandering womb," but when we remark that "Suzette is depressed because of a *biochemical imbalance,*" we are speaking with a Greek accent.

The pharmaceutical mantra—"You have a biochemical imbalance!" Each year, billions of advertising dollars are spent trying to convince you that your biochemistry is out of balance—in need of alterations. If the "black bile" of depression is drowning you in darkness, try Prozac. If road rage makes you see red or twists your stomach into knots, think of it as a "Maalox moment"—head for your local pharmacy and you'll soon be calm again. The most common advertising theme today is "Why struggle *behaviorally* or fret *mentally,* when a pill can restore balance to your personality."

"Depression," we are told, "is a disease—like diabetes." Even if you're having a great time already, it might be even better with a "This-Bud's-for-You" upgrade. In a pinch? A "pinch" of Skoals could give you the lift you need. Such highly financed theories of personality encourage you to see yourself in *deficit-compositional* terms ("biochemical imbalance"). Drug manufacturers, brewers, and tobacco growers remain eager for you to remedy your "deficit" with their particular mood-altering remedies.

A flawed theory of personality. There are two major flaws in the pharmaceutical model of personality. First, it insists on one-way traffic in the direction of "bad chemistry causes sad behavior," instead of acknowledging that it works both ways: "sadness can also cause bad chemistry." It is seldom clear, for example, whether depression causes a bad marriage or a bad marriage causes depression. Either may be true. Sometimes both are.

Secondly, although drug manufacturers love to say that "depression is like diabetes," we do not understand the biochemistry of mood swings as clearly as we understand diabetes. Even psychiatrists who utilize electroconvulsive therapy (ECT) to zap the brains of severely depressed patients *speculate* that ECT improves brain functioning by raising neurotransmitter levels and facilitating better synaptic firings, thereby resulting in more optimal behavioral functioning. However, they are *not* certain. The anatomy and physiology of diabetes is clearly understood, but the biochemical mechanisms of moods, emotions, and traits are *not*!

CONTEMPORARY COMPOSITIONAL THEORIES OF PERSONALITY

Scientists working in the *Physiological Zone* utilize high-tech instruments (e.g., MRIs, microscopes, computers, X-rays, EEGs, and centrifuges) to observe, process, or spin down bodily ingredients in the hopes of better understanding how biochemistry influences behavior. Although these "ingredients" have been upgraded from "wandering wombs" and "humors" to molecules, chromosomes, or neurotransmitters, the precise relationships between chemical constituents and observed behaviors still remain elusive. For example, in his book titled *The Biological Basis of Personality*, Eysenck (1967) speculated that introverts are characterized by high levels of cortical arousal in the brain, but the details of that relationship remained unspecified.

Modern researchers investigate *functions* more than *ingredients*. Although modern compositional theorists focus on brain *activity* (e.g., cortical arousal, inhibition, activation, etc.)—not a wandering womb—as the foundation for personality traits, the challenge remains in understanding *how* the living brain manages to provide a stable foundation for enduring personality traits while simultaneously firing off hundreds of thousands of neurological volleys in all directions. As we shall discover when we study trait theories (in Chapter 4), "the devil is in the details."

We won't concern ourselves with the details now, except to note that at the dawn of the twenty-first century, compositional theories of personality remain highly popular but still speculative. They remain blurry regarding the precise nature of the relationships between brain activities and those enduring patterns of behavior we call personality traits. Nonetheless, optimism among brain scientists is at an all-time high and shows no signs of subsiding. For example, in spite of the fact that there exist an estimated 20,000–35,000 genes in the human genome, one contemporary geneticist has suggested that " . . . we'll get genes for personality" (Plomin, 2002, p. 46).

That sort of "dammit-we'll-find-the-needle-in-the-haystack" optimism is apparently contagious, because a majority of the public also appears to believe that we are on the verge of discovering *the* genes that trigger everything from Parkinson's disease, asthma, and prostate cancer, to skydiving, prostitution, and (yes) even worship. The cover article of *Time* magazine (October 25, 2004) proclaimed discovering THE GOD GENE with a subtitle: "Does our DNA Compel Us to Seek a Higher Power? Believe It or Not, Some Scientists Say Yes."

In contrast to their ancient Greek predecessors, who explained personality in strictly compositional terms ("too much yellow bile"), contemporary compositionists emphasize *functions* more than *composition*. While many believe that behavior is best understood in terms of the biochemistry of the "wet mind" (Kosslyn and Koenig, 1992), modern neuroscientists focus on *functions*. It no longer suffices to say that depression is *inherent* in black bile. Such extreme reductionism—from behavioral symptom to chemical composition—no longer flies.

Some Contemporary Physiological Research Techniques

Noninvasive sensors. Many studies conducted by contemporary personality psychologists working in the *Physiological Zone* involve **noninvasive sensors,** or *sensitive electrical recording devices that attach to but do not generally penetrate the skin.* This is a great advance over older devices where participants were literally wired to a machine. Current studies also use **telemetry,** *a system whereby recordings made at the body site are sent by radio waves, instead of wires, to a central data processor,* which permits accurate physiological recordings to be made while a person carries on normal daily activities. Such technology allows researchers to study processes over longer periods of time, including in natural (outside the laboratory) settings.

Electrodermal activity (skin conductance). Sweat glands are highly sensitive to activation by the **autonomic nervous system (ANS),** which is *that part of the nervous system that prepares the body for "fight or flight."* Whenever the ANS is activated, sweat begins to spill out onto skin surfaces such as the palms of the hands. Since salty moisture greatly enhances the skin's ability to conduct current, researchers can directly measure such changes by passing a weak (nondetectable) electrical current over the skin and measuring changes in conductance.

Cardiovascular activity. Similarly, the heart and its associated blood vessels are also highly sensitive to activation by the ANS. They respond with increased activity whenever anxiety or other "fight-or-flight" responses occur.

Brain electrical activity. Brain activity has traditionally been measured using the **electroencephalogram (EEG),** *a device that measures electrical currents of the brain using electrodes placed on the scalp.* More recently brain researchers have used imaging techniques (e.g., **positron emission tomography—PET** for *tracking radioactive glucose metabolism in the functioning brain,* and **functional magnetic resonance imaging—fMRI** for *distinguishing different body tissues on the basis of their chemical compositions*) that are completely noninvasive, requiring no wires or electrodes to be attached to the person's body. Such techniques will be increasingly utilized in future personality research (Canlin et al., 2001).

Modern Compositional Theories

Donald O. Hebb (1904–1985)—Cell assemblies. One of the pioneer researchers in shifting from composition to function was Donald O. Hebb. He began his research career studying single neurons, but soon shifted focus to what he called the **cell assembly,** *a group of neurons that develop into a functioning unit through repeated stimulation.* Hebb believed that connections could be established either between single neurons to form cell assemblies, or between neurons connecting one assembly with another. Thus, cell assemblies could vary in size: "The assembly might be made up of perhaps 25, 50, or 100 neurons, and building it up in the first place could be a very slow process, requiring many repetitions of the stimulating conditions" (Hebb, 1959, p. 628).

According to Hebb, each environmental object we experience fires a *cluster* of neurons. If we look at a pen, we might shift our attention from the point to the pocket clip and back again. Meeting a person for the first time, we might focus on the individual's eyes, face, or hair and even glance at the shoes before reestablishing eye contact. As attention shifts, different neurons are stimulated, but the entire package of stimulated neurons corresponds to one environmental object.

Hebb also believed that *people are motivated to seek an optimal level of arousal.* His theory was controversial, because most researchers at that time believed *tension reduction* was the goal of all motives, yet Hebb was saying that some people actually *seek stimulation.* Hebb's ideas became more fully developed in Eysenck's (1973) theory of extraversion (which we will discuss more fully in Chapter 4) and Zuckerman's (1984) theory of sensation seeking, which we shall discuss shortly.

Gerald M. Edelman—Neural Darwinism. Edelman appropriated Hebb's cell assembly (renaming it *neuronal group*) as his primary structural construct, and added the evolutionary element of *selection.* According to Edelman (1987, 1992), the brain constantly "prunes" unused or outmoded neuronal circuitry in favor of establishing new, more efficient configurations of neuron clusters. Edelman believes that neuronal evolution occurs along the same lines as macro-evolution but proceeds much more rapidly. Edelman asserts that each person's brain evolves in accordance with the principles of natural selection, but what is selected is not a longer beak or a greater wingspan, but a more optimally functioning *group of neurons.* This occurs not over eons of evolutionary time, but within each person's own life span.

Neuronal groups become stronger and function more efficiently with practice. For instance, the *neuronal groups* that are utilized in learning to ride a bicycle or play golf become more precise and automatic with use, whereas neuronal groups associated with events that occur less frequently—falling off your bike or completely missing the golf ball when you swing—become "pruned" by nonuse as one's skills in cycling or golf increase.

In Edelman's *neural Darwinism,* your brain is comprised of constantly changing, rapidly shifting neuronal groups. This sort of evolution takes place throughout the entire body, but occurs most rapidly inside the brain. Under the transforming power of *neuronal group selection,* your brain "prunes" and reshuffles neuronal groups in the service of better efficiency. We can never step into the same neurological stream twice. Although Edelman vertically moves from molecular to macro—from cellular biology to language acquisition—he always does so within the context of *biological* functioning. He views the living brain as a "symbol manipulator and a semantic engine" (1992, p. 240) that operates on biological principles:

> We must incorporate biology into our theories of knowledge and language. To accomplish this we must develop what I have called a biologically based epistemology—an account of how we know and how we are aware in light of the facts of evolution and developmental biology. (Edelman, 1992, p. 252)

FACING THE TOUGH TWINS

Is it Testable?

Hebb's laboratory work was carried out with great care and precision at the molecular level of analysis; however, comprehension of how cell assemblies operate—or even proof of their existence—is much more complicated. The broader applications of Hebb's work are more difficult to test, as he himself recognized:

> It is clear that this theorizing is at several levels. The hypothesis about synaptic change is a very "molecular" one indeed. Each neuron might have up to a thousand such contacts with other neurons. The cell assembly might comprise something of the order of a hundred neurons. (Hebb, 1959, p. 630)

Similarly, although Edelman formulates a sweeping theory of brain functioning by integrating Hebb's cell assemblies with Darwin's evolutionary theory, testability becomes extremely difficult. Concepts like *cell assemblies* or *neuronal groups* have been mostly of *heuristic* value, encouraging further research and reminding researchers at higher levels of analysis not to ignore the *biomolecular* foundations of *macro-behaviors*. Contemporary personality researchers (e.g., Zuckerman, Cloninger, and others) continue to clarify the relationships between molecular variables and macro-behaviors.

Zuckerman's sensation seekers. Zuckerman's recent research (1991, 1994, 1995) on **sensation seeking,** or *the tendency to seek excitement, take risks, and avoid boredom* provides an excellent example of how contemporary personality psychologists seek to connect *molecular* research findings to *macro*–behaviors. During the mid 1960s, Zuckerman and his colleagues conducted a series of **sensory deprivation experiments** *where participants were isolated in total darkness in a soundproof chamber.* He and his colleagues noticed that some people found sensory isolation extremely upsetting and often quit the experiments early (Zuckerman & Haber, 1965). So, Zuckerman developed a questionnaire (Sensation-Seeking Scale) to measure how much a person seeks thrills, excitement, and risk. He found that persons scoring high on the SSS experienced sensory isolation as *very* unpleasant, while those scoring lower on the SSS were able to tolerate it for longer periods.

In the subsequent three decades, Zuckerman and others have reported numerous interesting findings: skydivers score higher on sensation seeking than non-skydivers, cops who volunteer for riot duty score higher on sensation seeking than those who don't. High sensation seekers also report having a larger number of sexual partners and engaging in a wider variety of sexual acts (Zuckerman, 1984, 1991).

Recently (1991) Zuckerman has focused his research on the role of **neurotransmitters,** which are *chemicals that facilitate transmission of nerve impulses from neuron to neuron.*

Other researchers have also emphasized the role of neurotransmitters in shaping and steering our personalities. Gray (1972, 1990) has outlined a theory of personality based on *activation* or *inhibition systems* of the brain, and Cloninger has proposed a tridimensional model of personality based on the levels of three neurotransmitters (dopamine, serotonin, and norepinephrine).

Cloninger's tridimensional personality model. According to Cloninger and colleagues (e.g., Cloninger, 1986, 1987, 1991, 1999; Cloninger; Cloninger, Sigvardsson, & Bohman, 1988; Svrakic & Przbeck, 1993), people low in *dopamine* seek novelty and thrills, people with low levels of *serotonin* are sensitive to punishment and pain, and persons low in *norepinephrine* tend to seek rewards by working long hours to win approval.

That's how many have come to understand personality in the *Physiological Zone:* neurotransmitters—not wandering wombs—are the reason we seek excitement, suffer from depression, or experience mood swings. Zuckerman says: "The Greek physicians had the right idea, but the wrong humors . . . . As the ancient Greek 'psychopharmacologists' surmised . . . . disordered personalities are a result of imbalances in humors" (Zuckerman, 1995, pp. 325, 331).

This sort of physiological research continues to gain momentum, and personality psychologists are at the forefront of investigating how such *molecular* processes translate into *macro*-behaviors. For example, if your favorite activities include bungee jumping, skydiving, or white water kayaking, Zuckerman would bet his money that you have low levels of MAO; Gray would suspect that your brain's behavior activation system is overly engaged; whereas Cloninger would wager that you seek novelty, thrills, and excitement to make up for low levels of the neurotransmitter dopamine. It's not necessary to remember the details of each *Physiological Zone* theory. Just be aware that researchers are actively seeking to understand how one individual's biochemistry nudges him to ride a roller coaster, while another fairgoer calmly eats cotton candy or visits with friends. Whether you're a bungee jumper or a "bookworm," it's not about a wandering womb anymore—it's your neurotransmitters!

Is it Useful?

Definitely—both heuristically and practically. Enthusiasm remains high in the *Physiological Zone,* even though it is difficult to connect *macro*-behaviors to their proposed *molecular* foundations. Nonetheless, even in the practical world of clinical treatment, Cloninger's theory has had some influence, proposing that not all alcoholics drink for the same reasons. Cloninger and his colleagues reason that alcoholics low in dopamine begin drinking for novelty and pleasure, while those with low levels of serotonin begin drinking to relieve the stress and anxiety they chronically feel. Similarly, they would argue, some smokers smoke to relieve stress, while others smoke primarily for pleasure (Cloninger, Sigvardsson & Bohman, 1988).

Clarifying the links between *molecular* neurotransmitters and the *macro*-behaviors of addiction will continue to challenge researchers; however, such findings could ultimately refine how we treat people struggling with addictions. Researchers in the *Physiological Zone* seem to have captured the mood of the current *zeitgeist:* we want the best of both worlds. We want to understand vast macro-achievements such as language acquisition or macro-problems such as addiction, and we want to do it with the precision of a microbiologist. Even theology is not immune to such reductionistic zeal, recently spawning a subfield dubbed "neurotheology," in which investigators have used the latest brain-imaging technologies to study cortical functioning during prayer or meditation.

We located this chapter's *compositional* theories of personality low on the vertical axis because of their reductionistic emphasis on biochemical composition. We placed them near the center of the horizontal axis because there is no *agentic self* operating; no decision-making center in the human organism. Unlike the behavioristic theories in the *Situational Zone,* the driving forces in the *Physiological Zone* come from *within* the person, not from the external situation. In this portrait of personality there is no *agentic self*. "*I*" exists only weakly, as a biological "landlord" whose behavior is driven by *my* biochemistry or *my* genes—not by "*me*."

THE SOCIOBIOLOGY OF E.O. WILSON—PERSON AS GENE CARRIER

Next we consider sociobiology, a biologically based theory of personality with extremely broad reaches into the *macro-behaviors* observed at the levels of culture and society. Sociobiologists study the biological roots of communication, aggression, altruism, and other kinds of social interactions, blending (some might say *bending*) modern theories of genetics, evolution, psychology, and sociology in purporting to show that the primary purpose of existence is to pass on one's genes. Sociobiology aspires to ascend our entire grid—from the genes in the *Physiological Zone* to society in the *Social Zone*.

From a personality perspective, sociobiology boils down to a person-as-gene-carrier *compositional* theory. According to sociobiologists, passing one's genes to the next generation is done in two primary ways: (1) by selective breeding (as Darwin suggested) but also (2) by protecting one's relatives (who share many of one's genes). Even the apparently altruistic act of sacrificing one's life for another is seen by sociobiologists as designed to pass on more of one's genes. For example, when a worker bee sacrifices its life by stinging an intruder to protect the queen, this act of apparent "altruism" insures that many of that worker bee's genes will be passed on to the next generation. Consistent with this theory, sociobiologists have found that the more closely two animals are related, the more likely one will sacrifice itself to protect the other.

According to the sociobiologists, nothing but passing on genes *really* matters; we may take music lessons, create great art, or win a Nobel prize, but the *real* purpose for our existence is to pass on our genes.

> So what does all this make us? Genetic caretakers? Temporary housings for chromosomes? Slaves to tiny, coiled molecules that operate us by remote control? . . . What about the fact that we are learning classical guitar? That we have an interest in tap dancing and may start lessons soon? . . . That we are fine people and our parents are proud of us? How about all that? Chromosomes make us do all that? "No," comes the answer from the mountain, "but they don't care if you do"—as long as it doesn't interfere with your reproduction. Being such a splendid person may even help you find a mate more easily and leave more genes. (Wallace, 1979, p. 183)

At first glance, sociobiology appears broad and *interactional* (genes interacting with the environment), but closer scrutiny reveals sociobiology's "center of gravity" to be located in the lower right part of the *Situational Zone*—along with Pavlov and other physiologcally based behaviorists. For sociobiologists it is the environment *out there* that works through Darwinian selection to make certain that organisms pass on their most adaptable genes. E.O. Wilson, one of the founders of sociobiology, said that natural selection favors the selfish, those who "benefit themselves and their immediate relatives . . . . Had dinosaurs grasped the concept they might have survived. They might have been us" (1978, p. 197).

Using a few basic evolutionary principles, and a sweeping *macro*-analysis, sociobiologists deftly move up and down the vertical axis, illustrating their concepts with bees, ants, dinosaurs, and humans. Differences between species are minimized, commonalities are emphasized. It makes little difference whether you're a beetle or a baboon, a dinosaur or a dog; all are members of a single gigantic gene pool, bound to one another by strands of DNA. Genes count for more than culture—genes *produce* culture.

Background Check—The Early Life of Edward O. Wilson (1929–)

In his autobiography, Wilson states that "I became determined at an early age to be a scientist so that I might stay close to the natural world. That boyhood enchantment remains undiminished . . . ." (Wilson, 1994, xxii). When Wilson was seven years old, his dreams took a turn downward. Fishing off a dock while vacationing, he yanked a fish out of the water and one of its spines pierced the pupil of his right eye. Although the pain was excruciating, young Eddie was so anxious to remain outdoors that he didn't complain, but continued fishing; He recalled that several months later, when he returned home to Pensacola,

> the pupil of the eye began to cloud over with a traumatic cataract . . . . I was left with full sight in the left eye only . . . . I was destined to become an entomologist, committed to minute crawling and flying insects . . . . The attention of my surviving eye turned to the ground. I would thereafter celebrate the little things of the world, the animals that can be picked up between thumb and forefinger and brought close for inspection. (1994, pp. 13–15)

How Wilson dealt with his loss of vision appears consistent with Alfred Adler's (Chapter 8) theory of *compensation*. Wilson *compensated* for his visual deficiencies by hard work, and by modeling after people who toil valiantly in the face of great odds:

> I find it easiest to admire . . . those who concentrate all the courage and self-discipline they possess toward a single worthy goal: explorers, mountain climbers, ultramarathoners, military heroes, and a very few scientists . . . . (1994, pp. 27–28)

ASKING THE BIG FOUR QUESTIONS

Sociobiological theory tries to explain *macro* issues (e.g., language, society, culture, racism) in *molecular* (chromosomal) terms. It is an ambitious project that leaps from genes at the bottom of our vertical axis to society at the top-and back down again-skipping a lot of levels in between.

What are the Parts?

Genes and chromosomes. Each cell in the body contains tens of thousands of **genes,** which are *infinitely small units of DNA (deoxyribonucleic acid) that determine which characteristics living organisms inherit from their parents* (e.g., shape and color of a flower petal, height and sex of a child). Genes are the reason a pregnant dog has puppies instead of kittens or goldfish. Just as architects use blueprints to specify the materials for building a house, *genes* contain the "blueprints" for constructing **proteins,** the *chemical building blocks of our bodies.* Additionally, special proteins known as **enzymes** *activate thousands of chemical reactions* constantly occurring in our bodies. Genes are so small that they cannot be observed under an ordinary light microscope and must be studied with advanced laboratory equipment such as electron microscopes.

Long strings of DNA are twisted into packets known as **chromosomes,** which are *tiny threadlike structures that form into pairs of rods just before a cell divides, at which time each new cell receives one of the "rods" containing an array of genes exactly like that found in the original cell.* Each species has a characteristic number of chromosomes in each body cell. Humans typically have 46 chromosomes (23 pairs) in each cell, dogs have 78 (39 pairs), and corn has 20 (10 pairs). As we learned earlier, the total number of genes carried by a species is known as its *genome.* According to recent estimates, the human genome (first mapped in 2001 C.E.) is thought to contain approximately 20,000–35,0000 genes. However, when we realize that *each gene* provides assembly instructions for as many as 20,000 different kinds of proteins, the number of possible combinations becomes unfathomable.

The mapping of the genes alone is enough to *fill 200 telephone directories at 1,000 pages each*! However, since each gene provides protein blueprints for as many as 20,000 different proteins, it becomes mentally impossible to imagine all the possible combinations. It requires numbers so vast our imaginations are rapidly left behind. We have to use terms like "exabytes" (all the words ever spoken by everyone who ever lived amount to *five* exabytes) to even think about mapping all the possible protein combinations.

Cultural universals. Sociobiologists attempt to establish connections between *genes* (anchored in the *Physiological Zone*) and **cultural universals,** or *symbols or behaviors found to exist in every society* (studied in the *Social Zone*). If a particular category of behavior occurs in every culture, sociobiologists believe chances are good that it is genetically transmitted. For example, dress and adornment are found in all cultures:

> They [cultures] may develop distinctive customs of dress and adornment, perhaps parrot feathers in one place, strange patterns of head shaving in another, the ritual carvings of deep scars on cheeks and foreheads in yet another, but some pattern of dress and adornment is always found. (Barash, 1979, p. 4)

Since this cultural characteristic is found in virtually every society, sociobiologists argue that a dress-and-adornment gene must exist in the human gene pool.

Inclusive fitness. First described by Hamilton (1964), **inclusive fitness** *maximizes the transmission of one's genes into subsequent generations by (a) producing offspring, (b) assisting relatives to survive, or <u>both</u>.* Defined in this way, *inclusive fitness* broadens Darwin's notion of **individual fitness,** the *success in passing on one's genes.* Silverman (1987, p. 214) described *inclusive fitness* as "undoubtedly the most heuristic sociobiological principle of the past two decades."

Suppose you are a prairie dog, peacefully nibbling grass at the edge of your colony. Suddenly you spot a hawk or a coyote. What should you do? The safest thing is to rush for the nearest burrow, and that's what most prairie dogs actually do. Some, however, sound an alarm call to alert others. The "altruistic" alarmist stands a greater chance of dying (and therefore not passing on its individual genes) than does the non-alarmist who quietly scuttles for cover. Darwin would have said that the alarmist is *reducing* its *individual fitness,* and that over time, alarmist genes would not survive. But that is not the case, and sociobiologists explain "altruism" in terms of *inclusive fitness.* Although the alarmist might die in the process of warning others, the benefit to the kinship group is so high that some of the shared alarmist genes are passed on to future generations.

Inclusive fitness is sociobiology's term for **nepotism,** or *favoritism toward relatives,* which is widespread not only in politics but in society in general. However, according to sociobiologists, the driving force behind nepotism is not love, devotion to family, or other such lofty values; the driving force is the *propagation of one's genes* as far into the future as possible.

What Makes a Person Go?

A powerful whisper—"Pass the genes, please." In his book titled *The Whisperings Within,* Barash describes passing on one's genes to be the master motive behind all behavior:

> We human beings like to think we are different. We introspect, we are confident that we know what we are doing, and why. But we may have to open our minds and admit the possibility that our need to maximize our [evolutionary] fitness may be whispering somewhere deep within us and that, know it or not, most of the time we are heeding these whisperings. (Barash, 1979, p. 31)

These "whispers" are not portrayed as compelling forces that push us around, like the reinforcers and punishers of the radical behaviorists, yet they are powerful because they are *persistent.*

"My genes made me do it." The first chapter of Wilson's classic text, *Sociobiology,* he writes: "Human behavior—like the deepest capacities for emotional response which drive and guide it—is the circuitous technique by which human genetic material has been and will be kept intact. Morality has no other demonstrable ultimate function" (Wilson, 1978, p. 167).

You might worry that such a gene-centered approach could lead to a loss of personal choice or responsibility, and your misgivings would be well founded. Wilson deftly dispenses with any semblance of an *agentic self,* portraying the organism as nothing more than a vehicle for transporting genes: "Its primary function is not even to produce other organisms; it reproduces genes, and it serves as their temporary carrier" (Wilson, 1975, p. 3).

In the world of sociobiology you are not a unique person; you are merely a temporary transporter of chromosomal cargo, contributing to an unfathomably immense gene pool in a way that contributes to the continuance of your species.

Yet, paradoxically, in the final chapter of his book, Wilson suggests that people have some ability to choose—even if it is genetically constrained: "Fortunately this circularity of the human predicament is not so tight that it cannot be broken *through an exercise of the will*" (Wilson, 1978, p. 196, emphasis added). In the end, even Wilson cannot coherently apply sociobiological principles without allowing for *personal agency* (Wilson, 1978, p. 196).

What Makes a Person Grow?

Describing the life cycle of *mosquitoes,* Wilson (1978) writes:

> The mosquito is an automaton. It can afford to be nothing else . . . . The only way to run accurately and successfully through a life cycle in a matter of days is by instinct, a sequence of rigid behaviors programmed by genes to unfold swiftly and unerringly to the final act of oviposition. (p. 56)

Although admitting that humans have a greater learning capacity than mosquitoes, Wilson nonetheless insists that "the learning potential of each species appears to be fully programmed by the structure of its brain, the sequence of release of its hormones, and, ultimately, its genes . . ." (Wilson, 1978, p. 65).

Prepared learning refers to *genetically programmed patterns of behavior* that used to be called "instinct." For example, newborn kittens are born blind and barely able to crawl; however, when it comes to behaviors necessary for survival, kittens show remarkable ability to learn. With the aid of either odor or touch, each newborn kitten can memorize the route along the mother's belly to its own preferred nipple, and in laboratory tests can quickly discriminate an artificial nipple from the real thing.

Wilson does not suggest that people are as uncomplicated as mosquitoes or as instinctive as newborn kittens, however he believes that human development is genetically programmed, and that human behavior only makes sense when "valuated in the coinage of genetic advantage" (Wilson, 1978, p. 70).

What Makes a Person Unique?

This discussion can be brief, because *personal* uniqueness is given short shrift by sociobiologists, who see the individual primarily as a vehicle to preserve and spread *genes.* "Samuel Butler's famous aphorism, that the chicken is only an egg's way of making another egg, has been modernized: the organism is only DNA's way of making more DNA (Wilson, 1975, p. 3)." Another modern biologist characterized persons as "gigantic lumbering robots," whose primary purpose for existence is gene transportation and preservation:

> Now they [genes] swarm in huge colonies, safe inside gigantic lumbering robots, sealed off from the outside world, communicating with it by tortuous indirect routes, manipulating it by remote control. They are in you and in me; they created us, body and mind; and their preservation is the ultimate rationale for our existence. (Dawkins, 1989, pp. 19–20)

Genes—not people—are forever. In Dawkins's vision, people exist briefly as "survival machines," whereas genes—like diamonds—"are forever":

> Individuals are not stable things, they are fleeting. Chromosomes too are shuffled into oblivion, like hands of cards soon after they are dealt. But the cards themselves survive the shuffling. The cards are the genes . . . . They are the replicators and we are their survival machines. When we have served our purpose we are cast aside. But genes are denizens of geological time: genes are forever. (Dawkins, 1989, p. 35)

In the end, sociobiologists reduce individual personality to a few droplets of chromosomal material in an oceanic gene pool: "The individual is an evanescent combination of genes drawn from this pool, one whose hereditary material will soon be dissolved back into it" (Wilson, 1978, p. 197). According to sociobiologists, we exist only fleetingly, for the purpose of contributing a few grains of genetic grit to the vast Darwinian dust storms that swirl down through landscapes of evolutionary time.

FACING THE TOUGH TWINS
Is It Testable?

Sociobiologists attempt to support their ideas by citing research based upon nonhuman species. However, this is precisely the sort of questionable *extrapolation* that most personality researchers seek to avoid. Seeking to bolster their claim that culture depends on chromosomes, sociobiologists frequently cite animal *analogies* rather than experimental data. "Homosexual rape among parasitic worms" or "adultery among bluebirds" (Barash, 1979, p. 2) makes for colorful writing, but it is no substitute for careful science. Furthermore, many of sociobiology's core assumptions are based upon field observations and naturalistic findings, where proving cause and effect relationships is extremely difficult. Consequently sociobiology has never suffered from a lack of criticisms.

Early a sampling of criticisms on, Gould and Lewontin (1979) criticized sociobiology, pointing out that factors other than adaptation (e.g., genetic drift and genetic mutations) can cause evolutionary change. Although certain characteristics may have evolved for specific reasons in the past, they may be used in totally different ways in the modern world. Whereas in the past one might run to flee enemies, now one might run to prevent a heart attack.

Too many limiting conditions. More recently, Schwartz (1986) has criticized the numerous constraints, or *limiting conditions,* surrounding sociobiology's central claim that organisms exist primarily to maximize their reproduction. In the real world, argues Schwartz, organisms don't really *maximize* their reproductive fitness, because "It is always possible to design a hypothetical creature that could do better" (1986, p. 185).

Limiting conditions in the real world, argues Schwartz, are the context within which sociobiology must be evaluated: "It might be wonderfully effective for a cockroach to produce an offspring that is as big as an elephant, as fast as a gazelle, and as smart as a person, while remaining as able to thrive amid squalor as a cockroach, but there is no chance that such a string of happy accidents could occur" (Schwartz, 1986, p. 185).

Too many constraints on fitness. A related criticism is that there exist too many "constraints on perfection." Schwartz lists four: (1) *natural characteristics*—not all of an organism's natural characteristics are the product of natural selection; (2) *time lags*—through language and culture, environments have changed so rapidly that classical Darwinian evolution (which requires eons of time) cannot possibly keep up; (3) *cost-benefit analysis*—every adaptation comes at a cost; having a heavy shell to protect against predators may result in moving too slowly to find food; (4) *capricious environments*—if an organism slowly adapts to an environment, cataclysmic changes may render these glacially developed adaptations obsolete. The number of opossums that end up as roadkill illustrates Dawkins's point.

The problem from a scientific perspective is that as such constraints become more numerous, it becomes logically impossible to falsify—or prove—sociobiology's original claims: " . . . there is no possible finding—no pattern of animal behavior in nature—that can embarrass sociobiology" (Schwartz, 1986, p. 191).

Schwartz summarizes his critique of sociobiology with an observation that is as applicable to Freud's theory as to Darwin's—indeed to many of the "grand old theories" of personality. It comes back to a point we discussed earlier, *falsifiability:* "Theories with this much flexibility can explain everything; as a result, they explain nothing" (1986, p. 190).

Is It Useful?

Sociobiology has proven itself remarkably *heuristic,* igniting intense criticism as well as stimulating research over a broad range of topics. We will illustrate this by looking at sexuality from a sociobiological perspective.

A sociobiological perspective on sexuality. Since sociobiology maintains that our main purpose in life is to pass on genes, it's hardly surprising that many of its core ideas involve sex. However, since sexual relations are among the most intimate encounters that take place between humans, sociobiologists have drawn some of their most intense criticism on this topic. We will briefly consider some of the criticisms and responses.

Critique: Sociobiology provides a built-in, genetic rationale for oppression and takes the romance out of sex:

> If men dominate women, it is because they must. If employers exploit their workers, it is because evolution has built into us the genes for entrepreneurial activity . . . Such a theory . . . serves at the personal level to explain individual acts of oppression and to protect the oppressors against the demands of the oppressed. It is "why we do what we do" and why we sometimes behave like cavemen. (Lewontin, Rose, and Kamin, 1984, pp. 236–237)

Response: A Johnny-Appleseed view of sexuality. Men behave not as "cavemen," brutalizing their victims into submission, but more like Johnny Appleseed, happily spreading their seed throughout the countryside.

Critique: Sociobiology makes it appear that females were designed to manufacture a few eggs and rear a few offspring, while men were designed to promiscuously propagate and leave child rearing to women. Even such unacceptable behaviors as rape and incest are seen to be "normal." To the dismay of many ethicists, feminists, and others who argue for equal treatment of women, sociobiologists seem to suggest that pleasure, intimacy, or fidelity are not the primary reasons for sexual relations; instead—no surprise here!—sexuality is about the *transmission of genes.* According to sociobiologists, the double standard of sexual fidelity is simply a biological given, necessary to insure widespread dissemination of genes. A woman produces only about four hundred eggs in her lifetime, whereas a man releases upwards of 100 million sperm with each ejaculation. In most species, assertiveness is the most efficient male strategy: "It pays males to be aggressive, hasty, fickle, and undiscriminating. Human beings obey this biological principle faithfully" (Wilson, 1978, pp. 123–125).

Response: Sociobiology simply "tells it like it is." Sociobiologists answer the last two criticisms—and a host of others like them—with the assertion that sociobiology simply tells it like it is:

> Evolution simply *is*—or better yet, evolution *does*. It says nothing whatever about what ought to be . . . . No one would think it awful to state that a man has a penis and a woman, a vagina. Or that a man produces sperm and a woman, eggs. But when we begin exploring the behavioral implications of these facts somebody is sure to cry "Foul." If male–female differences are sexist, we should put the blame where it really belongs, on the greatest sexist of all: "Mother" Nature! (Barash, 1979, pp. 89–90)

SUMMARY OF SOCIOBIOLOGY

Storytelling

Richard Lewontin (1998), an expert in both genetics and evolution, disagrees with Barash's assertion that "evolution *is*," insisting instead that "we will never know." Lewontin states that it is difficult to prove many evolutionary assertions, even when obvious anatomical differences exist between species. He points out the problem of origins is studied by attempting to reconstruct characteristics in long-extinct forms that lived in long-extinct environments. Although it is possible to exclude some explanations, it proves impossible to choose among the many available alternatives: "Did the dinosaur *Stegosaurus* use the large leaflike plates along its back for physical defense, for appearing deceptively large to potential predators, for sexual attraction, for thermoregulation, for all four, for some at one time and others at another, or none of the above? We will never know" (Lewontin, 1998, p. 119).

Lewontin concludes his analysis on a note designed to raise our cautions regarding the kind of grand theorizing seen in sociobiology:

> Finally, I must say that the best lesson our readers can learn is to give up the childish notion that everything that is interesting about nature can be understood. History, and evolution is a form of history, simply does not leave sufficient traces, especially when it is the forces that are at issue. Form and even behavior may leave fossil remains, but forces like natural selection do not. It might be interesting to know how cognition (whatever that is) arose and spread and changed, but we cannot know. Tough luck. (Lewontin, 1998, p. 130)

Harvard paleontologist Stephen Jay Gould (1978) observed that sociobiology, like Christian fundamentalism, is not *falsifiable*. In both cases it is possible to make up a "just-so story"—an explanation of behavior that sounds plausible, and may be true, but is not provable by solid evidence.

On the positive side, other scholars (Crawford, Smith & Krebs, 1987) see sociobiology to be a *heuristic* synthesis of ideas from population genetics, behavioral ecology, ethology, comparative psychology, and behavior genetics. They believe its eventual impact may be as great as that of psychoanalysis and behaviorism.

A fitting conclusion for our study of sociobiology as a theory of personality can be found in Barash's introduction to his *Whisperings* book, in which he informs the reader that he will be telling " . . . stories of rape in ducks, adultery in bluebirds, prostitution in hummingbirds, divorce and lesbian pairing in gulls, even homosexual rape in parasitic worms." Barash states that the real subject of his book is "human behavior, viewed from the perspective of sociobiology" (1979, p. 2).

However, by employing terms like "prostitution in hummingbirds" or "homosexual rape in parasitic worms" Barash invites his readers to gloss over the enormous species differences that must exist between "rape" among worms and rape among humans. Such analogizing hardly rises to the level of comparing apples with oranges, it's more akin to comparing apples with alligators.

For those wishing contemporary in-depth analyses, Alcock (2001) has written a positive critique entitled *The Triumph of Sociobiology,* and Segerstrale (2000) offers a negative critique entitled *Defenders of the Truth.*

EVOLUTIONARY PERSONALITY PSYCHOLOGY—THE "GRAND FRAMEWORK" OF DAVID M. BUSS

We conclude our chapter with a brief look at how evolutionary psychologists view personality. The broad sweep of evolutionary psychology appears similar to that of sociobiology, spanning our hierarchy from micro to macro—from genes to society. However, in place of sociobiology's attempt to explain all behavior as motivated by the urge to deliver one's genes to the next generation, evolutionary psychologists seek to explain how various personality traits have *evolved* over eons of time. They see personality as an "adaptive landscape" where certain *traits* (e.g., agreeableness) became a permanent part of human nature because of their adaptive value in promoting successful social relations within ancestral hunter–gatherer groups. Consequently, evolutionary psychologists are particularly interested in traits that influence mating, fighting, or fleeing.

What Is the Nature of Human Nature?

Intrinsically evil? In his novel *Lord of the Flies* (Golding, 1962), the author tells of a group of English schoolboys marooned on a deserted island following a plane crash. All starts out well enough, but by the end of the novel, most of the innocent schoolboys have become frenzied murderers. Shortly before his death, one of the boys concludes that there is no beast stalking the island, "It's only us" (p. 103). Other writers have painted a similarly dark portrait of human nature (e.g., Morris, D. *The Naked Ape* (1967). Ardrey, *The Social Contract,* 1970) in which humans are seen as aggressive beasts by nature.

We will discover in Chapters 6 and 7 that Freud's psychoanalysis had a similarly pessimistic tilt, as did Melanie Klein's revision. The Judeo-Christian concept of original sin and humankind's resultant "fallen nature" is consistent with the Buddhist belief that human desires are fundamentally flawed: permeated with selfishness, self-serving, and aggression. William James, in his classic work *The Varieties of Religious Experience* (1902), noted that nearly all religious viewpoints find something fundamentally wrong with human beings (which is why we inflict so much pain and suffering on one another). Religion calls us to renounce the beast within and to transcend our natural evil propensities through religious beliefs and practices.

Goodness and light? By contrast, Jean-Jacques Rousseau (1712–1778) argued that human beings are born fundamentally pure and good, but civilized society corrupts the natural goodness of such "noble savages." In our era, Carl Rogers and other humanists (Chapter 11) have embraced Rousseau's positive portrait, arguing that parents and teachers contaminate the natural goodness of infants and children by requiring them to meet societally derived "conditions of worth" before fully accepting them.

Survival of the aggressive? Aggression is central to Darwin's survival-of-the-fittest perspective, but it isn't the whole story. While it's believed that surviving hominids successfully outwitted or outran large predators, they also had to cope with tiny parasites as well. Not only did they have to contend with immediate life-threatening situations, they also had to successfully survive the more subtle threats of food shortages, harsh climates, and so on. In all this, Darwin saw *aggression* playing an important role, but he also saw *adaptation* as equally important. Ultimately, survivors were fighters, adaptors, and replicators—able not only to successfully defend themselves, but also adept at change and propagation. Darwin's final portrait of human nature was painted mostly in the dark colors of aggression, but it was complemented with the lighter tones of adaptation and creativity. And there was a halo in the picture that puzzled Darwin—*altruism.*

Darwin's dilemma—"whistle blowers" get eaten first. Altruism, *an unselfish concern for others,* was a riddle that Darwin's selectionism could not solve. Why would any organism put its own survival at risk to save another? As we just learned, Hamilton's (1964) concept of *inclusive fitness* provides at least a partial solution to Darwin's dilemma. Modern evolutionary theorists now argue that putting oneself at risk to protect *next of kin* frequently carries out evolution's imperative (to pass on one's genes) more efficiently than seeking one's immediate safety. If you save numerous members of your extended family (especially those most closely related to you, such as siblings, uncles, aunts, and first cousins) many of the genes you carry will effectively be passed on to future generations. Thus, in modern thinking *inclusive fitness* encompasses everything—even altruism—that enhances perpetuation of one's genes.

Evolutionary Personality Psychology—A Distal Perspective

Proximal versus distal perspectives. Evolutionary personality psychology, like sociobiology, begins with a strong biological base, but rapidly ascends to higher levels of abstraction (e.g., in the *Social Zone*). Not only does Buss move *up* several levels of abstraction (e.g., from genes to mating strategies), he also moves *back* (billions of years in time) seeking to connect **distal:** *(historically remote)* ancestral events with **proximal:** *(nearby or immediate)* personality variables.

Three goals. David Buss describes **evolutionary personality psychology** as *a "grand framework,"* providing *"tools for understanding the core of our human nature and the important ways in which we differ from one another,"* thereby linking the field of personality with *"what is known about the processes that govern all forms of life"* (1991, p. 486, emphasis added). Buss states that evolutionary personality theory has three main goals:

> 1. Identification of adaptive problems confronted by ancestral human populations . . . . 2. Correlation of currently observable personality factors with the proposed problems of ancestral populations . . . . 3. Identification of the major individual differences in the ways humans adapt and deploy dispositional strategies. (1991, pp. 476–477)

Notice that goal 1 is a *distal* goal, 2 is *proximal* and *distal,* and 3 is *proximal.* Buss carefully researches *proximal* individual differences in mating strategies, for example, but is forced to speculatively connect his research findings to imagined *distal ancestral societies.*

ASKING THE BIG FOUR QUESTIONS

What Are the Parts?

Personality—an adaptive landscape. Buss sees **personality** as *an adaptive landscape containing fundamental traits that underlie behavioral diversity.* For example, although humans in various cultures eat a diversity of foods, they share a worldwide preference for foods rich in sugar, fat, salt, and protein. Why does everyone, everywhere, love sweets? The reason is clear to evolutionists: "We are primates and some of our ancestors spent a great deal of time in trees, where they ate a great deal of fruit. Ripe fruit is more nutritious than unripe, and one thing about ripe fruit is that it contains sugars" (Barash, 1979, p. 39).

In much the same way, evolutionary personality psychologists argue that we have evolved "sweet" personality traits because of their survival value. Since our ancestors had to rely on group support to survive, traits such as friendliness, agreeableness, conscientiousness, and trustworthiness had survival value and were passed on. Thus certain "basic" personality traits (analogous to the universal preference for sweet foods) consistently emerge across the *adaptive landscape of personality* because they enhance survival and reproduction.

Evolved traits are *evaluative markers by which humans judge one another in terms of survival goals.* Thus, Peabody (1985) found that fewer than 3 percent of trait terms are evaluatively neutral, and Hogan (1983, 1996) asserted that traits represent evaluations of others as exploiters of, or contributors to, group resources. Considering the *Big Five* traits (Chapter 4) from an evolutionary perspective, Buss (1991) argues that traits such as *agreeableness* and *conscientiousness* "are the most important psychological dimensions of our social adaptive landscape" (p. 472). Graziano and Eisenberg (1997) assert that for animals living in groups, *agreeableness* is crucial for accomplishing coordinated, survival-enhancing action. Evolutionary personality psychologists seek to understand such traits in the broader context of evolutionary biology.

The giraffe's long neck—a model of the evolved mind. Evolutionary biologists cite the giraffe's long neck as an example of a genetic variation that got passed on because having a longer neck enabled the giraffe to obtain food elevated above the ground, and ultimately to survive and to reproduce. Evolutionary psychologists see a far greater achievement in the *evolved mind:* "The evolution of the human mind may be more subtle and more difficult to discern than the evolution of the giraffe's neck, but it is far and away more spectacular, and it is first and foremost what makes human beings distinctively human" (McAdams, 2000, p. 59).

Brain versus mind. Evolutionary psychologists distinguish between the **brain,** *a biological organ,* and the **mind,** *what the brain does.* Pinker captures this bio-cognitive evolutionary perspective in a single sentence: "The mind is a system of organs of computation, designed by natural selection to solve the kinds of problems our ancestors faced in their foraging way of life, in particular, understanding and outmaneuvering objects, animals, plants, and other people" (1997, p. 21).

Cognitive niche. Much as plants and animals survive by occupying a certain environmental niche, humans use their minds to carve out what Pinker (1997) calls a **cognitive niche,** or *sophisticated technologies and a language with which to synthesize it all.* Pinker contends that "All human cultures ever documented have words for elements of space, time, motion, speed, mental states, tools, flora, fauna, weather, and logical connectives" (pp. 188–189). This enables humans to incorporate these various words into grammatical sentences and to reason and speculate about invisible entities such as diseases, future weather, and absent animals (pp. 188–189).

What Makes a Person Go?

Mate selection—then and now. In *The Evolution of Desire* (1994) Buss uses contemporary patterns of mate selection—across a variety of diverse cultures—to illustrate evolutionary psychology. Over a period of five years, Buss enlisted the help of fifty collaborators from thirty-seven cultures on six continents and five islands to study how humans currently (*proximally*) choose mates. In all, he surveyed 10,047 people worldwide, and concluded that "sexual strategies do not require conscious planning or awareness" (1994, p. 6). He asserts that "just as a piano player's sudden awareness of her hands may impede performance, most human sexual strategies are best carried out without the awareness of the actor" (1994, p. 6).

This is hardly the "Harry-meets-Sally" amorous encounter we see in the movies or imagine in our own romantic fantasies; but Buss insists that in order to understand mating, we must "face our evolutionary heritage boldly and understand ourselves as products of that heritage" (1994, p. 16). So if it's not romance, what determines how we choose our mates? According to Buss, it's *sexual selection.*

Sexual selection. Over a century ago Darwin wondered why birds with bright feathers survived, since such coloration would make them more visible to predators. He concluded that the peacock's bright feathered displays led to *reproductive success,* because peahens preferred dazzling, colorful mates. However, it's not only brilliant plumage that bestows a sexual advantage. The male African weaverbird attracts a mate by first building a nest and then hanging upside down from the bottom of the nest flapping his wings to attract the attention of passing females. The female approaches and carefully examines the nest, poking and testing for as long as ten minutes. Only if the nest passes muster will she consider the builder as a potential mate.

Among animals, attracting potential mates, competing for them, and successfully retaining them involve a complex combination of genetic endowments, situational considerations, and strategic behaviors. Buss believes that much the same thing occurs with humans, but at an even more complex level:

> Today we are confronted with novel sexual circumstances not encountered by any of our ancestors, including reliable contraception, fertility drugs, artificial insemination, telephone sex, video dating services, breast implants, tummy tucks, "test tube" babies, sperm banks, and AIDS . . . . But we confront these modern novelties with an ancient set of mating strategies that worked in ancestral times . . . . Our mating mechanisms are the living fossils that tell us who we are and where we came from." (Buss, 1994, p. 222)

Such talk about "living fossils" may leave some less than convinced, because whatever *distal evolutionary* reasons theorists might propose for sexual activity (e.g., passing on genes), the *proximate* motivation for sexual activity is that it *feels good now!*

What Makes a Person Grow?

Integrating the person and the situation. Evolutionary personality psychologists attempt to connect the situational circumstances of the present with the biological structures and personality traits an organism has evolved over vast eons of time. From this perspective, emotions, moods, preferences, goals, and desires are seen as *codetermined* by natural selection and sexual selection.

Evolutionary psychologists believe that our various emotions and coping mechanisms evolved because of their adaptive features (Russell, Lewicka, & Niit, 1989). *Sadness* is socially adaptive because it elicits aid from others (Ellsworth & Smith, 1988). *Anger* alerts others that the angry person's strategies for adapting have been interfered with (Buss, 1989). *Jealousy*, among men, is a major source of intersexual violence— worldwide—because it has evolved to guard against paternity uncertainty (Daly & Wilson, 1988).

What Makes a Person Unique?

Darwin focused on how *individual* adaptations enhanced survival and procreation. Modern evolutionists have tended to focus on how *groups* or *species* survive. Evolutionary personality psychologists have again focused on the individual's unique psychological mechanisms, while at the same time putting it all under the big tent of evolutionary biology.

FACING THE TOUGH TWINS

Is It Testable?

History, science, or storytelling? *Distal evolutionary* variables, purporting to describe processes that occurred millions of years ago, belong in the domain of history rather than of science. Lewontin's "storytelling" critique of sociobiology is equally relevant for evolutionary psychology. He reminds us that "We should not confuse plausible stories with demonstrated truth. There is no end to plausible storytelling" (1998, p. 129).

The million-generation gap. E.O. Wilson called evolution one of three great mythologies (Marxism, religion, and evolution). In this context *mythology* does not necessarily mean *falsehood,* it simply means an unprovable epic story. Gould (1978) has argued that sociobiology, like Christian fundamentalism, is not *falsifiable.*

Although Buss and his colleagues describe evolutionary psychology as "a new and rapidly growing scientific perspective" (Larsen & Buss, 2002, p. 129), it might be more accurate to describe it as a rapidly growing *heuristic* perspective. Even Buss admits that the adaptations crucial to evolutionary theory were:

> forged over the long expanse of thousands or millions of generations, and we cannot go back in time and determine with absolute certainty what the precise selective forces on humans have been. Scientists are forced to make inferences about past environments and past selection pressures. (Larsen & Buss, 2002, p. 157)

No amount of contemporary research can overcome the fact that our ancestral origins are buried in the historical dust of thousands if not millions of generations. Whatever inferential theories we might insert into this chronological crevasse, they are not scientifically falsifiable. For example, although Buss's extensive cross-cultural research regarding mate selection was inspired by his evolutionary perspective and offers interesting insights into current mate selection strategies, it proves little about our *origins.*

Snakes, science, and stories. Based on the Darwinian story, evolutionary psychologists suggest that the universal fear of snakes is evidence that snakes "were hazards in our evolutionary past" (Larsen & Buss, 2002, p. 158). According to the Judeo–Christian story of origins, God cursed the serpent, making it crawl on its belly and putting "enmity" between it and humans (Genesis 3:15). Freud saw snakes as symbols of the penis and suggested that the widespread uneasiness about snakes reflects unresolved sexual conflicts. Clearly there are a number of possible explanations for snake phobias, few of them falsifiable. If it is this difficult to establish the origin of a simple snake phobia, think of the complexities involved in establishing the origins of human nature.

Heuristic myths? Seeking to understand human nature from an evolutionary personality perspective takes us beyond the realm of empirical science into the domains of history, philosophy, literature, and theology. If we assert that, "each living form can be viewed as an evolutionary experiment, a product of millions of years of interaction between genes and environment" (Wilson, 1978, p. 17), this would then turn out to be the longest running experiment ever conceived, with no hope of resolution in our lifetime nor in the lifetimes of our great, great . . . great grandchildren.

On the other hand, evolutionary theory can be seen as a heuristic program that highlights the importance of *distal ancestral contexts,* as a source from which more *proximal* theories of personality can draw ideas and inspiration. In the able hands of researchers like David Buss (1994), evolutionary theory has generated scientifically resolvable questions about *proximal* issues such as human mating strategies, but it will necessarily remain inferential regarding ancestral origins.

Contemporary work in the laboratory can never produce empirical data directly supporting or falsifying core inferences about ancestral origins. It is a long leap from finding common patterns of mating in contemporary cultures, to re-creating an ancestral mating ground.

Is It Useful?

Buss believes that evolutionary psychology enriches the study of personality by providing a framework within which the individual differences and unique behaviors of contemporary humans can be understood as evolving from a shared evolutionary history. Much of Buss's research has focused on the important but controversial area of human mating strategies. Evolutionary psychologists have frequently offended feminists and humanists in much the same way as sociobiologists did when they argued that rape is an efficient way for a man who cannot successfully compete for a mate to pass on genes. Reasoning about such emotionally charged behaviors from a solely biological perspective leaves the impression of insensitivity. Buss's analysis is more ethically sensitive and even suggests ways to reduce violence.

For example, Buss notes that women rate sexual aggression at 6.5 on a scale where 7.0 indicates maximum distress, whereas men rate the same behaviors performed by women as 3.2 or only lightly disturbing. Some men even indicate that such acts would be sexually arousing. Buss concludes that "men consistently underestimate how unacceptable sexual aggression is to women . . . . Consequently men may be prone to use aggressive sexual acts because they fail to appreciate how distressing such acts really are to women" (1994, p. 146).

SUMMARY OF EVOLUTIONARY PSYCHOLOGY

Evolutionary interactionism. Fuller (1994) criticizes sociobiology for stressing "the universals of human nature" while minimizing within-species differences, and Buss contends that every behavior—without exception—is a joint product of environmental influences *interacting* with *"evolved psychological mechanisms"* (1994, p. 16). Buss believes that both sociobiologists and behaviorists err in explaining individually based mechanisms in global terms, and he criticizes behaviorists for ignoring biological and psychological mechanisms inherent in humans.

The fundamental situational error–ignoring calluses. He illustrates the importance of biological givens by citing the biological adaptation system that produces calluses: "If I walk around on bare feet for a few weeks, my soles and heels develop thick calluses . . . . If I ride around in my car for a few weeks, however, my tires do not grow thicker" (Buss, 1991, p. 460).

Next, he refers to similar psychological givens:

If a person responds to the presence of a group by conforming (e.g. Asch, 1956) or by social loafing (Latane, 1981) but a cockroach, a rat, or a chimpanzee does not conform or loaf in response to identical environmental inputs, then there must be something about the *psychological mechanisms* of humans that differs from those of the cockroach, rat, or chimp. (Buss, 1991, p. 461)

Evolutionary personality psychology is seen by Buss and other advocates as providing a "grand framework" that is comprehensive enough to include biology and Darwinian evolutionary theory, yet individualized enough to avoid the "one-size-fits-all" broad-domain laws of sociobiology and behaviorism. The "superfactors" of trait theories are understood by evolutionary personality psychologists as evaluative markers, enabling persons to appraise one another in terms of characteristics deemed to be important for survival.

Levels of analysis. Buss analyzes human nature at three levels: genotypic (genetic), phenotypic (behavioral), and social. "Separate levels of analysis are often useful precisely because they provide insights not available through, or connected with, alternative levels" (Buss, 1984, p. 1143).

In a recent book, Larsen & Buss (2002, p. 137) proposed a three-tiered evolutionary hierarchy. At the top is modern evolution's *inclusive fitness theory* and underneath are middle-level and lower-level mini-theories (e.g., regarding altruism, jealousy, sex differences, universal emotions, and so on) from which hypotheses and predictions can be derived.

Chapter Summary

We began this chapter by discovering that personality theory began, not with Freud, but with the Egyptians, who first formulated a theory of the hysterical personality. This was the first recorded *compositional* theory of personality, which claimed that hysterical symptoms resulted from a wandering womb. Fifteen to twenty centuries later the Greeks expanded the notion of compositional causation, stating that everything in the universe was ultimately composed of earth, air, fire, or water. Galen transformed this into his theory of four personality types (melancholic, choleric, sanguine, and phlegmatic), each evolving from one of the four universal elements.

In modern times, compositional theories of personality have retained wide appeal, as people seem to intuitively believe that understanding our biochemical composition is the key to understanding behavior. This view is strongly promoted by pharmaceutical companies who have much to gain by convincing people to ingest various mind- and mood-altering drugs.

Contemporary researchers working in the *Physiological Zone* emphasize *process* more than *composition*. Beginning with Donald Hebb's *cell assemblies,* researchers have shifted attention from composition to processes. Edelman adapted this idea, calling them *neuronal groups* and maintaining that such groups were regularly "pruned" in accordance with Darwinian use-it-or-lose-it principles. Zuckerman, Cloninger, Gray, and other contemporary personality researchers have worked tirelessly in the *Physiological Zone* to understand the *molecular* foundations of sensation seeking, addictions, and other such *macro*-manifestations.

Next, we discovered that sociobiologists try to explain *all* behavior—from birds chirping and bees buzzing to human beings writing poetry and making love—in terms of one single principle: the biological imperative to *pass on one's genes*. Sociobiologists believe that this principle permeates the entire biosphere and is sufficient to explain all behavior. Critics (of whom there are many) disagree, but sociobiology has proven to be *heuristically* lively, generating spirited arguments about many important issues.

We concluded with a discussion of evolutionary personality theory, showing how it attempts to demonstrate that broad personality traits have survived because of their *adaptive value* during our ancestral past. Buss urges us to avoid separating behavior into biologically determined versus environmentally determined, and to seek "interactional" answers to the nature–nurture dichotomy: "human action is inexorably a product of both. Every strand of DNA unfolds within a particular environmental and cultural context" (1994, p. 17). Even evolved biological or psychological components must—like calluses—be acted on by the environment before change will take place; i.e., one must walk barefoot in order to develop calluses.

Although Buss appears to embrace an interactional view of persons versus situations, his balance is tilted in the direction of biology. Growing calluses is not the product of humanistic self-actualization or of existential choices. Calluses *happen*— indirectly, without our noticing them or choosing them.

Points to Remember

1. *Compositional* theorists emphasize that the makeup of a thing causes it to behave in a particular way. Rubber balls bounce because they're *composed* of rubber; cotton balls don't bounce because they're *composed* of cotton fibers. Eggs break instead of bouncing, and even a rubber ball won't bounce in a sand box. Ancient personality theories similarly emphasized *compositional causation*: you were depressed because you were composed of too much black bile, or irritable because you were made of too much yellow bile. Today, compositional researchers believe that someone is depressed because of a "biochemical imbalance."

2. The ancient Greeks believed the cosmos was composed of four *essential elements:* earth, air, fire, and water. Similarly, people were thought to be composed of four primary *fluids:* black bile, yellow bile, blood, and phlegm, which gave rise to the four basic *temperaments.* In this theory of personality, *composition* was king: birds flew because they were comprised of feathers and wings, fish swam because they had gills and fins, and melancholics wept because they contained too much black bile.

3. Hippocrates kept careful treatment records, carried out simple experiments, performed dissections, and utilized natural methods instead of temple mysticism in practicing the healing arts. Galen exhibited many of the same attitudes, employing experimentation and observation to enhance his understanding of anatomy, physiology, and disease processes. Although they were surrounded by ignorance, superstition, and tradition, these men helped to move the field of medicine out of the mystical shadows of the temples and into the mainstream of scientific inquiry.

4. Galen believed that persons are *composed* of four humors, which result in the four main personality styles: *sanguine* (enthusiastic, humorous) resulting from a preponderance of blood; *choleric* (irritable, quick-tempered) resulting from too much yellow bile; *melancholic* (depressive, having low initiative) as a result of

too much black bile; and *phlegmatic* (apathetic, listless) as the result of excessive phlegm or mucus. The *energy* or *motives* that fuel personality were "built in" to the composition of the humors.

5. Hebb believed that neurons, like members of a string quartet, *work in harmony.* Edelman renamed them *neuronal groups,* and asserted they follow Darwinian laws of natural selection. Groups that function together on a regular basis remain operational, while those that fire only occasionally are "pruned." As a result, the brain constantly evolves—endlessly changing and reconfiguring itself for greater efficiency.

6. *Sociobiology* is a modern compositional theory that attempts to explain all sorts of macro-social behaviors in terms of *genes.* People are designed primarily to spread their genes. All other goals, aspirations, intentions, and dreams function in the service of passing one's genes to the next generation.

7. Sociobiologists emphasize *cultural universals* (behaviors found in every society) because they believe that if something is universal it must be the result of genes. *Inclusive fitness* refers to behaviors that enhance the *kin group's* survival, even at the risk of endangering oneself. From a Darwinian point of view, it doesn't make sense for one member of a group to sound the alarm when an enemy is sighted, because this places the "whistle blower" at higher risk. However, it makes perfect sense in terms of *inclusive fitness,* because even if the "whistle blower" dies, its close relatives live another day to pass on much of the genetic material.

8. For the sociobiologist, all personal drives, motives, goals, and achievements are measured according to the Johnny-Appleseed yardstick of how much genetic material you pass on to the next generation. Everything else is secondary, nothing else really matters.

9. When criticized for being sexist and insensitive to issues of equality, justice, and fairness, sociobiologists reply, "Blame 'Mother' Nature; we just tell it like it is."

10. Sociobiology is difficult to prove or disprove. Testability and falsifiability are difficult enough in more narrow contexts (e.g., laboratory-derived theories of learning), but in the case of a theory that stretches across eons of time and multiple levels of analysis, "proof" is almost impossible to establish. Sociobiology serves an important *heuristic* function in attempting to explain personality functioning in both cultural and biological terms. But explaining far-reaching cultural macro-structures (e.g., kinship groups or political systems) solely in terms of the *reproductive imperative* (to pass on one's genes) seems questionable. As a theory of personality, sociobiology is reductionistic—ultimately compressing everything to DNA.

11. *Evolutionary personality psychology* examines personality within the broader context of *human nature,* seeking to correlate currently observable personality patterns with the adaptive problems of ancestral human populations. Although evolutionary theory proves to be *heuristically fertile,* it is difficult to *empirically*

prove or disprove the connection between our present experience and our ancestral past—between our *proximal* personality traits and our *distal* progenitors.

12. Evolutionary theory itself has evolved from Darwin's *natural selection* and *sexual selection,* to Hamilton's principle of *inclusive fitness,* to the *bio-cognitive synthesis* proposed by evolutionary personality psychologists. Using mate selection as an illustration, David Buss defines personality as an *adaptive landscape* of psychological mechanisms that have proven successful in the past, and have therefore evolved into the present. *Evolved emotions* and an *evolved mind* have enabled humans to occupy a particular *cognitive niche,* much as plants and animals occupy an environmental niche. Buss sees the sociobiological and behaviorist perspectives as too general, and proposes that evolutionary psychology has the capability *of integrating the person and the situation* (not a new idea among personality psychologists) with humankind's ancestral past.

Key Terms

Altruism   (34)

Autonomic nervous system (ANS)   (30)

Brain   (45)

Cell assembly   (30)

Chromosomes   (36)

Cognitive niche   (45)

Cultural universals   (36)

Distal   (43)

Electroencephalogram (EEG)   (30)

Enzymes   (36)

Evolutionary personality psychology   (43)

Evolved traits   (44)

Four basic elements   (25)

Four humors   (25)

Four temperaments (personality styles)   (26)

Functional Magnetic Resonance Imaging (FMRI)   (30)

Genes   (35)

Genome   (28)

Humor   (25)

Inclusive fitness   (36)

Individual fitness   (36)

Knockout mice   (55)

Mind   (45)

Nepotism   (37)

Neurotransmitters   (32)

Noninvasive sensors   (30)

Personality (according to Buss)   (44)

Positron emission tomography (PET)   (30)

Prepared learning   (38)

Proteins   (36)

Proximal   (43)

Sensation seeking   (32)

Sensory deprivation experiments   (32)

Telemetry   (30)

Web Sites

Galen

www.iep.utm.edu/g/galen.htm. The Internet Encyclopedia of Philosophy. This is a biography of Galen's life and training, as well as an explanation of his methodology.

www.collectmedicalantiques.com/bloodletting.html. **Collect Medical Antiques.** This interesting Web site provides pictures and description of some common instruments used in bloodletting.

Edelman

www.pbs.org/saf/1101/segments/1101-5.htm. PBS. Contains a synopsis of Edelman's interview with PBS, called "Monastery of the Mind."

www.nsi.edu. The Neurosciences Institute. Visit this Web site to get a peek into what life is like working as a neurobiologist and researcher. Click on the link that says "A Day at the Institute."

Zuckerman

www.bbc.co.uk/science/humanbody/mind/surveys/sensation/index.shtml. The BBC. Find out if you're a sensation seeker. Visit this Web site to take a quiz.

Wilson

psychologytoday.com/articles/pto-19950701-000024.html. Psychology Today. This fascinating article, titled "My Genes Made Me Do It," explores the personal and societal effects of blaming our behavior on our genes.

Learning on the Lighter Side

Are you biologically wired to be a dad or a cad? A mom or a madam? Personality researchers Simpson and Gangestad (1991) developed a measure of sociosexual orientation designed to differentiate between those seeking a single committed sexual relationship characterized by monogamy and high investment in children, and those characterized by multiple partners and less investment in children. The following three questions are typical. How would you answer them? (Answer them quickly, in the privacy of your own mind, before reading further).

1. **How often do you fantasize about having sex with someone other than your current partner? (circle one)**

   1. never
   2. once every two or three months
   3. once a month
   4. once every two weeks

   5. once a week
   6. a few times a week
   7. nearly every day
   8. at least once a day

2. **I would have to be closely attached to someone (both emotionally and psychologically) before I could feel comfortable and fully enjoy sex with him or her.**

1	2	3	4	5	6	7	8	9
I strongly disagree							I strongly agree	

3. **Sex without love is OK.**

1	2	3	4	5	6	7	8	9
I strongly disagree							I strongly agree	

Do you think differences in sexual styles are "hard-wired" into your personality, or do they reflect how you were raised? Are your preferences a matter of choice? Are differences gender related?

In what is arguably the best sex survey ever conducted (by interviewing randomly selected subjects from cities, towns, and rural areas throughout the entire country), Michael, Gagnon, Laumann, and Kolata (1994) reported that 59 percent of men said that sex with a stranger would be "very appealing" or "somewhat appealing," compared to 15 percent of women.

What do you think? Do such differences prove that sociobiology and evolutionary psychology are correct in arguing for "biologically built-in" differences in the urge to spread one's genes? Or do these disparities reflect dissimilarities in how we raise boys and girls? Would you want to share your responses to these three questions with your significant other? Do you think he or she would find your answers upsetting? Why or why not?

Movies

Lord of the Flies (1963, 1990) narrates experience of a group of schoolboys stranded on an island who descend into savagery. A dark view of human nature. Some viewers preferred the 1963 version as more true to the book and less laced with profanity.

Forrest Gump (1994) is the entertaining and embellished story of a mentally challenged man who transcends his *mental composition* to live a rich and fulfilling life. An optimistic perspective on human nature.

Human Nature (2002) is a good transition film to our next chapter (on conditioning and learning). It stars Tim Robbins as a behavioral scientist who conditions mice to have table manners. It also shows how Tim works with a man who was raised as a gorilla. Robbins conditions this man for entry into the world of complex social interactions.

Looking Ahead

It would be misleading to leave you with the impression that compositional theorists are the only ones who attempt to build theories bit by bit from the bottom up. Behaviorists, whom we will consider in the next chapter, are equally committed to a careful, bottom-up, piece-by-piece assembling of personality, but their building blocks aren't *internal (person-based)* biles or genes; they use *external (situation-based)* constructs such as reinforcement or punishment. Behaviorists believe that the environment engraves itself upon the person's mind, which is a *"blank slate" (tabula rasa)*, to form an aggregate of response tendencies that comprise the personality.

For behaviorists in the *Situational Zone,* personality is always *reactive*—always *responding to consequences dispensed by the environment*—never self-starting or self-steering. As with the sociobiologists, we will again find personal agency completely absent: "A person is not an originating agent; he is a locus, a point at which many genetic and environmental conditions come together in a joint effect" (Skinner, 1974, p. 168).

Conditioning/learning theories are formulated at a level of conceptualization somewhere above genes and neuronal groups, but well below the individual person or family system. Behaviorists see the individual as a trained animal, responding in predictable ways to stimuli in the environment. As we continue our vertical ascent, exploring personality theories at higher levels of analysis, we will see the importance of careful experimental work at each zone of the vertical axis. As we have just seen, sociobiology is not so much wrong as it is untested and unproved for the many levels of analysis that exist between *socio* and *biology*. With thousands of genes *interacting* with the environment in complex and unpredictable ways, a proper understanding will require hard work at all levels of analysis.

We conclude with an "appetizer" to illustrate the important role that psychologists in the *Situational Zone* fulfill when they intersect with other scientists at various levels of analysis. We could think of "knockout" mice as illustrating creative interaction between geneticists working in the *Physiological Zone* and behaviorists working in the *Situational Zone.*

"Knockout" mice—assisting in the understanding of alcoholism. Currently there exist thousands of different strains of **"knockout" mice:** *animals in which a single gene has been disabled or altered.* For example, Bowers et al. (2005) have analyzed genetically altered *"knockout"* mice (missing certain genes). They have discovered that such mice are more sensitive to alcohol than standard mice. While this may be a very small step toward understanding alcoholism among humans, it illustrates the kind of "multi-zone" experiments that are currently underway. Such studies would be impossible without the collaborative work of biochemists who understand proteins, biologists who create the "knockout" animals, behavioral psychologists who condition and test the mice for learning differences, and personality psychologists who study how impulsivity in humans relates to excessive drinking.

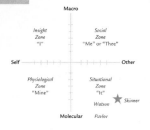

chapter 3

Conditioning/Learning Theories of Personality

Person as Trained Animal

Ivan P. Pavlov, John Watson, and Burrhus F. Skinner

IN THIS CHAPTER YOU CAN

1. Learn that *behavioral psychologists* (also known as *Stimulus-Response* psychologists or *Situationists*) are among the best animal trainers in the world—training pigeons to assist in rescue missions and goldfish to detect pollutants.

2. Recognize that behavioral psychologists focus on *situational triggers* and *consequences* of behavior, and view psychological problems *as learned/conditioned behaviors* that can be directly unlearned.

3. Find out that John B. Watson, the "father" of behaviorism, saw personality as *reactive*, rather than starting or steering the person. He once defined personality as a *"reaction mass."*

4. Discover that *systematic desensitization* and *learned helplessness* are modern applications of behavioristic principles.

5. Learn the **ABC**s of Watson's theory: **A**ssociated **B**ehaviors **C**onnect—behaviors that occur together become connected.

6. Learn the **ABC**s of Skinner's theory: **A**ntecedents lead to **B**ehavior, followed by **C**onsequences. Of these three, Skinner considered **C**onsequences to be the most important.

7. Realize that *immediacy* is one of the most powerful variables in psychology.

8. Notice that as a *method of conditioning*, Skinner's operant theory is without serious competitors; however, as a *theory of personality* it appears *overly simplistic*, viewing persons as trained animals without inner selves—relying completely on situational variables to account for behavior.

A PERSONAL PERSPECTIVE

Dave[1] Consults a Behavior Therapist

Dave is a 35-year-old man with a history of military service. While in the service, ten years previously, he was accidentally struck in the right eye with a rifle butt during training. At the time, Dave experienced pain and impaired vision in his right eye and was initially hospitalized for three weeks. He was followed as an outpatient for three months, but extensive ophthalmological and neurological assessments failed to find a physical basis for his continued visual problems. He returned home, lived with his

---

1. Not his real name—adapted from case studies by Brady & Lind, 1961; Bryant & McConkey, 1989.

parents, and held a succession of semiskilled jobs. Dave considered himself to be functioning pretty well considering how poor his vision was in his "injured" eye.

Ten years later he again sought treatment at a local V.A. facility, reporting that he was now "totally blind" in his right eye. After examination by an ophthalmologist, who could find no basis for Dave's blindness, he was referred to Dr. Mallory, a clinical psychologist, for **behavior therapy,** *a treatment that utilizes conditioning techniques to change specific problematic behaviors, rather than encouraging insight as a way of changing personality more generally.*

The following exchange illustrates the no-nonsense, pragmatic approach taken by behavior therapists. If one believes that "mental illness" is nothing more than faulty learning—and they do—it makes no sense to waste time exploring "psychological dynamics," so most behavior therapists focus on relearning more appropriate behaviors.

■ ■ ■

Dr. Mallory: According to your chart you had an eye injury while you were in the service, which recently got worse. Is that right?

Dave: Right.

Dr. Mallory: What happened recently to make it worse?

Dave: I'm not sure what happened, Doc. All I know is that three days before Christmas, I was out with my mother-in-law doing some last-minute shopping when all of a sudden I went totally blind in my right eye and I could barely make things out with my left eye. My left eye is OK now, but I still can't see anything with my right eye.

Dr. Mallory: Since Christmas—that was about three weeks ago—have you experienced any improvement in your right eye?

Dave: Nope, it's even worse.

Dr. Mallory: Worse?

Dave: Yeah, worse. After it first happened—I mean when I got hurt in the service—I could still see shapes and silhouettes, and it stayed that way for ten years, but now I can't see anything.

Dr. Mallory: According to your records, you have had all kinds of tests—vision tests, EEGs, CT scans—and nothing shows up.

Dave: (with slight irritation) I don't care what all the tests show—or don't show—I just know I can't see *anything* out my right eye.

Dr. Mallory: Dave, I'd like to work with you to retrain your right eye using some new technology. OK?

Dave: I guess, but I doubt it'll help.

Dr. Mallory: Well, let's give it a try anyway. . . . Over here I've got a video monitor with three triangles appearing on the screen and three indicator buttons on the panel under the screen. During your therapy sessions, a loud, obnoxious noise will come on at various times. If you press the correct button under the screen, it will immediately shut the noise off. If you hit the wrong button, the noise will continue until you find the correct switch. OK?

Dave: OK.

Dr. Mallory: All right then, let's get started. I'm going to cover your good eye with gauze so you have to rely only on your blind eye. It's a bit like kids with amblyopia, or "lazy eye," who wear a patch over the good eye in order to make the lazy eye work.

Dave: But my right eye isn't "lazy" or whatever fancy word you called it, Doc, it's *blind*! I can't see nothing out if it!

Dr. Mallory: I understand, but I'd like to try this anyway, sometimes we can "coax" some vision out of the blind eye. Let's go ahead and give it a try, OK?

Dave: I guess . . . You're the doctor.

Dr. Mallory: Any other questions before we get started?

Dave: Since I can't see, how will I know which button to press?

Dr. Mallory: Just keep trying until you hit the correct button.

■ ■ ■

At this time Dave's good eye was covered with a patch and he was seated in front of a video screen on which three triangles appeared. One of the three triangles on the screen was always rotated to be in a different spatial orientation from the other two. The button directly below the "odd" triangle would turn off the noise each time. Since Dave's good eye was covered with a patch, only his "blind" eye could benefit from visual cues.

Five Months Later

Dr. Mallory: Congratulations, Dave. Your accuracy in pushing the correct button on the first try has improved dramatically.

Dave: Really? I thought I was doing better, but I didn't know how much—and I'm not sure why.

Dr. Mallory: You have done a lot better. During the first couple of weeks you were correct on about 40 percent of your first tries. By the second month you were at about 60 or 65 percent, and now you're at about 95 percent. Pretty impressive, I would say.

Dave: I guess I'm a good learner, huh?

Dr. Mallory: But there's nothing to learn.

Dave: What do you mean, "Nothing to learn?"

Dr. Mallory: I mean that there was no pattern to learn, no rules or code to figure out, the button that shut off the noise was randomly programmed—different every time.

Dave: I don't get it. How come my scores kept improving?

Dr. Mallory: By using your right eye . . . it has gradually gotten strong again.

Dave: (visibly agitated) But that's impossible! I told you, I can't see anything out my right eye.

Dr. Mallory: Well, apparently you see more than you realize, because your left eye had the patch covering it, so the only way you could have pushed the correct button on the first try was by seeing which triangle was "tilted."

Dave: (visibly agitated) Couldn't I have guessed the right button?

Dr. Mallory: Sure you could have guessed, Dave, but you would have been right only about 30 or 35 percent of the time by guessing—not 90 or 95 percent. You're definitely seeing something with that right eye.

Dave: I'll have to think about that, Doc.

Dr. Mallory: Yes you will. Sometimes our minds can play tricks on us. Your eye must have improved so gradually that you didn't notice it.

Dave: Maybe so.

Commentary

Dave's blindness is a classic *hysterical* symptom. Behavioral clinicians have suggested that the parents of individuals who develop hysterical personality styles tend to be neglectful when the child is healthy and remorsefully overattentive when the child is sick or distressed, thus *reinforcing* the child's attention to somatic symptoms. Psychoanalysts have proposed that the hysterically inclined child comes from a home where dependency and passivity are encouraged or where sensual stimulation predisposes the child to develop bodily symptoms. In cases of inappropriate sensual stimulation, children frequently repress conscious awareness of the sexual features of such stimulation and what remains is an overinvestment in bodily functions (and/or ailments).

As illustrated in Dave's case, behavior therapists typically spend little time analyzing underlying or "unconscious" factors, choosing instead to focus on specific behavioral problems (hence the term *behavior* therapy). Also typical for behavior therapists is the manipulation of *situational* factors. Instead of using medical terms (e.g., health, illness, diagnosis, pathology, or therapy) and transporting these into the domain of psychology by adding a psychological prefix (e.g. *mental* health, *mental* illness, *psycho*diagnosis, *psycho*pathology, or *psycho*therapy), behavior therapists see "mental illness" as learned maladaptive habits. They do not refer to "symptoms" or "unconscious motivation," but focus instead directly on the obvious problem behavior. Thus, while Freudian therapists might see a child's bed-wetting as a "symptom" of anger toward mother, or an "unconscious regression" in order to extract nurturance from the parents, behavior therapists would treat bed-wetting as *the* primary problem and seek to directly modify it. This follows from their learning-theory orientation, in which all behavior is seen as learned or conditioned, and the job of the therapist is to rearrange the situational variables in such a way that desired behaviors are reinforced and unwanted behaviors become extinct. In Dave's case we saw how the behavior therapist essentially ignored (failed to reinforce) Dave's visual concerns and arranged situational conditions that reinforced correct visual responses while simultaneously ignoring "blindness."

By contrast, in Chapter 6 (psychoanalysis), we will learn how "Anna O.," a young woman with a hysterical personality style, was cured of her physical ailments by "talk therapy" that uncovered the underlying psychological causes. A young physician by the name of Sigmund Freud found the treatment of "Anna O." so fascinating that he subsequently founded psychoanalysis using similar techniques.

From the perspective of nearly four thousand years of treating hysterical problems, we see the pivotal importance of personality theories. Whether a therapist hunts for a wandering womb, opens a vein to drain off bad blood, sets up a video game, or encourages a person to talk depends directly on how the therapist views personality. In hospitals, schools, churches, corporations, and everyday life, theories of personality

"Oh, not bad. The light comes on, I press the bar, they write me a check. How about you?"

profoundly influence how we view others—and ourselves.

In this chapter we will learn how behaviorists have treated a wide variety of specific problems such as such as cigarette smoking (which is seen as learned behavior), bed-wetting (viewed as a the result of irregular conditioning), or phobias (resulting from past traumatic experiences). They have successfully treated aggressive behaviors such as biting, hitting, schoolyard bullying, or spousal abuse. Behavioral sports psychologists have used relaxation training, visualization exercises, and other behavioral techniques to help athletes overcome performance anxiety and enhance their chances of winning.

Much of what is called "sex therapy" is really behavior therapy designed to reduce anxiety about sexual "performance" and facilitate relaxing and pleasurable interactions. In fact, there is much overlap between hypnosis, relaxation training, biofeedback, and other direct, body-based treatment techniques. Later in this chapter we will discuss how behavior therapists use relaxation techniques to treat phobias. The success rates in treating phobias with behavioral techniques is so high that it is one of the few areas of clinical practice where therapists could offer money-back guarantees without fear of losing their shirts.

Person as Trained Animal

Behaviorists—or Stimulus-Response psychologists as they are sometimes called—think of people as similar to trained animals. The primary difference between "wild" and domesticated animals is *training*. You train your dog not to defecate on the carpet; you teach your cat to scratch a "kitty post" rather than your sofa. Behavioral psychologists utilize animals as *models* of *conditioning and learning,* and view people as simply "higher animals" (with language skills)—more complex than rats or pigeons, but essentially similar. Bypassing language and other human complexities, behavioral psychologists view their animal-based research as more "objective"—more "scientific"—than research conducted by personality psychologists at higher levels of analysis. And, compared with humans, conditioned animals *are* more predictable; so predictable that Yale psychologist Susan Brandon says, "I always tell the kids in my lab that if the session data looks strange, then search for research error or an error on the part of the apparatus because the error is virtually never in the animal's conditioning, unless the animal is ill" (Azar, 2002, p. 42).

No paradigm exerted a greater influence on American psychology during the twentieth century than behaviorism. While psychoanalysis and other influences dominated clinical practice, in academic circles behaviorism ruled. Much of behaviorism's appeal derives from its characteristically American combination of pragmatism, frontierism, and optimism. Behaviorists claimed nearly limitless possibilities for their conditioning technologies, which they declared were based upon "scientific laws of learning" (read: animal-based laboratory studies).

In America, at least, the twentieth century could be termed the "Century of Behaviorism," and that influence still remains strong. The American Psychological Association recently designated the beginning of the twenty-first century (2000–2010) the "Decade of Behavior."

Behaviorism's "Birth Announcement"

In 1913, John Watson famously proclaimed that behaviorism could shape your child into virtually any kind of adult you might desire:

> Give me a dozen healthy infants, well-formed, and my own specified world to bring them up in and I'll guarantee to take any one at random and train him to become any type of specialist I might suggest—doctor, lawyer, artist, merchant-chief and, yes, even beggar-man and thief, regardless of his talents, penchants, tendencies, abilities, vocations, and the race of his ancestors. (Watson, 1913, pp. 158–177)

But behaviorism hasn't proven quite that powerful. Watson couldn't take *any* baby *at random* and produce a mathematician. Notice a couple of the caveats that he slipped in: *healthy* infants, *well-formed*. Even the father of conditioners didn't promise to produce a rocket scientist or a brain surgeon from a baby born with Down syndrome. Watson wanted "well-formed" babies with correspondingly "well-formed" IQs before he promised that his conditioning factory could start turning out doctors and lawyers.

In our day, the branches of behaviorism's family tree have been significantly pruned by cognitive psychologists (Chapter 5), who highlight the importance of linguistic abilities and cognitive processing. Genetic researchers have demonstrated a significant inherited component in a wide variety of clinical problems such as ADHD (Eaves et al., 1997; Nadder, Silberg, Eaves, Maes, & Meyer, 1998; Rhee, Waldman, Hay, & Levy, 1999); autism (Rutter, Morley, & Graham, 1972; Szatmari, Jones, Zwaigenbaum, & MacLean, 1998); mood disorders (Farone & Tsuang, 1990; MacKinnon, Jamison, & DePaulo, 1997); and schizophrenia (Gottesman, 1991; Cannon, Kapiro, Lonnqvist, Huttunen, & Koskenvuo, 1998). Still, because of its reliance on research, behaviorism remains a redwood in a pine forest of less-investigated theories. As the following examples illustrate, behaviorists are the planet's most proficient animal trainers.

Rescue Pigeons, Goldfish, and "Robotic" Rats

Behaviorists have used their workhorse—conditioning—to take advantage of certain highly developed sensory systems in particular animals. For example, in the late 1970s, Navy psychologist Jim Simmons used conditioning techniques to train pigeons to assist the Coast Guard in rescue missions. Skeptical at first, the Coast Guard eventually described Simmons's project as "the best daylight search system" they had worked with (Azar, 2002, p. 43). The pigeons had a 93 percent accuracy rate, which, when combined with human searchers, increased to nearly perfect. At that time human flight crews were accurate 38 percent of the time. Pigeons can no longer outperform computer-aided searching, but with their excellent vision and a long history of conditioning, they are prime candidates for screening baggage, or performing other quality-control tasks. In the mid 1960s, pigeons trained to pick out defective drug capsules for a drug company were performing with 99 percent accuracy.

Goldfish have been conditioned to detect chemical pollutants present in water, and dolphins have been trained to recognize hostile movements near U.S. military operations. Recently, rats have been fitted with electronic "back packs," enabling researchers to steer the rats with radio signals, which the animals experience as a "touch" to either the right or left whiskers. This device also enables researchers to stimulate the pleasure centers of the rat's brain. Pairing such a guidance system with reward-based conditioning, researchers can train their "robo-rats" to assist in drug detection or to search through rubble for survivors, where the rodents' size, agility, and keen sense of smell enable them to outperform human rescuers (Azar, 2002, p. 42).

Behaviorist Theories of Personality

Behaviorists have not usually been considered personality psychologists, because they have emphasized the importance of the *situation*—often to the exclusion of the *person*. In place of individual differences (e.g., Allport's [1937] *ideographic* approach) behaviorists have emphasized *commonalities* across species in what they term *"laws" of learning*. They have followed a bottom-up, piece-by-piece, situationally based approach to analyzing behavior, and have shown a strong aversion for even speaking about internal constructs such as the *self*.

Behaviorists employ the term "personality" reluctantly—if at all—to mean nothing more than *consistent behavior resulting from conditioning history interacting with situational stimuli*. This is why the *Situational Zone* is at the bottom right quadrant of our grid—distant from higher-level formulations that include either *social situations* or the *self*. Still, we consider behaviorists to be personality psychologists because they aspire to explain why we behave as we do, and how we develop and change over time while still retaining our uniqueness and consistency—all areas of great interest for personality psychologists.

The *Situational Zone* provides a bridge between bottom-up chemical composition-ists and top-down humanists. Interestingly, some of the most celebrated humanists were trained in animal-based learning theories. For example, Abraham Maslow (Chapter 11), sometimes regarded as the "spiritual father" of humanistic psychology, was a graduate student at the University of Wisconsin when he was first "turned on" to psychology by Watson's behaviorism:

> I had discovered J. B. Watson and I was sold on behaviorism. It was an explosion of excitement for me. . . . Bertha came to pick me up and I was dancing down Fifth Avenue with exuberance; I embarrassed her, but I was so excited about Watson's program. It was beautiful. I was confident that here was a real road to travel, solving one puzzle after another and changing the world. (Maslow, 1968, p. 37)

About this same time another young graduate student by the name of Carl Rogers, who was also destined to become a giant in the humanistic psychology movement (Chapter 11), was completing his doctoral studies at Columbia University, where the emphasis was on measurement and statistics. "Freud," recalled Rogers, "was a dirty word" (1967, p. 356).

Ivan Pavlov—"Grandfather of behaviorism." Before turning to the study of John B. Watson's behaviorism in America, we pause to pay tribute to **Ivan Petrovich Pavlov** (1849–1936), the Russian physiologist who preceded Watson by nearly three decades. Pavlov is well known to psychology students for his work with salivating dogs, but few people realize that he formulated a theory of personality based on his work with animals (Pavlov, 1955).

Don't let sleeping dogs lie. Pavlov's theory of personality was sparked by a problem he confronted in his laboratory—sleeping dogs! Some dogs would fall asleep when put in a restraining harness prior to the conditioning experiments. Believing that he could predict which dogs had "sleepy personalities," Pavlov went into the kennel and selected dogs that were playful and active—barking and chasing other dogs. When he took these more frisky, emotional dogs into the laboratory, he found that they fell asleep more quickly. Pavlov theorized these dogs had "strong nervous systems," and were able to tolerate—in fact, sought out—strong stimulation. When required to stand quietly in the harness, they quickly became "bored" and fell asleep. These "emotional" dogs conditioned more slowly than their more sensitive counterparts, and Pavlov believed that these observed behavioral differences existed at the level of the neuron.

Such presumed physiological differences form the basis for a number of biologically based trait theories (which we will discuss in further detail in the next chapter). Eysenck's (1973) concept of *introversion,* Zuckerman's (1984, 1991, 1994) theory of *sensation seeking,* and Gray's (1964, 1972, 1990) *reinforcement sensitivity theory* all show significant debt to Pavlov's ideas. (See, I told you Molly has a personality!)

Background Check

The troubled, colorful life of John Watson (1878–1958). John Watson's lifelong fear of the dark, as well as his intense aversion to "states of consciousness" (which he compared to "so-called phenomena of spiritualism"), likely had their roots in his early childhood. His mother, Emma (described as "insufferably religious," [Karier, 1986, p. 111]), made her son vow to become a minister. Emma tied her family closely to the church, adhering strictly to prohibitions against drinking, smoking, or dancing.

By contrast, Watson's father drank, swore, and chased women, and when John was thirteen, his father left home. Almost immediately he became a troublemaker and was arrested for fighting and for firing a gun in the middle of Greenville. But if the breakup of his parents' marriage was profoundly unsettling to the adolescent Watson, it was probably "small potatoes" compared to the fears induced in him by the nurse his mother had hired to care for him when he was a young child. The nurse told little Johnny that the devil lurked in the dark, and that if he ever went out walking during the night, the Evil One might snatch him out of the darkness and off to Hell. This left Watson with a lifelong fear of darkness. He confessed that the reason he studied whether children were born with an instinctual fear of the dark was that he had never managed to rid himself of that phobia.

Education. At the University of Chicago, where Watson studied philosophy under John Dewey, he especially liked the writings of Hume because Hume held nothing to be fixed or sacred (in stark contrast to Emma Watson's fundamentalist views).

While at Chicago, Watson suffered an emotional breakdown, experiencing severe mood swings and sleeping only intermittently—and then only with a light turned on. However, he later characterized this as one of the best experiences of his university education, saying, "It taught me to watch my step and in a way prepared me to accept a large part of Freud, when I first began to get really acquainted with him around 1910" (Watson, 1936, p. 274). Precisely what Watson meant by "accepting a large part of Freud" was never clear, but it is of interest that the founding father of behaviorism had something positive to say about Freud.

In spite of his mood swings, Watson managed to complete his doctoral dissertation, which was entitled "Animal Education: The Psychical Development of the White Rat." At twenty-five, he graduated as the youngest student ever to attain a doctorate at the University of Chicago. In 1910 Watson confided to a colleague that he would like to remodel psychology by "putting consciousness in its place as an irrelevance" (Cohen, 1979, p. 62). In 1913 he published his famous article "Psychology as the Behaviorist Views It," after which he was publicly committed to radical behaviorism and thereafter showed no tolerance for any other brand of psychology.

While Watson was teaching at Johns Hopkins, his wife discovered that he was having an affair with his student, Rosalie Rayner, with whom he had been doing research on infant behavior. She divorced him, and the scandal was too much for Johns Hopkins, which asked for his resignation. For all practical purposes this ended Watson's meteoric career in academic psychology. For years he tried to gain another academic appointment, but the scandal took a toll and no one would hire him.

Behaviorist advertiser. Although Watson never regained his former academic reputation, he went into advertising, and must have felt some satisfaction in earning big bucks—even if it was by selling baby powder, Maxwell House coffee, and cigarettes. Watson was hired in 1921 for $10,000 a year and by 1930 he was earning over $70,000 a year (which translates to approximately $700,000 in today's dollars).

Behaviorism was one of the main reasons for Watson's success as an advertiser. Ever the researcher, Watson blindfolded smokers and discovered that they could not differentiate between various brands of cigarettes. Discovering that preferences were not based on taste, Watson concluded that sales could be influenced by manipulating the images associated with various products, and he increased the sales of everything from deodorants and cold cream to cigarettes and toothpaste. He hired pediatricians to vouch for the infection-fighting properties of Johnson & Johnson baby powder, and in one of the first uses of celebrity testimony, he got Queen Marie of Romania to endorse the beauty-enhancing properties of Pond's cold cream. He paid pretty models to suggest that it was OK for women to smoke, so long as they later brushed their teeth with Pebeco brand toothpaste (Fancher, 1990, p. 299).

Zeitgeist

The zeitgeist during the early twentieth-century was quite mechanistic; scientists like Watson perceived people to operate much like push–pull toys—responsive to external forces acting upon them. Just as a wagon has to be pulled, or a tricycle pedaled, your behavior requires pushing or a pulling to make it move. For behaviorists, personality is not a self-propelling device, it can only *react* when acted upon, only *respond* when externally stimulated. Mother nature might biologically influence personality through composition and temperament, but once a human being was born, personality played a minor role. For Watson and other early behaviorists, personality was not a pilot or a navigator, but merely a passenger—along for the ride—on a journey where external forces called the shots.

Purposive behaviorism. However, even in a zeitgeist where laboratory experiments were seen as the necessary foundation for learning theories, not all behaviorists saw persons as merely *reactive;* some saw behavior as guided by purpose. This difference was evident in the work of two of the most famous (and contentious) behaviorists of that era, John B. Watson and William McDougall (1871–1938). Whereas Watson believed behavior was always a *reaction* to a stimulus, McDougall argued that behavior was *purposive* and *goal-directed.* He explained human behaviors in terms of instincts and emotions, resembling Freud more than Watson.

The only thing Watson and McDougall appeared to agree upon was that **introspection,** or *the careful examination of one's subjective thoughts, sensations, and images,* was inadequate. But even here, they differed as to why introspection was deficient. McDougall saw introspection as an acceptable beginning step: "Psychology must not regard the introspective description of the stream of consciousness as its whole task, but only as a preliminary part of its work" (McDougall [1908], p. 15). Watson rejected introspection completely: "'States of consciousness,' like the so-called phenomena of spiritualism, are not objectively verifiable and for that reason can never become data for science" (1919, p. 1).

In the theoretical ferment of the early twentieth century, most American psychologists turned away from introspection as a scientific technique, and behaviorism and psychoanalysis emerged as the two most popular alternatives. On the issue of scientific objectivity, behaviorism claimed the high ground. However, Freudians and other personologists charged that behaviorism's objectivity was achieved by eviscerating a person's "inner" life, leaving only an empty organism or a conditioned ape.

ASKING THE BIG FOUR QUESTIONS

Defining personality as a "reaction mass." How did Watson go about constructing a model of personality from a few "objective" constructs? By reducing **personality** to nothing more than *a conglomerate of response potentials.* He criticized the "muddled writings" of others, defining personality as: ". . . an individual's total assets (actual and potential) and liabilities (actual and potential) on the reaction side" (1919, p. 427). Notice he ends his definition with *"on the reaction side."* Watson saw people as *reactors,* not *originators* or *initiators:* "Our personality is thus the result of what we start with and what we have lived through. It is the 'reaction mass' as a whole" (1919, p. 450).

What Are the Parts?

Stimulus and response. For Watson, *stimuli* and *responses* are the forces that shape personality. He described **S–R psychology** as follows: "The rule, or measuring rod, which the behaviorist puts in front of him always is: Can I describe this bit of behavior I see in terms of 'stimulus and response'?" (1930, p. 6). Watson wished to keep his theoretical constructs as "scientific" as possible, and that meant tilting toward Pavlov and the *Physiological Zone:* "We use the term *stimulus* in psychology as it is used in physiology. Only in psychology we have to extend somewhat the usage of the term" (Watson, 1919, p. 10).

And extend the term he did! As if to make up for simplistically reducing everything to two terms, Watson expanded the definitions of stimulus and response to cover nearly everything in the cosmos. **Stimulus** came to mean *"any object in the environment, or any change in tissues due to the physiological condition of the animal."* Equally broad was Watson's definition of **response:** *"anything the animal does—such as turning toward or away from a light, jumping at a sound, and more highly organized activities such as building a skyscraper, drawing plans, having babies, writing books, and the like"* (1930, pp. 6–7).

Recognizing that even with these elastic definitions of *stimulus* and *response* it still wasn't possible to account for all cases, Watson stretched the constructs even further by talking about *combinations* of stimuli:

> Life presents stimuli in confusing combinations. As you write you are stimulated by a complex system—perspiration pours from your brow, the pen has a tendency to slip from your grasp; the words you write are focussed upon your retinae; the chair offers stimulation, and finally the noises from the street constantly impinge upon your ear-drum. . . . The world of stimulation is thus seen to be exceedingly complex. It is convenient to speak of a total mass of stimulating factors, which lead man to react as a whole. . . . Situations can be of the simplest kind or of the greatest complexity. (1919, p. 11)

In spite of Watson's attempts to expand his handful of constructs to cover all imaginable behaviors (from having simple reflexes to building skyscrapers) radical behaviorists—from Watson to Skinner—have been widely criticized for oversimplifying complex human behaviors and for lacking the theoretical machinery to handle the convoluted everyday behaviors of ordinary life. For example, Chomsky (1959) roundly criticized Skinner for using simple laboratory terms in attempting to describe language acquisition, but the same kinds of criticism have dogged behaviorism from its earliest days. McDougall, in a famous debate with Watson, charged that S–R psychology was unable to account for some of the most satisfying human activities, such as the enjoyment of music:

> I come into this hall and see a man on this platform scraping the guts of a cat with hairs from the tail of a horse; and, sitting silently in attitudes of rapt attention, are a thousand persons who presently break out into wild applause. How will the Behaviorist explain these strange incidents: How explain the fact that the vibrations emitted by the cat-gut stimulate all the thousand into absolute silence and quiescence; and the further fact that the cessation of the stimulus seems to be a stimulus to the most frantic activity? (Watson & McDougall, 1929, p. 63)

What Makes a Person Go?

Association and repetition. Watson's associationistic theory of learning was similar to what Guthrie (1952, 1959) would call the **law of contiguity:** *when a pattern of stimuli is experienced along with a response, the two will become associated, so that when a similar pattern of stimuli is next encountered, it will tend to elicit a similar response.* Watson and

Guthrie both believed that conditioning occurred simply because events were closely *associated* in time. Additionally, Watson also believed that the more frequently the pairings occurred, the stronger would be the conditioning. So Watson's model was primarily based on two principles: *association* to couple the stimulus to the response, and *repetition* to strengthen or "stamp in" the connection.

ABCs of Watson's learning model. The following memory aid might help us to remember the basics of Watson's model: **A**ssociated **B**ehaviors **C**onnect. In this simple connectionistic model, Watson followed Pavlov who suggested that *pairing = conditioning*. But unlike Pavlov, Watson did not believe that *reinforcement* was necessary for conditioning to occur. Repeated pairings were enough.

Reacting protoplasm. It is apparent that in Watson's model of "personality," there is no hint of a *self*—no agent—only a "reaction mass" of response potentials. For radical behaviorists, personality has no internal "engine," it is simply a bundle of habits that have been conditioned by previous experience and that are triggered by stimuli mostly residing in the external environment. For Watson, the answer to "What makes a person go?" was quite straightforward: "When a human being acts—does something with arms, legs or vocal cords—there must be an invariable group of antecedents serving as a 'cause' of the act. For this group of antecedents the term situation or stimulus is a convenient term" (1919, p. 5).

Watson saw no need to go "deeper" in his analysis than to search for the external stimulus. His answer to "Why do men go to war? Why did George Smith leave his wife?. . . . or Why does John Doe live in the gutter . . ." was reductionistically plain:

> To answer any of the "whys" adequately about human activity we need to study man as the chemist needs to study some new organic compound. Psychologically, man is still *a reacting piece of unanalyzed protoplasm*. (1919, p. 6, emphasis added)

What Makes a Person Grow?

Development as situational conditioning. In the *Situational Zone*, the *stimuli and consequences in the surrounding situation* are all important. According to behaviorists, **development** *consists of the cumulative record that experience engraves on the tabula rasa of the person*. There is no "evolving" from within, no stages of development, no critical periods, only the *shaping* and *conditioning* of personality patterns by external events. Watson argued that "there is nothing from within to develop" (Watson & Raynor, 1928, pp. 40, 41). Not surprisingly, without an internally based theory of development, Watson made few distinctions between children and adults, emphasizing instead the importance of treating children "objectively" (read: *without emotionality*).

Rearing children "objectively." In 1928, Watson and his wife, Rosalie, published a book *(The Psychological Care of the Infant and Child)* that became extremely popular, selling 100,000 copies in the first few months. Their advice was behavioristic: blurring the distinction between children and adults, and urging parents to treat their children like little grown-ups, suggesting that affection or the "softer" emotions might "spoil" these miniature adults:

> Never hug or kiss them, never let them sit on your lap. If you must, kiss them once on the forehead when they say good night. Shake hands with them in the

morning. Give them a pat on the head if they have made an extraordinary good job of a difficult task. Try it out. In a week's time you'll find how easy it is to be perfectly objective with your child and at the same time kindly. You will be utterly ashamed at the mawkish, sentimental way you have been handling it. (Watson & Raynor, 1928, pp. 81–82)

Watson's aversion to parental expressions of affection may have been in reaction to his mother's emotional religiosity combined with an antipathy to the "progressive education" advocated by his former teacher, John Dewey. Whatever the roots, it seems likely that numerous aspects of Watson's own dysfunctional childhood seeped into his child-rearing advice and fueled his strong reaction to anything emotional. Nothing drew Watson's scorn more than what he considered the "coddling" of children: "When I hear a mother say, 'Bless its little heart' when it falls down, or stubs its toe, or suffers some other ill, I usually have to walk a block or two to let off steam" (Watson & Raynor, 1928, p. 82).

What Makes a Person Unique?

The only thing that counts toward uniqueness in personality is a *unique conditioning history*. Watson placed little weight on heredity, insisting that the external situation trumps all: "I would feel perfectly confident in the ultimate favorable outcome of careful upbringing of a healthy, well-formed baby born of a long line of crooks, murderers, thieves and prostitutes" (1926, p. 9). Or: "if we were able to obtain a new-born baby belonging to the dynasty of the Pharaohs, and were to bring him up along with other lads in Boston, he would develop into the same kind of college youth that we find among the other Harvard students (1919, p. 12).

Watson went even further, insisting that even structural differences were not of much significance when compared to environmental influence:

Some people are born with long, slender fingers, with delicate throat structure; some are born tall, large, of prize-fighter build; others with delicate skin and eye coloring. . . . But do not let these undoubted facts of inheritance lead you astray as they have some of the biologists. . . . Our hereditary structure lies ready to be shaped in a thousand different ways—the same structure mind you—depending on the way in which the child is brought up. (1926, p. 4).

Watson didn't care whether the newborn was the baby of a pimp or a pharaoh—it was all about conditioning.

FACING THE TOUGH TWINS

Is It Testable?

Although objectivity and testabililty are the touted hallmarks of behaviorism, Watson insisted his theoretical constructs were valid even when he knew that he was going beyond his laboratory data: "I am going beyond my facts and I admit it, but so have the advocates of the contrary and they have been doing it for thousands of years" (1926, p. 10). Watson insisted that his ideas were correct, even when he made applications at much higher levels of analysis than the "psychical development of the white rat" as outlined in his doctoral research.

Three basic emotions. According to Watson we inherit **three basic emotions:** *fear, rage,* and *love;* and through the process of conditioning, these emotions become attached to different stimuli. In a famous experiment demonstrating how emotions become conditioned to neutral stimuli, Watson and Raynor (1920) conditioned an 11-month-old boy named Albert to fear a rat. Originally Albert showed no fear whatsoever of the rat, but each time Albert reached for the rat, the experimenter struck a steel bar with a hammer, making a loud noise. After several such trials, the experiment was suspended for a week, so that Albert would not become too emotionally disturbed. When the experiment was resumed, and the rat again presented to Albert, he was very cautious of the animal. After several more conditioning trials, Albert developed a strong fear of the rat: "almost instantly he turned sharply to the left, fell over, raised himself on all fours and began to crawl away . . . rapidly" (p. 5). Albert also developed a generalized fear of objects such as a rabbit, dog, fur coat, and cotton—none of which were feared prior to the experiment—which raises an additional question:

Was it ethical? Although it is hardly fair to judge an experiment conducted in the 1920s by today's ethical standards, we must point out that in addition to illustrating the power of S–R conditioning techniques, Watson and Raynor also demonstrated why all such research nowadays must pass the scrutiny of a human subjects review committee. Today, we would not be allowed to traumatize subjects— certainly not infants—without numerous safeguards in place, such as requiring prior informed consent. Further, it would have to be demonstrated that any experimentally induced trauma was temporary and would be reversed before subjects were discharged.

Unfortunately, Watson and Raynor allowed little Albert to leave the hospital without attempting to decondition the fears they had so dramatically induced. Worse still, Watson and Raynor voiced no concerns or regrets. On the contrary, they used the case as an opportunity to ridicule psychoanalysis:

> The Freudians twenty years from now . . . when they come to analyze Albert's fear of a seal skin coat . . . will probably tease from him a recital of a dream which upon their analysis will show that Albert at three years old attempted to play with the pubic hair of the mother and was scolded violently for it. If the analyst has sufficiently prepared Albert to accept such a dream . . . he may be fully convinced that the dream was a true revealer of the factors which brought about the fear. (Watson & Raynor, 1920, pp. 12, 14)

Subsequently, Bregman replicated the experiment and found that conditioning occurred when a live animal was used, but *did not occur* with an inanimate object such as a bottle or a wooden animal. Bregman (1934) argued that his findings disproved Watson's claim that conditioning would occur with *any* object.

Removing fear. In fairness, it should be noted that Watson also used conditioning techniques to *remove* the fear of rabbits in a three-year old child named

Peter. Working together with Mary Cover Jones, he brought a caged rabbit into the forty-foot lunchroom where Peter was eating. Each day the researchers brought the rabbit a bit closer until it was sitting beside Peter as he ate his lunch. Finally Peter was able to eat while petting the rabbit at the same time. The healing generalized to other phobias as well, and Peter's fears of other objects (e.g., fur coats, rats, and frogs) also decreased. This was one of the first recorded cases of behavior therapy.

Is It Useful?

Behavior therapy. Traditional psychotherapists cultivate *insight* in their clients as a method of changing *personality* in order to bring about *behavior* change. Behaviorists tackle problem behaviors directly, assuming that personality will take care of itself. This was a highly heuristic notion during the last half of the twentieth century, spawning the field of **behavior therapy** or **behavior modification,** *treatments that use laboratory-derived "laws of learning" to directly change behaviors, in place of probing the unconscious or exploring the client's cognitions.*

Systematic desensitization. One of the most successful treatments for phobias ever developed was invented by **Joseph Wolpe** (1958), who used the ideas of Pavlov and Watson to decondition specific fears. **Systematic desensitization** is *a technique that repeatedly pairs relaxation with feared situations until phobias gradually lose their intensity.* For example, if Wolpe were treating someone for a fear of flying, he would first ask the client to construct an **anxiety hierarchy,** which is *a list of fear-inducing situations, in ascending intensity from slight to extreme fear.* An anxiety hierarchy for a flying-phobic client might resemble the following.

1. Talking with a travel agent about booking an airline flight.

2. Hearing the sound of an airplane.

3. Being in an airport.

4. Watching planes take off and land, from a distance.

5. Being close to a plane.

6. Boarding a plane.

7. Sitting in the plane while its engines revved.

8. Experiencing the plane gaining speed down the runway.

9. Flying.

After some training in progressive muscle relaxation, the client is instructed to imagine situation # 1 as vividly as possibly. Gradually working up the hierarchy, the behavior therapist assists the client in relaxation until situation # 9 can be imagined with little or no anxiety.

Systematic desensitization is based on Pavlov and Watson's notion that *repeated pairing* of two stimuli causes them to become connected. In the case of phobias, the sight of snakes, airplanes, dogs, or some other feared stimulus becomes *paired* with anxiety. Running away (and thereby reducing the anxiety) serves to *reward* or *reinforce* the fear, making it even stronger. Systematic desensitization uses *pairing* in the opposite way. Repeated pairings of the feared stimulus with deep relaxation results in the feared stimulus gradually losing its power to elicit anxiety. Repeated therapeutic pairings overcome the anxiety triggered by the original phobic pairing.

If you struggle with an unusually powerful fear you might like to try a series of such pairings to overcome your phobia. Or, even if your anxiety isn't at the phobic level, you might want to reduce your worries about speaking performances, sexual interactions, or athletic competitions. Whatever the nature of your anxieties or fears, simply construct an anxiety hierarchy describing your fears from least to greatest. Next, practice progressive relaxation (described in Learning on the Lighter side at the end of this chapter) until you are able to achieve a fairly deep level of relaxation. Then, focus on the least anxiety-provoking image in your hierarchy while maintaining your relaxed state. If you feel yourself tensing up, de-focus from the anxiety image and re-focus on relaxation. Spend about forty-five minutes pairing relaxed states with fear-producing images. Keep repeating this as you work your way up the hierarchy, until you can imagine your worst fear and still maintain a relaxed body. Now you're ready to take it on the road. If you've successfully worked your way up to the top of your "fear-of-flying" hierarchy, you might think of booking a flight for your next trip instead of taking the train or driving. If you've been phobic about going outside because you might see or step on a snake, take a walk in the woods. If you happen to spot a snake, you won't suddenly become totally relaxed (desensitization isn't *that* powerful!), but you'll probably be able to go outdoors without breaking into a cold sweat for fear of seeing a snake.

Numerous other examples of applying learning theory to the treatment of psychological problems could be given; however, they all share in common a focus on solving *specific* human problems using techniques first discovered in the animal laboratory. Unlike a traditional psychotherapist, who might help a client achieve "better adjustment" or "higher self-esteem," a behavior therapist would target a *specific problem* such as bed-wetting or a phobia, and employ laboratory-based learning techniques to "fix" (recondition or relearn) it.

From the animal laboratory to the psychiatric couch. Seligman's *learned helplessness theory of depression* (1975) provides an example of how laboratory analogs of "neurosis" in animals can sometimes lead to new understandings of complex human problems. In Seligman's studies, laboratory animals (dogs) were exposed to electric shock from which they could not escape. At first they showed signs of anxiety and discomfort, but eventually they simply lay down, whined, and accepted their fate in a manner that reminded Seligman of human depression. Noting that many depressed people experience losses and tragedies over which they have no control, Seligman then proposed a "learned-helplessness" theory of depression, which he subsequently investigated in the laboratory with human subjects (Hiroto & Seligman, 1975; Nolen-Hoeksema, Girgus, & Seligman, 1992; and Peterson, Maier, & Seligman, 1993). This is an excellent example of how personality researchers can move up the hierarchy from behavioral studies with animals to clinical applications with humans.

SUMMARY OF WATSON'S BEHAVIORISM

It is remarkable how many different areas of psychology have been influenced by Watson. He developed a significant theory of learning, wrote widely about child rearing, and had considerable influence on the field of advertising. Additionally he had a great deal to say about sex education, urging that children be given frank, *objective* information about sex, and even expressing gratitude for Freud's diffusing the secrecy surrounding sex.

Watson's accomplishments in psychology were significant and varied, but his theory of personality remained simplistic—recall his characterization of the person as a *"reacting piece of protoplasm."* Even many of his contemporaries took issue with what they considered Watson's extreme reductionism. Tolman (1952, p. 330), for example, referred to Watson's psychology as "twitchism" because it concentrated on isolated responses to specific stimuli.

Near the end of his career, Watson wrote:

> I honestly think that psychology has been sterile for several years. We need younger instructors who will teach objective psychology with no reference to the mythology most of us present-day psychologists have been brought up upon. I believe as firmly as ever in the future of behaviorism—behaviorism as a companion of zoology, physiology, psychiatry, and physical chemistry. (Watson, 1936, p. 281)

Fortunately for Watson, a "younger instructor" who would "teach objective psychology" appeared in the person of B. F. Skinner, who would rise to became behaviorism's most scintillating star.

As the twentieth century progressed, fewer and fewer psychologists embraced the core claim of **radical behaviorism**—that a *fully adequate explanation of human behavior can be achieved with a scientific analysis of situational stimuli.* Instead, a number of clinicians (e.g., Beck, 1967, 1973; Berecz, 1972, 1973, 1979; Meichenbaum, 1977; and Wolpe, 1958, 1969) included *cognitions* in their treatment models, utilizing the findings of laboratory-based behaviorism but capitalizing on the *human* capacity to *think, imagine,* or *visualize.* This led to a new variety of **cognitive behaviorism** *that sought to include the cognitive (subjective) dimensions of behavior along with the more obvious physiological or external measures.*

OPERANT CONDITIONING: THE BEHAVIORISM OF BURRHUS FREDERIC SKINNER (1904–1990)

Introduction

Skinner is to behaviorism what Tiger Woods is to golf—he didn't invent the game, but he raised it to a new level of excellence. The basics

B. F. Skinner.

of behaviorism (e.g., stimulus, response, reinforcement, and punishment) were not discovered by Skinner, but he refined them and added new distinctions, emphasizing the importance of *immediate consequences* in *shaping* behavior.

Background Check

Childhood. Skinner remembered his childhood home as "warm and stable . . ." (1967, p. 387). Early on, he got along well with his younger brother: "As a child I was fond of him. I remember being ridiculed for calling him honey, a term my mother used for both of us at home" (1967, p. 388). However, as the brothers grew older the sweetness dissipated, replaced instead by competition, in which his younger brother apparently excelled. Skinner recalled that his brother "proved to be much better at sports and more popular than I, and he teased me for my literary and artistic interests" (p. 388). This rivalry ended only when his brother died, and Skinner recalled that "When he died suddenly of a cerebral aneurism at the age of sixteen, I was not much moved" (1967, p. 388).

It seems remarkable that Skinner was "not much moved" by his brother's death—even considering their significant sibling rivalry. Skinner's emotional reaction to this brother's death is reminiscent of Watson's aversion to emotional relationships with one's child. For both of these preeminent behaviorists, one's inner emotional life appeared to count for little—might even be a sign of weakness—compared with the primacy of situational stimuli. Both of these behaviorists viewed persons as conditioned animals—organisms who are primarily propelled by external stimuli rather than by inner emotions.

Gadget builder. As a boy, Skinner was handy with making things:

> I was always building things. I built roller-skate skooters, steerable wagons, sleds, and rafts to be poled about on shallow ponds. I made see-saws, merry-go-rounds, and slides. I made slingshots, bows and arrows, blow guns and water pistols from lengths of bamboo, and from a discarded water boiler a steam cannon with which I could shoot plugs of potato and carrot over the houses of our neighbors. I made tops, diabolos, model airplanes driven by twisted rubber bands, box kites, and tin propellers which could be sent high into the air with a spool-and-string spinner. I tried again and again to make a glider in which I myself might fly. (1967, p. 388)

Education—English instead of engineering. In view of his creativity with gadgets, it seems surprising that Skinner chose to major in English rather than engineering. He states that "An old-maid school teacher named Mary Graves. . . . was probably responsible for the fact that in college I majored in English literature and afterwards embarked upon a career as a writer . . ." (1967, pp. 389–390).

After graduating from college, Skinner built a small study in the attic of his parents' home and began his career as a writer. He later described the results as "disastrous": "I frittered away my time. I read aimlessly, built model ships, played the piano, listened to the newly-invented radio, contributed to the humorous column of a local paper but wrote almost nothing else, and thought about seeing a psychiatrist" (1967, p. 394). Six months of bohemian living in Greenwich Village and a summer in Europe did little to unlock Skinner's writer's cramp, so after two years of trying, he concluded that he had failed as a writer.

From "firepigeons" to psychology. Since his writing had failed him, Skinner turned to science:

> The relevant science appeared to be psychology, though I had only the vaguest idea of what that meant. . . . Many odds and ends contributed to my decision. I had long been interested in animal behavior. We had no household pets, but I caught and kept turtles, snakes, toads, lizards, and chipmunks. . . . At a county fair I saw a troupe of performing pigeons. The scene was the facade of a building. Smoke appeared from the roof, and a presumably female pigeon poked her head out of an upper window. A team of pigeons came on stage pulling a fire engine, smoke pouring from its boiler. Other pigeons, with red fire hats rode on the engine, one of them pulling a string which rang a bell. Somehow a ladder was put up against the building, and one of the firepigeons climbed it and came back down followed by the pigeon from the upper window. (1967, pp. 395–396)

Skinner enrolled in the graduate program at Harvard where he single-mindedly pursued his studies, arising at 6 a.m. each morning in order to study before breakfast. He allowed himself no more than fifteen minutes of unscheduled time each day: "I saw no movies or plays, seldom went to concerts, had scarcely any dates and read nothing but psychology and physiology" (1967, p. 398).

"Baby box" anyone? Throughout his life, Skinner was always something of a showman, able to provoke controversy, which in turn focused attention on his work. He was not a dynamic speaker, but he was a genius at provoking discussion.

For example, when his youngest daughter was an infant, Skinner designed a glass-enclosed crib which he playfully dubbed an "Heir Conditioner." He later marketed it under the name of "Aircrib," but it was not a commercial success. Although the device's sole purpose was to provide a safe and comfortable alternative to traditional cribs and playpens, stories began to circulate that Skinner had raised his children like "rats in a box," and that they had become mentally ill or committed suicide. In fact, both daughters apparently turned out well; one became a professor of educational psychology, the other, an artist whose work was displayed at London's Royal Academy.

Aircrib

Zeitgeist

Skinner began his academic career teaching psychology at the University of Minnesota from 1936 to 1945. During this time he wrote his influential *The Behavior of Organisms* (1938). It was also during this World War II era that he presented a plan to the military for designing gliders that could use operantly conditioned pigeons as kamikaze pilots. Skinner and his coworkers trained pigeons to peck at discs when moving pictures of enemy targets were flashed on them. Skinner proposed that gliders loaded with high explosives could be piloted by pigeons, who could deliver their payloads to enemy targets without loss of pilots' lives.

It is a gauge of the zeitgeist that Skinner's pigeon-operated glider was rejected by the military. The reliability of animal behavior (now widely accepted, for example, in detecting illegal drugs at border crossings or in testing drugs in the laboratory) had not been well demonstrated. Military officials felt squeamish about trusting pigeon pilots to fly payloads of explosives to enemy targets. Skinner's subsequent research illustrated that animal behavior can be predictably "shaped" in almost any direction, so long as each behavior in the behavioral chain is immediately followed by reinforcing consequences. Most of Skinner's theory is summarized in the following sentence: "If the occurrence of an operant is followed by presentation of a reinforcing stimulus the strength is increased" (Skinner, 1938, p. 21).

ASKING THE BIG FOUR QUESTIONS

What Are the Parts?

Skinner box—the "wind tunnel" of operant conditioning. Aeronautical engineers fly small prototypes of airplanes in wind tunnels in order to study how these scaled-down planes perform in a variety of weather conditions. Then they *extrapolate,* or *generalize* their findings to the real world, presuming that actual planes will respond similarly during actual storms.

Skinner tried to do much the same thing. He designed an experimental apparatus that came to be known as the **Skinner box,** which is *a small compartment where experimental animals can be isolated from surrounding distractions, and conditioned to operate a key, bar, lever, or some other mechanical device that delivers rewards or avoids punishments.* The rat's behavior of pressing a lever or the pigeon's response of pecking a key is known as an **operant,** *a spontaneous behavior that an animal emits in order to "operate" on the environment.*

The Skinner box allowed animals a more active role—*operating* levers or pecking keys—instead of passively standing in a harness, like Pavlov's dogs, waiting for bells to ring and food to appear. Skinner's pigeons were free to walk about the compartment and *operate* on the environment, and when a desired behavior *(operant)* occurred, the experimenter immediately reinforced it by dispensing food or water, according to a prearranged plan.

First introduced in the 1950s, the compartment has been updated and modernized, with computer-based capabilities for dispensing reinforcers or punishers consistent with particular schedules. However, the essentials—an animal in an isolated environment performing simple tasks—have endured with little change. Behaviorists believe that the Skinner box provides a simplified—"purer"—model of how the world works.

Consequences. In Skinner's world, *consequences are king.* Although some effort is put into analyzing the *antecedent* stimuli, as well as the *target behavior,* the real focus is on **consequences,** *the emotional and situational changes that immediately follow the occurrence of a target behavior.* According to Skinner, what determines whether a particular behavior becomes a permanent part of your repertoire is nothing as slippery as the *self,* nothing so esoteric as *willpower;* it is *situationally dispensed consequences*—positive or negative—that ultimately "decide" how you will behave.

The ABCs of operant conditioning. The core of Skinner's theory is contained in the following sequence: **A**ntecedent → **B**ehavior → **C**onsequence. Operant conditioners have repeatedly shown that if a particular behavior (B) is *immediately* followed by pleasant or rewarding consequences (C), this behavior will almost certainly increase in frequency. Every teacher in the world knows that if children in a classroom laugh and applaud (reinforcing consequences) immediately following Courtney's "smart-aleck" remarks to a classmate, such remarks are highly likely to occur again. Conversely, if Cooper is ridiculed by his peers (punishing consequences) as he stammers his way through a reading selection, he is far less likely to volunteer to read aloud in the future. Numerous parents have learned the hard way that if you attempt to appease your tantruming child with a lollipop, the likelihood of your child throwing a temper tantrum the next time you're shopping at the mall will remain high.

Operant conditioners have carefully investigated all components of this **ABC** chain. Dieters are advised to avoid the *Antecedent* "triggers" for eating, by removing candy dishes from the coffee table and storing food in closed, opaque containers. People attempting to quit smoking are advised to engage in incompatible *Behaviors,* such as chewing on carrot sticks, or swimming. But by far the greatest emphasis has been on determining what kinds of *Consequences* increase or decrease particular target behaviors. Skinner and his students carefully studied what sorts of **contingencies** *("if–then" arrangements between behaviors and consequences:* **if** *you say "please,"* **then** *I'll pass you the sugar)* are most effective in promoting desired behaviors, or conversely, most efficient in eliminating unwanted behaviors.

Shaping new behaviors. Although in theory, one can wait for a "spontaneous" operant to occur (as when a rat "accidentally" rubs against or pushes the lever inside a Skinner box), in actual practice most conditioners reinforce **successive approximations,** or *beginning behaviors that partially approximate the final desired behavior.* For example, it would have taken a long time to teach Molly, my Black Lab, to retrieve a Frisbee if I had withheld her treat (reinforcer) until she chased the Frisbee, leaped into the air and caught it, brought it back to me, and dropped it at my feet (as she now does). Instead I used the process of **shaping,** *reinforcing gradually improving successive approximations.* I first rewarded Molly for even *looking* in the direction of the flying Frisbee I had thrown, then I required her to *run after it* before I would drop her a treat. Then, *run* and *pick it up.* Finally, she earned her treat only if she *looked, ran after, picked up, retreived, and dropped the Frisbee at my feet.*

In short, Skinnerians are *highly skilled environmental managers.* All behavior is seen to be the direct result of how situational contingencies are programmed and carried out.

What Makes a Person Go?

Reinforcement and punishment. Skinner's motivational constructs are all embedded in the *environment.* The person is seen as a *point of intersection*—a point where environmental forces and animal processes intersect to produce a behavior. By eliminating the *person* from his analysis, Skinner kept things simpler for the behaviorists, since all that remained to worry about was the *situation.* Almost everything of importance was ultimately boiled down to managing two major classes of situational consequences: *reinforcers* and *punishers.* And, in an ingenious theoretical sleight of hand, Skinner defined these concepts **circularly:** *any consequence which <u>increases</u> the likelihood of a response is termed a <u>reinforcer</u>, and any consequence which <u>decreases</u> the prob-ability of a response is a <u>punisher.</u>* This effectively short-circuited academic debates about the *true nature* of reinforcements or punishments, and provided a workplace definition that amounted to "if it works, use it."

A functional (experimental) analysis of behavior. In thus defining reinforcers and punishers by their *effects on the target behavior*—instead of presuming how they "felt" to the organism—Skinner and his followers emphasized a **functional (experimental) analysis of behavior** involving *experimental designs that carefully manipulate antecedents or consequences in order to show how they <u>functionally</u> relate to the target behavior. This is all done from a situational perspective that bypasses inner/personal "feelings" or"motives."* For example, Carr & Durand (1985) analyzed the behavior of children who exhibited behavior problems in the classroom. They carefully manipulated *task difficulty* and *social attention* while tracking problem behaviors. Their research revealed that some kinds of behavior problems were highest in the decreased-attention condition, while others were highest in the increased-task-difficulty condition. This sort of *functional analysis* gives teachers and other school personnel valuable information regarding what situational variables are influencing particular problem behaviors.

Reinforcement–punishment matrix. Skinner's *motivational constructs* are contained primarily in the situation—not in the person—and living animals mostly seek reinforcers and avoid punishers. Students sometimes find it difficult to distinguish between positive reinforcement, negative reinforcement, direct punishment, and punishment by withdrawal, but take heart, there's an easy way to keep it straight.

Reinforcement. Whether you are conditioning with lollipops or loud noises—positive or negative stimuli—**reinforcement** *always increases the likelihood of the target behavior's occurring.* Whether it's *positive reinforcement* or *negative reinforcement* doesn't really matter. To understand this a bit more personally, a cognitive behaviorist would say that a **positive reinforcer** *is a stimulus that feels, smells, or tastes good when it is presented to you.* A **negative reinforcer** *is an aversive stimulus that feels sounds, smells, sounds, or tastes good when it is terminated or turned off.* You positively reinforce yourself for mowing the lawn when you give yourself a candy bar after you are finished. You

TABLE 3.1

Reinforcement/Punishment Matrix

CONSEQUENCES

	Dispense or **Make Available** whenever the target behavior occurs	**Take Away** or **Terminate** whenever the target behavior occurs
Positive Stimuli: food, drink, candy, sex, smiles, praise, rest, recreation, TV, music, attention, etc. (*anything* experienced as pleasant)	Positive **Reinforcement**	Indirect **Punishment**
Negative Stimuli: noise, cold, hunger, electric shock, hitting, yelling, teasing, insults, etc. (*anything* experienced as negative)	Direct **Punishment**	Negative **Reinforcement**

negatively reinforce yourself if you jump into your swimming pool, effectively "shutting off the heat" when you have finished mowing.

Positive reinforcement is easy for most people to understand because it involves receiving something that tastes good or experiencing some sort of gratification. However, *negative reinforcement* is frequently confused with *punishment*, because it involves aversive stimuli. But it won't confuse you if you remember that *reinforcement* (positive or negative) *always feels good*. Whenever you *turn off* something noxious, the consequence feels good (i.e., will be negatively reinforcing). Zipping up your jacket on a cold day (to turn off the cold), putting up your umbrella (to turn off the rain), closing your window (to terminate the obnoxious sound of your neighbor's stereo), or loosening your shoelaces (to turn off the pain of pinched toes) are all examples of *negative reinforcement*, because they bring relief from something annoying, obnoxious, or painful.

Escape and avoidance behaviors. When discussing *negative reinforcement*, behaviorists make a distinction between **escape behavior,** or *action that terminates an already-present aversive stimulus* (for example, running rapidly across hot asphalt onto the grass *escapes* the burning heat to one's feet); and **avoidance behavior,** or *action that prevents or avoids an aversive stimulus.* Putting money into a *parking meter* is an example of *avoidance* behavior—you *avoid* the financial punishment of getting towed or ticketed (or both!) by regularly putting smaller amounts of money into the meter. Behaviorists see this as roughly analogous to the laboratory rat that presses a switch that delays shock for ten seconds. By regularly pressing the bar (at least once every ten seconds) the rat can completely *avoid* an electric shock or a loud noise. Similarly, if you put on shoes before walking across hot asphalt, you can *avoid* getting the bottom of your feet burned. Getting up and moving away from a group of noisy teenagers in a theater *escapes* their noise; walking into a theater and choosing a seat far away from teenagers *avoids* their noise.

Examples of positive reinforcers. Positive reinforcers include water (when you're thirsty), food (when you're hungry), or sex (when you're horny). In Skinner's box, the term "reinforcer" usually meant that the animal received a morsel of food or a sip of water, but the following list of reinforcers illustrates how broadly the term *reinforcement* has come to be used when applied to humans in real life situations:

praising oneself	putting on makeup
taking bubble baths	not going to work
making love	"doing anything I want to do"
going to a movie or a play	going to parties
going to the beach	being alone
mountain climbing	"doing only the things I want to
spending time on a favorite hobby	do, all day"
spending money	"not doing my duty sometimes"
playing records	goofing off
listening to the radio	watching TV
eating favorite foods	gardening
going out "on the town"	making long-distance calls
playing sports	playing with the parrot
getting to "be the boss" with a	buying a present for someone
boyfriend	spending extra time with a friend
pampering oneself	reading erotica
taking long breaks from work	reading mystery stories
taking a "fantasy break"	lip-synching (pretending to be a
window shopping	rock star in front of a mirror)
(Watson & Tharp, 1993, p. 212)	

Notice that although most of these are *positive reinforcers* (e.g., taking bubble baths, eating favorite foods, reading erotica, or pampering oneself), others have the *negative reinforcing* quality of achieving pleasantness by *turning off something unpleasant* (e.g., not going to work, goofing off, or "doing anything I want to do").

This list also illustrates both the *broadness* and the *individuality* of reinforcers. For some people, gardening or putting on makeup might be a chore (mild punisher), whereas for others it could be "fun" (reinforcing). Although most of us would find "eating favorite foods" or "goofing off" to be reinforcing, some might suffer great guilt for "indulging" in such gratifications. Similarly, people vary considerably when it comes to such activities as "being alone" or "going to parties." Here it is entirely possible that precisely the same circumstances that are reinforcing to one individual may be punishing to another. I recall that when my sons were young, I couldn't simply say "Clean up your rooms (or whatever else I wanted them to do) and we'll go out for ice cream." Two of the boys would have responded positively, but for the one with cold-sensitive teeth, biting into an ice cream cone was a painful (punishing) experience.

Punishment. Conditioning by **punishment** *always hurts—sometimes directly, sometimes indirectly.* At the age of eight or nine, Skinner studied the piano for a year with an old man, who, he recalled, ". . . jabbed me in the ribs with a sharp pencil whenever I made a mistake" (1967, p. 390). Skinner recalled that his mother only punished him once, but that it was pretty direct: "She washed my mouth out with soap and water because I had used a bad word" (1967, p. 390). He remembered that his father, an attorney, never missed an opportunity to inform his son of the punishments that were awaiting him if he became a criminal. He took his young boy to a lecture, illustrated with colored slides, describing life in Sing Sing. "As a result," confessed Skinner, "I am afraid of the police and buy too many tickets to their annual dances" (1967, pp. 390–391). It's not surprising that when Skinner grew up to become a psychologist, he disliked using direct punishment, and demonstrated how to reduce unwanted behaviors without poking someone with a pencil or taking them on a tour of the local jail.

Punishment by withdrawal *reduces the likelihood of a behavior by taking away something pleasant each time the behavior occurs.* For example, if your child has recently discovered profanity, you can reduce the frequency of the f__ word through indirect punishment:

Child: "This is the best f__king ice cream I've ever tasted!"
Parent: "Hand me your dish and get down from the table, we don't use that word in our house."

If such punishment-by-withdrawal procedures are consistently followed, the frequency of that particular verbal behavior will decrease. Washing the child's mouth with soap, as Skinner's mother did, would be *punishment by presentation;* whereas removing the pleasant stimulus (ice cream) from the child would be *indirect punishment.* **Time out** (a well-known term for the indirect punishment) *removes a misbehaving child from a pleasant situation.*

When your mother told you "No more TV until your arithmetic grade comes up," or your father said "I'm taking your car keys if you get another speeding ticket," they were using indirect punishment.

Factors influencing the effectiveness of consequences. There are a number of factors that influence how efficiently reinforcers or punishers influence behaviors. We will briefly discuss four.

(1) Immediacy. Immediacy is among the most powerful variables known to psychologists. Behaviorists have conducted thousands of laboratory experiments that have proved beyond any doubt that *the longer the delay between a behavior and its consequences, the less influence the consequence will have on the target behavior.* For example, when Molly was a puppy, if I had rewarded her for "rolling over" by giving her a treat *five minutes later,* she would never have learned this behavior. Such a "too-delayed-for-a-dog" interval would have sabotaged the effect on the trick I wanted to teach her. Instead, the treat might have inadvertently reinforced whining, begging, tail-wagging, or whatever behavior *immediately* preceded it.

When it comes to immediacy, people aren't *that* different from Molly. A child might work quickly to mow the lawn if she knows that within half an hour of finishing, she'll get to watch TV or receive some other reinforcer. By contrast, working to get good grades in school because "someday you can be a brain surgeon" seldom works. Immediacy ("a bird in the hand . . . ") typically trumps the future. For example, the brevity of the interval between inhaling on a cigarette and experiencing a nicotine "high" to the brain (about seven *seconds*), compared with the gestation period for lung cancer (five to fifty *years*), is the reason that smokers "choose" cancer over health. *Immediacy* is a common thread among all addictions; thoughts about long-term, undesirable consequences (e.g., obesity or cirrhosis of the liver) are erased by the more immediate pleasures of eating chocolate pie or drinking cognac. Cognitive slogans (e.g., "A moment on the lips, a lifetime on the hips") do not suffice to outweigh immediate gratification. Nor does scientific information (e.g., "The surgeon general has determined that smoking is hazardous to your health").

And it's not just addictive behaviors that are shaped by immediate consequences. Consider how important immediacy is in social relationships. You're exquisitely attuned to the *immediate* smiles, nods, eye contact, laughter, or touches from others that reinforce what you say or do. You're equally alert to frowns, yawns, wandering eyes, or other indicators of boredom or disapproval. If you tell a joke or story that draws immediate laughter, you're likely recycle it in the future; however, even a slight delay in laughter will likely send it to the "delete" file.

(2) Contingency. Contingencies refer to the "if–then"aspects of behavior. A **contingency** *states that "if" a certain behavior occurs, "then" a particular consequence will follow.* Thus, we could say that your car engine's starting is *contingent upon (or dependent upon)* your turning the ignition key: it starts when—and only when—you turn the key. If your car started up "on its own" some of the time, or if it started only "occasionally" when you turned the key, we wouldn't say that engine starting was *contingent* upon key turning. Behaviorists say that reinforcement is most effective when it is delivered *contingent* upon the target behavior.

(3) Deprivation, satiation, and other "establishing operations." Behavior conditioners are able to change the power of a reinforcer or a punisher through **establishing operations,** that is, *manipulating situational factors in a way that either intensifies or decreases the power of consequences* (Michael, 1993). Thus, deprivation increases the effectiveness of many reinforcers, while satiation renders them less potent. Food, for example, is an effective reinforcer *before* Thanksgiving dinner, but loses most of its power after a large meal. Liquids effectively reinforce drink-seeking behaviors in thirsty organisms, which is why many bars provide "free" (and that's not "salt-free") pretzels and popcorn. That cold beer you buy is going to taste a lot better (read: be more reinforcing) if your mouth is dry and salty.

(4) Characteristics of consequences may vary considerably. Every parent has discovered the truth of Lincoln's aphorism that you "can't fool all the people all the time." Stimuli intended by parents to be reinforcing do not affect all children similarly. Although most children find M & Ms reinforcing, the child with a chocolate allergy or the kid with cavities might not.

What Makes a Person Grow?

Growth and development seen as situational shaping. For operant conditioners, the answer to "What makes a person grow?" is (not surprisingly!) the *situation*. The person is not a tulip bulb growing from within, nor a baby chick pecking its way out of a shell. For radical behaviorists there are no unique developmental stages, no psychological crises that occur in a specified chronological order. Really, there is no developmental theory as such—only the shaping and acquisition of new behaviors as a result of the *environment engraving experience onto the tabula rasa, in accordance with the principles of operant conditioning.*

The same basic techniques that are used to teach Ben to use the potty are employed when teaching Rachel how to read. Even in counseling and clinical settings the emphasis is on acquiring new behaviors through conditioning. The behavioral marriage counselor might instruct a husband to do little favors for his wife, and simultaneously instruct the wife to "reinforce" her husband's behavior by thanking him for his efforts, or by reciprocating with favors of her own. The couple might perceive themselves as suffering from a "marriage problem," but the behaviorist's approach to solving it would be similar to what might be recommended to a parent trying to teach a child to pick up toys before bedtime: *reinforce desirable behaviors, ignore or (mildly) punish undesirable behaviors.*

In other words, behaviorists tend *not* to place great stock in developmental distinctions; whether they are working with infants or the elderly, their methods remain similar. Whatever the age of the organism, the operant conditioner begins by undertaking a *functional analysis* to determine precisely how situational variables are related to the target behavior. Next, the operant conditioner attempts to adjust situational variables to insure that *consequences* will bring about the desired change in the target behavior. In all of this, the age or developmental stage of the person plays only a minor role.

For Skinner and modern behaviorists, **acquisition** *involves more than Watson's "stamping in" of S–R connections; it consists of acquiring new responses through shaping and reinforcement.* The strength of the responding is behaviorally measured through resistance to extinction (RTE).

Schedules of Reinforcement

Table 3.1 outlines the basic characteristics of reinforcement and punishment, but experimenters (as well as parents and teachers) must *schedule* how and when reinforcers or punishers are dispensed. On a **continuous reinforcement schedule,** *reinforcement occurs every time the target response occurs.* A candy vending machine is an example of continuous reinforcement—every time you put in money you get candy out. A slot machine illustrates an **intermittent schedule of reinforcement,** in which *you do not get rewarded each time you perform the behavior.* Skinner illustrated intermittent reinforcement by saying "We do not always win at dice. Nor do we always get an answer when we telephone a friend. Reinforcement for these responses occurs intermittently" (Holland & Skinner, 1961, pp. 121–122). There are numerous ways in which reinforcement can be intermittently delivered—each affecting behavior in different ways—but it has been found that *intermittent* reinforcement is even more effective than *continuous* reinforcement for maintaining behavior, i.e., it creates high **resistance to extinction (RTE).**

Thus, a parent who gives in to a child's whining demands "once in a while" unwittingly conditions the child to become a *more persistent whiner.* If you *occasionally* feed your dog a few scraps of food from the table, you are training your pet to become a tenacious, unrelenting beggar. That's why, as a practical matter, you should be scrupulously consistent with dogs or children. Bottom line: if you want a dog that incessantly begs for table scraps or a child who incessantly whines for a toy, all you have to do is reinforce this *once in a while* (not *some* of the time, not even *most* of the time)—just *occasionally*. The *RTE* of intermittently reinforced behaviors is the main reason casinos stay in business and lottery sales remain brisk.

Next, we will briefly consider four of the most common schedules of reinforcement.

Fixed ratio (FR) schedule. **In a fixed ratio (FR) schedule**, *a specified (fixed) number of responses must occur before reinforcement is delivered.* This is similar to Janelle working "piecework" in a factory where she is paid $10.00 for assembling a 24-part rocking chair. FR schedules produce high rates of behaving that include a significant pause following reinforcement.

Variable ratio (VR) schedule. **A variable ratio (VR) schedule** *is similar to a FR schedule in that reinforcement is based on the number of responses that occur, but in this case it is the <u>average</u> number of responses.* Janelle still earns $10.00 for each chair assembled, but the number of parts in each chair might vary (*averaging* about 24 parts/chair), and Janelle might not be immediately paid for each chair. VR schedules produce high, steady rates of behavior with no pause after reinforcement. Slot machines in casinos have been described by behaviorists as operating on VR schedules of reinforcement.

Fixed interval (FI) schedule. With interval schedules of reinforcement (either *fixed* or *variable* intervals) responses are reinforced only after a certain *interval of time* has elapsed. On a **fixed interval (FI) schedule,** *the interval is fixed—it stays the same each time.* For example, on a fixed-interval thirty minutes (FI thirty minute) schedule, responses that occur *before* thirty minutes have elapsed are not reinforced; only responses that occur thirty or more minutes after the previous reinforcement are rewarded. In this case Janelle's supervisor would come by every half hour and give her a ten-dollar bill for the first part of the chain Janelle put together after the supervisor appeared in her workplace.

Using a FI schedule of reinforcement with pigeons, Ferster and Skinner (1957) encountered substantial pauses in responding immediately after reinforcement, after which the pigeons would again began responding—speeding up as they neared the end of the time interval. Thus, we might expect that after Janelle receives a ten-dollar bill and the supervisor walks away, she might take a break, get some coffee, chat with a friend, then return to work, speeding up near the end of the next half hour.

Variable interval. **On a variable interval (VI) schedule,** *reinforcement is delivered only after a certain <u>average</u> interval of time has passed since the last reinforcement*—each time interval is of a different length. In this case, Janelle's supervisor would show up—ten-dollar bill in hand—at unpredictable intervals of time (e.g., thirty-five minutes, twenty-two minutes, five minutes, forty-five minutes) making it impossible to anticipate when she might appear. Not surprisingly, such schedules result in *steady rates* of responding, without pauses or accelerations.

In short, operant conditioning is mostly about *environmental management*—mostly focused on the *situation* rather than the *person* or *personality*. The essential thrust of Skinner's work was to program *environmental consequences* in such a way that desirable behaviors were reinforced, and destructive or undesirable behaviors were ignored or punished. As a consequence, desirable behaviors were shaped, acquired, and maintained, while undesirable behaviors were punished or underwent extinction due to lack of reinforcement.

What Makes a Person Unique?

It follows from what we've just learned that behaviorists view uniqueness primarily in terms of a historically unique conditioning history. Behaviorists believe that a few general "laws of learning" can be applied across a wide spectrum of animal behaviors with little concern for individual differences or **species-specific behaviors,** that is, *instinctual behaviors*. Although fish swim, birds fly, and dogs bark, Skinner believed all were subject to similar laws of conditioning.

Personal *uniqueness* fares poorly in the hands of the behaviorists. Humans lose their "special" standing among the animals of the planet, as well as any humanistic or existential splendor that might result from such specialness. Lost is the similar-yet-different, snowflake-like uniqueness of each personality. Gone is the one-of-a-kind, finger-print distinctiveness of each human being. Unlike the humanists and existentialists (Chapters 11–12) who make personal uniqueness, choice, and responsibility the core of personality, behaviorists view personal uniqueness as mere historical happenstance—chance combinations of people and situational consequences.

FACING THE TOUGH TWINS

Is It Testable?

No psychological theory has generated more research than Skinner's operant conditioning, and, at the ("Skinner-box") laboratory level, none has achieved greater consistency or proven more reliable. As a technology for training animals, operant conditioning has no serious competitors. However, when Skinnerians move beyond the laboratory and attempt to apply their findings across a broad range of species or in higher-level applications, operant theory loses power. By disregarding cognitive variables in humans and minimizing species differences among animals, radical behaviorists have left themselves open to serious criticisms.

Skinner *extrapolated* from the precise data generated by rats and pigeons in his laboratory to all sorts of higher-order behaviors in human beings, such as language acquisition, without changing the simple, straightforward, behavioristic essentials of his theory and without seriously taking such basic parameters as species differences into account.

Instinctual drift—"messiness" in real life. Two of Skinner's associates, Marian and Keller Breland, moved from Minnesota, where they had worked closely with him, to Arkansas, where they embarked on a business called Animal Behavior Enterprises, training animals to perform a wide variety of tricks. Their animals appeared at fairs, conventions, amusement parks, and on television. By the early 1960s, the Brelands had conditioned over 6,000 animals of 38 different species, including pigs, chickens, reindeer, cockatoos, porpoises, and even whales.

At first, all seemed to go relatively well, but soon the Brelands began to experience breakdowns of conditioned behavior. The problems became so significant that they reported them in an article wryly titled *The Misbehavior of Organisms* (Breland & Breland, 1961), a parody on the title of Skinner's first book *The Behavior of Organisms* (1938).

The Brelands reported that although most of their animals were, at first, highly conditionable, instinctive behavior frequently appeared and interfered with what had been learned. Racoons, for example, were trained to pick up coins and deposit them into a five-inch metal box. Training racoons to pick up a single coin was no problem, but racoons experienced difficulties letting go of the coin. The racoon would rub the coin inside the box, take it back out, grasp it firmly for a few seconds, and *finally* let go of it—not the most efficient way to earn a reinforcer! During the next phase of training the racoons were required to place *two* coins in the box in order to receive reinforcement, and the animals would *not* let go of the coins. Instead, they rubbed the coins together, dipped them into the box, and then removed them completely. The rubbing behavior became more and more pronounced, even though this behavior delayed or prevented reinforcement. The trainers concluded that conditioning a racoon to place two coins into a metal box was not commercially feasible. Apparently the racoons' instinctual tendencies to wash and manipulate their food were too powerful to be overcome by operant conditioning techniques.

The Brelands also encountered difficulties in training pigs to pick up big wooden coins and deposit them in a large "piggy bank." The wooden coins were positioned several feet from the bank and the pig was required to transport the coins to the bank in order to receive reinforcement. At first, conditioning seemed successful, and the pigs appeared eager to transport their coins to the "piggy bank." As time went on, however, the pigs began to perform more slowly, repeatedly dropping the coins and rooting them along the ground with their snouts on the way to the "piggy bank." Thinking the rooting behavior was a result of insufficient drive on the part of the pigs, the Brelands intensified motivation by increasing food deprivation prior to conditioning. However, this only intensified the rooting "misbehavior" of the pigs. Eventually it took the pigs about ten minutes to transport their coins a distance of six feet—hardly an exciting show for an audience of humans! The trainers concluded that these animals were "trapped by strong instinctive behaviors," which were prepotent over conditioned behaviors. The Brelands termed this **instinctual drift,** stating that after a period of initial conditioning, *"Learned behavior drifts toward instinctive behavior"* (1961, p. 185).

Language acquisition. "Verbal behavior" is how behaviorists refer to language, and it is the area where the limitations of learning theory stand out most starkly. It shouldn't surprise us that a theory which grew out of work with rats, pigeons, monkeys, and other language-deficient species would turn out to be inadequate in accounting for language acquisition—the characteristic that most clearly differentiates humans from other species.

Chomsky's critique. In arguably the most cogent critique of operant conditioning ever written, MIT linguist Noam Chomsky took Skinner to task for overgeneralizing his laboratory work when attempting to explain language acquisition:

He [Skinner] utilizes the experimental results as evidence for the scientific character of his system of behavior, and analogic guesses (formulated in terms of a metaphoric extension of the technical vocabulary of the laboratory) as evidence for its scope. This creates the illusion of a rigorous scientific theory with a very broad scope. . . . The phrase "**X** is reinforced by **Y** (stimulus state of affairs, event, etc.)" is being used as a cover term for "**X** wants **Y**", "**X** likes **Y**", "**X** wishes that **Y** were the case," etc. Invoking the term "reinforcement" has no explanatory force, and any idea that this paraphrase introduces any new clarity or objectivity into the description of wishing, liking, etc., is a serious delusion. . . . (Chomsky, 1959, p. 38)

Given the persuasiveness of Chomsky's argument, it's not surprising that Skinner claimed: "I have never actually read more than half a dozen pages of Chomsky's famous review of *Verbal Behavior*" (1967, p. 408).

However, in fairness to Skinner, we find the phrase "X is *reinforced* by Y" to be a significant improvement over saying "X *wants, likes,* or *wishes* Y were the case," because it encourages us to study "reinforcement" in behaviorally measurable ways such as *resistence to extinction*. Few personality psychologists would argue that operationally defining terms in experimentally testable ways is not a significant improvement over the common vocabulary of "wanting, wishing, or liking." The main quarrel here is about whether situationally based, behavioristic theories are adequate for explaining such high-level processes as language acquisition.

Relational Frame Theory (RFT). The debate about how language is acquired is still very much alive. Pinker (1984), (1999), Chomsky, (1959), (1987), Hauser, Chomsky, and Fitch (2002) and others contend that when young children acquire language, they use innate, grammatical categories similar to those used by adults. Chomsky calls this a **language-acquisition device (LAD):** *the inherited ability of children to learn the rules of language.* Behaviorists disagree, using **relational frame theory (RFT)** to argue that *early syntax is built around relational frames, not built-in grammatical categories.* RFT theorists (e.g., Tomasello, 2000; Seidenberg & MacDonald, 1999) have created a "Verb-Island" model suggesting that early language acquisition begins around *verbs.* The details of these arguments and rebuttals are too complex to concern us here; we need only to understand that behaviorists believe that the learning of language is ultimately traceable to situational contexts rather than to representations in the mind. In this way, behaviorists have utilized RFT to bounce back from what many considered to be Chomsky's death arrow to Skinner's behavioristic analysis of language.

Currently, the debate rages hot and a "winner" has not been declared; however, some time in the future, it is likely that both sides will be declared "winners," because like other variations of the nature–nurture debate, language acquisition will likely be seen to result from biologically built-in capacities *interacting* with environmental stimulation.

A recent study, for example Mayberry, Lock, & Kazmi (2002), found that both deaf and hearing adults who experienced language in early life (signed or spoken—it made no difference) had little difficulty learning a new language later in life, whereas adults who were born deaf and had little experience with language early in life showed low levels of American Sign Language performance later. Apparently if the young brain does not experience language-rich stimulation, the capacity to learn a language later remains impaired.

In a recent refinement of the *LAD*, Chomsky and his colleagues assert that:

> . . . although bees dance, birds sing, and chimpanzees grunt, these systems of communication differ qualitatively from human language. In particular, animal communication systems lack the rich expressive and open-ended power of human language. . . . we take as uncontroversial the existence of some biological capacity of humans that allows us (and not, for example, chimpanzees) to readily master any human language without explicit instruction. (Hauser, Chomsky, & Fitch, 2002, pp. 1570–1571)

Chomsky and colleagues assert that human language has at its core the computational mechanism of **recursion,** or *the capacity to repeat and/or recombine,* which gives humans—and no other species—capacity for limitless expressive power:

> It seems relatively clear, after nearly a century of intensive research on animal communication, that no species other than humans has a comparable capacity to recombine meaningful units into an unlimited variety of larger structures, each differing systematically in meaning. (Hauser, Chomsky, & Fitch, 2002, p. 1576)

In short, by insisting on the primacy of the situation, and ruling out *personal agency, innate predispositions,* or *internal representations,* Skinner left himself vulnerable to the criticism that operant theory lacks adequate tools for dealing with complex behaviors such as acquiring a language or maintaining a happy marriage—not to mention writing poetry or eliminating poverty.

Is It Useful?

By emphasizing the importance of immediate reinforcement, Skinner has done us all a great service. Operant techniques have become accepted strategies in areas too numerous to list. Whether you are a parent, teacher, advertiser, therapist, politician, jogger, or long-haul truck driver, operant techniques have likely influenced your behavior. From dolphin training to drug testing, from baby boxes to teaching machines, Skinner has had a profound influence on how we live our lives. Let's consider a few examples.

Training dolphins—immediacy at the water park. If you've ever visited a water park and attended a dolphin show, you have unwittingly witnessed how "the most powerful variable in psychology is immediacy." It probably didn't make an impression on you, but next time you'll be more aware and you'll notice that as the dolphin comes lunging out of the water to hurtle over a pole held several feet above the surface, the trainer blows a whistle at the *exact instant* the dolphin crosses over the pole. Then, the dolphin immediately swims to where the trainer is hanging over the water in a small cage ready to reward the dolphin's performance with a fresh fish—the **primary reinforcer,** *the actual food the animal consumes.*

In teaching animals (or people), *immediacy* is so important that the trainer doesn't want a delay of even a couple seconds, so before beginning to teach the dolphin a series of tricks, the trainer conditions the sound of the whistle to be a reinforcer. *Pairing* the sound of the whistle with the taste of fish, over and over again, makes the two become connected (recall Pavlov's dogs and Watson's "Little Albert"), and the *sound of* the whistle takes on much the same stimulus value as the *taste* of fish. In technical terms, the sound of the whistle becomes a **secondary reinforcer,** *a conditioned signal that food is available.* Now it becomes possible to blow the whistle (deliver this secondary reinforcer) *immediately following* the desired behavior. The trainer can now deliver a reinforcer at the *exact instant* the dolphin clears the hurdle. Notice this the next time you attend one of those performances, and it will *reinforce* your study of personality theory.

Immediacy in the classroom. We've already seen how behaviorists have applied their ideas to a variety of clinical problems in a field that has come to be known as *behavior therapy.* Much the same has happened in the field of education. Skinner's emphasis on immediate reinforcement led to teaching machines (Skinner, 1958) and foreshadowed computerized learning programs. In a famous article entitled "Good-Bye Teacher" (Keller, 1968) one of Skinner's early associates, Fred Keller, outlined **PSI,** which is a *personalized system of instruction,* in four basic steps: (1) Determine the material to be covered in the course, (2) Divide the material into self-contained segments, (3) Create methods of evaluating the degree to which the student has conquered the material in a given segment, and (4) Allow students to move from segment to segment at their own pace. Today computers have replaced teaching machines, making immediate reinforcement even more easy to apply.

Operant theory has led to more effective instructional methods in a number of areas—especially in dealing with students previously thought to have been "unteachable" because of severe intellectual limitations. During the past four decades, persons with developmental disabilities have been taught self-help skills in the areas of toileting, feeding, dressing, social skills, vocational skills, and many other survival behaviors (Carr, Coriaty, & Dozier, 2000; Cuvo & Davis, 2000).

Pop cans—reinforcing my running. The Michigan legislature passed a refund law a few years ago, "reinforcing" picking-up-trash behavior at the rate of ten cents a bottle or can. A dime isn't a lot of money any more, but it was enough to modify my behavior. Now when I go jogging, I typically pick up a pop can or two along the roadside to help defray the costs of my overpriced Nike running shoes. To the chagrin of environmentalists, I must admit I didn't bother to slow my running pace until my legislature (undoubtedly inspired by a Skinnerian study demonstrating the effectiveness of reinforcement in reducing litter) passed a law making it worth my while.

Roadside punishment. Similarly (although Skinner didn't much believe in it), punishment also works. When I was growing up as a kid, we thought nothing of throwing bits of trash out the car window—nothing drastic, just napkins and leftover pieces of hamburger or french fries. Now, when I see signs threatening to punish me (to the tune of $100 to $500) for such misbehavior, I put my leftover french fries in the litter bag of my car or in litter barrels alongside the highway.

I suspect we have all been operantly conditioned to lessen our littering, but additional operant programs have been instituted to counteract the effects of those who still persist in tossing trash out car windows. We reinforce people to pick up after others by publicly posting the names of the "picker-uppers" on signs alongside the road. In my state it's called the "Adopt a Highway" program. You know, you've seen it: "The next mile of this highway has been adopted by the Dan Goodwin family."

Drug research. One of the most impressive applications of operant theory is in testing new drugs. If you take a tranquilizer once in a while to steady your nerves, a pain killer to soothe those sore muscles, or an antihistamine to assuage your allergies, your life will have been influenced by operant conditioning. In former times, drug testing was largely an unscientific procedure. An experimental drug would be administered to a few rats or monkeys who would be observed to see if they got sleepy or sluggish, or exhibited bizarre behaviors. Operant conditioning changed all that. After Skinner and Ferster published *Schedules of Reinforcement* (1957), demonstrating that behavioral baselines could be predictably established with rats, pigeons, and other nonhuman species, this provided a behavioral yardstick by which new drugs could be measured. With this new technology, even slight changes in behavior could be precisely measured, providing a performance grid on which the behavioral effects of new experimental drugs could be mapped. Drug companies hired large numbers of researchers trained in operant techniques, and the field of behavioral psychopharmacology was born.

Now, when a new drug is developed it can be tested on animals who are known to behave in very predictable ways under standardized conditions. Since it is easy to train rats to press a lever for food or to avoid shock by pressing a lever, it becomes practical to establish baselines of how animals respond to different levels of shock, different amounts of reinforcement, etc. After such behavioral baselines are carefully established, researchers can evaluate to what extent a new tranquilizer induces *calmness* without *sleepiness*. It becomes possible to assess new drugs with rigorous precision—against well-established baselines. An optimal antianxiety agent should relax an animal, yet not sedate it so much that it fails to successfully avoid punishment. This sort of fine-grained analysis evokes the metaphor of *behavioral microscope*. Prior to Skinner, drug testing was crudely carried out with the "naked eye"; operant theory provided the pharmaceutical industry a behavioral "microscope."

Operantly redefining "mental illness." We began this chapter with Dave visiting a behavior therapist, who treated his hysterical blindness by using an *escape* conditioning procedure similar to what might be carried out in the laboratory with pigeons or rats. Behavior therapists have redefined "neurotic" problems (e.g., hysterical blindness, bed-wetting, thumb sucking, stuttering, sexual perversions, cigarette smoking, blushing, and phobias, to name but a few) as *learned maladaptive habits*. Forty years ago, behavior therapists optimistically declared an end to *"mental illnesses,"* insisting that all behavior problems were learned habits that could be unlearned (reconditioned).

Introducing a section in their widely read *Case Studies in Behavior Modification* (1965), Ullmann and Krasner's optimism was evident:

> All the papers in this section deal with severely disturbed subjects who are labeled "schizophrenic." . . . The major theme running throughout these first thirteen articles is the direct manipulation of behavior by response contingent reinforcement. . . . there is a feeling of optimism and confidence that effective means for modifying severely maladaptive behavior are available. (1965, pp. 65–67)

Nearly half a century later, numerous clinical problems have been successfully treated using behavioral techniques. However, in spite of these reported successes, workers in other areas of clinical practice (e.g., marriage and family therapists, psychoanalysts, existential therapists) have asserted that laboratory-derived operant techniques are inadequate to address many of the more complex problems people experience. But whatever the deficiencies of behavioral techniques for dealing with complex behaviors, their value has been demonstrated in a wide variety of settings (e.g., juvenile detention centers, drug treatment programs, pain management clinics, schools, and homes) with a vast array of problems, ranging from toilet training to teaching arithmetic.

Skinner's influence on theories of personality. Skinner would not have wanted to be remembered as a personality theorist. In fact, he disavowed theory of any kind:

> Much useless experimentation results from theories, and much energy and skill are absorbed by them. Most theories are eventually over-thrown, and the greater part of the associated research is discarded. . . . It is argued that research would be aimless and disorganized without a theory to guide it. . . . But this is not the way most scientists work. It is possible to design significant experiments for other reasons. . . . (1950, pp. 194–195)

But in spite of his antitheory rant, Skinner *was* a theorist, enthusiastically espousing some constructs such as *reinforcement,* and eschewing others like the *self.* Just because he insisted on *operational definitions* does not change the fact that Skinner was a psychologist, not a carpenter or a plumber. To be a psychologist is to be a theorist, and claiming to conduct "atheoretical" experiments appears to be an exercise in self-delusion. Skinner could no more conduct an experiment without theorizing than a fish can swim without becoming wet. Although Skinner tried to distance himself from theory, others ascertained the obvious, and included his work in books on *theories* of learning, in which Skinner's name has become synonymous with the constructs of operant conditioning.

Feisty to the end. Skinner enjoyed baiting theologians and philosophers into arguing with him about whether human beings were free to choose (as active agents) or merely to live with the *illusion* that they were free. The title of his book *Beyond Freedom and Dignity* (Skinner, 1971) seemed designed to incite just such discussions, and the contents were consistent with the title. Not surprisingly, Skinner reached the scandalizing conclusion that freedom and dignity were mere illusions.

Skinner understood the notion that if people throw enough stones at you while you're alive, when you die you will leave a monument behind. In the following passage, published three years before he died, we see how Skinner purposely *incited* controversy by his use of the provocative term "accuse" (which *he*—not I—italicized for emphasis):

> I *accuse* cognitive scientists of misusing the metaphor of storage. The brain is not an encyclopedia, library, or museum. . . .
>
> I *accuse* cognitive scientists of speculating about internal processes which they have no appropriate means of observing. Cognitive science is premature neurology . . .

I *accuse* cognitive scientists of emasculating laboratory research. . . .

I *accuse* cognitive scientists of reviving a theory in which feelings and state of mind observed through introspection are taken as the causes of behavior rather than as collateral effects of the causes.

I *accuse* cognitive scientists as I would accuse psychoanalysts of claiming to explore the depths of human behavior, of inventing explanatory systems. . . .

I *accuse* cognitive scientists of speculation characteristic of metaphysics, literature, and daily intercourse, speculation perhaps suitable enough in such arenas but inimical to science. . . .

Let us bring behaviorism back from the Devil's Island to which it was transported for a crime it never committed, and let psychology become once again a behavioral science. (1987, p. 111)

Clearly, this was not written to win Skinner friends in the community of cognitive psychologists who rejected his bare-bones behaviorism for more complex models, or among counselors and therapists who found his empty-organism approach lacking the emotional richness of more dynamic models; but it was vintage Skinner—feisty to the end—who was apparently "reinforced" by criticism.

Person without a personality. In spite of their many contributions to research and practice, the *self*less model of personality created by behaviorists appears much like the rubber puppet you played with as a child. Lacking a life of its own, your puppet appeared alive and animated so long as it was powered by your hand, but as soon as you removed your hand, its rubber face lost expression and its voice went dead. At the end of the day, all the articles you endowed with personality and made alive with your childish energy (e.g., trucks, tricycles, dolls, and dishes) became just a "pile of toys" that needed to be picked up before bedtime.

So it is with the behaviorism. At the end of the day, in spite of their impressive scientific contributions, behaviorists create a person without a personality—a complex gadget without an engine, a plane with no pilot. The energizing, steering *inner self* is missing. However, as personality psychologists, we are not forced to choose *either* radical behaviorism or humanistic self theories. It is possible to *look both ways*: upward to the *Insight* and *Social Zones,* while maintaining ties to the *Situational Zone.*

Just as Larsen and Buss (2002) reminded us in the previous chapter that the nature–nurture controversy evaporates at the personal level, much the same is true of the determinism vs. freedom issue. At the experiential level, we experience ourselves as *both* determined *and* free. When playing poker, for example, *determinism* describes what we are dealt, *choice* describes how we play our cards. The behavioral outcome is inextricably determined by *both*:

Being the product of conditioning and being free to change do not war with each other. Both are true. They coexist. . . . We must affirm freedom and responsibility without denying that we are the product of circumstance, and we must affirm that we are the product of circumstance without denying that we have the freedom to transcend that causality to become something which could not have been previsioned from the circumstances which shaped us. (Wheelis, 1973, pp. 87, 88)

Chapter Summary

Focusing exclusively on the situation. By shifting attention away from the *person* (where philosophers and scholars had focused for centuries) to the *situation*, Watson and Skinner brought about a "sea change" of thinking, resulting in a genuine paradigm shift. Few areas of human functioning have been untouched by the behaviorists' single-minded insistence that the *situation*—not the *person*—is where the action is. For Skinner, all of the essential "scientific" variables were seen to reside in the environment or the situation, not the *person* (or personality). There was no internal agency—none! Stimuli *out there* reinforced operant behaviors emitted by the organism.

Respectability for single-subject research. Behaviorists brought scientific respectability to the single-case experiment. Prior to operant conditioning studies, experiments tended to be judged by the number of subjects involved. By demonstrating that careful study of a single subject is a valid technique, Skinnerians have done personality psychologists a service as well. In their famous ABAB design, the experimenter records the *baseline frequency (A)* of a target behavior (such as smoking cigarettes). Next an *intervention (B)* utilizing some sort of smoking-cessation therapy (relaxation training, biofeedback, punishment, etc.) is begun and frequencies of the behavior (smoking) are carefully recorded. Then the treatment is stopped and the frequency of smoking is carefully recorded to see if it "returns to baseline." If the behavior returns to the original baseline (A), treatment procedures (B) are restarted. Such an on-again-off-again study clearly demonstrates the effects of treatment on smoking. Such experiments can be carried out with single subjects, and are sometimes referred to as "own-control studies." This sort of careful work made single-subject studies acceptable to the scientific community while allowing for the study of individual differences.

Behaviorist *philosophy* vs. behaviorist *techniques*. We do well to differentiate behaviorist *techniques* from behaviorism as a *philosophy*. This is a distinction that Skinner, himself, frequently failed to make. When Skinner was conditioning rats or teaching pigeons to peck keys, his work was science at its best—empirical, elegant, and convincing. When he *extrapolated* his laboratory findings to language acquisition, social engineering, and a host of other complex human problems, he sometimes lost credibility with many scholars even within his own profession.

For both Watson and Skinner, the person was always a reactor, never an agent. We've seen how behaviorism eviscerates the self out of the person and removes the *person* from the *Person X Situation* interaction. But we need to remind ourselves that it is possible to utilize the *techniques* of behaviorism without necessarily adopting behaviorism as a *philosophy of life*. An existential personality psychologist, for example, might be completely turned off by Skinner's philosophical notion that people are mere reactors—animal reactors at that!—but could still utilize behavioral *techniques* in losing weight, stopping smoking, or maintaining an exercise program. There is no genuine conflict between Watson and Skinner's science and other good science; the conflict arises only when we fail to distinguish between the *techniques* of behaviorism and the *philosophy* of behaviorism.

Points to Remember

1. Behaviorists think of persons as *trained animals,* so they see no problem with studying animals in the laboratory under controlled conditions in order to find out more about how people think and learn. Just as engineers use wind tunnels and scale models in order to discover how actual airplanes will perform in the real world, *behaviorists use animals as simpler models* upon which to test their theories about *human learning and behavior.*

2. *Operant conditioners are among the most skilled animal trainers in the world.* They have trained pigeons to assist the Coast Guard in rescue missions. Operant techniques have enabled trainers to teach guide dogs to assist their vision-impaired owners in traveling along traffic-crowded streets without danger. Police dogs have been taught to detect drugs or to assist in apprehending criminals; dolphins have been conditioned to respond to hostile movements in waters near military installations; and goldfish have been taught to recognize pollutants—all using principles of operant conditioning.

3. Behaviorists carefully analyze behavior from the bottom up—bit-by-bit—but they largely eliminate the *person* from their theories, treating humans as animals with language. Persons are seen primarily as *responders.* A well-trained animal doesn't think for itself, it *responds* to the trainer's commands. Similarly, the well-conditioned person *responds* and *acts upon* stimuli in the surrounding situation. By altering *triggering stimuli* as well as *consequences,* behaviorists have been highly successful in training animals and people to respond in predictable ways.

4. When treating clinical problems, behavioral clinicians (known as *behavior therapists) focus directly on the presenting complaint, instead of attempting to understand the family or personal dynamics surrounding a problem.* In "Dave's" case, for example, the behavior therapist used a laboratory-like procedure to confront Dave with the fact that he was not *biologically* blind, no matter what his conscious experience might be.

5. As a child, John B. Watson was *deeply frightened of the devil,* and he retained a lifelong fear of the dark. It's not surprising that the *behaviorism* he founded *avoided all mention of "spirit"* and *refrained from anything referring to an "inner" life.* For Watson, *personality* was simply an accumulation of learned responses—a *"reaction mass,"* as he put it.

6. Like other behaviorists who would follow, Watson did *not* put much stock in *developmental stages.* He didn't believe that children were much different from adults, and advised parents to use "objective" (emotion-free) techniques to rear their children. Humans are born pretty much as "blank slates," say the behaviorists, and development consists of experience making its marks on the "blackboard" of personality in the form of habits or other learned behaviors.

7. For watson, emotional life consists of the three basic emotions—fear, rage, and love—becoming connected to various situational triggers. He demonstrated this by

producing a fear of furry objects in baby Albert, and removing a fear of rabbits in three-year-old Peter.

8. Contemporary behavior therapists use similar techniques (e.g., a process called *systematic desensitization*) to eliminate phobias. *Learned helplessness* is a contemporary *theory of depression,* originally derived from behavioral research with animals.

9. In Watson's world, learning took place by the *association* or *connection* of elements that occurred together in time. Thus, in the case of little Albert, *fear* (a natural emotion) became *connected* to furry objects because Albert experienced a frightening noise in the presence of a furry object; hence the two became *connected.* Remember the ABCs of Watsonian conditioning as **A**ssociated **B**ehaviors **C**onnect.

10. B. F. Skinner fizzled as a writer, but succeeded splendidly as a psychologist breathing new life into Watson's behaviorism by highlighting the importance of *consequences* for *shaping and reinforcing new behaviors.*

11. The greatest memorial to Skinner is not some flowery obituary or an elegant tombstone; it is rather the fact that even as you read this sentence, somewhere in the world, in a Skinner box, there is a pigeon pecking a key, or a rat pressing a lever—much as a gambler in some casino somewhere is pulling down on a handle—in order to earn some reward or escape some stress.

12. The *ABCs of operant conditioning* follow a temporal sequence: **A**ntecedents precede the target **B**ehavior, which is followed by **C**onsequences. The *immediate consequences* are the *most crucial elements* in shaping the acquisition of desirable behaviors or eliminating unwanted ones.

13. Although laboratory animals perform predictably, in the real world things sometime get "messy," and other influences, such as genes or instinct, interfere with learning.

14. Skinner's theory has no serious competitors when it comes to training animals. In the case of *complex human behaviors* such as *language acquisition,* operant conditioning proves too simplistic. Chomsky's critique is the most devastating ever leveled at operant theory, and cautions us not to apply findings from the animal laboratory to complex human situations without doing the bridging research.

15. Behaviorists have demonstrated that *immmediacy is one of the most powerful variables in psychology.* Working with both animals and human beings has proved immediacy to be a crucial factor in the acquisition of new behaviors. From water parks to the classroom, whether you're teaching an animal or a person, learning will take place most rapidly, and remain intact longest, if you make certain that your subject *experiences positive consequences as quickly as possible following the desired response.*

16. As a description of animal learning, operant conditioning theory is without rivals; however, as a theory of personality, it fails to account for higher-level human functioning such as language acquisition and usage, cognition, etc. By eliminating

the *self* or any other *agency or internal processors,* Skinner was left to explain the complexities of higher human functioning in animal-behavior terms. This, as Chomsky pointed out, proved disastrous.

17. Nonetheless, Skinner has influenced personality psychologists by emphasizing the importance of the situation as a determinant of behavior. Mischel (chapter 4) cogently argued Skinner's position in his famous "situationist critique." This was a wake-up call to the field, and has resulted in a sharpening of issues and a compromise *interactionist* position where both persons and situations are taken into account. Additionally, with careful experimental designs and detailed accounts of their findings, behaviorists have endowed single-subject studies with a level of scientific respectability never before achieved. In turn, case studies in personality psychology are more acceptable to the scientific community—especially if procedures and findings are carefully documented.

Key Terms

Acquisition   (82)

Anxiety Hierarchy   (70)

Avoidance Behavior   (78)

Behavior Therapy   (57)

Behavior Therapy/Behavior
   Modification   (57, 70)

Circularly   (77)

Cognitive Behaviorism   (72)

Consequences   (76)

Contingencies   (76)

Contingency   (81)

Continuous Reinforcement Schedule
   (82)

Development   (67)

Escape Behavior   (78)

Establishing Operations   (81)

Fixed Interval (FI) Schedule   (83)

Fixed Ratio (FR) Schedule   (83)

Functional (Experimental) Analysis of
   Behavior   (77)

Immediacy   (80)

Instinctual Drift   (85)

Intermittent Schedule of Reinforcement
   (82)

Introspection   (65)

Language-Acquisition Device (LAD)   (86)

Law of Contiguity   (66)

Negative Reinforcer   (77)

Operant   (75)

Personality (According to Watson)   (65)

Positive Reinforcer   (77)

Primary Reinforcer   (87)

Psi   (88)

Punishment   (79)

Punishment By Withdrawal   (80)

Radical Behaviorism   (72)

Recursion   (87)

Reinforcement   (77)

Relational Frame Theory (RFT)   (86)

Resistance To Extinction (RTE)   (82)

Response   (66)

Secondary Reinforcer   (88)

Shaping   (76)

Skinner Box   (75)

Species-Specific Behaviors   (84)

S–R Psychology   (65)

Stimulus   (66)

Successive Approximations   (76)

Systematic Desensitization   (70)

Three Basic Emotions   (69)

Time Out   (80)

Variable Interval (VI) Schedule   (83)

Variable Ratio (VR) Schedule   (83)

Web Sites

Skinner

www.bfskinner.org/. B.F. Skinner Foundation. The Web site gives a full bibliography of Skinner's books, and students can get copies of his articles free of charge by e-mailing the Foundation at bfsf@wvu.edu. Also included is a small biography written by Skinner's daughter, a Foundation newsletter, and other publications of the Foundation.

Watson

www.psy.pdx.edu/PsiCafe/KeyTheorists/Watson.htm. The Psi Café. This Web site boasts a small biography, links to other Web sites about Watson, a listing of and links to his papers and selected books, and even some overhead illustrations of the famous little Albert study!

alpha.furman.edu/~einstein/watson/watson1.htm. The personal Web site of Gil Einstein. A visually stimulating biographical site that follows John Watson's life from womb to tomb. It also contains references students can look up for more information on Watson.

Pavlov

www.cshl.edu/PDogs/37.html. Cold Springs Harbor Laboratory. Here you can see pictures of Pavlov's dogs with their names and charts that indicate their retention rates. You can also navigate to the site's Library and Archives to view the James Watson archive.

Learning on the Lighter Side

Watching Nanny 911

If you watch episodes of the TV series "Nanny 911," you will see how Skinner's principles of operant conditioning enable parents to regain control of their unmanageable children. Hopefully, the information you've learned in this chapter will help you to be the kind of consistent parent who never has to call "911" for help with out-of-control little brats!

Movies

Owning Mahowny (2003) is based on a true story about a bank executive with an addiction to gambling. It is an interesting portrait of the power of schedules of reinforcement in shaping personality.

Teaching Your Dog to Ring the Doorbell or to Play the Piano

If you have a dog, you can teach it to ring a bell to let you know when it would like to go outside (for play or potty purposes). Following these four simple steps:

1. Hang a small "jingle bell" on the knob of the door you want your dog to use when entering or exiting the house.

2. Begin conditioning your dog by sounding a "click" (produced by your mouth or by a small "cricket" type of novelty noise maker) each time you toss a small

piece of food or some other "doggy treat" into your pet's food dish. Repeat this until your dog approaches the dish as soon as the noise is sounded (this is *conditioning by pairing,* similar to what Pavlov and Watson used). Now you can use the "click" as an *immediate* reinforcer, signaling that food is available.

3. Start by "click" and rewarding *any* behavior your dog makes that *resembles touching the bell with its nose* (successive approximations); but gradually require your dog to come closer and closer to touching the bell in order to receive reinforcement. You may assist your pet by gently pushing or pointing it in the direction of the door (*shaping).*

4. Finally, click and reward only when your dog rings the bell with its muzzle or paw. If you choose to reward muzzle ringing, it will mean you won't have scratch marks on your door.

This entire process should take less than an hour.

You can use a similar procedure to shape your dog to "play the piano." Begin by purchasing a small toy piano. By shaping and reinforcing successive approximations, as illustrated in the example above, you can condition your dog to approach and "play" the piano by striking the keys with one of its front paws. Then pair your dog's name with the word "piano" in an authoritative voice (*"Duke, play the piano")* each time you dispense the reward. When you pair your pet's name with the word "piano," your dog should approach the piano and begin "playing." Finally, require the animal to "play" for ten or fifteen seconds before dispensing the reward. Now you can treat visiting friends to a "piano concert," courtesy of Duke.

■ ■ ■

Teaching Yourself Progressive Relaxation—"Raggedy Ann (or Andy)" at the Beach[2]

Ask a friend with a soothing voice to record the following instructions, pausing for approximately five seconds for each asterisk. Do not read the numerals. Or, you may read and record the instructions yourself; but since most of us don't like how we sound when we record ourselves, it will probably work best if you have a friend do the reading. Then, listen to the recording while you lie on a sofa, bed, recliner, or a carpeted floor.

1. Lie down and close your eyes *** I want you to imagine that you are lying on the beach * Notice how the warm sand cradles your body and feel how the sun gently warms your face * Listen to the ocean waves rhythmically breaking on the sand. * In the distance you can hear seagulls squawking softly as they fly overhead.* Notice how good the warm sand feels beneath your body **

2. Now, I want you to clench your *right* fist—make it into a tight ball * Hold it and notice how the tension feels ** Now relax * Notice the contrast—notice how much better relaxation feels **

---

2. Adapted from Hammond, 1990; Jacobson, 1938; Martin & Pear, 2003, and the author's own clinical experiences.

3. Now I want you to clench your *left* fist—tight, into a hard ball * Feel the tension * Now relax—just let go and notice how loose and heavy your hand feels **

4. Now clench *both* fists into hard balls and feel the tension * Hold it and notice how the tension spreads into your forearms and even into your shoulders * OK, relax ** Just let your arms become totally relaxed—loose and heavy **

5. Now I want you to squeeze both fists and also bend your arms at your elbows * That's right, bring both clenched fists up to your shoulders * Now feel the tension spreading from your fists into your arms, shoulders, and chest * Now let go—just let your arms flop down by your side and notice how loose and heavy they feel ** Notice that relaxation isn't something you have to "do," it just happens naturally * Your body knows how to relax on its own **

6. Again, clench both fists, bend both arms and feel the tension in your fists, arms, shoulders, chest—hold it tight, feel the tension * OK, relax, let your arms drop to your sides and notice how nice and heavy they feel **

7. Now, wrinkle your forehead and squint your eyes shut very tight * Squeeze those eyes—tight and hard * Wrinkle your forehead up like a crumpled-up piece of newspaper * OK, relax ** Just let the relaxation flow and notice how your face smooths out like a quiet pond with just a few ripples around the edges **

8. OK, wrinkle up your forehead * squint your eyes shut * Now I want you to clench your jaw * That's right, just clamp your teeth together as hard as you can * Hold it and feel the tension in your jaw * Squeeze your lips together really tight * Now relax ** just totally relax and enjoy how good it feels **

9. Now all together—wrinkle your forehead, squint your eyes, clamp your jaw, make your lips tight * Hold them all and feel the tension throughout your forehead, eyes, jaw, neck, and lips. Hold it. Now relax **

10. Now do it all again—wrinkle your forehead, squint your eyes, clench your jaw, tighten your lips, and now I want you to push your head back against the sofa (floor) and feel the tension in your neck * Slowly turn your head from left to right and feel the tension in your neck shift ** OK, relax, just let it all go limp ** Feel the relaxation from your entire head as if it's flowing down through your arms and out your fingertips like water ** Good * Notice how good relaxation feels **

11. Now I want you to shrug your shoulders—pull them up as high as you can and feel the tension throughout your upper back, neck, and head ** Now relax * Just let those shoulders go limp

12. Now squeeze both your shoulders forward as hard as you can until you feel your back muscles pulling tightly across your back like a belt—especially between your shoulder blades * Now relax ** Feel all the tension just dissolve **

13. Once more, squeeze your shoulder blades forward again, and at the same time suck in your stomach as far as you can. Suck in your stomach until it feels like

your tummy is touching your backbone * Hold it and feel the tension throughout your entire upper body * Now relax ** Feel the difference enjoy the relaxation **

14. Now I want you to combine everything we've done so far: clench your fists, bend your arms, shrug your shoulders, wrinkle your forehead, squint your eyes, clench your jaw * Hold it and feel the tension * Now, in addition I want you to take a deep breath and hold it * Feel the tension * Keep holding your breath * Keep holding your breath * Feel the tension * OK, relax ** Notice how the air rushes into your lungs and how your breathing automatically resumes massaging your body with its rhythmic inhalations and exhalings ** It all happens automatically, you don't have to "do" anything—except relax * Enjoy how good relaxation feels **

15. Now, focus on your pelvis * I want you to squeeze your buttocks together as if you were pinching a dime between them that you didn't want to lose * Feel the tension * Hold it * OK, relax **

16. Next let's go to your legs * Push your heels into the sofa (floor) as hard as you can and feel the tension throughout your legs and lower body * Hold it * Feel the tension * Now relax * feel the difference **

17. Now I want you to point your toes toward your head as far as you can * Feel the tension all throughout the back of your legs * Keep pointing them and feel the tension—even the pain * Now relax * Just allow your legs to be nice and heavy and loose and relaxed **

18. Now take three deep breaths ** Now, tense all the muscles as I name them, just as we've practiced: fists, arms, forehead, eyes, jaw, lips, neck, shoulders, stomach, legs; hold it * Now relax **Breathe in deeply and exhale two times * Once more, but on the third time, hold your breath ** Hold it and feel the tension beginning to build * Hold it a little longer * OK, relax * Resume breathing normally—without thinking about it, let the breathing massage your body **

19. Now think of yourself totally relaxed ** Feel the warm sand under your body ** Feel the relaxation flowing, like a gentle stream from the top of your head throughout your entire body ** Feel the relaxation flowing down your arms and out your fingers—down your legs and out your toes **

20. Think of yourself as a rag doll lying in the warm sand. Lift one of your arms just a little and let it drop as if it were the arm of a Raggedy Ann (or Andy) doll ** Lift your other arm just a little and let it drop * Feel how loose and heavy and floppy it feels ** Do the same with one of your legs—lift it just a little and then let it flop down ** Now the other leg * That's right * Now your entire body should feel loose and heavy, warm and comfortable—like a floppy rag doll, warming in the sun ***

Looking Ahead

We have now learned that neural circuits are essential in the *Physiological Zone,* and external stimuli, reinforcers, and punishers are the foundation for behaviorists in the *Situational Zone.* Next we will discover that *trait theorists* believe personality is a package of *predispositions.*

Our journey has catapulted us across forty centuries—from the Egyptians and the Greeks, to Pavlov, Watson, and Skinner. We have ascended the vertical axis with remarkable speed, from analyzing amoebas and neural synapses to exploring such broad concepts as Wilson's sociobiology. If you're feeling a bit dizzy or discouraged, don't despair. Remember how after experiencing that first stomach-wrenching drop of a roller coaster ride, you can handle the subsequent slopes more easily? It will be much the same with this text. If you've managed to hang on up to this point—and I hope you have—the following chapters will become easier to negotiate. As we move to higher levels of abstraction you will be less challenged by the vocabularies of biochemistry and neuroanatomy. Although the mathematics of factor analysis may at first appear intimidating, you will discover that the basic ideas behind traits are not difficult to comprehend.

chapter 4

Trait Theories of Personality

Person as Dispositions

Gordon Allport, Hans J. Eysenck, Raymond B. Cattell,
Paul Costa & Robert McCrae

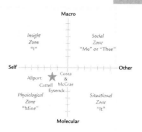

IN THIS CHAPTER YOU CAN

1. Wonder whether your pet has a personality. Does an amoeba?

2. Discover how trait theorists construct personality bit by bit, a trait at a time.

3. Understand that *correlation* is a mathematical description of how two things *co-relate*, or *vary together*.

4. Learn how *factor analysis* reduces a large number of correlations to a few basic *clusters of correlations*, known as *factors*.

5. Wonder how many "basic" factors are needed to explain personality. This is a packaging decision—are two or three *broad factors* best, or are thirty more *specific factors* preferable?

6. Realize that *traits* mean *different things at different levels of analysis.* For some theorists, traits are *real biological entities;* for others, traits are *linguistic descriptors* or *mathematical coordinates.*

7. Learn that Gordon Allport pioneered American trait theory, beginning in the *Physiological Zone* and defining a trait as a *real biological entity:* a

"neuropsychic system." However, in addition to traits, Allport subsequently added a *holistic self,* moving up into the *Insight* and *Social Zones* to deal with values, prejudice, and religious experience.

8. Understand how Hans Eysenck, working mostly in the *Physiological Zone,* concluded that personality is best understood in terms of *three superfactors* (**P***sychoticism,* **E***xtraversion,* and **N***euroticism).* Notice the first letters spell **PEN.**

9. Find out why Raymond Cattell named *sixteen personality factors,* and distinguished among three different kinds of data: *Life records* (L-data), *Questionnaires* (Q-data), and *Tests* (T-data), warning that different kinds of data should not be haphazardly combined.

10. Wonder why it took half a century of research to convince many personality psychologists that *five factors* is a natural number for describing personality. The currently popular *Five-Factor Model (FFM)* includes: **O***penness,* **C***onscientiousness,* **E***xtraversion,* **A***greeableness,* and **N***euroticism.* Notice the first letters of these factors spell **OCEAN.**

A PERSONAL PERSPECTIVE

Does an amoeba have a personality? Does Molly?

As we begin to study trait theories, we might wonder whether distilling people down into basic traits can further our understanding of personality. Earlier, we might have questioned how molecular research in the *Physiological Zone* would help us understand

THE FAR SIDE® BY GARY LARSON

© 1986 FarWorks, Inc. All Rights Reserved/Dist. by Creators Syndicate

The Far Side® by Gary Larson © 1986 FarWorks, Inc. All Rights Reserved. The Far Side® and the Larson® signature are registered trademarks of FarWorks, Inc. Used with permission.

"Stimulus, response! Stimulus, response! Don't you ever *think?*"

such macro behaviors as visiting Austria or hosting a Super Bowl party. Can we possibly learn anything about ourselves from single-celled organisms or from the statistical bits and pieces that trait theorists boil personality down to? Is smaller better? Some investigators think so:

> Curiously enough, the most primitive response to stimuli we know, that of the amoeboid cell, is directed in space, either at the stimulus or away from it . . . . The amoeboid cell's one motor pattern serves locomotion, feeding, and escaping . . . making it retract and flee from noxious stimuli and "effusively" run toward promising ones. Whoever has watched an amoeba in near-natural surroundings will have been surprised at the seeming "intelligence" of its behavior—in other words, at the wealth of innate and environmental information on which it acts. (Lorenz, 1996, pp. 13–14)

Notice that Lorenz puts quotation marks around *"intelligence"* when referring to the navigation of an amoeba. I doubt that he would attempt to measure the *"IQ"* of his one-celled friends, and we might chuckle if he were to boast that "Amy," his pet amoeba, performs "above grade level." Still, we might wonder, Does an amoeba have a personality? Does a dog? Could an amoeba "change its mind"? Does an amoeba even *have* a mind? Could an amoeba ever be *self-actualized*? Is an amoeba that rapidly sprouts "feet" (pseudopodia) in the direction of "goodies" displaying a *hedonistic personality*?

To humanistic or existentialist psychologists, the idea of a "self-actualizing amoeba" sounds like a bad joke, but to researchers working in the *Physiological Zone*, there is continuity to all of life, and they remain unperturbed by Gestaltists who insist "the whole is greater than the sum of the parts"; by existentialists who assert "people make choices, amoebas do not"; or by theologians who say that "souls, not cells, should be the focus of our concern." A zonal perspective allows us to study amoeboid *movements* without insisting they comprise an amoeboid *mind*. We can study single-celled organisms while remaining clear that amoebas do not exhibit the uniquely individual, cross-situationally consistent behaviors that characterize *personality*.

I am quite willing to say that Molly, my Black Lab, *really does* have a personality! For example, she has a canine's "conscience," which causes her to "guiltily" slink away if I catch her eating from the cat's food dish. She "remorsefully" hangs her head when I catch her trying to sneak off to visit the neighbors. Nonetheless, Molly's personality isn't a *human* personality. She has far less freedom than I to transcend her immediate surroundings. Although I'm convinced that Molly "walks" and "talks" in her sleep (her muffled barks and rapid paw movements lead me to infer she is dreaming about chasing rabbits or retrieving a Frisbee), I'm equally convinced that she does not analyze her dreams for symbolic meanings upon awakening. I doubt that her behavior is truly **teleological:** *motivated by future goals.* Molly never refuses food because she's "on a diet." She lives in a world dominated by proximal stimuli; which is to say that Molly is exquisitely sensitive to her immediate surroundings, rather than to past regrets or future plans, as are we.

At various points along the phylogenetic footpath from amoebas to Molly to you and to me, the essentials of mind and personality successively emerge. In the higher *zones* that we will explore in successive chapters, personality constructs increasingly reflect greater complexity and higher levels of abstraction. No personality psychologist seriously speaks of "self-actualized" amoebas, because a single cell does not have adequate complexity to form a *self*, let alone engage in introspection about the place of such a "self" in the universe. Dogs, not snakes, are deemed "humankind's best friend" because dogs possess brains with sufficient complexity to forge emotional bonds with their owners through *limbic resonance* (Lewis, Amini, & Lannon, 2000).

So, as we ascend our vertical axis, *personality* evolves from molecules, chromosomes, and single cells to broader constructs in the form of traits, superfactors, and persons. Although personality is absent in amoebas, its precursors appear in Skinner's pigeons, emerge with tail-wagging exuberance in Molly, and approach a philosophical/spiritual pinnacle in you and in me.

In summary, we can answer our earlier question: amoebas do not have personalities, dogs do. Nonetheless, Molly's personality differs substantively from yours and mine. She has limited ability to transcend her immediate circumstances in order to focus on distant goals. She has limited choices, reduced responsibility, and little capacity for ethical reflection.

PERSON AS PREDISPOSITIONS

In the previous chapter we learned that behaviorists view personality as a collection of conditioned habits, locating their most important constructs (e.g., punishers and reinforcers) in the *Situational Zone*. Previously (in Chapter 2) we discovered that psychologists working in the lower regions of the *Physiological Zone* view personality as an envelope of biochemical molecules or as combinations of chromosomes. Now, somewhat higher in the *Physiological Zone*, we find theorists looking inward, seeking to understand people in terms of their **traits:** *inner predispositions to think and act in characteristic ways.*

A bottom-up approach. Trait theorists are methodologically similar to compositionists and behaviorists in utilizing a bottom-up, bit by bit (trait by trait) approach to the study of personality. Did you ever wonder how a windup clock works? I did, back when I was in the fourth grade. Taking the clock apart wasn't hard, but putting it back together again—well, I learned firsthand what the Humpty Dumpty poem was really about.

In a way, that's how trait theorists operate. They know personality works—they have seen that people can be consistent and unique, and maintain a certain behavioral rhythm—but they are *curious* about what *really* makes people "tick." So they disassemble personality into the thousands of bits of behavior (habits and traits) that comprise a person's daily life and then they measure individuals' rankings on a large variety of traits. Then they sort these traits into clusters *(factors),* and portray personality as a conglomerate of such clusters. It's somewhat like putting together a 1,000-piece puzzle: gathering the sky-blue pieces in one corner of the table, the earth tones in another, and the red pieces that comprise the "old red barn" in yet another cluster. Trait theorists statistically sort the "pieces" or traits of personality into clusters *(factors)* and then assemble these into a meaningful portrait.

Predicting on the basis of predispositions. Trait theorists use traits to predict future behaviors. Thus, if ten-year-old Tommy scored high on a trait for aggression, we would not be surprised to find out that he is frequently in trouble for fighting on the playground. Conversely, since we would not expect someone scoring high on traits linked to femininity to slug another person in the face, we would predict that Tommy would score low on femininity. Adding other traits to our list, we could come up with a trait-based description of Tommy based on his rankings on such traits as warmth, sensitivity, perfectionism, self-reliance, conscientiousness, suspiciousness, friendliness, self-confidence, and shame (to list only some of the possibilities). Each trait has a *range,* so Tommy could be seen as *mildly* aggressive, *moderately* aggressive, or *extremely* aggressive.

Newspapers create pictures in much the same way. If we view pictures in our daily newspaper using a magnifying glass, we notice that each picture is composed of hundreds of little dots of ink—each particular ink spot ranging in intensity from *light* to *medium* to *dark.* Trait theorists form their personality "portraits" in much the same way; by ranking a person as "light, medium, or dark" along numerous traits ("dots") that combine to form a composite portrait of personality.

Before considering trait theories in more detail, we need to understand two statistical operations, *correlation* and *factor analysis,* that are commonly used by trait theorists in their research.

Correlation *is the <u>co-relation</u> of two things that vary together.* Your hands, for example, are positively co-related: they vary together. If, as a human being, you have a left hand there is a very high probability that you also have a right hand. If it weren't for accidents or birth defects, the *correlation* would be perfect and could be mathematically expressed as a *positive correlation coefficient* of +1.0. In other words, we could say that for every 25,000 left hands at an athletic stadium, we could expect to find 25,000 right hands. Even taking tragedies into account, the correlation is still extremely high (probably +.99 or thereabouts).

The *size* of the correlation indicates the *strength* of the co-relationships, while the *sign (+ or −)* indicates the *direction.* A *negative* correlation simply means that two things vary together in *opposite* directions. For example, in outdoor athletic stadiums, we expect to find a *negative* correlation between mittens and temperature; i.e., you expect to see few mittens during a July baseball game when temperatures are high, but many mittens during a November football game when temperatures are low. The correlation of mittens with outdoor temperatures is strong but negative: high temperatures, few mittens; low temperatures, many mittens. Of course, this would not be a perfect correlation because some people with cold hands use their pockets as hand warmers and others simply tough it out; but I suspect the correlation would be in the $-.50$ to $-.75$ range during a late-November Green Bay Packers home game.

Correlation is <u>not</u> causation. What's really important to remember is the famous phrase taught to beginning statistics students: "Correlation is *not* causation." Sometimes there *might be* a causal relationship, but frequently there is *not*. Left hands don't *cause* right hands, even though cold temperatures *do* cause people to wear mittens. A *correlation coefficient* is a number that tells you how strongly two things vary together, but it does not tell you if there is any *causal* relationship between them. When people plunge to their deaths by jumping off skyscrapers (a correlation of $+1.0$) we don't conclude that the skyscrapers *cause* suicide.

Church steeples and murder rates. Similarly, although we could probably show a positive correlation between the height of church steeples and the number of homicides in a large metropolitan area, we would intuitively guess that church steeples do not *cause* homicides. We would likely find that in the inner city, where urban blight and homicides are more prevalent, a number of grand old church steeples still stand—relics from a more splendid past. As we move outward toward suburbia, we encounter more modern churches (with shorter steeples) and lower murder rates. However, the *causal* factors would likely be found in more jobs and affluence, less drug addiction, more effective law enforcement, and a whole variety of socioeconomic factors—not in the height of church steeples.

In science our findings are seldom as obvious as church steeples, and frequently our intuitions can mislead us. For example, when researchers find correlations between specific genes and certain behaviors, we are inclined to believe there *must* be some sort of biological causation at work, but this is not necessarily true. Consider, for example, the strong positive correlation between X chromosomes and hair length. The correlation is not perfect, because some women wear short hair, and some men wear long hair; but it is probably in the $+.90$ range, because *on the average,* women (with two XX chromosomes) wear long hair, and men (with a single X chromosome) wear short hair. Although X chromosomes and hair length are strongly and positively correlated, we intuitively know that this correlation has little to do with biology and is rather a result of social customs.

This is a persistent problem for trait-theory researchers. When sifting through vast arrays of correlations in search of "basic" personality factors, it is difficult to decide which variables are *causally* connected (e.g., temperature and mittens) and which are serendipitous correlations (e.g., church steeples and homicide rates).

Factor Analysis: A few good factors? Like a Marine recruiter, searching for "A Few Good Men," the typical trait theorist is hoping to find "A Few Good Factors" as he or she uses *factor analysis* to sort through a vast array of correlations. **Factor analysis** *is a mathematical procedure for reducing a large collection of correlations to a small number of core factors.* Consider, for example, an Olympic decathelete who competes in ten different events (e.g., 100-meter, the javelin and discus throws, shot put, pole vault, etc.). We might describe such an all-around athlete by enumerating *specific* skills: sprinting, running, jumping while running, leaping, lunging, springing, aiming, throwing, twirling, pitching, hurling, etc. Alternatively, we could describe the same athlete in terms of a *few basic factors:* speed, strength, and agility. Similarly, a personality psychologist might describe a person as outgoing, gregarious, friendly, cheerful, optimistic, and empathic; or simply as *sociable.*

Choosing factors was subjective. Deciding how to arrive at a *few basic factors* was frequently a highly subjective process. Nowhere is this more apparent than in the disagreements between Eysenck and Cattell, two of the leading trait theorists of the twentieth century. Although both used factor analysis, they dramatically disagreed on how many "basic" factors were needed to describe personality. Since no one was certain precisely what personality "looks like," deciding on which factors to use in describing it was *highly subjective.* Calculators and statistical techniques helped to boil things down, but in the end they offered these early investigators little help in deciding which clusters mattered most. It was not simply a matter of "counting noses," it was a matter of deciding whether to count noses, ears, toes, or tonsils! Each personality researcher had to decide *which* variables to investigate, *where* to look for them, and *how many* correlations to combine into clusters. With so many cooks in the kitchen, and no recipe to follow—only measuring cups and a pantry full of ingredients—it's not surprising that there was little harmony regarding which traits best describe personality.

Finding what you're searching for. If you believe (as did Eysenck) that you must begin low in the *Physiological Zone* searching for a *few* basic biological factors, it wouldn't be surprising that you might conclude that *extraversion-introversion* is one of three basic personality dimensions. Consequently, you would design test questions and assessment devices to measure a person's "outgoing" or "turning-inward" attitudes and behaviors. On the other hand, if you believe (as did Cattell) that personality is composed of more than a dozen different factors, your measuring devices will be designed to find them. Bottom line: factor analysis is a measurement technique, it doesn't tell you *what* to measure. Consequently, *your ideas about the composition of personality will profoundly affect <u>what</u> you try to measure and <u>how</u> you try to assess it.* Mapping someone's chromosomes requires different assessment techniques than measuring *introversion.* Since there are no identity tags like a kangaroo's pouch or a pelican's bill to help you know if you're dealing with a marsupial or a feathered vertebrate, much of what you "see" in hunting down personality depends on the theoretical lenses you peer through and the measurement techniques you employ:

> The researcher must also remember that factor analysis will always produce factors. Thus, factor analysis is always a potential candidate for the "garbage in, garbage out" phenomenon. If the researcher indiscriminately includes a large number of variables and hopes that factor analysis will "figure it out," then the possibility of poor results is high. (Hair, Anderson, Tatham, & Black, 1998, p. 97)

Because of different starting assumptions regarding basic traits, two of the leading trait theorists of the twentieth century arrived at very different numbers when it came to "boiling down" personality, Cattell ending up with *sixteen* personality factors, Eysenck boiling it down to *three*.

Are we hunting for unicorns or platypuses? There is a delicate balance to be struck between creativity and skepticism. Sometimes when a personality theorist claims to have discovered a "furry fish," or a "flying lobster," others are inclined to be critical. However, just because you have never seen a "unicorn" in your backyard does not mean such a creature could not exist. In fact, a unicorn (an animal with the body of a horse, the tail of a lion, and a single horn in the middle of the forehead) seems to me a more likely creature than a platypus (a furry creature shaped like a beaver, with a thick, flat tail, webbed feet, and a duck's bill). Problem is, unicorns don't exist but platypuses (platypi—if you prefer) *do*. If you look up *platypus* in your dictionary, you will probably find a picture, because even Webster can't define this creature in words alone. Platypuses blur our usual boundaries between beavers and ducks—appearing as a blend of both. Baby platypi hatch from eggs but feed on their mothers' milk. An egg-laying, milk–producing mammal? Go figure!

Similarly, in our hunt for personality there is no "moose-have-antlers, zebras-have-stripes" certainty. On this scientific safari, one hunter looks for personality to "walk" on three legs, another expects five, while someone else says it takes sixteen legs to support this creature. Who is right? Are we looking for a unicorn or a platypus? Where's a photo?

In short, correlation, factor analysis, and other statistical techniques cannot guarantee that we will arrive at an accurate portrait of personality. Statistical tools can assist us in *quantifying* and packaging *whatever* we focus upon, but packaging doesn't change the commodity—whether we purchase milk by the glass or by the gallon, milk is still milk. However, *what* we measure does makes a great deal of difference (the "garbage in garbage out" principle). If we statistically equip ourselves to search for unicorns, we may be prepared to saddle up and ride should we happen upon a horse with a horn; however, we may be ill equipped to analyze platypus milk.

Structural Equation Modeling (SEM): Contemporary antidote to subjectivity. Although subjective judgement will always play a crucial role in analyzing and interpreting data, new statistical tools are now available to help researchers decide among competing claims for basic factors. **Structural equation modeling** *includes a family of advanced statistical techniques that allow researchers to simultaneously study multiple relationships within a single model, using* <u>statistical</u> *rather than* <u>subjective</u> *judgements.* SEM provides contemporary personality psychologists with the tools to study multiple relationships (e.g., such as those existing among biochemical components, personality traits, and observed behaviors). SEM allows researchers to rely more on statistical techniques and less on subjective biases in sorting out which clusters of traits deserve further study.

"Trait" Means Different Things in Different Zones

A *trait* refers to an inner tendency or predisposition for a person to act in a certain way; however, the term *trait* means different things at different levels of analysis. In the *Physiological Zone,* we might describe someone as high in epinephrine or low in serotonin—energetic or sluggish. In the *Insight Zone* we might characterize someone as

BOX 4.1 ■ The Best-kept Secret in Psychology: If You Really Want to Know, Be Square!

Personality psychologists have been keeping a little secret to themselves. They have not always informed the public of the "Be-Square" secret, so the average person intuitively thinks of a correlation as a percentage. The average person thinks that if A and B are correlated at .50 that accounts for about 50 percent of what is happening. **Wrong!** If you want to think in percentages you must *square the correlation coefficient.*

It's very natural to think in percentages—from the earliest years in school, you were proud when you got 100 percent, or even 90 percent on a spelling test, probably not as happy with 70 percent or 50 percent. Thinking in percentages is perfectly natural and totally legitimate, but in order to think that way you have to transform correlations. From now on—for as long as you live—whenever you see a correlation coefficient, **square it.** Thus, a correlation of .50, when squared (.50)(.50), yields 25 percent. A correlation of .30 becomes (.30)(.30) = (9 percent). Notice how drastically this changes your thinking. Now instead of looking at a correlation of .30 and thinking "I can

account for about 1/3 of the relationship," you realize "I can account for less than 10 percent." Or, equally accurate, "More than 90 percent of what's going on is unaccounted for."

Since personality researchers sometimes report correlations in the .30 to .40 range, it is not surprising that they are reluctant to tell the world that in such cases they have accounted for approximately 10–15 percent of the relationship. Or to put it more drearily, they cannot account for 85–90 percent of what is happening. To state it technically, when you square a correlation coefficient, you discover the *percent of variance accounted for.* That indicates to what extent knowledge about one variable allows you to make good predictions about the other. But, as we've already seen, even when correlations are high, we can't be certain precisely how the variables relate to each other. Accounting for how strongly two variables correlate is only a beginning step in the process of understanding such relationships.

Now you know. The secret's out. *Be square!*

psychologically sensitive or thoughtful. In the *Social Zone,* as friendly, sneaky, or trustworthy. At an even higher level on the vertical axis, in the *Transpersonal/Spiritual Zone,* we might describe an individual as spiritual or wise.

In whatever zone we focus, *traits* are relatively stable predispositions by which people can be ranked—*all* people. *Everyone* can be ranked as low, moderate, or high in "musical ability," just as everyone can be ranked as short, medium, or tall in height. From among a nearly limitless number of dimensions, personality researchers have focused on those traits that appear to help us *go, grow,* or become *unique.*

(1) Traits as the biological "bricks" of personality. Many trait theorists maintain strong ties to biology. As Zuckerman put it: "The Greek physicians had the right idea, but the wrong humors . . ." (Zuckerman, 1995, p. 325). Eysenck and Zuckerman are kindred spirits with the Greeks in seeking to reduce personality to biology. For these theorists, traits are the biological "bricks" used in building a theory of personality solidly based on biological foundations.

(2) Traits as statistical coordinates. In this chapter we will also consider Cattell's statistically derived theory as well as the more recent formulations of

Costa and McCrae. In these models, biology is not predominant. Cattell was less concerned with discovering the underlying biological foundations of traits, and more interested in *predicting* how a particular person would respond in a given circumstance. This is reflected in his definition: "Personality is that which permits a prediction of what a person will do in a given situation" (Cattell, 1950). For Cattell, traits were *mathematical coordinates* helping us to predict how a person with certain underlying dispositions (source traits) will respond behaviorally (surface traits) in a specific situation.

(3) Traits as the biological foundations of humanistic psychology. We will begin our discussion by considering Gordon Allport because he was the first American trait theorist. Allport insisted that traits are *actual biological entities*— "really there"; however, he did not remain in the *Physiological Zone,* but climbed several levels to integrate biologically based traits with *humanistic strivings* in the *Insight* and *Social Zones.*

GORDON ALLPORT: TRAITS AS BIOPHYSICAL FOUNDATIONS FOR HUMANISM

Gordon Allport, one of the earliest and most influential trait theorists, was also one of the most upward-reaching. His doctoral dissertation in 1922 was the first American study of personality traits, and he is also credited with coining the term *humanistic psychology* (DeCarvalho, 1991). He was a man for all seasons (and zones), not limiting himself to the investigation of traits (which he considered *real* biological structures), but ascending upward and ranging widely to study the psychology of radio, rumor, race relations, and religious experience.

Background Check

Childhood—the kid who swallowed a dictionary. Gordon Allport (1897–1967), the fourth son of a schoolteacher and a country doctor, remembered himself as socially shy, an isolated child who aspired to be the "star" among a small group of friends. He described himself as "quick with words, poor at games," a view apparently shared by one of his schoolmates who said, "Aw, that guy swallowed a dictionary" (Allport, 1966, p. 4).

Meeting with Freud. After graduating from Harvard, Allport spent a year abroad, teaching English. During this time, he arranged to meet Freud. Entering the famous red burlap office, Allport found that Freud, true to psychoanalytic form, said nothing, but simply waited in silence for Allport to state his mission. Scrambling for a topic to break the silence, Allport told Freud about a small boy whom he had observed while riding the streetcar to Freud's office. The little boy, apparently suffering from a dirt phobia, found everything to be dirty; he didn't want to sit in a certain place, didn't want to sit next to a dirty man, etc. Allport thought the cause of the four-year-old's phobia was obviously apparent in the form of his "well-starched . . . dominant and purposive looking" mother (1966, p. 8), but he was surprised by Freud's interpretation. When Allport finished his story, he recalled that "Freud fixed his kindly therapeutic eyes upon me and said 'Was that little boy you?' " (1966, p. 8).

Put off by Freud's implication that Allport saw himself in the boy, he later recounted that "The experience taught me that depth psychology, for all its merits, may plunge too deep, and that psychologists would do well to give full recognition to manifest motives before proving the unconscious" (1966, p. 8).

Zeitgeist

However, if he was put off by Freud's "depth" psychology, Allport was also disenchanted with the behaviorism of his day. He warned against wholeheartedly accepting behaviorism, fearing its methods were too restrictive: "The irrelevance of much present-day psychology to human life comes from its emphasis on mechanical aspects of reactivity to the neglect of man's wider experiences, his aspirations, and his incessant endeavor to master and to mould his environment (1966, p. 23)." Embracing what he termed "systematic eclecticism," Allport identified himself most closely with humanists such as Carl Rogers and Abraham Maslow (see Chapter 11).

ASKING THE BIG FOUR QUESTIONS

What Are the Parts?

Allport defined **personality** as *the dynamic organization within the individual of those psychophysical systems that determine his unique adjustments to the environment* (Allport, 1937, p. 48, emphasis in original). This definition allows for "inner" predispositions (traits) as well as taking into account "adjustments to the environment." He criticized the psychology of his day for being too preoccupied with the past: "People, it seems, are busy leading their lives into the future, whereas psychology, for the most part, is busy tracing them into the past" (1955, p. 51).

With his emphasis on traits, inner motivations, social variables, and spiritual values, Allport touched all the *zones* of our grid, but he was most strongly anchored in the trait domain where his ideas influenced subsequent workers such as Eysenck, Cattell, and the Big Five theorists. Although Allport was the pioneer American trait theorist, he never got lost in statistics, but always emphasized **personology**—*the study of persons as unified, conscious, whole individuals.*

Habits. Allport defined **habits** as *specific, low-level behaviors that form the foundation for higher-level traits.* Whenever you shower, wash your hair, brush your teeth, clean your nails, or change your underwear, you are engaging in a specific *habit* under the control of the higher-level *trait* of cleanliness.

Traits. According to Allport, a **trait** is *"a generalized and focalized neuropsychic system (peculiar to the individual), with the capacity to render many stimuli functionally equivalent, and to initiate and guide consistent (equivalent) forms of adaptive and expressive behavior"* (Allport, 1937, p. 295, italics added).

To translate this into more understandable English, the "capacity to render many stimuli functionally equivalent" means that if you have a *trait for anxiety*, it translates numerous stimuli into anxiety triggers: flying, driving, talking, boating, skiing, painting, writing—even falling asleep—might be permeated with anxiety. Meeting new people would almost certainly make you anxious. On the other hand, if you have a strong *trait for friendliness*, you might, like Will Rogers, never meet a person you didn't like. Or, in place of feeling anxious around others, you might share the experience of Samuel Johnson who said, "The feeling of friendship is like that of being comfortably filled with roast beef . . ." (Brussell, 1988, p. 219).

From a zonal perspective, Allport's definition of *trait* as a "neuropsychic system" implies a physiological (compositional) base. For him, a trait referred to something *concrete*, not merely to a consistent way of looking at things: "A trait . . . has more than nominal existence; it is independent of the observer, it is *really* there . . ." (Allport, 1937, pp. 337–338). However, defining traits as "neuropsychic systems" in purely biological terms proved too limiting and too concrete to explain the complexities of personality, so Allport (like Eysenck and Cattell, who came later) formulated other kinds of traits in higher zones. That's how the term *trait* came to mean different things at different levels of analysis.

What Makes a Person Go?

Proprium. Allport created the construct *proprium* to encompass the energizing, motivating aspects of *personality as a whole*. Seeking to avoid a *homunculus* ("little man") or a *self* inside the personality, Allport defined the **proprium** as *the totality of the person as process, as an entity that is becoming* (1955, p. 53; 1961, p. 130). He created the term *proprium* (from the prefix "pro") to capture the idea of *growth and forward movement of the entire person*. *Propriate functions* are Allport's holistic way of blending motivation, development, and uniqueness into his model of personality. With *propriate functions*, he was able to move beyond his biologically based trait theory to address higher-level humanistic and transpersonal concerns. Instead of an *agentic self*, Allport described seven propriate functions that involve the *entire personality*, not only the *self*. The easiest way to keep this straight is simply to think of *proprium* as a synonym for *personality-functioning-as-a-whole*.

What Makes a Person Grow?

Allport's seven *propriate functions* develop gradually over time—none of them is innate—in a holistic, harmonious way. Each of the seven propriate functions is an emerging aspect of the developing person-as-a-whole. In this way Allport's seven stages of propriate development are consistent with the zonal perspective of our text, moving from viewing the person as a biological composition at the molecular level (Chapter 2) to perceiving the person as a spiritual seeker at the transpersonal levels (Chapter 13).

TABLE 4.1

Developmental Eras of the Proprium

1. BODILY SELF:	Develops during the first year; a realization of the body and a discovery of sensations.
2. SELF-IDENTITY:	Develops during the second year; a sense of inner sameness and continuity.
3. SELF-ESTEEM:	Develops during the third year; a sense of pride and accomplishment in mastering tasks.
4. SELF-EXTENSION:	Develops between ages four and six; a sense of ownership outside of the self.
5. SELF-IMAGE:	Develops between ages four and six, in response to an awareness of how one's behavior measures up to the expectations of others.
6. SELF-AS-RATIONAL-COPER:	Develops between ages six and twelve; a sense of one's rational problem solving capacities.
7. PROPRIATE STRIVING:	Develops between age twelve and adolescence; a sense of one's purpose and goals in the long-term future.

Allport's seven propriate functions. Allport believed that development occurs in gradual stages and involves the entire personality. Allport saw the proprium as evolving in seven developmental stages which all merged in the final stage—adulthood.

(1) Bodily self (first year). The first propriate function to emerge is a *dawning awareness of sensations in the body and a discovery of body.* Where is *your* propriate self located? Probably somewhere in your head region—perhaps behind your eyes. Certainly not beneath your *toes!* Your propriate self is not evenly distributed across your body. As a child, when your mom told you to wash your hands and face, you likely washed the front of your hands and the front of your face, but hardly ever the back of your hands or behind your ears. The bodily self is the primary propriate experience during the first year of life.

(2) Self-identity (second year). The second propriate function to emerge is the *awareness of inner sameness and continuity.* Even toddlers feel some sense of sameness from day to day, and this sense of continuity is further facilitated by language development.

(3) Self-esteem (third year). Between the ages of two and three, self-esteem blossoms as a child experiences a *sense of pride in accomplishing and mastering tasks.* This is also when independence and negativism develop alongside the pride and self-esteem.

(4) Self-extension (four to six). Between the ages of four and six *self-extension,* or a *sense of ownership,* develops as the child identifies "my tricycle" or "my ball."

(5) Self-image (four to six). Self-image develops as *a result of an awareness of how one's behavior measures up to the expectation of others.* "Good" and "naughty" selves emerge.

(6) Self-as-rational-coper (six to twelve). Between the ages of six and twelve, *self-as-rational-coper* flourishes as children discover and develop their rational capacities to solve problems.

(7) Propriate striving (twelve through adolescence). During adolescence, *propriate striving, the development of long-term purposes and goals,* takes place. Owning and accepting one's feelings, needs, thoughts, and goals provides the foundation for adulthood.

(8) Self-as-knower (adulthood). During adulthood, the totality of all previous experiences is integrated into an awareness of self.

Functional autonomy. Allport's controversial notion of **functional autonomy** suggests that *adult motives and behaviors are not necessarily tied to earlier childhood experiences.* Imagine, for example, that Jamie's father was an avid hockey fan. During kindergarten he bought Jamie his first pair of skates and arranged for him to play in a preschool hockey league. During the early grades and middle school Jamie continued to play hockey at every opportunity available, and Dad was always on the sidelines encouraging him. It made Jamie happy to make his father proud. However, by the time Jamie reached high school he was genuinely "into" hockey for his own pleasure and Dad (who had been promoted) was frequently unable to attend games because of business-related travel. After attending college on a hockey scholarship, Jamie was recruited to play for the Colorado Avalanche. Allport would argue that although Jamie's hockey career was *historically* related to his father's enthusiasm for the sport, by the time Jamie reached high school—and certainly during college—his motives for playing hockey were entirely free of his original motives to please Dad. In other words, his motives had become *functionally autonomous.*

What Makes a Person Unique?

Allport was a strong advocate for the uniqueness of the person, at a time when behaviorism appeared bent on blotting it out. Allport believed that personality was so complex that all legitimate methods of study should be employed in seeking to understand it:

> How shall a psychological life history be written? What processes and what structures must a full-bodied account of personality include? How can one detect unifying threads in a life, if they exist?. . . . What then is my personal idea? I suppose it has to do with the search for a theoretical system—for one that will allow for truth wherever found, one that will encompass the totality of human experience and do full justice to the nature of man. (1966, pp. 3, 23)

FACING THE TOUGH TWINS

Is It Testable?

Nomothetic vs. idiographic research methods. Allport believed in research—his whole life was spent in academia—but he believed that personality psychologists ought to conduct research that preserves the uniqueness of each person, so he introduced a distinction that is still recognized today. **Nomothetic research** *(from the Greek <u>nomos</u>, meaning laws) is the attempt to discover general laws that apply to all people.* Allport also emphasized the importance of **idiographic research** *(from the Greek <u>idios,</u> meaning one's own, and graphein, to write), an approach that emphasizes individuality and employs techniques designed to highlight the uniqueness of each person.* It is this *idiographic* emphasis that characterizes Allport's personology.

Although Allport was one of the earliest trait theorists, his diverse contributions also had significant influence in the *Insight, Social,* and *Transpersonal Zones.* Differing from the psychoanalysts of his day, he did not ignore the societal influences in the *Social Zone.* Motivated by concerns about rumors that circulated following the Japanese attack on Pearl Harbor in 1941, Allport and his colleagues (Allport & Postman, 1947) carried out social psychological research regarding rumors and advised the federal government.

One classic study demonstrated how racism influences rumors. The experiment begins with a subject viewing a slide in which a white man holding a knife is apparently arguing with a black man in a subway car. By the time the story is passed on to several subjects, in over half the replications, the black man is erroneously reported to be holding the knife (Allport & Postman, 1947).

In the *Transpersonal/Spiritual Zone,* Allport criticized the psychologists of his day for ignoring the role of religion in personality (Allport, 1950). He was interested in how religion relates to racial prejudice. He distinguished between people who have an **extrinsic religious orientation** *and who use religion for self-serving purposes such as increasing status in the community,* and those of **intrinsic religious orientation**, *who incorporate religious values of loving other people into their own belief system* (Allport & Ross, 1967).

Is It Useful?

Allport was not a practicing psychotherapist and did not develop specific treatment techniques; however, many of his ideas have been assimilated into mainstream psychology via other theories. His thinking ranged widely across several zones, and his research stimulated lines of investigation that are still active today.

He was an important forerunner of Cattell, Eysenck, and the Big Five theorists. The influence of his research in the *Social Zone* is still seen today. Some investigators have confirmed his finding that extrinsic religious orientation predicts higher racial prejudice (e.g., Donahue, 1985; Herek, 1987). However, the picture is not clear, because *intrinsically* religious people showed higher than average prejudice against homosexuals (Herek, 1987).

Religious orientation also appears to interact with gender biases in complex ways. Burris and Jackson (1999) found that undergraduates with high intrinsic religious orientation scores were more tolerant of a male's abusive behavior toward a girlfriend who had rejected his marriage proposal, saying she might be a lesbian. In another study, however, intrinsically religious subjects were less likely to devalue a rape victim (Joe, McGee, & Dazey, 1977).

Again, these relationships appear complex and the findings difficult to interpret, but such studies illustrate the *heuristic* power of Allport's thinking across a wide range of issues.

SUMMARY OF ALLPORT

A Man for All Seasons

Allport was a man for all seasons—and all *zones*. His influence lives on, not only in trait theories, but also in social, humanistic, existential, and spiritual psychologies with their emphases on meaning and values. His distinction between nomothetic and idiographic continues to stimulate debate and research. Recently, Pelham (1993) asserted that within-subject research designs and idiographic techniques are able to capture the truth of *phenomenological reality* (personal, ongoing experience) in a way that between-subject designs fail to grasp. Lamielle (1981) has argued against "continued adherence to the long dominant 'nomothetic' paradigm for personality research," arguing instead for what he terms an **idiothetic approach** *that combines the best features of both idiographic and nomothetic approaches* by utilizing norms while still respecting individuality. Allport's distinctions between *extrinsic* and *intrinsic religious experience* appear as relevant in the postmodern, post-911 twenty-first century as when he first discussed them.

THE GREEK CONNECTION: HANS J. EYSENCK'S THREE-FACTOR MODEL

Background Check

Childhood. Hans J. Eysenck (1916–1998), the only child of theatrical parents, was born in Berlin, on March 4, 1916. Eysenck remembered his mother as a beautiful actress who starred in the silent films of her era. She fell in love with and married Anton Eysenck, a star of stage and operettas. Hans Jurgon was born soon thereafter, but by the time he was two, his parents had divorced, because his father was a "womanizer" (Eysenck, 1990, p. 11).

A "motherless" child. Eysenck had few positive memories of his mother, and regarded her as an inadequate parent: "I don't think nature intended her to be a mother. I saw very little of her, except occasionally on holidays, and she never managed to treat me as a child, or show much interest in what I was doing." (1990, p. 7).

A distant father. Eysenck remembered his father as less than satisfactory. He recalled how his father taught him to ride a bike: "He took me to the top of a hill, told me that I had to sit on the saddle and pump the pedals and make the wheels go round." Then, leaving his son to struggle on his own, the elder Eysenck went off to do some target practice. Meanwhile, Eysenck recalls, "I got on it, started to pedal, and promptly fell off. But after an hour, and many similar discomfitures, I managed to wobble along. A good training in independence, but not perhaps the behaviour of a loving father." (Eysenck, 1990, p. 12)

From biting student to tough-minded scientist. Eysenck's distaste for his father was undoubtedly reactivated (Freud called it *transference;* see Chapter 6) by Herr Meier, an authoritarian music teacher who demanded that Eysenck come to the front of the class and sing. When Eysenck persisted in refusing, Herr Meier tried to hit him with a ruler, but Eysenck quickly withdrew his hand, causing the teacher to miss. This served to infuriate Meier further, and he raised his arm and was about to strike again when Eysenck took matters into his own hands (or teeth):

> I leaned forward and sank my teeth into the fleshy part of his hand, underneath his thumb. I have always been tall and strong, and I bit him very hard indeed. He dropped the ruler, blanched (I have never seen anybody's face go so white so quickly) and tried to withdraw his hand. I hung on like a bull terrier. . . . (1990, p. 16)

This incident was, perhaps, a metaphor of Eysenck's psychology career, during which he relished attacking authorities and ideas such as Freud, psychoanalysis, traditional psychiatry, established views of intelligence, and traditional approaches to psychotherapy. He admitted as much: "In many ways what I did then [biting his music teacher] was prognostic of what I was to do later on, though in rather less physical fashion. You cannot let people get away with wrongdoing just because they are strong and powerful; whatever the cost, you have to stand up for yourself" (1990, p. 17).

And stand up for himself he did! Over his long and influential career, Eysenck wrote seventy-nine books and more than a thousand journal articles, in addition to mentoring several hundred students through completion of their doctoral degrees.

Zeitgeist

Education. Eysenck left Germany because of the rise of Nazism and enrolled in the psychology program at London University, where he earned both a bachelor's degree and a Ph.D. by the age of twenty-three. When Eysenck entered psychology in the 1930s, the field of personality was dominated by psychodynamic (Freudian) approaches. Measurement-based approaches were not well represented, and research was not very comprehensive in range. While still in his twenties, Eysenck began an ambitious program of research, measuring a wide array of *molecular* variables in the *Physiological Zone,* and seeking to relate them to *macro* measures of behaviors and traits in the *Situational* and *Social Zones.* His stands as a twentieth-century bridge, connecting the compositional theories of the ancient Greeks with contemporary measurement-based personality theories such as the Five-Factor Model.

Although Eysenck criticized Galen's theory of four temperaments for being "almost entirely of a subjective character" (1967, p. 34), he nevertheless felt that "this system still has much to teach us" (1964, p. 284), and he presented a figure integrating Galen's typology with factor analytic studies.

From categories to dimensions. Eysenck's quarrel with Galen was not that his typologies were wrong; it was that Galen treated the four temperaments as *discrete categories* instead of *calibrated dimensions.* Modern trait theorists see types as composed of *normally distributed* characteristics. In measurement terms, the Greeks thought of

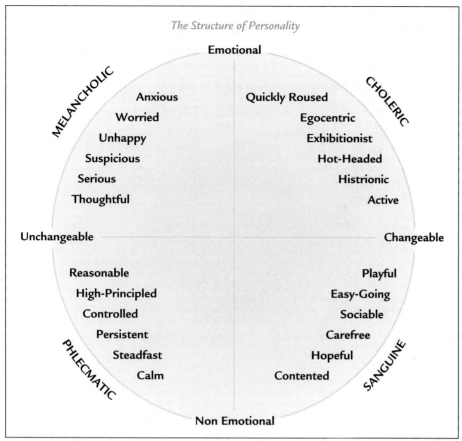

Figure 4.1 ■ *Integrating Galen's and Eysenck's Typologies.* (Adapted from Eysenck 1967 Biological Basis of Personality)

types as *nominal* categories, whereas contemporary personality psychologists think of types as made up of countless *ordinal* traits.

> The ancient Greeks and the psychoanalysts conceived of types as unique constellations of traits with no gradations between them; a person is either an introvert or an extravert, for instance. Psychologists who measured traits found that they are distributed in a normal bell-shaped curve . . . with most persons falling close to the mean and fewer persons near the extremes of the distribution. . . . Most persons are ambiverts, rather than introverts or extraverts, in the sense that their measured tendencies fall near the mean rather than at the two extremes. (Zuckerman, 1991, p. 4)

ASKING THE BIG FOUR QUESTIONS

What Are the Parts?

Traits, "superfactors," and personality. Eysenck concluded that personality was comprised of three broad "superfactors," each made up of narrower traits. Persons high on **(P) psychoticism** show *aggressive, cold, egocentric, impersonal, impulsive, antisocial, unempathic, creative, tough-minded* traits. Persons high on **(E) extraversion** are seen as *active, assertive, carefree, dominant, lively, sensation seeking, sociable, surgent,* and *venturesome.* Individuals high on **(N) neuroticism** are described as *anxious, depressed, irrational, moody, emotional, shy, tense,* and experiencing *guilt* and *low self-esteem.*

E covers the more "normal" range of traits, while *N* and *P* encompass traits more commonly encountered in clinical problems such as neurosis, psychosis, and psychopathy. Eysenck formulated a hierarchical model of personality, moving from *specific responses* to *habitual responses, traits,* and *types*—all combining to form *personality.*

If Figure 4.2 were illustrating "biking with friends," **specific responses** might include such behaviors as *grasping the handle bars, pumping the pedals,* and *balancing your body by leaning into turns.* These would coalesce into the **habitual response,** or *riding a bicycle,* which would be quite different from *playing golf* or *going out to eat.* At a still higher level of abstraction, all of a person's habitual responses might contribute to the *trait* of *sociability* in an *extraverted type* of person who plays golf at a country club, rides bike with other members of a bike club, and frequently goes out to movies and dinner with friends. For Eysenck, **personality** *is composed of specific responses, habitual responses, and traits—all organized into more or less stable and enduring configuration of a person's temperament, intellect, and physiology that characterizes unique adjustment to the environment.*

Eysenck had a similar hierarchal conception of the relationship between genes and behavior (see Figure 4.3). At Level 1: *level of the gene,* Eysenck was unable to obtain direct measurements, but with recent advances in genetics and molecular biology this is beginning to change. At Level 2: *laboratory studies,* Eysenck carried out experimental studies on speed of conditioning, sensory thresholds, vigilance, etc. and related these to Level 3: *behavioral habits,* which then fed into traits, types, and personality as a whole.

Whatever one might fault about Eysenck's theories, he is a splendid model of the scientist-practitioner, systematically investigating phenomena at the laboratory level and then attempting to apply his findings at the more abstract levels of typology, personality, and clinical practice.

Temperament types. Whereas Galen originally proposed four types of temperament, Eysenck proposed only two: "At the highest and most inclusive level of personality description, we are apparently dealing with two main dimensions . . ." (1967, pp. 36, 40). However, since Eysenck saw temperament in terms of *dimensions*

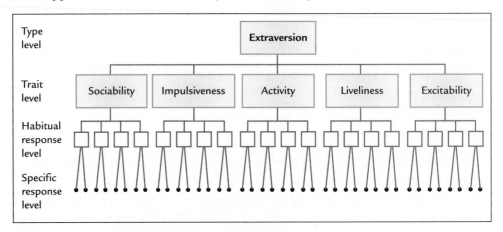

Figure 4.2 ■ *Eysenck's Hierarchical Model of Personality*

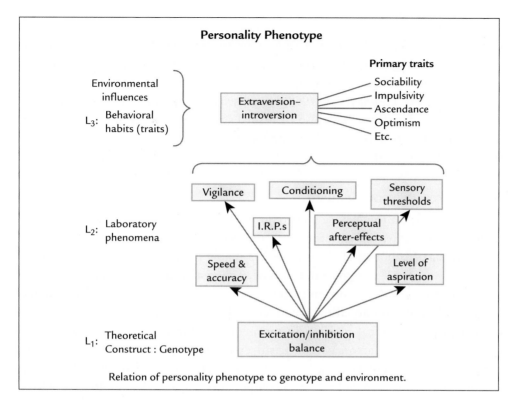

Figure 4.3 ■ *Personality Phenotype (Eysenck 1967, p. 220)*

rather than *categories,* one can superimpose these two dimensions, like a template, over Galen's four temperaments, and the similarities are obvious (see Figure 4.2).

Eysenck and his coworkers (1976, 1985) later formulated a third superfactor, *psychoticism (P),* which included a degree of psychopathy in the form of asocial and impulsive behaviors, absence of guilt, and egocentricity. Unlike Eysenck's other two superfactors, psychoticism is not a dimension with an opposite pole; rather it is a single factor, thought to be present in varying degrees.

What Makes a Person Go?

For Eysenck, as for earlier compositional theorists, there was no need to formulate a motivational force such as Freud's *libido.* According to Eysenck, body and personality are so closely connected that activating the body motivates the personality. According to Eysenck, "It is not only sensible but obligatory for us to search for underlying neurological, physiological, biochemical, and other causes for the observed behaviour patterns . . ." (1967, p. 225).

Eysenck spent his entire career investigating the relationship of his superfactors to a wide spectrum of behaviors, ranging from the molecular sensations involved in sensory and pain thresholds, to the macro behaviors seen in a habitual life of crime. He believed behavioral differences were surface manifestations of biologically based, genetically determined, compositional differences in traits: "Here we will rest content with arguing that some form of 'personality predisposition' theory . . . is in good agreement with the facts" (Eysenck, 1967, p. 39).

What Makes a Person Grow?

Unlike Freud, Erikson, Piaget, or other famous developmental theorists, Eysenck did not formulate stages of development. Instead, he argued that the consistency of behavior from a very early age supports compositional rather than environment-reactive theories: "Thomas *et al.* (1964) have discussed the reasoning underlying this proposition in detail, and have also furnished strong evidence to suggest that even during the first two years of life infants show consistent behaviour patterns" (Eysenck, 1967, p. 219).

What Makes a Person Unique?

Like Sir Francis Galton, whose picture hung in his study, Eysenck believed in the importance of individual differences, but he studied differences from a statistical rather than a personological perspective. His answer to "What makes an individual's personality unique?" was given in terms of varying amounts of his three superfactors. Like trait theorists before and after him, Eysenck focused more on basic ingredients and core commonalities than on individual uniqueness. He described individual psychological makeup in terms of biological composition, and then related it to his superfactors psychoticism, extraversion-introversion, and neuroticism. Like the ancient Greeks, he believed *individual uniqueness* resided in each person's peculiar *balance* of biological components. For Eysenck, biological reductionism was the royal road to truth.

FACING THE TOUGH TWINS

Is It Testable?

Eysenck ceaselessly sought to reduce the higher-level, macro formulations of personality found in the *Insight* and *Social Zones* to the molecular basics of biology found in the *Physiological Zone*. He tried to do this in scientifically rigorous ways, rejecting his own hypotheses if they could not be experimentally verified. His theory of personality rests on an extensive foundation of psychobiological research barely touched by most trait theorists. Never one to mince words, Eysenck said that if other personality theorists were not biological reductionists like himself, they didn't deserve to be called scientists: "Personality theories have much to lose by pretending to greater coverage or rigour than they in fact possess; in following this time-honoured primrose path to damnation they easily leave the field of science altogether" (Eysenck, 1967, p. 340).

Although Eysenck acknowledged that environment always plays a significant role, he believed that his three major superfactors were mostly genetically determined and would be found across most cultures. He carried out cross-cultural studies and reported that

> Identical factors have been found cross culturally in over 35 different countries covering most of the globe, from Uganda and Nigeria to Japan and mainland China, from the Capitalist countries of the West and the American continent to Eastern-bloc countries such as the Soviet Union, Hungary, Czechoslovakia, Bulgaria, and Yugoslavia. (Barrett & Eysenck, 1994)

Is It Useful?

Eysenck's theory proved to be one of the most heuristic of trait theories, due in large part to his own relentless efforts to connect *macro* personality constructs to a few *molecular* biological factors. Whereas Cattell (whom we shall discuss shortly) tended to lose readers with his complex mathematical formulas, Eysenck tried to distill everything to a few superfactors. He even outdistilled Galen and the ancient Greeks, who condensed everything in the universe to *four* elements (earth, air, fire, and water); Eysenck got it down to *three* broad superfactors. He spent his entire career in this sort of "top-down" reducing of higher level abstractions to one of his three all-encompassing biologically-based factors. His curiosity seemed limitless ranging from cigarettes to crime, including education and behavior genetics.

Cigarettes, school, and crime—a sampling of Eysenck's research interests.

Cigarettes and cancer. In the early 1920s, several researchers (Ludlum, 1918; Starr, 1922; and Rich, 1928) found evidence to suggest that individuals with alkaline saliva and urine are more emotionally unstable than those with acidic excretions. Eysenck (1965) reviewed evidence showing that lung cancer is associated with acidic smoke and with tobaccos grown in acidic soil; he concluded that "there is quite a strong correlation between neuroticism/emotionality and freedom from lung cancer," and suggested that "the relationship between neuroticism and greater alkalinity in saliva and urine may be in part responsible for this relationship between neuroticism and absence of lung cancer" (Eysenck, 1967, p. 58).

Education. In the field of education there has been considerable discussion about whether *discovery learning* (students are encouraged to explore on their own) is superior to *reception learning* (students are taught in a traditional manner). It turns out that *extraverted* children learn best with discovery learning while introverted children benefit most from a traditional approach (Leith, 1974). Such applications of Eysenck's personality model have tremendous implications for bettering schools. If personality styles could be matched with teaching methods—as research suggests—learning might become easier and more effective for all concerned.

Eysenck's lifelong commitment to buttressing higher-level abstract constructs with biologically based findings has exerted a corrective influence on a field that mainly considered personality to be the product of family and social influences. Today, personality psychologists are seriously examining the role of heredity in forming personality by comparing characteristics of identical and fraternal twins with nontwin siblings. By comparing twins adopted out and reared apart *(nonshared environment)* with those reared in the same family *(shared environment)*, researchers attempt to separate the effects of genes and environment.

Crime. Eysenck (1977) argued that a life of crime is strongly influenced by genetic factors because (1) cross-cultural studies show that criminal, psychopathic behaviors are strongly related to *P (psychoticism)*, a factor that has been shown to have a large genetic component; (2) twin studies show a higher rate of *concordance* or *similar criminal behavior* between identical twins than between fraternal twins or nontwin siblings; and (3) adopted children resemble their biological parents more than their adoptive ones in a whole array of traits. Clearly, there appears to be something going on here, but as contemporary researchers have found, the relationship between genes and personality is not simple:

> We do not inherit behavior, habits, personality traits, intelligence, or even height. . . . Genes interact with the environment from conception onward. A person has genes that are "programmed" for large bone growth . . . but a lack of protein and calcium in pre- or postnatal environments will stunt the growth regardless of genetic coding. Genes assemble the building materials. . . . Genes affect behavior in a probabilistic fashion; they are not deterministic in themselves. (Zuckerman, 1991, p. 90)

Reviewing a large number of genetic studies, Zuckerman concluded, "There is little or no influence of a shared family environment in most personality traits" (1991, p. 128). This is especially true of *broad traits* such as *E* or *N:* "Scales that reflect specific interests, values, and beliefs are more likely to be influenced by family environment than are broader personality traits" (Zuckerman, 1991, p. 120).

Although such conclusions go against much of what has been taught over the past fifty years, Zuckerman maintains that "only a third of the similarities between parents and their biological children can be attributed to environmental influences, the rest comes from the parental genes" (1991, p. 128).

Contemporary echoes of Eysenck. Part of the success of Eysenck's work can be measured in terms of its heuristic value. His insistence that personality is biologically based and can best be understood in terms of a few superfactors has been echoed by other contemporary theorists. We have previously reviewed Zuckerman's research with *sensation seekers,* who show a strong positive correlation with Eysenck's *extraverts.* In the preface to his 1979 book, Zuckerman states, "Hans Eysenck was the inspiration to my biological approach to personality . . . I will always be indebted to him for the inspiration of his work on the 'biological basis of personality'" (1979, p. xiii).

Similarly, Gray's (1964, 1972, 1990) **reinforcement sensitivity theory** *postulates two biological systems in the brain:* The *Behavioral Activation System (BAS)* is sensitive to rewards and has much in common with Eysenck's extraversion (Pickering, Corr, & Gray, 1999); and the *Behavioral Inhibition System (BIS)* is responsive to punishment and shares similarities with Eysenck's neuroticism factor. Finally, as we discussed earlier, Cloninger's tridimensional personality model (Cloninger, 1986, 1987; Cloninger, Svrakic, & Przbeck, 1993; Cloninger, 1999) *relates three "superfactors" to lowered levels of major neurotransmitters.* Clearly all of these theories echo Eysenck, who drew upon Hebb's theory of *optimal level of arousal,* which, in turn, was related to Pavlov's notions of "strong" and "weak" nervous systems.

SUMMARY OF EYSENCK

Hans J. Eysenck was one of the most prolific and influential psychologists of the twentieth century. He brought the methodological rigor of the hard sciences to personality psychology, providing what one admirer described as "a breath of fresh air in a field awash in untestable theories" (Farley, 2000, pp. 674–675). The unquestioned leader in biologically based personality research, Eysenck once described his theoretical journey as continually moving down from higher-level abstractions to the firm footing of the *Physiological Zone:* "I have tried to go deeper still and find biological causes underlying the psychological concepts of emotion, excitation, and inhibition which formed the building stones of my earlier efforts" (Eysenck, 1967, p. xii).

Next, we will consider the classic work of Raymond Cattell, as well as the more recent formulations of Paul Costa and Robert McCrae. Our discussion will become more mathematical, but the logic behind the math will not be difficult to understand.

CATTELL'S SWEET 16

Background Check

Raymond B. Cattell (1905–1998) was born in England and remembers a happy childhood; however, when Cattell was nine years old England became involved in World War I, which made life much more difficult. Majoring in chemistry and physics, Cattell graduated from the University of London at the age of nineteen, and earned his Ph.D. by the time he was 24. He studied under Charles Spearman, the distinguished psychologist who invented factor analysis.

The next several years were difficult for Cattell due to the depressed economy, poor health, poverty, and the breakup of his marriage. Nonetheless, he never flagged in his dedication to research, and less than 10 years after he received his doctorate, the University of London awarded Cattell an honorary doctor of science for his research in personality.

Zeitgeist

Cattell's life chronologically parallels Eysenck's, so both of them share a similar zeitgeist: a time when behaviorism and psychoanalysis were considered the North and South poles of psychology. Freud's psychoanalysis was seen as *the way* to understand the "inner life," while behaviorism was seen as offering the only rigorous road to scientific discovery. Cattell's theory of personality was dominated by his desire to use traits to *predict* behavior, so it satisfied neither the behaviorists nor the psychoanalysts. Although the behaviorists were committed to scientific rigor, they had little use for Cattell's "inner" constructs (traits).

We have just seen how Eysenck provided a conceptual bridge from the ancient Greek compositionists to modern molecular biology. Cattell's trait theory ascended a couple steps higher on the vertical axis, because he focused more on mathematically describing complex situations in the *Social Zone*, and less on biology: "Personality is that which permits a prediction of what a person will do in a given situation" (Cattell, 1950). Since Cattell derived his traits from *verbal* rather than *biological* sources, he preferred linguistic and mathematical analyses over biologically based research.

Boiling Down the Dictionary

Cattell took his cue from Allport and Odbert (1936), who concluded that there are approximately 4,500 English words describing personality traits. Cattell grouped these words into synonyms, reducing the original 4,500 words to 171 terms. Then he used these 171 terms to classify a normal population of subjects. Factor analyzing his results, he arrived at thirty-six "natural clusters" of descriptors, which he termed the *standard reduced personality sphere* (1957, p. 72). It was from this "standard sphere" that Cattell derived his final sixteen source traits. As we learned earlier, however, there is nothing "natural" about how one decides on the "final" traits—especially in Cattell's day when modern multivariate techniques such as *Structural Equation Modeling (SEM)* were not yet available.

It's not important that you remember exact numbers or technical terms; but it's essential to realize that Cattell's reductionism is very different from Eysenck's boiling-down process. Eysenck sought to reduce things to their *biological essentials,* and then to build his three superfactors with these bio-bricks; Cattell began with a higher-level, more abstract *linguistic distillation.*

Eysenck and Cattell differed not only about the *number* of factors, but about the content as well. Comparing Eysenck's and Cattell's traits is like comparing apples and oranges; or, after all the factor analytic processing, like comparing applesauce and orange juice.

ASKING THE BIG FOUR QUESTIONS
What Are the Parts?

Surface traits vs. source traits. Cattell—like Eysenck—proposed a hierarchical model of personality, but he did not define his underlying traits in solely biological terms. Cattell distinguished between **surface traits,** or *clusters of observable behaviors such as cheerfulness, spontaneity, friendliness, and outgoingness, which usually occur together in an individual,* and **source traits,** *the underlying factors (in this case "sociability") that shape and determine the surface traits.* For Cattell, the term *"trait"* is a unifying term, pulling together common clusters of surface behavior (he chose thirty-six) and relating them to underlying *source traits (sixteen).*

Different varieties of source traits. Cattell believed that **constitutional source traits** are *genetically determined,* whereas **environmental-mold traits** are the *products of experience.* Fine-tuning source traits even further, Cattell designated **dynamic source traits** as *traits that set the individual into action to accomplish a goal;* **ability** traits as *traits that facilitate how or whether people effectively pursue their goals;* and **temperament traits** as *genetically determined source traits that shape a person's energy, tempo, and emotional reactivity.*

Cattell pictured these interconnections among traits as a **dynamic lattice,** *a diagram of the relationships among the various levels of traits.* **Subsidiation** means that *lower-level traits are subordinate or subsidiary to more comprehensive traits.* This is a "levels" analysis much like we saw with Eysenck, which is also cosistent with our current zonal analysis.

In naming his sixteen source traits, Cattell used terms that sound as if they were lifted from a science fiction movie: *threctia* or *parmia* to describe the shy or the socially bold; *Harria* and *premsia* to differentiate between self-reliant versus clinging; and *praxernia* and *autia* to delineate between practical, down-to-earth individuals, and absent-minded ones.

Syntality—group traits. Cattell used the term **syntality** to describe *personality "traits" of the group as a whole.* In the case of national cultures, for example, Cattell (1975, p. 415) described about a dozen "syntality factors" or "group traits" that he believed accounted for most of the variance among groups. Among the most important are cultural pressure, group size, morale, economic-educational level, and patriarchal structure. Possibly *syntality* could prove useful in today's global village where understanding (possibly even measuring) the "personalities" of various cultures might assist in resolving or preventing wars or other conflicts.

What Makes a Person Go?

Motive. Cattell defined **motive** *"as something that exists in the here and now, at the moment of acting"* (1957, p.439, emphasis added). Cattell was not impressed with how other personality theorists formulated their motivational constructs: "Dynamic psychology talks of drives, complexes, sentiments, interests, super ego structures, habits, etc. Nearly all of these are complex patterns, the nature of which must be inferred, in the last analysis, from observation of more trivial, manifest habits or attitudes . . ." (1957, p. 442). Cattell much preferred his own here-and-now approach.

    Attitude. He then proposed that the optimum level of analysis "would seem to be that at which the unit can be defined as an *attitude.*" An **attitude** is *"a tendency to act in a particular way to a situation. And it is not only a tendency, because, in fact, it issues in <u>action</u> from time to time"* (1957, pp. 442–443, emphasis added). For Cattell, a motive is not some sort of internal trigger, but rather involves the entire person–situation complex. He illustrates this with the following sentence:

"In these circumstances	I	want so much	to do this	with that."
(stimulus situation)	(organism)	(interest-need, of a certain intensity)	(specific goal, course of action)	(object concerned in action)

    This appears straightforward enough, but according to Cattell, assessing motivation is no simple matter. He devoted fifty pages to this topic and concluded by listing fifty-five (that's right—*fifty-five!*) principles for measuring motivation! These fifty-five principles include every imaginable aspect of motivation that might possibly be measured (e.g., preferences, skills, memory, inhibitions, conflicts, fluency, endurance, learning, warming time, reminiscences, autonomic responses, physical responses, sensory thresholds, fantasies, reasoning, and expectancies). No one ever accused Raymond Cattell of not being thorough!

What Makes a Person Grow?

In spite of his encyclopedic meticulousness when measuring traits and motives, Cattell said very little about development. He stated that age-related changes are influenced by four major factors; we will list two (imprinting and equity) as examples. **Imprinting** means that *environmental experience has a greater influence at earlier ages;* and **equity** means that *the older person is treated more "fairly" because things "even out" over a lifetime.*

What Makes a Person Unique?

Whereas Eysenck settled on three personality superfactors, Cattell thought it took sixteen to adequately describe personality. Based on how one answers various test questions, a person can be ranked on each of these sixteen factors. In typical trait-theory style, Cattell believed that a person's distinctiveness is captured in the *pattern* of rankings on each of these sixteen traits.

FACING THE TOUGH TWINS

Is It Testable?

Testable but mathematically complex. Is Cattell's theory testable? Yes; however, his theory is so mathematically complex that even many (dare we say *most?*) psychologists are intimidated by his complex statistical formulas and elaborate mathematical operations.

Distinguishing among different kinds of data. Cattell made some important distinctions regarding the collection of personality-related information. He warned that data from different levels of analysis should not be indiscriminately mixed together for comparisons. He identified three kinds of data (Q-Data, T-Data, and L-Data) that should not be indiscriminately "mixed."

Questionnaire (Q-Data). **Q-Data** is *obtained from questionnaires or other self-report instruments providing information about behavior, feelings, and personality characteristics.* Examples of *Q-data* include problem checklists or health-screening checklists. Modern personality psychologists have further subdivided Cattell's *Q-data* category into **self-report data (S-Data),** or *the information people reveal about themselves through questionnaires, interviews, personal journals, or other self-disclosing procedures,* and **observer-report data (O-data)** whose sources are *family, friends, casual acquaintances, or teachers who provide information about an individual's personality.*

S-Data. *Self-report data* is a type of *Q-Data* that occur in a variety of forms, ranging from unstructured, *open-ended questions,* such as "Tell me about yourself," to structured, *"yes–no"* questions such as "Do you like loud, noisy parties?" The *Twenty Statements Test* (Kuhn & McPartland, 1954) is an example of an open-ended device for gathering personal information. Participants are asked to complete the phrase "I am ____" twenty different times.

The Twenty Statements Test has been used recently to investigate the role culture might play in self-definition. Ma and Schoeneman (1997) found, for example, that

TABLE 4.2

Data Types: Q, (S&O), T, & L

QUESTIONNAIRE (Q-Data):	This type of data is obtained by self-report instruments. There are two kinds of Q-Data, **Self-report Data (S-Data)**, which is usually a questionnaire about feelings, behaviors, etc., and **Observer-report Data (O-Data)**, which is gathered about a person from others, such as family or friends.
TEST VARIABLES (T-Data):	This type of data gets collected under tightly controlled laboratory conditions. T-Data can be from physiological feedback devices, video monitoring, etc.
LIFE RECORD (L-Data):	The final type of data is sampling taken from a person's life situation, such as peer personality evaluation, and is used to see what predictive outcomes it has for the person's future life and behavior.

Kenyan university students mentioned social groups 17 percent of the time, compared to American college students who referred to social groups 12 percent of the time. However, when rural tribespersons made self statements, they referred to social groups 80–84 percent of the time.

Experience sampling requires people to answer questions about their physical symptoms or moods, every day for several weeks or longer (Hormuth, 1986; Larsen, 1989). When experience-sampling was employed with college students to measure mood fluctuations during the week, it was found that Monday was *not* the worst day of the week. Positive moods peaked on Friday and Saturday (no big surprise there!) and "tanked" on Tuesday and Wednesday (Larsen & Kasimatis, 1990). However (consistent with Eysenck's theory) introverts showed a much more stable cycle than extraverts. Probably introverts are less likely to alter their moods through weekend partying, etc.

The important point to remember is that *questionnaire data (Q-data),* whether in the form of *self-reports (S-data)* or *other reports (O-data),* provide important information about how personality variables interact with real-life situations.

Test variables (T-data). **T-data** is *information obtained under precisely controlled conditions such as in the laboratory, or during carefully administered paper-and-pencil tests, or through videotaping or tape recording.* Psychologists have a long history of utilizing tests to evaluate personality. **Projective tests** *require a person to describe what something is, or to make up stories in response to relatively unstructured stimuli such as the ambiguous pictures of the Thematic Apperception Test (TAT), or the inkblots of the Rorschach.* Presumably, the person being tested has the freedom to "project" his or her personality into the ambiguous, vaguely defined stimuli. For example, a person who perceives biting animals or sees mean faces in ambiguous inkblots is thought to be more aggressive than someone who sees flowers or friendly elves. In more **structured psychometric tests,** *individuals are limited to answering "yes" or "no," or to rating themselves on some clearly defined dimensions (e.g., I am <u>not at all,</u> <u>mildly,</u> <u>moderately,</u> or <u>extremely</u> **depressed**).* The Minnesota Multiphasic Personality Inventory-2 (MMPI-2) is one of the most widely used structured personality tests, consisting of 567 true-false items.

As electronic circuitry has become miniaturized, mechanical recording devices have become more practical. In one study (Buss, Block, & Block, 1980), children ages three and four wore *actometers (electronic devices used to measure movement)* on their wrists, and experimenters also collected observer evaluations regarding whether the children were talkative, deceitful, submissive, high-energy, etc. Not surprisingly, there was a strong positive correlation between the T-data and O-data.

Paralleling this increased utilization of mechanical devices, there has been a resurgence of interest in **physiological assessment devices,** which are *sensors that can detect minute changes in blood pressure, heart rate, muscle contraction, electrical activity of the brain, etc.* When data from different domains converge, it strengthens our confidence in conclusions. For example, in Epstein's (1967) sky-diving study of anxiety that we discussed in Chapter 1, physiological measures and subjective ratings (*T-data and Q-data*) showed similar patterns, thus strengthening the study's conclusions. However, Cattell cautioned that we must be careful how we synthesize our findings; simply combining data without regard for how it was derived is dangerous. As he aptly put it, "ten men and two bottles of beer cannot be added to give the same total as two men and ten bottles of beer . . ." (1957, p. 11).

Life Record (L-data). **L-data** *is sampled from the person's life situation, such as ratings of children in the classroom, or peer ratings of personality.* Cattell referred to it as *Life-data,* modern personality psychologists call it *Life-outcome data.* S-data and O-data are frequently used to predict L-data. For example, Caspi and his colleagues (Caspi, Elder, & Bem, 1987) initially interviewed mothers of children ages eight, nine, and ten, collecting O-data regarding such behaviors as kicking, biting, throwing things, and verbal aggression. Later, during adulthood, when the children were thirty to forty years old, the researchers gathered L-data about life outcomes such as marriage, education, work, and parenting.

The results—three decades in the making—were remarkable. Men who had displayed temper tantrums as boys experienced negative life outcomes in a number of areas. They attained lower ranks in the military, experienced less stable employment, and experienced less satisfying marriages than their more even-tempered cohorts. By age forty, some 46 percent of them were divorced, compared with only 22 percent of their milder cohorts. This study illustrates how L-data provides important real-life information about personality across the life span.

Is It Useful?

The 16 PF. Cattell developed the **Sixteen Personality Factor Questionnaire (16PF),** *a test of 187 questions designed to assess a person's rank on each of sixteen source traits.* The test taker chooses among two alternatives posed by each question: e.g., During a social occasion, would you rather "come forward" or "stay quietly in the background"? Answers provide information regarding which source traits are dominant in the personality, and Cattell (1990) claimed that he could predict behavior by combining trait scores into a **specification equation,** *which weighted each trait according to relevance for a particular situation.* For example, in predicting a salesperson's annual earnings, Cattell might use the following *specification equation:* Earnings = .21 outgoingness + .10 emotional stability + .10 dominance + .21 easygoingness + .10 conscientiousness − .10 suspiciousness − .31 imaginativeness, and + .21 shrewdness.

> However, Cattell's optimism appeared overstated. A respected expert on testing wrote: Despite the extensive research conducted by Cattell and his associates for more than three decades, the proposed traits must be regarded as tentative. . . . Factor analysis provides a technique for grouping personality inventory items into . . . clusters . . . . But they are not substitutes for empirical validation" (Anastasi, 1988, pp. 542–543).

SUMMARY OF CATTELL

Hopefully, you have caught the flavor of Cattell's work (mathematically complex, exhaustively thorough, and encyclopedically comprehensive) without drowning in details. If you feel overwhelmed, welcome to the club! Even experienced personality psychologists despair when trying to summarize his work. Writing in the 1968 *Annual Review of Psychology,* Wiggins noted that in the three years under review (1964–1967) Cattell had written four books, 40 articles, and 12 chapters for a total of almost 4,000 pages. "The appearance of so many major works . . . has once again forced an evaluation of a body of literature so vast, uneven, and demanding that many American workers have simply tended to ignore it" (p. 313).

So you see, it's not just you! Most of us feel overwhelmed by Cattell, which is probably why his work has not had greater influence. If you have to keep in mind *fifty-five principles* just to study motivation, the theory might feel like it's more work than it's worth.

THE TRIUMPH OF THE FIVE-FACTOR MODEL (FFM)

Zeitgeist

The current version of the Five-Factor Model (FFM) is associated with the work of McCrae and Costa (1985a); however, Five-Factor models have been around for half a century and represent work by many different people. So we will skip our usual "background check" of theorists and review the history of the FFM itself.

Early roots of the FFM. As early as 1932, William McDougall proposed that "Personality may to advantage be broadly analyzed into five distinguishable but separable factors" (1932, p. 5). A couple years later, L. L. Thurstone, another heavyweight of that era, factor analyzed a list of sixty adjectives and reported his surprise at finding that "the whole list of sixty adjectives can be accounted for by postulating only five independent factors" (Thurstone, 1934, pp. 1–42).

A half-century gestation period. Digman (1994) expresses surprise at how long it took before the FFM came into its own. He concludes that it wasn't so much theoretical differences that kept people from accepting the FFM, it was *technological difficulties.* The ordeal of carrying out a factor analysis in the precomputer era is almost beyond imagination: "Analysis of even a 30-variable problem was a daunting task that could suggest many weeks of clerical work filled with the possibility of errors of calculation at every turn" (Digman, 1994, p. 13).

The "Big Five"—plus or minus two. Support for five factors of personality has been gradually building steam since the 1930s; however, the most recent version of the FFM originated in a paper, first published in 1961, by Tupes and Christal, and later summarized and expanded by Norman (1963). Now, more than forty years after the original Norman article, the FFM appears to have gained supremacy. Zuckerman suggests that the popularity of the FFM "probably reflects disillusion with the complicated and unreliable Cattell multifactor system and the feeling that Eysenck's big three are not enough dimensions to account for the complexity of personality" (1991, pp. 17–18).

Still, even with current popularity of the FFM, personality psychologists are far from agreed on how many factors best describe human functioning. Instead of five factors, some researchers insist on seven, while others settle for three or four (e.g., Church & Burke, 1994; Zuckerman, Kuhlman, Joireman, Teta, & Kraft, 1993). This led Briggs (1989) to refer to "The Big Five, plus or minus two."

ASKING THE BIG FOUR QUESTIONS

What Are the Parts?

From a zonal perspective, we need to remember that traits mean different things in different zones. Allport and Eysenck saw traits were *real physiological entities,* whereas FFM theorists (in the tradition of Allport and Cattell) derived their traits from hundreds of linguistic descriptors. Five-Factor Model theorists are more concerned with prediction and reliability than with anchoring their traits to molecular biology in the style of Eysenck. However, FFM theorists share Eysenck's zeal for condensing hundreds of behavioral habits and traits into a few basic *factors*; even the "Big Five" can be further subdivided. Costa and McCrae (1985b) suggested that each of the five factors can be divided into six facets or categories. Then, instead of the *big five*, we would have the *not-so-big thirty!* So, as we noted earlier, your number of "basic" traits boils down to a packaging choice—you can purchase milk by the glass or by the gallon. Similarly, whether you purchase a personality model with five factors or thirty may be more a matter of convenience than reality; it's more a decision about which level of analysis you wish to pursue.

Next, let's look more closely at the "Big Five" superfactors, noticing that the first letters of each can be combined to spell **OCEAN,** reminding us that a vast "ocean" of personality traits has been distilled down to five.

Openness to experience (O). *O* has been called by many different names. Cattell, in his original formulation of sixteen basic factors (1943), referred to this factor as a dimension of intelligence, whereas Norman (1963) identified it as a dimension of culture having to do with a person's refinement and contemplative qualities. According to Norman, high scorers on **O** are *insightful, imaginative,* and *intellectually well-rounded,* whereas low scorers are seen as narrow, unimaginative—possibly even crude and boorish.

In the FFM, **O** refers to the *depth, breadth,* and *flexibility* of a person's conscious experience. **Open people** *are curious, imaginative, and willing to explore novel ideas and hold unconventional values.* By contrast, low scorers on *O* tend to be conventional and conservative in their tastes and rigid and dogmatic in their beliefs. They are the kind of people who are commonly described as "set in their ways." Not surprisingly, people high on *O* appear to welcome change and challenges. In one study of career changes in adults over fifty-five, 71 percent of women and 64 percent of men who changed jobs scored above the midpoint on *O* (McCrae and Costa, 1985b).

Among the FFM traits, *O* appears most directly related to political beliefs and attitudes, with persons scoring low on *O* tending to be moderate-to-conservative in their views. The *authoritarian personality style* was first suggested by Erich Fromm (1941), and later clarified by an ambitious program of research, resulting in the development of the California F ("Fascism") scale, and the publication of a landmark book, *The Authoritarian Personality* (Adorno, Frenkel-Brunswik, Levinson, and Sanford, 1950). The authoritarian personality is one manifestation of the low end of the *O* continuum.

Conscientiousness (C). McCrae and Costa (1997) subdivided the *C* domain into six facets: competence, achievement striving, dutifulness, order, self-discipline, and deliberation. People high on **conscientiousness** *are hard-working, self-disciplined, organized, reliable,* and *persevering.* They tend to be *goal-directed, ambitious, and careful.* At the low end are those who might be described as lazy, aimless, unreliable, careless, lax, negligent, and hedonistic. It is difficult to predict what they will do, since they are erratic and inconsistent. *Low-C* people might appear spontaneous and "alive," but since they show little regard for serious standards of work or morality, and seem to have little inclination to stand by principles, they are poor risks in love or friendship.

Extraversion (E). Carl Jung (Chapter 13) first introduced the term *extraversion* into psychology in 1913, and his original descriptions seems fairly consistent with the FFM use of the term, although Jung's usage conveys a more histrionic and narcissistic flavor:

Extraversion is characterized by . . . a ready acceptance of external happenings, a desire to influence and be influenced by events, a need to join in and get "with it," the capacity to endure bustle and noise of every kind, and actually find them enjoyable . . . the cultivation of friends and acquaintances, none too carefully selected, and finally by the great importance attached to the figure one cuts, and hence a strong tendency to make a show of oneself. . . . (Jung, 1936/1971, pp. 549–551)

Whereas Jung saw extraversion and introversion as two sharply demarcated *types,* Eysenck viewed them on a continuum, suggesting that people who fell in the middle of the distribution might be seen as "ambiverts" combining qualities of both extraversion and introversion. Research with the FFM is in agreement with Eysenck's view of factors as continuous dimensions.

E, in the FFM, refers to the intensity and quantity of interpersonal interactions, as well as to the person's need for stimulation and capacity for joy. People high in **extraversion** *are seen to be sociable, talkative, active, people-oriented, optimistic, fun loving, and affectionate.* Conversely, those low in *E* tend to be more reserved (but not necessarily unfriendly), aloof, independent, sober, and quiet. Introverts are not necessarily unhappy or pessimistic, but they are less given to the exuberant high spirits typical of extraverts.

Research finds that extraverts talk more and sooner when they meet someone (Carment, Miles, & Cervin, 1965), and that they engage in more eye contact (Rutter, Morley, & Graham, 1972). They do more gambling (Wilson, 1978), and they are more sexually active than introverts (Giese & Schmidt, 1968). Extraverted college students like to study in places that provide opportunities for social interaction, whereas introverts seek secluded spots (Campbell & Hawley, 1982).

Agreeableness (A). *A* is an *interpersonal* scale (like *E*), measuring the kinds of interactions a person prefers, ranging along a continuum from compassion to antagonism. People high on **agreeableness** *tend to be soft-hearted, good-natured, trusting, helpful, forgiving, and empathic.* Individuals who score low on *A* are called *antagonistic* and tend to be rude, abrasive, suspicious, cynical, uncooperative, and irritable. They can be manipulative, ruthless, and vengeful. Other personality inventories have variously referred to this trait as sociability, empathy, and tolerance. This construct is undoubtedly related to Adler's notion of *social interest,* and to what Graziano and Eisenberg (1997) term *prosocial tendencies.*

Since agreeable people are easier to enjoy than disagreeable people, they are usually more successful in life, forming better friendships, and being more collegial colleagues and consistent caregivers. McCrae and Costa (1991) found that high scores on *C* and *A* were positively correlated with psychological well-being. Since agreeable people are loving, generous, and warm, and conscientious people are competent and hardworking, it's not surprising that such people tend to get along well with others. "This is perhaps what Freud meant when he suggested that *Liebe und Arbeit,* love and work, are the keys to psychological health and happiness" (McCrae & Costa, 1991, p. 228).

Neuroticism (N). *N* is strongly related to various kinds of stress, and is generally described as *a continuum from emotional instability to emotional stability.* Persons high on **neuroticism** *are prone to psychological distress measured on such facet scales as anxiety, angry hostility, depression, self-consciousness, impulsiveness, and vulnerability.* Individuals high on *N* tend to be hot-tempered, easily frustrated, and unable to resist impulses. They are worriers who tend to feel hopeless, guilty, and blue. Guilt, shame, and feelings of inferiority are pervasive.

Such persons frequently experience escalating spirals of anxiety and panic, which tend to become self-sustaining. In counseling or clinical settings, they respond best to treatments that assist them in managing their "out-of-control" emotions. Relaxation training, biofeedback, and hypnosis may be usefully employed in interrupting the spiral of anxiety and allowing such persons to "settle down" and work on other issues as well.

What Makes a Person Go? What Makes a Person Grow?

As we saw in Eysenck's model, as well as in other compositional theories, little effort was expended in formulating *motivational* or *developmental* constructs; trait theorists have devoted the major portion of their energy to creating, explaining, and measuring *structural constructs*. They seem to assume that *traits*—like acorns—contain within themselves the necessary motivational and developmental ingredients to transform themselves from acorns into oaks.

From Hippocrates and Galen to Eysenck and Cattell, compositional theorists have mostly provided an "ingredients list," and in this respect the FFM is not radically different. Perhaps the "ingredients" are more precisely specified, and the investigations more carefully designed, but research in motivation and development still remains modest. A recent book entitled *The Developing Structure of Temperament and Personality from Infancy to Adulthood* (Halverson, Kohnstamm, & Martin, 1994) is an attempt to address such issues.

Trait psychologists are able to tell you whether you're extraverted or introverted, whether you are agreeable or antagonistic, but they have little information about how you came to be that way, or how you might go about changing your undesirable behaviors. They are more helpful in the "hire-or-fire" department than in the "fix-it" clinic.

What Makes a Person Unique?

It shouldn't be surprising that trait theorists consider *personality* to be *a package of assorted traits*. This is the classical compositionist formulation of personality. Distinctiveness resides in the particular combination of trait "ingredients" you happen to contain.

FACING THE TOUGH TWINS

Is It Testable?

Yes, the FFM is testable, which is why it is among the more popular theories at the current time; but the relationships among the Big Five traits, or their connection to other traits, is far from clear. Zuckerman (1994), for example, has proposed an "Alternative Five": *sociability, neuroticism-anxiety, impulsive sensation seeking, aggression-hostility,* and *activity*. Cloninger (1987), who initially developed a three-factor model of personality based on the traits of *novelty seeking, harm avoidance,* and *reward dependence,* subsequently expanded it to seven factors by adding the traits of *cooperativeness, persistence, self-determination,* and *spirituality*.

So the search for "basic" traits goes on, along with the accompanying discussion of how many are needed (three, five, seven, sixteen, thirty or more) to accurately describe human personality. The liveliness of the discussions is testimony to the fact that personality psychologists are talking about *models* of personality, not palpable entities. One could scarcely imagine a conference of hand surgeons devoting symposia to discussing whether the "basic hand" is composed of three, five, or sixteen fingers.

Eysenck and Cattell believed that their proposed traits were hierarchically ordered—from basic or source traits to surface traits and behavior. Although this is logically appealing, the empirical evidence supporting this sort of orderly "lattice" or hierarchy is not very compelling. With so many different traits, under various names, at different levels of abstraction, personality sometimes seems like a grocery bag filled with apples, squash, bottles, cans, chicken breasts, and cereal boxes.

Such an eclectic smorgasbord of traits should no longer surprise us, since we now know that what comes out of a factor analysis is dependent on what goes in. Each theorist has his or her "pet" traits. Some personality psychologists contend that much of the statistical relationship found among various traits results from the subjective process of finding what you are searching for. Digman and Takemoto-Chock (1981) argue that many of Cattell's factors have not been confirmed by other researchers; and Goldberg (1981) says that when Cattell's data is analyzed by others, they typically find five factors, not sixteen.

Is It Useful?

Trait theories have spawned tests specifically designed to assess the proposed traits and factors. The FFM is typical in this respect. Costa and McCrae (1992) designed the Neuroticism Extraversion Openness Personality Inventory, Revised **(NEO-PI-R)** to assess these factors. To the extent that it proves valid, the NEO-PI-R might be of assistance in the corporate world by providing information to decision makers regarding hiring and firing or promotions, for example. Valid information about personality can be of value to educators and clinicians as well.

Personality disorders—categorical versus dimensional models. The *Diagnostic and Statistical Manual of Mental Disorders, Fourth Edition (DSM-IV)* describes nearly a dozen different personality disorders. Understanding personality disorders is extremely important to a wide variety of people including clinicians, law enforcement authorities, educators, and human resources personnel, to name but a few. However, most authorities agree that "No other area in the study of psychopathology is fraught with more controversy than the personality disorders" (Davis & Millon, 1999, p. 485). Personality psychologists believe that much of the confusion results from the fact that DSM-IV utilizes a *categorical* approach:

> The diagnostic approach used in this manual [DSM-IV] represents the categorical perspective that Personality Disorders represent qualitatively distinct syndromes. An alternative to the categorical approach is the dimensional perspective that Personality Disorders represent maladaptive variants of personality traits that merge imperceptibly into normality and into one another. (American Psychiatric Association, 1994)

Personality researchers from Eysenck onward have discovered that traits vary along *dimensions,* meaning that the boundaries among personality disorders (and between normal and abnormal) are more like the "boundaries" between twilight and darkness, or dawn and daylight—no bright lines. It shouldn't surprise us that users of DSM-IV frequently find themselves confused by co-occurring symptoms in allegedly different personality disorders.

For example, clinicians working with *borderline, histrionic,* or *antisocial* personality styles are likely to encounter unstable, emotional, impulsive, narcissistic—sometimes grandiose—behaviors in all three categories! The FFM and similar research-based theories are beginning to bring some clarity to this confusing arena. According to FFM researchers, borderline personalities show substantial elevations on neuroticism; histrionic personalities are characterized by excessive extraversion; while antisocial personalities are characterized by low agreeableness. A clinician could administer the NEO-PI-R in order to assess the underlying *dimensions* of personality and not be confused by parallel behaviors in overlapping diagnostic *categories*.

Hysteria in the age of computers. According to the Egyptians and Greeks, hysterical symptoms were caused by a wandering womb; according to behaviorists it results from parents' reinforcing sick children with attention but being neglectful when they are healthy. In Chapter 6 we will learn that psychoanalysts see hysterical symptoms as resulting from intense, repressed emotions. Trait theorists (e.g., Eysenck, 1957; Millon, 1981; Widiger, Trull, Clarkin, Sanderson, & Costa, 1994) see the hysterical personality as an extreme variation of *extraversion*. No wandering womb, no repressed memories, just *excessive extraversion:* histrionics exaggerate emotions, crave excitement, and quickly form superficial—but intense—relationships.

Mischel deals a near-fatal blow to trait psychology. The FFM has proved itself heuristically vigorous, and has contributed significantly to the rehabilitation of trait theories after their "near-death" experience in the late 1960s. This is a result of Walter Mischel's **situationist critique,** according to which *situational variables are far more powerful than traits in determining behavior.* In dealing a near-fatal blow to the trait theory establishment, Mischel wrote: "It is evident that the behaviors which are often construed as stable personality trait indicators actually are highly specific and depend on the details of the evoking situation and the response mode employed to measure them" (1968, p. 37).

This debate has been settled as a draw, with each side focusing on the importance of its favorite variables, but begrudgingly admitting that other variables also have a role to play. The *person X situation interaction* is now the currency of the realm.

Chapter Summary

We began our chapter by learning that factor analysis and other statistical techniques used by trait theorists involve subjective judgments. This was especially true during the days when Eysenck, Cattell, and other early pioneers were formulating their theories. It is less true today with the availability of advanced techniques such as Sequential Equation Modeling (SEM), but personal judgement still plays a significant role in theory building.

We explored the pioneering work of Gordon Allport, who believed traits were real biological entities, but who expanded his theories to include the study of higher-level humanistic and spiritual concerns. Next we learned how Hans Eysenck spent his entire life seeking to establish personality traits on a solid biological footing. Numerous contemporary trait theorists (e.g., Zuckerman, Cloninger, and Gray) continue to focus on the biological foundations of personality.

Raymond Cattell and the Five-Factor advocates derived their traits from linguistic descriptors, so they were less concerned with connecting traits to biology. Cattell's goal was to *predict* behavior on the basis of situational variables. The Five-Factor Model (FFM) is *the* dominant personality model among contemporary academic and research personality psychologists. Among clinical, counseling, corporate, and educational psychologists the FFM is less popular, and many prefer the broad contexts provided by such traditional paradigms as behaviorism, psychoanalysis, humanism, and existentialism. Nonetheless, researchers and academicians appear to favor the *molecular* work being carried out in the *Physiological* and *Situational Zones.* As new generations of clinicians and consultants emerge from graduate programs with heavy emphases in multidisciplinary areas such as *physiological psychology* and *cognitive behaviorism,* the FFM will likely become more and more connected with biochemical foundations. The carefulness with which trait theorists have carried out their research will facilitate connecting their mathematically derived traits (in the *Insight* and *Social Zones*) with underlying biochemical foundations (in the *Physiological Zone*). It will also become increasingly possible to understand how long-term dispositions (traits) are influenced by proximal situational variables (in the *Situational Zone*).

Points to Remember

1. Does an amoeba have a personality? Not really. A single-celled organism lacks the "neuronal software" found in higher species that provide the undergirding for authentic personality functioning. Does a dog have personality? Of course— ask any dog owner! Like numerous other mammals, dogs have the ability to connect emotionally with their human caretakers through *limbic resonance.* Yet a dog's personality lacks the richness and complexity of the human personality because the canine brain lacks some of the essential human features such as the ability to generate and understand grammar.

2. *Trait theorists attempt to construct personality piece by piece* or trait by trait. They disassemble personality into the thousands of bits of behavior (habits and traits) that comprise a person's daily life; then, with the help of mathematical analyses, they sort the pieces into piles that appear similar. Have they been successful? Will they be successful in the future? Can personality be disassembled into component parts for study, and successfully reassembled? You'll have to decide that on your own; you might even choose to become part of the enterprise. Hopefully this chapter has served as a progress report.

3. *Correlation* is a mathematical indicator of how strongly (or weakly) things *co-relate* or *co-occur.* We have learned that just because things happen to coexist doesn't *necessarily* mean they have a *causative* relationship. Sometimes they do and sometimes they don't. Church steeples and crime coexist but they don't have a causative relationship. That's where subjectivity comes into trait theories of personality; just because traits are correlated, we don't know *how* they are related—coincidentally or causatively.

4. *Factor analysis* is a useful tool for sorting traits into similar piles; but again, it doesn't tell us what we have in each pile. After the most mathematically sophisticated cluster analysis, we are still left to *decide subjectively* what a particular cluster of correlations means—or how many piles (factors) there really ought to be. "Garbage in = garbage out" is how the old saying goes, to remind us that statistics are only for *counting* things, they can't tell us *what* to count, or how to interpret our findings.

5. Although trait psychologists appear remarkably *objective* when "crunching numbers," or devising tests, they are necessarily *subjective* when formulating factors and delineating traits. This has led to a lively debate regarding the correct number of "basic" factors. What do you think? Three? Five? Seven? Sixteen? Thirty? The field seems to have come full circle from Galen's *four*, to Eysenck's *three*, to Norman's Big *Five* (or *thirty*, if you count facets), to Cloninger's *seven*, to Cattell's *sixteen*, back to Eysenck's *three*, or Digman's *Big Two*. *Five* is probably the most popular number at the present moment, but it is clear that in the trait department of the personality store, you can still buy your milk by the glass, pint, quart, half-gallon, or gallon. Choose the size that best fits your need, it's up to you.

6. Traits mean different things at different levels of analysis. Eysenck and Zuckerman saw traits as real biological structures, whereas Cattell began his factor analyses with *words,* instead of body fluids, so his traits are more linguistically based. The FFM researchers have also used a linguistic base.

7. Allport pioneered American trait theory, completing his doctoral dissertation on the topic in 1922. Like others who followed him, Allport proposed a hierarchical order of traits, ascending from specific behavioral *habits* (e.g., brushing one's teeth, washing one's face, combing one's hair), which combined to form a *secondary trait* (cleanliness), which might be part of a *central trait* (healthful living or social attractiveness), which might feed into a *cardinal trait* (living an exemplary life before others).

8. However, Allport was more than a trait theorist; by formulating the *proprium,* he hoped to avoid the *agentic self* or *homunculus-like* formulations of other theories while still including such things as self-identity, self-esteem, self-extension, and striving under the umbrella of *propriate functions*. He wanted to capture a sense of self, but make it a part of the total personality—not a homunculus inside, pulling strings. But with his concept of *propriate functioning,* Allport moved up several levels of abstraction beyond the traditional trait theorists, to deal with such abstract issues as values, prejudice, and religious experience.

9. Allport's emphasis on *idiographic research* methods—coming during an era when psychoanalysis and behaviorism were on the throne—had the twin effects of bringing personality psychology more solidly into the scientific arena, and paving the way for what Rychlak (1994, 1995) terms "rigorous humanism."

10. Eysenck's model of personality is *hierarchical,* with *specific responses* at the bottom, leading to *habits* at the next level, which make up *traits* at a higher level, which finally combine into *three superfactors* or *types* (psychoticism, extraversion-introversion, and neuroticism) at the top level of abstraction. The first letters of these superfactors form the word **PEN**. Eysenck and other trait theorists have emphasized the *structure*

of personality and said less about motivation, development, or uniqueness. Genes are seen as the most basic of building blocks, containing within themselves the necessary ingredients to shape motivational and developmental predispositions. But unlike the sociobiologists, Eysenck and the trait theorists were much more meticulous and bottom-up in analyzing personality.

11. Several contemporary theories echo Eysenck: Zuckerman's *sensation seekers,* Cloninger's *novelty seekers,* and Gray's *reinforcement-sensitive* persons all share much in common with Eysenck's *extraverts*. Like Eysenck, these personality psychologists have proposed theories based on two or three biologically based superfactors.

12. Cattell was more interested in *prediction* than in tracking down biochemical correlates. *Linguistic distillation* was how he boiled things down; but since he was willing to use *oblique* (overlapping) factors, he ended up with *sixteen personality factors* that he considered essential, instead of three or five. He distinguished between *surface traits* (clusters of observable behaviors: smiling, laughing, talking, or "partying") and the underlying *source trait* (e.g., *sociability,* in the above example). Cattell believed that by assigning weights to traits in accordance with their relevance for specific actions or situations, he could predict behavior. Thus, a salesperson's yearly earnings could be predicted by assigning appropriate weights (or degrees of importance) to such source traits as outgoingness, dominance, shrewdness, etc. Cattell used a *dynamic lattice* to show relationships among the various levels of traits.

13. Cattell distinguished among three kinds of data: *L-data* (life records), *Q-data* (questionnaires), and *T-data* (tests). This distinction is valuable for researchers and students alike. It's the personality psychologists' version of, "You can't compare apples and oranges," or, to be more correct, "You should compare them *carefully*."

14. The most popular trait theory today is the Five-Factor Model (FFM). Many believe that *three* is too few, *sixteen* is too many, and *five* is just the right number of basic traits for capturing the complexity of human personality. And who knows, maybe they're right. Five fingers work well for grasping the world around us, so maybe five is the right number of factors for grasping personality. With *OCEAN* as a memory aid, they're easy to remember, and factors like "Openness" and "Agreeableness" make sense to the average person, compared with Cattell's sci-fi names for his traits (e.g., threctia, premsia, or abculion), which are intimidating.

Key Terms

Ability Traits (124)
Agreeableness (131)
Attitude (125)
Circadian Rhythms (140)
Conscientiousness (130)
Constitutional Source Traits (124)
Correlation (104)
Dynamic Lattice (124)
Dynamic Source Traits (124)

Environmental-Mold Traits (124)
Equity (125)
Experience Sampling (127)
Extraversion (117, 131)
Extrinsic Religious Orientation (114)
Factor Analysis (105)
Functional Autonomy (113)
Habits (110)
Habitual Response (118)

Idiographic Research   (114)
Idiothetic Approach   (115)
Imprinting   (125)
Intrinsic Religious Orientation   (114)
Life Record (L-Data)   (128)
Morning-Eveningness Trait   (140)
Motive   (125)
Neuroticism   (118, 131)
Nomothetic Research   (114)
Observer-Report Data (O-Data)   (126)
Open People   (130)
Personality   (110, 118)
Personology   (110)
Physiological Assessment Devices   (127)
Projective Tests   (127)
Proprium   (111)
Psychoticism   (117)
Questionnaire Data (Q-Data)   (126)

Reinforcement Sensitivity Theory   (122)
Self-Report Data (S-Data)   (126)
Situationist Critique   (134)
Sixteen Personality Factor Questionnaire (16 PF)   (128)
Source Traits   (124)
Specific Responses   (118)
Specification Equation   (128)
Structural Equation Modeling   (107)
Structured Psychometric Tests   (127)
Subsidiation   (124)
Surface Traits   (124)
Syntality   (124)
Teleological   (103)
Temperament Traits   (124)
Temporal-Isolation Design   (140)
Test Variables (T-Data)   (127)
Trait   (103, 110)

Web Sites

Cattell

www.psy.pdx.edu/PsiCafe/KeyTheorists/Cattell.htm The Psi Cafe. The all-inclusive stop on the Web for Raymond B. Cattell! There are helpful links about his life, research, and writing, as well as an interview with him.

Allport

www.findarticles.com/m0341/3_55/issue.jhtml. Journal of Social Issues. In this Fall 1999 issue, there are several articles on Allport's ideas and even a tribute to his life and work.

Buss

http://homepage.psy.utexas.edu/homepage/Group/BussLAB./ This is Dr. Buss's class Web site, but it includes photos, his books, selected papers, links to a 10-part radio series he did for ABC Radio's National Science Shows, and an interview in *The Evolutionist*. An excellent research resource.

Costa & McCrae

www.outofservice.com/bigfive. The Big Five Personality Test. Visit this Web site to take a brief online personality test and see your results instantly. Learn about yourself and contribute to research at the same time!

The Myers Briggs

www.personalitypathways.com/type_inventory.html. Personality Pathways. This Web site offers a lot of information about personality testing and the Myers Briggs Personality type. You can take a simplified online test to discover how you score in the areas of the Myers Briggs.

Learning on the Lighter Side

The Lemon Test—Are You an Extravert or an Introvert?

Before moving on, why don't you have some fun figuring out who, among your friends and yourself, are extraverts or introverts. But remember, Eysenck considered this a normal superfactor, so labeling someone an extravert or an introvert is merely a statement about whether they prefer private time to socializing—it's not classifying them as normal or abnormal. Furthermore, since this is a *continuous dimension*, numerous people will also be in the middle and could be classified as "ambiverts," so don't take your "diagnoses" too seriously. Have a little fun, and take the **five-step lemon test:**

1. Tie a length of thread or a piece of string about 18″ long to the *exact center* of a cotton swab. Adjust the string if necessary so that the swab hangs *exactly horizontally* when you dangle it from the string.

2. Swallow three times and immediately place the swab under your tongue, just like you would a thermometer. Keep it there for exactly 30 seconds.

3. Remove the swab and have a friend squirt 4 drops of lemon juice directly onto your tongue.

4. Swallow three times and immediately place the dry tip of the cotton swab under your tongue for exactly 30 seconds.

5. Remove the swab and let it dangle from the string.

This test provides a rough measure of Eysenck's superfactor *introversion-extraversion*. According to Corcoran (1964), if you are an *introvert,* one end will hang noticeably lower, indicating that you have produced a significant amount of saliva in response to the lemon juice. Conversely, if the swab remains roughly horizontal, you are probably an *extravert.* The test is based on the compositionist idea that the same physiological processes that control salivation also determine introversion/extraversion personality traits.

Later: What do you think? Are you a believer or a skeptic? Either way, you'll probably remember Eysenck's introversion/extraversion superfactor now, so it won't have been time wasted. Learning tip: an easy way to remember all three of Eysenck's superfactors is to think of a **PEN** (**P**sychoticism, **E**xtraversion, and **N**euroticism). Then if you think of losing your **PEN** while sailing on the **OCEAN,** you'll have two of the major theories covered. Probably no one but Cattell could remember sixteen personality factors, so you should be in pretty good shape when it comes to trait theories.

Are You an Owl or a Lark?

Cupid pours coffee—how "larks" can learn to live with "owls." Many contemporary personality psychologists carry out biologically based research. Although such experiments don't result in full-blown theories of personality in the tradition of Freud, they follow Eysenck's example of carefully researching the biological basis for a specific behavior and then relating that behavior to *macro* traits. For example, the

morning–eveningness trait refers to *stable differences between persons in their preferences for different times of day.* In the laboratory, researchers have utilized a **temporal-isolation design** that *totally eliminates time clues,* to study **circadian rhythms,** which are *24-hour fluctuations.* Since there are no clocks, windows, live television, or regularly scheduled meals, participants have no clues whether it is day or night. For entertainment, they watch videotapes or listen to prerecorded music. Volunteers live in this environment for several weeks or longer while researchers track various biological rhythms (e.g., body temperature, alertness levels, mood changes) on an hourly basis.

Researchers have found that although a 24- to 25-hour cycle is the average, wide differences exist between individuals, ranging from short cycles of 16 hours to long cycles of 50 hours. Such research led to the development of a 19-item **Morningness–Eveningness Questionnaire (MEQ)** (Horne & Ostberg, 1976) designed to assess biorhythms through questions such as the following:

1. **Considering only your "feeling best" rhythm, at what time would you get up if you were entirely free to plan your day.**

    1. between 11:00 A.M. and noon
    2. between 9:30 A.M. and 11 A.M.
    3. between 7:30 A.M. and 9:30 A.M.
    4. between 6:00 A.M. and 7:30 A.M.
    5. before 6:00 A.M.

Similar questions inquire about preferred bedtimes, preferred times to take a test, etc. Another question asks the respondent to indicate at what single hour of the day they reach their "feeling best" peak.

Working with first-year college students at Michigan State University, Watts (1982) found that the greater the differences in roommates' MEQ scores, the lower they rated the quality of their relationship. Findings from research conducted by Revelle and his colleagues (1980) suggest that morningness–eveningness differences can be reduced through the use of stimulants such as caffeine.

So, you see, personality research can make a difference in your life. If you're a "lark" living with an "owl," you can assist Cupid by pouring your roommate a cup of freshly brewed java rather than resenting the fact that he or she is refusing to get out of bed.

Looking Ahead

In the next chapter we will move beyond the trait theorists who view personality as a package of predispositions. We will continue ascending our vertical axis: moving above the *Physiological Zone,* where theorists believe personality is the product of biochemical ingredients, and climbing beyond the *Situational Zone,* where persons are seen as conditioned animals. At a level slightly above the trait theorists, we will encounter *cognitive scientists* who believe that the mind operates somewhat like a giant "wet" computer, with the capacity to process enormous amounts of information.

chapter 5

Person as Processor

Person as Neural Processor, Cognitive Processor, Social Processor, and Cosmic Processor

Karl Pribram, Steven Pinker, Walter Mischel,
Albert Bandura, & Chaos Theorists

IN THIS CHAPTER YOU CAN

1. Ponder Pribram's proposal that the brain operates like a *hologram* (a three-dimensional image produced by a split beam of light).

2. Understand that *cognitive science* is a multidisciplinary approach that seeks to describe the mind in terms that capture the complexities of inner life, yet remain scientifically rigorous.

3. Discern that while some cognitive psychologists believe the mind operates according to *computational principles* similar to those followed by computers, others emphasize the unique features of the "wet mind" that enable it to perform more efficiently than computers.

4. Learn how Steven Pinker views the mind as made up of *mental modules,* each specialized to process certain kinds of information.

5. Discover how Walter Mischel began his career declaring that *situations* are more decisive than inner *traits* in determining behavior, but nearly four decades later, he has come full circle, proposing a *Cognitive–Affective Personality System (CAPS)* in which situations and persons are seamlessly blended into a single processing system.

6. Notice how Albert Bandura emphasized the importance of the *Self* with such concepts as *self-efficacy* and *observational learning.*

7. Wonder if *Chaos Theory (CT),* using such dynamic concepts as *attractors, repellors, basins, bifurcations,* and *fractals* to describe how the universe operates, might be *heuristically* helpful in understanding personality theories from various zones.

A PERSONAL PERSPECTIVE

"Thinking Meat"

Imagine that you're listening in on the following radio conversation between the leader of an interplanetary explorer fleet and his commander in chief as they discuss their research on humans:

"They're made out of meat."

"Meat?". . .

"There's no doubt about it. We picked up several from different parts of the planet, took them aboard our recon vessels, probed them all the way through. They're completely meat."

"That's impossible. What about the radio signals? The messages to the stars?"

"They use the radio waves to talk, but the signals don't come from them. The signals come from machines."

"So who made the machines? That's who we want to contact."

"They made the machines. That's what I'm trying to tell you. Meat made the machines."

"That's ridiculous. How can meat make a machine? You're asking me to believe in sentient [thinking, feeling] meat."

"I'm not asking you, I'm telling you. These creatures are the only sentient race in the sector and they're made out of meat."

"Maybe they're like the Orfolei. You know, a carbon-based intelligence that goes through a meat stage."

"Nope. They're born meat and they die meat. We studied them for several of their life spans, which didn't take too long. Do you have any idea [of] the life span of meat?"

"Spare me. Okay, maybe they're only part meat. You know, like the Weddilei. A meat head with an electron plasma brain inside."

"Nope, we thought of that, since they do have meat heads like the Weddilei. But I told you, we probed them. They're meat all the way through."

"No brain?"

"Oh, there is a brain all right. It's just that the brain is made out of meat!"

"So . . . what does the thinking?"

"You're not understanding, are you? The brain does the thinking. The meat."

"Thinking meat! You're asking me to believe in thinking meat!"

"Yes, thinking meat! Conscious meat! Loving meat. Dreaming meat. The meat is the whole deal! Are you getting the picture?" (Bisson, 1991)

As we climb our vertical axis, somewhere between the *Physiological* and *Insight Zones* we encounter theories that view the person as an *information processor*. Working at this level of analysis, cognitive scientists—like our imaginary interplanetary explorers—seek to explain how personality can emerge from "meat." They conclude that the crucial difference between ordinary "meat" and minds is the ability of minds to *process information:*

. . . brain tumors, the brains of mice, and neural tissue kept alive in a dish don't understand, but their physical-chemical properties are the same as the ones of our brains. The computational theory explains the difference: those hunks of neural tissue are not *arranged* into patterns of connectivity that carry out the right kinds of information processing. For example, they do not have the parts that distinguish nouns from verbs, and their activity patterns do not carry out the rules of syntax, semantics, and common sense. (Pinker, 1997, p. 95)

Person as information processor. From a cognitive science perspective, personality emerges from *mind,* and **mind** is *what the brain does.* "The human mind is a complex system that receives, stores, retrieves, transforms, and transmits information" (Stillings, Feinstein, Garfield, Rissland, Rosenbaum, Weisler, & Baker-Ward, 1987, p. 1). Cognitive scientists do not separate personality from how the mind operates. To understand how the mind works is to understand personality. Although some of the scientists in this chapter are biologists or information-theory researchers—not personality theorists in the traditional sense—we have included them in our text because they look at behavior in broad terms, asking higher-level questions: How do biochemical processes function within the "wet" computer we call mind? How do people process information in a way that leads to the emergence of personality?

We begin with the work of Karl Pribram, a physiological psychologist who carried out investigations spanning both *Physiological* and *Insight Zones.* Then, we consider the theories of Steven Pinker, who views the mind (and personality) as an information processor. Walter Mischel's cognitive social learning theory sees the person processing the *social situation,* while Complexity Theorists seek to understand rules for processing the *entire universe.*

What all these theorists hold in common is their view of the person as an information processor. Here, our earlier distinctions between *description, explanation,* and *integrated understanding* seem particularly relevant. Utilizing information technology metaphors, the cognitive scientists in this chapter *describe* personality as a complex communications network. They even *explain* how the various components appear to interact, but *understanding* precisely how "meat" thinks remains elusive.

Perhaps a more mystical understanding in the *Transpersonal/Spiritual Zone* might encompass how the human brain self-assembles, self-repairs, and even grows while simultaneously carrying on millions of neurological "conversations" at synaptic junctions throughout the organism. Such complexity is—pun intended—"mind boggling"; and it would appear arrogant to claim that finding appropriate *analogies* is equivalent to *understanding.* Still, it is to models and metaphors we must turn; and here we find that biology, information technology, and complexity theory offer some of the most heuristic analogies regarding how "meat" thinks.

Background Check—The Birth and Development of Cognitive Science

In this chapter, instead of tracing the childhood and educational background of various theorists, we will examine the birth and development of the "cognitive revolution" itself.

The birth of cognitive science. George Mandler recalls that cognitive science emerged "in the 5-year period between 1955 and 1960" from the confluence of a number of disciplines: artificial intelligence, anthropology, cybernetics, communications theory, linguistics, and psychology. Prior to the mid-nineteen fifties, only tenuous connections had existed among them, but during the next ten to twenty years, "they would be identified as the components of the newly emerging discipline of cognitive science" (Mandler, 1985, p. 7).

Others have pinpointed the date and birthplace of cognitive science even more precisely, stating that: "there is some consensus that it was born on September 11, 1956 at the Symposium on Information Theory held at MIT" (Gardner, 1984). George Miller, one of the "midwives" at that birthing, left the symposium with a feeling of exhilaration:

I went away from the symposium with a strong conviction . . . that human experimental psychology, theoretical linguistics, and computer simulation of cognitive processes were all pieces of a larger whole, and that the future would see progressive elaboration of their shared concerns. (quoted in Gardner, 1984, p. 29)

This might remind us of how the Internet evolved out of a system of loosely connected computers. And indeed, a sampling of recent university bulletin descriptions defining cognitive science seems to bear out the accuracy of Miller's intuition. The following is typical:

> *Cognitive science is the scientific study of the mind, the brain, and intelligent behavior, whether in humans, animals, machines, or the abstract.... It is a multidisciplinary approach to the study of cognition that blends anthropology, computer science, psychology, neuroscience, linguistics, sociology and philosophy.* (University of California, San Diego)

It is frequently asserted that cognitive psychology was sired by the emergence of Noam Chomsky's (1957) **transformational grammar,** consisting of *rules for converting the "deep structure" of a language to the "surface" language* within the field of linguistics; however, it can be shown that many psychologists were on the cognitive track long before they heard of transformational grammar. The "new look" in perception (e.g., Postman, Bruner, & McGinnies, 1948) began in the late forties and was an important forerunner of today's cognitive science. Research psychologists in the areas of perception, memory, and concept learning (e.g., Bousfield, 1953; Bruner, Goodnow, & Austin, 1956; Hovland, 1952; Miller,1956; and Rock, 1957) were laying the foundations for what is known today as cognitive psychology. Perhaps this diversity in pedigree accounts for the vigor of the offspring, but whoever "started it," cognitive psychology has come of age and is clearly here to stay—for the betterment of all—most would agree.

Zeitgeist

Living the *zeitgeist*. When we first encountered the German word *zeitgeist* in Chapter 1, we had to settle for a dictionary definition. Now we can *experientially* understand what *zeitgeist* means, because we are *living* it! Each time we send or receive an e-mail, play a computer game, or surf the Internet, we are immersed in the *zeitgeist*—the spirit of the times—in the age of computers.

The current expressions of the computer revolution (e.g., the Internet, digital cameras, e-mail, mp3 player, cellular phones) have changed the way we do business, communicate with one another—even how we meet and romance potential spouses or lovers. But has this changed the human personality? Do terms like id, ego, and superego now seem anachronistically anchored in a psychoanalytic Stone Age? Do we need new theories of personality to account for love in cyberspace?

Computer-based theories of personality. Yes, computers have changed how we view personality. How could it be otherwise? Science is—and always has been—part of the culture of a given era, and we are living in the zeitgeist of the computer age. People worried during the industrial revolution that persons would become dehumanized, replaced by machines; and some still worry about many of the same issues at the present time.

We even **anthropomorphize,** *attributing human qualities* to our computers. How many times have you heard the following:

"The computer did it."

"Sorry the computer fouled up, you'll receive your check a week late."

Although we frequently suspect that such statements are an attempt to shift blame, the mere fact that one can transfer blame to a machine illustrates the anthropomorphizing of silicon chips to a degree that was previously unthinkable. Today we don't merely operate our computers, we *interact* with them. Any parent who has tried to pry a child loose from a video game to do homework or prepare for bed knows how powerful such *interactions* can be. Perhaps that's why the notion that our brains operate similarly to computers has such intuitive appeal. The hours we spend interacting with our computers makes it easy to anthropomorphize their operations. It is easy to experience our computers—like our contact lenses and jewelry—as extensions of our own personalities.

The computer as a metaphor of the "wet mind." Cognitive scientists *do not* conceive of the mind as a literal computer; however, many believe that the mathematics behind computers (technically known as *computability theory*) provide an appropriate conceptual model for theories of the mind. What Turing demonstrated was that machines can be used to create symbols that process information—machines that "think." One computer scientist even demonstrated how to build a rational machine, using a single die, some rocks, and a roll of toilet paper (Pinker, 1997, p. 68). Although no one would use rocks and toilet paper to build a real computer, the primary idea that launched the computer revolution was that *some* arrangement of gadgets could function as an intelligent symbol processor.

One cognitive psychologist even saw the computer metaphor as a way of resolving the centuries-old dualism debate:

> In the past, the mind had been likened to a wax tablet, to a hydraulic system, and to a telephone exchange. "Now, there was a new reaction to Dualism: brain and mind are bound together as computer and program. . . . (Johnson-Laird, 1988, p. 23)

Having briefly explored the foundations of the computer age and learned of the circumstances surrounding the birth of cognitive science, we now consider the work of physiological cognitive scientist Karl Pribram.

PERSON PROCESSING NEURO-FEEDBACK— THE HOLOGRAPHIC MIND

Karl Pribram (1919—) began his career by examining the physiological structure and function of neurons, but he soon shifted to investigating how clusters of neurons encode, store, and communicate information. He ultimately came to view the brain as a kind of biological supercomputer. In his classic book, *Languages of the Brain* (1971), Pribram climbs steadily upward, from the *Physiological Zone* where he analyzes the *molecular biology* of neural circuits and biochemical pathways, to the *Insight Zone* where he seeks to understand the *macro* dynamics of signs, symbols, talk, and thought. But this is not an easy climb, because in moving from molecular biology to the macro-behaviors of personality, the reader can easily become lost in a blizzard of neurological details. Although most of Pribram's experimental work was carried out in the *Physiological Zone,* his theoretical applications transcend both neurology and behaviorism, culminating in his model of the *holographic mind.*

ASKING THE BIG FOUR QUESTIONS

What Are the Parts?

Hologram. Pribram's primary metaphor is the **hologram,** which is *a three-dimensional image, produced by a split beam of light.* The *hologram* (from the Greek *holos* meaning "whole") is a type of lensless photography for which Dennis Gabor won a Nobel Prize in 1971. Unlike a photograph, which stores a two-dimensional image, a holographic plate stores a three-dimensional representation that is created by two beams of light. In holography a laser beam is split by a prism so that half the beam shines directly onto a holographic plate, while the other beam illuminates an object. By encoding the differing patterns of these two beams, a pattern can be stored from which a three-dimensional portrait of the object can be projected into space (or onto a screen). You might be carrying a credit card that projects a holographic, three-dimensional image when you hold it at a certain angle to the light.

Neurological "holograms." Pribram suggests that the brain uses parallel *feedback* and *feed-forward* nerve impulses to form "neurological holograms" in much the same way that holography uses two laser beams (each shining on the object from a different angle) to form an image. Remarkably, if a holographic plate is broken into small pieces, the *entire* three-dimensional portrait can be recovered from a *single shard* of the shattered plate. This is consistent with what neuroscientists know about how the brain recovers from massive injuries by reassigning various functions to parts of the brain that have not been traumatized. This sort of redundancy and plasticity is consistent with holographic storage of information.

What Makes a Person Go?

Feedback and feed-forward systems. Pribram conducted experiments on nearly 2,000 monkeys, using implanted electrodes to measure activity in the *visual cortex* and other related brain areas. Pribram concluded that the brain utilizes **feedback systems,** *returning a part of the output signal to the control device for purposes of "fine-tuning" behaviors.* In both machines and monkeys, feedback systems monitor signals, which are compared to a reference signal and fed back to a control device. In the case of a furnace, for example, the sensor (a thermostat) feeds back information about room temperature to a device that controls the furnace, turning it on or off. Similarly, when we stand upright in a moving boat,

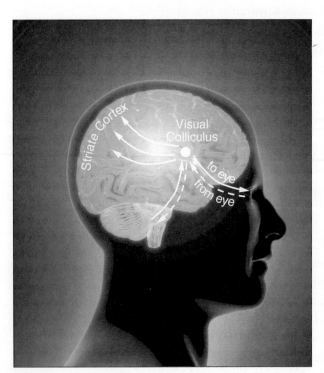

Figure 5.1 ■ *The Holographic Mind*

information from sensors in our feet and ankles continuously feeds back to the muscles and postural mechanisms by which we maintain our upright position.

Feed-forward systems *control behaviors or processes by providing advance information* instead of feedback. To catch a ball it is necessary to *predict* its trajectory and to place one's hands at a point that will intercept that path. In catching a ball, the feed-forward control system must accurately interpret visual cues and correspondingly flex the appropriate muscles in anticipation of the ball's impact.

Pribram discovered that in the visual system of monkeys, incoming impulses from the retinas of both eyes are relayed to a processing center in the brain where they are compared with *feed-forward* impulses from the visual colliculus. From these *converging* systems the brain accumulates information that allows it to produce something analogous to a *hologram* of the correct response sequence.

What Makes a Person Grow?

Pribram did not specify developmental stages, but we can assume that biological maturity and growth fine-tune the feedback and feed-forward neural mechanisms, possibly providing a foundation for experiencing one's *self*. For example, if vibrators designed to simulate the human eardrum are placed on each of your forearms, you will at first experience these sensations as jumping back and forth between your arms, but as you fine-tune the frequencies and become familiar with the feelings, you will begin to experience your "feeling self" as somewhere in the middle. This is similar to how you can tinker with the balance adjustment of your stereo, moving the music from left to right, until you can listen to the musical performers "seated" directly in front of you.

From a personality perspective, it is possible that our sense of a central *self* emerges as the result of a potpourri of childhood experiences that "converge"—like laser beams—from multiple social encounters to form our own unique "me-myself-and-I" image.

The kinds of social "feed-forward" and "feedback" processes necessary for our *holographic self* to form might take place as naturally as inhaling and exhaling—without awareness or effort. Do you recall "feed-forward" thoughts the last time you were on your way to a party: Wonder who will be there? What will I say if Cooper asks me out? Should I tell that joke about how many Freudians it takes to change a light bulb? Do you remember your "feedback" thoughts on the way home: Why did Cooper avoid me? Everyone except Emily laughed at my Freud joke—I wonder, did she get it or did she think I was "out of line"?

Of course, by asking such questions we've leaped several rungs up our vertical axis from neurons to social encounters—from the *Physiological* to the *Social Zone*—but that's in the spirit of Pribram's work.

What Makes a Person Unique?

A holographic plate does not simply store a one-image code, so by altering the angles at which light strikes a target object, and by altering the frequency of the laser beam, *one cubic centimeter* of plate can store *ten billion* codes! Clearly, if the brain is organized along holographic lines, there is plenty of capacity for individuality and uniqueness.

FACING THE TOUGH TWINS

Is It Testable?

In the *Physiological Zone,* Pribram's investigation of feedback and feed-forward neural impulses was elegant and carefully carried out; however, at higher levels of analysis, the task of demonstrating that the human brain encodes information *holographically* becomes extraordinarily difficult. Nevertheless, the holographic hypothesis is consistent with much that is currently known about brain behavior. For example, the brain is able to store huge amounts of information in a small space, in a way that is highly redundant and extremely resistant to destruction. People are able to survive significant brain injuries with many functions still intact, while computers, by comparison, are frequently disabled by the malfunctioning of a single circuit.

The brain as a "wet" supercomputer. Numerous cognitive scientists agree with Pribram's perspective that the brain is a "wet" (biologically based) information processor. Living in the computer age, it appears reasonable to think that a person provides a biochemically balanced habitat for a living information processor that floats within the protective custody of the cranium. From this perspective, personality is embodied by, and emerges from, the brain or "wet computer" inside our skulls.

Critiques of "wet computer" theories. Some of the most vigorous critiques of the brain-as-computer have come from neuroscientists who insist that it is impossible to understand the mind apart from understanding its underlying biology. Edelman, for example, argues that although physics is "the mother of all sciences," it is not a good model for understanding how the brain works. "What is missing is . . . an account of real psychology, of real brains, and of their underlying biology" (1992, pp. 213, 217). However, most cognitive scientists do not insist that all cognitive processes must be *reduced* to physiological components (i.e., "behind every twisted thought is a twisted neuron").

Billions of possible connections. The human brain has 100 to 200 *billion* neurons, many of which have up to 10,000 direct connections with other neurons. Even though *billion* has been italicized in order to grab our attention, it is probably a safe bet that we don't *really* comprehend what that number means. When we hear of government budgets with their millions, billions, and even trillions of dollars it simply means "lots of taxpayer dollars." But let's try to understand what this means in terms of how our brains are constructed.

How much is a billion? Think of each brain neuron as equivalent to a *second* of time. How long do you think it would take to tick off a *million* seconds?

About $11\frac{1}{2}$ days.
How long would it take to tick off a *billion* seconds?
About 32 *years!*

Let's do the math. Since there are 100 to 200 *billion* neurons in a human brain, it would take somewhere between three and six thousand *years* to build a human brain, constructing it at the rate of one neuron per second! But that's not all. Since we know that most neurons are interconnected with hundreds and even thousands of other neurons in a communication network, the number of possible connections becomes—literally—unimaginable.

Critiques of the brain as "wet computer." Not only biologists, but cognitive psychologists as well, remind us that the brain-as-computer metaphor cannot be taken literally. Only in the most general sense that both computers and nervous systems *encode and process information* does it make sense to think of the brain as a computer. However, such metaphors—even if compelling—do not provide us the cognitive theories necessary to relate physical composition to conscious mental experience. Moving from analyzing the composition of "meat" to understanding the functions of mind requires more elaborate theories.

Is It Useful?

Summary of Pribram's theory. Pribram's theory is both practically and heuristically useful. His holographic hypothesis is based in neurobiology, but he ascends several levels to explain higher-order psychological functions. One personality psychologist had this to say:

> Pribram's holographic model is potentially the stuff of scientific revolution, resolving at a stroke the sterile dualisms of mind and matter, humanities and sciences, existentialism and essentialism. . . . He posits an open, intentional, cybernetic system of organism *plus* environment wherein consciousness is heightened by disparities between "feedback" and "feed-forward". . . .
> (Hampden-Turner, 1981, p. 97)

Since Pribram's theory is deeply rooted in neurobiology, it is not usually considered a personality theory in the traditional sense; however, it provides a conceptual bridge from Galen's humor-based temperaments, Eysenck's physiologically based traits, and Skinner's billiard-ball behaviorism to the information-rich analyses of cognitive psychologists. With the notable exception of Eysenck's work, the biological foundations of personality remained marginalized throughout much of the twentieth century. Now, with the molecular structure of the nervous system more clearly understood than ever before, Pribram's *holographic hypothesis* shimmers as one of the brightest stars in the constellation of early biological theories. Whether Pribram's theories ultimately turn out to be validated or falsified, they have heuristically energized one of the hottest areas of research today: investigating how a living human brain encodes and employs information.

STEVEN PINKER'S COMPUTATIONAL THEORY OF MIND

Few psychologists have contributed more to the computational theory of mind than has Steven Pinker. His engaging writing style and scientific pragmatism appeal to professionals and public alike. Pinker begins with a solid neuroscience base in the *Physiological Zone* and then moves to higher levels of analysis in the *Insight Zone*. He investigates such areas as language development and visual cognition, and disagrees with the postmodern, poststructural notions currently in vogue that *all* categories of knowledge are socially constructed and *all* definitions of reality are socially relative.

Such thinking, says Pinker, is politically motivated ("a convoluted way of getting to the conclusion that oppression of women, gays, and minorities is bad" [1997, p. 57]). Confusing political goals with scientific psychology leads many to believe in what Pinker calls a "structureless mind" (1997, p. 57). Pinker insists that reality *is* definable, and he urges us to avoid the "poverty of imagination" that leads to a dichotomy between what is "in nature" and what is "socially constructed." He proposes that "some categories are products of a complex mind designed to mesh with what is in nature" (1997, p. 57).

ASKING THE BIG FOUR QUESTIONS

What Are the Parts?

The stuff of life: springs, hinges, and trapdoors—no quivering, glowing, wondrous gel. For Pinker, the mind (and by extension, personality) is neither intangible nor socially constructed. Instead, according to his **computational theory of mind,** *mind consists of mental modules, supported by multiple layers of biochemical machinery, capable of processing memory, thoughts, emotions, desires, and other information.* Notice that although Pinker sees the mind as arising out of biological "machinery," this is machinery specially organized to *process information.* In this way he resolves Descartes's ancient mind–body dualism. Pinker views the brain and its attached nervous systems somewhat as a "meat"-based computer, capable of processing and acting upon information, transforming such odorless, tasteless, touchless intangibles as "wanting to visit Paris" into such "meaty" activities as actually moving one's bones in the direction of an airport from which planes fly to France!

Mechanical metaphors. According to Pinker, our minds are composed of real biological parts: "The stuff of life turned out not to be a quivering, glowing, wondrous gel but a contraption of tiny jugs, springs, hinges, rods, sheets, magnets, zippers, and trapdoors, assembled by a data tape whose information is copied, downloaded, and scanned" (1997, p. 22).

From this perspective, even the ordinary *hand* (to say nothing of the brain, heart, lungs, or Freud's centerpiece—the penis) is a marvel of mechanical engineering. Nearly twenty centuries ago, Galen noted that the hand can manipulate an astonishing range of objects from a millet seed to a log: "Man handles them all," he noted, "as well as if his hand had been made for the sake of each one of them alone" (quoted in Williams, 1992). Pinker elaborates:

> The hand can be configured into a hook grip (to lift a pail), a scissors grip (to hold a cigarette), a five-jaw chuck (to lift a coaster), a three-jaw chuck (to hold a pencil), a two-jaw chuck (to turn a key), a squeeze grip (to hold a hammer), a disc grip (to open a jar), and a spherical grip (to hold a ball). Each grip needs a precise combination of muscle tensions that mold the hand into the right shape and keep it there as the load tries to bend it back. Think of lifting a milk carton. Too loose a grasp, and you drop it; too tight, and you crush it; and with some gentle rocking, you can even use the tugging on your fingertips as a gauge of how much milk is inside! (Pinker, 1997, p. 12)

Pinker's computational perspective of mind (and personality) ascends far beyond mechanical reductionism in the *Physiological Zone,* and it would be misleading to leave the impression that getting inside the mind could be accomplished by getting inside the cranium and untangling a few trillion neurological circuits—like removing the cover of a computer to expose the hard drive.

Computers can't compare with your brain. Although Pinker views the mind as "a set of modules," he quickly adds that "the modules are not encapsulated boxes or circumscribed swatches on the surface of the brain." Although he asserts that "thinking is computation," he explains that the computer is not a good metaphor for the mind:

> Computers are serial, doing one thing at a time; brains are parallel, doing millions of things at once. . . . Computers have a limited number of connections; brains have trillions. . . . Computers are assembled according to a blueprint; brains must assemble themselves. . . . The claim is not that the brain is like commercially available computers. Rather, the claim is that brains and computers embody intelligence for some of the same reasons . . . *the mind is not the brain but what the brain does.* . . . The brain's special status comes from a special thing the brain does, which makes us see, think, feel, choose, and act. *That special thing is information processing and computation.* (1997, pp. 23–26, emphasis added)

Patterns of information, not compositional ingredients. Notice that even though many cognitive scientists have strong roots in the *Physiological Zone,* they insist that differences of composition exist only to serve the main purpose of the mind: *processing information.* Just as the content of a book or a movie is embedded in the *patterns of information* encoded in the marks on a page or the magnetic charges on a segment of celluloid tape, the essence of mind exists in the *patterns of information* encoded in the nervous system, not in the *composition* of the biological substrates. All the information, in all the books of the world, is contained in patterns created from approximately seventy-five different characters:

> There are millions of animal species on earth, each with a different set of cognitive programs. *The same basic neural tissue embodies all of these programs,* and it could support many others as well. Facts about the properties of neurons, neurotransmitters, and cellular development cannot tell you which of these millions of programs the human mind contains. Even if all neural activity is the expression of a uniform process at the cellular level, it is the arrangement of neurons—into bird song templates or web-spinning programs—that matters. (Tooby & Cosmides, 1994)

Although neural tissues kept alive in a specimen dish or inside a mouse's brain exhibit the same biochemical characteristics as our brains, they lack "human intelligence" because they are not arranged into modules that can carry out the appropriate information processing.

According to cognitive scientists, "mind" does not emerge from the *composition* of neural components, but evolves when the brain and nervous system *process information* and *cause further changes*. That means that most "parts" of this theory of personality are interchangeable with almost any other "parts"—so long as replacement parts have a similar capacity to carry information and cause further events. Thus, one might use meat instead of metal, Jello instead of silicon, or toilet paper instead of typing paper to process information. As they say these days, "It's all good."

What Makes a Person Go?—Information

Turing's typewriter as a model of the "computational mind." For cognitive scientists information does not function as a *motive* or an *instinct*—driving the organism as libido propelled Freud's patients, or hunger motivated Skinner's pigeons. Instead, information is built into the environment much as "wetness" is built into the ocean, requiring organisms to process information about moisture and seaweeds in order to adapt and survive.

If cognitive scientists talk about "motivation," it usually has to do with how data flows through a network of information-processing components. One doesn't find descriptions of the type of "fuel" the cognitive "engine" requires; no talk of libido, self-actualization, or existential angst. "Motivation" is already built into **cognitive science's foundational assumption:** *the human mind receives, retrieves, stores, transforms and transmits information.* Most of the discussion is about architecture—how various information-processing modules are arranged, and the direction and volume of informational flow.

Churchland and Churchland (1994) view the brain as the most complex and highly sophisticated thing on planet earth. Kolb and Whishaw note that "if there were no order in [the brain's] complexity, it would be incomprehensible" (1990, p. 4).

Simplifying features. Some simplifying features are *compositional* or *structural:* for example, electrical signals are virtually identical in all nerve cells in the human body; neurotransmitters released at synapses to send chemical signals to other neurons are common to many different species of animals. "In this sense, nerve impulses can be considered stereotyped units. They are the universal coins for exchange of communication in all nervous systems that have been investigated" (Nicholls, Martin, & Wallace, 1992, p. 2).

Other simplifying features are *organizational:* neuroscientists have discovered that neurons function in systems or networks. The pioneering work of Hebb, 1949, 1959; Hubel & Wiesel, 1959, 1962; Pribram, 1971; and others led to the realization that there is a hierarchy of organization in neural connections. The work of these early investigators laid the foundation for two core assumptions in modern neuroscience: (1) the basic building blocks of the nervous system are *relatively uniform* in their composition and mechanics, and (2) the *pattern of connections* among neurons is central to understanding how the brain functions.

Four representational formats. Laboratory research has revealed that most people use four major formats for representing and processing information: (1) **visual image:** *a two-dimensional, picturelike mosaic in the "mind's eye";* (2) **phonological representation:** *stretches of syllables* that enable us to hold four to seven "chunks" of information in short-term memory for three to five seconds; (3) **grammatical representation:** *hierarchical trees of verbs, phrases, clauses, stems, roots, phonemes, and syllables* that determine how we compose sentences and communicate through language; and (4) **mentalese**: *the language of thought* (cf. Pinker, 1997, pp. 89–90).

Modularity of the mind. Equipped with the ability to represent information in different formats, the mind *modularizes* its operations, in the spirit of an anthill or a beehive. Each module is designed to do one thing well. "Complex systems are hierarchies of modules," writes Pinker, "because only elements that hang together in modules can remain stable long enough to be assembled into larger and larger modules" (1997, p. 92).

Four but no more. Recent research (Verhaeghen, Cerella, & Basak, 2004) has confirmed that the human brain utilizes *modularity* in short-term memory tasks. For example, when you sort coins, you naturally sort them into separate piles of pennies, nickels, dimes, and quarters—keeping track of how many of each there are in each pile, rather than trying to keep a running total of all the coins in whatever order you receive them. With training you could learn to keep track of up to four piles at the same time, but never more than four. It appears to be a fundamental characteristic of human memory: four but no more.

What Makes a Person Grow?

The role of the family in personality development. Pinker's views on personality development as well as his computational theory of mind both grow out of his evolutionary perspective of adaptation. Much as Buss views personality as an "adaptive landscape" (Chapter 2), Pinker views the human brain as a conglomerate of modules that have evolved because of their adaptive functions. Pinker believes about 50 percent of the variation in personality is due to genetic causes, while another 45 percent results from other environmental events impinging on the growing brain (e.g., viruses, physical trauma such as being dropped on one's head when a baby, or emotional experiences such as being chased by a dog or being treated with kindness by a teacher). According to Pinker, only about *5 percent* of personality differences among people can be attributed to parental influence (1997, p. 448).

Peers, not parents. Citing the work of Judith Harris (1995) that children are primarily socialized by the peer group rather than by parents, Pinker, nevertheless, states that "Young children surely need the love, protection, and tutelage of a sane parent" (p. 449). Pinker is not saying that parents are unimportant, only that personality *differences* seen in adults would probably have developed in much the same manner even if you had left children in their original homes and switched parents around in a "musical chairs" manner. This is simply an evolutionary psychologist's way of saying that parents contribute ten times more to their offsprings' personalities through genes than through parenting.

What Makes a Person Unique?

Although cognitive scientists emphasize *processes* more than persons, they do not completely obliterate uniqueness from personality. Pinker states that "Our obsession with individual personhood is not an inexplicable quirk, but probably evolved because every human being we meet . . . is guaranteed to house an unreplicable collection of memories and desires owing to a unique embryological and biographical history" (1997, p. 117).

Falling in love with a twin—*not!* To illustrate the importance of uniqueness, Pinker asks us to imagine falling in love with a twin. Whatever attracts us to one twin—the way she talks, the way she walks, the way she looks—should, according to associationistic theory, attract us to the other twin as well. In real life, this doesn't happen. Spouses of identical twins are not attracted to their spouse's sibling. As Pinker summarizes it: "Love locks our feelings in to another person *as that person,* not as a *kind* of person, no matter how narrow the kind" (1997, p. 117).

Variant of a variable. Not all cognitive scientists value uniqueness; for many investigators, individuals are only part of a larger whole. This is usually the case in studies with insects or other nonhuman species. In such instances, *individuals* count for little, it is *process* that matters. When you study population genetics, for example, the *individual organism* is not your primary interest; uniqueness is not what it's about. Each organism is only a variant of a variable. Some investigators have pointed out that information processing capacities (thus a "mind") is by no means limited to the human species.

The computational mind of insects. Gallistel (1998) convincingly showed that wasps, ants, bees, birds, and locusts have brains with capabilities not unlike the *global position sensors (GPS)* currently available to help you find your way back home when you're "lost," or to precisely judge your distance from a green, if you're playing a round of golf at an upscale country club. Honeybees dance to communicate to their hive mates the approximate distance and angle of flight to the food sources. Ants know the distance home, traveling, when released, to within 10 percent of the distance from their nest at the time of capture. A locust computes distance by "peering" at a target while slowly shifting its upper body back and forth, counterrotating its head as it shifts in order to keep oriented straight ahead. This allows the locust to calculate the precise distance to the target by a surveyor's technique known as triangulation.

Analyzing his results, Gallistel writes:

> What makes this of interest to cognitive scientists is that it suggests that the brain of an insect is a symbol-processing organ. It suggests that the brain uses computation to construct a cognitive map and to compute courses from the positional values stored in that map. . . . Thus the homing abilities of insects might be taken as strong evidence in favor of a computational-representational theory of mind. (1998, p. 6)

FACING THE TOUGH TWINS

Is It Testable?

As you have no doubt concluded by now, research is the heart of cognitive science. As we learned earlier, cognitive psychology has filled the "empty organism" left behind by behaviorism. Cognitive science is the *new mentalism*; but it is a *rigorous mentalism*, a *research-based mentalism*. Progress has not come easily, however. It has been extremely difficult to program computers to solve higher-order problems like learning a language the way people do. Children, for example, easily "pick up" language from their playmates; but programming a computer to "learn" a language has proven a daunting task.

Recently, however, artificial intelligence researchers have been tackling the more difficult problems. Clark (1997) and his colleagues have been working on building a knowledge base for a computer with hundreds—even thousands—of commonsense notions (e.g., "underwater = wet"; "in the rain without an umbrella = soaking wet or dripping wet," and thousands more). Their attempt is to provide computers with the comparable experiences of an infant actively using its senses, thoughts, and perceptions to interact with the surrounding world. Presumably, with a broad enough set of such "experiences," computers might be able to "think" in a way that more closely mirrors humans' ordinary use of language.

Is It Useful?

In our computer-permeated society, the ways in which a *computational approach to thinking* has altered our lives are too numerous to mention there are no signs of a slowdown. Unlike the "grand" theories of behaviorism, psychoanalysis, or humanistic psychology, cognitive science has been interdisciplinary from the start, and has been enlivened by the controversies that such mixed pedigrees foster. Research, controversy, and new applications tend to accelerate knowledge.

Summary of Computational Models of Mind and Personality

Seen from a *zonal perspective,* the *computational mind* consists of a complex array of information-processing modules that are biochemically based *(Physiological Zone)* and capable of integrating information from our conditioning histories *(Behavioral Zone)* with traits, thoughts, dreams, and desires *(Insight Zone)* as well as interpersonal relationships *(Social Zone).* These information-processing modules function to provide us the cognitive and psychological foundations that allow us to experience our *selves* and significant *others* in ways that feel coherent and seamless.

Pinker puts it picturesquely: "A human being is simultaneously a machine and a sentient free agent, depending on the purpose of the discussion, just as he is also a taxpayer, an insurance salesman, a dental patient, and two hundred pounds of ballast on a commuter airplane, depending on the purpose of the discussion" (1997, p. 56).

Science versus ethics. Although ethical worries swirl rampantly whenever one begins to talk about machines that "think," Pinker articulately argues that there is no essential clash between science and ethics:

> Science and ethics are two self-contained systems played out among the same entities in the world, just as poker and bridge are different games played with the same fifty-two card deck. The science game treats people as material objects, and its rules are the physical processes that cause behavior through natural selection and neurophysiology. The ethics game treats people as equivalent, sentient, rational, free-willed agents, and its rules are the calculus that assigns moral value to behavior. . . . (Pinker, 1997, p. 55)

Next, we move to a higher level of analysis where whole *persons*—not cognitive modules—are seen as processing complex social situations.

PERSON PROCESSING SOCIAL SITUATIONS—THE SOCIAL LEARNING THEORY OF WALTER MISCHEL

Introduction

Walter Mischel has played a prominent role in the recent history of personality theories. He first tried to pry other personality theorists loose from what he saw as a one-sided preoccupation with the "inner" person by insisting that the *Situational Zone* was *the* prime shaper of personality. However, over time, he shifted from insisting on the primacy of the situation to a more balanced *interactionist* approach, including the *Insight* and *Social Zones* as well.

Background Check

Walter Mischel (1930–) was born in Vienna, within walking distance of Freud's house. When he was nine years of age, because of the looming Nazi threat, his family left Europe and relocated in New York City, where Mischel eventually became a social worker. He became disillusioned with Freud's theory when working with juvenile delinquents and subsequently enrolled at Ohio State University, where he completed doctoral work in psychology under the influence of such eminent personality psychologists as Julian Rotter and George Kelly (Chapter 10).

Rotter is famous for developing the **Rotter Incomplete-Sentences Blank** (Rotter & Rafferty, 1950), a test consisting of *forty open-ended sentences (e.g., "I like ——" or "When I was younger ——" or "My greatest worry is ——") that respondents are asked to complete in their own words.* Rotter is also known for his research (1990) on **internal versus external locus of control,** *a personality construct referring to whether an individual locates responsibility for behavior or events internally (within oneself) or externally (in luck or fate).* Kelly is famous for formulating a theory of personality that focuses on each individual's **personal constructs,** which are *psychological "templates"—unique to each person—through which they view the world.* We will examine Kelly's theory in more detail later (Chapter 10), but here we notice how Rotter's and Kelly's ideas influenced Mischel's theory of personality. Rotter emphasized the importance of *expectancies* in human behavior, while Kelly emphasized the active role a person plays in creating an internal network of *personal constructs.* Both of these influences remain strong in Mischel's most recent (1995, 1999) theory.

Zeitgeist

The *zeitgeist* in psychology during the 1950s and 1960s was strongly influenced by the work of Clark Hull (1884–1952), a learning theorist who loved logic, geometry, and machines. Hull's heroes were men like Newton (who described the universe as a huge machine), and people like Pavlov and Watson (who believed that "consciousness" was an obsolete holdover from medieval metaphysics and theology). As part of a course he taught at the University of Wisconsin, Hull invented a machine that could automatically compute correlations among test scores. Later, at Yale, Hull again studied the creation of machines that could learn and think.

Other important contributors to the *zeitgeist* included Neal Miller and John Dollard, who developed their own laboratory-based social-learning theory. They agreed with Freud's theory of instinctual aggressive urges, but reframed the problem of aggression in behavioral and social terms (Dollard, Doob, Miller, Mowrer, & Sears, 1939). According to their **frustration-aggression hypothesis,** *the more an organism's goals are blocked, the greater will be the resultant frustration and subsequent aggression.* Miller and Dollard believed that aggression—like all behaviors—is *learned* in a particular social and cultural context, but that it is powered by *drive.* They integrated Freud's idea of instinct with Hull's (1943) notion of drive, and recast many of Freud's classic defense mechanisms, such as repression, displacement, and ambivalence, as social-learning processes.

The behaviorist traditions of Pavlov, Watson, Hull, Skinner, and others all emphasized the importance of the *situation* as the source of rewards, punishments, and other essentials of learning—almost to the complete exclusion of *persons as agents.* However, under the influence of early cognitive learning theorists like Rotter and Kelly, things were beginning to shift slightly, and graduate students like Mischel were becoming increasingly uncomfortable with the limited scope of traditional learning theories as well as the broad but difficult-to-test umbrella of Freudianism. Mischel sought to translate the mechanistic aspects of behaviorism into a broader social-learning theory. In attempting to "cognitivize" the radical behaviorists, Mischel moved toward the domain of higher-order personality issues, but he continued to insist on the primacy of the *Situational Zone.*

Situationism—a pipe bomb in the camp of trait theorists. Mischel is famous for his vigorous (1968) exposition (many saw it as an attack) regarding the limitations of traditional theories of personality. In the behaviorist tradition of Watson and Skinner, Mischel argued for the supremacy of *situation variables* in determining and predicting behavior, while simultaneously challenging the value of both psychoanalytic and trait theories. Since personality theorists had traditionally emphasized *inner-person variables (e.g., instincts, traits, self-esteem)* as primarily responsible for initiating, guiding, and energizing behavior, it wasn't surprising that Mischel's critique set off a firestorm of controversy.

"Personality" defined as a field of study. Shortly following his initial critique, Mischel took the position that the term *personality* did not refer to an individual's inner psychological structure; instead, it indicated a *field of study:* "The term 'personality' has numerous meanings. To psychologists, personality is a field of study rather than a distinct aspect of people" (1971, p. 7).

Few personality psychologists—then or now—would disagree with Mischel's emphasis on the importance of research. However, many were critical of his "piecemeal" approach:

> To study the "total individual" or the "whole person" may be a worthy goal, but it is a practical impossibility. To progress beyond recognizing and admiring the complexity of man, the researcher must select things about people that he can study. (Mischel, 1971, p. 1)

Person as situation processor. However, by the late 1970s, Mischel was sounding more like his graduate school mentor, George Kelly, in emphasizing the importance of the *person* as a *constructor* of meanings:

> I prefer to stress the active cognitive *constructions* that underlie complex social perceptions, not to belittle the "reality" of personality but to underline its

complexity. . . . Consequently, it may not be possible to assign the residence of dispositions exclusively either to the actor or to the perceiver; we may have to settle for a continuous interaction between observed and observer, for a reality that is constructed and cognitively created but not fictitious. (Mischel, 1977, pp. 333–334)

In the end, Mischel had morphed into an *interactional constructivist,* emphasizing the importance of *both* situations *and* persons:

Recognizing that the question "Are persons or situations more important?" is misleading and unanswerable, one can now turn to the more interesting issue: When are situations most likely to exert powerful effects and, conversely, when are person variables likely to be most influential? (Mischel 1977, p. 346)

Interactionism. By 1979, Mischel's shift from situationism to interactionism seemed complete. Having thrown his situationist pipe bomb into the camp of the trait theorists, Mischel now seemed inclined to wave the olive branch of interactional reconciliation:

In the previous decade many of us realized the incompleteness of a personality psychology that failed to include and consider seriously the role of *specific situations* in the analysis of behavior. In the decade now ending, many of us

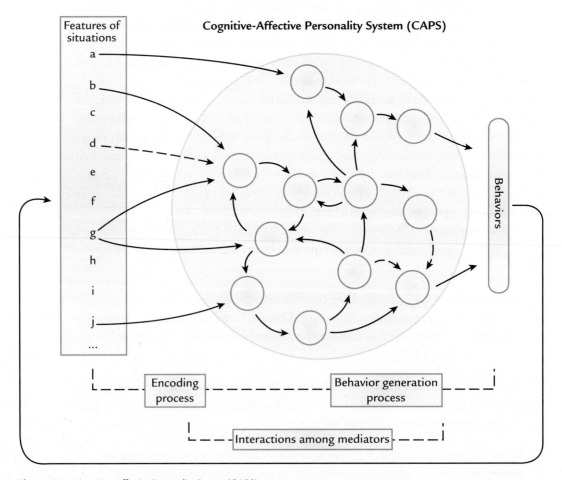

Figure 5.2 ■ *Cognitive-Affective Personality System (CAPS)*

have come to recognize increasingly that an adequate analysis of behavior cannot proceed without serious attention to the cognitive processes of *both* the actors and the observers. . . . (Mischel, 1979, p. 1752, emphasis added)

Cognitive–Affective Personality System (CAPS)—Mischel's final formulation. Over a period of more than three decades, Mischel softened his "hard line" on the primacy of the situation and embraced an *interactional* approach (1977, 1979), which most recently has evolved into a *systems* model. Mischel and Shoda (1995) formulated what they term a **Cognitive-Affective Personality System (CAPS)** *in which person and situation are seamlessly blended into a single processing system.*

In formulating the CAPS model, Mischel has moved considerably beyond his 1971 position that it was impossible to study the "whole person. In the CAPS model, Mischel and Shoda not only undertake to study the "whole person," they attempt to comprehensively blend persons, situations, and mediating strategies into one holistic *system*.

Levels of analysis. Most recently, Mischel has incorporated a "levels" perspective, suggesting that personality includes *personal tendencies, psychological* processes, and *biological-genetic processes,* interacting at different levels "to influence the individual's distinctive patterns of adaptation throughout the life span" (Mischel, Shoda, & Smith, 2004, p. 4).

ASKING THE BIG FOUR QUESTIONS

What Are the Parts? and What Makes a Person Go?

With Mischel & Shoda's model the "Big Four" questions tend to merge because the CAPS model of personality is not so much a theory of the person as it is a *system* for integrating the study of persons and situations in what we have called *zones of analysis*. The closest that Mischel and Shoda come to listing personality "parts" or discussing how they might motivationally energize the person is their enumeration of five types of **Cognitive–Affective Units,** which are *dynamic person variables that mediate, define, and process the situation and shape behavior.*

Five Kinds of Cognitive–Affective Units

(1) Encodings are categories (constructs) for characterizing self, others, events, and situations. Here we see the influence of George Kelly (see Chapter 10), who suggested that any given event can be *construed* or *interpreted* in any number of different ways. The particular symbols, words, or concepts that people use are unique to each person. Each person has her own way of construing or encoding events. Furthermore, since these encodings are dynamic—not static—they frequently change over time so that not only will a situation be construed differently by two different people, the same situation may be construed differently on separate occasions by the same person.

A professor, for example, might chastise his students for their poor performance on the first exam, and threaten them with daily quizzes in order to press them to better performance. But since each student *encodes* the professor's threats differently, one might decide to drop the course after the "No more Mr. Nice Guy" lecture, while another might, indeed, study harder. Still another student might decide the professor was bluffing or just having a "bad day," and not take the threats seriously—neither dropping the class nor studying harder.

(2) Expectancies and beliefs. Julian Rotter was the mentor who developed in Mischel an appreciation for importance of expectancies. In Mischel's theory **expectancies** *include speculations about the likely outcomes for behavior in particular situations, estimates about self-efficacy, and surmises about the social world.* In a *behavior–outcome expectancy* the person thinks, "If I act in a certain way, it will have the following result." In a *stimulus–outcome expectancy,* anticipate that if *A* occurs, *B* is likely to follow. Thus if I hear a siren (A) nearby, I expect (B) an emergency vehicle to appear. A *self-efficacy expectation* is my estimate of how efficiently I am likely to perform in a certain circumstance. Thus, it is one thing to *know* that a drowning person needs rescuing; it is another to be *able* to swim to their aid.

(3) Affects are feelings and emotions (including physiological reactions) that vary from person to person and influence how an individual responds to a given situation. Here Mischel is primarily concerned with how emotions influence a person's interaction with situational stimuli (recall, from Chapter 1, Mischel's investigations of "hot" or "cool" emotional responses to marshmallows, pretzels, or other "temptation" foods).

(4) Goals and values play a crucial role in determining which personal or situational variables will be translated into action. A student may *know* that it is necessary to write an excellent term paper in order to receive an "A" in a particular class, but he may put a higher *value* on helping his fiancée move into her apartment, and neglect doing the paper until it is too late in the semester to do a superior job.

(5) Competencies and self-regulatory plans. According to Mischel and other social learning theorists, people acquire information about their physical and social worlds and about their abilities to deal with the environment. **Competencies** *are what a person knows and what he or she is capable of doing.* Mischel and Shoda see these competencies not merely as static memories, but as active processes—dynamic tools—that allow a person to make a wide variety of creative responses to any given situation.

Social learning theorists believe that much of human behavior is **self-regulated;** for example, *a person sets for herself certain standards and when she meets or exceeds them, she feels good about herself.* According to this view, behavior is influenced more by *intrinsic* reinforcements or punishments than by *external* rewards or punishments.

Person-as-processor, not as agentic self. Mischel's theory is informed by the excellent experimental work he has pursued on various personality variables. However, CAPS is a *system* for interconnecting the *person-as-processor* with the *situation-as-perceived.* It is not a theory of personality in the classical sense of explaining individual peculiarities or characteristics in terms of an *agentic self.* Although Mischel has moved a considerable distance from his early days of radical situationism, he has stopped short of creating a genuinely agentic self. For him personality remains a *system*—somewhat like the mass transit systems of Chicago or Boston—where humans are whisked about to various destinations within a labyrinth of interconnected paths. CAPS provides us with an intricate mapping of human beings traveling about in a complex cybernetic system where persons and situations interact to create, shape, and change behaviors and environments, but we are still missing, for the most part, the *person.*

The specific connections shown in Figure 5.4 illustrate:

(a) there are many possible relations among the units but only some are functionally important; (b) units become activated in relation to situations and to other units in the personality system; (c) feedback activations occur that produce and sustain patterns of activation over time: and, most important, (d) units that become activated in the personality system activate other units through their distinctive organization in a network of relations, ultimately generating observable behaviors. (Mischel & Shoda, 1995, pp. 254–255)

Mischel has moved from the far right of the *Situational* Zone, where he previously shared much in common with Skinner and other behaviorists, to a more centrist position of viewing the *person* as a processor. Nonetheless, in CAPS the person remains a *processor* more than a *person*. Make no mistake, this is no "empty-organism" brand of behaviorism; Mischel's model of personality portrays the individual as a complex processor having remarkable capacities for *encoding, valuing, self-regulating*, etc., but this individual still lacks an *agentic self*, which we will encounter in the *Insight Zone*.

What Makes a Person Grow?

CAPS presents little in the way of developmental constructs. To the extent that social-learning theories are tilted toward emphasizing the situation more than the person, they have not included carefully articulated theories of development. In the tradition of Watson and Pavlov, learning trumps innate blooming ("Give me a dozen healthy infants . . . ," said Watson, "and I'll guarantee to take any one at random and train him to become any type of specialist"). Learning theory's developmental model has traditionally been quite simple: the experiences of life engrave themselves upon the *tabula rasa* of the mind.

Mischel and Shoda are not quite that drastic. They provide a flow chart (Figure 5.3) in which development is nested in a box that connects the situation and the person by

Figure 5.3 ■ *CAPS Model of Developmental Influences*

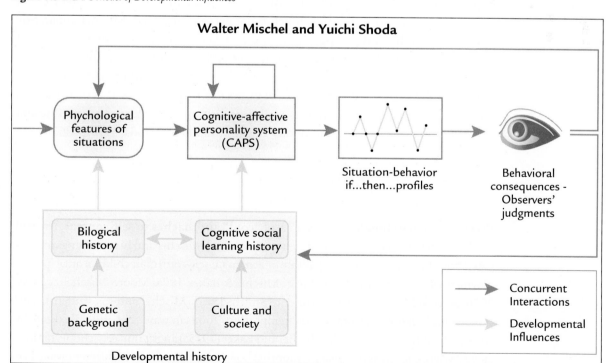

The Cognitive-Affective Personality System (CAPS) in relation to concurrent interactions and developmental influences (see text).

means of hatch-lined arrows. Their explanation of developmental constructs is brief to the point of barrenness: "Developmentally, the organization of the relations among the cognitive–affective units reflects the individual's cognitive social learning history in interaction with the biological history, such as the temperamental and genetic–biochemical factors" (Mischel & Shoda, 1995, p. 262). In the domain of development, CAPS doesn't take us much beyond the nature–nurture truism that all behavior is a joint function of learning and biology.

What Makes a Person Unique?

Every person a processor—every processor unique. CAPS is a useful model for integrating social-learning theory, cognitive psychology, and systems theory; but it is not a theory about *unique personal characteristics* (the sort studied by personologists). Instead, we are presented with a system for studying person-by-situation *interactions*.

Uniqueness from the CAPS perspective has a taken-for-granted, built-in quality that reflects the influence of Mischel's teacher, George Kelly, who proposed that every person is a "scientist" *construing* his or her own unique version of the world.

Differing from Allport. Gordon Allport asserted that personologists ought to decontextualize personality in order to avoid the "confusion of surrounding variables" (Allport, 1937, p. 61). Quite the contrary, Mischel and Shoda embrace the situation: "rather than being dismissed as noise, psychological contexts—far from obscuring personality—become part of the essence of coherence and the route to capturing the person's distinctiveness" (Mischel & Shoda, 1995, p. 263).

Balancing the person and the situation. In formulating their CAPS model, Mischel and Shoda hope to provide a mechanism for integrating two divergent streams in personality study—traits and circumstances. They attempt to strike an interactional balance by making the situation much more person-processed. Mischel apparently hopes to eclipse his earlier reputation as a staunch advocate of the situation over and against the person. By means of their *Cognitive–Affective Units,* the authors couple the situation with the person and the person with the situation: "Rather than dichotomizing personality research into the study of dispositions *or* processes, this theory allows one to pursue concurrently both personality dispositions and processes—structure and dynamics—as aspects of the same unitary system" (Mischel & Shoda, 1995, p. 263).

FACING THE TOUGH TWINS

Is It Testable?

Pretzels and marshmallows—"hot" and "cool" approaches to self-control. You will recall that in Chapter 1, we alluded to studies in which Mischel and his colleagues investigated how different mind-sets facilitate or attenuate self-control in children anticipating playing with toys or eating snacks (e.g., Mischel & Baker, 1975; Moore, Mischel, & Zeiss, 1976; Schack & Massari, 1973; Toner & Smith, 1977). Mischel and his students have taught children how to think about "temptation" foods in ways that either facilitate or erode self-control. For example, Mischel and Baker (1975) taught nursery school children (aged 3 years, 4 months to 5 years, 5 months) how to visualize foods in different ways. For example, "hot" visualizations of pretzels emphasized how crunchy, salty, and toasty brown they were; "cool" visualizations viewed them as long, thin, and brown— like logs, trees, or telephone poles. Children employing "cool" thoughts were able to delay consuming pretzels for significantly longer than those thinking "hot" thoughts. Mischel and Baker concluded that "the results demonstrate the powerful role of such cognitive transformations and support the theoretical view that the cognitive encoding of stimuli significantly and predictably influences their impact on behavior" (1975, p. 261).

Social cognitive neuroscience. The kind of person–situation blending suggested by the CAPS has recently been expanded even further. Ochsner and Lieberman (2001) go even beyond Mischel and Shoda's *system* for studying person-situation interactions to suggest a new *discipline* that they propose to call *Social Cognitive Neuroscience.* They

"I'm neither a good cop nor a bad cop, Jerome. Like yourself, I'm a complex amalgam of positive and negative personality traits that emerge or not, depending on circumstances."

state that neuroscientists have traditionally tried to understand the world from the *bottom up,* identifying the basic neural systems used to recognize, remember, and process social situations (e.g., facial expressions) or emotionally relevant stimuli (such as odors, danger signals, etc.). By contrast, social psychologists have studied a broad range of complex, socially relevant phenomena from the *top down.* Advocating an approach that is consistent with our text, Oschner and Lieberman call for two-way traffic on the vertical axis of our grid:

> In recent years, there has been increased appreciation that the top-down and bottom-up approaches cannot be researched independently because they are intimately linked to one another. . . . From the social cognitive neuroscience perspective, each approach provides a necessary but individually insufficient piece of a bigger psychological puzzle. By joining forces, social psychologists and cognitive neuroscientists will no longer be strangers passing on the street but colleagues walking together toward a brighter future. (Ochsner & Lieberman, 2001, pp. 727–729)

Is It Useful?

In the CAPS model, Mischel did not abandon his strong affinity for situational variables, but he also included sizable segments of the person's "inner life" for making sense of and processing situations:

> Thus, what constitutes a situation in part depends on the perceiver's constructs and subjective maps, that is, on the acquired meaning of situational features for

that person, rather than being defined exclusively by the observing scientist . . . The theory views the person not as reacting passively to situations, nor as generating behavior impervious to their subtle features, but as active and goal-directed, constructing plans and self-generated changes, and in part creating the situations themselves. (Mischel & Shoda, 1995, 251–253)

Summary of situation-processing models. Mischel and Shoda's CAPS model as well as Ochsner and Liberman's Social Cognitive Neuroscience model both reflect an emerging zeitgeist in the study of personality. Increasingly it is recognized that the "grand" theories of psychoanalysis and humanism were too global in their reach, whereas laboratory-based behaviorism was too narrow. However, since human behavior is too complex to allow researchers to simultaneously focus on all the relevant issues at the same time, the zonal approach of our text as well as the broadly integrative programs advocated by CAPS and Social Cognitive Neuroscience provide integrative frameworks within which personality psychologists can work either side by side at the same level, or cooperatively at different levels. It is increasingly clear that each of us can grasp only a piece of the elephant and that cooperative, multidisciplinary efforts will best promote our understanding of personality.

THE SOCIAL-COGNITIVE PSYCHOLOGY OF ALBERT BANDURA

Albert Bandura (1925–) is a giant figure in the field of personality psychology, and the brevity of our discussion is possible only because much of the spirit of his work is reflected in what we have just encountered in the CAPS and Social Cognitive Neuroscience models. Here we will briefly summarize the highlights of Bandura's work to illustrate how consistent it is with the current multidisciplinary zeitgeist emphasizing the *interaction* of persons and situations. In his earlier work (1977, 1986) the *self* was a social *processor* (as it is in CAPS), but in his more recent work (1997) the *self* appears more genuinely agentic.

Reciprocal determinism. Bandura's answer to the controversy that threatened to divide the field of personality into personologists and situationists was **reciprocal determinism,** *the view that human behavior emerges from the <u>dynamic interplay</u> among internal factors, external factors, and the behaviors themselves—all reciprocally influencing one another*. For example, if someone you don't much like *(internal thoughts/feelings)* asked you to play golf, you would probably "pass." However, if this person offered to pay your green fees at an expensive country club *(external incentive),* you might decide to play. Finally, if you were well matched and played an enjoyable game together the experience itself *(behavioral factors)* would increase the likelihood that you would play golf with this person again—even if she didn't pay your fees.

Observational learning—beating up on "Bobo." In his earliest writings, Bandura rejected classical behaviorism's exclusive emphasis on *association* as the prime mechanism of learning. Bandura believed that humans learn as much—perhaps more—by *observing.* In perhaps his most famous study, Bandura showed nursery school children a video clip in which an adult model aggressively punched, kicked, and threw balls at a life-sized, inflatable "Bobo doll" (1965, pp. 589–595). Children viewed three different endings: one in which the aggressive behavior was rewarded with candy, soft drinks, and praise; another in which the model was spanked with a rolled-up magazine and warned not to be aggressive again; and a third group in which no information was given about consequences. Subsequently, when left alone in a room with a "Bobo doll," children who had seen the aggressive model rewarded were significantly more likely to act aggressively than those who had seen the model punished.

Self-efficacy. Most recently, Bandura has emphasized the importance of **self-efficacy,** or *the extent to which a person believes that she can successfully bring about a particular outcome.* Here we see the *self* acting as an *agent,* capable of making things happen. According to Bandura, *self-efficacy* is influenced by four main sources: (1) mastery experiences, (2) vicarious mastery experiences, (3) verbal persuasion/encouragement, and (4) physiological/emotional states. Bandura believes that successful behavior-change programs work by enhancing self-efficacy. The most effective sources involve mastery experiences.

Thus, in a procedure known as **guided mastery,** *a therapist arranges a situation and offers guidance that practically guarantees success.* For example, people who are afraid of snakes are helped to overcome their fears by learning to approach and touch snakes (Bandura, Adams, & Beyer, 1977). People afraid to drive alone in traffic learn to master their fears by first driving short distances down secluded streets. These techniques are described in detail elsewhere (Bandura, 1997).

We conclude here by noting that both Mischel and Bandura have resolved the person–situation dilemma with *interactional* ideas. Bandura has recently shifted the balance even more in the direction of the *self* with his emphasis on self-efficacy. Next, we consider one of the broadest processing systems of all—chaos theory.

CHAOS THEORY—MATHEMATICAL MODELS FOR PROCESSING THE UNIVERSE

Introduction

Chaos Theory is not so much a personality theory as a *trans*personality theory—including not only the person and the situation, but the entire universe. It is cosmic in scope, and therefore somewhat impersonal. Yet, we have included it in our consideration of personality, because it provides metaphors for understanding patterns that might prove valuable to future personality researchers.

Chaos/Complexity Theory (CT)—processing the universe from molecules to galaxies. In whatever zone they work, personality psychologists look for *patterns* of consistency. We conclude this chapter by considering *Chaos Theory (CT),* which provides mathematical models for describing *patterns of consistency* not only within a person's brain, or in social situations, but across the entire universe. CT seeks to discover underlying *patterns* of behavior in both living and nonliving systems. Chaos Theory reaches even into the *Transpersonal/Spiritual Zone* (Chapter 13), where it is consistent with the "New Physics" that sees God/gods in everything. Zohar & Marshall describe this Divine Vacuum in the following words:

> When Buddhists speak of "emptiness" or "void" they mean that nothing is separate, that all things are *interconnected.* This vacuum has been described as: "a vast sea of all

else that is—the stars, the earth, the trees, ourselves, and the particles of which we are made. . . . The vacuum is all of physics. . . . In more religious language, the vacuum is *the* All of everything. . . . If we were looking for "God" within physics, the vacuum would be the most appropriate place to look. . . . (1994, pp. 238–239, 240)

From a personality perspective, we will consider CT not so much as a spiritual quest, but rather as a *heuristic* way of thinking about the *patterns* of repetitive behaviors that constitute what personality psychologists term *consistency*. Once we leave the *Situational Zone*, with its emphasis on carefully controlled external variables, we also leave behind billiard-ball analogies regarding causality. The higher we ascend up our vertical axis the more "messy" become our understandings of causality and consistency. It no longer suffices to say that *stimulus A* caused *behavior B*—much as the cue-ball striking the eight-ball causes it to drop into the corner pocket. At higher levels of analysis, it may be heuristically helpful to replace our tendency to think linearly—from left to right—with metaphors from Chaos Theory: attractor, repellor, bifurcation, and fractal.

Chaos and complexity. Before beginning, we need to understand that the term *"chaos"* as used in *Chaos Theory* does not mean confusion or disorder; **chaos** *refers to nonlinear, difficult-to-predict patterns (e.g., faucets dripping, ocean waves breaking offshore, or volcanoes erupting) that appear random or chaotic, but nonetheless follow mathematically predictable patterns.* We will use the terms *Chaos Theory* and *Complexity Theory* as approximate synonyms, abbreviating both with *CT*. In his book entitled *Chaos: Making a New Science*, James Gleick writes with near religious zeal, outlining what he calls "a revolution in seeing":

> Believers in chaos—and they sometimes call themselves believers, or converts, or evangelists—speculate about determinism and free will. . . . They feel that they are turning back a trend in science toward reductionism, the analysis of systems in terms of their constituent parts: quarks, chromosomes, or neurons. They believe they are looking for the whole. . . . Now that science is looking, chaos seems to be everywhere. A rising column of cigarette smoke breaks into wild swirls. A flag snaps back and forth in the wind. A dripping faucet goes from a steady pattern to a random one. Chaos appears in the behavior of the weather, the behavior of an airplane in flight, the behavior of cars clustering on an expressway, the behavior of oil flowing in underground pipes. . . . The simplest systems are now seen to create extraordinarily difficult problems of predictability. Yet order arises spontaneously in those systems—chaos and order together. Only a new kind of science could begin to cross the great gulf between knowledge of what one thing does—one water molecule, one cell of heart tissue, one neuron—and what millions of them do. (1987, pp. 5–8)

Complexity or Chaos Theory (CT) *focuses on the self-organizing dynamical systems that lead to adaptation. Such systems range in size from molecules of slime mold to global weather systems.* Since *CT* transcends the traditional lines that separate scientific disciplines it might provide a heuristic frameworks for interrelating personality theories ranging from molecular neurobiology to transpersonal or spiritual.

No single person is responsible for CT, and since the *zeitgeist* is *now,* we will skip our usual background checks and move directly to the theory, learning how molecules "talk" to each other.

ASKING THE BIG FOUR QUESTIONS
OF CHAOS/COMPLEXITY THEORY

What Are the Parts?

Cell-adhesion molecules (CAMs)—nature's communicational glue. Nerve cells transmit signals throughout the body by chemically converting the electrical impulses at the synapses into *ion-gated protein channels*. Incredibly, this happens hundreds of billions of times *each second* in the human brain. In multicellular organisms, individual cells must become aligned in precise patterns in order to form the organs and systems of a fully functioning organism. This sort of *large-scale communication is accomplished with the help of one of nature's ingenious biological glues* called a **cell-adhesion molecule (CAM)**.

CAMs are the reason blood circulates freely throughout the body, whereas cardiac cells and lung cells stick together to form structures. While it is critically important that some cells stick together to make lungs and livers, it is equally important that others flow freely. Somehow cells "talk" to one another, and each is "told" whether to "network" with its neighbors to form organs, or to "go with the flow." Communication in the human body takes place through neural networks that are composed of over 100 *trillion* interconnected, intercommunicating pathways that function to preserve and propagate an entire lifetime of memories, experiences, learning, and behavior.

In the light of such communicational complexities, the compositional theories of the ancient Greeks appear as fossilized bones scattered across a prehistoric landscape. Even "modern" formulations like behaviorism, psychoanalysis, and humanism seem ill equipped to deal with systems composed of trillions of such sending-and-receiving stations. Here *Complexity Theory* provides a conceptual framework that appears especially well suited for focusing on microscopic constituents without losing the big picture of macro-behavioral functioning.

An **attractor** *is a force that pulls things toward it.* Gravity is an attractor, pulling rain, planes, skiers, skateboarders—literally everything and everyone—toward earth. The end of your vacuum sweeper hose is an attractor, as is your mouth when you're sucking on a lollipop. Physicists recognize several kinds of attractors. A pendulum has a *fixed-point attractor* and will ultimately come to rest where the weight of the pendulum is closest to the pull of gravity. Your heart is an example of a *limit cycle attractor*, varying its beat frequency between an upper and lower limit, but doing so in a regular and predictable fashion, dictated by your body's blood needs.

Complexity theorists are interested in *strange/chaotic attractors,* those that have multiple pendulum-like resting points, and unpredictable, irregular patterns. Yet, in spite of their complexity and variability, these strange/chaotic attractors *do* have patterns. *Attractors* in complex systems tend to organize themselves into *larger clusters* known as **basins of attraction,** which in turn assemble into even larger conglomerations known as **attraction landscapes**. This sort of behavioral "ski map" allows a more complex understanding of the behavioral landscape. Returning to our example of gravity as an attractor for snow or rain, think of ponds, lakes, and oceans as *basins* of attraction, which, when considered along with rivulets, creeks, rivers, and waterfalls make up a *landscape of attractors.*

A Variety of Attractors

A pendulum represents a system where the pendulum is "attracted" to zero motion at rest.

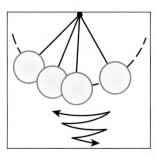

This is similar to someone in a swing or a hammock.

A roller coaster illustrates an attractions landscape, a series of attractors and repellors

Illustrations of Self Similarity

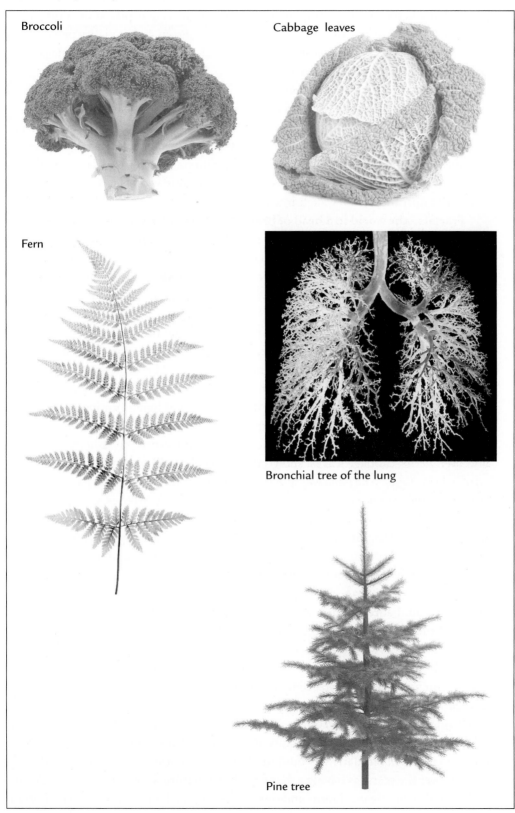

Broccoli

Cabbage leaves

Fern

Bronchial tree of the lung

Pine tree

A **repellor** *is a state from which a system tends to move away.* If you're a golfer, you know that when you are putting on a green where the flag is placed on a ridge, the ball wants to roll *away* from the cup, not toward it. From a personality perspective, *repellors* are *transient* or *unstable moods*—like laughing in the midst of a traffic jam, or being temporarily in a foul mood at the beach.

A **bifurcation** *is a sudden and discontinuous change in the dynamics of a system when a certain point is reached.* A pan of water gradually accumulates heat until the point at which it *suddenly* begins boiling. The proverbial camel driver loads straw onto his beast of burden until—with one final straw—the camel's back *suddenly* collapses. Waking and sleeping states are behavioral bifurcations. You lie in bed relaxed, thinking about how good the soft pillow feels, when—abruptly—you begin snoring. You've crossed a bifurcation from wakefulness to sleep.

Fractals—the world in a head of broccoli. A **fractal** *is a geometric figure whose large-scale and small-scale structures resemble each other.* Mathematical equations can be used to describe fractal regularities that occur in complex patterns or objects. A characteristic feature of fractals is what complexity theorists call **self-similarity,** referring to *an object or process in which the same pattern is repeated at larger and larger (or smaller and smaller) scales.* Broccoli is an excellent example of a fractal-patterned vegetable. If you disobeyed your mother when you were a kid ("Quit playing with your broccoli!"), you might have noticed that each portion of the green vegetable on your plate appeared a "miniature" of the entire head of broccoli. A *fractal* object (e.g., head of broccoli) is comprised of a lot of smaller (broccoli-like) *fract*ions. *Fractal* objects are characterized by *self-similarity*—the units all resemble each other, even at different levels of magnification or scale.

Fractal objects and processes are regularly found in natural systems. Nature frequently constructs things—besides broccoli—by duplicating the same pattern over and over. Ferns, cabbage leaves, snowflakes, seashells, and your own lungs are constructed through *fractal branching* and *fractal folding* patterns. A fractal pattern can be seen throughout your circulatory system in the network of arteries, veins, and capillaries. Similarly, your lungs appear to be composed of a branching system of "little lungs." Fractal branching patterns are also found in the network of filters and bile ducts that make up your kidneys. Fractal *folding* patterns are found in the furrows of your intestines and the fissures of your brain.

Less obvious, perhaps, but equally prevalent is nature's fractal pattern of *tubes* and *sheets.* Your neurons, veins, arteries, intestines, and lymphatic system are all comprised of tubes, so it's no exaggeration to say that "Human beings are tubes within tubes" (Furman & Gallo, 2000, p. 69).

Thinking *fractally* about objects or processes means that we attempt to understand them not in terms of size dimensions (inches, degrees, or pounds), but in terms of their *fractal patterns* that recur at many different levels of scale. We adopt a kind of "the-world-is-a-head-of-broccoli" attitude and look for patterns of self-similarity. We might heuristically think of personality as a *landscape of attractors* toward which behaviors tend to settle. Similarly we could think of "friendliness" (in the moment, during the day, over the years) as having a *fractal* quality. If nature widely employs fractal patterns in constructing our brains and our bodies, might she use *self-similar behaviors* in constructing the *fractal* consistencies we call personality? In the complex world of interrelated causes and consistencies that we call *personality,* perhaps broccoli is a better metaphor than billiard balls or dammed-up libido.

What Makes It Go?

Entropy vs. pattern. In classical physics, the second law of thermodynamics describes **entropy**—*all physical processes flow toward disorder, randomness, equilibrium, or death.* Consequently, the heat in your steaming cup of coffee gradually dissipates until the energy is equally distributed throughout the system, and the coffee and cup both reach "room temperature" (which is then slightly higher than it was before). *Entropy* is seen as the fundamental process driving everything in the universe—from the microscopic to the macroscopic.

Chaos theorists believe that the *law of entropy* strictly holds only in closed systems—which are extremely rare. Most complex systems do *not* degenerate (as the law of entropy would predict) to randomness and disorder; instead, they appear to be in constant flux, dynamically *balanced* between *pattern* and *chaos.* Complex systems *self-organize* as a way of overcoming entropy by gaining energy from the surrounding environment:

> . . . these complex, self-organizing systems are adaptive, in that they don't just passively respond to events the way a rock might roll around in an earthquake. They actively try to turn whatever happens to their advantage. Thus, the human brain constantly organizes and reorganizes its billions of neural connections so as to learn from experience. (Waldrop, 1992, p. 11)

Self-organization *means that the components of nonlinear dynamical systems engage in joint transactions to form adaptive organizations.* That's quite a string of big words—probably as clear as the directions that come with a bicycle in a box—but let me illustrate with an example.

From slime to slugs, and back again. Biologists are familiar with an organism that demonstrates self-organization at the most elemental levels. Slime mold, aka *dictyostelium discoideum,* is at various times in its life a single-celled organism that feeds on its own self and multiplies by direct cell division; and at other times one that morphs into a multicellular organism (Briggs & Peat, 1989, pp. 138–139; Prigogine & Stengers, pp. 147–150, 1984). When there is a food shortage, for reasons not yet clearly understood, some of the slime cells begin emitting rhythmic pulses of a chemical known as *cyclic adenosine monophosphate (CAMP).* Neighboring cells receiving the CAMP messages are attracted to the cells sending the messages, and begin manufacturing more CAMP. Soon a pulsating, concentric spiral of slime mold cells forms into a multicellular slug, with a head and a tail, that slithers around searching for a new food source. Once food is found, the slug forms a hard stalk with a head filled with spores at the top. The head subsequently breaks open and the spores are dispersed to continue independent lives as single-celled organisms.

If slime and slugs can self-organize, it doesn't seem like too much of a stretch to think your brain can do the same.

What Makes a Person Grow?

Whereas some personality psychologists have tended to view development as resulting from linear causal processes, CT suggests that causes are seldom simple and rarely linear. According to notions of multiple causality, human behavior shows recurrent patterns that are never independent of context. Thus *attractors* take the place of *traits,* and development is seen in terms of increasingly adaptive forms of *self-organization.* For complexity theorists, the developmental landscape is permeated with attractors, repellors, and bifurcations. Development is not a linear process moving forward in time; rather, maturity involves increasingly efficient *self-organization* that takes place through processes involving *cognition, emotion, feedback,* and *appraisal.*

From a CT perspective, "stages" are replaced by **developmental bifurcations** *wherein some regions of the personality landscape suddenly shift and reorganize.* Some attractors fade while new ones take their place. For example, the childhood *repellor,* eggplant, becomes the adult's gourmet *attractor* in the form of eggplant parmigiana. From a CT perspective, development could be seen as the process of continuously refining *self-organization.* According to complexity theory, chaos is not pathological; it is, rather, a state of optimal openness to the self-organizing patterns of behavior that we call personality.

What Makes a Person Unique?

Complexity Theory is concerned with general processes more than individual uniqueness; nonetheless, it provides metaphors that allow plenty of room for personal distinctiveness in the unique combinations of attractors, repellors, bifurcations, and the like, that grow out of each person's unique history.

SUMMARY OF COMPLEXITY/CHAOS THEORY (CT)

In the preceding chapters we have moved up several levels of abstraction and have seen how models of personality have evolved from the humoral theories of the ancient Greeks, to the highly sophisticated systems theories (e.g., CAPS) of today. As technology has become more sophisticated, scientific theories have blended composition/ structure with function, much as Einstein famously blended matter and energy in $E = mc_2$. It has been suggested that Einstein's equation "will have to be extended to account for the hypothesis that information, too, can be converted into energy and matter, through the resulting property of their continued interaction . . ." (Furman & Gallo, 2000, p. 77).

CT is not a theory of personality; rather, it is a mathematically based *method for discerning patterns* in all sorts of objects and organisms ranging from microbes to galaxies. CT provides a nonlinear, dynamical alternative to the linear causality of the "hard" sciences. Chaos theory replaces the *associationistic causality* of Pavlovian conditioning, the *linear causality* of operant conditioning, and the *dispositional press* of trait theories with dynamic, nonlinear metaphors. Even at the higher levels of analysis, CT goes beyond the *communicational flow* of cognitive theory, the *hydraulic causality* of psychoanalysis, or the *self-actualizing* causality of humanism to propose models broad enough to conceptualize the breakup of the former Soviet Union, yet precise enough to analyze slime mold. CT seems heuristically promising as a context for thinking about personality theories in various zones of analysis.

Chapter Summary

In this chapter we have moved up and to the right from Pribram's biological "holograms" to Pinker's cognitive science, to Mischel's social learning theory, to Oschner and Lieberman's social cognitive neuroscience, to Bandura's emphasis on self-efficacy, and finally to Chaos/Complexity Theory. Where does it leave us? Breathless? Bored? Tired? What possible difference could all these theories make in our lives?

Frankly, I'm more breathless than bored, and I hope you're feeling the same way. Cognitive scientists have revitalized psychology's inner mental life with a contagious freshness that reminds me of how families grow and develop. Parents and grandparents age, become rigid, and ultimately pass on the torch, even as new packages of protoplasm bound onto center stage. Children (Jackie Kennedy once referred to them as "our visible immortality") pick up where their parents' generations have faded away. Similarly, cognitive science, cognitive–affective personality systems, and social cognitive neuroscience are the new faces of mentalism—the grand children of Gestalt grandparents and introspectionist forebearers—boldly filling the vacuum left by radical behaviorism with a host of information-processing operations made respectable by the rigor of their research programs.

Chaos Theory represents a paradigm shift from the mechanistic, reductionistic, positivist linearities of twentieth-century thinking, in which uncertainty and unpredictability were viewed as noise, confusion, or error. Now, chaos and complexity are seen as necessary conditions for the self-organization that characterizes complex systems. As Niels Bohr put it, "if you're not confused by quantum mechanics then you haven't understood it" (quoted in Cohen & Stewart, 1994, p. 266).

So, if you have been disappointed by the apparent lack of agreement among the theorists of this chapter, take heart! It comes with the turf. Psychologists seldom agree—even when casually "chatting" over coffee. One psychologist recalled the coffee room of his graduate days:

> Conversation is what the coffee room was all about. . . . there was a generous amount of "shop talk." Faculty would test research ideas out on each other, would describe their latest results, and would discuss problems that were arising with one project or another. (Dawson, 1998, p. 1)

Dawson then asks the question that might be puzzling you at this point in your study of personality psychology:

> Imagine, for instance, that Sigmund Freud and B. F. Skinner were both members of the same psychology department. Would they have enough in common to engage in "shop talk"?. . . .
>
> My suspicion is that in view of their wildly different worldviews, and in the interest of our imaginary department's peace, Freud and Skinner would arrange their coffee-room visits to occur at different times. (Dawson, 1998, p. 2).

Recall how, early on, we suggested that instead of asking which theory is "right" or "wrong," it would be more appropriate to ask which is most "useful" for your purposes. Psychology is so permeated with diversity that there is little agreement upon what constitutes the "core" of knowledge. So, if you've been stunned by the kaleidoscopic range of topics under the umbrella of personality theories, or discouraged by the lack of a clearly defined core, it might help to celebrate the diversity:

> No doubt many psychologists were drawn to their field because of its diversity of subject matter. Biologists and chemists can find a home in psychology. Physicists can find much interest in contemporary work in perception. Anthropologists, sociologists, economists, and political scientists could be happy in social psychology, cognition, development, and other psychological subfields. Business people, educators, and healers all can find a home. The quantitatively inclined are welcomed, as are the computer scientists. Sports fans too can pursue their love in psychology. Even historians can find work in this field. (Benjamin, 2001, p. 740)

And you can find a home too! Personality theorists are like a gathering of relatives at a family reunion. Some won't speak to each other; others can't stop talking. Some are old and can barely move; others are young and can't sit still. Yet they're all part of the family, just as you, taking your first course in theories of personality, are now a kind of "distant cousin" to Skinner and Freud. Welcome to the family! We're a family with little agreement about anything—a "large, sprawling, confusing human undertaking" (Leahey, 1987, p. 3)—but that is, for most of us, a positive thing. As one "family member" put it nearly half a century ago:

> Perhaps psychologists are the last of the rugged individualists. It is quite apparent that we value variability, experimentation, and educational freedom far more than we value conformity and standardization. It will be a sad day when we agree on the content of the core curriculum. (Ericksen, 1958, p. 58)

As we continue our ascent up the vertical axis, I can't promise you clarity, I can't promise you consensus, but I can promise you *fun*, and I can promise that as you analyze numerous theories, in different zones, at various levels of abstraction, you will begin to form your own opinions regarding where theories belong on the grid. You will gain a deeper sense of the continuity that connects diverse theories of personality; and you will be able to communicate at different levels of conceptualization without becoming confused or cantankerous.

Points to Remember

1. Based on experiments with nearly 2,000 monkeys, Pribram accumulated evidence that the brain processes and stores information in ways that are analogous to *holograms*. By the parallel processing of *feed-forward* and *feedback* neural impulses (much as holograms are based on simultaneous processing of split beams of light), the brain is able to compactly store "mental" holograms.

2. Cognitive science is a multidisciplinary approach to understanding the mind that draws upon psychology, computer science, philosophy, linguistics, and neuroscience. It is a modern, *rigorous mentalism*, filling the void left by behaviorism's scooping out of inner life.

3. Although some cognitive scientists view the brain as a supercomputer, with personality emerging as a kind of behavioral "printout," most see the computer only as a metaphor, emphasizing that our biologically based *"wet mind"* has unique features enabling it to operate far more efficiently than silicone-based computers.

4. Steven Pinker believes the mind works according to *computational principles.* He proposes that the *mind consists of multiple layers of mental modules* capable of processing memory, thoughts, emotions, desires, and other information into physical bits of matter. In Pinker's model, *patterns of information* are far more important than *composition.* Thus the computational mind is present not only in humans but also in ants, bees, birds, and other mammals.

5. Walter Mischel became famous as a *situationist,* insisting that the situation was primary in determining behavior and that inner variables (collectively known as *traits*) were far less influential. Recently he has taken a more balanced approach emphasizing the *interaction* of persons and situations. He has proposed a *Cognitive–Affective Personality System (CAPS)* in which *person variables* (such as expectancies, emotions, goals, values, and competencies) are seen as *crucial for processing situations.*

6. Similarly, Ochsner and Lieberman have called for a *Social Cognitive Neuroscience* focus where investigators would attend simultaneously to neural systems, cognitive processing, and social situations. They say that *top-down and bottom-up* approaches are intimately linked and ought not to be independently researched.

7. *Complexity Theory (CT)* is about *self-organizing systems* in nature. CT discerns patterns in seemingly chaotic events. Utilizing such concepts as **attractors,** *repellors, basins, bifurcations,* and *fractals,* CT offers a dynamic, nonlinear theory of systems that is in sharp contrast to linear, billiard-ball models of causality that have been prevalent in the "hard" sciences. Since personality theories are typically broad in scope and involve recursive behaviors, complexity theory may provide a heuristic model for the field.

Key Terms

Affects   (160)

Anthropomorphize   (144)

Attraction Landscapes   (167)

Attractor   (167)

Basins of Attraction   (167)

Bifurcation   (170)

Cell-Adhesion Molecule (CAM)   (167)

Chaos   (166)

Cognitive–Affective Personality System (CAPS)   (159)

Cognitive–Affective Units   (159)

Cognitive Science's Foundational Assumption   (152)

Competencies   (160)

Computational Theory of Mind   (150)

Developmental Bifurcations   (172)

Encodings   (159)

Entropy   (171)

Expectancies   (160)

Feedback Systems   (146)

Feed-Forward Systems   (147)

Foundational Assumption   (152)

Fractal   (170)

Frustration—Aggression Hypothesis   (157)

Goals and Values   (160)

Web Sites

Pinker

http://pinker.wjh.harvard.edu. This is the best all-around Web site for Steven Pinker. It truly is great for serious research and serious laughs! Students can access Pinker's books and papers, and read articles about him. When you read his personal page be sure to click on his "Silly" link for some more fun.

Mischel

http://jocn.mitpress.org. *The Journal of Cognitive Neuroscience.* This is a great place to look for articles and read about groundbreaking research and current issues in the field. Students can read abstracts, and some articles are full-text.

Shoda

http://shodalab.psych.washington.edu/Shoda%20Lab.htm. The Yuichi Shoda Lab. See pictures and review their current research projects.

Bandura

www.des.emory.edu/mfp/bandurabio.html. This Web site offers an amazingly extensive biography of Albert Bandura. The document has many embedded links to find more information about his work and personal life.

Chaos Theorists

www.jessiegietl.com/theorypage.html. This is sure to pique your interest. Follow the art gallery links and see some truly amazing art inspired by Chaos Theory. Enjoy!

wws.societyforchaostheory.org. The Society for Chaos Theory in Psychology and Life Sciences. Visit this Web site if you want to understand this mysterious theory a little better.

www.abarim-publications.com/artctintro.html. This is a Web site on Chaos Theory for beginners. It helps to elaborate and explain the principles more clearly and engages the reader with provocative illustrations and interesting stories.

Chomsky

www.personal.kent.edu/~pbohanbr/Webpage/New/newintro.html. For those who like to wax philosophical about linguistics, the Chomsky for philosophers Web page is for you! Here several papers on Chomsky's work can be found, along with a little publicized interview.

Learning on the Lighter Side

You might want to rent the movie *Matrix,* because it illustrates what a crucial role the cognitive mind-set of a person plays in understanding reality. This is somewhat similar to Mischel and Choda's CAPS, in which internal variables profoundly influence interactions with the external situation. *A Beautiful Mind* is another movie that illustrates how profoundly internal perceptions shape external reality.

Looking Ahead

As we move up the vertical axis to employ broader units of analysis, *Self* will begin to play a more pivotal role in personality. Among the theorists of our current chapter, we have seen less emphasis on the molecular constructs of the *Physiological Zone* and less focus on the external stimuli of the *Situational Zone.* Personality is no longer the product of biles, biochemicals, genes, or traits. For example, although Steven Pinker began with a strong physiological base, he quickly emphasized that mind is what the brain *does;* and what the brain does best is *process information.* Similarly, although Mischel began his career by exclusively focusing on the *situation,* he has come to a much more balanced *interactionism,* which is consistent with Bandura's *reciprocal determinism.*

In future chapters personality will not be seen as shaped primarily by stimuli located "out there" acting upon the person with billiard-ball-like effectiveness. For example, in Freud's classical psychoanalysis, *libido* is seen as a powerful, but unconscious, *life force* that functions much like a fluid in a closed hydraulic system. However, even in Freud's "hydraulic" model, *libido* is channeled and balanced by an *agentic ego.* In the *Insight Zone* personality will no longer be pushed about *solely* by biochemistry, the environment, internal predispositions, or an internal computer. In Freud's agentic *ego,* we will encounter an "I" that chooses or decides *for the sake of* something.

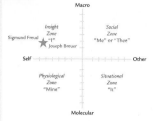

chapter 6

The Surrounded Self (Ego) of Psychoanalysis

Josef Breuer and Sigmund Freud

IN THIS CHAPTER YOU CAN

1. Discover that it was Josef Breuer—not Sigmund Freud—who first utilized the "talking cure" that formed the foundation for psychoanalysis.

2. Appreciate that although Freud insisted psychoanalysts should "operate with the objectivity of a surgeon," his own blind spots were evident when he attempted to psychoanayze his daughter, Anna.

3. Learn that the psychoanalytic couch was Freud's way of *minimizing his direct emotional connection* with patients by requiring them to lie down out of sight. He candidly admitted that he didn't like to be "stared at . . . for eight hours a day."

4. Wonder how growing up with a doting mother and a distant father might have shaped Freud's psychoanalysis.

5. Find out that Freud intensely focused on *singular facts*, but failed to rigorously evaluate his ideas using scientific methods.

6. Understand how Freud combined his *topographic, structural, economic, genetic,* and *adaptive models* into one all-encompassing *metapsychology.*

7. Learn that Freud's final *metapsychology* featured the *id, ego,* and *superego* as the major parts that were energized by *libido.* Freud used a hydraulic metaphor, treating *libido* as if it were a liquid in a closed system or electricity flowing into appliances.

8. Evaluate research findings to discover that there is less support for some ideas than psychoanalysts like to admit, but considerably more than critics care to concede.

9. Understand how profoundly psychoanalysis has influenced clinical practice through the careful training of psychoanalysts as well as by emphasizing the importance of *unconscious feelings—on the part of both the patients and psychoanalysts.*

10. Appreciate how Freudian theory has so permeated Western culture that we interpret dreams, analyze Freudian "slips," and look for what is "below the surface" almost automatically.

A Clinical Case that Changed History

Although Sigmund Freud is the undisputed father of psychoanalysis, Josef Breuer (1842–1925) could be designated *grandfather,* since he was the first to employ the "talking cure" that Freud later developed into psychoanalysis. His treatment of the hysterical "Anna O." is arguably the most important case study in the history of psychiatry.

"Chimney-sweeping" with "Anna O."[1] A few days before Christmas in 1880, Dr. Josef Breuer began treating Bertha Pappenheim (1859–1936), more famously known as **"Anna O."** After climbing two flights of stairs, Breuer was shown to the parlor, where Anna's mother reported that for the past two weeks her daughter had refused to get out of bed. Anna O.'s right arm and both legs were paralyzed. However, it wasn't the paralysis that worried Anna's mother most. "I'm so worried about Anna O.'s cough," she told Breuer. Anna's mother lived in terror of tuberculosis—as did nearly everyone else in the city.

Breuer's famous patient "Anna O." (Bertha Pappenheim)

"Anna O." was in a real sense, the founding patient of psychoanalysis. Following her treatment, she became one of the first advocates for women's rights.

Shown to the young woman's bedroom, Breuer found his twenty-one-year-old patient lying motionless as a corpse, her long dark hair tied with a ribbon to keep it from tumbling over her features. Breuer noticed that her eyes were slightly glazed.

"Is anything particularly upsetting Anna today?" Breuer asked. A look of anguish crossed the mother's face as she replied, "Her father—he's in the room down the hall. She's been caring for him, but the doctors say he has an abscess on his lung that won't heal."

Breuer realized immediately that Anna's father was dying of the dreaded tuberculosis.

"At first Anna and I took turns nursing him," continued the mother. "I stayed with him during the day, she watched at night, but since December 11th Anna has been in bed herself."

Suddenly Anna's cough shattered the silence. Her mother winced, as if in pain, but Breuer's experienced ear immediately recognized the sound of a nervous cough—*tussis nervosa*—and he sighed in relief; this was not the cough of an infected lung. Pulling his chair alongside Anna's bed, Breuer gently placed his hands on her forehead, and softly began his hypnotic induction:

"Close your eyes. Breathe deeply and evenly. Allow yourself to feel peaceful. You are now falling asleep . . . deeper and deeper . . . asleep . . . asleep."

Anna's eyelids fluttered temporarily, as if trying to fight off Breuer's suggestion, but then they slowly closed and her breathing became deep and regular.

"Now tell me," Breuer said softly, his hand still on Anna's forehead, "is something troubling you?"

Anna shook her head from side to side, as if denying that anything was bothering her. It *is* hysteria, thought Breuer, she can move her neck muscles when she is relaxed under hypnosis. Breuer was certain his young patient's paralyses were of psychogenic origin, since they vanished when she was hypnotized. He surmised that all of Anna's symptoms—especially her cough—were psychologically connected to her father, who lay dying two doors down the hallway.

Day after day, week after week, Breuer visited his youthful patient, "Anna O." Sometimes he found that she had entered a state of "autohypnosis," intensifying

---

1. Adapted from Breuer and Freud (1893–95), Ellenberger (1972), and Freeman (1972).

her daydreams into trance-like experiences that Breuer would "relieve" with talk therapy:

"I used to visit her in the evening," Breuer recalled, "when I knew I should find her in her hypnosis, and I then relieved her of the whole stock of imaginative products which she had accumulated since my last visit. . . . She aptly described this procedure, speaking seriously, as a 'talking cure,' while she referred to it jokingly as 'chimney-sweeping'" (Breuer & Freud, 1893–95, p. 30).

Using hypnosis in combination with his **cathartic method,** which meant *encouraging the patient to discharge tension or anxiety by talking it out,* Breuer discovered that Anna's "nervous cough" had occurred for the first time when she was sitting at her father's bedside and heard the sound of dance music coming from a nearby house. Experiencing a sudden wish to be dancing, she simultaneously felt guilty about the wish. "Thereafter," reported Breuer, "throughout the whole length of her illness, she reacted to any markedly rhythmical music with a *tussis nervosa* [nervous cough]" (Breuer & Freud, 1893–95, p. 40).

Using his talking cure, Breuer subsequently removed symptom after symptom; Anna O.'s cough, blurred vision, deafness, speech problems, and paralysis were all "talked away." This astonished even Breuer, who reported, "It took me completely by surprise, and not until symptoms had been got rid of in this way in a whole series of instances did I develop a therapeutic technique out of it" (Breuer & Freud, 1893–95, p. 46).

Commenting on Anna O.'s case nearly thirty years later, Freud credited Breuer with launching psychoanalysis:

> Never before had anyone removed a hysterical symptom by such a method or had thus gained so deep an insight into its causation. It could not fail to prove a momentous discovery. . . . When, some years later, I began to employ Breuer's method of examination and treatment on patients of my own, my experiences entirely agreed with his. . . . I should like to formulate what we have learned so far as follows: *our hysterical patients suffer from reminiscences.* (Freud, 1910, pp. 13–16)

Since Anna O's treatment has been extensively discussed by others (e.g., Breuer & Freud, 1893–95; Freud, 1910; Jones, 1953; Pollock, 1968; Ellenberger, 1970, 1972; Freeman, 1972; and Gay, 1988), we will forego further details and skip to the startling conclusion.

"Pregnant" with Breuer's baby. Freud was intensely interested in Anna O.'s case and urged Breuer to publish his findings, but ten years passed before Breuer reluctantly agreed to publish (with Freud as coauthor). He reported that he had cured Anna of her illness, adding only a brief hint that all had not ended well: "The final cure of hysteria . . . was accompanied, as I have already said, by considerable disturbances and a deterioration in the patient's mental condition" (Breuer & Freud, 1893–95, p. 47).

Years later, Freud reported that although Anna's symptoms had completely subsided by the end of treatment, Breuer was summoned again shortly afterward, and found Anna confused and writhing with abdominal cramps. "Asked what was wrong, she replied: 'Now Dr. B.'s child is coming!' " (E. L. Freud, 1960, p. 413). According to this account, Breuer was "seized by conventional horror . . . took flight and abandoned the patient to a colleague." (E. L. Freud, 1960, p. 413). Ernest Jones (1953) claimed it was Breuer's jealous wife, not the cure of Anna's symptoms, that brought treatment to a halt: "his wife became bored at listening to no other topic, and before long jealous" (p. 224). However, recent scholarship warns that Jones's account is "fraught with impossibilities . . . based on hearsay, and should be considered with caution" (Ellenberger, 1970, pp. 483–84).

Whatever happened, all accounts agree that Anna's treatment ended abruptly, with Breuer viewing Anna as "excessively demanding and downright embarrassing," vowing that he would "not go through such an ordeal again" (Gay, 1988, p. 69).

Comment on case study of Anna O. This case reveals the intrapsychic model of mind in its embryonic stages. The notion that *memories of emotional experiences* could trigger *physiological symptoms* such as coughing or paralysis was revolutionary, and formed the basis for Freud's "iceberg" view of the mind as a powerful force with much of its mass below the surface of awareness. For subsequent generations of psychoanalysts, conscious awareness was only the "tip of the iceberg," with repressed memories, buried guilt, "forgotten" experiences, phobic dreads, disjointed dreams, and compartmentalized anxieties making up the greater portion of the mind's psychological mass. As we have just seen in Breuer's treatment of Anna O., the *unconscious* exerts a powerful influence on healers as well as on their patients.

The terms *Freudian* and *psychoanalytic* will be used interchangeably throughout this text. Strictly speaking, **psychoanalysis** *refers to a treatment method conceived by Freud for the alleviation of emotional problems.* However, Freud's life was so intertwined with his methods that his name has come to be synonymous with psychoanalysis (much as Kleenex is synonymous with facial tissue). Although few psychoanalysts today describe themselves as orthodox (pure) Freudian, most have been profoundly influenced by Freudian ideas both in their training and in practice.

Freud's volcanic perspective. As we ascend higher on the vertical axis, using the broader analytic tools of psychoanalysis, we find that Freud shifts the direction in which psychological forces are presumed to push. Behaviorists have emphasized the power of the *situation* to act upon the person from the *outside in,* much as the moon acts upon the ocean to cause tides. By contrast, Freud's psychoanalysis is an *inside-out* theory of mind where internal forces flow upward and outward to produce external behavior, much as interior pressures cause volcanoes to erupt.

Freud's model of personality is composed of opposing forces (e.g., conscious versus unconscious, id versus superego) surrounding a *self* within a closed system. These forces constantly push against one another, like tectonic plates (continental-sized slabs of rock beneath the earth's crust) building up pressure that eventually causes earthquakes to occur and volcanoes to erupt. Similarly, in Freud's "geology" of the mind, psychological forces below the surface collide with one another, generating the energy and pressures that erupt in observable symptoms.

For Freud, all behaviors, even the most complex human experiences such as falling in love, sculpting a statue, or building a rocket, result from the collision of forces within a closed system. Just as Earth does not change size in order to accommodate pressure from colliding tectonic plates, but erupts in volcanoes or earthquakes instead, the mind at first attempts to repress or bury unacceptable impulses, but eventually releases the buildup of internal pressures through a "volcano" of symptoms, slips, dreams, or defense mechanisms that relieve pressure—if only temporarily. In this chapter we will study the vast mental "geology" created by Freud to explain how human personality operates; but first, a brief historical overview to help us understand how it all began.

Background Check—In Love with Mom

Personality of the personality theorist. Nowhere is the personality of the theorist more significant than in Freud's case. As Gay put it, "This entanglement of autobiography with science has bedeviled psychoanalysis from its beginnings" (1988, p. 89). Freud's theories were co-mingled with his own issues (e.g., his attraction to his mother, enchantment with older male authority figures, and intolerance of divergent opinions on the part of his followers). Freud was a private, autonomous, and somewhat conflicted person; not surprisingly, his theory of personality views the mind as similarly private, autonomous, and conflicted.

Childhood and youth. Sigmund Freud was born at 6:30 P.M. on the sixth of May, 1856, in Freiberg, Moravia, and died on the twenty-third of September, 1939, in London. Except for his first four years, and his final one, Freud lived his entire life in Vienna, Austria.

Favoritism toward the firstborn. In Jewish culture, favoritism toward a firstborn son is not only acceptable, it is mandated by the Torah. A practice known as the birthright requires that firstborn sons be given a double portion of the father's inheritance. Freud's sister, Anna, remembered her brother as a favored son (he was the only child in the family to have his own room and an oil lamp—a luxury at that time). She also saw her brother as a tyrant who forbade her to read Balzac and Dumas (Freud-Bernays, 1940). In short, it is apparent that Freud, the father of psychoanalysis, was not beyond the reach of his own family-of-origin dynamics, nor was he untouched by his Jewish heritage.

Doting mother, distant father. Freud's mother, Amalia, had just turned nineteen when she became Jacob's third wife, and was barely twenty-one when Freud was born. All accounts seem to agree on the following three characteristics of Freud's youthful mother: (1) her beauty, (2) her authoritarian personality, and (3) her boundless adoration of her firstborn son. Doubtless reflecting his childhood experiences, Freud wrote: "A man who has been the indisputable favorite of his mother keeps for life the feeling of a conqueror, that confidence of success that often induces real success" [Freud, 1940–52, Vol 12, p. 26 (quoted in Jones, 1953, p. 5)].

By contrast, Freud remembered his relationship with his father primarily in terms of authority and conflict. When Sigmund was two, he was still wetting his bed and it was his father, not his indulgent mother, who reproved him. Freud remembered saying, on one such occasion, "Don't worry, Papa. I will buy you a beautiful new bed in Neutitschein" (the chief town of the district) [Freud, 1940–52, Vols. 2 & 3, p. 221 (quoted in Jones, 1953, p. 7)].

From family dynamics to theoretical universals. Freud's position as his mother's favorite son, accentuated by his father's age and emotional distance, probably provided the emotional underpinnings for his dominant developmental construct, the

Oedipus complex, *(named for the Greek myth about King Oedipus who unknowingly married his mother and killed his father) the core assertion in psychoanalytic theory that the little boy wishes to sexually possess his mother and replace his father.* Freud's fervent love for his mother led him to believe that the *Oedipus complex* was a universal phenomenon, failing to consider that, unlike himself, not *every* boy has the hots for Mommy.

Freud acknowledged his tendency to generalize to others on the basis of personal experiences, admitting that whenever he became aware of a personal quirk or complex, he would think: "This cannot possibly be an individual peculiarity of my own. . . . I have reasons for supposing that other people are in this respect very similar to me" (Freud, 1901, p. 24).

Freud's early career—faltering at science, flirting with cocaine. Freud's great strength was in the extraordinary value he placed on a *singular fact.* Whereas other investigators might dismiss a single instance as an artifact or a mere blip on the radar screen, Freud held single instances in high regard and his mind would not dismiss them until he had worked out a satisfactory explanation. That was Freud's genius— his intense study of the singular—but it was also his greatest shortcoming as a scientist. Even his admiring biographer admitted that Freud was deficient as a scientist:

> When he got hold of a simple but significant fact he would feel, and know, that it was an example of something general or universal, and the idea of collecting statistics on the matter was quite alien to him. . . . When, for example, Freud experienced certain attitudes toward his parents, he immediately felt that they were not peculiar to himself and that he had discovered something about human nature in general: Oedipus, Hamlet, and the rest soon flashed across his mind. (Jones, 1953, p. 97)

Freud's initial enthusiasm for cocaine illustrates this tendency. Cocaine made him feel vital and more alive, so he was puzzled when others experienced cocaine as addicting. Freud, who suffered from periodic depression as well as from anxiety attacks, found that cocaine calmed his agitation, dispelled his depression, and gave him a sense of energy and vigor. Writing to Martha, his fiancee, he said: "In my last severe depression I took coca again and a small dose lifted me to the heights in a wonderful fashion. I am just now busy collecting the literature for a song of praise to this magical substance" (Jones, 1953, p. 84).

In fairness, we need to remember that cocaine was an accepted medical treatment during that era, not an illegal substance as it is now.

Reevaluating cocaine. Freud finally reevaluated the "wonders" of cocaine after he unsuccessfully used it to treat a friend. Although treatment with cocaine at first relieved his friend's severe insomnia, pain, and other symptoms, increasingly larger doses became necessary to bring about relief. This led to chronic intoxication and finally to delirium tremens with white snakes creeping all over his friend's skin (Jones, 1953, p. 91).

The dual picture that emerges of Freud early in his career is that of a dedicated— sometimes brilliant—investigator of the *single fact,* but a marginal scientist who relied on his own personal experience at the expense of scientific evaluation. Although, in the late nineteenth century, statistics were not yet an integral part of scientific inquiry, Freud fell short even when measured by the scientific standards of his day.

Speaking of the only experimental study Freud ever published, Jones (1953) described it as an illustration that "this was not his real field. The ideas are all good, but the facts are recorded in a somewhat irregular and uncontrolled fashion that would make them hard to correlate with anyone else's observations" (p. 92). Even Jones, ever ready to lionize his hero, gave Freud barely passing grades as a scientist.

Freud's personal blind spots—massaging Ms. Emmy, analyzing Anna. Freud's behavior as a clinician also testifies to the power of the unconscious mind. Although he may have been reasonably objective about Breuer's treatment of Anna O., Freud had his own blind spots. In the same volume in which Breuer presented Anna O.'s case (Breuer & Freud, 1893–95), Freud described his treatment of "Emmy Von N." without even a passing reference to the erotic emotions he had likely awakened in her.

Ms. Emmy. Following her husband's death, fourteen years earlier, Ms. Emmy had been experiencing varying degrees of illness, and on the evening of May 2, Freud visited her in the nursing home, reporting: "I ordered her to be given warm baths and I shall massage her whole body twice a day . . ." (pp. 50–51). In his account, Freud describes numerous instances of using massage therapy with Emmy.

It is hardly surprising that after seven weeks of intensive, twice-a-day full-body massages by her thirty-three-year-old physician, Ms. Emmy told Freud that "she had not felt so well since her husband's death" (p. 77). Although such treatments were regarded as appropriate medical practice during that era, Freud apparently failed to appreciate that giving full-body massages to a lonely widow might evoke erotic feelings. Not surprisingly, Freud's subsequent attempt to refer Ms. Emmy to another physician "failed completely. From the very first she [Emmy] seems to have been at cross-purposes with the [new] doctor" (Breuer & Freud, 1893–95, p. 78).

In fairness, we need to remember that in Freud's day, such massage therapy was innovative, and it anticipated by half a century some later findings (e.g., Spitz, 1945) regarding the importance of touch in nurturing the human psyche. Even today many people utilize massage as a way of managing stress.

Analyzing Anna. The power of the unconscious in Freud's own life is, perhaps, most vividly illustrated in his attempts to psychoanalyze his youngest daughter, Anna. Although he insisted that other psychoanalysts must "model themselves during psycho-analytic treatment on the surgeon, who puts aside all his feelings . . ." (1911–13, p. 115), Freud put his own daughter on the analytic couch. Anna's psychoanalysis was a drawn-out affair that began in 1918, continued for more than three years, and resumed again for another year in 1924.

Freud appeared worried that his daughter chose to remain single, yet he was unable to acknowledge how much he might have contributed to her reluctance to marry. His unconscious need for Anna's undivided affection is revealed in the following letter to a friend:

Anna & Sigmund Freud
Freud with Anna in the fall of 1928, in Berlin to be fitted with a new prosthesis. (*Mary Evans/Sigmund Freud Copyrights, Wivenhow*)

. . . she has just passed her 30th birthday, does not seem inclined to get married and who can say if her momentary interests will render her happy in years to come when she has to face life without her

father? . . . Sometimes I urgently wish her a good man, sometimes
I shrink from the loss. (Gay, 1988, p. 438)

And the feeling was apparently mutual, as Anna expressed in a letter to her father:
"You surely can't imagine how much I continually think of you" (Gay, 1988, p. 438).
Indeed, late in life, Freud admitted to the addictive quality of his relationship with
Anna. Helplessly entangled with his favorite child, Freud lamented: "With all these in-
soluble conflicts it is a good thing that life at some time comes to an end" (quoted in
Gay, 1988, p. 440).

Zeitgeist

From biology to psychology. Freud began his career by attempting to create "a psychology that shall be a natural science . . ." (Freud, 1895, p. 295). Gradually he became more social in orientation, however, and in his last work (the posthumously
published *Outline of Psycho-Analysis),* Freud completely abandoned his early neurological framework, declaring that mental investigations must start with "consciousness"
(Freud, 1937–39, p. 157). At that time, Freud also rejected behaviorism's empty organism: "One extreme line of thought, exemplified in the American doctrine of behaviourism, thinks it possible to construct a psychology which disregards this
fundamental fact [consciousness]!" (Freud, 1937–39, p. 157).

Subsequently, all of Freud's followers—admirers and dissenters alike—reformulated
psychoanalysis upward, away from the *Physiological Zone* in the direction of *insight,
awareness,* and *interpersonal relations (Insight and Social Zones).* Even Freud's most loyal
disciple—his daughter, Anna—tilted psychoanalysis away from her father's concentration on biology and unconscious processes by focusing her attention on the adaptive functions (defense mechanisms) of the *ego.* Virtually all of Freud's earliest
disciples-turned-dissenters (e.g., Jung, Adler, Horney, Erikson) moved from his early
biological reductionism to embrace broader social constructs. As these theorists
moved in the direction of the ego and rationality, their theories engendered greater
degrees of personal agency and responsibility, preparing the way for the humanists
and existentialists.

Brain mythology. In Freud's day, prior to the emergence of statistical techniques
and brain-imaging technologies, loose analogies and mixed metaphors were freely accepted as starting points for science. Few scientists grasped the distinction between a
bright idea and a carefully researched conclusion, and in comparison, brilliantly conceived speculation was often more admired. Consistent with the trends of his time,
Freud wrote: "Instead of starting from a definition, it seems more useful to select . . . a
few specially striking and characteristic facts to which our enquiry can be attached"
(1921, p. 72). Nor did he think it necessary to synthesize his observations into a coherent
whole: "I so rarely feel the need for synthesis. The unity of the world seems to me something self-understood, something unworthy of emphasis" (Freud, E. L., 1960, p. 310).

In this way, Freud mirrored his mentors—men who pioneered scientific break-
throughs in brain anatomy and physiology, while simultaneously indulging in what
was sometimes called *Hirnmythologie* (brain mythology). One of Freud's early mentors,
Theodor Meynert (considered one of the greatest brain anatomists in Europe at the

time), was a prime example of this scientific-mythologic tradition. One student told of his disappointment upon discovering that many of the "brain tracts" allegedly "discovered" by Meynert were the creation of his imagination (Forel, 1935, p. 64). Such a mix of biology and mythology was typical for thinkers of that time.

Ready to kill or be killed. Early in his career, Freud's commitment to biological materialism was so intense that once during a debate, Freud "behaved very rudely to his philosophical opponent and obstinately refused to apologize; *there was even for the moment some talk of a duel*" (Jones, 1953, p. 43, emphasis added). One can assume that if Jones (the biographer who painted Freud's portrait in the most glowing colors) said he "behaved very rudely," Freud must have acted quite nastily. As indicated by his willingness to fight to the death, Freud was not necessarily the dispassionate scholar one might picture the father of psychoanalysis to have been. On the contrary, Freud was so convinced of his correctness that he typically experienced disagreement with his formulations as a personal attack.

Mechanistic versus humanistic images. Freud struggled with what one scholar described as two images of persons. Freud's *mechanistic* model views the person as an object differing little from other organisms in the universe. All needs, longings, wishes, etc., are conceived as energies seeking discharge. As he once put it, reality contains "only masses in motion and nothing else" (Freud, 1895, p. 308). Freud's *humanistic* image views persons as composed of a *dual nature*: one part being carnal, destructive, selfish, greedy, and lustful, the other with a capacity for art, literature, religion, science, and philosophy. Inner conflict is inevitable because of the clash of the higher and lower natures. Throughout his career, Freud struggled with these two images. Although he saw people as differing from animals or machines, they nonetheless remained subject to the same forces of nature: electrical, mechanical, chemical, magnetic, light, heat, etc.

A "decalogue" for studying Freud—and others. Holt (1973) suggests the following ten principles for studying Freud. We list them here because they are applicable to other theorists as well.

1. Beware of lifting statements out of context. There is no substitute for reading enough to get the theorist's full meaning.

2. Don't take extreme formulations literally. Treat them as the author's way of getting your attention.

3. Watch out for inconsistencies. Don't trip over them, nor seize on them with glee, but take them as incomplete formulations.

4. Be alert for figurative language, and rely most on statements that are least poetic and dramatic.

5. Don't expect rigorous definitions; try to understand how terms were used over a period of time.

6. Be skeptical about assertions of proof that something has been established beyond doubt. Remember that we have much higher standards of proof than in former times.

TABLE 6.1

Freud at a Glance

MODEL OF PERSONALITY	DESCRIPTION	DYNAMICS
What Are the Parts?	**Id:** "seething cauldron" of raw emotions–sex, aggression, hunger, thirst. **Ego:** carries out thinking, planning, mediating, and reality-testing. **Superego:** the moral arm of personality, in endless conflict with the *id*.	Tripartite model has *conscious awareness* as "tip of the iceberg." *Unconscious* processes comprise the bulk of mental functioning. *Ego* is sandwiched between the *id* and *superego*, ceaselessly mediating their conflicts.
What Makes a Person Go?	**Libido:** not simply "sex drive." For Freud, *libido* is broader, including a wider range of life instincts or life forces.	*Libido* is Freud's primary *instinct*, bridging the gap from body to mind. Beginning as bodily urges, instincts become psychic forces in the mind, urging the person toward gratification.
What Makes a Person Grow?	The newborn grows by passing through a series of **psychosexual stages:** *oral, anal, urethral, phallic,* and *genital.* Stages are designated by the anatomical location where *libido* is presumed present in high concentrations.	*Libido* is *cathected* (*focused*) at body locations of high activity. During the *oral* stage, the infant sucks intensely; during the anal stage, fous is on "holding in" or "letting go." Spending too much or too little time "sucking" may lead to *arrest* or *fixation* at the oral stage; the person may remain excessively "oral" throughout life—eating, drinking, smoking, or talking too much.
What Makes a Person Unique?	**Biological determinism is strong**—each infant passes through similar stages. However, *libido* is distributed differently for each person and *defense mechanisms* also operate uniquely for each person.	Each individual develops a *unique pattern* of libido distribution, arrests, or fixations; along with a characteristic configuration of defense and coping mechanisms. Much of this remains *unconscious*, and the goal of psychoanalysis is to raise a person's level of awareness.

7. Freud was fond of opposites and dichotomies, even when his data might better have been conceptualized as continuous variables.

8. Be wary of Freud's persuasiveness. Although he was frequently right, it was not always for the reasons he gave.

9. Don't take every sentence as a profound truth.

10. Don't become so offended by Freud's lapses from methodological purity that you dismiss him altogether. We can learn a lot from Freud if we carefully consider his work and not take each pronouncement too seriously.

ASKING THE BIG FOUR QUESTIONS

Freud's psychoanalytic theory is so elaborate and so complex that before asking the Big Four questions, we need to understand the overarching themes that recur throughout his multiple models.

Constructs in conflict. Freud *loved* creating **opposing constructs,** or *contrasting pairs of components.* Freud viewed the mind as a cauldron of conflict, and conflict is most easily conceptualized as occurring between *two* antagonists. Thus, Freud tended to emphasize opposing *pairs:* conscious versus unconscious regions of the mind, Eros (life instincts) versus Thanatos (death instincts), pleasure principle versus reality principle.

Freudian constructs are like kites. We might think of Freudian constructs as behaving like kites—*dynamically suspended between opposing forces*—achieving some sort of equilibrium. If a wind blows our kite west, we pull the string east; if a gust lifts the kite up, we pull down. Like kites, Freudian constructs achieve a sort of dynamic stability, *suspended between equal, opposing forces.* In our own personal lives, we frequently find ourselves is awash in opposing forces: conflict with our impulses, conflict with our consciences, even conflict with unconscious urges that are revealed only in dreams or **Freudian slips,** which are *unconsciously motivated "accidents" or "errors" that reveal underlying truths about personality.*

Merging a succession of models into a final metapsychology. Asking the "Big Four" is difficult with Freud, because he constantly revised his theories, creating new models to correct earlier deficiencies. So if someone asks you, "What do you think of Freud's theory?" you might well respond "Which one?" Over the course of nearly half a century, Freud formulated *six* major models: the **neurological model** *(Phi, Omega, and Psi neurons);* **topographic model** *(conscious, preconscious, unconscious);* **structural model** *(id, ego, superego);* **economic model** *(instincts, drives);* **genetic model** *(psychosexual stages);* and **adaptive model** *(defense mechanisms).* During the last twenty-five years of his life, Freud synthesized all of these models into what he called his metapsychology: *a comprehensive theory that incorporated all earlier models but surpassed, or went "beyond" them—hence, the prefix "meta" from the Greek "beyond."* Although Freud's ever-evolving theories frequently appear overwhelming to first-time readers, our *zonal* perspective will help us follow the changes that took place in his thinking.

Finding our way to Freud's final metapsychology. Recall that earlier we discussed three levels of learning: *description, explanation,* and *synthesis.* Freud's theory of personality followed a similar sequence. He first *described* a neurological model, next he *explained* how various components of the mind interacted (topographic, tripartite, and economic models), and finally he *synthesized* all his previous models into one overarching *metapsychology.* We will trace the evolution of Freud's thought from biological beginnings to his final model. In this way we will develop a clear understanding of the essentials of psychoanalysis—one of the most important intellectual influences of the twentieth century.

What Are the Parts?—Neurological and Topographic Models

Biological beginnings. Freud's first attempt at theory building (*Project for a Scientific Psychology,* 1895) was a combination of the reductionist scientific methods of his day,

TABLE 6.2

Models of Freud's Metapsychology

NAME	COMPONENTS	UTILITY
Neurological Model	Phi, Omega, and Psi neurons	Freud attempted to explain complex psychological processes in strictly neurological terms. He wanted a purely descriptive and scientific model.
Topographic Model	Conscious, Preconscious, and Unconscious	Still a descriptive model, the description of personality as having depth and being multilayered moved beyond the neurological model, because it allowed for qualitative distinctions to be made.
Tripartite Model	Id, Ego, and Superego	Reaching above the realm of description, the tripartite model provided the structural foundation for his subsequent models. Here three different agencies captured the interplay of forces within personality.
Economic Model	Instincts and Drives	This model outlines Freud's motivational system for libido distribution. Regulating mental forces through the pleasure–unpleasure principle, he created fuel for his metapsychology, which focuses on psychic forces in conflict.
Genetic Model	Psychosexual Stages	The psychosexual stages show how a fixed amount of libido is distributed in a closed system. Here psychic energy becomes cathected at various bodily orifices. The genetic model was steeped in dualism, with stages unfolding in the mind, but deriving their psychological power from the body.
Adaptive Model	Defense Mechanisms	Finally, following from the genetic model, Freud explored how libido arrest during the childhood stages informs coping and defense mechanism that adults will use throughout their lives. This adaptive model showed how individuals will react and what attitudes they will hold; in essence, their personal style.

intermixed with speculative brain mythology of his own making. He attempted to correlate psychological processes with presumed quantities of energy circulating throughout hypothetical brain structures containing three different types of neurons: *Phi, Psi,* and *Omega* neurons. Stimuli from the outside world, he said, encountered *Phi* neurons, which either responded to the stimulation, stored the signal in memory, or buried it deep within what would later come to be known as the *unconscious. Psi* neurons provided long-term memory by storing experience, and *Omega* neurons facilitated reality testing by differentiating between external stimuli and those arising from needs within the person.

Freud was intent on creating a *scientific* model of psychological processes—one that carried the "serious stamp of science." Soon, however, he realized the futility of attempting to explain complex psychological processes in solely neurological terms, and he abandoned the *Project* almost as soon as it was completed, keeping it from publication during his lifetime. Although Freud subsequently tried to move away from biology toward social relations, near the end of his life he concluded that all psychological processes were derived from two biological drives: libido and aggression—*Eros* and *Thanatos*.

In the *Project*, Freud erroneously conceptualized the nervous system as a *passive processor* of nervous energy that arose either from the external environment or from bodily needs. Freud conceptualized neurons as *processing* stimulation, but never *generating* energy on their own, as we now know they do. As McCarley and Hobson put it: "The absence of self-generated activity and energy . . . for neuronal systems leads directly to the notion of lack of autonomy for psychological systems" (1977, p. 1217).

From a zonal perspective we could say that even though Freud tried to ascend vertically—moving from the *Physiological Zone* to awareness and social relations—he never fully escaped his early love affair with biology; he never gave up trying to be *scientific* by reducing things to physiology. In the end—shortly before his death—Freud concluded that the ultimate goal of all life was *death* (1920, p. 38). Thus, he ended his career as he had begun, more a biologist than an existential philosopher. Birth and death—and all the experiences in between—were regarded primarily as manifestations of the biological life cycle.

Although Freud's Phi, Psi, and Omega neurons have gone the way of kerosene lamps and horse-drawn carriages, they serve to remind us of his theoretical foundations. Freud was not a sexist "dirty old man" as some have concluded; he was, at heart, a biologist whose twin theoretical errors consisted of overgeneralization from his own private experiences, and biological reductionism. Freud's psychoanalysis was not so much a theory of *pansexualism* as it was *reductionist biology*.

Topographic Model—"Depth" Psychology

After abandoning his neurological model, Freud constructed a *topographic model* (also known as the *"depth"* model) in which he described a multilayered "geography" of the mind, much as a cartographer might construct a topographic map using different colors to distinguish among mountains, plains, and valleys. In the *Interpretation of Dreams* (1900), Freud located the *unconscious* at the deepest level, the *preconscious* as the next layer, and the *conscious* at the top. This model was an improvement over the *Project* because it allowed Freud to make *qualitative* distinctions (e.g., between conscious and unconscious thoughts) in a way that transcended his earlier neurological reductionism.

Conscious (Cs). In Freud's topographic "depth" theory, **the conscious (Cs)** *is the part of your mind that is immediately aware of your surroundings and your thoughts at any given moment, and is experienced by you as your own private "stream of consciousness."* Freud felt that consciousness was so obvious as to hardly need defining:

Figure 6.1 ■ *Freud's "corrected" topographic map of the mind*

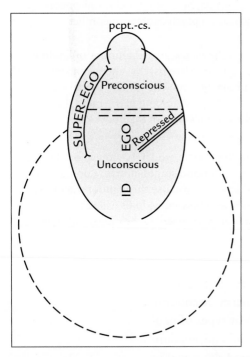

Freud presented this map of the mind with the following comment:

It is certainly hard to say to-day how far the drawing is correct. In one respect it is undoubtedly not. The space occupied by the unconscious id ought to have been incomparably greater than that of the ego or the preconscious. I must ask you to correct it in your thoughts. (Freud, 1932, pp. 78, 79)

Hatched lines indicate my "correcting" it as suggested by Freud.

"There is no need to characterize what we call 'conscious': it is the same as the consciousness of philosophers and of everyday opinion. Everything else psychical is in our view 'the unconscious'" (Freud, 1937–39, p. 159). Elsewhere, Freud described consciousness as a "searchlight" illuminating the darkness of the unconscious: "Without the illumination thrown by the quality of consciousness, we should be lost in the obscurity of depth-psychology . . . " (Freud, 1933, p. 70).

   Unconscious. According to Freud, **the unconscious (Ucs)** *is the largest part of your mind, containing repressed impulses, emotional conflicts, or painful memories that you want to keep out of awareness. It is only indirectly accessible to you or your analyst through dreams, "slips," or free associations.* Although Freud is frequently credited with "discovering" the unconscious, it was not entirely his invention. Centuries earlier, Plato had described the soul as two spirited horses—one noble, the other nasty—pulling in opposite directions. Christian theologians pictured human nature as both divine and carnal, and the apostle Paul's first-century description of his own conflicts is consistent with Freud's notion of the unconscious: "I do not understand what I do. For what I want to do I do not do, but what I hate I do" (Romans 7:15 NIV). Goethe found the idea of "depths beyond depths" highly appealing, and Nietzsche and Schopenhauer warned against overestimating the conscious at the expense of unconscious forces of the mind.

   Freud's genius was in developing a comprehensive model of the *unconscious* that explained such diverse phenomena as dreams, defense mechanisms, hypnotism, "slips" (of the tongue, pen, hands, or feet). Freud described the unconscious as an "untidy storehouse for the most explosive materials old and new . . . laden to the brim with wishes, quite unable to entertain doubts, tolerate delay, or understand logic" (Gay, 1988, p. 367).

   For Freud, the *unconscious* is broad, powerful, far-reaching, and influential; yet, it remains inaccessible to the individual—that's why you have to pay an analyst to help you probe it! Additionally, Freud recognized that many things normally remain outside awareness even though they are not deeply repressed. To account for this, he formulated the *preconscious.*

   Preconscious. Your preconscious (Pcs) *is a kind of "twilight zone" where, at any given moment, you are not thinking about something, but you easily could; these are not thoughts, emotions, or actions that you try to keep out of awareness, but many have simply become "automatic," such as brushing your teeth or steering your automobile.* Freud defined the *preconscious* as what "easily becomes conscious" (Freud, 1933, p. 71). *Preconscious* thinking includes such things as your awareness of breathing, the sensation that your mouth is coated with saliva, the sound of "background" noise, or the pressure you feel on your buttocks from the chair in which you are sitting—thoughts that you can easily bring to mind but usually don't. With the *preconscious* in place, Freud felt he had created an adequate model: "We now have three terms, 'conscious,' 'preconscious,' and 'unconscious,' with which we can get along in our description of mental phenomena" (Freud, 1933, p. 71).

Summary of Parts

Freud was fond of dichotomies. His most important dichotomy (conscious versus unconscious) is the foundation upon which psychoanalysis rests. Freud was awestruck by his science professors and attempted to emulate their tough-minded

ScienceCartoonsPlus.com

science—Newtonian physics—when he first tried to formulate a model of the mind. Although he abandoned the *Project* (1895) early in his career, realizing he could not explain complex psychological processes while adhering to radical biological reductionism, he never strayed far from Newton's third law of motion: "For every action, there is an equal and opposite reaction." His topographic or "depth" model moved slightly beyond the various neurons he postulated in the *Project*, but still remained a *descriptive* metaphor that was limited in its ability to explain higher psychological processes. Next, Freud formulated Newton's law of opposing forces into still other models of the mind, where opposing forces dynamically held each other in equilibrium: *tripartite* and *economic* models.

What Makes a Person Go?

Tripartite model. Freud was dissatisfied with his topographic ("depth") model, because it failed to adequately depict the *interplay* among various forces within the personality; so he subsequently formulated a model in which personality was composed of three agencies (id, ego, and superego) holding each other in balance. Among this trio, the *self* or *ego* is surrounded on all sides by opposing forces. Sandwiched between the biological impulses of the *id* and the societal restraints of the *superego,* the *ego* experiences conflict as ceaseless and unrelenting. Only death or insanity brings tranquillity. Let's look more closely at how Freud used these "big three" to fire up the engine.

The tripartite model—Freud's enduring foundation. Writing in *The Ego and the Id* (1923), Freud presented his new **tripartite model,** *in which the mind consists of three agencies or operating systems: id, ego, and superego.* Now, instead of picturing the mind as comprised of sharply separated, geographically distinct subsystems, he portrayed personality as a *fusion* of forces that blend and merge into one another. These three newly created agencies included all the functions previously assigned to the unconscious, preconscious, and conscious: "For we picture the unknown apparatus which serves the activities of the mind as being really like an instrument constructed of several parts (which we speak of as 'agencies') . . ." (Freud, 1925–26, p. 194).

Here, Freud moved beyond his concrete geographical metaphor to create what Schafer (1976, p. 86) described as an "assembly of minds." In this model Freud described each "agency" as if it were a separate personality with feelings, motives, wishes, blind spots, and goals of its own. For example, he described the ego not only as a "helper to the id," but also as a "submissive slave who courts his master's love" (1923, p. 56). In another place Freud described the ego as subject to "three tyrannical masters . . . the external world, the superego, and the id" (1923, p. 77). The net effect of these colorful metaphors is to convey Freud's conviction that personality is comprised of three loosely partitioned subsystems, each powered by biological forces.

Id—a "seething cauldron" of emotions. The **id** (literally "it") *contains our instincts, impulses, and irrational feelings.* Freud referred to the *id* as "a chaos, a cauldron full of seething excitations . . . " (1933, p. 73). Although the *id* is bursting with energy, it has no organization or goals except the immediate satisfaction of instinctual needs. Freud described the *id* as operating by the **pleasure–unpleasure principle:** *the two-pronged desire of the organism to seek <u>immediate</u> gratification of pleasure and <u>instant</u> relief from pain.*

Given how intensely we experience our passions and how little control we often feel over our emotions, it's no wonder that we frequently refer to our emotions in *id* ("it") terms: "*It* makes me crazy when people turn left in front of me!" "*It* feels empty inside." "*It* tickles my funny bone when. . . ." "*It* feels like I'm about to explode!" According to Freud, the *id* is illogical, immoral, and timeless. "The logical laws of thought do not apply in the id . . . contrary impulses exist side by side, without canceling each other out or diminishing each other. . . . The id of course knows no judgements of value: no good and evil, no morality (1933, pp. 73-74).

In our own lives we experience these *id impulses* in the form of "rubber necking" at the site of an accident (secretly excited by the misfortunes of others); voyeuristically looking at something "naughty" on the Internet; or yearning to slap someone or "punch their lights out" when they provoke us.

Ego—the mind's "I". We learned earlier that Freud viewed the mind as constantly in conflict. Yet, amid all this conflict, Freud's central agent (*ego*) organizes behavior and anchors experience: "We call this organization their '*Ich*' ['ego'; literally, 'I']" (1925–26, p. 195). At the center of Freud's tripartite model of the mind is the **ego,** *a reality-oriented, thinking agency that promotes harmony within the mind and good relations with the external world.* Although Freud did not use the term *self* in constructing his mental apparatus, the *ego* operates as the thinking, directing agent of personality. When we speak of *ego* functions we can usually substitute "I" for ego: "*I* decided to work for a year before starting college," or "*I* arranged to visit Hawaii." Freud said, "The ego represents what may be called reason and common sense, in contrast to the id, which contains the passions . . . ." (1923, p. 25).

Ego functions both as a pilot and as a peace negotiator. The *ego* struggles to find socially acceptable ways for the *id* to gratify impulses. In one of his most famous passages, Freud described how the ego valiantly struggles to steer behavior in socially acceptable directions in spite of being powerfully pushed around by the id:

> The ego's relation to the id might be compared with that of a rider to his horse. The horse supplies the locomotive energy, while the rider has the privilege of deciding on the goal and of guiding the powerful animal's movement. But only too often there arises between the ego and the id the not precisely ideal situation of the rider being obliged to guide the horse along the path by which it itself wants go. (1933, p. 77)

Here we see illustrated Freud's belief that the biological forces are the ultimate source of all psychological processes. Even the ego—the rational navigator of personality— is frequently forced to follow the "horse" of biological impulses.

Superego—the parent within. The **superego** (literally "above-I") is *the moral arm of the personality.* According to Freud, the *superego* is the last portion of personality to develop and results from the long period of interactions between parents and child:

> The superego is the successor and representative of the parents (and educators) . . . it carries on their functions almost unchanged. It keeps the ego in a permanent state of dependence and exercises a constant pressure on it. (Freud, 1937–39, p. 117).

Freud further subdivided the superego into two portions: **Conscience** is *that portion of our personality that scolds, shames, or "guilts" us into remedial action when our biological impulses get out of control or we appear in danger of violating society's expectations.* Freud saw the role of the *ego* as negotiating the incessant conflict that exists between our raw impulses and society's expectations: "It is as important for the ego to remain on good terms with the super-ego as with the id. You will already have guessed that the super-ego is the vehicle of the phenomenon that we call conscience" (Freud, 1925–26, p. 223).

However, the *superego* does more than point out wrong or censure unacceptable impulses, it also holds up standards for us to strive for. The **ego-ideal** *is the second portion of the superego, consisting of our ideal self-image—those aspects of ourselves that we value and prize—those portions of our personality that we are proud of and seek to enhance.* When you act or think in a way that would make your Mama smile, your *ego-ideal* is probably at work; when you behave in a way that would make your Daddy frown, you've probably violated your *conscience.*

Tripartite foundation for Freud's final metapsychology. This tripartite model provided the foundation for Freud's final metapsychology. Building upon the triad of forces contained in the *id, ego,* and *superego,* Freud fine-tuned his theory of

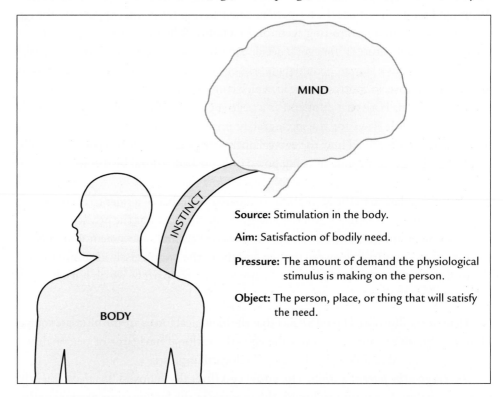

Figure 6.2 ▪ *Instinct: Freud's Mind–Body Bridge*

personality to include a *motivational* (economic) model, a *developmental* (psychosexual stages) model, and an *adaptive* (defense/coping) model. This allowed him to explain how psychological forces ebb and flow, change over time, and are utilized by defense or coping mechanisms to keep anxiety at bay. These additional models provided a rich supply of additional constructs for understanding personality, but they did not change the essential biological foundations.

Economic model for libido distribution. *Economics* refers to the production, distribution, and consumption of goods and services. Freud's **economic model** *outlines his system for the production, distribution, and use of libido—the motivational fuel of personality.* Freud sometimes spoke of *libido* as if it were a stream of water that could be dammed up, diverted, or allowed to flow freely. At other times he referred to libido as if it were electricity, flowing into objects and energizing them. Freud's economic model regulated mental forces through the *pleasure–unpleasure principle* and provided the groundwork for his final dynamic metapsychology, which focused on psychic forces in conflict.

Instincts—Freud's bridge between soma and psyche. In describing motives, Freud found himself astride the dualism of his day, caught between the mind and the body—between psychoanalysis and physics. He solved this by defining **instincts** *as inborn biological drives (such as hunger, thirst, sex, aggression, and elimination) that bridge the gap between body and mind.* At first, Freud was clear on the multiplicity of instincts: "The forces which we assume to exist behind the tensions caused by the needs of the id are called *instincts*. They represent the somatic demands upon the mind.... It is possible to distinguish an indeterminate number of instincts . . ." (1937–39, p. 148).

In the end, however, Freud's fondness for dichotomies won out and he reduced the "indeterminate number of instincts" to only two: "After long hesitancies and vacillations we have decided to assume the existence of only two basic instincts, *Eros* and *the destructive instinct*" (1937–39, p. 148). He even sought to connect his final two with the Ancient Greeks: "I came upon this theory of mine in the writings of one of the great thinkers of ancient Greece. . . . The two fundamental principles of Empedocles . . . are, both in name and function the same as our two primal instincts, *Eros* and *destructiveness* . . . " (1937–39, p. 246).

Four components of an instinct: source, aim, object, and impetus. Freud described instincts as having four characteristics: **(1) the source** *is the physical deficiency such as thirst;* **(2) the aim** *is to* remove the bodily *deficiency;* **(3) the object** *is something, such as* a glass of water, *with the capability of fulfilling the need,* and **(4) the impetus** *is a measure of how urgently the organism seeks gratification*—"I'm *dying* for a drink!" Freud viewed instincts as arising from within the body:

> Its source is a state of excitation in the body, its aim is the removal of that excitation; *on its path from its source to its aim the instinct becomes operative psychically*. We picture it as a certain quota of energy which presses in a particular direction. (1933, p. 96, emphasis added)

Notice that here, at the very heart of his theory, Freud struggled with the dualism of his day—how to reconcile *physical* and *psychic* forces. An instinct begins as a *physical* energy, having force and direction, but "on its path from its source to its aim," it magically morphs from a *somatic* into a *psychic* "force." Apparently, Freud wanted to have his Cartesian cake and eat it too! He wanted both the scientific respectability of biological reductionism and the flexibility of psychological agencies.

Libido—king of instincts. *Libido* is the fuel Freud used to fire up the entire personality. All of Freud's mental mechanisms *derived* their power from the *id*—the chief biological instinct: "The power of the id," wrote Freud, "expresses the true purpose of the individual organism's life" (1940, p. 148). The enduring limitation of this thinking was to tether all of Freud's subsequent models to the power of the id. Freud viewed the ego and superego as *derivatives* or *by-products* that grew out of the *id.* As we will see shortly, it took years of psychoanalytic squabbling to break free of Freud's fascination with the power of the *id.*

As commonly used today, *libido* means *sex drive.* If during a physical exam, a physician inquires, "How's your libido?" we assume that she is asking about frequency of intercourse and things related to sex drive. However, for Freud, **libido** *is a life force that includes sexual love, but also transcends biological urges.* It is a far-reaching form of sexual energy that includes "all the activities of the tender feelings which have primitive sexual impulses as their source, even when those impulses have . . . exchanged this aim for another which is no longer sexual" (1910, pp. 222–223). Freud defined *libido* broadly enough to include friendship and love for humanity as well as for children and parents. He even included devotion to concrete objects and to abstract ideas. Freud used the term *psychosexual* to emphasize that the psychological factors of sexuality should never be underestimated.

Freud wasn't a sex pervert. As we will see shortly, Freud's psychoanalytic theory of development is a process in which intellect triumphs over impulse. During development, the id relinquishes its primitive impulses to the ego for refined expression and fulfillment, while the superego softens its demands for perfection. Although Freud emphasized the importance of sexual instincts—even in the life of children—he was not the pansexualist some mistakenly portray him to be. He expanded the sexual instinct, *libido,* to include a wide range of tender feelings.

Cathexis and anticathexis. Sexuality run amok would cause chaos, so Freud invented the construct *cathexis* for containing or channeling libido. Much as pipes deliver water or wires transmit electricity, *cathexis channels libido.* Freud first introduced *cathexis* in his *Project* to express the idea of physical energy being lodged in the ego, and sent out to adhere to external objects somewhat like an electrical charge. According to Freud, libidinal "energy" was stored in the ego, from where it was sent out, or to where it could return, much as an amoeba sends out or withdraws its pseudopodia, or foot-like appendages.

Cathexis is derived from the Greek *cathexo,* meaning "I occupy," and Freud used it to refer to the sum of psychic energy that occupies or is contained in particular objects or channels. We might think of various light bulbs around the house as being *cathected* with electricity. The 10-watt bulb inside the refrigerator is *cathected* with less energy than the 250-watt floodlights that illuminate the deck. Freud retained this idea of "filling up" an object with energy even after he abandoned the biological aspects of his *Project.* In later use, *cathexis* came to mean a *focus of mental interest on a given object.* Thus, if a woman falls in love with a man, she might mentally "fill up" her mind with his image: daydreaming about him, fantasizing about him, even having imaginary conversations with him. In this way she is *cathecting* or engulfing him with her libidinal energies.

Motives. In Freud's system, *motives* channel libido to *cathect* specific objects or persons. In the illustration just cited, a woman might be motivated to form a friendship or a dating relationship with this man of her dreams, consummating in a sexual relationship. However, in some instances this sequence might be blocked by *anticathexis*. Although the id might *cathect* a desired object, the ego might *anticathect* this lustful longing with its own supply of libido ("He's not the right guy for you—don't waste time with him"). In other words, the ego might censor, suppress, or sabotage the id.

In Freud's economic model, conflicts frequently arise when libido being focused *(cathected)* in one direction is blocked by libido driving in the opposite direction *(anticathexis)*. Freud used these forces and counterforces to explain a wide variety of sexual, aggressive, or otherwise repressed behaviors, including humor. We will illustrate Freud's economic model by considering his theory of humor.

Freud's theory of humor—what's so funny about aggression and sex? Early in his career, Freud wrote a book titled *Jokes and their Relation to the Unconscious* (1905a), in which he described laughter as a mechanism for releasing thoughts or feelings that have been repressed or pushed down into the unconscious. Does such a theory make sense to us a hundred years later?

Recall watching a "Three Stooges" episode? Why was it funny when Larry poked Moe in the eye, or Curley hit Larry on the head with a frying pan? What makes "slapstick" aggression funny? Or, consider the following:

Question: What is this sound? Clop, clop . . . bang, bang. Clop, clop . . . bang, bang.
Answer: Amish drive-by shooting.

Why would anyone laugh at the image of drive-by shootings? Is killing ever funny?

Consider this: on January 28, 1986, the space shuttle *Challenger* exploded shortly after liftoff, sending flaming debris into the Atlantic Ocean while the world watched in shock. All seven crew members died. Yet, within a couple of days half a dozen *Challenger* jokes were making the rounds. Why do highly publicized tragedies typically breed such tasteless jokes? Who comes up with Helen Keller jokes or the "dead baby" variety? And all those forbidden jokes about "Polacks," gays, blacks, or red necks—what makes them funny?

According to Freud, parents/society ordinarily suppress the free expression of aggression or sexuality, and jokes provide a temporary lifting of such inhibitions—the intensity of the laughter being directly proportional to the inhibition. So whether it's one of the Three Stooges poking the other in the eye, a racist story, or a *Challenger* joke, what these jokes share in common is their ability to release the listener from inhibitions by evoking laughter. Freud put it like this:

In laughter . . . the cathectic energy used for inhibition has now suddenly . . . been lifted, and is therefore now ready to be discharged by laughter. . . . the hearer of the joke laughs with the quota of psychical energy which has become free through the lifting of the inhibitory cathexis; we might say that he laughs this quota off. (Freud, 1905a, pp. 148–149)

This sort of push–pull explanation sounds, perhaps, more like a description of how a hydraulic jack operates, but Freud's concern with being "scientific" frequently led him to mechanistic descriptions—even of laughter. Nonetheless, we might wonder whether the notion that laughter serves to "release" inhibited impulses coincides with our daily experience. If Freud were right, we might expect most humor to contain aggressive, sexual, or similar usually repressed content. What do you think? Is this the case? Have you ever heard a stand-up comedian who did *not* use sex or hostile putdowns as part of his or her monologues?

According to Freud's *economic model, Challenger* jokes would relieve the tension generated by such a graphic reminder of our vulnerability to death and disaster. Lawyer jokes, Freud would say, express our aggression toward those we perceive as powerful and possibly threatening: "By making our enemy small, inferior, despicable or comic we achieve in a roundabout way the enjoyment of overcoming him" (Freud, 1905a, p. 103). Freud would probably have considered Jay Leno's political jokes as a healthy exercise in democracy because they release the tension we feel "against persons in exalted positions who claim to exercise authority. The joke then represents a rebellion against that authority, a liberation from its pressure" (Freud, 1905a, p. 105).

Researching Freud's theory of humor. Does research support Freud's ideas about humor? You decide. When participants in a study were "insulted" by the experimenter, those who were given the opportunity to read a series of hostile jokes "got over" their anger more than those who read nonhostile jokes (Leak, 1974). In another experiment, participants viewed cartoons expressing hostility toward women. They were subsequently asked to administer shocks to women as part of a "learning experiment." Compared with participants who had not viewed the hostile cartoons, they administered less intense, shorter shocks (Baron, 1978). In another study, black Americans who listened to a black comedian make fun of white racists felt less aggressive than those who listened to a nonhostile comedian (Singer, 1968).

When you laugh loudly do you release more tension? Does how loudly people laugh indicate how much "pressure" they are releasing? Freud thought so—what do you think? Ever notice how skilled storytellers build tension by elaborating on details as they work their way toward the "punch" line? As the tension builds—especially if it's a sexual joke—listeners may smile or even begin to blush as they anticipate the climax is nearing. According to Freud, the longer the buildup, the greater will be the tension generated and the funnier will people find the punch line. This seems to occur in daily life, but does it hold up in the laboratory? An experiment by Shurcliff (1968) suggests that it does.

Participants were all told they would be working with a laboratory rat. In the *low-tension* condition they were told they would be required to hold the rat for five seconds. "These rats are bred to be docile and easy to handle," the experimenter assured them. In the *high-tension* condition they were told they would be required to draw a small sample of the rat's blood and warned that the rat "might bite." The "punch line" occurred when they reached into the cage and discovered a toy rat. The high-tension participants found this to be much funnier than did those in the low-tension condition.

A humanistic/existential perspective on humor. We will be studying humanistic and existential theories in later chapters; here—as an "appetizer"—we'll briefly compare Freud's "libido-release" theory of humor with a humanistic perspective. Abraham

Maslow, a cofounder of the humanistic psychology movement (Chapter 11), saw humor in a broader context:

> The real point is that it [the joke] is a solution of the human predicament—it integrates & bridges the discrepancy between hope & actuality, between aspirations & limitations. It is an integrating mechanism very profoundly, & I must add it to love, art, & reason.
>
> It makes it possible for man to be puffed up & humble at the same time, because he can laugh at his bloat—that makes it right & not paranoia or megalomania. Then it's not a sin. Therefore it *allows* us to retain the pride we need in order to do anything. . . . (Maslow, quoted in Lowry, 1982, pp. 10, 11)

What Makes a Person Grow?—The Genetic Model

We're about to explore Freud's famous *psychosexual stages,* but first we need to understand a few things about how a fixed amount of *libido* gets distributed within a closed system. In the *economic model,* we have just seen how *cathexis* and *anticathexis* do a "dance" that keeps aggression, sex, and other forbidden urges safely below the surface of consciousness. Now, in Freud's *developmental/genetic* model, we will again find *cathexis* and *anticathexis* doing their "dance," but this time it involves either arresting *libido* into *a fixation* or *regression,* or channeling it into further *development.*

Psychic energy, in the form of *libido,* becomes *cathected* or invested at assorted body orifices during various psychosexual (e.g., oral, anal, urethral, phallic) stages. If too much libido is cathected at a particular developmental stage there is danger of *developmental arrest* or *fixation.* When just the right amount—not too much, not too little—is cathected at a particular stage, development proceeds smoothly.

We might think of Freud's psychosexual stages as resting places (benches) along a pathway illuminated by lightbulbs that are lighted with libido instead of electricity. Imagine we have a fixed amount of libidinal "wattage"—say 1000 watts. The optimal personality might have 200-watt bulbs lighting each of five stages ("benches") along the way, but the person who had spent too much (or too little) time at Mommy's breast might be libidinally overinvested at the oral stage and be burning a 600-watt bulb at the first bench, leaving only 100-watt bulbs for each of the remaining stages. Similarly, the person whose parents obsessed about toilet training, cleanliness, or punctuality might have an 800-watt bulb at the anal–muscular stage, leaving only 50-watt bulbs for the other benches. Freud would say this person was *fixated* or *arrested at* the anal stage of development.

Fixation. A person is said to be "arrested" or **fixated** *if too much libido is invested at one particular psychosexual stage, making it difficult to move on to higher levels of psychological achievement.* A person who is *fixated* at the oral stage, for example, has too much energy invested in seeking to satisfy oral needs. Activities involving the mouth, lips, or tongue such as eating, drinking, kissing, or smoking occupy a disproportionate amount of such a person's time and interest, making it difficult to move forward with a balanced development in other stages.

Regression. This appears similar to fixation, but **regression** *means slipping backward and becoming "stuck again" at an earlier stage that had previously been left behind.* When we experience stress, we frequently *regress* to earlier forms of behavior, investing excessive amounts of libido in places where we previously felt comfortable. For example, the fourth grader who begins sucking her thumb (even though she hasn't done so since kindergarten) upon learning that her parents have decided to divorce, is exhibiting *regression,* whereas a fourth grader who never stopped sucking her thumb in the first place would be *fixated.*

Erogenous zones. Each stage has its own particular **erogenous zone,** which is *an area of the body (such as the mouth, anus, or genitals) where libido is concentrated and where gratification is most likely to occur.* Freud's developmental considerations revolved mostly around how, and in what proportions, libido became invested at particular *erogenous zones.*

Now that we understand cathexis, anticathexis, fixation, regression, and erogenous zones, let's turn to a more detailed consideration of Freud's psychosexual stages.

Oral stage (first year of life). During the **oral stage** *the mouth is the primary source of gratification.* The neonate's mind is *all id,* because the ego has not yet begun to differentiate itself from the id, and superego development is still far in the future. Since the id is completely self-centered or narcissistic, Freud sometimes referred to the *oral stage* as the **stage of primary narcissism,** *when the libido is directed inward toward the infant's own body,* instead of turning outward toward external "objects" like parents or caretakers.

Oral eroticism. Freud believed that newborns experience little real consciousness, and that their primary desire is **oral eroticism** or *seeking pleasure through the mouth (the erogenous zone of this stage).*

Primary process. At this earliest stage of development, newborns operate according to the **primary process,** which is *seeking immediate gratification.* When a newborn is hungry he insists on eating *"NOW!"*

Oral incorporation and *identification* are terms that have been used somewhat interchangeably to describe the infant's earliest, most elemental forms of "taking in." However, there are differences. **Incorporation** *means taking in actual physical supplies (such as mother's milk) or experiencing real physiological sensations from the inner world of experience;* **identification** *means "taking in" the behavioral or cognitive styles, beliefs, and attitudes of others.*

During these earliest stages of life, the infant reflexively removes some internal tensions (e.g., through urination or defecation); however, an external **object** *("object" is the psychoanalytic term for "parent" or "caretaker")* is necessary to assist in removing many tensions such as hunger, thirst, or wetness. If the caretaker is physically absent, emotionally unavailable, or slow in responding, the infant may resort to **wish fulfillment,** that is, *hallucinating (literally seeing, smelling, or hearing) what is desired through an act of fantasy.* Freud designated this as *primary process* thought, believing it was identical to the mechanisms at work in dream formation.

Freud saw *identification* as the earliest, most primitive form of psychological attachment: "Identification has been not unsuitably compared with the oral, cannibalistic incorporation of the other person. It is a very important form of attachment to someone else, probably the very first . . ." (Freud, 1933, p. 63).

Thus, for Freud and his followers, *incorporation* referred to the earliest "taking in" of external supplies (air, water, food) from the external world, whereas *identification* referred to "taking in" another person's behavioral or psychological characteristics. In current usage, *incorporation* refers to a primitive process of "taking-in-whole" of nourishment or of another person, whereas *identification* refers to a higher-level, more selective attachment to another person. Thus, the "groupie" who attends *every* Britney Spears concert, owns *every* CD she's released, and yearns to get close enough to literally touch her, would be *incorporating* or *introjecting* Britney-as-a-whole, whereas a young musician who sings and practices guitar for hours each day hoping to "sing like Britney" would be *identifying* with her.

Anal/muscular stage (second year of life). Sometime during the second year of life, known as the **anal/muscular stage,** *libido cathexis shifts from the mouth to the anal-buttocks region, the primary erogenous zone of this period.* During the *anal/muscular stage* the infant is confronted by societal demands to regulate urination and defecation. According to Freud, significant sensual energy is invested in "holding on" or "letting go" of feces or urine. Retention and elimination occur in regular cycles of tension accumulation and release, and learning to regulate one's bladder and bowels is one of the first significant accomplishments of the newly emerging *ego.* Additionally the toddler begins learning to control the muscles used in eating, dressing, walking, and talking.

Reality principle and secondary process thought. Until now, the baby has assimilated the surrounding world by incorporation or introjection; now he is called upon to live more in accordance with the **reality principle:** *the ego's process for regulating, delaying, or foregoing immediate gratification in favor of culturally acceptable alternatives.* The toddler now begins using **secondary process thought,** *the ego's style of realistically thinking, planning, evaluating, and solving problems.* The anal/muscular stage begins the lifelong process of striving to fulfill one's impulses while still taking into account the prohibitions of one's elders that are embedded in the larger culture.

Urethral stage (third year of life). Freud did not draw a hard line between the *anal* and *urethral* stages, and many authors combine them. During the **urethral stage,** *libido cathexis shifts from the anus to a new erogenous zone, the urethra.* Like the anal stage, which precedes it, the urethral stage is a time of buildup and release of tension—specifically bladder tension. Learning to release urine in appropriate ways and places helps to consolidate the developing ego's sense of mastery. Children of this age sometimes take pleasure in playing games which involve the retention and release of urine. Boys sometimes engage in competitions to see who can shoot a stream of urine the farthest.

Oedipal/phallic stage (three to five years). In psychoanalytic theory, **phallus** *refers to the penis or to a symbol of the penis; it may also refer to the clitoris.* Freud used *phallus* primarily in reference to the penis. During the **Oedipal** or **phallic stage,** *little boys experience erotic feelings for the mother accompanied by hostility, fear, and rivalry toward the father.* Freud believed this stage to be a universal phenomenon: "The Oedipus complex, as far as we know, is present in childhood in all human beings. . . . Its essential characteristics, its universality, its content and its fate were recognized long before the days of psycho-analysis" (Freud, 1927–31, p. 251). Freud quoted Diderot as saying: "If the little savage were left to himself . . . adding to the small sense of a child in the cradle the violent passions of a man of thirty, he would strangle his father and lie with his mother" (Freud, 1927–31, p. 251).

Male Oedipus complex. Likely because of his attraction to his own mother, Freud believed that all three- or four-year-old boys lust for their mothers. Freud said the boy "becomes his mother's lover. He wishes to posses her physically in such ways as he has divined from his observations and intuitions about sexual life . . ." (1937–39, p. 189).

Castration anxiety. According to Freud, such lustful longings result in the boy's suffering **castration anxiety**—*fear that his father will cut off his penis, or his testicles, or both.* With each increase in sexual longing for Mommy, Junior feels a corresponding rise in castration anxiety. Just when castration seems inevitable (because the lusting-for-Mommy *id* does not heed the warnings of the ego), a solution is found. Rather than risk losing his prized penis, the little boy sells out his interest in Mom and *identifies* with Dad, *introjecting* his father's superego standards. According to Freud, the male conscience is born of fear. Although Junior might previously have had warm feelings toward Dad, this final act of *paternal identification* is more a matter of self-defense—even cowardice—than a high moral achievement. The kid simply caves in to the societal standard: "Conform or be castrated!"

Primacy of the penis. Freud left himself vulnerable to the feminist criticism that he was a male chauvinist, because he emphasized the primacy of *masculine* sexuality: "What is present, therefore, is not a primacy of the genitals, but a primacy of the *phallus*" (Freud, 1923, p. 142, emphasis in the original). Nearly a decade later, approaching the end of his life, Freud still insisted on the primacy of the penis for the psychosexual development of *both* genders: "With their entry into the phallic phase the differences between the sexes are completely eclipsed. . . . We are now obliged to recognize that *the little girl is a little man*" (1932, pp. 117–118, emphasis added).

Female Oedipus complex. Freud believed that all little girls develop a **female Oedipus complex:** *intense longing for a penis.* This begins with what Freud termed "a momentous discovery which little girls are destined to make": Noticing the "strikingly visible" penis of a playmate or a brother, Freud believed that girls "at once recognize it as the superior counterpart of their own small and inconspicious organ, and from that time forward fall a victim to envy for the penis" (Freud, 1923–25, p. 252).

Freud's penis-centered theory of psychosexual development holds true for both genders, but works in opposite directions. For a boy, the fear of losing his penis is the core concern, whereas for a girl, not having a penis (perceiving herself to have already been castrated) is the central dynamic: "When the little girl discovers her own deficiency, from seeing a male genital, it is only with hesitation and reluctance that she accepts the unwelcome knowledge. . . . it follows that femaleness—and with it, of course, her mother—suffers a great depreciation in her eyes" (Freud, 1927–31, p. 233).

Freud's chauvinistic view of female sexuality. Finally, in what appears another deflation of female psychosexual development, Freud concluded that since the conflicts of the Oedipal period are not so intense for girls as for boys, women develop a less vigorous superego. Consequently, women show:

> . . . less sense of justice than men, that they are less ready to submit to the great exigencies of life, that they are more often influenced in their judgements by feelings of affection or hostility. . . . We must not allow ourselves to be deflected from such conclusions by the denials of the feminists, who are anxious to force us to regard the two sexes as completely equal in position and worth . . . (1923–25, pp. 257–258).

It is hardly surprising that many modern feminists, like their forebearers, find Freud's theories offensive. In fairness to Freud, however, we need to realize that his conclusions did not arise from hostility toward women or disrespect for the "weaker sex," as they were known during his era. Rather, Freud was entrapped by his reductionist notion that *biology shapes destiny*. From there, it was but a short step to *anatomy determines destiny,* and the resulting phallo-centric view that females are the lesser gender because they lack penises. Not only fervent feminists, but many males as well, have questioned the validity of Freud's view that "the little girl is a little man" (1932, p. 118).

Likewise, Freud's description of the clitoris as an "atrophied penis" (1932, p. 65) is understandably offensive to women, much as describing the penis as a "jumbo clitoris" would likely be distasteful to men. Subsequently, many (even psychoanalysts) have questioned the *universality* of Oedipal feelings. Karen Horney (Chapter 7), for example, viewed Oedipal dynamics (in either gender) as a result of provocative behavior on the part of parents. Recall how Freud's own doting mother showered her "beloved Ziggy" with an extraordinary amount of affection and special privileges.

Normality, neurosis, and psychosis—all rooted in the Oedipal/phallic stage of psychosexual development. For Freud the Oedipal/phallic stage was the most pivotal of all the psychosexual stages. The foundations of normality, as well as the roots of neurosis and psychosis, can all be found in the resolutions (or failures) of this stage.

Normality. According to Freud, *normality differs from neurosis only by degrees:* "the boundaries between the two [normal versus neurotic] are not sharply drawn, their mechanisms are to a large extent the same . . ." (Freud, 1937–39, p. 125). Convinced of the universality of the Oedipal conflict, Freud believed that few children reach adulthood without some traces of neuroses being present in their personalities: "The neuroses . . . shade off by easy transitions into what is described as the normal; and, on the other hand, there is scarcely any state recognized as normal in which indications of neurotic traits could not be pointed out" (Freud, 1937–39, p. 183).

Whereas humanistic psychologists (see Chapter 11) have suggested that a person's normal condition is health, and that the average person seeks to actualize a healthy self, psychoanalysis was conflict-ridden and tilted in the direction of pathology. For Freud, the mind was more a war zone than a flower garden. Thus, he concluded that "a normal ego . . . is, like normality in general, an ideal fiction" (1937–39, p. 235).

Neurosis. According to Freud, **neurosis** *consists of conflict between the impulses of the id and the repressions of the ego.* Instead of successfully *mediating* this conflict, as it usually does, the ego becomes overwhelmed and withdraws, leaving itself "permanently narrowed in its sphere of influence" (1925–26, p. 203). Thus weakened, the ego is no longer able to effectively mediate the inevitable conflicts between the id and the superego:

> In what did we find the essence of a neurosis? In the fact that the ego, the higher organization of the mental apparatus . . . is not able to fulfill its function of mediating between the id and reality, that in its feebleness it draws back from some instinctual portions of the id. . . . (Freud, 1925–26, p. 241)

Freud viewed neurosis as a nearly universal phenomenon that could always be traced back to childhood: "It seems that neuroses are only acquired during early childhood (up to the age of six), even though their symptoms may not make their appearance until much later" (1937–39, p. 184). According to Freud, the conflicts between the "I-want-to-have-sex-with-Mommy" urges of the id, and the "Daddy-will-cut-off-your-penis!" warnings of the ego, peak in their intensity during the Oedipal period.

Psychosis. The most serious disturbance of personality—in any theory of personality—is **psychosis,** which is *distorting or turning away from the real world.* Freud said this occurred in one of two ways: (1) unconscious repressed material becomes excessively strong, overwhelming the ego, or (2) reality became so intolerably distressing that the ego caves in to "unconscious instinctual forces" (Freud, 1933, p. 16). In other words, psychosis is the result of a complete collapse of the ego's mediating function with reality. Freud saw a direct analog between dreaming (in which the influence of the external world is absent or greatly diminished) and psychosis: "The state of sleep involves a turning-away from the real external world, and there we have the necessary condition for the development of a psychosis" (Freud, 1933, p. 16).

The importance of the ego. The balance and resilience of the *ego* establishes whether the personality will function normally, neurotically, or psychotically. As a mediator of conflict, and a touchstone to reality, the *ego* is preeminent among Freud's personality trio. The *id* contains powerful impulses that energize personality, and the *superego* strives to implant cultural values, but it is the *ego* that carries out the "balancing act" that determines the quality of personality.

In short, a *neurotic* ego becomes so beleaguered by the urges of the id or the demands of the superego that it *partially withdraws* and no longer performs its mediating functions effectively. Subsequently the untamed impulses of the id crash headlong into the guilt-inducing moral searchlights of the superego. If the conflict between impulse and conscience becomes too agonizing, the ego may become *psychotic,* turning *completely away* from reality and leaving the mind vulnerable to takeover by the primitive impulses of the unconscious.

Latency stage (from six or eight years to about twelve). Beginning sometime between the ages of six to eight and lasting until puberty, children pass through a **latency stage,** *a time of dramatic decline in sexual interests and activities.* Although Freud did not insist that latency was inevitable in every child's life, he believed that for most children this was a time for establishing one's identity as male or female: boys solidifying their masculinity by joining gangs or playing with other pals, girls forming cliques and preferring the company of other girls. Freud saw the latency period as something of a "rest stop" between the intense dynamics of the Oedipal stage and the sexual awakenings of adolescence. In real life, however, most parents or professionals working with children of this age seldom find it to be a time of tranquillity.

During my internship, I spent some time working at a residential treatment home for latency-aged boys, and I recall the director (Albert Trieschman, who had been psychoanalytically trained) making the comment that "The only thing *latent* about the latency period is the parents' awareness of what's going on!" Or, "I would love to do dream interpretation, but first we've got to figure out how to get these kids to bed so they can dream!" Granted, some of this was said with humor, but life at this group home was far from tranquil, and the libidos of these boys far from latent.

Adolescence (twelve to eighteen). Surprisingly, adolescence receives scant attention in Freud's writings. This seems puzzling, since puberty is a time of obvious sexual awakenings. However, since Freud (1933, p. 147) placed primary emphasis on the early years ("Those [first five] years include the efflorescence of sexuality which leaves behind it decisive instigating factors for the sexual life of maturity"), it follows that by the time a child reaches adolescence, personality is pretty much a "done deal."

As Freud saw it, adolescence is a time when suppressed Oedipal conflicts flare up again, but now the adolescent may resolve them by falling in love with an older person of the opposite sex. The teenaged girl, for example, might get a "crush" on her high school coach or be "gaga" about a rock singer.

Balancing life and death. In keeping with his fondness for opposites, Freud viewed adolescence as a time when the peaking of libido instincts is counterbalanced by a heightening of aggressive instincts, as revealed in aggressive fighting, reckless driving, delinquency, and other forms of antisocial behavior. It is hardly surprising to psychoanalysts that the three leading causes of death among teens are motor vehicle collisions, homicide, and suicide. Part of this is because adolescence is a time of peak health, so relatively few teens die of coronaries or cancer. Still, Freud believed that aggression peaks during the adolescent years, accounting for the violent quality of many adolescent deaths.

Adulthood—the genital stage. During the **genital stage,** *the average person achieves the ability to reproduce and to enjoy heterosexual lovemaking.* Freud did not view homosexual adjustment as fully mature. This puts him at odds with gays and lesbians, much as his penis-envy views bring him into conflict with feminists. Freud felt that homosexuality, like other sexual problems or accomplishments, had roots in the Oedipal dynamics of the phallic psychosexual stage.

The homosexual male as "Mother." Freud saw the homosexual male (he had little to say about lesbians) as a child who had been pampered, doted over, and greatly protected by a maternal figure. Consequently, instead of *lusting* for Mommy as a sexual object during the Oedipal stage, *the homosexual male strongly identifies with (introjects) his mother.* Subsequently, during adolescence and adulthood, such a male becomes a *psychological mother* to other males in reenacting the mother–son love dynamics of the Oedipal period. In this way, Freud saw homosexuality and narcissism as closely related. By loving other males, the gay man is both a *maternal figure* and a *narcissistic lover of himself.* In this way, Freud would likely have described the disproportionate number of gays in theater and dance as indications of narcissism turned into creativity.

Beyond early adult life. Late in his life, affected by the destructiveness of WW I and his own struggles with cancer of the jaw, Freud introduced one of his most controversial constructs, the **death instinct:** *the "goal" of life is death.* In *Beyond the Pleasure Principle* (1920) Freud first introduced the *death instinct* construct, which some of his followers subsequently called *Thanatos* (a term Freud, himself, never liked). This idea was received with mixed reactions even by many psychoanalysts, perhaps because it was seen as a return to the reductionism of his long-abandoned *Project for a Scientific Psychology* (1895). Freud now balanced his *pleasure principle (id seeking immediate gratification)* with the "tendency to stability," which physicists call *entropy.* Freud referred to the ultimate reduction of tension in death as the **Nirvana principle:** *extinction is the goal of all life* (from the Sanskrit word *nirvanah,* which means the "blowing out" of a light).

Accordingly, Freud's final metapsychology combined his commitment to biology with his fondness for pairs. Now the two primary instincts *libido* and *thanatos* (life and death). frequently appeared *fused* in their expressions. Thus, sadism was seen as a fusion of hostility (death) and sex (eros). Even the basic mammalian response of fighting to protect oneself was seen as a fusion of self-love (eros) and hostility (death). Freud said that "the two classes of instinct hardly ever appear in a pure form, isolated from each other . . ." (Freud, 1927–31, pp. 138–139).

Developmental dualism. Psychoanalysis is a deeply divided dualism, and near the end of his career, we find Freud still struggling with the dualism of his day. Although his psychosexual stages unfolded in the realm of the *mind*, they derived their emotional color and psychological characteristics from the regions of the *body* where they first emerged. As we saw earlier, Freud used *instinct* as a mind–body bridge, performing a psychoanalytic sleight of hand whereby an instinct somehow morphed from a *physical* force in the body to a *psychic* "energy" in the mind.

By retaining the *unconscious id* as the backbone of psychoanalysis, in combination with his heavy reliance on *instinct theory,* Freud remained imprisoned by the logical positivism and "hard" sciences of his early mentors. We might say that Freud suffered, not from penis envy, but from *physics envy.* Above all else, he wished for his formulations to be regarded as "scientific," so near the end of his career—even after developing his dynamic, inclusive *metapsychology*—we find him returning to the biological reductionism of his earlier years, reducing everything to *eros* or *thanatos.*

What Makes a Person Unique?—Adult Personality Styles as Manifestations of Childhood Fixations

According to Freud, each person's **uniqueness** *is determined by the kinds of defense mechanisms or coping strategies an individual develops during childhood and carries over into adult life.* In the next chapter we will study defense/coping mechanisms in greater detail; here we need only understand that they are the ego's method for minimizing anxiety. Freud saw adult personality as characterized by the psychological features that were prominent during the particular psychosexual stage at which someone became *arrested,* or to which he *regressed.*

Since personality development follows the pathways of libido distribution, psychological differences among adults largely result from differences in libido allocations during infancy and childhood. Just as libido cathected at the mouth differs in quality from libido cathected at the anus or the phallus, the "oral" personality style differs in significant ways from the "anal" or "phallic" styles.

Libido—instinctual "tidal wave" of infancy. For Freud, *libido* distribution during infancy and early childhood determines the unique characteristics of each person's adult personality. Although *now* we might experience our *ego ("I")* as thinking, choosing, or steering ourselves, that was not our experience when we were toddlers. *Then* the id *("it")* employed its brawny biological determinism to make certain that *libido* got *its* way. We pretty much had to "go with the flow"—wherever libido took us.

Picasso, potty training, and loan officers. Freud believed that virtually all of the differences among adults could be traced back to infancy and early childhood when libido was first focused at the mouth, anus, genitals, or other body locations. Thus, if a miserly *(anal-retentive)* loan officer refuses to approve your mortgage request, he is merely reenacting with you his early potty-training conflicts with his parents. *Witholding* money from borrowers is simply an adult version of the toddler's stubbornly *withholding* feces from parents.

Today, few analysts strictly hold to such libido-based explanations, preferring instead a more inclusive social framework, in which a toddler's unresolved *autonomy–shame conflicts* around "holding" or "letting go" during toilet training might carry over into childhood as a reluctance to share toys, or into adult life as qualms about "letting go" of money. Many contemporary psychologists have difficulty accepting the idea that libido cathected at the anus affects one's lending behavior later in life, or that Picasso's paintings are simply an adult sublimation of his infantile urges to smear feces.

Personality styles as "recovery" from early hangups. Freud viewed adult personalties as shaped primarily by repression, fixation, or developmental arrests from the earliest years of life. For psychoanalysts, there are few "accidents"; nearly everything is determined (mostly *unconsciously*) during the first few years of life. Since those early days are frequently difficult for infants, psychopathology is always lurking around the next developmental corner. For Freud, the adult personality is "in recovery" from the past—tending to deal with the world in ways that worked during infancy and childhood. The following examples illustrate how adult functioning grows out of early experiences.

Oral personality styles. The **oral personality style** *includes fixations dating back to the oral stage of life (first year), when sucking was the engrossing, fulfilling, all-sufficient behavior.* Freud viewed mothers in general (and probably his own mother, in particular) as the primary source of all good feelings. Since the mother is the provider of nourishment as well as pleasure, she becomes the infant's first love object: "Sucking at the mother's breast is the starting-point of the whole of sexual life, the unmatched prototype of every later sexual satisfaction . . ." (Freud, 1916, p. 314).

This powerful oral cathexis of libido, established during the earliest months of life, remains a fountain of pleasure for adults who are fortunate enough to experience intimate sexual relations. For those who do not have access to sexual opportunities, other oral activities (e.g., eating, smoking, singing, chewing gum, sucking lollipops, talking, laughing, etc.) provide alternative, if less satisfying, sources of pleasure. According to Freud, either too much sucking or too much deprivation can result in *fixation* and formation of an *oral personality style* in adulthood.

As an aside, we might note how difficult it is to scientifically "falsify" or investigate a condition that is said to have been caused by either *too much* or *too little* of something.

Oral-incorporative versus oral-sadistic. If the fixation occurs relatively early in the oral stage, the adult might manifest an **oral-incorporative** or **oral-receptive personality** and be *characterized as a cheerful, overly dependent "Santa Claus type" who might tend to be intellectually naive and gullible—willing to "swallow" anything.* If fixation occurs later—after the infant has begun to teeth—the adult might manifest an **oral-sadistic personality** *characterized by cynicism, pessimism, or "biting" sarcasm.* This type of personality is more rare, however, and the more common oral personality is a jovial, talkative, affectionate person who responds to your attention by taking an interest in your activities, and by seeking your advice on many of his life's problems.

Gerald Ford's oral-incorporative/receptive personality style. Gerald Ford, thirty-eighth president of the United States, illustrates the oral-incorporative personality, known today as *dependent personality style*. In his memoirs, Ford said: "Throughout my political life, I always believed what I was told" (Ford, 1979, p. 5). Ford was the "Mr. Nice Guy" of politics. Even in his sleep he was Mr. Nice Guy. His wife, Betty, recalled that "One night I woke up and Jerry was talking in his sleep—he kept saying 'Thank you, thank you, thank you,' He was in a receiving line" (Vestal, 1974, p. 21).

Ford loved the campaign trail, where people saw and adored his benign, earnest, smiling exterior. In the brief eight months of his vice presidency, Ford visited forty states and flew 118,000 miles. From a St. Patrick's Day dinner in Charleston, South Carolina, to a lunch with seventh graders in Honolulu, no event was too small for Ford to attend. "There was a joke during this period that if you were having a banquet and couldn't get the local police chief to speak, ask Vice-President Ford" (Nessen, 1978, p. 5).

Anal personality styles. The **anal personality style** develops when *excessive amounts of sensual energy are devoted to issues of control ("holding on" or "letting go") during the second year of life.* The infant who masters the cycles of tension buildup and release gains a sense of mastery, autonomy, and self-control. Conversely, failure to do so, or prolonged efforts without success, jeopardize self-esteem.

Anal retentive versus anal expulsive. Two types of personalities develop around issues of toilet training. When parents focus excessively on cleanliness, toilet training, rules, or perfection, children sometimes grow up to become excessively preoccupied with orderliness, rules, details, perfection, punctuality, and control. They are sometimes stubborn, stingy, and withholding of goods or affection. Some children defecate in inappropriate places or at improper times. The child who soils himself may be unconsciously "getting even" with parents regarding issues of control, neglect, or harshness. In adults such "soiling" may become more refined (not literally in one's pants) but the psychological meaning may remain similar.

Since toilet training is the first time societal expectations intrude on the young child, a bowel movement becomes a kind of psychological barter between parent and child, in which the child who feels loved produces feces while on the potty, while the rejected child may withhold feces in retribution or stubbornness. Children in this stage frequently save their "gift" in the potty until all the family members can admire and congratulate them for so fine a production. Freud thought that fecal content in dreams symbolized something valuable like money, or in the case of females, a baby.

Jimmy Carter's anal-retentive personality style. We noted in an earlier chapter that Jimmy Carter, thirty-ninth president of the United States, illustrates the obsessive–compulsive or anal-retentive personality style. As president, Carter's engineering mind focused intensely on details—sometimes at the expense of the big picture—failing to see the forest because of the trees. During the final days of his presidency, for example, Carter remained obsessively focused on the sixty-six American hostages, even while Russia sent 85,000 troops into Afghanistan, 20,000 Moslem demonstrators stormed the American embassy in Pakistan, and his approval ratings languished at about 22 percent—lower than Nixon's during Watergate.

Lyndon B. Johnson's anal-expulsive personality style. Another type of anally fixated toddler may grow up to become the kind of person who impulsively "lets go" of control in unsuitable ways, at improper times, or in unbefitting circumstances. This kind of person may be disorderly and disorganized, often acting in cruel and destructive ways—"sh_tting on others," so to speak.

Lyndon B. Johnson, thirty-sixth president of the United States, manifested—quite literally—some of the characteristics of the anal-expulsive personality style. One visitor to the White House recalled the following incident:

> From the Oval Office he [LBJ] went into the bathroom adjacent, leaving the door open behind him. Around the corner from me loud expulsive sounds mixed in with his continuous talking. One of his young men squatted down just outside the open door and made notes. Another was hovering around him somewhere inside the bathroom. (Dugger, 1982, p. 21)

Some journalists attempted to put a positive spin on Johnson's crudities, referring to this as LBJ's "naturalness," but others described it as an abusive method of control, a way of diminishing the status of his subordinates.

Summary of Freud's Final Theoretical Synthesis: Metapsychology

We have now touched on most of the major aspects of Freud's vast creation known as psychoanalysis. Wrapping one's mind around such a profusion of theories is not easy—especially since Freud constantly created new models. It helps to synthesize these theories by *zones*. After discarding his biologically based *Project*, Freud subsequently evolved a series of increasingly higher-level models. Following his geographic "depth" model, he developed a *tripartite* model in which personality was the result of interactions among three agencies: *id, ego,* and *superego*. Now the mind could no longer be described in terms of sharply delineated layers with distinct boundaries, but appeared, instead, as a fusion of forces with indistinct boundaries.

However, even this trio of "agents" proved insufficient for representing the complexities of the mind, so near the end of his career, Freud formulated a *metapsychology* incorporating multiple variables (e.g., structural parts, economic motives, genetic stages) co-mingling with one another in the unique developmental experiences of a particular person. This is why Freudian theory is referred to as *dynamic* psychology, and why Freud is sometimes ranked with Einstein as one of the great thinkers of the twentieth century.

Thus, although Freud never completely overcame his "physics envy," his final metapsychology was more Einsteinian than Newtonian—more relative than absolute. Just as Einstein's theory of relativity blurred the once-distinct boundaries between matter and energy, psychoanalysis blurred the once-distinct boundaries between conscious and unconscious thought, between love and hate, between self and the external world, between dreams and reality. Freud's final portrait of personality was not painted with the primary pigments of Newtonian certainty, but rather with rainbow fusions of Einsteinian relativity.

SUMMARY OF FREUD'S FINAL CLINICAL SYNTHESIS: PSYCHOANALYSIS

From masseur to Buddah behind the couch. We learned earlier that when Anna O.'s relationship to her doctor became sexually overheated, Breuer allegedly "retreated in a cold sweat." Freud's response to erotic intensity was to ensconce himself behind the couch and formulate a theory of treatment that strictly regulated the boundaries between doctor and patient. He confessed that one of the reasons he had abandoned the use of hypnosis was to avoid "painful discussions" with female patients who made passes at him:

> As she woke up on one occasion [from hypnosis], she threw her arms round my neck. The unexpected entrance of a servant relieved us from a painful discussion, but from that time onwards there was a tacit understanding between us that the hypnotic treatment should be discontinued. I was modest enough not to attribute the event to my own irresistible personal attraction. . . . (1925–26, p. 27)

Following that incident Freud no longer used hypnosis, only "requiring the patient to lie upon a sofa while I sat behind him, seeing him, but not seen myself (1925–26, p. 28)." He candidly confessed that he didn't like to be stared at by other people for eight hours a day.

Freud retreated from the hands-on intensity and latent eroticism of massage and hypnosis, even seeking to avoid direct eye contact. Stationing himself behind the couch for the remainder of his career, Freud advised others to operate with the objectivity of surgeons (even while he ignored his own advice in the case of his daughter).

In short, although Freud began his career as a hands-on masseur, he quickly distanced himself from intense emotionality, taking up his permanent professional place behind the couch, where he described therapy changes in theoretical terms.

Key ingredients of psychoanalysis. In spite of the fact that very little "pure" psychoanalysis is practiced today, Freud's ideas have had such a profound influence on clinical practice that we will conclude our discussion with a brief outline of how orthodox psychoanalysis was first practiced.

Free association—the "fundamental rule." **Free association** means *saying whatever comes to mind* and is the core requirement of psychoanalysis. Freud explained it to patients in the following way:

> So say whatever goes through your mind. Act as though, for instance, you were a traveler sitting next to the window of a railway carriage and describing to someone inside the carriage the changing views which you see outside. Finally, never forget that you have promised to be absolutely honest, and never leave anything out because, for some reason or other, it is unpleasant to tell it. (Freud, 1911–13, p. 135)

Evenly suspended attention. In response to the patients' free associations, analysts were instructed to maintain *evenly suspended attention:* "It will be seen that the rule of giving equal notice to everything is the necessary counterpart to the demand made on the patient that he should communicate everything that occurs to him without criticism or selection . . ." (1911–13, p. 112, 114–115).

Attitude of the analyst. Freud advised analysts to keep their own emotions detached from the encounter so as not to intrude on the patient's free flow of psychic material: "I cannot advise my colleagues too urgently to model themselves during psycho-analytic treatment on the surgeon who puts aside all feelings, even his human sympathy, and concentrates his mental forces on the single aim of performing the operation as skillfully as possible . . ." (Freud, 1911–13, p. 115).

Freud's ideal psychoanalyst differed considerably from today's popular image of the counselor as a warm, caring person who listens empathically and responds by offering advice and suggestions for problem solving. Freud believed that by remaining neutral, the analyst provided a screen or mirror onto which patients could project unconscious fantasies, perceptions, and impulses: "The doctor should be opaque to his patients and like a mirror, should show them nothing but what is shown to him" (1911–13, p. 118).

Freud felt that such opaque objectivity was desirable for both the patient and the analyst: "for the doctor a desirable protection for his own emotional life and for the patient the largest amount of help that we can give him to-day" (1911–13, p. 115).

"Purification" of the analyst. Freud insisted (although he did not submit himself to anyone else for analysis) that personal analysis was a necessary preparation for clinical work. It was not enough, he wrote, that the analyst be an "approximately normal person." More was required: "It may be insisted, rather, that he should have undergone a psycho-analytic purification and have become aware of those complexes of his own which would be apt to interfere with his grasp of what the patient tells him" (1911–13, p. 116).

The ideal psychoanalyst is not so much cold or distant as *nonintrusive.* The analyst-in-training undergoes personal psychoanalysis to increase self-awareness, and thereby to minimize unconscious intrusions into the patient's material.

Summary of key ingredients of psychoanalysis. According to Freud, four key ingredients for successful psychoanalysis are (1) *frequent meetings* between a (2) *patient who follows the fundamental rule of free association,* and (3) an *analyzed ("purified") psychoanalyst,* who maintains (4) *evenly suspended attention.* As Freud described it, the analyst "lets the patient do nearly all the talking and explains nothing more than what is absolutely necessary to get him to go on with what he is saying" (1911–13, p. 124).

Further factors influencing the psychoanalytic process. Even under the best of circumstances, psychoanalysis invariably encounters "speed bumps" in the form of resistance, transference, and countertransference.

Resistance and working through. Freud used the term **resistance** to mean *"whatever interrupts the progress of analytic work . . ."* (1900–01, p. 517). Resistance makes its appearance in the form of a conflict with the analyst or a distraction of some kind. The analyst counteracts resistance by **working through:** *talking, examining, and reexamining the ways in which the patient "resists" treatment by unconsciously trying to obstruct or divert the analysis.* Although in common language "resistance" usually means obstinacy, stubbornness, or inflexibility—especially toward change—in psychoanalysis it means *anything* that threatens to derail the analytic process. Resistance can include the entire range of emotions from sleepiness and boredom, to excitement and erotic feelings, on the part of either the analyst or the patient.

Transference, countertransference, and transference neurosis. Therapy arrangements were designed by Freud to optimize **transference,** *the unconscious projection of emotions and perceptions from past relationships onto a significant person, such as the therapist),* and to minimize **countertransference,** *the unconscious projection of the therapist's emotions and perceptions onto the client.* Freud believed that when these conditions were met, the patient would unconsciously relate to the analyst in much the same way that he had related to significant adults earlier in life. Freud referred to this reenactment of early parent–child dynamics as the **transference neurosis:** *the emotionally intense connection of analyst and client.*

Freud saw *transference neurosis* as the main vehicle for healing. Through the re-creation of the child–parent dynamics with the analyst, an opportunity for re-parenting was present. Freud also viewed the transference neurosis as an important diagnostic tool, describing it as "a stereotype plate (or several such), which is constantly repeated—constantly reprinted afresh—in the course of the person's life . . ." (1911–13, pp. 99–100). Understanding such recurrent, stereotypic behaviors provided the analyst a psychological portfolio of how a particular person functioned with significant others.

Summary of the process of psychoanalysis. For Freud, the skillful management of resistance, transference, and countertransference constituted the essence of psychoanalytic treatment. Although "pure" psychoanalysis is rarely practiced today, Freud's theories emphasized the importance of maintaining appropriate boundaries with patients and the importance of understanding one's own unconscious before attempting to heal others.

FACING THE TOUGH TWINS

Is It Testable?

Recent investigations of psychoanalysis have been carried out at three different levels of analysis: in physiological, insight, and social zones.

Research in the physiological zone. Although psychoanalysis has historically moved *upward* from Freud's biological reductionism toward higher-level social considerations, recent advances in molecular biology and neurophysiology have led some researchers to investigate the biological correlates of classic psychoanalytic constructs. Levin (1991), for example, notes that neurological pathways connecting the left and right brain hemispheres by means of the corpus callosum are usually established at about three and one-half years of age. He postulates that *repression* is the process of blocking the input of the left cerebral hemisphere.

Gedo (1991) writes that "the weight of evidence suggests that the sense of self is originally a cerebellar function: the cerebellum forms maps of the body-in-space very early. . . . Later these maps are duplicated in the central parietal cortex" (p. 8). Gedo continues, "From the viewpoint of therapeutics, the cardinal implication of the new brain science is that treatment should be aimed at improving the information-processing skills available to the patient" (p. 9).

Research in the insight zone: Silverman's "Mommy and I are one" studies. Lloyd Silverman and his coworkers (1976, 1982, 1983, 1985) conducted a long-term research program investigating the role of unconscious thoughts in normal and patient populations. They used a device known as a tachistoscope (which flashes words or pictures so briefly—4 milliseconds—that they can presumably be recognized only at an unconscious level). Some phrases were designed to *reduce* anxiety (e.g., MOMMY AND I ARE ONE), some were designed to *increase* anxiety (e.g., CANNIBAL EATS PERSON), and some were *neutral* (e.g., PEOPLE ARE WALKING). These phrases were presented to normal subjects as well as to patients suffering from such disorders as schizophrenia, obesity, and depression. The findings are too vast to review in detail, so we will only discuss some studies carried out on seven groups of schizophrenics (total N over 200). When patients' responses to messages were compared, it was found that presentation of MOMMY AND I ARE ONE led to a temporary decrease of pathology in schizophrenic patients, while the I AM LOSING MOMMY intensified pathology. Silverman suggests that the fantasy of oneness with mother implies her "continual and unconditional presence" as well as the constant presence of "oral supplies." He concludes that the results "can be viewed as providing further experimental support for the psychoanalytic view of psychopathology" (Silverman, 1976, p. 630).

However, when Balay and Shevrin (1988) reviewed a large number of studies, they concluded that there was not a single instance of a real replication of one of Silverman's studies. They further suggested that whenever Silverman and his students suspected that a study might turn out to falsify or disconfirm a Freudian hypothesis, they would change their measures until the results lay in the predicted direction.

Research in the social zone: dancing with Mama. Other researchers (e.g., Condon & Sander, 1974) studied the mother–infant relationships by carefully analyzing movies (frame-by-frame) of mothers and their newborns. They found that as early as the first postnatal day, the neonate "dances" in precise synchrony with adult speech rhythms. By twelve to twenty-one days, infants copy adults' facial and manual gestures (Meltzoff & Moore, 1977). This is in contrast with the classical psychoanalytic notion of the newborn as an "unhatched" person. After reviewing numerous studies of infants and their caretakers, Lichtenberg (1983) concludes that neonatal research highlights the importance of object relations theory, but with a new twist: "The postnatal baby is a participant in and an activator of the dialogue, not simply a recipient" (1983, p. 17).

Transference in everyday life—reenacting earlier relationships. Although Freud's concept of *transference* referred mainly to unconscious dynamics occurring in the treatment situation, subsequent researchers have studied it more broadly—as it relates to daily life. Consistent with Freud's notions of *transference* and *repetition compulsion*, Swann (2005) found that people choose to interact with evaluators who affirm and verify their long-held self-images—*even when such images are negative*! Apparently people reenact earlier relationships by seeking out and maintaining relationships with others who affirm their beliefs about themselves.

Is psychoanalysis alive and well? Not surprisingly, the answer depends on whom you ask. Eysenck and Wilson (1973), two investigators known for their anti-Freudian biases, investigated 19 empirical studies of psychoanalytic concepts ranging from castration anxiety to oral sexuality, and identified serious methodological flaws that they claimed invalidated the findings. Kline, a psychologist with a more favorable estimate of Freudian theory, reviewed several hundred studies; while admitting that many concepts such as the death instinct and the pleasure principle are unscientific, he concluded that

"Many of the Freudian concepts most important to psychoanalytic theory have been supported, for example, repression and the Oedipus complex" (1972, p. 358).

No lack of research. Critics commonly claim that psychoanalysts practice by "faith," because there is little research about psychoanalysis. However, when Fisher and Greenberg (1977, 1985, 1996) evaluated over 2,000 studies, they concluded that many of Freud's "minitheories" are supported by research findings. For example, Freud asserted that *paranoia* was related to homosexual impulses, which in turn resulted from unresolved issues with the same-sexed parent. A majority of the better studies seem to support the validity of this idea. Freud postulated a relationship between early loss experiences and *depression* in adult life. Research did not support this idea but did confirm Freud's portrayal of the depressed person as passive or "orally fixated." Similarly, Freud's description of the "anal" personality as orderly and obstinate found strong research support. Research regarding the Oedipal dynamics of attraction between opposite-sexed parent and child and tension between same-sexed parent and child reported mixed results. The predicted attractions and tensions were in the directions suggested, but seemed to have little relationship to subsequent sexual adjustment. Finally, Freud's notion that dreams are disguised fulfillment of forbidden wishes was contradicted by current dream research.

Fisher and Greenberg conclude by pointing out that "Freud's statements and speculations add up to a series of minitheories rather than a grand integrated structure. . . . Overall, we are impressed how robust many of Freud's minitheories have shown themselves to be. Significant chunks of his theorizing have held up well to probing" (1996, pp. 266–267).

Still, since Freud formulated most of his ideas in metaphorical terms that are difficult to translate into operational definitions, psychoanalysis remains difficult to prove or disprove. As one personality psychologist put it, ". . . it is likely that no research will ever substantially affect what the adherents or the foes of psychoanalysis do or think about this theory" (Monte, 1999).

Is It Useful?

Psychoanalysis in schools. Not surprisingly, Freud's psychoanalysis, with its emphasis on childhood sexuality and "depth" analysis, has not been widely utilized by educators. The teaching of sexuality in schools is almost always a political nightmare, and many of the constructs of classical psychoanalysis are not classroom-friendly. Freud's notion that character development results from the fact that little boys want to "get it on" with Mommy, but are frightened that Daddy will castrate them, does not play well in Peoria. Kohlberg's six stages of moral development (Kohlberg, Levine, & Hewer, 1983) are much more classroom-friendly and have eclipsed Freud's Oedipal theories as an explanation for conscience development.

As we shall learn in subsequent chapters, educators have been far more interested in utilizing Erikson's (Chapter 8) psychosocial stages, or applying Piaget's (Chapter 10) cognitive stages. We could say that in school settings, Piaget gets an "A," Erikson and Kohlberg get "Bs", and Freud barely passes.

The workplace. Psychoanalysis hardly fares better in the workplace. When it comes to evaluating a worker's personality for purposes of hiring, firing, or promotion,

Freudian theory or techniques have seldom played a significant role. Corporations are more interested in job analysis than dream analysis, more concerned with measuring their own bottom line than in exploring an employee's unconscious. Consequently, *research-based personality tests* such as the MMPI or the Myers-Briggs Type indicator have been far more popular with businesses than the Freudian-based *projective tests* such as the Rorschach or the TAT.

Clinical or counseling settings. Freud's influence has been greatest in clinical or counseling settings, but even here psychoanalysis appears to be losing ground. The most important practical consideration has been *cost*. Even the most generous insurance carriers might pay for psychotherapy at the rate of one session per week, but Freud saw his patients *six days a week*, and even referred to the "Monday crust" (1911–13, p. 127) he had to break through after the Sunday layoff. No insurance carrier today would dream of subsidizing daily treatment, consequently, unless your last name is Rockefeller, Kennedy, or Gates, psychoanalysis—as Freud practiced it—is not going to be an option. In the real world, most psychoanalytically oriented psychotherapists see their clients twice weekly.

Psychoanalysis in everyday life. Psychoanalytic theory has become so much a part of Western culture that, like fish who are unaware of being wet, we frequently fail to realize how "soaked" we are in Freud. As a result of his work, most of us have more than a passing interest in our dreams. Although prophets and seers in all ages placed a high value on dreams, ordinary working people didn't put much stock in their own dreams until Freud came along and devoted over seven hundred pages (*The Interpretation of Dreams, Volumes 1 & 2,* 1900, 1900–01) to convincing people that dreams were *"the royal road to a knowledge of the unconscious activities of the mind"* (1900–01, p. 608). Freud found that "instead of bringing forward their symptoms," his patients "brought forward dreams." And, he said, "on this discovery the psycho-analytic method of treatment was founded" (1915–16, p. 83).

On the occasion of his lectures at Clark University, Freud again described dream interpretation as "the surest foundation of psycho-analysis, if I am asked how one can become a psycho-analyst, I reply: 'By studying one's own dreams' " (1910, p. 33).

Chapter Summary

Much of modern dynamic psychiatry is a reformulation of Freud. Unconscious motivation, defense mechanisms, transference, and countertransference are considered psychological bedrock by psychoanalytic clinicians. Until quite recently, however, psychoanalytic concepts have not been tested in the "wind tunnels" of academic research laboratories. It has been mostly in the turbulent crosswinds of clinical practice that psychoanalytic formulations have proven useful. Clinicians treating clients over extended periods of time repeatedly feel the powerful tugs of transference and the tempting entanglements of countertransference of which Freud warned. Resistance, in its myriad forms, is everywhere present, eager to sabotage and derail the healing process.

Historically, there has been little communication between academically based researchers and practicing clinicians, or between behaviorists, analysts, and humanists. Recently, however, this seems to be changing, and analysts are beginning to look at their discipline with more candor. *The Psychological Birth of the Infant* (Mahler, Pine, & Bergman, 1975); *Psychoanalysis and Behavior Therapy* (Wachtel, 1977); *Psychoanalysis and Infant Research* (Lichtenberg, 1983); *Contexts of Being* (Stolorow and Atwood, 1992); and *The Prisonhouse of Psychoanalysis* (Goldberg, 1990) are but a few of the books written by psychoanalysts themselves, seeking to evaluate Freud's insights in the light of current research findings.

Points to Remember

1. Over the course of his career Freud shifted from his biologically based beginnings to broader relationship and social issues. Even his most loyal of followers—his daughter Anna—tilted psychoanalysis away from Freud's focus on the unconscious processes of the id, to the more adaptive, coping functions of the ego.

2. Josef Breuer successfully removed Anna O.'s hysterical symptoms, utilizing *hypnosis* and *catharsis*. Anna developed a strong *erotic transference* for Breuer, who reportedly fled the house in a cold sweat and vowed to "never go through such an ordeal again" (Gay, 1988, p. 69). Freud improved upon Breuer's techniques (dropping hypnosis, utilizing catharsis, and elaborating on how to handle powerful transference–countertransference feelings) and founding *psychoanalysis*.

3. Freud developed a possessive relationship with his youngest daughter, Anna, whom he made the intellectual heir of psychoanalysis although she had no formal academic training in psychology or medicine.

4. Freud escaped the emotional intensity of his patients by discontinuing the use of hypnosis (which functioned to make them more uninhibited), and taking up his position behind the couch, from where he could analyze from a distance, avoid eye contact, and minimize emotional entanglements. He admitted that he didn't like to be "stared at . . . for eight hours a day."

5. Freud was undoubtedly attracted by the energy and beauty of his young mother and disappointed by what he perceived to be his father's nonassertiveness. It is not surprising that the Oedipus complex, castration anxiety, and repression became central components in his theory of personality development.

6. Freud had the ability to intensely focus in on a single fact, and then to generalize it into a larger context. His initial enthusiasm for cocaine illustrates how he assumed that his own experience—without further testing—would be the experience of others.

7. Like his admired mentors, Freud struggled to build psychoanalysis on a firm biological foundation. He soon abandoned his *Project,* and gave up trying to reduce everything to neurology. Although his subsequent theories were much more psychological in nature, using higher-level concepts, even in his later works we can detect a certain "physics envy."

8. Freud combined his early *topographic, structural, economic, genetic,* and *adaptive models* into a more encompassing *dynamic metapsychology.* He loved opposing pairs

and balanced psychoanalysis on the teeter-totter of *unconscious* versus *conscious*. Numerous other paired constructs permeate his theories (e.g., libido versus Thanatos, pleasure principle versus reality principle, etc.) Even his *tripartite* model of the mind (id, ego, and superego) ultimately boiled down to a major duel between id and ego.

9. Freud's final *tripartite* model of personality channeled energy (in the form of *libido* instincts) from sources in the body to agencies of the mind—*id, ego,* and *superego.* Freud was not obsessed with sex per se, but used *libido* to broadly include a variety of life energies. *Cathexis* and *anticathexis* were terms Freud formulated to describe libido distribution, much as we might describe the flow of fluid in a closed hydraulic system, or picture electrical current energizing lightbulbs or appliances.

10. Freud saw development occurring in stages characterized by the region of the body where a major concentration of energizing *libido forces* was located at a particular age: *oral* (birth to one year), *anal/muscular* (second year), *urethral* (third year), *Oedipal or phallic* (three to five years), *latency* (six or eight years to about twelve), *adolescence* (twelve to eighteen), and *adulthood.* Individuals might become *fixated* or *arrested* at any given stage of development by either too much or too little gratification. In times of stress, people tend to *regress* to earlier stages.

11. Uniqueness of personality is determined by the stage at which *arrest* or *fixation* occurs. A person with an *oral* personality style is focused on the sucking, eating, talking, or chewing pleasures of the earliest months of life. *Anal/muscular* personality styles may show *withholding* or *expulsive* behaviors corresponding to early toilet-training experiences, etc. Such dynamics importantly shape how one will relate to members of the opposite sex.

12. Rigorous research evaluating psychoanalysis is difficult to carry out because many of Freud's theoretical constructs were presented as metaphors. Recently, however, there has been renewed interest in experimentally evaluating core components of psychoanalytic theory. The results have been mixed, depending on the biases of the investigators, providing some support for analysts, as well as ammunition for their critics.

13. Although not a major influence in schools or corporations, psychoanalysis has profoundly influenced clinical techniques in a number of paradigms. Dealing with issues of *transference/countertransference, resistance,* and *working through* have become important aspects of training clinicians of a variety of schools of thought—the major exception being behavior therapists.

14. Freud's "iceberg" theory of the unconscious has had a profound influence on Western civilization. In daily life, we interpret dreams, analyzing Freudian "slips," and assert that those who disagree with our interpretations are "in denial." No other personality theory has had a greater impact on the way we see ourselves and others.

Key Terms

Aim   (195)
Anal/Muscular Stage   (201)
Anal Personality Style   (208)
Castration Anxiety   (202)
Cathartic Method   (180)
Condensation   (219)
Conscience   (194)
The Conscious   (190)
Countertransference   (212)
Death Instinct   (205)
Dreamwork   (219)
Economic Model   (195)
Ego   (193)
Ego-Ideal   (194)
Erogenous Zone   (200)
Female Oedipus Complex   (202)
Fixated   (199)
Free Association   (210)
Freudian Slips   (188, 220)
Genital Stage   (205)
Id   (193)
Identification   (200)
Impetus   (195)
Incorporation   (200)
Instincts   (195)
Latency Stage   (204)
Latent Content   (219)
Libido   (196)
Manifest Content   (219)
Metapsychology   (188)
Neurosis   (203)
Nirvana Principle   (205)

Object   (195, 200)
Oedipus Complex   (183)
Opposing Constructs   (188)
Oral Eroticism   (200)
Oral-Incorporative/Oral-Receptive
   Personality   (207)
Oral Personality Style   (207)
Oral-Sadistic Personality   (207)
Oral Stage   (200)
Parapraxis   (221)
Phallic Stage   (201)
Phallus   (201)
Pleasure–Unpleasure Principle   (193)
Preconscious   (191)
Primary Process   (200)
Psychoanalysis   (181)
Psychosis   (204)
Reality Principle   (201)
Regression   (199)
Resistance   (211)
Secondary Process   (201)
Source   (195)
Stage of Primary Narcissism   (200)
Superego   (193)
Transference   (212)
Transference Neurosis   (212)
Tripartite Model   (192)
The Unconscious   (191)
Uniqueness   (206)
Urethral Stage   (201)
Wish Fulfillment   (200)
Working Through   (211)

Web Sites

http://nyfreudian.org/index.html. The New York Freudian Society. This site is a solid resource for researching and finding specific topics on Freud's writings. It contains a list of all of his books.

www.freud.org.uk/index.html. The Freud Museum in London. This Web site is loaded with information about Freud. Read descriptions of his personal dreams and his interpretation of them, see hundreds of pictures, visit the museum store and buy funny and interesting gifts, and see the archives of research and letters Freud wrote and received.

www.enhypniomancy.com/Default.aspx#home. Dream Interpretation. If you're intrigued or plagued by a mysterious dream, visit this Web site to submit your dream for interpretation. While this Web site is not a scholarly resource, it's worth a visit.

Learning on the Lighter Side

As wise as Solomon? Understanding your dreams and slips may seem almost impossible (isn't that why people pay psychoanalysts?). Nevertheless, if you study your dreams and slips, it will deepen your self-awareness and might stimulate you to further study. This summer, instead of packing your beach bag with Tom Clancy, John Grisham, or Stephen King, you might try reading *New Introductory Lectures on Psychoanalysis, The Psychopathology of Everyday Life, and The Interpretation of Dreams.* That's a good cross section of Freud, and although you might find some of his notions outrageous or even offensive (like all that penis-envy stuff), you won't likely be bored, and you will come away from that reading more sensitive to the extraordinariness of the ordinary: "To the observer of human nature they [slips] often betray everything—and at times even more than he cares to know. A person who is familiar with their significance may at times feel like King Solomon who, according to oriental legend, understood the language of animals" (Freud, 1901, p. 199).

Analyzing your dreams. After you've had a dream that you can recall, take a few moments to analyze the meaning. Although analyzing your dreams won't earn you a diploma from a psychoanalytic institute, it might prove enlightening about your own personality, providing you another avenue for self-awareness. The following guidelines will help you.

1. Write down a brief summary of your dream(s) immediately upon awakening. Freud believed that the dreams of a single night make up the parts of an integrated whole. In attempting to make sense of your dreams, analyze them a piece at a time, allowing your mind to free-associate to various aspects of the night's dreams.

2. Distinguish between the **manifest content,** which is *apparent or obvious meanings,* and the **latent content,** which is *hidden elements in need of interpretation.* Remember there is a process Freud called the **dreamwork,** whereby the *usually censored impulses and emotions of the latent dream are converted into a more acceptable manifest dream.* Don't get too caught up in the *manifest* contents, which frequently occur as disconnected fragments or visual images. In order to derive the latent (true) meaning of your dreams you need to be aware that dreams undergo **condensation** (forming *new configurations from elements that in our waking state we would keep separate, but which have dynamic commonality*), and displacement (by which the *manifest content of the dream reproduces only a distorted picture of the underlying wishes, anxieties, or emotions*).

3. *Free-associate* to the various segments of your manifest dreams, letting your mind wander in the general area of your dream. Since dreams are constructed by your unconscious during a time when the normal censoring processes are less active, it shouldn't surprise you if you frequently come up with unintelligible associations at first; but stay with your associations—"go with the flow"—and don't worry about "making sense" of it all at first.

4. Be sensitive to symbolic representations. Freud saw the latent dream as comprised of "unacceptable, unconscious wishful impulses" (1915–16, p. 149), which are censored and thus appear only in *symbolic* or *distorted* form in the manifest dream. So, try to analyze your *associations* to various symbols, rather than searching for a single, true meaning. It's possible to free-associate to your dreams and learn about yourself, without necessarily buying the "whole nine yards" of Freud's interpretive scheme.

Analyzing your "Freudian slips" (more than verbal misstatements). Along with dreams, Freud felt that "slips" of the tongue, or other "accidental" behaviors, provide important clues to a person's inner thoughts. When the average person refers to a **Freudian slip,** he or she usually means *verbal errors that reveal an underlying (unconscious) wish, worry, or motive.* For example, a client, who was extremely worried that her

TABLE 6.3

Freudian Slips

Bungled behaviors: breaking a flower vase, using the wrong keys, interchanging medicines, having a carriage accident, pinching one's thumb, and taking the elevator to the wrong floor.

Errors: a child's name wrongly registered, husband and lover wrongly addressed, train missed, and a mother who "erroneously" said an expensive silver tea-service (a wedding gift) belonged to her youngest daughter (whom she wished would marry as well)

Forgetting impressions and intentions: a book not sent, committee meetings missed, postcard repeatedly not mailed, watch repeatedly left at home

Forgetting names and words: Freud forgot the names of Italian towns after war broke out between Germany and Italy

Misreading, misprinting, and slips of the pen and tongue: addresses wrongly written, substituting "insult" for "consult," or the woman who said that her soldier son was part of the 42nd "Murderers" instead of the 42nd "Mortars"

Losing or mislaying objects: A man who did not want to attend a certain social function unlocked a trunk and removed his formal attire, then went to shave. Upon his return he found the trunk locked, and with no available locksmith, he was forced to cancel the social function. When the lock was later sprung, the keys were found inside where they had been "mislaid"

Symptomatic and chance actions: lights left burning, watch not wound up, forgotten wedding dresses or lost wedding rings daughter's diagnosed melanoma was going to be fatal, told me that her daughter was going into the hospital for an *autopsy* (when she meant to say *biopsy*). There can be little doubt that this "slip" was a revealing indicator of the mother's anxiety about her daughter's prognosis.

The term **parapraxis** is translated from the German *fehlleistungen* and literally means *"faulty acts" or "faulty functions"*; it covers much more than verbal slips. The concept was invented by Freud, who used it broadly to refer not only to slips of the tongue, but to misreading, mishearing, forgetting, mislaying or losing objects, and other "mis" behaviors. Table 6.2 summarizes some of the parapraxes Freud covered in his book *The Psychopathology of Everyday Life* (1901).

Analyzing my own dream. Last evening, my wife and I shared a quiet supper together. She's a busy attorney, often arriving home after seven, and yesterday was typical. I had been working on this textbook for several hours, and had seen five clients in therapy, so by the time we finished eating we both felt "fried," and decided to unwind by watching a TV episode of "The Education of Max Bickford."

Max Bickford is a slightly crusty college professor, played by Richard Dreyfus, who believes in the old educational values of hard work, truth seeking, etc., and who is frequently at odds with administrators and colleagues. This episode centered around Bickford's nine-year-old son, Lester, who was working on a class assignment about Abraham Lincoln. Bickford, a history professor, was perturbed to discover that his son was writing the usual vanilla stuff about Lincoln: that he was the great emancipator of slaves, a sort of pre–Civil War Martin Luther King, Jr. So, in a fatherly way, Bickford pulled a few books from his library and showed his son that preserving the union—not freeing slaves—was Lincoln's primary concern. Keeping the country united was the issue he was willing to fight a war over. Lester revised his paper, trotted happily off to school, and promptly got in trouble with his teacher for his revisionist views regarding Lincoln.

After watching the Bickford episode, I decided to check my e-mail—assuming it wouldn't take much effort. I was wrong. There was a message from my senior editor expressing some concerns about an earlier chapter. So much for "relaxation." I promptly sat down and sent off an e-mail addressing the concerns. It was now nearly 11:00, and as I trudged upstairs to bed, I was concerned about what I felt was a misunderstanding, but I felt reasonably confident (at a *conscious level*) that my e-mail had cleared everything up. I tossed and turned, finally falling asleep; but awakening from a dream early the next morning, I decided to interpret it:

I wrote down all I could recall immediately upon awakening: Lester (Bickford) and I are riding in the back seat of a car together. It's an older automobile, somewhat like the Chrysler PT, with high-back front seats and a cavernous rear seat where a little boy could feel lost and separated from the driver and front-seat passenger. As we sit in back together, I am acutely aware that Lester feels small and alone, and that he is concerned about how the people in the front seat evaluate his performance. We are traveling home from Lester's first day at work—never mind that he is only nine years old!—and he thinks he has "blown it." I somehow omnisciently understand that the people in the front seat found him not only competent but "cute," so I reassure him that all is well. The end.

Free-associating to the *manifest content* of the dream, I recall how as a little boy, I occasionally rode in the back seat of a big Buick sedan. I remember how it left me feeling distanced from the folks up front. Another association: earlier in the week, Monty, my son, had left the corporate law firm where he had been working to begin a new job in the prosecutor's office. I had spoken with him by phone several times during the transition, reassuring him that he was doing the right thing by following his intuitions (he disliked practicing corporate law, and was taking a significant pay cut to work in the prosecutor's office).

Symbolism in this dream moves us from the *manifest* to the *latent content* of the *dreamwork*. The *manifest* dream appears to be a replay of the previous evening's TV episode, but there is a crucial difference. The Lester on TV was self-confident, almost cocky, as he went off to school to read his Lincoln report; and when the teacher challenged him, he stood his ground, defending his thesis, and dramatically telling his teacher "My dad knows more about history than you do!" In my dream, Lester was deeply concerned with how the people in the front seat were evaluating him, and not nearly so confident of his performance. I was confident Lester had done well his first day on the job, and I reassured him that he was OK with the people up front, but he was much more restrained than in the television episode.

Interpretation: My unconscious used the *happenings of the day and segments of the TV episode* to compose the *dreamwork*. Sitting in the back seat of that sedan, I was *both* Lester and his father. As Lester's father, I was reassuring and confident, as I had been with Monty earlier in the week—as Professor Bickford had been with his son during the previous evening's television episode. That's the *manifest* content: "Daddy is here, everything is going to turn out fine." But in the *latent* dream, I was the worried little boy, feeling small and alone in the back seat of that huge Buick sedan, concerned that the people up front (my senior editor and other high-level decision makers) were not pleased with my job performance. In real life, I believed I was a capable writer, and assumed that I was doing a good job; but the previous evening's e-mail had reminded me that I was definitely a passenger, not the driver of this huge sedan driven by my publisher.

Looking Ahead

In the next chapter we will see how Freud's late-career shift in focus—from the id to the ego—was reinforced and expanded by his daughter Anna in her classic work *The Ego and the Mechanisms of Defense* (1946). Since then, there has been no turning back, and subsequent generations of psychoanalysts have spent more of their theoretical efforts elucidating the ego than tracing the unconscious currents of the id.

Melanie Klein, a mother of three, expanded psychoanalytic theory from an *intrapsychic* system designed to deal with internal conflicts of the mind, to an *interpersonal* theory concerned more with the interactions between infants and their caretakers. By including mothers in the analytic equation, Klein brought about a shift that became known as *object-relations theory*. This emphasis on infant–caretaker interactions has been continued in more recent times by theorists who have blended *self* psychology with psychoanalysis (e.g., Mahler, Kohut, Kernberg, and others). We will examine their work in more detail shortly.

chapter 7

The Relational Self of Object-Relations Theories

The *Coping Self* of Anna Freud, the *Persecuted Self* of Melanie Klein, and the *Conflicted Self* of Karen Horney

(With Cameo Appearances by Heinz Kohut, Otto Kernberg, Donald W. Winnicott, and Margaret Mahler)

IN THIS CHAPTER YOU CAN

1. Discover that Anna Freud, Melanie Klein, Erik Erikson, Donald Winnicott, and Margaret Mahler all worked with children, which nudged psychoanalysis in a more *interpersonal* direction.

2. Learn how *coping strategies* (historically known as *defense mechanisms*) are used by people to protect themselves from being overwhelmed by anxiety.

3. Realize that Melanie Klein saw *weaning* as a pivotal *interpersonal milestone*. Klein emphasized the importance of *early interpersonal relations* between the infant and the mother (caretaker), making her one of the pioneer founders of *object-relations theory*. She also invented *play therapy*.

4. Guess that it was probably because of her own encounters with death and war that Klein perceived the minds of infants and children to be *permeated with images of death, destruction, sadism, and murder*—hardly a picture of childhood "innocence."

5. Appreciate how Kohut's object-relations contrasted with Klein and agreed with Mahler in emphasizing the *warm bonding* that occurs between mothers and newborns.

6. Learn how Karen Horney, the first feminist psychoanalyst, grew up amid *conflict* and *rejection*, because her father strongly believed women to be inferior to men.

7. Understand why practicing psychoanalysis during the Great Depression led Horney to conclude that *culture*—not libido—was the most important influence on personality.

8. See if it makes sense to describe personality as composed of *four selves: (1) despised real self, (2) positive real self, (3) idealized self*, and *(4) actual self*.

9. Admire Horney for challenging Freud by asserting that *womb envy* and *breast envy* in little boys are the counterparts of *penis envy* in little girls.

10. Learn how Otto Kernberg, like Klein, emphasized sex and aggression.

11. Explore the meaning and importance of Winnicott's notion of the *transitional object*.

12. Discover how Margaret Mahler, a pioneer investigator of object-relations theory, used a standardized setting to carefully study interactions between infants and their mothers.

13. Realize that *defense/coping mechanisms* have stood the test of clinical practice and research scrutiny.

How *Sublimation* Worked for Me

Most of us can recall times when we successfully reduced our anxiety by "not thinking" about something or by mastering a task. We can probably remember occasions when we effectively managed our sexuality or redirected our anger. In this chapter we will learn how coping/defense mechanisms function to keep anxiety at bay, aggression from becoming brutal, or sexuality from running amok. When adequate coping mechanisms are in place, such managing of impulses takes place automatically, unconsciously—without thinking it through.

I recall an occasion during my graduate studies when the coping mechanism of *sublimation* worked particularly well for me. I had been working for weeks on a term paper that would constitute my entire grade in a child psychopathology course. When I finally finished the paper and received my semester grades, I was outraged to discover that the professor had given me a "B+" instead of the "A" I felt I clearly deserved. I was so agitated, I barely slept for an entire night. Early the next morning, I decided I would "show him," and I promptly began rewriting the paper. After making some of the changes he suggested, I submitted it to a leading psychology journal for possible publication. Months passed, I heard nothing, but finally I received word that it had been accepted for publication. I don't know who was more excited, I or my professor. *Sublimation* of rage had transformed my "B+" term paper into my first professional article (Berecz, 1968).

Freud viewed sublimation as one of the highest forms of redirecting instinctual impulses: "Sublimation . . . is what makes it possible for higher psychical activities, scientific, artistic, or ideological, to play such an important part in civilized life" (1927-31, p. 97). Sublimation (when you can pull it off) is *sublime*. Instead of going to my professor's office and punching his lights out, I rechanneled all this energy into something that ultimately made us both happy.

From Freud's Biological Reductionism Toward the Beginnings of an Agentic Self

Freud's lifelong goal was to create a scientific model of the mind that was consistent with the *biological reductionism* embraced by his mentors. Throughout his career, he focused primarily on the biologically based *id* instincts of aggression and sex. It remained for others to move psychoanalysis toward a broader concern with *adaptive functioning of the self (ego)* in the real world of *interpersonal relations*. This revolution gained momentum from the most surprising quarters—within Freud's own family. Whereas many of Freud's earliest and most promising disciples (e.g., Alfred Adler and Carl Jung) left psychoanalysis because of theoretical squabbles, the real revolution was an "inside job" led by such "loyalists" as his daughter Anna and a housewife named Melanie Klein. Together with Karen Horney, the first feminist psychoanalyst, and an art teacher named Erik Erikson, they shifted psychoanalysis away from Freud's biologically based *intrapsychic* analysis of the *id* (in the *Physiological Zone*) to focus more broadly on the *ego* and on *interpersonal dynamics* in the *Insight* and *Social Zones*.

Unwitting "midwives" for the births of object-relations and ego psychology.
Anna Freud (1895–1982) began her career teaching at a small school attended by the
children of her father's patients and friends. While there, she hired, befriended, and
trained an erstwhile art teacher named Erik Erikson (1902–1994), who subsequently
became a luminary among the new wave of ego analysts. Working mostly with children, Anna Freud (along with her rival, Melanie Klein, and her protege, Erik Erikson)
rerouted Sigmund Freud's psychoanalysis in directions that focused less on intrapsychic conflicts and more on how a child copes in the real world. As Anna Freud put it:
"If in the outer world the level of good relations with the parents rises, so does the
prestige of the Super-ego. . . . If the former is lowered, the Super-ego is diminished as
well . . . " (A. Freud, 1926, 1927, pp. 48–50).

Anna Freud and Erik Erikson both emphasized the ego's ability to *cope* and *adapt*.
Anna's theory and terms sounded similar to her father's psychoanalysis; however,
instead of focusing on the id and unconscious processes, she emphasized how the
ego copes with anxieties by using defense mechanisms. Similarly, Erikson also
remained close to Freud's original terms and vocabulary, but he infused them with
an *interpersonal, adaptive* emphasis (which we will discuss in the next chapter). This
new emphasis, promoted by Anna Freud and Erik Erikson, came to be known as *ego
psychology*.

Object-relations theory. In a related development, two women—also working
with young children—broadened Freud's psychoanalysis into what would become
known as **object-relations theory,** which is the *developmental psychology of early relationships with parents or caretakers*. (Note: the "object" in *object relations* usually refers to the
mother, but may include favorite toys, teddy bears, blankets, or other nonhuman
"objects" with whom a baby interacts.) Melanie Klein (1882–1960) saw the mother's
breast as the primal source of all things—both good and evil. For Klein, *weaning* was
the fulcrum of early development and *relationship* with the mother—not instinctual
conflicts—became her primary focus.

Margaret Mahler (1897–1985) also emphasized the importance of the close relationship between the newborn and the caretaker, borrowing the term *symbiosis* from
biology to describe this relationship. **Symbiosis** is the association or living together of
two dissimilar organisms where neither is harmed, and one or both benefit from the
relationship.

Together, Klein and Mahler cofounded what became known as *object-relations theory*.

Object relations versus ego psychology. We need not draw too fine a distinction
between object-relations theory and ego psychology; both see the baby's personality as
shaped by the surrounding interpersonal world. *Object-relations* theorists placed great
emphasis on the parent-child relationship as the fountainhead of all later psychological achievements and/or problems. *Ego analysts* also recognized the importance of early
relationships, but emphasized the work of an *adaptive ego* within a more classical
Freudian framework. Both ego analysts and object-relations theorists moved beyond
Freud's biological determinism that designated the id as the engine of personality. Instead, they saw the earliest relationships between newborns and their caretakers as setting the tone for all later development. In this new emphasis, *relationships* replaced
libido as the center of personality.

Research with infants has supported this view. When researchers use video cameras to record interactions between mothers and newborns, they find that babies are primed for social relationships. From the earliest days of neonatal life, babies carefully study and imitate their caretakers' facial expressions, voice rhythms, and other social cues. In short, babies are far more socially oriented and much less biologically driven than Freud thought. More about this later.

A blossoming agentic self. This shift from id to ego was accompanied by an emerging *agentic self.* Freud's *ego* was caught between biologically driven urges and social constraints—a *surrounded self* that was pressed on one side by the biological urges of the id for instant gratification, and circumscribed on the other by the superego's counter-demands for social conformity. Still, even amidst all this conflict, Freud's ego (self) functioned as a mediator or peacemaker between biological urges and societal values. Anna Freud took this further, highlighting the ego's *coping* and *adaptive* capacities. Similarly, Melanie Klein emphasized the ego's ability to survive an inner world permeated with persecution, chaos, and violence by "splitting" trouble into manageable portions and working out the conflicts with a caretaker in the real world. Karen Horney believed that the child's *self* responds to feelings of helplessness and hostility by first forming a *despised self* and then replacing this with an *idealized self.* Margaret Mahler concluded that the newborn's success in forming a *self* depends mainly on the quality of the mother-infant bond.

Taken together, these shifts facilitated the blossoming of a more vibrant *ego* in the ensuing work of psychoanalysts and provided a foundation for the fuller flowering of *self theories* in the subsequent work of constructivists, humanists, and existentialists, whom we will consider in later chapters.

Background Check

Anna Freud—a very special daughter. Born the last of his six children, **Anna Freud**—"little Annerl"—became her father's favorite. He once described her to Ernest Jones as "the most gifted and accomplished of my children . . . full of interest for learning, seeing sights, and getting to understand the world" (Gay, 1988, p. 434).

Freud's relationship to Anna had a protective quality that might have been appropriate when she was a child, but appeared overly possessive as she entered adulthood—reaching a peak during Freud's later years when he was struggling to survive cancer. As Anna grew to maturity, she became firmly installed as her father's secretary, confidante, representative, colleague, and nurse. "She became his most precious claim on life, his ally against death" (Gay, 1988, p. 442).

Carrying the psychoanalytic torch. Trained as a teacher, Anna taught in a girls' school during her early twenties, but even as a young child, she had listened with interest to her father's discussions with visitors and she subsequently decided to earn a medical degree and become a psychoanalyst. Freud, however, encouraged her to become a lay (nonmedical) analyst instead, and sometime in 1918 he took her into analysis. Subsequently she began to appear with her father at various international conferences and by 1923, friends began commenting (much to Freud's delight) that his daughter's style was indistinguishable from his own.

Protecting the flame. The latter part of Freud's career included a series of painful surgeries necessitated by cancer of his jaw. During these years Anna functioned not only as her father's caretaker and nurse, but also as guardian of the psychoanalytic flame. She, of all the women in Freud's life, best understood his mind and supported his work. As her father became increasingly weakened by his illness and surgeries, Anna grew correspondingly more protective, both of his health and of his psychological formulations. In developing her more ego-oriented approach to psychoanalysis, Anna was not attempting to undermine her father's orthodoxy nor to supersede him; she would have done nothing to sully her father's reputation or subvert his theories. On the contrary, she always remained her father's protector, caretaker, and ardent admirer.

Inadvertently opening the dam. Anna was trained as a teacher before becoming an analyst, so it's not surprising that she was one of the first to apply psychoanalysis to children. Anna's first patients were the orphaned little sons of her deceased sister, Sophie. By getting them to share their dreams and stories, and by questioning them about such mysteries as where babies come from, she concluded that six-year-old Ernstl's fear of the dark had been triggered by his mother's warnings that if he did not stop playing with his penis, he would become very sick.

Anna began working with other children as well, and by the mid-1920s she had established herself as a leading child analyst, upstaged only by the spirited Melanie Klein (if, indeed, the apple of Freud's eye could be upstaged by another analyst).

Anna's application of psychoanalysis to children reshaped her father's theory in more practical and interpersonal directions. Anna also trained and psychoanalyzed Erik Erikson, an art teacher with only a high school diploma, who became a leading figure in modifying psychoanalysis into a more interpersonal, social-psychological theory.

Zeitgeist

During the 1920s and 1930s psychoanalysis was awash in conflict, but it was a creative, heuristic conflict. Two of the major players were Anna Freud and Melanie Klein, both child analysts who saw themselves as loyal to Freud, but who disagreed sharply regarding key issues. This created a climate of intellectual ferment that ultimately freed psychoanalysis from the biological constraints of Freud and his authoritarian mentors.

Innovative child analysts—in conflict. Anna Freud and Melanie Klein disagreed sharply on how treatment ought to be conducted with children. Klein treated children much as she might have psychoanalyzed adults, viewing a child's play activities as similar to an adult's free associations or dreams. She believed that a child's play provided direct access to the deeper layers of the unconscious. Anna Freud passionately disagreed. Child analysis, she asserted, could not be carried out with the usual tools of free association or dream analysis. Instead, a long preparatory phase was necessary to establish the analyst as a special sort of teacher, assisting the young patient in understanding herself and in coping with a puzzling outer world: "The child analyst who interprets exclusively in terms of the inner world is in danger of missing out on his patient's reporting activity concerning his—at the same time equally important—environmental circumstances" (A. Freud, 1965, pp. 50–51).

Controversy stimulated creativity. Anna and Melanie's disagreements stirred lively debate and the net effect was to attenuate the importance Sigmund Freud had placed on anatomy and biology and to shift attention to higher levels of analysis—*object-relations* and *adaptive ego functions*. By their example, Anna Freud and Klein communicated that it was permissible to modify psychoanalysis in more practical, ego-oriented directions. Anna specifically stated that analyzing *conscious* processes did not mean one was rejecting her father's psychoanalysis: ". . . whenever . . . research was deflected from the id to the ego—it was felt that here was a beginning of apostasy from psychoanalysis as a whole. . . . But the definition immediately loses all claim to accuracy . . ." (Anna Freud, 1946, pp. 3–4).

Subsequent generations of psychoanalysts saw their goal as understanding the mind from the perspective of the *ego* instead of the *id*—i.e., most modern psychoanalysts are *ego analysts* or *object relations theorists*. In this, they took their cue from Freud's own daughter, who opened the dam that allowed psychoanalytic theory to flow in the direction of the ego, effectively draining the id of the power and preeminence it had held in her father's formulations.

Changing the rules when working with children. In her first book, *An Introduction to the Technique of Child Analysis* (1926, 1927), Anna Freud consolidated her reputation as a child analyst and intensified her controversy with Klein by insisting that psychoanalysis with children ". . . follows its own rules, determined by childish nature and temporarily independent of analytical theory and technique" (1926, 1927, p. 45). She said that a child analyst must present herself or himself to the child as interesting, useful, and protective, thereby creating "a tie between us, which must be strong enough to sustain the later analysis" (1926, 1927, p. 13). Although Anna agreed with her father that psychoanalysts working with adults ought to "remain impersonal and shadowy. . . . a blank page on which the patient can inscribe his transference-fantasies, somewhat after the way in which at the cinema a picture is thrown on an empty screen," she insisted that "the children's analyst must be anything but a shadow" (1926, 1927, pp. 37, 41). Anna asserted that the child analyst must also address issues with "living persons, existing in the outer world and not enshrined in memory. . . . Here again is a double work, from within and from without" (1926, 1927, p. 61).

ASKING THE BIG FOUR QUESTIONS

Having discussed the "Big Four Questions" in relation to Sigmund Freud's classical theory, we will consider them only briefly in the case of Anna's formulations, since she attempted to conduct her work in a way that was congruent with her father's theories. Her work differed from her father's primarily because she worked with children and found it necessary to *actively cultivate a positive transference* (Anna was no Buddah-behind-the-couch). In addition to her work with children, Anna extensively elaborated the notion of **ego defense mechanisms,** or *unconscious strategies that the ego employs for keeping anxiety, guilt, unacceptable impulses, and other threats to the ego out of awareness.*

What Are the Parts?

Although Anna's "parts" list includes most of her father's terms (e.g., id, ego, and superego), she shifted emphasis, concluding that analyzing the *ego* was more helpful in understanding children than tracking the arrests or regressions of their unconscious libido instincts.

What Makes a Person Go?

Anna Freud's shift toward the ego meant that she viewed personality as shaped more by ego-based coping mechanisms than by id-driven instincts. The first subheading in her classic book on defense mechanisms (1946) is entitled: "The Ego as the Seat of Observation." Anna did not reinvent her father's theory—she still used the same vehicle, but she changed chauffeurs. The publication of her book put the *ego* in the driver's seat, while the *id* was relegated to the passenger seat.

What Makes a Person Grow?

On the surface, Anna did not appear to deviate from her father's theory of psychosexual stages (oral, anal, phallic, genital). However, by emphasizing *ego* defenses and coping strategies, she transformed her father's biopsychology into a more social psychology. This trend flowered even more fully in the work of her student Erik Erikson.

What Makes a Person Unique?

We learned in the previous chapter that Sigmund Freud understood uniqueness mostly in terms of early fixations and arrests (sometimes referred to as *"originology"*). Thus, the meat cutter would be seen as having sublimated his infantile aggressive urges to cut and kill into a profession that puts meat on your table. In other individuals, the same urges to cut might take the form of pursuing a career in surgery or wood carving. In any event, Sigmund Freud traced personality variations seen in adult life to libidinal fixations of the past—mostly the first six years. By contrast, Anna Freud—focusing more on the present and the future than on the past—saw uniqueness in how each person's *ego adapted and coped* with current stresses and anxieties.

DEFENSE MECHANISMS—ANNA FREUD'S BRIDGE FROM CLASSICAL PSYCHOANALYSIS TO EGO ANALYSIS AND OBJECT RELATIONS

Introduction to Defense Mechanisms

Anna Freud's lasting legacy is her elaboration of defense mechanisms. She originally discussed ten defense mechanisms *(regression, repression, reaction-formation, isolation, undoing, projection, introjection, turning against the self, reversal,* and *sublimation)* to which we will add *denial, intellectualization, rationalization, displacement,* and *substitution,* bringing our total to fifteen. Although Sigmund Freud was the first to discuss defense mechanisms, he did so mostly in relation to the *id*. Anna saw defense mechanisms not only assisting the *ego* in dealing with forbidden *instinctual urges,* but also in coping with *real* anxiety arising from outside: "In the same early period in which it [the ego] becomes acquainted with dangerous internal instinctual stimuli it experiences also 'pain' which has its source in the outside" (A. Freud, 1946, pp. 73–74).

Do "defense" mechanisms or "coping" strategies differ? Defense mechanisms were originally formulated by Sigmund Freud to explain how neurotic individuals struggled to function effectively in spite of their hangups; however, as psychoanalysis became more ego-oriented, defense mechanisms expanded beyond their clinical meanings to include **coping mechanisms,** *or adjustment strategies used by normal persons to cope with anxiety.*

Recent studies comparing *defense* mechanisms and *coping* strategies find that they do *not* appear to differentially affect experimental outcome measures. Cramer (1998) carefully differentiated between defense and coping mechanisms on the basis of theoretical variables (e.g., conscious versus unconscious, or intentional versus unintentional), but when she searched for differences in how *defense* or *coping* affected psychological or physical health, she found none. Throughout the remainder of our text, we will consider defense mechanisms and coping strategies as referring to similar processes.

Understanding Defense/Coping Mechanisms

Repression and regression—defense/coping mechanisms that span the rest. *Repression* and *regression* span the entire developmental range and form the foundation for *all* other coping/defense mechanisms. Defense mechanisms are *unconscious* strategies for reducing anxiety, and it is through *repression* that forbidden urges and thoughts get pushed out of awareness. So, repression isn't just one of a dozen different defense mechanisms, it is *the* "grand daddy" of them all! Without repression there would be no other defense mechanisms.

Regression constitutes a return to earlier forms of defense or coping, and it also spans the entire range of coping/defense mechanisms. Let's look at both of these in more detail.

(1) Repression reduces anxiety by *excluding awareness from consciousness,* as in the case of an aging father who fails to recognize his feelings of jealousy and hostility toward a young, athletic son. Freud referred to repression as the "cornerstone" of psychoanalysis: "The theory of repression became the corner-stone of our understanding of the neuroses . . ." (1925, pp. 29–30).

(2) Regression *psychologically transports oneself back to a previous time in which former fixations and bygone defenses were prevalent.* Like repression, regression functions in combination with all other defense mechanisms. Operating somewhat like a shuttle bus at a "psychological antique mall," *regression* transports the user back in time, allowing him to reuse coping "tools" from earlier eras. During times of stress, people typically return (regress) to familiar coping/defense strategies from earlier days.

TABLE 7.1

Summary Table of Defense/Coping Mechanisms

NAME AND DEFINITION

Primitive/ Narcissistic Mechanisms	**Identification:** reduces anxiety by excluding awareness from consciousness	An inner-city child overwhelmed with anxiety about his future "becomes" Michael Jordan
	Denial: distorts reality to protect ego from external threats	Bill Clinton's Famous Phrase "I did not have sex with that woman!"
	Reversal: reverses both aim and content of an instinct to make impulses acceptable	Sadism turning to masochism, with the self becoming a passive, dominant lover
	Turning Against the Self: turns hatred or other unacceptable emotions against the self, instead of others	The little girl who hates her mother, but redirects the hatred toward herself
Intermediate Mechanisms	**Undoing What Has Been Done:** attempt by symbolic or motor action to make a past happening nonexistent	An adolescent scrubs his hands compulsively after masturbating in an attempts to "undo" his guilt-producing behavior
	Isolation: removes an instinctual impulse from its emotional context, so the idea is isolated from feelings	A parent springs into action to remove his or her child's implied finger from barbed wire
	Reaction-Formation: holds off unacceptable impulses by emphasizing opposite thoughts and behavior	A person attracted to pornography might become a moralistic leader against it, but get unconscious gratification from having to "investigate" it
Sophisticated/ High-level Mechanisms	**Intellectualization:** copes with instinctual conflicts by translating them into intellectual terms	A celibate priest spends inordinate amounts of time writing about or studying sexuality in order to control strong impulses
	Rationalization: devises a plausible explanation for engaging in forbidden behavior	A woman married to an unfaithful man keeps finding reasons for his persistent affairs to protect her own self-esteem
	Projection: unconsciously projects one's unacceptable impulse onto others	A closet homosexual may accuse everyone around him of being gay
	Displacement: allows unacceptable parts of the unconscious to bypass resistance and appear in dream thoughts	A man who is abused by his boss targets his anger at his wife and children
	Substitution: leaves the source, aim, and energy of an impulse the same, but changes the target	An adolescent male dances or masturbates instead of fulfilling his sexual impulses with another person
	Sublimation: transforms unacceptable impulses into socially prized behaviors	A gay artist redirects his sexual impulses into acclaimed sculptures of the male body

(3) Identification means *incorporating another person's values, opinions, ideas, and skills as a whole—"lock, stock, and barrel."* The key to understanding *identification* is in realizing how undiscriminatingly and holistically this process occurs in the very young. The baby or young child simply *takes in* another's entire personality—*becomes* that other person. The beleaguered inner-city child, overwhelmed with anxiety about his future, *becomes* Michael Jordan. The daughter of physician parents about to divorce *becomes* Brittany Spears. Freud described identification as "the assimilation of one ego into another, as a result of which the first ego behaves like the second" (S. Freud, 1933, p. 63). Freud believed that identification was the very first attachment to another person. Some see the Christian practice of the Eucharist as a similar form of identification in which believers incorporate the "body of Christ."

Freud believed that at a later stage of development, the Oedipal boy coped with lust for his mother and the accompanying anxiety that his father would castrate him by *identifying* with his father—by *becoming* Dad. In the boy's *identification* with his father, Freud saw the foundations of the *superego,* which he described as "the representative for us of every moral restriction, the advocate of a striving towards perfection . . ." (Freud, 1933, p. 67).

During adolescence, *identification* is based on attitudes, goals, opinions, and other aspects of life that the young person takes on—e.g., the qualities of sports heroes, media stars, or admired teachers. Thus, we can see that *identification* is used differently—means different things—at different ages. This shouldn't surprise us, because we are aware of how drastically language usage changes from two to sixteen.

(4) Denial (in words, actions, play, or fantasy) *defends the ego against external threats,* as compared with repression, which defends against threatening *internal instincts.* Denial is a coping mechanism of the psychologically immature, no longer useful when the ego becomes mature enough to realize others "see through" the crude distortions of reality that denial attempts. When confronted with an empty cookie jar and crumbs on the kitchen counter, the toddler remains resolute in her denial—"No eat cookies Mommy!"

"I'm doing a lot better now that I'm back in denial."

(5) Reversal is a process that *reverses both the aim and the content of an instinct.* The sadomasochism lover uses *reversal* when he or she substitutes a passive aim (to be dominated or tortured) for the original less-acceptable active aim (to dominate or torture). Reversal of *content* is accomplished by changing (unacceptable) hatred into love. Thus the man who visits the female dominatrix is seen by psychoanalysts as having reversed his own anger and urges to dominate by becoming a punished, compliant lover.

(6) Turning against self involves *turning hatred or other unacceptable emotions that the child feels toward others, against the self, instead.* Anna Freud (1946, pp. 48–50) wrote about a young girl who experienced hatred toward her mother, but who assuaged her guilt by redirecting this hatred away from her mother and turning it on herself. As this girl grew older and entered adolescence she began using the process of *projection.* Her self-hatred was now transformed into the conviction that she herself was hated or persecuted by others. She thus found relief from her guilt and self-loathing, but at the cost of adopting a paranoid attitude that Anna Freud reported "was a source of very great difficulty in her both in youth and adult years" (1946, p. 49).

(7) Undoing is a defensive maneuver by which a person uses *symbolic rituals or motor actions to magically make past happenings nonexistent.* The adolescent who feels guilty about masturbating and compulsively scrubs his hands until they are raw—allegedly to make certain there are no germs present—might be trying to magically *undo* the guilt surrounding erotic self-stimulation.

(8) Isolation removes *an instinctual impulse from its emotional context, thereby isolating an idea from its accompanying feelings.* By dissolving the links between thoughts and feelings, a person can keep a frightening or horrible idea in mind without seeming to be upset by it. Thus, a psychotic person might believe that his intestines are rotting, yet not be emotionally upset by it. Normal persons sometimes cope with intense anxiety by *isolating* thoughts from emotions, as when a parent extricates a child's bleeding finger from a fence on which it has become impaled. The parent "does what has to be done," trying not to experience the horror that would normally accompany seeing a piece of fence protruding from the child's finger.

(9) Reaction-formation holds *unacceptable impulses at bay by emphasizing opposite thoughts and behaviors.* Reaction-formation is a high-level defense that is used in a variety of ways to keep forbidden impulses at bay. A person who is attracted to forbidden sexuality might become a leading figure in fighting pornography, experiencing some unconscious sexual gratification while investigating the "detestable rubbish."

The author of the following letter (written to a researcher who used cats in experiments to study alcoholism) attempts to contain his unconscious aggressive impulses toward alcoholics and animal researchers alike by focusing on his tender concern for cats:

> I am surprised that anyone who is as well educated as you must be to hold the position that you do would stoop to such a depth as to torture helpless little

cats in the pursuit of a cure for alcoholics. A drunkard does not want to be cured—a drunkard is just a weak minded idiot who belongs in the gutter and should be left there. Instead of torturing helpless little cats why not torture drunks. . . . (Masserman, 1961, p. 35)

(10) Intellectualization, which is among the most sophisticated of defense mechanisms, helps persons *cope with instinctual conflicts by translating them into intellectual terms.* The adolescent, the celibate priest, or the closet homosexual might all spend inordinate amounts of time studying, writing, or thinking about sexuality in an effort to contain powerful sexual impulses.

(11) Rationalization *devises plausible explanations for engaging in forbidden behaviors or gratifying objectionable instinctual impulses.* Thus, a man who dislikes another person in his circle of acquaintances might *rationally* find all kinds of reasons for avoiding this person: "I'm too busy," "She's never home and I don't like to leave messages," etc., when the real reason is unconscious hatred or jealousy. The woman married to a philanderer devises a series of "reasonable" explanations for why he persists in having affairs (e.g., an unfortunate childhood, poor parental examples, etc.) in order to protect her own self-esteem.

"Sour grapes" is a famous illustration of rationalization found in Aesop's fable of the fox who, after trying and failing several times to secure a cluster of grapes hanging from a trestle, exclaims, "They were probably sour anyhow!" Probably everyone who has ever been spurned by a would-be lover has uttered some variation of the fox's lament: "She's so stuck on herself that I'd have broken up with her in a couple months anyway." "He's such an arrogant jerk I wouldn't *really* want to date him anyhow!"

(12) Projection allows a person to *project unacceptable impulses or feelings outward (onto someone else).* Projection has come to have a broader meaning than defense. It is used as a *coping* mechanism at various stages of life. As a higher-level defense mechanism, projection distances forbidden impulses or unwanted feelings by projecting them onto someone else (e.g., the man who barely resists being unfaithful to his spouse becomes chronically suspicious that *she* is having an affair behind his back; the adolescent male typically deals with any hint of homosexual attraction to another guy by suddenly "noticing" how some guys are coming on to him).

Even more broadly, Freud saw projection as the dynamic process behind *transference* and *countertransference,* two of the most central processes in psychoanalysis. He warned other psychoanalysts about the dangers of projecting their own issues onto their patients: "But anyone who has scorned to take the precaution of being analysed himself. . . . will easily fall into the temptation of projecting outwards some of the peculiarities of his own personality . . ." (1911–13, p. 117).

Thus, although projection functions as a defense/coping mechanism at various steps along the developmental journey, it has acquired broader meanings.

(13) Displacement *allows unacceptable aspects of the unconscious to bypass the censoring superego and appear in dream thoughts.* Freud first introduced displacement as a defense mechanism that operates primarily during dreaming. Since Freud's time, however, the meaning of *displacement* has evolved to become almost synonymous with *substitution,* the defense mechanism by which hostility or some other unacceptable impulse is *displaced* onto a safer target.

(14) Substitution is a defense or coping strategy in which *the source, aim, and energy of an instinct remains the same, and only the <u>target</u> changes.* If, for example, the religiously devout adolescent diverts his overpowering sexual urges into petting or masturbation, this is *substitution*, because only the *target* has changed. Similarly, when the frustrated middle manager comes home and yells at the dog, the kids, or his wife, he is venting his rage at his boss on a variety of different "safer" targets. If he regularly *substitutes* in this way he may obtain a promotion at work but a divorce at home.

(15) Sublimation *is the highest form of defense or coping, consisting of transforming unacceptable impulses into societally prized behaviors.* The gay artist who redirects his sexual energies into creating acclaimed male sculptures, has, in Freud's view, successfully sublimated his forbidden homosexual impulses. The sexual-assault survivor who pursues a career as a rape counselor, or becomes an attorney who specializes in prosecuting pedophiles, is unconsciously sublimating her rage.

Sublimation is the "Everest" of defense/coping mechanisms. As we have just learned, substitution changes the bull's-eye for discharging instinctual libido, blunting the intensity of murderous rage by spreading the passion among a variety of innocent targets. We also learned that reaction-formation, intellectualization, rationalization, and projection are pretty good coping mechanisms, but compared with all other defense or coping mechanisms, *sublimation is sublime* because it allows a person to discharge powerful emotions in a societally acceptable way. This is, in short, the goal of parents and teachers who socialize and educate their children to "express their feelings," but to do this in a way that doesn't harm or hurt others. When you add to that an artistic or cultural contribution it becomes not only a safe discharge, but a contribution.

Summary of Defense/Coping Mechanisms

Sigmund Freud's ego-based concepts emerged late in his career, when he had little interest or energy to devote to their expansion, so it fell to Anna Freud, Erik Erikson, and others (e.g., Heinz Hartmann, 1939; Robert White, 1960, 1981; and Heinz Kohut, 1977) to develop ego psychoanalysis more fully. Prior to this new generation of ego analysts, psychoanalysis was essentially a "depth psychology" that evolved out of Freud's unrelenting focus on unconscious forces. However, when it came to the everyday problems of treating patients—especially children—such "depth" considerations gradually gave way to more practical issues. Ego analysts remained concerned with how the ego mediates unconscious conflicts among the id, ego, and superego, but they also wanted to know how the ego develops out of a child's relationship to parents and caretakers in the real world—how competency and self-reliance develop as a result of coping with the challenges of living.

The heuristic value of defense and coping mechanisms is seen in the number of new coping strategies that have been elaborated since Anna Freud's (1946) classic ten.

We have briefly reviewed fifteen, but the current diagnostic manual of the American Psychiatric Association lists *thirty-one!* The important concept to remember is that all defense/coping mechanisms are unconscious psychological processes employed by the ego to protect the person from anxiety.

FACING THE TOUGH TWINS

Is It Testable?

Research regarding defense/coping mechanisms. Holmes (1968, 1978) asserted that there is no research evidence for unconscious *projection*. However, Vaillant (1994) subsequently concluded that "defenses provide a diagnostic template for understanding distress and for guiding the clinical management of psychology's most baffling and frustrating clients" (p. 49). More recently, Cramer (2000) reevaluated Holmes's assertion:

> Holmes did not say the phenomenon of projection did not exist. . . . Rather, he believed that the same process was more parsimoniously labeled *attribution*. The study of this process, sans its connotation as a defense mechanism, was taken up by social psychologists and incorporated into attribution theory. (Jones & Davis, 1965; Kelly, 1967). (Cramer, 2000, p. 638)

Cramer (2000) then discussed how defense mechanisms have been researched by a broad range of contemporary psychologists:

> Virtually every leading cognitive psychologist today accepts the premise that mental processes go on outside awareness (e.g. Greenwald, 1992; Jacoby, 1991; Kihlstrom, 1987; Roediger, 1990). . . . There is an extensive body of research showing that memories unavailable to consciousness nevertheless influence conscious memory and task performance (Cramer, 1965; Marcel, 1983). . . . Computer simulations of the defensive process of projection have been written and tested by Colby (1981). . . . Further studies have provided evidence for erroneous nonconscious inferential processes (Lewicki, Hill & Czyzewska, 1992). . . . Recent studies have demonstrated that children's use of defense mechanisms changes in a developmentally predictable pattern (Cramer, 1991) a finding that has been validated both cross-sectionally (Porcerelli, Thomas, Hibbard, & Cogan, 1998) and longitudinally. (Cramer, 1997; Cramer, 2000, pp. 638–639)

Although Anna Freud felt that a developmental ranking of defense mechanisms would have been "premature" (in 1946), she acknowledged that the various defenses arose at different points along the developmental pathway. Cramer's (2000) view is consonant with Anna Freud's:

> Relying on the immature defense of denial is normative for a five-year-old but is developmentally out of phase in a young adult. . . . When children and adolescents use age-characteristic defenses, they protect themselves from undue psychological stress. When individuals use age-inappropriate defenses, there is

often evidence of maladaptive functioning (Cramer & Block, 1998; Vaillant, 1977, 1992, 1994). (Cramer, 2000, p. 643)

The scientific Achilles' heel of psychodynamic research. The problem in researching defense mechanisms is that we cannot directly measure "unconscious" processes; ironically, most research on "unconscious" processes relies on the *conscious* self-report of experimental subjects. So, Holmes's (1978) assertion that defense mechanisms can be more parsimoniously explained in terms of attribution theory is likely true—as is Cramer's (2000) observation that research shows that memories unavailable to consciousness nevertheless influence conscious processes. This is apparently why defense and coping mechanisms have proven so useful. A wide variety of workers (e.g., psychoanalysts, brain scientists, and clinicians of various stripes) appear to agree that unconscious processes influence our behavior. They differ primarily on how to study and explain such "unconscious" processes, but not on their existence.

Is It Useful?

Defense mechanisms, as elaborated by Anna Freud and expanded on by subsequent generations of clinicians, have stood the test of time. Defense and coping mechanisms have provided guidance for clinicians of varying stripes—including many who are far from being "true believers" in Freudian theory. Such ideas have been widely assimilated into Western culture; for instance, we regularly hear people say "You're in denial," or "That sounds like rationalization to me."

Defense mechanisms have gradually expanded to include normal, socially based coping styles. In Sigmund Freud's earliest portrait of the mind, the *ego* was constantly fighting to keep the urges of the *id* from flooding the conscious mind with raw libido. Defense mechanisms rushed to the rescue, "arresting" primitive libido's unconsciously redirecting them. Contemporary clinicians view defense mechanisms (especially the higher-level variety) as functioning to "rewire" or "reprogram" the mind with a variety of *coping circuits*. Today, not only psychoanalysts, but cognitive scientists and social psychologists as well are interested in understanding how processes outside awareness influence behavior.

OBJECT-RELATIONS THEORY OF MELANIE KLEIN
The Hand That Rocks the Cradle

An "inside job" by a mother of three. The work of Melanie Klein marks a major turning point in psychoanalysis, because in spite of retaining Freud's instinct theory and psychosexual terminology, she punctured the heart of classical psychoanalysis by asserting that conflict between a baby and its caretakers begins almost from the moment of birth—much earlier than the anal and oedipal stages suggested by Freud. By pushing such interpersonal conflicts back to the earliest days of neonatal life, Klein and her followers diminished the importance of Freud's biologically based libido theory. Now, the *interpersonal relationship between the infant and its caretaker—not libido—*was seen as the primary influence that shapes personality.

Background Check

Melanie Klein (1882–1960), the "mother" of object-relations theory, was born Melanie Reizes, on March 30, 1882, in Vienna, Austria. Reared in an orthodox Jewish family, Melanie was the youngest of four children, born when her father was in his fifties. The last of four children, Melanie was told by her mother that she was "unexpected," and she was acutely aware that her father preferred his oldest daughter Emile to her. Melanie was the only child of the four who was handed over to a "wet nurse" for nursing (Grosskurth, 1986, pp. 10–11). In addition to the rejection she may have experienced from her parents, she suffered the death of two of her three siblings, her "father" analyst (Franz Alexander), and her own son.

Death—the earliest enemy. Four-year-old Melanie was closely bonded with Sidonie, her eight-year-old sister, who became seriously ill in 1886 and spent much of the subsequent year in bed. During this time, Sidonie taught Melanie reading, writing, and the rudiments of arithmetic. The following year Sidonie died, inflicting on five-year-old Melanie the first in a series of sorrows that would puncture her life.

A few years later, young Melanie developed a similarly close bond with her brother, Emmanuel, a gifted young man who was skilled both as a writer and a pianist. Melanie shared her brother's literary and artistic interests, and her self-confidence was heightened by Emmanuel's open admiration of her evolving talents. However, Emmanuel suffered from heart trouble and died at the age of twenty-five, leaving twenty-year-old Melanie devastated. Death continued to pummel Melanie, not only with the loss of her siblings during childhood and adolescence, but also during adulthood, when she would lose her "father" analyst (Franz Alexander) to death, and subsequently her own son.

Zeitgeist

Although Klein has been described as "one of the great creative minds of psychoanalysis" (Guntrip, 1971, p. 65), she never perceived herself as anything but loyal to Freud. Her theory was shaped by the practical considerations that grew out of working with children, as well as by her own experiences with death. She never intended to distance herself from Freud.

Analyzed and sponsored by the happy Hungarian. Sandor Ferenczi (1873–1933), Freud's distinguished Hungarian disciple, enjoyed a celebrated reputation in his native land, and sometime during World War I, Melanie Klein was psychoanalyzed by him. Ferenczi's approach to psychoanalysis was more permissive than Freud's, emphasizing the healing aspects of love and acceptance. Favorably impressed by her ebullient analyst, Klein said that "the remarkable *rapport* he had with the minds of children, have had a lasting influence on my understanding of the psychology of the small child" (Klein, 1932, pp. x–xi).

Psychoanalysis begins at home. Following her training analysis with Ferenczi, Klein began to apply the principles of psychoanalysis to the rearing of her youngest son, Erich. She wrote of this experience using the pseudonym "Fritz" for her son: "My first patient was a five-year-old boy. I referred to him under the name 'Fritz' in my earliest published papers. . . . Between 1920 and 1923 I gained further experience with other child cases . . . " (Klein, 1955, pp. 122–124). Moving to Berlin in 1921,

Klein continued the "psychoanalysis" of her son, and began treating other children at a clinic.

More death, and the "depressive position." In those days it was not unusual for someone to follow up their training analysis with subsequent analyses, and in 1925 Klein entered psychoanalysis with Karl Abraham. However, it was interrupted after fourteen months when Abraham suffered an attack of bronchial pneumonia and shortly thereafter, died. Klein, who had lost two of her three siblings to death, and her husband to divorce, now lost her analyst as well. Her mourning was extended and painful. The usually energetic Klein read no papers and published no articles until the end of 1928.

A few years later, in 1934, death struck again, snatching Melanie Klein's oldest son, who died in Switzerland in a mountain climbing accident at the age of twenty-seven. It was probably not coincidental that later that year Klein presented a paper at that Congress introducing one of her central theoretical constructs, the **depressive position,** *a developmental stage, peaking at about six months, when the infant fears either losing or destroying the beloved caretaker.*

Death hovered ominously over Klein's life, stalking her from early childhood onward. Growing up in Vienna, she was undoubtedly affected by the deaths and privations of World War I, but it was the death of her siblings, her analyst, and finally her own son that likely shaped her view of life as well as her theoretical formulations. Whereas few psychoanalysts rushed to embrace Freud's late-in-life, half-hearted introduction of the death instinct, Klein saw the death instinct as primary, even assigning it precedence over libido. Given her own life experiences, this hardly seems surprising.

ASKING THE BIG FOUR QUESTIONS

Klein employed Sigmund Freud's vocabulary, but reinterpreted his terms, infusing them with her own distinctive *object-relations* meaning. Viewed from Klein's perspective, the inner life of the infant and young child is replete with images of death and destruction—permeated with murder, mayhem, and cannibalism. The profusion of death in Klein's own life probably contributed to the violence-permeated pessimism that colored her view of the child's inner world, however, an equally important factor may have been that most of her initial theories were based on the same half dozen cases (Rita, Trude, Ruth, Peter, Erna, and "Fritz"—her own son). Generalizing to all children on the basis of these war-frightened children likely led to distortion.

What Are the Parts?

Introjected objects (internal images). In Klein's theory, a child's internal images were accorded equal rank with reality. She viewed the young child's mind as brimming with **introjected objects,** *internal images of parents and other adults.* Such images coexist and coalesce with the *actual encounters* a child experiences with adults. Klein envisioned the child's inner world as savage and sadistic, filled with persecution and fear.

TABLE 7.2

Klein at a Glance

MODEL OF PERSONALITY	DESCRIPTIONS	DYNAMICS
What Are the Parts?	***Introjected Objects:*** internalized images of parents and other adults ***Whole and Parts Objects:*** whole objects are internal images of entire persons, whereas part objects are images of separate organs or products ***Early Superego:*** sadistic and severe introjected parental object that comes before the oedipal conflict ***Id:*** sadistic center of protection against death and frightening objects ***Ego:*** functions in sorting out "good" and "bad" part and whole objects	A child creates internalized objects of parents or caretakers, beginning with part objects, like a "good" or "bad" breast, and developing into whole objects or entire persons. This is how the early Superego is born, though it is a harsh internalized object not always consistent with the reality of the parent. The Superego causes conflict, and the Id answers with impulses to protect the child from perceived threats. The ego attempts to resolve conflict by *splitting* objects and relationships into more-manageable "good" and "bad" pieces.
What Makes a Person Go?	***Splitting:*** advances development by *splitting* whole objects into more-manageable "good" or "bad" parts ***Death Instinct:*** anxiety about death ***Epistemophilic Instinct:*** desire to know ***Weaning:*** the pivotal developmental event, triggering intense sadistic impulses ***Sadistic impulses:*** the child's means of protection from the threatening "enemies" such as parent/caretakers and others "out there"	In Klein's theory, fear of death was a primary force, sort of dethroning Freud's libido. Although she did include it in her theory, it was seen through object-relational eyes. The epistemophilic instinct was usually repressed when it came to sexual issues, and this caused conflict and increased sadistic impulses as the child fought against the image of the combined parent. Klein saw the height of sadism as brought about by weaning.
What Makes it Grow?	Here the infant passes through two "positions": the paranoid position, which spans from birth to three months and the depressive position, which begins at three to six months. This helps them develop tools for using in the adult life.	The paranoid position finds the infant making relationships with part objects and not yet recognizing whole objects. The infant sees these objects as persecuting and is terrified of them. In the depressive position, triggered by the weaning process, the infant develops the ability to relate to whole objects or entire persons. Fantasies of reparation with parents and the mechanism of splitting allow the infant to enter and finally four years later to exit this stage.

continued

TABLE 7.2 *(continued)*

Klein at a Glance

MODEL OF PERSONALITY	DESCRIPTIONS	DYNAMICS
What Makes it Unique?	Object relations are unique because no two infant-caretaker relationships are alike. Each infant brings a unique blend of splittings, emotions, attacks, counterattacks, and reparations to the relationship. Similarly, caretakers bring a plethora of expectations, projections, and reality distortions to the table as well. Consequently, there are few constraints on uniqueness.	Klein's theory is infused with unique possibilities from the relationship of the child to his parents, to the child's internal fantasies and projections. The distinctive developmental history will be markedly varied for each infant.

Early, harsh superego. Whereas Freud saw superego formation as a late-childhood development, resulting from the resolution of oedipal conflicts (3–5 years), Klein believed the superego appeared much earlier—composed of *introjected parental images* that were characterized by severe strictness and frequently bore little resemblance to the child's actual parents. She noted that one of her child patients developed a harsh superego on the basis of his own internal images, despite the fact that his parents were "unusually kind and loving." Klein said that "The contrast between his tender and loving mother and the punishment threatened by the child's super-ego is actually grotesque and is an illustration of the fact that we must on no account identify the real objects with those which children introject" (Klein, 1927, p. 155).

According to Klein, babies and very young children frequently experience adults as menacing and sadistic, and respond by developing a paranoid attitude toward these "persecuting" parents. In Klein's object-relations reformulation of psychoanalysis, libido fixations and cathexes were no longer the driving forces in development; it was the *superego*—not the id—that became the child's chief tormenter. Object relations superseded biological instincts.

Id. The *id* lost stature in Klein's theory in direct proportion to the gains of the superego. For Klein, the main enemy of the child's ego is not the id, but the harsh superego. Klein also insisted that in the formation of early object relations the primary motive was *sadism* not sexuality, and libido developed primarily to counterbalance the death instinct. It was a grim picture—death dominating life—consistent with Klein's own developmental experiences.

Ego—the great splitter. Whereas for Freud, the ego is the *mediator* of id and superego conflicts, for Klein the ego functions as the great *splitter*. Present from the earliest days of life, the ego first *splits* internal images into **good objects**, or *internal representations of good relationships,* and **bad objects**, or *internal representations of persons seen as dangerous or threatening.* The violent and sadistic fantasies of young children do not arise from forbidden *id* impulses, but are, instead, responses of the *ego* to the perceived threats of introjected objects. In Kleinian theory, the ego also functions to *split part objects* from *whole objects.*

Splitting *whole objects* into manageable parts. The **whole object** consists of *the internal image of the entire person,* whereas a **part object** consists of *separate organs or products—breasts, penis, milk, blood, or feces.* Klein viewed the newborn as incapable of visualizing its mother's entire body, so the infant introjects the mother piece-by-piece as a *good breast* or a *bad breast*—mostly *bad* since reality is filled with so much sorrow. As psychological development advances, the infant *splits* the mother-image into a "good mother" and a "bad mother." This allows the baby to attach the hatred it feels onto the "bad" mother, "while it directs its restorative trends to its 'good' mother and 'good' father" (Klein, 1932, p. 222).

Ambivalence. In Freud's theory, **ambivalence**, *love and hate for the same object,* has a negative connotation, occurring during phases of development when love and destructive tendencies are found side by side. Klein, by contrast, viewed ambivalence as positive, because through the mechanism of *splitting,* love and hate could be sorted out and dealt with separately:

> This process of relating to objects is brought about by a splitting up of the mother-image into a good and a bad one. The existence of this type of ambivalence towards the object indicates a further step in the development of object-relations . . . " (1932, p. 222).

Summary of parts. If repression was the "cornerstone" of psychoanalysis for Freud, *splitting* is the essential process for Klein. In fact, since splitting begins almost at birth, it shapes everything that follows—even repression. For Klein, even the adult defense mechanism of repression is seen as a kind of *splitting* whereby a well-developed adult ego splits itself off from unconscious threats.

What Makes a Person Go?

Primacy of the death instinct. Freud's theory of motivation primarily focused on the distribution of the libido's life forces. He formulated the *death instinct* late in his career and never appeared as fully enamored with it as he was with libido. For Klein, death was primary. Or, putting it more precisely, *anxiety* about death was Klein's central driving force. She saw her little patients not so much bubbling with sexuality as afraid of death and destruction—which they ferociously fought in fantasy by attacking the enemy (adults). As one historian of psychoanalysis aptly put it:

> According to Klein, the internal world of the small child is a mass of destructive and anxious fantasies, redolent with unconscious images of mayhem and death. For Freud, the child is a selfish savage, for Klein, it is a murderous cannibal. If anyone took Freud's death drive with all its implications seriously, it was Melanie Klein. (Gay, 1988, p. 468)

It is understandable that someone who lost two beloved siblings, an analyst, and finally, her own son to death might conclude that death is more basic than life. In Klein's theory, the child lives in terror of his or her death instinct. But such children need not have experienced bad mothers in reality, because they *project* this basic death instinct into the breast, creating the ubiquitous "bad breast" or "bad mother" that one finds everywhere in Klein's theories. Guntrip put it well: "I cannot see how, on Klein's assumptions, a baby can ever experience a really good breast at all . . . the death instinct must always ruin it" (1971, pp. 67).

Of course, Klein wasn't the first to come up with the idea of a death instinct (Freud proposed it in *Beyond the Pleasure Principle,* 1920), but she was among the first to give it a central role in her theories. How much of this anxiety actually existed in the children she analyzed and how much was her own projection is difficult to disentangle, but no personality theorist before or since has made death such a primal force in theory or practice.

Transcending libido with an interpersonal twist. Klein saw libido as progressively invested in wider and wider regions of the body—beginning with the fingers and extremities and eventually including the entire skin surface. However, instead of accepting Freud's cathexis-anticathexis ideas about libido distribution, Klein saw libido in *object–relational terms*. In psychoanalyzing her son, she concluded that her body and his body were symbolically experienced by Erich as geographically related towns and countries, connected by a complicated railway system on which "pipi-trains" and "khaki-trains" ran, and where railway terminals and platforms represented the mouth, anus, and penis.

Body geography. Klein used geography as a metaphor for describing the spread of libido through fantasy sex play. One day, for example, Erich took one of his toys, a little dog which he referred to as *"Son"* in his games and fantasies, and slid it over his mother's breasts (mountains) and genital region (big river). But the trip ended badly because other toys accused the little dog of committing a crime, and it was beaten or killed. Klein saw this as clear evidence for Erich's oedipal conflicts: "Thus we found that his sense of orientation . . . was determined by the desire to penetrate the mother's body and to investigate it inside, with the passages leading in and out and the process of impregnation and birth" (Klein, 1923a, p. 98). By viewing all of a child's play as a direct expression of unconscious or preconscious fantasies, Klein retained Freud's classical emphasis on the importance of unconscious motivation, but transcended his biological reductionism by infusing everything with an object-relations perspective.

Weaning triggers sadistic impulses. Within Klein's system, *sadistic impulses* play a key role. She frequently used the phrase "by means of every weapon which sadism can command" to denote this phenomenon, which included the urge to bite, soil with excrement, cut up, burn, etc. Sadism becomes the fantasy weapon of choice to be used for the annihilation of a threatening "object." According to Klein, sadistic impulses and the oedipal conflict are both triggered by *weaning*. At first, sadism is confined to part objects (especially the breast), but later, it includes the whole parent.

What Makes a Person Grow?

Positions instead of stages. As we have seen, Melanie Klein drastically revamped Freud's biology-based motivational constructs along more interpersonal lines. Similarly, she reformulated Freud's psychosexual stages as *positions,* based on the status of the *object relationships* between infant and caretakers. **A position** *describes the basic flavor* *of the interpersonal relationships—including the accompanying coping or defense mechanisms.* A position is *the psychological arena in which the ego operates.* This is not an anatomical site such as the mouth or anus; rather, it is an *interpersonal arena.* Different arenas can be exchanged or blended, and it also becomes possible to occupy several positions or sites within a larger arena. Thus, within the broad scope of the *depressive position,* the ego could simultaneously assume an *obsessional position* of control, an *empathic position* of identification or reparation, as well as a *position of overwhelming despair.*

Put more simply, we can experience several different emotions at the same time, and we can correspondingly utilize a blend of different defense/coping mechanisms. Let's briefly examine one of Klein's earliest and most important positions—the depressive position.

Depressive position—three to six months. The depressive position is triggered by *weaning,* combined with the infant's capacity to *synthesize part objects* into *whole persons.* During the **depressive position,** *the inner world of the child becomes object-relational, and involves real and fantasized relationships with other whole persons, not merely body parts.* During these early phases of the depressive position *splitting* is not yet present, so the "good" and "bad" aspects of whole objects are not well differentiated, but weaning dramatically imposes the differentiation of part from whole on the infant: "Since the concept of the breast extends to that of the mother, the feelings of having lost the breast lead to the fear of having lost the loved mother entirely . . ." (Klein, 1936, p. 295).

Earlier, the infant experienced a mini-loss each time the breast or bottle was removed or whenever the possession of the breast was interrupted, the baby was uncertain of its return. Subsequently, weaning came as a cumulative climax to these numerous mini-losses along the way, making the final weaning momentous: "the crucial point is reached at the actual weaning when the loss is complete and the breast or bottle is gone irrevocably" (Klein, 1936, p. 295).

Weaning precipitates what Klein referred to as *primal mourning,* triggering the depressive position. In light of the depressive significance of weaning, Klein felt that the mother "must do everything she can to help the child to establish a happy relationship with her" (1936, p. 297), and to help her baby to "develop a strong attachment to the nipple and to the breast" (p. 297). This was a theme also expounded by Klein's student, Winnicott (1951, 1962, 1966), and later developed by Bowlby (1969) as well.

From our *zonal* perspective, it is worth emphasizing that although Klein was not the first psychoanalyst to emphasize the near mythical virtues of breast-feeding, she was among the first to emphasize that *mothering was more than feeding.* Freud emphasized the importance of the breast for feeding and for the cathexis of sexual libido, but it was Klein who first interpreted the breast in truly object-relational terms—as part of a *whole person*—highlighting the relationship with the *whole* mother as the fulcrum upon which everything of significance turned.

What Makes a Person Unique?

Uniqueness abounds in Kleinian psychology. Object relations are seen as the basis for growth, and since no two people are alike, it comes as no surprise that each infant–caretaker relationship is distinctive. Since Klein's construct of *position* includes the infant's unique personality as well as the individually distinct personalities of the parents/caretakers, the resulting mix produces a one-of-a-kind "cocktail" of splittings, emotions, defense mechanisms, attacks, counterattacks, and reparations. Add to this array of internal fantasies and projections a variety of *real people* interacting with the young child, and there are few constraints on individual uniqueness.

FACING THE TOUGH TWINS

Is It Testable?

Perhaps there is no better illustration of how a lack of scientific grounding can foster bizarre notions than Melanie Klein's theories. Her play therapy with children *heuristically* stimulated the field of psychoanalysis to broaden its focus, but her scientifically unexamined belief that play directly reveals a child's unconscious processes led her to conclusions that are almost certainly wrong. I say "almost certainly wrong" because how can one scientifically investigate whether drawings of starfish really do represent, as Klein suggested, "Daddy's starfish genital inside Mummy" (1961, p. 79)?

Without experimental studies or scientific checks and balances, Klein created her own vision of the child's unconscious world. Consequently, she frequently interpreted the meaning of her young patients' play to fit her own preexisting theories. It is impossible to disentangle how much of what Klein perceived actually existed in the minds of her young patients and how much of what she "saw" was a result of her own theoretical biases.

Additionally, the situational realities of the war profoundly influenced what occupied the minds of children and adults alike during the early 1940s. Brief excerpts from Klein's sessions with Richard illustrate how she intermingled her own theoretical ideas with Richard's fantasies—all of this taking place in a war zone:

> Richard's attacks on the flies stood for attacks on the babies inside her. . . . Richard wished to cuddle Mrs. K., but he felt afraid of her genital and her inside, because it was soiled and poisoned by the dirty and dead babies (the squashed flies) and by the Hitler-Daddy. Richard might, therefore, be terrified— even if he were grown up—of putting his genital into such a dangerous place, in spite of also wishing to do so. (1961, pp. 397–398)

When in their final (ninety-third) session Richard was killing flies with a "V for Victory vengeance," Klein interpreted this to mean "His killing 'all the flies' was to protect Mrs. K.—and Mummy—against the bad babies whom Richard felt she contained and who could endanger her" (1961, p. 463).

While Klein's interpretation regarding Richard's killing of flies was consistent with her own theoretical formulations, other—more parsimonious—interpretations also fit. Richard, both anxious and angry about his final analytic session, was probably shifting his anger from his psychoanalyst to the flies in her office. By terminating the flies, Richard sublimated his aggression (killing flies is a societally valued behavior) and reassured himself of his strength by dominating these insects in a way that felt powerful in a war torn country. Interpreting the dead flies as representing "dirty and dead babies" inside Mrs. Klein's "soiled and poisoned genital" is a more Kleinian—but not necessarily more correct—interpretation.

Klein's attempts to explain personality development in terms of the internal fantasies of infants and young children proves extremely difficult to experimentally investigate. If Freud's formulations have sometimes been difficult to operationalize, Klein's are even more challenging. Klein was a careful observer of behavior and gifted in her ability to establish rapport with children, but *objective* she was not. She was a housewife with no scientific training who apprenticed to two Freudian loyalists (Ferenczi and Abraham), and her interpretations appear to reflect her own theoretical predilections as much as they do the children's dynamics. Additionally, she was practicing in a war zone, and the children she analyzed likely experienced genuine situational anxieties regarding their safety or destruction.

Is It Useful?

Play therapy—Klein's lasting legacy. During the summer of 1923, Klein invented **play therapy,** *a treatment method that encourages children to use puppets, finger paints, clay, blocks, and other toys to "play out" their feelings.* Play therapy was not so much a stroke of intellectual genius on Klein's part as it was the natural outcome of how she began her clinical practice—psychoanalyzing her own son (at home, by asking him questions while he played with toys). When she subsequently agreed to analyze a young patient named Rita (2 years, 3 months of age), the analysis took place in the toddler's home, where Klein observed her spontaneously playing with toys. In this sense, play therapy was brought to psychoanalysis by children.

Feuding with the Freuds. When Klein observed children's play, she found both negative and positive ingredients, and came to believe that both kinds of fantasies were part of all childrens' transferences and should be addressed in treatment. Anna Freud differed sharply, arguing that negative transference always interfered with the treatment of children and that the child analyst must actively cultivate a positive transference in order to facilitate treatment. On this, and numerous other points, Melanie Klein and Anna Freud disagreed vigorously; however, such foment seemed to help, rather than hurt, psychoanalysis during the decades of the 1920s, 1930s, and 1940s.

Klein moved up the vertical axis from a more biologically based instinctual emphasis to an object-relational zone. Although she retained much of Freud's terminology, Klein pushed the oedipal struggles back to the earliest months of existence, thereby changing the metaphor used to describe the inner lives of little children from a seething cauldron, bubbling with sexual instincts and biological drives, into a theater stage upon which the dark dramas of object-relational struggles are played out.

Klein's profound differences from both Freuds is likely related to the fact that as a mother of three she nursed her own children for significant periods of time. She undoubtedly experienced the pleasures of breast-feeding, as well as some of the "biting" and other irritations that accompany early feeding experiences. Weaning, with its accompanying disappointments and distress, was also part of the personal experience she wove into her theories of development.

In the end, in spite of remaining verbally loyal to Freud's classical psychoanalysis, Klein found herself orbiting in a different galaxy. Navigating by her stars, the breast was the "milky way" of the child's universe, leaving the Oedipus complex a distant constellation.

KAREN HORNEY: THE CONFLICTED SELF IN FAMILY AND SOCIETY
Background Check

Conflict-permeated childhood with a beautiful mother and a Bible-throwing father. Karen Horney (pronounced "HORN"—"eye") (1885–1952) was born in a small village near Hamburg, Germany. Her father was a Norwegian sea captain with four children from a previous marriage when he married Karen's mother—eighteen years younger. He was a tall, handsome, stern, God-fearing person who strongly believed that women were inferior to men. Since Eve had first succumbed to temptation in the Garden, he saw her (and women in general) as the source of evil in the world.

Karen's mother was beautiful, intelligent, proud, and freethinking. Not surprisingly, these two parents with powerful personality differences frequently clashed, and sometimes after reading the scriptures at length, Karen's father would explode in a fit of anger and throw the Bible at his wife, earning the nickname "Bible thrower" from his children (Rubins, 1978, p. 11). It is hardly surprising that Horney developed a negative attitude toward authority figures and a skepticism toward religion. However, Karen's feelings about her father were deeply conflicted. She was intimidated by his strict, self-righteous manner, disappointed by his preference for her brother, and dismayed by his derogatory comments about her appearance and her intelligence. Yet, he enchanted her by taking her on at least three lengthy sea voyages, and he frequently brought her exotic gifts from distant lands.

Seeking to please. In a family constellation saturated with conflict, young Karen tried at first to cope through compliance and pleasing, behaving, according to her own account, "like a little lamb" (Rubins, 1978, p. 13). She even placed some of her toys on the street for poorer children to find, hoping by such altruism and charity to win the love of her parents (Horney, 1942, p. 190; 1950, p. 20). By the time she was nine years old, Karen began openly competing with her schoolmates as a way of compensating for the inferiority she felt as a result of her father's critical belittling. As she explained to her daughter, years later, "If I couldn't be beautiful, I decided I would be smart" (Rubins, 1978, p. 14).

Adult life. After being treated by a physician when she was twelve, Karen decided she wanted to become a physician herself, a decision opposed by her father but enthusiastically endorsed by her mother. At the age of twenty-one, she began her studies at the medical school in Freiberg, Germany, one of the few that allowed women to enroll at the time. Shortly thereafter, she met Oskar Horney, a strong, stern, intelligent, independent young man—not unlike her father—whom she married about three years later. Oskar became a lawyer, and a year later, Karen was pregnant with the first of their three daughters. Shortly before the birth of this infant, Karen's mother died of a stroke.

Nearly suicidal. A short time later, Karen's brother, Berndt, died of pneumonia, reawakening the myriad childhood conflicts she had struggled to suppress. His death fulfilled Karen's darkest childhood wishes and simultaneously triggered the most intense guilt. Caught in conflict—as she had been for most of her life—she sank into a deep depression, nearly taking her own life. While vacationing at the beach with her family following Berndt's death, she went for a swim, and when she failed to return after more than an hour, her husband found her clutching a piling in deep water, trying to decide whether to let go and end it all, or swim back to shore (Rubins, 1978, p. 87). After much pleading by Oskar and his friends, Karen swam back to shore, but she wrestled with depression most of her life.

A failed marriage and difficult professional life. Not long afterward, her marriage began to disintegrate. The firm for which Oskar worked went bankrupt, his investments failed, and he suffered a near-fatal attack of meningitis. He became emotionally withdrawn and depressed, and family life became increasingly difficult. In 1926, Karen and their three daughters moved into a small apartment; however, the divorce wasn't final until thirteen years later.

Zeitgeist

The Great Depression and the primacy of culture. After teaching at the Berlin Institute for Psychoanalysis from 1918 to 1932, Horney came to the United States and was associate director of the Chicago Institute of Psychoanalysis. However, she found it difficult to apply classical Freudian psychoanalysis during those Depression years in America. She found people were more worried about losing their jobs and not having enough money to pay the rent or provide for their families, than they were concerned with sexual problems. Horney came to believe that neuroses were culturally rather than biologically driven. Increasingly, she emphasized family and cultural influences over the intrapsychic conflicts of id, ego, and superego. Horney's revisionist views—especially of the psychology of women—created a degree of divisiveness at the Chicago Institute, which was among the reasons she left after only two years. Following her brief stint at Chicago, Horney moved to New York City, where she established a private practice and trained analysts at the New York Psychoanalytic Institute.

Old patterns in a new place. Horney's life in America replicated many of the same patterns she had experienced as a child. Just as she had failed to meet the expectations of her biological father, she failed to please her analytic "fathers." Much as her relationship with her brother had been permeated with conflict and guilt, and ended tragically when he died, her marriage to a man of similar personality ended in divorce.

The conflicts that Horney experienced during her childhood, marriage, and professional life sensitized her to a multiplicity of relationship dimensions that others might easily have overlooked. Her theory is a pioneering *self* psychology that includes a sequence of selves that develop in response to numerous conflicts—many of which appear to mirror her own life.

TABLE 7.3

Horney at a Glance

MODEL OF PERSONALITY	DESCRIPTIONS	DYNAMICS
What Are the Parts?	**Despised Real Self:** experiences the self as unworthy and detestable **Ideal Self:** strives for perfection **Positive Real Self:** authentic core with the potential for growth and health **Actual Self:** the sum of everything a person *actually is,* disregarding judgment by oneself or others	These personality "parts" develop out of the difficulties of childhood. The despised real self carries parental conditions of worth, while the ideal self works endlessly to attain perfection. The positive real self is a sort of reservoir of innate qualities and gifts that allow for growth and adaptation. The actual self is seen as objective, the reality of what one is, instead of all other subjectively held views about oneself.
What Makes a Person Go?	**Basic Anxiety:** child's feeling of isolation in a potentially hostile world **Basic Evil:** parent's lack of genuine warmth and affection **Hostility:** child's natural response to mistreatment by parents/caretakers	Although these motivational drives might appear similar to the conflicts of libido distribution in Freud's model, Horney's emphasis is on *interpersonal relations* instead of intrapsychic conflicts. These relations arise between child and parents or caretakers, not primarily as biological impulses.
What Makes a Person Grow?	Horney did not delineate developmental stages, but emphasized the importance of early family dynamics	Horney, like Adler, focused on how early family dynamics equip individuals with *characteristic coping strategies* as they live their lives.
What Makes a Person Unique?	**Moving Toward People:** compliant people-pleasing interpersonal style **Moving Against People:** a manipulative style from a "me against the world attitude" **Moving Away From People:** a style marked by defeat and withdrawal from human affairs	These personality styles accompanied by Horney's theories on the four selves, ten needs, and seven auxiliary approaches make for an abundance of unique personality combinations. In these three interpersonal styles we see an anticipation of the three DSM-IV personality clusters.

ASKING THE BIG FOUR QUESTIONS

What Are the Parts?

Horney was a pioneer *self* theorist, describing four different selves that sequentially evolve as the growing child traverses the traumas and difficulties of development.

(1) Despised real self and idealized image of self. Caught in conflict between a sense of helplessness and unexpressible hostility toward their parents, many children develop a **despised real self,** *experiencing their self as unworthy, unlovable, imperfect, and detestable.* This occurs when parents are coercive, inconsistent, or indifferent to a child. Added to this, the child's repressed hostility toward the parents is turned inward and the *real self* morphs into the *despised real self.* Children who thus despise their real selves frequently create an **idealized image of the self,** *a renovated portrait of the despised real self—revised along lines they believe will be acceptable to parents.* The child attempts to live according to parental "shoulds," rather than by the yardstick of an authentic inner self. Here Horney anticipated what Rogers (Chapter 11) would later describe as *incongruence* between experience and self, resulting in *conditions of worth* being implanted in the child by adults. Eric Berne (Chapter 9) described Horney's *idealized image of self* as the *adapted child,* and Albert Ellis (Chapter 10) termed Horney's *"tyranny of the should,"* as *"musterbation."* Horney, herself, described the discrepancy in the following way:

> . . . the neurotic . . . holds before his soul his image of perfection and unconsciously tells himself: "Forget about the disgraceful creature you actually *are*: this is how you *should* be; and to be this idealized self is all that matters. You should be able to endure everything, understand everything, to like everybody, to be always productive"—to mention only a few of these. Since they are inexorable, I call them "the tyranny of the should." (Horney, 1950, pp. 64–65)

A shrine in place of a goal. In Horney's view, the *idealized image of self* functions as a shrine, rather than a goal—as an object of worship, rather than an incentive to move ahead. "Shoulds" and wishful thinking are substituted for genuine motivation in a case of self-actualization gone awry.

(2) Ideal Self: the "search for glory." Over time, this idealized *image* of the self evolves into a more substantive *ideal self,* which then dooms the person to strive incessantly and compulsively to reach unattainable goals. Such a person loses awareness that perfection is a *fiction*—at best, a goal toward which one might aim but will never attain. Horney termed this compulsive striving for perfection as a "search for glory" (1950, p. 23). In reading Horney's writings about the "tyranny of the shoulds" and the "search for glory," one can almost visualize her father sternly coercing the family into following his rigid standards of decorum and impossible moral codes of conduct.

(3) Positive Real (authentic) Self. In her later writings, Horney used the term **real self** *to refer to a person's authentic core that contained the potential for growth and health.* Anticipating the human-potential movement and the self-actualizing theories of Rogers, Maslow, and other humanists, Horney suggested:

> You need not, and in fact cannot, teach an acorn to grow into an oak tree, but when given a chance, its intrinsic potentialities will develop. Similarly, the human individual, given a chance, tends to develop his particular human potentialities. . . . And this is why I speak . . . of the *real self* as the central inner force, common to all human beings and yet unique in each, which is the deep source of growth. (1950, p. 17)

(4) Actual Self. Horney defined the **actual self** *as the objective sum total of everything a person really is at a given moment, irrespective of judgments by others or by one's self.* This was to clearly differentiate the *actual self* from all other subjectively held views of oneself.

Summary of Horney's four selves. We will conclude this "parts" section by summarizing Horney's four selves: (1) *Despised Real Self* contains self-derogatory ideas about one's weakness, helplessness, incompetence, and general unlikeability—spawned and reinforced by parental coercion, neglect, or indifference. (2) *Ideal Self* begins as an *image* one strives to become in order to please the adults, and gradually it evolves into a more substantive *ideal self,* which drives the person toward unattainable perfection. (3) *Positive Real Self* contains the growth core innate to humankind, providing the potential for self-actualization. (4) *Actual Self* is the *real* self as objectively measured, in contradistinction to the other three *subjectively perceived* (by oneself or by others) selves.

What Makes a Person Go?

For Horney, as for Freud, *anxiety, hostility,* and *conflict* are powerful forces within the personality. However, in Horney's theory, although conflict is ultimately experienced as intrapsychic conflict (*Insight Zone*) among the various *selves,* this conflict first originates in the *Social Zone* as *interpersonal* and *social* struggles before becoming internalized. In this sense Horney resembled Melanie Klein and other object-relations theorists more than Freud.

Basic anxiety. According to Horney, the true core of neurosis is **basic anxiety:** *"the feeling a child has of being isolated and helpless in a potentially hostile world"* (1945, p. 41, emphasis added). In another place Horney described *basic anxiety* as *"a feeling of being small, insignificant, helpless, deserted, endangered, in a world that is out to abuse, cheat, attack, humiliate, betray, envy"* (1937, p. 92, emphasis added). This portrait of the helpless and deserted child in a world that is out to abuse, cheat, and attack is reminiscent of Klien's notion that the infant perceives a persecutory world, and also shares much in common with Adler's description (next chapter) of *inferiority.*

Basic evil. Horney defined **basic evil** as *"a lack of genuine warmth and affection"* on the part of the parent. She adds that "A child can stand a great deal of what is often regarded as traumatic—such as sudden weaning, occasional beating, sex experiences—as long as inwardly he feels wanted and loved" (1937, p. 80). Horney believed it was the parents' own neuroses that prevented them from showing compassion and affection toward their children, but that in most cases "the essential lack of warmth is camouflaged, and the parents claim to have in mind the child's best interest" (1937, p. 80).

Basic hostility. Horney saw **basic hostility** as *the child's natural response to mistreatment by parents or caretakers,* but since little ones are dependent on the adults for survival, such hostility must be repressed: "I have to repress my hostility because I need you. . . . I have to repress hostility for fear of losing love. . . . I have to repress hostility because I would be a bad child if I felt hostile" (Horney, 1937, p. 86).

In what appears to be a page from her own childhood, Horney wrote: "Furthermore, we find various actions or attitudes on the part of the parents which cannot but arouse hostility, such as preference for other children, unjust reproaches, unpredictable changes between overindulgence and scornful rejection, unfulfilled promises . . . (1937, pp. 80–81). After enumerating these triggers for hostility, Horney describes "the child's sense of lurking hypocrisy in the environment: his feeling that the parents' love, their Christian charity, honesty, generosity, and so on may only be pretense" (1945, p. 41).

Alienation between the real self and the idealized self—the core neurotic conflict. When the *basic anxiety* of the child is coupled with *unexpressible hostility* toward parents and other adults, it causes *alienation* from the child's real self. According to Horney, this creates the **core neurotic conflict**—*alienation between the real self and the idealized self*. This conflict depletes the self of spontaneity and energy, leaving the person feeling "driven" or compelled instead of in the driver's seat. This *intrapsychic* conflict between the ideal self and the real self usually leads to *interpersonal* conflict with others because of compulsive behaviors and resentment on the part of the person who is working so hard to be loved by others:

> As soon as, for instance, his need to be liked by everybody becomes compulsive, the genuineness of his feelings diminishes; so does his power to discriminate. As soon as he is driven to do a piece of work for the sake of glory, his spontaneous interest in the work decreases. . . . In other words, the tyranny of the should drives him frantically to be something different from what he is or could be. (Horney, 1950, p. 159)

Results of intrapsychic alienation. As a result of this inner alienation, neurotic individuals tend to abandon self-responsibility, feeling "I am driven instead of being the driver" (Horney, 1950, p. 159). Additionally, they actively move away from the real self, while inner creative forces lie dormant, subverted by the "search for glory" embodied in the effort to fulfill all the "shoulds" of the idealized self.

Horney reverses the Freudian order of things. Instead of the usual inside-out sequence where *intrapsychic* conflict leads to social maladjustments, Horney—like Klein and other object-relations theorists—argued that personality conflicts are first formed in the matrix of *interpersonal* relationships, and subsequently become *internalized*:

> Freud had been increasingly aware of the significance of inner conflicts; he saw them, however, as a battle between repressed and repressing forces. The conflicts I began to see were of a different kind . . . they originally concerned contradictory attitudes toward others, in time they encompassed contradictory attitudes toward the self. . . . (Horney, 1945, p. 15)

Ten Neurotic Trends

Disconnected from one's real self, the neurotic person copes with life in compulsive but unsatisfying ways. Horney did not draw a sharp contrast between normal and neurotic needs, viewing them as differences of *degree* more than differences of *kind*. Whereas a normal person shows a healthy need for affection, the neurotic is *obsessed* with finding love. The normal person seeks an intimate partner for companionship, the neurotic wants someone to *completely take over* his life. Normal needs can be met with reasonable effort; neurotic needs, because of their contradictory nature, are impossible to satisfy. As Horney saw it: "The neurotic person engulfed in a conflict is not free to choose. He is driven by equally compelling forces in opposite directions, neither of which he wants to follow. . . . He is stranded, with no way out" (1945, p. 32).

Horney (1942, pp. 54–60) described the following **ten neurotic trends**:

1. **The neurotic need for affection and approval** manifests itself as an indiscriminate desire to be loved and approved by everyone, coupled with a dread of self-assertion and a dread of hostility on the part of others, or within oneself.

2. **The neurotic need for a "partner" who will take over one's life** is what we might today call a *dependent personality disorder*. The person with this disorder is not looking for a "complementary" partner; the neurotic wants someone who will take responsibility for success or failure, for good or evil, someone who will fulfill all the expectations the neurotic holds but feels doomed to fail in achieving. The "center of gravity" is entirely in the partner, with accompanying dread of desertion and fear of being left alone.

3. **The neurotic need to restrict one's life within narrow borders** is found in a person who tries to remain inconspicious, dreads making any demands, and tries to be content with little—the opposite of the more healthy trends to take responsibility and rely on one's own strength to achieve and acquire.

4. **The neurotic need for power** is the opposite of the trend just discussed, and manifests in an individual who is "power hungry," seeks to dominate others, admires strength and authority, and dreads loss of control or helplessness.

5. **The neurotic need to exploit others and by hook or by crook get the better of them:** This fits what we might diagnose as the *sociopathic or antisocial personality disorder*. Others are evaluated primarily in terms of how they can be "used." Exploiters take pride in their manipulative skills and dread being victimized themselves, as this would show them to be "stupid."

6. **The neurotic need for social recognition or prestige:** Self-evaluation is primarily made in terms of how others perceive oneself. There is a dread of losing status or being humiliated.

7. **The neurotic need for personal admiration:** Like the trend just discussed, this one involves a narcissistic need to be admired, not so much for what one actually *is,* but for what one *imagines oneself to be.* Narcissistic persons want to be treated in accordance with their own grandiose self-image.

8. **The neurotic ambition for personal achievement** is present in a person whose self-esteem depends on being the *best possible* athlete, lover, worker, or writer—especially in one's own mind. This person strives mightily to fulfill all the "shoulds."

9. **The neurotic need for self-sufficiency and independence** is the opposite of what is found in the dependent personality. A person with this trend attempts

never to need anyone, never to be "tied down," never to "fall in love," or in any other way become entangled with another. He equates needlessness with freedom.

10. **The neurotic need for perfection and unassailability** is characterized by a relentless driving for perfection, self-recriminations regarding even the smallest personal "flaws," and feelings of superiority because of being (at least attempting to be) perfect.

"Auxiliary" Neurotic Mechanisms for Resolving Conflict

In addition to these ten trends, Horney believed neurotics also attempt to resolve conflict by externalization and other "auxiliary means." She believed that various defense mechanisms are used in concert: "A combination of defenses is developed in every neurosis; often all of them are present, though in varying degrees of activity" (1945, p. 140). However, since these unconscious strategies are frequently in conflict with one another, neurotics can only hope to gain partial relief, which is why Horney titled her chapter on this topic *"Auxiliary Approaches to Artificial Harmony"* (1945, pp. 131–140).

Externalization *is the tendency to experience internal processes as if they were outside oneself.* Thus, it is not unusual for a depressed mother to complain that her child is "hyperactive." Horney referred to externalization as a way of eliminating intolerable inner tension by eliminating self from the loop. In contrast with the *intrapsychic* quality of Freudian defenses (e.g., denial, projection, rationalization) Horney's defense of *externalization* has a decidedly *interpersonal* flavor: "making the person more reproachful, vindictive, and fearful in respect to others" (Horney, 1945, p. 130).

Blind spots *create a discrepancy between a neurotic's idealized picture of himself or herself, and actual behavior.* Sometimes, according to Horney, such discrepancies are: ". . . so blatant that one wonders how he himself can help seeing it. But far from doing so, he is able to remain unaware of a contradiction that stares him in the face" (Horney, 1945, p. 132).

Compartmentalization, in classical psychoanalytic theory, is *the defense mechanism whereby incompatible thoughts or feelings are stored* as if in psychologically sealed containers, allowing them to exist side by side without influencing one another. Notice how Horney's definition adds an *interpersonal* flavor:

> There is a section for friends and one for enemies, one for the family and one for outsiders, one for professional and one for personal life, one for social equals and one for inferiors. Hence what happens in one compartment does not appear to the neurotic to contradict what happens in another. (1945, p. 133)

Rationalization is *"self deception by reasoning"* (1945, p. 135, emphasis added). This seems similar to a Freudian definition, but in psychoanalytic theory *rationalize* means to intellectually justify expressing or acting out forbidden instinctual impulses. For Horney, *rationalization* is not primarily about explaining to onself and others why an instinctual impulse was acted upon; rather rationalization functions as inner "self-talk," seeking to achieve harmony between the real self and the idealized image: ". . . discrepancies between the actual self and the image must be reasoned out of existence" (1945, p. 135).

Excessive self-control: Another auxiliary strategy for bolstering "artificial harmony" is excessive self-control:

> Persons who exert such control will not allow themselves to be carried away, whether by enthusiasm, sexual excitement, self-pity, or rage. . . . In short, they seek to check all spontaneity. . . . The exertion of will power then, consciously or unconsciously, is needed to keep the conflicting impulses under control. (Horney, 1945, pp. 136–137)

Arbitrary rightness: In what was probably a portrait of her own father, Horney stated that *arbitrary rightness* "has the twofold function of eliminating doubt from within and influence from without" (1945, p. 137). Uncertainty detracts from one's ability to cope with life, and certain individuals—those in whom a lot of unresolved conflict exists—find additional ambiguity and uncertainty intolerable:

> The more a person sees life as a merciless battle, the more will he regard doubt as a dangerous weakness. . . . It [arbitrary rightness] constitutes an attempt to settle conflicts once and for all by declaring arbitrarily and dogmatically [echoes of Daddy?] that one is invariably right. (Horney, 1945, pp. 137–138)

Elusiveness is nearly the polar opposite of rigid rightness. In Horney's description, people who use this defense sound eerily like contemporary politicians in the midst of campaigns to win public office:

> . . . [they] often resemble those characters in fairy tales who when pursued turn into fish; if not safe in this guise, they turn into deer; if the hunter catches up with them, they fly away as birds. You can never pin them down to any statement; they deny having said it or assure you they did not mean it that way. . . . (Horney, 1945, pp. 138–139)

Cynicism: Horney believed that *cynicism* operates by

> . . . denying and deriding of moral values. . . . a deep-seated uncertainty in respect to moral values is bound to be present in every neurosis. . . . thereby relieving the neurotic of the necessity of making clear to himself what it is he actually believes in. . . . (Horney, 1945, pp. 139–140)

Summary of Horney's motivational constructs. Horney's motivational constructs and defense strategies appear, at first, to have a familiar psychoanalytic flavor; however, closer inspection reveals significant differences. For Sigmund Freud, defense mechanisms were primarily *intrapsychic*—mostly concerned with impulse control and libido distribution. After Anna Freud's elaboration, defense mechanisms took on a slightly more relational flavor; however, Horney saw defense/coping strategies as *interpersonal*—played out at the broadest personal and societal levels. In Horney's hands, motivational theory escapes the hidden recesses of the unconscious mind, shakes off the handcuffs of libidinal cathexes, and blooms in the interactional milieu of the home, office, church, shopping mall, and everywhere that people interact.

What Makes a Person Grow?

Horney did not delineate a series of psychosocial or cognitive stages in the style of Erikson or Piaget. Nor did she view development as a series of bus stops along a pre-arranged Freudian route. Instead, like Adler, she focused on how early family dynamics predispose a child to cope with the challenges of life. Her developmental formulations were more far-reaching than detailed. What she thought was foundational was the *quality* of early family life, and her own experiences of having been treated unfairly as a child—especially by her father—were never far distant from her theoretical formulations.

What Makes a Person Unique?

Horney painted psychological development with broad strokes and a wide brush, finding uniqueness in the way each person deals with the familial, social, and cultural forces seeking to shape personality. Recall that in the "parts" department Horney formulated *four selves;* in the "fuel" department she introduced *ten needs* along with *seven auxiliary approaches;* and we are about to study *three broad interpersonal styles.* So with four selves, ten trends, seven auxiliary approaches, and three interpersonal styles (as well as extensive variation *within* each category), the number of possible personality configurations is quite high.

Three interpersonal styles. In grappling with chaos in the environment and alienation within themselves, Horney saw children developing one of three major coping styles:

> A child can move *toward* people, *against* them, or *away from* them. . . . When moving *toward* people he accepts his own helplessness, and in spite of his estrangement and fears tries to win the affection of others and to lean on them. . . . When he moves *against* people he accepts and takes for granted the hostility around him, and determines, consciously or unconsciously, to fight. He implicitly distrusts the feelings and intentions of others toward him. . . . When he moves *away from* people he wants neither to belong nor to fight, but keeps apart. He feels he has not much in common with them, they do not understand him anyhow. . . . (Horney, 1945, pp. 42–43)

DSM-IV-TR (American Psychiatric Association, 2000) lists nearly a dozen different personality styles, which are further categorized into three major *clusters: A, B,* & *C.* It is interesting to notice the correspondence between Horney's three ways of relating to people and these three diagnostic clusters. *Moving toward* people is similar to the shy and dependent personality styles contained in Cluster C, *moving against* people reminds one of the manipulative personality styles found in Cluster B, and *moving away from* people resembles the withdrawn personality styles of Cluster A. Horney appears to have anticipated these clusters about fifty years earlier.

Moving toward people. This *self-effacing interpersonal strategy* is followed by persons who are compliant, cooperative, and so eager to comply with the wishes of significant others that the relationship is virtually guaranteed to remain intact. Horney said:

> This type needs to be liked, wanted, desired, loved; to feel accepted, welcomed, approved of, appreciated; to be needed, to be of importance to others, especially

to one particular person; to be helped, protected, taken care of, guided. (1945, p. 51)

Moving against people. This is the *expansive/manipulative interpersonal strategy* founded on the belief that the world is a hostile place and that life is a "struggle of all against all" (Horney, 1945, p. 63). These people tend to be "slick" operators, socially skilled in getting what they want, facile in exploiting others for their own benefit: "Any situation or relationship is looked at from the standpoint of 'What can I get out of it?'—whether it has to do with money, prestige, contacts, or ideas" (Horney, 1945, p. 65).

Horney also included in her description of this style much that today would be included under narcissistic personality disorder: ". . . the individual prevailingly identifies himself with his glorified self. When speaking of 'himself' he means . . . his very grandiose self. Or, as one patient put it, 'I exist only as a superior being'" (Horney, 1950, pp. 191–192).

Moving away from people. This is a *strategy of withdrawal or resignation*. Such persons withdraw and largely become detached from human affairs, creating an inner, isolated world of their own. Although most of us experience times when we want to be left alone to "chill out," the neurotic's need to be alone is *persistent*, based on the "intolerable strain in associating with people." Horney says, "He is like a person in a hotel room who rarely removes the 'Do-Not-Disturb' sign from his door" (Horney, 1950, pp. 73, 76).

When followed in a neurotically rigid way, these three patterns are incompatible—you can't move *toward* others and *away* from others at the same time. In normal individuals such trends are balanced and used alternately—sometimes we seek to move toward others, at times we yearn for solitude. The neurotic tends to rigidly utilize only one of these strategies, to the exclusion of the other two. Neurotic needs are characterized by their disproportionate intensity, disregard for reality, indiscriminate application, and a tendency to evoke intense anxiety.

FACING THE TOUGH TWINS

Is It Testable?

Horney's theory, like Freud's and other early analysts', was not formulated in a way that easily lends itself to validation by empirical testing. Her generic constructs and sweeping social generalizations are difficult to operationally define and empirically test. Nonetheless, some of her ideas have been *indirectly validated*. For example, in her early writings, Horney noted cultural trends toward hypercompetitiveness, and devoted two chapters to discussing competitiveness (1937, pp. 188–230).

Subsequently, Ryckman, Hammer, Kaczor, and Gold (1990) developed the *Hypercompetitive Attitude Scale* to investigate the validity of Horney's ideas. They found that among college students, those scoring higher in hypercompetitiveness had less self-esteem and were more poorly adjusted than those scoring lower. Kaczor, Ryckman, Thornton, and Kuelnel (1991) found that hypercompetitive males were more likely to view rape victims as responsible for having been raped.

Another example of indirect support for Horney's theories comes from the work of Albert Ellis (1994), whose Rational Emotive Behavior Therapy incorporated Horney's (1950) "Tyranny of the Should." Ellis, in his typically flamboyant style, called this "musterbation," but the idea that maladjusted people live by lots of irrational "shoulds" is central to both the work of Horney and Ellis. Considerable evidence (Ellis & Greiger, 1977; Smith, 1983) supports the effectiveness of challenging clients' irrational beliefs and replacing them with more realistic thoughts and feelings.

Is It Useful?

Self-analysis. Horney used Freud's techniques of free association and dream analysis, but instead of utilizing them to uncover the unconscious, she gave them a more interpersonal emphasis, utilizing them in her efforts to scout out neurotic coping strategies. Although Freud discouraged self-analysis (except in the case of himself), Horney actively encouraged self-analysis, devoting an entire book to the topic. As she saw it, self-analysis increases self-confidence: "This effect is the same in analysis as in other areas of life. To find a mountain path all by oneself gives a greater feeling of strength than to take a path that is shown. . . . " (1942, p. 36).

Pioneer feminist—putting womb envy on a par with penis envy. In the area of feminine psychology Horney's work was truly groundbreaking. Although she agreed with much of Freud's theory, she disagreed with almost every conclusion Freud reached about girls and women. Horney's rebellion wasn't simply an angry "It-isn't-true!" challenge to the centrality of penis envy in Freud's formulations. Instead, she stood psychoanalysis on its head, contending that **womb envy,** or *the male's envy of pregnancy, childbirth, motherhood, breasts, and the act of suckling,* is as intense in males as penis envy is in females.

Summary of Horney

From psychoanalyst to humanistic social psychologist. Although Horney began her career as a classical psychoanalyst operating in the *Insight Zone,* she subsequently moved diagonally toward the *Social Zone*—to broader levels of analysis and a more interpersonal focus. Moving beyond her traditional training as a psychoanalyst, she first evolved into an object-relations theorist, analyzing how interactions between infants and caretakers shape personality development. In attempting to correct Freud's (and her own father's) antiwomen biases, Horney evolved further into the *Social Zone* to became the first feminist psychoanalyst. She was interested in much broader forces than libido: "Freud's disregard of cultural factors not only leads to false generalizations, but to a large extent blocks an understanding of the real forces which motivate our attitudes and actions" (1937, pp. 20–21). She was also one of the first humanistic *self* theorists, anticipating the "third force" movement in psychology by emphasizing the *self-actualizing* potential in all humans.

Insisting that *interpersonal* neurotic trends were the real forces energizing personality, Horney's evolving formulations foreshadowed much that followed in the field of personality. For example, Horney's *Moving Against People/Expansive* interpersonal style appears to share much in common with Eysenck's *extraversion,* which in turn was incorporated into the Five Factor Model (Chapter 5) as well as into Cluster B of DSM-IV-TR.

Although Horney used many of the traditional psychoanalytic terms, she gave them distinctly *interpersonal* meanings. Just as she reinterpreted "penis envy" in broad cultural terms, she did the same with Freud's pivotal concept, the oedipal situation, viewing it as a clash of *interpersonal attitudes:*

> The typical conflict leading to anxiety in a child is that between dependency on the parents . . . and hostile impulses against the parents. . . . The resulting picture may look exactly like what Freud describes as the Oedipus complex. . . . But the dynamic structure of these attachments is entirely different. . . . They are an early manifestation of neurotic conflicts rather than a primary sexual phenomenon. (1939, pp. 83–84)

Once again we see Horney desexualizing or dephysiologizing a classic Freudian construct and moving to a higher level of analysis—explaining it in terms of conflicted *interpersonal* relations.

KOHUT, KERNBERG, AND WINNICOTT: THEORIES THAT ECHO AND EXPAND

Next we will briefly examine the work of Kohut, Kernberg, and Winnicott, theorists who followed in the footsteps of the earliest ego analysts and object-relations theorists, but expanded and elaborated their ideas. Like Anna Freud, Kohut focused on the importance of warmth and empathy in relating to infants and children; and like Klein, Kernberg focuses on aggression and splitting. Winnicott was supervised by Melanie Klein for the better part of six years, but he viewed children in much friendlier terms. First trained as a pediatrician and then as a child psychoanalyst, Winnicott retained a lifelong playfulness in relating to his young patients. His ability to form relationships with children (he metaphorically termed it *"holding"*) was legendary.

Heinz Kohut—Mother as Self-object

Heinz Kohut (1913–1981) shared Klein's conviction that object-relations are the most important influence in early development; however, his was a much kinder, gentler portrait of the baby and the mother. His portrait of this relationship was filled with fondness rather than aggression; he saw the infant not as persecuted and seeking retaliation, but as warmly bonded with the mother. Under such conditions of tenderness the mother becomes for the infant a **self-object.** "Self-objects are objects [people] which we experience as part of our self . . . "(Kohut & Wolff, 1978, p. 414).

    Empathic attunement. Kohut differed from Freud, who pictured the mother-infant relationship primarily in terms of drive satisfactions; and he replaced Klein's dark portrait of the infant under attack, developing a portrait that emphasized empathy, warmth, and affectionate responsiveness between the infant and caretaker. In response to this sort of **empathic attunement,** *the accurate reflection of another's emotional state,* the child grows to experience herself as a joyful, competent, and prized person:

> The essence of the healthy . . . relationship for the growing self of the child is a mature, cohesive parental self that is in tune with the changing needs of the child. It can, with a glow of shared joy, mirror the child's grandiose display one minute, yet perhaps a minute later, should the child become anxious and

overstimulated by its exhibitionism, it will curb the display by adopting a realistic attitude *vis-a-vis* the child's limitations. (Kohut & Wolff, 1978, p. 417)

Mirroring and merging. In Kohut's brand of interpersonal psychoanalysis, the mother serves as a **mirroring self-object:** *a mother who empathically affirms her infant's sense of health, happiness, greatness, joy, and strength.* It is through the empathic "mirroring" of their caretakers that infants and children gain the self confidence to construct what Kohut termed a **cohesive nuclear self:** *a self that is formed not so much by conscious encouragement and praise but by* "deeply anchored responsiveness of the self-objects [caretakers]" (Kohut, 1977, p. 100).

Somewhat later in development, the mother also serves as an **idealizing self-object:** *allowing the child to merge with her own strength, calmness, and competence as an adult.* This provides for the developing child a model of power, perfection, and soothing which comes to be experienced as part of the child's own interpersonally-affirmed personality.

Thus, both by *absorbing* the affirming mirroring of an empathically attuned caretaker, and *merging* with her/his competence and values, the developing child develops a *cohesive nuclear self* that resists *fragmentation* under the stresses of life. Kohut summarized it in these words: "In the last analysis, only the experience of a firmly cohesive nuclear self will give us the conviction that we will be able to maintain the sense of our enduring identity, however much we might change" (1977, p. 182).

Otto Kernberg—the Primacy of Aggression

Otto Kernberg (1928–) shares Klein's emphasis on aggression and rage as major emotions contributing to the development of personality. Like Klein, he uses the notion of *splitting* to explain the intense emotional reactions of people (especially those with *borderline* personality styles) who fluctuate between intense rage and fervent love for significant others—failing to integrate both the attractive and frustrating aspects of a whole person.

Kernberg begins with a somewhat Freudian emphasis on instinctual drives, but agrees with other object relations theorists that early interpersonal relations modify and shape such drives. Kernberg agrees that personality is profoundly influenced by early object relations, but his emphasis is not—like Kohut's—on the empathic mirroring of the caretakers, but on how sexuality, aggression, and rage are *neutralized* under the influence of caretakers.

Donald W. Winnicott—Cofounding "Mother" of Object Relations

Donald Winnicott (1896-1971) was trained *both* as a pediatrician and as a psychiatrist, and blended both professions throughout his career: "I am a paediatrician who has swung to psychiatry," he wrote, "and a psychiatrist who has clung to paediatrics" (1948, p. 157). At first, he was strongly influenced by Melanie Klein, whom he retained as a clinical supervisor for the better part of six years. Although he found much of value in Klein's ideas, he worked to depathologize her positions. In sharp contrast to Klein, Winnicott saw infants not as sadistic savages but as collaborators in the interpersonal enterprise of becoming human.

He replaced Klein's dark, persecutory, aggression-permeated view of children with a much more playful portrait that grew out of his pediatric/psychiatric consultations with upwards of 20,000 children and their mothers. In conducting such consultations, Winnicott followed a standardized interview (which he termed a "set situation") that functioned as a near-standardized experimental situation. This led to a much more reality-based view of the child as compared with Klein's inferences about the child's inner mind.

Writing of the differences that emerged between Klein's classical views and his own interpersonal ideas, Winnicott said: "Since those days [of supervision] a great deal has happened, and I do not claim to be able to hand out the Klein view in a way that she would herself approve of. I believe my views began to separate out from hers" (1962, p. 176).

Contrasting sharply with Klein, Erikson, and Horney, who felt alienated in their childhood families, Winnicott was enveloped in maternal warmth. He grew up in a family that included his mother, two older sisters, a nanny, sometimes a governess for his sisters, his aunts, a cook, and several parlor maids who doted on him. Winnicott grew up *surrounded* by nurturing females. With so many females around to *mother* him, he hardly missed his father who was apparently preoccupied with business matters most of the time. On the positive side,

. . . . because young Donald received so much affection from so many women with whom he interacted in a reliable manner, he felt protected, safe and secure, and this emotional stability provided him with a solid foundation for a sturdy, productive, and creative adult life. (Kahr, 1996, p. 6)

On the negative side, Winnicott's strong female identification included a squeaky, high pitched voice that he detested. Once, after doing some radio broadcasts for the BBC, he received numerous letters addressed to "Mrs. Winnicott" (Kahr, 1996, p. 7).

Another personality psychologist concluded that because of "Winnicott's affinity for and empathy with mothers. . . . and his own impressive talents 'mothering' and 'holding' his patients. . . . Winnicott must share with Anna Freud. . . . the title of *mother of object relations theory*" (Monte, 1999, p. 354).

The primacy of holding. Beginning with the literal *holding* of the infant by the mother during diapering, dressing, and nursing interactions, Winnicott metaphorically expanded the meaning of *holding* to include a wide array of caring behaviors and communications that take place between caretakers and infants. Winnicott saw *holding* as providing the opportunity for the infant to integrate a sense of self and a personality out of fragmented sensory experiences: "The tendency to integrate is helped by . . . the technique of infant care whereby an infant is kept warm, handled, and bathed and rocked and named. . . . Many infants are well on the way toward integration during certain periods of the first twenty-four hours of life" (1945, p. 151).

Babies begin life as part of a "nursing couple." Winnicott believed that babies are born—literally—with no individual personality: "What is there is an armful of anatomy and physiology, and added to this a potential for development into a human personality" (Winnicott, 1987, p. 89). However, unlike Anna Freud and Klein, who saw the developing child mostly from an *intrapsychic* perspective, Winnicott saw the newborn as an inseparable part of a *dyad*. He famously said: *"'There is no such thing as a* *baby.'*. . . if you show me a baby you certainly show me also someone caring for the baby, or at least a pram with someone's eyes and ears glued to it. One sees a 'nursing couple.'" (D. W. Winnicott, 1952/1992, p. 99).

Dyadically "in synch." Winnicott described the interpersonal dynamics of the mother–infant dyad in vivid terms: "mother has a breast and the power to produce milk, and the idea that she would like to be attacked by a hungry baby. These two phenomena do not come into relation with each other till the mother and child *live an experience together*" (1945, p. 152).

Transitional objects. During the earliest hours of life, a baby experiences the mother's breast as part of himself or herself. As Winnicott put it:

> The mother, at the beginning, by an almost 100 per cent adaptation affords the infant the opportunity for the *illusion* that her breast is part of the infant. . . . The mother's eventual task is gradually to disillusion the infant, but she has no hope of success unless at first she has been able to give sufficient opportunity for the illusion (1971, pp. 12–13).

Soon, however, babies begin to dimly recognize that Mother's breast is *not* part of one's self, not something that can always be produced upon demand; rather, the breast is something "out there" that sometimes disappears and cannot be successfully retrieved, something that might vanish when you need it most. Donald Winnicott was the first to describe how *transitional objects* assist newborns in forming a differentiated self. When Mother's breast is not available, other external "objects" such as a teddy bear, a favorite blanket, or a cuddly toy help to make the *transition* from the inner world of needs and tensions to the external world of supplies and suppliers.

Transitional Objects

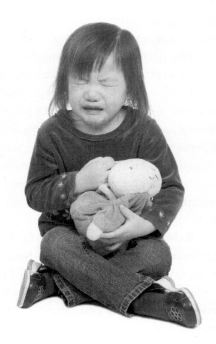

Whether at rest or in distress, children find security in their transitional objects.

Though *not* part of one's self, such soft, soothing *transitional objects* assist the baby in differentiating between what is *me* and what is *not me*.

The *transitional object* must never change, unless changed by the infant. It can never be replaced, unless replaced by the infant. It must survive both intense love *and* intense hatred—serving as a focus for rage as well as affection. The *transitional object* provides the infant a sense of warmth and security, appears to have life and vitality of its own, yet is capable of accommodating the baby's emotional projections without disappearing or ceasing to exist.

Confirming research: A breathing teddy bear. The importance of transition objects was experimentally demonstrated by researchers who found that "breathing" teddy bears exert a calming influence on premature infants. Using a specially designed pump, Ingersoll and Thoman (1994) created a "breathing" bear, whose rate of respiration could be altered by the researchers. An important characteristic of these bears was that they were designed to "breathe" quietly in order to avoid imposing a constant and unavoidable sound on the premature infants. The researchers studied low-birth-weight infants by randomly placing a breathing bear in half the infants' cribs. They then set the breathing rate of each breathing teddy bear at one-half the normal breathing rate of the baby, to study whether the bear's slower "breathing" would exert a calming effect on the preterm baby with whom the bear shared a crib. In optimal development, breathing rates become slower from premature periods to later ages.

After two weeks of sleeping with a slowly breathing bear, premature infants showed statistically significant decreases in their breathing as compared to babies who slept alone. Since slower respiration is seen as a sign of developmental maturity, the experimenters concluded that "the results of this study provide further evidence that exposure to the breathing bear has a positive impact on the neurobehavioral development of infants" (1994, p. 859).

Good-enough mothers. Another major theme in Winnicott's theories was that of the *good-enough mother.* This notion is, perhaps, the most reassuring thought professional psychiatry has ever offered to generations of worried, guilt-ridden mothers. Winnicott's writings are sprinkled with frequent references to the "ordinary devoted mother" or the "good enough mother" (e.g., 1966, 1971). Winnicott flatly stated:

> *The ordinary good mother is good enough.* If she is *good enough* the infant becomes able to allow for her deficiencies by mental activity. . . . The mental activity of the infant turns a *good-enough* environment into a perfect environment. . . . that releases the mother from her need to be near-perfect in the infant's understanding. (1948, p. 245)

Summary of Winnicott—a reassuring psychiatrist. Following Klein, Winnicott shifted focus from a Freudian analysis of intrapsychic conflict in the *Insight Zone,* to the study of mother–infant relationships in the *Social Zone,* picturesquely describing this dyad as the "nursing couple." He trusted the newborn to a *good-enough mother*, believing in her ability—both physically and psychologically—to *hold* her baby in a manner that promoted healthy development. He mostly encountered mothers and their children in a standardized "set" situation, which, as in Mahler's experimental work, helped to rescue object-relations theory from the quicksands of Kleinian subjectivity.

MARGARET S. MAHLER: PIONEER OBJECT-RELATIONS RESEARCHER

Mahler began her research career with a major study of infantile psychosis—severe cases in which infants remained attached to their mothers instead of separating and individuating as normal two-year-olds do (M. S. Mahler, 1968). Following this study of psychotic children, Mahler and her colleagues carried out a five-year study of "average mothers and their normal babies" (Mahler, Pine, & Bergman, 1975). She saw her research as "supplementing" Freud's drive theory by "showing the growth of object relationship . . . in parallel with the early life history of the ego" (1975, p. 6). Thus, although Mahler and her colleagues shared Freud's psychoanalytic perspective, theirs was a more *object-relational, ego-oriented* approach. For Mahler, development was less about libido and more about *differentiation* and *individuation*—both interpersonal concepts.

Working with normal children and their mothers at the Masters Children's Center in New York, Mahler and her coworkers used a specially equipped "waiting room," which included one-way mirrors and playrooms, to unobtrusively observe mother–infant interactions. Their stated goal was to "strike a balance between free-floating psychoanalytic observation and pre-fixed experimental design" (1975, p. 17).

Object-relations theory. From their careful observations of children ages four months to four years, Mahler and her colleagues (Mahler, Pine, & Bergman, 1975) detailed the *"psychological birth"* of infants as they matured through what they termed the **separation–individuation process**—*six stages of object-relational development, comprised of two "forerunner" phases (autism and symbiosis), and four subphases (differentiation, practicing, rapprochement, and emotional object constancy).*

What is important for us to remember about Mahler's theory is not the details of each developmental subphase, but the overall portrait of the infant entering the world symbiotically attached to the mother, hardly aware of her existence as a separate person—and subsequently "hatching" into an independent person.

Interpersonally speaking, it can be said that over the first three years of life, the child *individuates* by *differentiating* from mother. The first subphases are all heavily **dyadic**, *with mother and infant fused in a kind of psychological cocoon.* It is only during the fourth and final subphase that the consolidation of individuality begins to take place, facilitating the formation of genuinely **triadic relationships** *that include others in addition to the primary parent.* Mahler's model is thoroughly object-relational (interpersonal). Little is said about libido forces, cathexes, or intrapsychic conflicts; the focus of interest is the mother–infant interaction. However, in place of Klein's unverified inferences, Mahler and her colleagues carried out behavioral investigations of their ideas. Interestingly, some of Mahler's formulations (such as the earliest stage of "symbiosis") have been *falsified* by recent research. This is, perhaps the greatest compliment that can be paid to someone's work—that it is scientific enough to be carefully investigated and falsified.

Recent research reformulations. Neonatal research has reinforced this object-relations shift from biological determinism to social relations by demonstrating that babies are more socially oriented and less biologically driven than we originally thought. In place of a *passive* newborn that Freud once compared to a bird's egg, we now know that from the first days of neonatal life the babies are spring-loaded for socialization.

Searching for Mama. Researchers have found that infants do far more than sleep and feed. They actively seek stimulation, proactively pursuing social interactions with their caretakers (Roffwarg, Muzio, & Dement, 1966). By two weeks, infants will look at the mother's face longer than at a stranger, and they will gaze even longer if she is talking to them (Carpenter, 1974). Beebe and Stern (1977, pp. 35–55) reported a "visual violation" experiment in which mothers were instructed to keep their faces expressionless and immobile. Infants actively tried to recapture the mother's expected response by moving their hands and eyes, and by reaching with their arms, legs, and entire body. If mothers failed to respond, the infants showed increasing signs of distress.

Dancing with Mama. Neonates are primed for social interaction. As early as four weeks of age, researchers can tell whether the baby is interacting with his mother or with an inanimate object: "You could indeed tell from looking at a toe or a finger whether the infant was in an interaction with an object or a parent—and by 4 weeks of age, even which parent it was" (Brazelton & Als, 1979, pp. 357–359).

Such findings strongly support Erikson's view (next chapter) that psychological development is shaped by *mutual regulation* between the infant and caretaker from the earliest moments of life. Lichtenberg (1983) notes that babies aged twelve to twenty-one days consistently copy adults' manual and facial gestures, and he concludes that "the postnatal baby is a participant in and an activator of the dialogue, not simply a recipient. As early as the first postnatal day, microkinesic movie analysis reveals that the neonate moves in precise synchrony with the articulated structure of adult speech" (p. 17).

In terms of our zonal perspective, this means that nearly all reformulations of classical psychoanalysis have been diagonally upward: from id to ego, from biology to psychology, from libido to object relations. However, this has been balanced with renewed interest in the *Physiological Zone* as well.

Contemporary prenatal research. We learned that Klein shifted emphasis from the oedipal crisis, at around ages four or five, to the weaning process taking place during the first two years of life. Neonatal researchers have focused on the earliest hours of life. Now, researchers have focused on even earlier events—those taking place *in the womb*. Recent studies of humans and nonhuman primates have revealed links between maternal hormone levels during pregnancy and subsequent caregiving behaviors on the part of the mother. Maestripieri & Zehr (1998) showed that in pigtail macaques (monkeys), increased caregiving behaviors in females were correlated with an increase in estradiol concentrations in the blood. Maestripieri (2001) also showed that there seems to be a *sensitive* period shortly after birth when it is especially important for mothers and their infants to be in close contact.

Other prenatal researchers have sought to clarify the relationship between prenatal maternal stress and child development. Although data is still somewhat scanty, Welberg & Seckl (2001) documented changes in brain structure as a function of prenatally stressed animals. The relationships appears complex, however, because other researchers (e.g., Fujioka, T., Fujioka, A., Tan, N., Chowdhury, G., Mouri, H., Sakata, Y., & Nakamura, S., 2001) found that mild stress *benefits* rather than damages later learning in rats. In the case of humans, DiPietro concluded that "At this time there is too little scientific evidence to establish that a woman's psychological state during pregnancy affects her child's developmental outcomes. It is premature to extend findings from animal studies to women and children . . ." (DiPietro, 2005, p. 37).

However, new, noninvasive technologies for assessing fetal functioning promise to increase our knowledge of infant development—including not only neonatal socialization and weaning but studying personality formation during the stages of fetal development as well.

Chapter Summary

Anna Freud—a favorite daughter opens the floodgates. In this chapter we discovered how far modern psychoanalysis has moved from Freud's instinct-driven, conflict-ridden model of the mind to ego-oriented, interpersonal emphases. Although Anna Freud remained her father's most loyal supporter, her work with children and her focus on ego defense mechanisms shifted her father's theory away from instinctual drives to coping processes—from the id to the ego.

Melanie Klein—"Mother" of object-relations theory. Melanie Klein moved interpersonal issues back to the earliest months of life by emphasizing *weaning* (instead of oedipal conflict) as the most crucial interpersonal encounter. Although Klein used many of Freud's terms, she painted development in object-relational hues. She supplanted Freud's anatomy-is-destiny, phallocentric view of development with more gender-neutral concepts such as weaning, splitting, part versus whole objects, and "good" versus "bad" caretakers. We briefly examined how Kohut and Kernberg built upon but transcended the work of Klein and Anna Freud.

Karen Horney—first feminist. If Klein was the "mother" of object-relations theory, Horney was the founder of feminist psychoanalysis. She saw psychological development as a result of family dynamics, not anatomy. Practicing psychoanalysis during the Great Depression, impressed upon Horney the importance of cultural influences; consequently, many see her as a cultural psychoanalyst. While that is partially true, we have seen that she believed the development of *self* is primarily the result of early object relations, not culture. Although she applied her insights at the societal level (in the *Social Zone*), at the core Horney is an object-relations theorist.

Winnicott and Mahler—research "mothers" of object-relations theory. Winnicott used his "set situation," and Mahler and her colleagues utilized one-way mirrors in a "waiting room" to standardize observation-based research for the purpose of validating or disproving psychoanalytic ideas. Their work was a shining counterpoint to Klein's subjectivity and laid the groundwork for the scientific investigation of subsequent theories.

Points to Remember

1. Anna Freud, Melanie Klein, and Erik Erikson moved psychoanalysis in a more *interpersonal (object-relations)* direction. This came about not as an intentional rebellion, but primarily because they worked with children, and children demand more than an "opaque mirror" from their analysts.

2. Additionally, Anna Freud's work with children caused her to shift her focus from her father's favorite topic—unconscious processes of the id—to more practical considerations, such as *defense mechanisms of the ego*. Through her training and analysis of Erik Erikson, she further facilitated this movement in the direction of a more child-friendly, socially oriented, interpersonal psychoanalysis.

3. *Defense mechanisms* (also known as *coping strategies* when used by normals) serve to protect persons from becoming overwhelmed by anxiety. They vary, according to the developmental level of the person, from primitive to highly sophisticated.

4. Sigmund Freud first described the process of unconscious defense mechanisms, but it remained for his daughter, Anna, to develop his ideas more fully by describing and elaborating *ten defense mechanisms*. All defense/coping mechanisms are automatic (unconscious) psychological processes designed to protect the person from anxiety.

5. Melanie Klein, a mother of three, with no academic training in psychoanalysis, was first analyzed by Freud's famous Hungarian disciple, Sandor Ferenczi, who tutored her in his own brand of "active" psychoanalysis. This proved especially beneficial in her work with young children.

6. According to Klein, infants use *splitting* to sort "good" or "bad" internal images that result from *interpersonal relationships* with a "good" or "bad" mother (parent or caretaker). This is followed by distinguishing between "part" objects (nipple, breast, or penis) and the "whole" objects (mother, father, caretaker) they represent.

7. Klein emphasized *weaning* as *the* pivotal developmental event. Since weaning is an *interpersonal* milestone, occurring much earlier than the oedipal crisis, attention was turned to interpersonal relationships at a much earlier age than emphasized in Freud's psychoanalysis. Klein preferred the term *position* in place of *stage*. She defined *position* to include both the flavor of the *interpersonal relationships* as well as the characteristic *defense or coping strategies*.

8. Klein insisted that *early interpersonal relationships*—not libido concentrations—were crucial in the formation of personality. This fostered a more ego-oriented focus that undermined Freud's preoccupation with early instinctual processes.

9. Klein's legacy is twofold: (1) she began what is now known as *object-relations theory*, emphasizing *interpersonal relationships* between the infant and its caretakers; and (2) she *invented play therapy*, utilizing children's play (instead of free association) as a way of gaining access to a child's unconscious.

10. Probably because of her own personal encounters with death and destruction, Klein saw the *baby's mind as filled with internalized images of death and destruction, sadism and humiliation, cannibalism and killing, murder and mayhem*—hardly a warm and fuzzy place.

11. Karen Horney grew up amid family conflict and rejection by her father. Her brother's death as a young man left Karen feeling guilty and depressed nearly to the point of suicide.

12. Horney emigrated to the United States, where, practicing psychoanalysis during the Great Depression, she concluded that people's problems were related more to losing their jobs and worrying about food than to arrested libido. Her subsequent theories emphasized the broader influences of culture on personality functioning.

13. One of the first psychoanalysts to use the term *self,* Horney described personality as composed of *four selves: despised real self, idealized self, positive real self,* and *actual self.*

14. Like Klein, Horney had a dark view of the inner life of the child. Undoubtedly influenced by her own unhappy childhood, she saw most parents as *lacking warmth or neglecting their children—basically evil*—and their children becoming *hostile* and *anxious* as a result.

15. Caught between their *unexpressible hostility* and *basic anxiety*, children develop a *core neurotic conflict*, consisting of *alienation* between the *real self* and the *idealized self.*

16. Having lost touch with the *real self,* a neurotic person tries—unsuccessfully—to find happiness using *ten neurotic strategies* as well as seven *auxiliary approaches.* Additionally, Horney outlined *three interpersonal styles: moving toward, against,* or *away from others.*

17. A pioneer feminist, Horney challenged the validity of Freud's *penis-envy* formulations, arguing that *womb envy* and *breast envy* on the part of little boys was as prevalent as penis envy on the part of girls.

18. Heinz Kohut, a more contemporary object-relations theorist, contrasted with Klein and agreed with Mahler in emphasizing the *warm bonding* that occurs between mothers and newborns. Otto Kernberg disagreed with Kohut and focused on sex and aggression more in the style of Klein.

19. Donald Winnicott is remembered for his incisive description of *transitional objects,* his *playful* view of children, and his encouraging view of mothers, whom he generally regarded as "good enough."

20. Margaret Mahler was a pioneer investigator of object-relations theory, using a standardized research setting to study interactions between infants and their mothers.

21. Research has generally supported the Freudian idea of *unconscious defense mechanisms;* however, the classical Freudian notion that the infant enters the world as drowsy "eater" and "sleeper" has not fared so well. Infant research has revealed the baby to be an *active socializer,* vigorously seeking contact with caretakers.

22. Traditional psychoanalysis has provided many valuable clinical perspectives, but due to managed care and other market forces, it appears possibly headed for extinction. However, object-relations theories and ego-analytic approaches appear likely to endure.

Key Terms

Actual Self   (251)
Ambivalence   (242)
Arbitrary Rightness   (255)
Bad Objects   (241)
Basic Anxiety   (251)
Basic Evil   (251)
Basic Hostility   (251)
Blind Spots   (254)
Cohesive Nuclear Self   (260)
Compartmentalization   (254)
Coping Mechanisms   (230)
Core Neurotic Conflict   (252)
Cynicism   (255)
Denial   (232)
Depressive Position   (239, 244)
Despised Real Self   (250)
Displacement   (234)
Dyadic   (264)
Ego Defense Mechanisms   (228)
Elusiveness   (255)
Empathic Attunement   (259)
Epistemophilic Instinct   (240)
Excessive Self-Control   (255)
Externalization   (254)
Good Objects   (241)
The Height of Sadism   (240)
Idealized Image of the Self   (250)
Idealizing Self-Object   (260)
Identification   (232)
Intellectualization   (234)

Introjected Objects   (239)
Isolation   (233)
Mirroring Self-Object   (260)
Object Relations Theory   (225)
Part Object   (242)
Play Therapy   (246)
Position   (243)
Primitive/Narcissistic Defenses   (231)
Projection   (234)
Rationalization   (234, 254)
Reaction-Formation   (233)
Real Self   (250)
Regression   (230)
Repression   (230)
Reversal   (233)
Self-Object   (259)
Separation–Individuation Process   (264)
Sophisticated/High-Level Defenses   (231)
Sublimation   (235)
Substitution   (235)
Symbiosis   (225)
Ten Neurotic Trends   (253)
Triadic Relationships   (264)
Turning Against Self   (233)
Undoing   (233)
Whole Object   (242)
Womb Envy   (258)

Web Sites

Anna Freud

www.annafreudcentre.org/history.htm. The Anna Freud Center, London. This page explains the history of this wonderful child therapy center started by Anna Freud. Follow the link at the bottom of the page to read Anna's biography.

Klein

www.melanie-klein-trust.org.uk/. The Melanie Klein Trust. This organization is dedicated to promoting training and research in the psychoanalytic techniques and theory of Melanie Klein. Read some fascinating interviews with people who know and remember Klein.

www.webster.edu/~woolflm/women.html. This is the homepage of Dr. Linda Woolf who, in addition to several other subjects, has compiled an extensive body of knowledge on women who have contributed to the fields of anthropology, psychology, psychoanalysis, sociology, and social work. This page includes links to three articles about Melanie Klein.

Horney

http://plaza.ufl.edu/bjparis/. The International Karen Horney Society. This provides students a link to a world of Horney disciples along with information about Horney and the reason her work was so groundbreaking. It includes her bibliography and information on how to procure her papers from Yale.

www.psyking.net/id164.htm. King's Psychology Network. This page, devoted to humanistic psychology and Karen Horney, has short, interesting bites of information about her life and work.

Learning on the Lighter Side

In the movie *Cast Away*, Tom Hanks plays the role of a recently shipwrecked person who successfully creates fire and manages to survive on a remote island. He also becomes "buddies" with a volleyball. Previously, you might have thought his forming a personal "relationship" with a volleyball a sign of insanity, or at the very least, a scriptwriter's unrealistic fantasy. Now that you understand *regression* as a coping mechanism, and realize that under stress *everyone* regresses, you find the portrayal more realistic. Yes, this movie illustrates the power of Winnicott's *transition object* in times of stress—not only for toddlers, but for adults as well.

Looking Ahead

In this chapter we discovered how *psychoanalysis* evolved into *ego analysis* and *object relations theory*. Neonatal research has reinforced this shift, revealing that newborns are far more socially oriented than originally thought. In place of a *passive* newborn, which Freud once compared to a bird's egg, we now see the baby as spring-loaded for socialization. In terms of our levels-of-analysis perspective, this means that nearly all reformulations of classical psychoanalysis have moved toward a broader perspective: from id to ego, from biology to psychology, from libido to object relations.

In the next chapter we will further broaden our perspective by switching to the "wide-angle" lens of *society*, considering how the developing child interacts not only with Mommy or family, but with peers and teachers. We will begin with the theories of Erik Erikson, who was trained as a psychoanalyst, but who broadened his thinking to include culture at every step of development. We will continue by examining the work of Alfred Adler, who left Freud's inner circle to develop his own theory of *Individual Psychology,* which focused on the complexes, life style, and goals of persons as members of a larger society. Adler believed that people continually evolve toward higher and higher levels of *social interest* in a kind of social Darwinism.

The chapter will conclude by examining the work of Erich Fromm, who believed that social/political currents were far more important than *libido* flow in shaping personality. He attempted to blend Freud and Marx, utilizing Freud for understanding the individual's alienation from self, and Marx for describing the person's alienation from fellow humans.

chapter 8

Social Self in Cultural Context

Erich Fromm, Erik Erikson, and Alfred Adler

IN THIS CHAPTER YOU CAN

1. Discover how Erich Fromm tried to *synthesize the theories of Freud and Marx* to create a Marxist theory of psychoanalysis.

2. Surmise that since Erik Erikson experienced an early *identity crisis* as a fair-haired Danish boy in a Jewish family, the achievement of *identity* became an important component of his developmental theory. Erikson retained much of Freud's language but infused the terms with *interpersonal* and *social* meanings.

3. Learn how Erikson used *mutual regulation* to replace *libido* as the motivating force in personality development. He also replaced Freud's psycho*sexual* stages with his own psycho*social* stages.

4. Discover that Erikson moved beyond Freud's *originology (explaining development in terms of origins)* to formulate an *epigenetic* approach in which each

new stage of development *incorporates—in expanded and enriched forms—all the previous stages.* Far ahead of his time, Erikson mapped development over the *entire* lifespan.

5. Wonder whether Alfred Adler was correct in believing that most of us suffer from some sort of *organ inferiority,* and that we *compensate* by developing a counterbalancing skill.

6. Realize that *fear of death* was conspicuous in Adler's childhood as well as in his later theories.

7. Find out how Adler combined *structure* and *motivation* into forward *movement* toward *goals.*

9. Determine the importance of *birth order in the family constellation.*

10. Evaluate Adler's four major personality styles: *ruling, getting, avoiding, and socially useful.*

A PERSONAL PERSPECTIVE

Dying for Daddy and Dying for Country

Erich Fromm was about twelve years old when an attractive young woman—a friend of the family—committed suicide. This tragedy profoundly affected him:

> Maybe she was 25 years of age; she was beautiful, attractive and in addition, a painter, the first painter I ever knew. I remember having heard that she had been engaged but after some time had broken the engagement; I remember that she was almost invariably in the company of her widowed father. . . . Then one day I heard the shocking news: her father had died, and immediately afterwards she had killed herself and left a will which stipulated that she wanted to be buried together with her father. (Fromm, 1962, p. 4)

Young Erich, who had found this woman "beautiful" and "appealing," and her father "old, uninteresting, and rather unattractive-looking" (1962, p. 4), was deeply shaken by what appeared to be such senseless behavior: "I was hit by the thought 'How is it possible?' How is it possible that a beautiful young woman should be so in love with her father, that she prefers to be buried with him to being alive to the pleasures of life and painting?" (1962, p. 4)

About this same time, World War I was beginning and German nationalism was running high. Erich was especially disturbed by his Latin teacher, who showed a genuine fondness for the whole idea of war:

> How is it possible that a man who always seemed to have been so concerned with the preservation of peace could be so jubilant about the war?. . . . How is it possible that millions of men continue to stay in the trenches, to kill innocent men of other nations, and to be killed and thus to cause the deepest pain to parents, wives, friends?" (1962, pp. 6, 8)

Commentary

Fromm found the answer to his adolescent dilemma in his early twenties when he first discovered Freud's formulation of the Oedipus complex. The young woman's suicide, previously an undecipherable enigma, suddenly made sense, and psychoanalysis appeared a clarifying lens for viewing human behavior: "When I became acquainted with Freud's theories, they seemed to be an answer to a puzzling and frightening experience" (1962, p. 4).

Similarly, Fromm felt that Marx's social theories provided an alternative to war. He concluded that both Freud and Marx were necessary for a clear understanding of human behavior:

> Freudians saw the individual unconscious, and were blind to the social unconscious; orthodox Marxists, on the contrary, were keenly aware of the unconscious factors in social behavior, but remarkably blind in their appreciation of individual motivation. . . . one cannot separate man as an individual from man as a social participant—and if one does, one ends up by understanding neither. (Fromm, 1959, pp. 110–111)

In this chapter we will consider the personality theories of Fromm, Erikson, and Adler. All three transcended Freud's *self* in a closed system by placing more emphasis on how society shapes personality.

In formulating his theory of personality, Fromm did not carefully define "parts," nor were his motivational and developmental constructs clearly articulated. Instead, he blended psychoanalysis and Marxist political theory into a personality theory that was primarily socially constructed from the outside. Although Fromm was trained as a psychoanalyst, the *self-as-agent* was lost along the way—not to Freud's biological determinism, but to Marx's sociopolitical constructions.

ERICH FROMM'S MARXIST PSYCHOANALYSIS

Erich Fromm (1900–1980) was psychoanalytically trained and deeply conversant with Freud's family dynamics, peer relationships, and religious and political convictions. His book, *Sigmund Freud's Mission* (1959) is a masterpiece of psychohistorical analysis.

However, most of Fromm's writings sought to synthesize Freud and Marx: "I tried to see the lasting truth in Freud's concepts. . . . I tried to do the same with Marx's theory, and finally I tried to arrive at a synthesis which followed from the understanding and criticism of both thinkers" (1962, p. 9). Even the titles of his books (e.g., *Escape from Freedom,* 1941; *The Sane Society,* 1955; *Beyond the Chains of Illusion: My Encounter with Marx and Freud,* 1962; *Social Character in a Mexican Village,* by Fromm & Maccoby, 1970) reveal the strong sociopolitical tilt of Fromm's thinking. Here we will briefly touch on some of the main themes of his work.

The illusion of individuality. Fromm was skeptical of Western democracy's ability to provide adequate nurturing for the self. He referred to the *illusion of individuality,* by which he meant that in modern industrial societies most people feel "powerless and alone, anxious and insecure" (1941, p. 240). The healthy self for Fromm was always societally shaped and culturally embedded: "One can call a person normal or healthy if he is able to fulfill the social role he is to take in that given society" (1941, p. 138). Fromm described what he considered to be an optimal personality—the **social character:** " . . . it is the social character's function *to mold and channel human energy within a given society for the purpose of the continued functioning of this society*" (1962, pp. 78–79).

Alienation—the fundamental pathology. Marx's influence is seen most clearly in Fromm's adoption of *alienation* as the core of human motivation: ". . . he speaks of one form of psychic crippledness [alienation] which to him is the most fundamental expression of psychopathology and which to overcome is the goal of socialism: *alienation*" (1962, p. 43). According to Marx, as the worker produces more wealth, she becomes spiritually poorer because she becomes alienated and distanced from the products of her labors. "Alienation then, is, for Marx, *the* sickness of man" (Fromm, 1962, p. 48).

Is It Testable?

We have seen that as theories become broader—moving up the hierarchy and utilizing more far-reaching constructs—they become correspondingly more difficult to precisely define and validate. This is certainly the case with Erich Fromm, who blended psychoanalysis and Marxist political theory. To empirically test Fromm's theory would be somewhat similar to scientifically investigating Marx. Fromm was a social and political critic who relied on what has sometimes been called the "coherence theory of truth." For Fromm the "proof" of a theory emerges from its internal coherence and ability to shed light on the human condition.

Nonetheless, Fromm and Maccoby (1970) utilized an interdisciplinary team of psychologists, historians, anthropologists, and other experts to study a Mexican village that had been lured away from a traditional craft-oriented, land-based, village life by the advent of technology and industrialization. Fromm and his colleagues trained Mexican interviewers to conduct in-depth assessments. Not surprisingly, Fromm found support for his theory that personality development is significantly affected by social structure. Maccoby subsequently studied 250 managers in large corporations and identified a "company man" style of manager, similar to Fromm's *marketing* character (Maccoby, 1976).

Fromm wrote little about his clinical techniques, indicating only that he was a more "active" therapist than Freud, but offering few details. His writings have not been highly influential in the clinical realm, but have been widely read by the public. His book, *The Art of Loving* (1956), became an inspirational best seller, and books like *To Have or to Be?* (1976) highlight how a technological society may subvert self-actualization.

ERIK ERIKSON'S PSYCHOSOCIAL, CULTURALLY CONNECTED, *MUTUALLY REGULATING SELF*

Background Check

Jew or Gentile? Erikson's personal identity crisis. Erik Erikson (1902–1982) was born to Danish parents living in Frankfurt, Germany. His biological father left the family before Erik was born, and three years later his mother married Erikson's pediatrician, Dr. Theodore Homberger. Although this was kept secret from young Erik, he apparently developed a sense of "not belonging" in this family. This intensified as he grew to be a tall, blond, blue-eyed Scandinavian, in a family where both his mother and stepfather were Jewish. At school he was known as a Jew, but at his stepfather's synagogue he was referred to as a "goy," a Yiddish term for Gentile.

As an adult, Erikson's "outsider" complex was, no doubt, intensified by the fact that his formal schooling ended when he graduated from the gymnasium (approximately the European equivalent of an American high school). Yet, he spent much of his professional life in some of America's most renowned academic institutions (e.g., Harvard, Yale, and Berkeley) rubbing shoulders with colleagues who mostly held earned doctorates.

An outsider's lucky break. Rebelling against his stepfather's wish for him to become a physician, Erik studied art and roamed around Europe instead. His lucky break came in 1927 when an old school buddy, Peter Blos, invited him to work at a small school attended mostly by the children of Freud's patients and friends. Erikson accepted the offer, first working as an artist and then as a tutor. And, in his luckiest break of all, Anna Freud subsequently offered to train him as a child psychoanalyst. Although he later enrolled at Harvard as a Ph.D. student, he dropped out within a few months. Since he had been trained by Anna Freud, and had subsequently been voted a full member of the Vienna Psychoanalytic Society, he apparently didn't consider further training necessary. Thus equipped with the credentials of having been trained by Freud's daughter, and bolstered by his own incisive writing, Erikson achieved eminence as an unschooled, but brilliant, psychoanalyst.

Between 1936 and 1939 Erikson was affiliated with the Yale University Medical School, where he worked with normal as well as emotionally disturbed children. At this time, he became acquainted with anthropologists Margaret Mead and Ruth Benedict, and accompanied them on a field trip to study the child-rearing practices of Sioux Indians in South Dakota. During this trip his awareness of the importance of social and cultural factors in personality development flourished. A little over a decade later, he published his famous book *Childhood and Society (1950)* in which he highlighted the importance of social and cultural factors in personality development.

In this book he also expanded and elaborated on the functions of the ego, making him one of the earliest ego analysts.

Zeitgeist

For Erikson, psychoanalysis was both his identity and his prison. Without his Anna Freud training and credentials, it is certain that he would not have achieved the professional recognition that he did; but, he also felt imprisoned by the biological reductionism of Freudian theory and by what he considered its excessive emphasis on early childhood:

> In its determination to be sparing with teleological assumptions, psychoanalysis has gone to the opposite extreme and developed a kind of originology . . . a habit of thinking which reduces almost every human situation to an analogy with an earlier one. . . . Psychoanalysis has tended to subordinate the later stages of life to childhood. (Erikson, 1958, pp. 18–19)

ASKING THE BIG FOUR QUESTIONS

Introduction

Erikson shook off the shackles of Freud's biological determinism and historical originology, but he still managed to remain inside the boundaries of the psychoanalytic institutions of his day. He translated his own personal identity crisis into a theory of development that was lucid and far-reaching. Using the identity crisis of adolescence as his launching pad, Erikson propelled his version of ego analysis beyond the early childhood years (which had been so intensely scrutinized by Freud and object-relations theorists) to span the entire life cycle. His students at Harvard informally renamed his popular Human Life Cycle course "From the Womb to the Tomb."

Erikson at first appears loyal to psychoanalysis by defining the "parts" of his model in biological ways that sound much like Freud; e.g., "I do not think that psychoanalysis can remain a workable system of inquiry without its basic biological formulations, much as they may need periodic reconsideration" (Erikson, 1963, p. 70). However, as we shall discover shortly, he "rewired" Freud's biologically based psycho*sexual* stages of development with his own culturally enriched psycho*social* "circuitry." He energized his system not with libido, but with the interpersonal fuel of *mutual regulation.*

What are the Parts?

Id. Erikson viewed the *id* much as did Freud, defining **id** as *the animal side of our nature, the repository of all the raw, biological forces evolutionarily implanted within the organism:*

> The id is everything that is left in our organization of the responses of the amoeba and of the impulses of the ape, of the blind spasms of our intrauterine existence, and of the needs of our postnatal days—everything which would make us "mere creatures". . . . (Erikson, 1963, pp. 192–193)

Superego. Erikson saw the **superego** as *the core of conscience:* " . . . the oppressive force of conscience. . . . a kind of automatic governor which limits the expression of the id by opposing to it the demands of conscience. . . . the sum of all the restrictions to which the ego must bow" (Erikson, 1963, pp. 192–193). "So we would not want to make the superego appear to be expendable. It is an essential part of man's inner structure" (quoted in Evans, 1964, p. 107).

Ego. Like Freud, Erikson saw the **ego** as the *touchstone to reality and mediator of intrapsychic conflict:*

> Between the id and the superego, then, the ego dwells. Consistently balancing and warding off the extreme ways of the other two, the ego keeps tuned to the reality of the historical day, testing perceptions, selecting memories, governing action, and otherwise integrating the individual's capacities of orientation and planning. . . . (Erikson, 1963, pp. 193–194)

Here it might appear that Erikson simply reiterates Freud, but for Erikson the *ego* is far more than a "referee" supervising an unending boxing match between the *id* and *superego.* Erikson's *ego* functions more as a *dance instructor,* choreographing a dance of *interpersonal mutuality:* "I would call mutuality a relationship in which partners depend on each other for the development of their respective strengths" (Erikson, 1964, p. 231).

What Makes a Person Go?

In 1890, one of the founders of modern psychology, William James, picturesquely described the newborn baby's experience as "one great booming, buzzing confusion." James believed that babies are faced with the daunting task of differentiating themselves from this surrounding "confusion" and forming a unique and enduring identity. Recall that Winnicott also saw newborns as utterly void of any sense of personal identity (" . . . an armful of anatomy and physiology," 1987, p. 89). Erikson agreed, describing the first developmental step was differentiating *self* from *other,* by "constant tasting and testing of the relationship between inside and outside" (Erikson, 1963, p. 248).

Freud's prime motivational fuel, *libido,* was too biologically deterministic to suit Erikson: "we must become sensitive to the danger of forcing living persons into the role of marionettes of a mythical Eros—to the gain of neither therapy nor theory" (1963, p. 64).

Mutual regulation. Erikson's alternative to Freud's biologically based libido was **mutual regulation,** *a process of reciprocal, complementary interpersonal exchanges in which each participant is able to retain autonomy and exert self-control.* Instead of viewing persons in terms of their "libido economy," Erikson saw the psychoanalyst's task as facilitating *mutual regulation* between child and parents:

> Babies control and bring up their families as much as they are controlled by them; in fact we may say that the family brings up a baby by being brought up by him. Whatever reaction patterns are given biologically and whatever schedule is predetermined developmentally must be considered to be a series of *potentialities for changing patterns of mutual regulation.* (Erikson, 1963, p. 69, emphasis in original)

Erikson described the difference between mutual regulation and classical psycho-analysis as the difference "between last century's preoccupation with the economics of energy and this century's emphasis on complementarity and relativity" (Erikson, 1997, p. 21).

What Makes a Person Grow?—Erikson's Psychosocial Stages

Maturation: personality's balancing act. Abandoning Freud's "libido economy," and even moving beyond object-relational concerns within the mother-child dyad, Erikson proposed a broader synthesis that included *whole persons interfacing with culture*. What he saw was not a concentration of biological libido at the baby's mouth, but a sequence of mutually satisfying interactions between infant and caretaker, occurring within the framework of a "welcoming" culture. Notice how broadly Erickson defines the "oral" stage to include infant, mother, and culture:

> His [the baby's] inborn and more or less co-ordinated ability to take in by mouth meets the breast's and the mother's and the society's more or less co-ordinated ability and intention to feed him and to welcome him. At this point he lives through and loves with his mouth; and the mother lives through and loves with her breasts. (Erikson, 1963, p. 72)

As we learned previously, this description is consistent with recent research that finds the baby "dancing" with the caretaker.

Polarities of personality development. Erikson defines psychological maturity as the successful *balancing* of **polarities:** *e.g., trust versus mistrust, autonomy versus shame, initiative versus guilt, industry versus inferiority, identity versus confusion.* During optimal development, negatives are not vanquished but are synthesized into a dynamic balance where positives prevail. During the earliest stages of normal development, the infant's *trust* provides the foundation for the toddler's subsequent *autonomy, initiative, and industry.* These cumulatively blend with the adolescent's *identity,* and the adult's *intimacy* and *generativity*, to endow life with *integrity* and *meaning.*

Virtue—a product of personal synthesis. According to Erikson, this balancing of polarities is an "active" and "spirited" process that results in a *virtue* (1964, p. 113). Other psychologists have referred to similar processes as *ego strength,* but according to Erikson, *virtue* is more than ego strength or moral consciousness. Virtue means *synthesis:* "Virtue is that active capacity for synthesis which enables one to take due account of the negative aspects of each of these nuclear conflicts while still tilting the crises in favor of the positive" (Browning, 1973, pp. 160–161).

With *virtue,* Erikson broadens the scope of his object-relational vision (moving into the *Social Zone*) to include not only the infant and the mother, but all of society—not only in the present, but including the past and anticipating the future as well: "Every virtue involves a synthesis of psychosexual, psychosocial, and cognitive stages of development, as these epigenetic elements not only shape but are shaped by external, familial, institutional, cultural, and historical factors" (Browning, 1973, p. 161).

Ritualizations—the products of cultural syntheses. Erikson views personality as developing in concert with—rather than at war against—society. Whereas Freud conceptualized the ego as endlessly entangled in conflict between the id and the superego (culture's "enforcer"), Erikson saw culture wearing a friendlier face. According to Erikson, **ritualizations** *are recurring patterns of behavior that reflect the values, customs, and beliefs of a particular culture that serve to make life meaningful.* Each child must become "familiarized by ritualization with a particular version of human existence. He thus develops a distinct sense of corporate identity" (1977, pp. 79–80).

In each person's own culture—where things are familiar—rituals do not stand out as something strange or special; they are simply experienced as "the way we do things." In American society, for example, a man is permitted to touch a woman's body on a dance floor, but not while walking on the street. A woman can appear in a bikini on the beach, but not at the office. Jokes can be told at work but not at funerals. Such customs do not seem strange, it's simply "the way things are."

Avoiding "originology"—the importance of endings. In mapping the developmental journey, Erikson reversed Freud's emphasis that the child is the father of the man—that the end of life must be understood primarily in terms of beginnings. Instead, said Erikson, beginnings must be understood in terms of how they facilitate later development; late-in-life developments are just as pivotal as those appearing earlier. For Erikson, the cardinal sin of classical psychoanalysis was not biological reductionism, it was **originology**—*attempting to understand phenomena primarily in terms of beginnings.* Erikson was willing enough to consider biological roots, but only as the beginning—not the end—of development. Rieff (1959) made a similar point: "while an oak does originate in an acorn, the mature tree cannot be held to be still 'essentially acornish'" (p. 49). In this emphasis Erikson was far ahead of his time (when developmental psychology focused almost exclusively on infancy and childhood), anticipating our contemporary emphasis on development across the entire lifespan.

Epigenetic analysis. Erikson's developmental map follows his **epigenetic principle,** *according to which the rudiments of earlier stages are found—transformed, enriched, and expanded—in later stages.* For example, in speaking about the relationship of childhood rituals to adult behaviors, Erikson said: "In all epigenetic development, however, a ritual element, once evolved, must be progressively reintegrated on each higher level, so that it will become an essential part of all subsequent stages" (1964, p. 218).

Object-Relations Emphasis. Erikson's final reformulation of psychoanalysis was clearly object-relational in flavor; and, like Anna Freud and Melanie Klein, he was nudged in that direction by his work with children. But it was more than object-relational, it included families and society; it was culturally embedded and societally sensitive. His wife, Joan recalled:

> It was in the seminars dealing with child patients . . . that the reductionist language of scientistic theory moved into the background, while the foreground became vivid with innumerable details illustrating the patient's mutual involvement with significant persons. Here, instead of the single person's inner "economics" of drive and defense, an *ecology* of mutual activation within a communal unit such as the family suggested itself. . . .
> (J. Erikson, 1997, p. 21)

The Eriksons' Nine Psychosocial Stages

Table 8.1 summarizes Erikson's *developmental polarities* as well as the *virtues* and *rituals* that result from successful resolutions. During each of Erikson's stages, the maturing individual encounters a distinct *interpersonal* challenge that shapes future development. If she stumbles, development is delayed or regresses, but if the challenge is successfully mastered by learning the appropriate psychosocial skills, development proceeds to the next stage. Speaking of the oral stage, when the interpersonal polarities are *trust versus mistrust,* Erikson said:

> . . . when these stages are quoted, people often take away mistrust and doubt and shame and all of these not so nice, "negative" things and try to make an Eriksonian achievement scale out of it all, according to which in the first stage trust is "achieved." Actually, a certain ratio of trust and mistrust in our basic social attitude is the critical factor. When we enter a situation, we must be able to differentiate how much we can trust and how much we must mistrust, and I use mistrust in the sense of a readiness for danger and an anticipation of discomfort. (Evans, 1964, p. 15)

TABLE 8.1

The Eriksons' Nine Stages of Development

STAGE	NUCLEAR CONFLICT	VIRTUE	RITUALIZATION
1. Infancy: Birth–1	Trust vs. Mistrust	Hope	Numinous Presence vs. Idolism
2. Early Childhood: 1–3	Autonomy vs. Shame	Will	Judiciousness vs. Legalism
3. Play Years: 3–6	Initiative vs. Guilt	Purpose	Authenticity vs. Impersonation
4. School Age: 6–11	Industry vs. Inferiority	Competence	Formality vs. Formalism
5. Adolescence: 12–20	Identity vs. Role Confusion	Fidelity	Ideology vs. Totalism
6. Young Adult: 20–24	Intimacy vs. Isolation	Love	Affiliation vs. Elitism
7. Adulthood: 25–64	Generativity vs. Self-absorption	Care	Generationalism vs. Authoritism
8. Old Age: 65–89	Integrity vs. Despair	Wisdom	Integralism vs. Sapientism
9. Very Old Age: 90+[1]	Despair vs. Integrity	Gerotranscendance	

[1] Stage 9 was created by Joan Erikson after her husband's death.

Stage 1 (Infancy: birth to 1 year) *Trust versus Mistrust.* Erikson reformulated Freud's *oral stage* in object-relational dimensions of *trust versus mistrust.* Whereas according to Freud the neonate was a biological bundle of *id,* Erikson regarded the mother–infant nursing experience as the earliest instance of *mutual regulation:*

> The mouth and the nipple seem to be the mere centers of a general aura of warmth and mutuality which are enjoyed and responded to with relaxation not only by these focal organs, but by both total organisms. (1963, p. 76)

Over a decade later, Erikson maintained the same object-relational perspective, defining *orality* as a complex of experiences that are centered in the mouth and that take place "in relations with the mother who feeds, who reassures, who cuddles, and keeps warm . . . " (Evans, 1964, p. 14).

Numinous Presence versus Idolism. Erikson defines the culture's primary ritualization for this earliest stage as **numinous presence:** the *various ways that society prescribes how mothers care (are present) for their babies.* In our culture this includes how mothers are expected to touch, handle, feed, bathe, and play with their babies. If, through either overindulgence or neglect, the infant's normal love and respect for the parent becomes excessive, turning into a kind of blind hero worship, this ritualism can become *idolism.* The infant who successfully maintains a balance of trust and mistrust during this stage achieves the virtue of *hope.*

Thus, we see that from the very earliest stage of life, Erikson views the mutual regulation between infants and caretakers as occurring in a specific cultural context. In this way he seamlessly synthesizes object relations with culture.

Stage 2 (Early Childhood: 1 to 3 years) *Autonomy versus Shame.* Freud's anal–muscular stage is described by Erikson as a time during which the toddler experiences intense interpersonal challenges:

> The rages of teething, the tantrums of muscular and anal impotence, the failures of falling, etc . . . not even the kindest environment can save the baby from a traumatic change . . . because the baby is so young and the difficulties encountered are so diffuse. . . . The matter of mutual regulation now faces its severest test. (Erikson, 1963, pp. 78, 79, 82).

During this stage, the baby's bowels begin to function more efficiently in processing solid foods, and the result is better formed stools, making the tasks of *retention* and *elimination* more possible and more conscious. But the balancing of *holding on versus letting go* is not restricted to bladder and bowel control. The musculature also becomes more skillful in guiding the arms, hands, and legs in walking, running, holding, throwing, dropping, etc. The balancing act of this era— *holding on* or *letting go*—involves the entire body, and colors interpersonal relations as well.

Autonomy and pride versus shame and doubt are the polarities the ego seeks to balance during the anal–urethral–muscular stage in order to develop a healthy *will.* Using new motor skills and mental awareness, the toddler discovers how to decide and choose for herself. Autonomy is fostered when caretakers permit reasonable choices and do not coerce or shame the young child. As Erikson explained it: "From the sense of inner goodness emanates autonomy and pride; from the sense of badness, doubt and shame" (1963, p. 84). Yet, even here, Erikson believed "a ratio is necessary to development" (Evans, 1964, p. 19).

Judiciousness versus Legalism. Because society permits some behaviors and forbids others, the toddler must learn the rules, laws, and honored practices of his culture. He must learn to anticipate how others will judge him, and act accordingly. If all proceeds in a balanced way, the child learns to be **judicious**, that is, *wise to the rules and regulations of his culture*. Blind adherence to a set of rules without accompanying understanding is characterized by Erikson as **legalism**, or "the victory of the letter over the spirt of the word and the law" (1977, p. 97). *Legalism* is typically manifested by an excessively harsh and morally superior approach to punishment of rule breaking.

Stage 3 (Play Years: 3 to 6 years) ***Initiative versus Guilt.*** Erikson described Freud's phallic stage interpersonally as the *play years*. The three-year-old not only walks, but walks easily. This period is characterized by the toddler's pervasive *intrusiveness*, which Freud associated with the boy's growing awareness of his penis. Erikson, however, described such intrusiveness in broader, object-relational terms: intruding into another's space with vigorous locomotion, intruding into another's ears by aggressive talking, and intruding into other bodies by physical attack or other kinds of body contact.

According to Erikson, successful "intrusions" form the foundation for developing *initiative*. However, following hard on the heels of intrusion successes, the newly acquired attitude of initiative is threatened by the archenemy: *guilt*. Such guilt may arise in connection with the exuberant enjoyment of new locomotor skills or may result from the hopes and fantasies of the young child.

A boy's oedipal wish to "marry Mommy," or a girl's wish to "marry Daddy," inevitably meet with delay, disappointment, and displacement. If prohibitions are too rigorously enforced, the balance tilts toward excessive guilt; but if the child's emerging sexuality is appropriately affirmed, along with other "intrusions," the balance will shift toward vibrant *initiative*, with a sense of *purpose* instead of crippling guilt. According to Erikson, "The problem, again, is one of mutual regulation. . . . as some of the fondest hopes and the wildest phantasies are repressed and inhibited" (Erikson, 1963, pp. 256–257).

Authenticity versus Impersonation. In addition to playing with toys, toddlers play with roles—trying on costumes, imitating people, even pretending to be various kinds of animals. Through this "trying on" process, the child begins to discover the blend of roles that fits best. **Authenticity** *is a ritualization that blends those societal roles that allow a child to develop and express his or her unique personality in authentic ways.* By contrast, **impersonation** *is a ritualism that confuses the true self with the various roles society expects one to play.*

Stage 4 (School Age: 6 to 11 years) ***Industry versus Inferiority.*** The early school years are described by Erikson as "only a lull before the storm of puberty" (1963, p. 260). These are years when the child sublimates earlier libidinal urges into *producing things.* Expanding his or her ego boundaries to include skills and tools, the child seeks to master the fundamentals of technology and to gain affirmation for the products of his or her labor. However, this is not merely preparation for later entry into the workforce, it is a socially decisive period as well; a time when children begin to understand their future possibilities in society and develop an optimal balance of *industry versus inferiority,* with the accompanying virtue of *competence.*

Formality versus Formalism. Erikson described **formality** *as the ritualization whereby a child learns how to do things "properly."* Whether at home, school, or play, children are expected to behave appropriately—in line with cultural expectations. **Formalism** *is an exaggerated ritualization in which overconcern with doing a thing "properly" eclipses the purpose and meaning of the activity.*

Stage 5 (Adolescence: 12 to 20) Adolescence *Identity versus Role Confusion.* Adolescence corresponds to Freud's *genital psychosexual stage*—a time when Erikson sees the ego reaching its fullest bloom: "I would say that you could speak of a fully mature ego only after adolescence, which means, after all, becoming an adult" (Evans, 1964, p. 31). With some mastery of tools and skills and the beginning of puberty, "childhood proper comes to an end. Youth begins" (Erikson, 1963, p. 261). However, as parents of adolescents frequently discover, teenagers are prone to revisit the battles of earlier years, even if they have to "artificially appoint perfectly well-meaning people to play the roles of adversaries" (Erikson, 1963, p. 261).

Identity—the fulcrum of development. Probably because of his own identity struggles ("All through my earlier childhood they kept secret from me the fact that my mother had been married previously and that I was the son of a Dane who had abandoned her before my birth" [Erikson, 1970, p. 742]), Erikson was exquisitely sensitive to the importance of *identity*. He made *identity* the fulcrum of his developmental theory, asserting that the successful synthesis this polarity, and its consequent virtue, *fidelity,* were the crowning achievements of adolescence, providing a psychological bridge to authentic adulthood.

So important was the challenge of knowing *who I am,* and *who I am to become,* that Erikson avoided a narrow definition of **identity**, including synthesizing aspects of the Physiological, Insight, and Social Zones.

> I can attempt to make the subject matter of identity more explicit only by approaching it from a variety of angles. . . . At one time, then it will appear to refer to a conscious *sense of individual identity;* at another, to an unconscious striving for a *continuity of personal character;* at a third, as a criterion for silent doings of *ego synthesis;* and finally, as a maintenance of inner *solidarity* with a group's ideals and identity. (1959b, p. 102, emphasis in original)

However, even *identity,* the centerpiece of Erikson's developmental theory, is not a homogenized, "it's-all-good" kind of process. Here as with all of Erikson's developmental constructs we find polarities. Just as newborns experience the polarities of trust versus mistrust, and toddlers balance autonomy versus shame, adolescents seek to synthesize the positive and negative aspects of identity:

> Mixed in with the positive identity, there is a negative identity which is composed of what he has been shamed for, what he has been punished for, and what he feels guilty about: his failures in competency and goodness. Identity

means an integration of all previous identifications and self-images, including the negative ones. (Evans, 1964, pp. 35–36)

Work and play. *Work* serves a crucial identity-clarifying function for the adolescent, much as *play* did during earlier years. For the young child, *play* is "a function of the ego, an attempt to synchronize the bodily and social processes with the self" (Erikson, 1950, p. 211). *Work* fulfills a similar function, serving to integrate the adolescent's previous biological development with current and future societal opportunities and expectations: "The *work role* which we begin to envisage for ourselves at the end of childhood is . . . the most reassuring role of all, just because it confirms us in skills and permits us to recognize ourselves in visible works" (Erikson, 1977, p. 106).

Conversely, the failure to successfully identify with a work role is one of the more common problems of adolescence: "In most instances . . . it is the inability to settle on an occupational identity which disturbs individual young people" (1950, p. 262).

Ideology versus Totalism. Adolescents search for an **ideology**, *a "game plan" that synthesizes previous development and promises to provide meaning for life.* Such ideologies may be philosophical, spiritual, political, or career-oriented, but they must be congruent with both the individual's goals and cultural expectations. By contrast, **totalism** *is the unquestioning commitment to oversimplified ideologies.* Cults, gangs, music groups, or film stars may be attractive to the adolescent tilted toward exaggerated ritualization of ideology.

Stage 6 (Young Adult: 20 to 24) ***Intimacy versus Isolation.*** Early adulthood is a time when people seek to establish *intimate relationships* that can be filled with *love* and can serve to sustain them as they enter life as fully formed adults. For individuals unable to find intimacy, *isolation* may become a way of life. Such individuals are seen by others as "painfully shy" or "withdrawn," and clinicians see them as suffering from avoidant personality disorders, paranoid personality disorders, or schizoid personality disorders, all personality styles of isolation. Such people have difficulty forming loving relationships with others because they are unwilling to risk the give-and-take of a genuinely intimate relationship—preferring the "safety" of isolation.

Affiliation versus Elitism. Society's ritualization for the young adult is **affiliation**, *a variety of ways in which culture provides for close, caring, loving relationships between adults.* The marriage ceremony, with the exchange of rings, vows of faithfulness, and subsequent honeymoon, is one of the ways society ritualizes affiliation between adults. Churches, service clubs, and other community organizations offer opportunities for the ritualization of affiliation. When such affiliations are exaggerated or made exclusive, **elitism**, or *surrounding oneself with small groups of like-minded individuals,* may take the place of genuine affiliation.

Stage 7 (Adulthood: 25 to 64) ***Generativity versus Self-absorption.*** This is a time when life revolves around one of the most crucial of Erikson's polarities, *generativity versus self-absorption.* For Erikson, the artist-turned-psychoanalyst, **generativity** *is an artistic synthesis that builds upon several earlier syntheses.* When a person successfully balances the polarities of childhood, youth, and early adulthood, *generativity* is the synthesizing process that endows the last years with integrity and meaning instead of despair.

It should come as no surprise that for the mature, generative person *care* is a cardinal virtue. According to Erikson, if a man and a woman have successfully negotiated all the earlier stages of childhood, adolescence, and early adulthood, they will "soon *wish* . . . to combine their personalities and energies in the production and care of common offspring" (Erikson, 1959b, p. 97). *Care* is the emergent virtue during adulthood, just as *hope, will, purpose, competence*, and *fidelity* synthesized infancy, childhood, and adolescence.

Stage 8 (Old Age: 65 to 89) *Integrity versus Despair.* The senior citizen who successfully balances the polarities of *integrity versus despair* emerges with *integrity* as the "ripened fruit" of the previous stages, and *wisdom* as the defining virtue. Admitting that he lacked a "clear definition" of *integrity,* Erikson includes several ingredients in definition: "postnarcissistic love . . . acceptance of one's one and only life cycle . . . a different love of one's parents . . . comradeship with the ordering ways of distant times" (1963, p. 268).

In this final stage—as in his first—Erikson remained true to his object-relational roots, defining the important elements more in terms of relationships than biological changes. Building on previously mastered polarities, and energized by previously synthesized virtues, this final stage of development becomes not only the ultimate synthesis of a person's life, but also includes the integration of this individual with his or her culture. True to the epigenetic principle, Erikson comes full circle and concludes by relating his final stage to his earliest:

> Webster's Dictionary is kind enough to help us complete this outline in a circular fashion. Trust (the first of our ego values) is here defined as "the assured reliance on another's integrity," the last of our values. . . . And it seems possible to further paraphrase the relation of adult integrity and infantile trust by saying that healthy children will not fear life if their elders have integrity enough not to fear death. (1963, p. 269)

Integralism versus Sapientism. Erikson views the ritual of **integralism** *as a final synthesis of all earlier ritualizations*—a ritualization that puts life and death into perspective, diminishing the dread of mortality "by tying life cycle and institutions into a meaningful whole . . . " (Erikson, 1977, p. 112). Erikson defines **sapientism** *as "the unwise pretense of being wise"* (1977, p. 112). Some older persons, faced with despair over impending death but unable to place their lives in meaningful context, might pretend to have "all the answers" in a vain attempt to allay their existential anxieties.

Stage 9 (Very Old Age: 90 to death) *Despair versus Integrity—a reversing of polarities.* A *ninth stage* was introduced by Joan Erikson, with the comment that her husband, Erik, had written *The Life Cycle Completed* before reaching his nineties; and hence before they had really experienced the completion of the life cycle. She stated that in their eighties they had begun to acknowledge their elderly status, but they had not really faced its challenges until they were close to ninety.

> At ninety we woke up in foreign territory. . . . we soon began to face unavoidable—and certainly not amusing—realities. . . . At ninety the vistas changed; the view ahead became limited and unclear. Death's door, which we always knew was expectable but had taken in stride, now seemed just down the block. . . . (J. Erikson, 1997, p. 4)

Joan Erikson wrote eloquently about the difficulties encountered in the last decades of life:

> In spite of every effort to maintain strength and control, the body continues to lose its autonomy. Despair, which haunts the eighth stage, is a close companion in the ninth because it is almost impossible to know what emergencies and losses of physical ability are imminent. (J. Erikson, 1997, pp. 105–106)

Writing with unvarnished candor from her perch near the end of the ninth stage, Joan noted that in the previous eight stages, the synthesizing polarities were mentioned first (e.g., *trust* before mistrust, *autonomy* before shame, *intimacy* before isolation, etc.). However, during the ninth stage, she experienced a reversal of these polarities. Joan cast a backward glance and reversed polarities with the grace of one who is willing to face reality without bitterness, despair, self-absorption, or loss of integrity.

Experiencing reversed polarities without despair. *Mistrust versus Trust:* Remarking that "Time takes its toll even on those who have been healthy," Joan observed that "Hope may easily give way to despair in the face of continual and increasing disintegration, and in light of both chronic and sudden indignities" (1997, p. 107).

Joan Erikson reviewed the remaining six stages in much the same manner, showing how old age tilts polarities in a negative direction. Yet she didn't leave the person merely struggling to stay alive, but moved into the *Transpersonal/Spiritual Zone,* challenging the very old to **gerotranscendence**, which she described as "cosmic communion with the spirit of the universe," which includes a sense of self that "expands to include a wider range of interrelated others" (1997, p. 124). Joan said that life need not be limited to gradual loss of functions, but could be activated into transcen*dance* [her italics], which might include "a regaining of lost skills, including play, activity, joy, and song, and, above all, a major leap above and beyond the fear of death. It provides an opening forward into the unknown with a trusting leap" (1997, p. 127).

What Makes a Person Unique?

In Erikson's model, *uniqueness* is folded into the epigenetic stages, which describe maturation in a comprehensive way that includes biological, personal, social, and societal variables. Each person *balances polarities* in a distinctive way, blending biological givens, social experiences, and ecological peculiarities. Like snowflakes that appear identical to the casual glance, newborn babies—especially twins—appear to share common features. However, closer scrutiny reveals that no two neonates are precisely identical, and their subsequent developmental journeys accentuate these differences.

Summary of Erikson

Erikson's theory is a comprehensive synthesis of biological development, interpersonal relationships, and cultural expectations coalescing to shape personality. He avoids the handcuffs of originology on the one hand and social construction on the other. In this way he anticipated modern systems theories (e.g., Bateson, 1971; Bowen, 1978; Minuchin, 1974, and others) that seek to understand individuals in terms of their families, communities, and cultures. Erikson's theory is not a social psychology of the person primarily being shaped and molded by societal forces; his is a truly interactionist model that sees behaviors emerging from the *mutual regulation* occurring between infants and their caretakers, and from the *interaction* between persons and their cultures. Unlike some behaviorists who narrowly define "situation" in terms of eliciting stimuli or reinforcing consequences, Erikson's situational landscape is permeated with people and includes *cultural rituals*. In this way, he presents a truly comprehensive theory of personality—simultaneously synthesizing the *Physiological, Insight,* and *Social Zones*.

FACING THE TOUGH TWINS

Is It Testable?

Research evaluating Erickson's theory has produced mixed results. Although his early conclusions regarding gender differences in constructing play spaces have been criticized, his assertions regarding the importance of identity formation and mutual regulation have been supported by recent research.

Toys are us? Erikson's most famous study was conducted during the early 1950s. He invited 150 children to construct "movie scenes" with a variety of toys and blocks. Much to his surprise the children seemed to disregard his instructions and went about constructing their scenes "as if guided by an inner design" (Erikson, 1950, p. 98). Since there were drastic gender differences (see Figure 7.1), Erikson concluded that a child's creation of play space parallels the structure of his or her genital equipment: " . . . in the male, an external organ, erectable and intrusive in character . . . in the female, internal organs, with vestibular access, leading to statically expectant ova" (1968, p. 271).

However, Caplan (1979) failed to replicate Erikson's findings and criticized the notion that the arranging toys and blocks into play spaces corresponds to anatomy:

> The most important physiological factor to take into account is that there is no inner space. The walls of the uterus touch each other, as do the walls of the vagina. They are open only when separated by and filled with substances, as in intercourse or pregnancy. If girls' play constructions were to represent their uteri, they should look more like folded flapjacks than enclosures. (Caplan, 1979, p. 101)

If the Freudian "anatomy-is-destiny" aspects of Erikson's theory have not held up to research scrutiny, his more general ideas have fared better. Ciaccio (1971) asked 120 children to make up stories about five pictures, which were then analyzed for content. The five-year-olds showed the greatest number of themes corresponding to stage two, eight-year-olds gave the greatest number of stage-three sentences, while eleven-year-olds showed the greatest number of themes corresponding to stage four.

Identity achievement. Researchers (e.g., Bourne, 1978; Rosenthal, Gurney & Moore, 1981) have devised ways to quantify *identity achievement* so that it can be experimentally investigated. In general, such studies have been supportive of Erikson's model. Researchers (e.g., Adams & Fitch, 1982; Waterman, Geary, & Waterman, 1974) found that many college students achieve both occupational and ideological identities some time between their freshman and senior years, as predicted by Erikson. Waterman, Buebel, and Waterman (1970) found that the identity achievement is much more likely if trust, autonomy, industry, and initiative have previously been attained. Similarly consistent with Erikson's theory was the finding that identity achievement increases the probability of achieving intimacy during middle age (Kahn, Zimmerman, Csikszentmihalyi, & Getzels, 1985; Schiedel & Marcia, 1985; Tesch & Whitbourne, 1982).

Cross-cultural research regarding racial identity achievement. Cross-cultural researchers have explored Erikson's psychosocial stages in relationship to the development of personal *identity*. Such research has underscored the importance of ethnicity in the identity of Mexican Americans (Bernal, Knight, Garza, Ocampo, et al., 1990), African Americans (Aries & Moorhead, 1989; Cross, 1971, 1991) and other groups (Markstrom-Adams, 1992). Parham and Helms (1985) developed a Racial Identity Attitudes Scale (RIAS) to measure how African American identity forms, and Phinney (1992) developed a model of ethnic identity explicitly based on Erikson's psychosocial stages.

Assessing generativity. According to Erikson, the midlife balancing of *generativity versus self-absorption* is the primary task of the adult years. Others agree: "Generativity is the normative center of Erikson's thought" (Browning, 1973, p. 181). McAdams and his colleagues developed a self-report scale for assessing generativity (McAdams & de St. Aubin, 1992), and have conducted considerable research comparing generative and less generative adults (e.g., McAdams, Diamond, de St. Aubin, & Mansfield, 1997). McAdams says that in middle age we develop a "generativity script" linking our individual lives with the collective myths of humankind. Generative adults—more than less-generative adults—told life stories that frequently turned negative events into positive outcomes. Such generative themes also figure prominently in the stories of recovering addicts (Singer, 1997).

Erikson's ideas appear to be very much alive, heuristically generating significant amounts of research on such topics as generativity, achieving identity, and comparing identity achievement among various ethnic groups and cultural settings.

Is It Useful?

Most contemporary psychoanalysts practice what Freud might have disdained as unorthodox technique—a sort of psychoanalysis lite. They utilize some of Freud's methods, but—like Erikson and other ego analysts—they are less concerned with unconscious impulses and more focused on the coping capabilities of the ego. Like the object-relations therapists of our previous chapters, they focus on family relationships more than libido, and most do not necessarily require their clients to lie on a couch. Like Fromm, Erikson, and Adler, they place great importance on the role of society in shaping our lives; and like Horney, they replace Freud's male-centered constructs with feminine-friendly, nonsexist alternatives.

So, the opinion that "psychoanalysis will die out in our lifetime" is, perhaps, too pessimistic. Although behavior therapy, cognitive therapy, and other such "active" therapies are currently quite popular, Glen Gabbard, a psychoanalyst and professor of psychiatry at Baylor University, notes, "If you look at good therapists on videotape, you'll find that the cognitive therapists and analysts do many things in common" (Grossman, 2003, p. 73).

Next, we will study the work of Alfred Adler, a theorist who considered societal influences of great importance, but who avoided the sweeping generalizations of Fromm's Marxism, and felt no compulsion to retain much of Freud's vocabulary, as did Erikson.

ALFRED ADLER—THE COMPENSATING SELF IN FAMILY AND SOCIETY

From organic to social evolution—transcending Darwin and Freud. Nearly a century ago, Alfred Adler began on a biological pathway, but added a social twist—**social interest,** the *"striving for a form of community that must be thought of as everlasting, as . . . if mankind had reached the goal of perfection"* (Adler, in Ansbacher & Ansbacher, 1964, pp. 34–35). Adler added *social interest* to each of the four Greek temperament types, thus seeking to integrate biological and social factors. Accordingly, the *melancholic,* whom the Greeks said had too much black bile, was seen by Adler as also *low in social interest.* The *sanguine* not only had plenty of blood, as the Greeks asserted, but was *high in social interest.*

Adler illustrates our zonal perspective particularly well, because over the course of his career his theories traversed three zones: from biological determinism in the *Physiological Zone,* to psychoanalysis in the *Insight Zone,* to social evolution in the *Social Zone.* Beginning with his biologically based notion of **organ inferiority** characterized by *a weak, vulnerable, or frail physical system,* Adler saw psychological development shaped by the attempt to **compensate,** or *counterbalance one's organic inferiorities by developing an offsetting skill or system (e.g., the stuttering child becomes a great orator, the skinny kid becomes a body builder).* Next, after a brief sojourn as a member of Freud's inner circle, Adler developed his own theory, synthesizing Darwin, Freud, and Marx into his own version of social Darwinism.

BACKGROUND CHECK

A childhood permeated with competition, inferiority, anxiety, and compensation. When Sigmund Freud was not quite fourteen, **Alfred Adler** (1870–1937) was born of Hungarian Jewish parents in a suburb of Vienna. Like Freud, Adler was adept at transforming his childhood experiences into theoretical universals. Born second in a family of six, Adler lived in the shadow of his older brother, who invariably defeated him in numerous boyhood competitions. There can be little doubt that the importance Adler accorded **birth order,** *the child's position in the family constellation,* had its roots in this lifelong competitive relationship with his older brother. Near the end of his life, Adler confessed that "My eldest brother is a good industrious fellow—he was always ahead of me—and for the matter of that, he is *still* ahead of me!" (Bottome, 1957, p. 27).

Chronic sense of inferiority. As a child, Adler suffered from rickets, a disease that caused softening and malformation of his bones. His chronic physical disability left Adler feeling envious and inferior:

> I remember sitting on a bench bandaged up on account of rickets, with my healthy elder brother sitting opposite me. He could run, jump, and move about quite effortlessly, while for me, movement of any sort was a strain and an effort. (Bottome, 1957, pp. 30–31)

Numerous near-death experiences. Additionally, from his earliest years, Adler encountered death and near-death experiences close at hand. When he was only three, his younger brother died in the bed beside his. As a young boy, Alder was twice run over by carriages in the streets (*where* were his parents?) and recalled recovering consciousness on the living room sofa (Orgler, 1963, p. 2). Adler's most memorable near-death experience occurred at four or five years of age, when he became so ill with pneumonia that the family physician gave him up for lost. Fortunately, another physician took over his treatment, and in a few days the "lost" patient was on his way to recovery. Alongside his recovery there was much talk about how close to death he had been, and young Alfred *compensated* by deciding to become a physician: *"I came to choose the occupation of physician in order to overcome death and the fear of death"* (cited in Ansbacher & Ansbacher, 1956, p. 199).

Successful compensations. Near the end of his life, Adler recounted how he had successfully compensated throughout his entire career:

> I would say I was born a very weak child suffering from certain weaknesses, especially from rickets which prevented me from moving very well. Despite this obstacle, now, nearly at the end of my life, I am standing before you in America. You can see how I have overcome this difficulty. (Stepansky, 1983, p. 9)

Achieving his life goal. Although Adler accomplished his **life goal**—*the dominating, overarching goal that colors one's whole life*—by becoming a physician, this did not completely allay his anxieties about death: "I posited a goal, expecting it to put an end to my infantile worry and fear of death. It is obvious that I anticipated more from the choice of this profession than it could grant" (Orgler, 1963, p. 204). In those days before insulin, Adler became overwhelmed by the death of several of his young diabetic patients, and eventually gave up the practice of general medicine, specializing in neurology instead.

The connections between Adler's childhood experiences and his subsequent theoretical constructs are more transparent than for most personality theorists. *Birth order, compensation, ambition, and striving for superiority* appear clearly related to his childhood experiences: "It is these physical trends, which even in my childhood have assumed form and style-of-life, to which I am indebted also for my insight into psychological manifestations" (cited in Bottome, 1957, p. 33).

Zeitgeist

A Russian wife. In addition to the influence of his childhood experiences, Adler's social theorizing was undoubtedly shaped by the intellectual and political currents that swirled about him and by his choice of a wife. In college he joined a group of socialists and met a Russian student, Raissa Timofejewna, whom he married. Raissa's independence, political activism, and general liveliness undoubtedly played a role in Adler's theoretical formulations in which he sought to synthesize Darwin, Freud, and Marx, while also advocating for equality of the sexes.

Horrors of war. Although Adler had already been drifting in the direction of *social interest,* World War I (1914–18) was a turning point in his life. After spending two years caring for soldiers near the Russian front, he returned to civilian life a changed man—intent on doing all he could to cultivate *social interest* among all humans. He said that psychologists must work against those forms of nationalism that harm the community of nations, against hopelessness, against widespread unemployment, and against anything that disturbs the spreading of social interest throughout the family, school, and social institutions.

Overshadowed by Freud. Fairly or unfairly—then as now—Adler was overshadowed by Freud. Their brief period of compatibility began about 1900, when Adler wrote an article in a Viennese newspaper defending Freud's recently published *Dream Analysis*. Freud wrote Adler a postcard of thanks and subsequently asked him to join a discussion circle of psychoanalysis. The honeymoon ended about a decade later because of widening theoretical and personal differences.

Adler and Freud—family constellations destined to clash. If Adler's notions of birth order have any validity whatsoever, he and Freud were doomed to disagree. Adler with his "ain't-gonna-live-in-the-shadows" qualities of the secondborn child was destined to quarrel with Freud, the quintessential eldest child (ambitious and authoritarian) who was pampered as his mother's favorite and as the Jewish beloved "firstborn" son.

In addition to their personality differences, Freud and Adler's theoretical differences predestined them to divorce. Although Freud was creative and innovative at the *intrapsychic* level of analysis, he never moved far beyond the *Physiological* and *Insight Zones,* never developing a genuinely *social* psychology. Adler, by contrast, kept broadening his perspective, ultimately adopting a societal level of analysis and making *social interest* the cornerstone of his theory.

Divorcing Freud. Having decided to clear the air of the underlying tension between the two principles, the Psychoanalytic Society invited Adler to systematically present his ideas, which he did in a series of sessions beginning on January 4, 1911, and concluding on February 22nd. Following this, Adler resigned from the presidency of the Society—a post he had held for less than a year—and by May 24th he had withdrawn from all contact with the group. At this time, Freud criticized Adler for being what today we would call an "ego psychologist" or an "object relations" theorist. Freud said that Adler's theory "presents surface ego psychology. Lastly, instead of the psychology of the libido, of sexuality, it offers general psychology" (Nunberg & Federn, 1974, p. 147). Writing to Jung, Freud said: "what really alarms me—is that he [Adler] minimizes the sexual drive and our opponents will soon be able to speak of an experienced psychoanalyst whose conclusions are radically different from ours" (Freud & Jung, 1974, p. 376).

Despised by Freud. Freud did not tolerate dissenters well and he maintained a lifelong hostility toward Adler. It was Adler he had in mind when he said: "I made a pigmy great." Corresponding with Jung, who had not yet defected, Freud described Adler as paranoid: "I have finally got rid of Adler. . . . The damage is not very great. Paranoid intelligences are not rare and are more dangerous than useful. As a paranoic of course he is right about many things, though wrong about everything" (Freud & Jung, 1974, p. 428).

Substantive differences. Adler's differences with Freud involved far more than personality differences or theoretical wrangling. Adler felt that Freud had fragmented personality into segments that were in conflict with one another, and this went against Adler's conception of the *whole person,* which was similar to the Gestalt psychologists' emphasis on wholeness. Adler called his system **Individual Psychology** *in order to emphasize each person's unique qualities.* He sought to understand each individual as a seamless garment—an undivided whole—embedded within an even larger whole (society).

TABLE 8.2

Adler at a Glance

MODEL OF PERSONALITY	DESCRIPTION	DYNAMICS
What Are the Parts?	**Inferiority complex:** exaggerated feelings of inferiority that tend to immobilize a person **Body Language:** the way people carry themselves, nonverbal communications **Goals:** the forward-leaning concept giving humans purpose **Lifestyle:** the plan by which a person attempts to achieve goals **Creative Self:** the element of personality that allows humans to choose certain goals or lifestyles	Adler believed that structure and movement were one and cannot be separated. Therefore the "parts" of his theory are permeated with a forward thrust. The creative self chooses his goals and then finds a lifestyle that is compatible with them.

TABLE 8.2 *(continued)*

Adler at a Glance

MODEL OF PERSONALITY	DESCRIPTION	DYNAMICS
What Makes a Person Go?	*Law of Movement:* combines both physical and psychological *movement*—functioning as both a "part" and a motive *Lifestyle:* is both a "part" and a plan by which the person seeks to fulfill goals *Compensation:* strives to make up for physical or psychological inferiorities by striving harder. *Will power:* refers to infant's reaching out and grasping of objects and people *Creative power:* totally psychological/motivational construct; moves away from *libido* or other biological determinants. *"As-if" goals:* goals, even "fictional" goals, that provide powerful motivation.	"Parts" function as motives. Adler sees forward movement occurring as a result of diverse physical and psychological influences, such as birth order, physical inferiorities, and "fictional" goals. Compensation, will power, and creative power assist the individual in achieving a satisfactory *lifestyle*.
What Makes a Person Grow?	The child's growth is not seen in stages, but is thought to be affected by the family constellation. For Adler, birth order profoundly shapes personality, and parents also influence the process by showing affection or by "spoiling." The child's own innate striving for superiority, and social interest, also play an important role.	The child is an active participant in his or her own development—not merely acted upon by outside influences. Optimally, the family constellation provides enough affection—without pampering—to create a well-adjusted individual high in social interest.
What Makes a Person Unique?	Each person experiences a unique combination of influences such as one's birth order, genetic endowment, and family constellation. Additionally, a person's inferiorities, compensations, and goals are shaped by the creative self into a distinctive lifestyle.	A person born, for instance, without legs, might compensate by becoming a skilled writer. Her birth order as the second child might provide her a competitive edge. Attitudes shaped by such life experiences form the creative self, which seeks to accomplish the desired goals. There are millions of such combinations, which gives each individual a unique quality.

Over the course of his career, Adler moved steadily toward broader levels of analysis—beginning with the biological, tarrying for a time in the psychoanalytic, ultimately shifting to the societal. In the end, Adler replaced Freud's *intrapsychic* conflict model with a *societal* model of the person embedded in a community.

ASKING THE BIG FOUR QUESTIONS

What Are the Parts? and What Makes a Person Go?

Mind, body, and movement are inseparable. In the following discussion, we merge our "parts" and "motives" questions because they are so blended in Adler's theory. He resisted describing people as "parts," bridging Descartes's mind–body gap with his **law of movement:** *movement is both physical and psychological.* For Adler, *movement* was critical in distinguishing between plants and animals. He noted that if a flower was about to be trampled by a horse, it could do nothing to avoid this fatality, whereas a person could move: "All moving beings . . . can foresee and reckon up the direction in which to move; and this fact makes it necessary to postulate that they have minds or souls. . . . This foreseeing the direction of movement is the central principle of the mind" (Adler, 1958, p. 26).

Body language. Since he believed that it was impossible to separate "structures" or "parts" from movement, Adler took *body language* very seriously: "Movement," he wrote, "becomes moulded movement—form. Thus it is possible to gain a knowledge of mankind from form, if we recognize in it the movement that shapes it" (1964b, p. 95). He asserted that we can learn much about others by the way they carry themselves or in the steadiness of their gaze. Nowadays, we refer to Adler's **organ dialect** (1964a, p. 156) as *body language, or nonverbal communication.*

Adler believed that Freud erred in assuming that when an older child wet the bed, for example, he was *regressing* to earlier times and acting in a way that was prompted by *unconscious* forces. Adler saw it instead as *communication* through *organ dialect.* The child might be angrily communicating "Piss on you!" to a parent, or could be communicating a wish to be nurtured: "I still want to be a baby, will you care for me if I wet myself?"

Inferiority complex. Among Adler's most famous constructs is the **inferiority complex,** or *exaggerated feelings of inferiority that dominate a person's lifestyle so much that it becomes difficult to initiate or accomplish anything.* The difference between normal feelings of inferiority and an *inferiority complex* is a matter of degree. A child who suffers an *inferiority complex* feels overwhelmed by feelings of inadequacy, tends to be shy, and shows an increased need for support. Such a child seeks ways to *avoid* challenges, rather than *overcome* or *compensate.* Adler's *inferiority complex* functions less as a "part" and more as a funnel for motives and energy, illustrating the blending of structure and motives.

Goals motivate people and give life meaning. Goals are a key ingredient of Adlerian theory, flavoring everything with a forward-leaning tilt: "We cannot think, feel, will, or act without the perception of some goal" (Adler, 1968, p. 3). Adler avoided the term *causation* because he felt it was backward-looking. Instead, he highlighted the importance of goals in steering our lives. We've all experienced how excitedly little children "look forward" to events: attending a birthday party, going to the zoo, playing a video game. Adler believed that without goals people would not know what to do with themselves; lacking objectives toward which to move, they would be psychologically lost: "The psychic life of man is determined by his goal. . . . No human being can think, feel, will, dream, without all these activities being determined, continued, modified, and directed towards an ever-present objective" (Adler, 1927, p. 29).

Unconscious goals. According to Adler, goals need not be *conscious* in order to influence the direction of one's life. This is about as close to Freud's theory of the unconscious as Adler comes: "The goal, although unknown to the individual, directs unobtrusively and unshakably all psychological expressive forms" (cited in Ansbacher & Ansbacher, 1956, p. 72).

Fictional goals. The **fictional final goal** *is a goal that, even if it proves to be unattainable, nonetheless guides and influences one's lifestyle.* Such goals may be conscious, but they are frequently unconscious. *Fictional final goals* function to guide and direct the lives of individuals, providing purpose and unity for the personality. Even young children are guided by fictional goals (which may or may not eventually be realized) such as becoming firefighters, astronauts, or professional athletes. Frequently, such goals serve to compensate for inferiority feelings, as in Adler's case, when he consciously determined early in life to become a physician, hoping to overcome his fear of death and to compensate for feelings of inferiority with respect to his older brother.

Turning from Freud to Vaihinger—from libido to "as if." Adler's emphasis on the importance of fictional goals grew out of Vaihinger's book *The Philosophy of "As If"* (1911), which he read about the time he and Freud were breaking up. Vaihinger said that many of the goals and ideals we live by turn out to be "fictions"—created for our convenience and edification. Vaihinger emphasized the *subjective nature* of people's perceptions. For example, physicists sometimes function "as if" light were comprised of waves, at other times "as if" it were discrete packets of energy.

Many social "fictions" such as "all men are created equal" serve to shape ethical behavior regardless of whether they are literally true. Vaihinger used concepts such as *guiding fiction* or *fictional final goal* to emphasize how various fictions serve to guide behavior—regardless of whether they turn out to be "true." Vaihinger even acknowledged that some fictions were "carried on in the darkness of the unconscious" (Ansbacher & Ansbacher, 1956, p. 88), a notion that was congruent with psychoanalysis.

Adler adapted Vaihinger's three main characteristics of "fictional" goals for his own goal-based theories: (1) "fictional" goals are subjectively created and personally meaningful; (2) "fictions" are created by individuals to navigate the obstacles of existence; and (3) "fictional" goals are sometimes unconscious.

Lifestyle. Goals and goal orientation infuse Adler's entire theory, but his broadest construct is **style of life** or **lifestyle:** *the means by which a person attempts to achieve real or fictional goals.* Adler used several different terms to refer to a person's unique strategy for reaching goals. In 1913 he spoke of it as an *ego line* (Adler, 1968, p. 126); in 1914, he referred to it as a *life line;* and later, as a *life plan* (Adler, 1968, pp. 3, 6). It wasn't until the 1920s that he coined the term *style of life,* which has been absorbed into the mainstream of our culture.

Primed to move forward. Adler's forward-leaning, goal-oriented approach was also influenced by the French philosopher Henri Bergson, from whom Adler adopted the concept of ***elan vital:*** *persons thrust or fling themselves forward on the basis of experience* *and memories.* Whether one labels this "forward thrust" as creativity, power, striving, or self-actualization, Adler concluded that *all humans have a vital urge to move forward.* Such goal-oriented, forward-leaning constructs give Adler's theory a pull-yourself-up-by-your-bootstraps quality. Dependency on others is the curse to be avoided, the root of all feelings of inferiority.

From organ inferiority to creative power. As a medical practitioner, Adler believed that disease attacks at the body's Achilles' heel—at the point of inferior body organs. The cause of the organic infirmity might be genes, accidents, or disease, but the body frequently compensates for weakness in one organ system by strengthening another. For example, when a kidney is removed, the remaining kidney usually enlarges to compensate for the loss of the diseased one.

Adler originally defined *organ inferiority* and *compensation* primarily in biological terms: *"As soon as the equilibrium . . . appears to be disturbed due to inadequacy of form or function, a certain biological process is initiated in the inferior organs. . . . until the deficit is made up through growth of the inferior organ"* (Ansbacher & Ansbacher, 1956, p. 24). However, he soon adopted a much more *holistic/psychosomatic* approach that emphasized psychological creativity over physiological compensation. During this same era, the psychoanalyst Franz Alexander also emphasized the close relationship between physical and psychological functioning in what he termed *psychosomatic medicine* (1950).

An honor roll of overcomers. Demosthenes overcame stuttering to become a great orator, and children with visual difficulties grew up to become famous painters. Homer was supposed to have been blind, and Beethoven wrote his greatest music when totally deaf. And, of course, there was Helen Keller, blind and deaf at an early age, who learned to experience the world through her sense of touch, and who later graduated from Radcliffe. Adler also applied his theory to Napoleon, who became a great leader in spite of (or because of) his short stature. To this list of overcomers we might add cyclist Lance Armstrong, who—given less than a 50 percent chance of overcoming testicular cancer that had spread to his lungs and brain—not only beat the odds and *lived,* but came back to win an unprecedented seventh *Tour de France!*

Although Adler began with an organic orientation, he came increasingly to emphasize that it was not the organ inferiority per se that determines one's lifestyle, but the *attitude* one took toward it. "The fundamental law of life," wrote Adler, "is that of overcoming" (1964b, p. 71). Early in his career, while still in psychoanalytic circles, Adler had toyed with the same sorts of biologically based, conflict-generating, oppositional drives of which Freud was so fond. Adler spoke of *aggression* and *affection* as two opposite drives, but this did not last long, for Adler soon substituted the *will to power* (Ansbacher & Ansbacher, 1956, p. 111) for the aggressive drive, and creative power for libido (Adler, 1964b, p. 219). This made his break with Freud inevitable.

Will to power. Adler adapted the German philosopher Friedrich Nietzsche's (1844–1900) concept, *will to power.* For Adler, **will to power** *meant the infant's attempt to reach out, grasp, and hold on to objects for selfish purposes.* He used *will to power* to describe the six-month-old's *interpersonal* relationships: "under the pressure of a will-to-power, it seizes hold of people who take an interest in him" (Adler, 1968, p. 50). Thus, instead of defining *will to power* in physiological or philosophical terms, Adler turned it into an object-relational construct of grasping for, and holding on to, another *person.*

Creative power. After his break with Freud, Adler increasingly shifted his emphasis away from biological determinism and past experiences toward the future: "the psychic life of man is determined by his goal" (1954, p. 29). Breaking with Freud's biologically based motivational fuel—libido—Adler emphasized **creative power,** *a totally psychological/motivational construct with no physiological analogs, that focuses on the end product—not the mechanics of the artist's brushstrokes or the cuts of the sculptor's chisel.* For the remainder of his career, Adler continued moving away from the *Physiological Zone* toward the *Social Zone.* After this shift, emotions (e.g., inferiority feelings and social feelings) played the central role in energizing the drive toward goal attainment.

Neurotic behavior. According to Adler, **neurotic behavior** *results from a combination of the inferiority complex and a lack of social interest.* Since neurotics feel incapable of coping with the challenges of life they employ a variety of what Adler calls "cheap tricks" to avoid responsibility. Neurotics blame their shortcomings on others, seek revenge, or experience exaggerated feelings of guilt, shame, or other negative emotions.

Superiority complex. The **superiority complex** *is a neurotic way of disguising intolerable feelings of inferiority.* The person with a *superiority complex* tries to portray that he is better than others—in all ways, in all circumstances. This is not to be confused with a normal *striving for superiority,* which Adler felt was a healthy motivational force in personality development and functioning.

Masculine protest. During an era when women had few rights and privileges, Adler coined the term **masculine protest** to mean a *striving to be powerful and strong—especially on the part of girls and women—in order to achieve the power, status, and strength of their male counterparts.* This was one of Adler's earliest motivational terms and it has frequently been misunderstood, because during this prefeminist era, masculinity was equated with strength and femininity with weakness. This was congruent with attitudes toward women nearly a century ago, when women were routinely seen as the "weaker sex." Not until 1920 did women win the right to vote, and when Adler was growing up, one of the worst insults you could hurl at a boy was to accuse him of "acting like a girl." Seen in historical context, Adler was ahead of his time, because although he recognized differences in physical strength, he considered women to be *psychologically equal* to men.

Understood within the zeitgeist of Adler's era, *masculine protest* is not so much about gender conflicts as it is a form of *compensation.* Although Adler did not emphasize sex in the manner that Freud did, we can see similarities in *masculine protest* and Freud's notion of *penis envy.* Adler did not limit *masculine protest* to women; "macho" men—the kind of guys who consider women to be men's playthings—were also seen as displaying masculine protest. The main characteristic of masculine protest (whether seen in women or men) is: ". . . a needlessly domineering attitude towards the opposite sex" (Adler, 1964a, p. 42).

Safeguarding tendencies—psychological "sideshows." According to Adler, **safeguarding tendencies** *are strategies to protect self-esteem from external (usually interpersonal) threats.* This is about as close as Adler gets to Freud's unconscious defense mechanisms, but there are significant differences. Unlike Freud's *intrapsychic* defense mechanisms—utilized by the ego to protect itself from the urges of the id or the censure of the superego—Adler saw the *entire person* as protecting himself or herself against threats to the *physical self* (we may get sick or hurt, or even die); threats to the *social self* (we may be humiliated, embarrassed, or punished); or threats to *how we see ourselves* (we want to look good in our own eyes).

Six psychological "sideshows." Adler (whose clientele included a number of carnival performers) referred to *safeguarding tendencies* as "sideshows," which distract attention from the "main performance"—the "tasks of life."

(1) Symptoms. Symptoms help people avoid responsibilities. If I'm "ill," I may not have to take a scheduled examination, or show up for work. Whether conscious or unconscious—which is difficult for others to prove—such benefits are referred to by contemporary clinicians as "secondary gain."

(2) Excuses. Excuses are another way persons avoid responsibility. Although many Adlerians don't hesitate to use the word *excuse,* some prefer the more neutral term *rationalization,* as it seems to convey a less moralistic meaning.

(3) Aggression. One of Adler's early contributions to psychoanalysis (Sicher & Mosak, 1967) was to consider aggression a *strategy* or *secondary* phenomenon—a choice a person makes to move toward a goal. In an early anticipation of attribution theory, Adler delineated three variants of aggression: *depreciation* as a way of reducing feelings of inferiority by putting others down; *idealization,* which puts down real people by comparison, and *accusation,* a common form of aggression, in which we hold others responsible for our own shortcomings.

(4) Distance seeking. Another way that people seek to safeguard self-esteem is by restricting or avoiding participation with others. The distance seeker reduces the risk of rejection or ridicule by avoiding or withdrawing from "risky" interpersonal interactions. Adler (1983) described four styles of distance seeking (moving backward, standing still, hesitation or "back and forth," and creating obstacles).

(5) Anxiety. Anxiety is another way people avoid meeting challenges. Adler claimed that certain panic conditions and phobias functioned to allow people to sidestep responsibilities. Like other safeguarding mechanisms, fear frequently allowed people to evade challenges. For Adlerians, fear is no exemption; otherwise one would never learn to walk or cross the street.

(6) Exclusion Tendency. The *exclusion tendency* refers to the narrowing down of one's approach to life. For example, if one socializes only with admirers, it is never necessary to change or grow.

From World War I to social utopia. Following World War I, *social interest* became Adler's master motive. Intermingling his own ideas regarding the primacy of goals with concepts taken from Darwin and Marx, Adler concluded that through *social interest,* humans could evolve into higher and higher states of social living. Leaving behind the horrors of world wars, humans could naturally *become* better. Now, in place of *inferiority* and *compensation,* Adler emphasized *fulfilling* or *becoming,* clearly anticipating the humanistic psychology of Rogers and Maslow (Chapter 11).

In the end, Adler's biologically based concepts of *organ inferiority* and *compensation* evolved into a broader vision of *cooperation* among individuals for the good of the group: "Social life became a necessity because through the community and the division of labor in which every individual subordinates himself to the group, the species was enabled to continue its existence" (1927, p. 36).

Lifestyle. Adler's final overarching motivational concept was **lifestyle,** referring to *the strategy by which individuals seek to fulfill their life goals.* One of Adler's contemporary interpreters defines *lifestyle* as "the rule of rules" (Schulman, 1973). *Lifestyle* rule refers to the subjective, sometimes unconscious set of guidelines that individuals develop and use as they move toward their goals.

What Makes a Person Grow?

Children actively participate in their development. Adler's view of development is distinctively *constructivist* in the spirit of Kelly and others (Chapter 10) who highlight each person's ability to participate in shaping his or her own destiny. According to Adler, the *creative self* actively constructs personality from the raw materials of biological givens and environmental circumstances. Whereas other developmental theorists of his era saw the child being *acted upon* either by the environment or by other people, Adler endowed the child with *agency* and *responsibility*. Instead of being a *victim* of circumstances or a *tabula rasa* onto which the environment stamped its imprint, the child was seen as an active participant in the developmental process: "*Nobody really permits experiences as such to form, without their possessing some purpose.* Indeed, experiences are moulded by him . . . by the way in which he thinks they are going to aid or hinder him in the attainment of his final goal" (Adler, 1968, p. 62).

Adler paid more attention to the *family constellation* than to developmental stages. He viewed the newborn as essentially a reflexive organism, with little ego identity, and no *goal* toward which to progress. Consequently, he did not view the first few months of life as very important in psychological development. This is in contrast to developmental theorists who weight the early experience quite heavily. More about birth order shortly.

Children need affection. Adler viewed the mother as a prime influence in the life of her children, and he stressed the importance of *tenderness* on the part of parents. He underscored the child's *need for affection:* "Children want to be fondled, loved, and praised. They have a tendency to cuddle up, always to remain close to loved persons, and to want to be taken into the bed with them" (Adler, 1908, p. 40).

Such wanting to be touched and taken to bed with parents would have been seen by Freud as inappropriately sexual, but Adler saw the child's striving for affection as the parents' opportunity to educate their young in the direction of social interest and affection for their fellow humans. Consistent with his emphasis on tenderness, Adler discouraged the use of corporal punishment, scolding, or nagging, because these, he believed, would only lead to discouragement and would intensify feelings of inferiority. Praise and encouragement, on the other hand, instilled hope, as well as that all-important quality of *social interest*.

Spoiling and pampering. Although Adler spoke of the importance of tenderness and love, he also warned against **spoiling** and **pampering** *by doing too much and expecting too little. Such children are in danger of growing up dependent and with a sense of entitlement.* In Adler's terms, *"spoiling"* means approximately what we mean today by **codependency,** that is, *taking responsibility for another's life to such an extent that they do not fully experience the consequences of their own actions.* It means depriving a child of the opportunity to accomplish things on his or her own initiative, because of overinvolved parenting. The *spoiled* child is likely to grow up to become a dependent adult. The *pampered* child (often the last-born "baby" of the family) is in danger of becoming a selfish adult, expecting everything to be handed to him or her on a silver platter.

Children actively shape their own development. Adler was not very explicit in specifying what developmental tasks were likely to be mastered at specific months or years of age. According to Adler, during the first few weeks or months of life, the infant was mostly "reflexive"; thereafter, he viewed the child as actively shaping his or her own development. Between three and five years of age, the child assesses his or her life circumstances and develops a *prototype or lifeline (game plan).* Then, as the child matures in understanding and gains experience, he or she strives to cope with circumstances in a way that succeeds: *striving for power, striving for superiority,* and developing *social interest.*

From minus to plus. Adler believed that each person has an inborn tendency to *strive for superiority.* Thus, whether a child tries to succeed in basketball, mathematics, art, or music, each person yearns to be outstanding—or at least a bit better than the next person—in something. Adler referred to this innate tendency as going **from minus to plus:** *"The impetus from minus to plus never ends. The history of the human race points in the same direction. . . . it represents the fundamental fact of our life"* (Adler, 1956, p. 103).

In optimal development, our inborn strivings for superiority—for moving from minus to plus—are developed and nurtured until they mature into the highest form of striving: *social interest.* As Adler saw it, most maladjusted individuals—criminals, drug addicts, alcoholics, prostitutes, and neurotics—display a *lack of social interest,* whereas well-adjusted people manifest social interest by showing a concern for children, families, friends, the needy, the homeless, and others in need of social support. To Freud's twin criteria of mental health (the ability to work and to love), Adler added a third: *social interest.*

Creative self—Adler's "crowning achievement." One of Adler's major developmental constructs is not well known, but is nonetheless important in his theory. The **creative self** is *the free element of personality that allows the person to choose among alternative goals and lifestyles.* The eminent personality psychologists, Hall and Lindzey, described the *creative self* as Adler's "crowning achievement": "Here at last was the prime mover, the philosopher's stone, the elixir of life, the first cause of everything human for which Adler had been searching" (1978, pp. 165–166).

Indeed, for Adler, the *creative self* synthesizes all the factors in a person's life, and moves the individual in a goal-seeking direction. Although heredity and environment provide a person the raw materials from which to construct goals, it is the *creative self* that provides the energy, strategies, and motivation to achieve goals.

What Makes a Person Unique?

Uniqueness is a core component in Adlerian theory, which he called *Individual Psychology*. Persons are seen to be actively in charge of shaping their lifestyles. Whatever the inferiority—whether organic or psychological—the person's *attitude* ultimately determines destiny. Adlerians see the *creative self* as the great synthesizer of everything else that comprises the personality of the individual. Each person is composed of differing organic materials, a unique coalition of chromosomes, and distinctive attitudes. Additionally, each individual grows up within a distinctive family constellation—even *birth order* means different things in different families. For example, a "middle child" might be in the middle of two siblings or ten. The home may have been swarming with siblings, parents, grandparents, uncles, aunts, cousins, and playmates, or it may have been empty except for the child and a single parent. So much varies from home to home that each family member emerges with a finger-printishly unique combination of inferiorities, superiorities, and social interests, which are *synthesized* by the *creative self* into a one-of-a-kind lifestyle.

Four personality styles. Adler formulated uniqueness at two levels: typological and individual. We've already seen how he builds uniqueness into his *Individual* theory. Next, we will briefly look at his typological classification. Adler connected his favorite concept, *social interest,* with the four temperaments proposed by the ancient Greeks, coming up with a refurbished typology.

Ruling type. Adler described **rulers** *as high in activity and low in social interest.* "Thus we find individuals whose approach to reality 'shows'; from early childhood through their entire lives a more or less dominant ruling attitude. This attitude appears in all their relationships" (Adler, 1929, p. 68). By today's diagnostic criteria such a person would likely be seen as narcissistic or even sociopathic (e.g., alcoholics, drug addicts, delinquents, tyrants, and sadists). *Rulers,* according to Adler, attempt to achieve superiority by hurting or exploiting others.

Getting type. Persons described by Adler as **getting types** *are low in both activity level* and *social interest.* Known as "takers," these are people who expect much from others but give little in return—the *entitled,* as we refer to them today. Since their relationships with others are ordinarily dependent and passive, we sometimes think of them as *passive–aggressive* or *hostile–dependent* personality styles.

Avoiding type. Another group, **avoiding types**, *are low both in activity levels* and *social interest;* however, instead of struggling with their problems, or even trying to manipulate others, as *getting types* are prone to do, *avoiders* simply withdraw, leaving a gulf between themselves and others. Adler placed neurotics and psychotics in this group.

Socially useful type. A fourth type, the **socially useful,** *display a high level of activity combined with high social interest.* Prepared to work hard and cooperate with others, such persons use their abilities and energy for the betterment of humankind. Conscientious and diligent, they make contributions that benefit the entire community. Of the four types, this is the only one that Adler considered psychologically healthy—poster persons for his theory of social evolution: "It is useful, normal, highly embedded in the stream of evolution of mankind" (1956, p. 168).

Adler's typologies might appear quaint and too moralistic for modern tastes, but they can be seen as forerunners of today's widely used personality styles listed in the diagnostic "bible" of clinical practice, *Diagnostic and Statistical Manual of Mental Disorders,* fourth edition (American Psychiatric Association, 1994) commonly referred to as DSM-IV.

Although these typologies give general clues to each person's uniqueness, it is through the lenses of *earliest memories, birth order (family constellation),* and *lifestyle* that Adlerian therapists bring each person's uniqueness into focus.

Earliest memory. The **earliest memory,** *the very first experience a person can consciously recall,* was seen by Adler as a gateway into the mind. Because he saw children as actively involved in their own psychological development, Adler attributed great significance to the earliest memories that they retained as older children or adults.

For example, one woman's earliest memory was of receiving a pony as a gift from her father when she was three years old. Her sister, who also received a pony from their father, rode her pony down the pathway in great triumph. This woman's pony followed her sister's but ran too fast, throwing the three-year-old rider into the dirt. She never forgot the humiliation of being surpassed by her sister, and eventually became the better equestrian of the two.

Adler surmised that this patient hadn't been particularly happy in her home life because her earliest memory was of her father, not her mother, as would have been the case for most people. Furthermore, the initial triumph of her sister probably indicated an unhealthy level of competition between them. Her later surpassing of her sister as an equestrian did not extinguish her initial feelings toward her. This case also illustrated the constant strivings of the second child to overcome.

Birth order in the family constellation. A child's position in the family constellation provided what Adler felt were among the most important clues to personality. He focused on four major positions: firstborn, second-born (frequently called the "middle child"), last-born, and only child.

First born. Firstborn children occupy a unique position; beginning life as the only child, they are frequently showered with love and attention. A "pioneer," this child is not only the first to pass through the birth canal, she is also the one on whom the parents "learn" how to parent. At first the sole object of the parents' (and grandparents') attention, this child is sometimes rudely "dethroned" when another sibling is born. Unless carefully prepared by the parents for the arrival of a new "king," the eldest child's feelings of inferiority and competitiveness may intensify, leading to excessive striving for power in an attempt to regain the lost kingdom.

On the positive side, the firstborn is more likely to become a leader, since he will understand the significance of authority, power, and competition; according to Adler, the firstborn is more likely to become a *ruling type* than a *socially useful type.* Recall that both *ruling* and *socially useful* types have high energy, differing primarily in *social interest.*

Second-born or middle child. This child is the one most likely to be *competitive.* Such individuals frequently spend their entire lives running to "catch up." Adler reported that second-born people commonly dream about running. If the competitive attitude is too strong, such persons might become revolutionaries, but generally, they are in a favorable position to become *socially useful* (an observation that might have been colored by Adler's own position as a second-born).

Last-born. These are the children most likely to be *pampered*. Frequently, parents—especially older ones—realize that this will be their last "baby," and since they are generally better off financially than when they first began having children, they tend to shower the last born with indulgences. The risk of "spoiling" is greatest in the youngest.

On the positive side, Adler cites cases where the last-born strives to surpass all the older ones and becomes a conquering hero. Many fairy tales follow such a theme, with the youngest ultimately overcoming. Adler believed that the "second largest proportion of problem children come from the youngest" (1931, p. 151).

Only child. The only child, like the youngest, is likely to be pampered. Afraid of losing her only child, the mother may become hypervigilant in parenting. The only child is not likely to become a competitor because there is no one with whom to compete. As the center of attention, such children often develop exaggerated estimates of their own importance. Adler believed that *only children* tend to be anxious, timid, and dependent, because their mothers' anxieties about losing an only child are communicated to them.

Multiple Family Influence. Was Adler right in placing birth order and family constellation among the primary shapers of lifestyle? The answer is complex, in that many psychologically significant differences exist even among those born into the same position.

Harry S. Truman (1884–1972) was a *firstborn* who was surrounded by loving women, so he didn't feel particularly "dethroned" by his sisters. According to Adler's theory, the combination of his small stature and poor eyesight must have made Harry feel *inferior*, but he *compensated* by studying diligently, working hard, and faithfully practicing the piano. Like Donald Winnicott (Chapter 7), Truman loved the warmth and bustle of the kitchen and the comforting presence of women, so he sought to faithfully follow his beloved Mama's words: "Now Harry you be good" (Truman, 1955, p. 54). Nonetheless, as president, Truman made difficult decisions with a firmness and integrity that led the news anchor, Eric Sevareid, to eulogize him in the following words: "remembering him reminds people what a man in that office ought to be like. It's character, just character. He stands like a rock in memory now" (Sevareid, quoted in McCullough, 1992, p. 992).

Lyndon Baines Johnson (1908–1973) was the quintessential "dethroned" *firstborn*. So thrilled were his parents when he was born that they hired a photographer to come to the farm and take pictures. When Lyndon's mother suggested ordering ten prints for various family members, his politician father ordered fifty, sending them to his friends in the legislature as well.

However, at the age of two, little Lyndon was dethroned by the birth of his sister. During the next six years, three more children were born, further depleting his mother's energy and involvement. Whether in direct response to his "dethroning," his mother's depression, or as a result of his own lively hyperactivity, little LBJ began toddling off down the road to "see Grandpa" or to explore the countryside. "Every time his Mamma turned her back seems like, Lyndon would run away" (Caro, 1983, p. 68). "He wanted attention," recalled Jesse Lambert, the maid who worked for the Johnsons at the time. "He would run away, and run away, and the minute his mother would turn her back he would run away again, and it was all to get attention" (Dallek, 1991, p. 34).

As an adult, Johnson showed the high activity and low social interest of Adler's *ruling type*. On the campaign trail, the energetic LBJ was oblivious to anything but getting to the next stop on time. When his pilot expressed concern about flying their small plane into a late-afternoon Texas thunderstorm, whose black clouds rose some thirty or forty thousand feet into the air, Johnson's standard comment was "Well, just keep on going, we've got to get there" (Caro, 1990, p. 263).

Gerald Rudolph Ford (1913–2006) was the *firstborn (only)* child of a marriage that dissolved when he was two. His mother remarried, but Jerry wasn't told that "Dad Ford" wasn't his "real" father until he was twelve or thirteen. He grew up with three half brothers, the oldest of whom was five years his junior. Soon after his new half brother's birth, Jerry began stuttering, and he continued stuttering for the next four years. Being "dethroned" must have generated feelings of inferiority and anxiety in young Jerry, who coped by stuttering, until he learned that he could get along by being "Mr. Nice Guy." Ford achieved prominence as a politician not because of his leadership abilities, but because he avoided offending anyone. The stuttering stepson who was dethroned by three "real" sons successfully *compensated* for his stuttering speech and stepson status with his "Aw-shucks, I'm-an-ordinary-guy" niceness. This contrasted favorably with the abrasive arrogance of Spiro Agnew, whom Ford replaced as vice president, and with the paranoid perspectives of Nixon, whom he replaced as president.

James Earl Carter, Jr. (1924—) was a *firstborn* child whose sister dethroned him twenty months later. Although Carter had been healthy up to this time, shortly after his second birthday (and shortly after being dethroned), Jimmy developed bleeding colitis and was hospitalized at a nearby sanitorium.

Jimmy's father "Earl" was a shy, almost timid man, known for working harder than anyone else and always seeking new ways to make money. His mother, Lillian, was a nurse; and with no doctor in the county, Lillian served as a physician to blacks and whites alike. Highly dedicated to her career, Jimmy's mother turned over most of the child-rearing responsibilities to a thirteen-year-old black girl named Annie Hollis. When she wasn't working as a nurse, Lillian liked to play bridge, go to auctions, or attend the Missionary Society. "Mothering" was not high on her "to do" list.

As a boy, Carter felt inferior about his small physique, his crooked teeth, and probably his inability to live up to his father's expectations and his neglect by his mother. Not one to give up, Jimmy *compensated* for his felt *inferiorities* through conscientiousness, hard work, and moral uprightness.

Multiple familial influences. Psychohistorical analysis (Berecz, 1999) suggests that, in addition to birth order, numerous other variables come into play. From our brief analysis above, it appears that Truman was never "dethroned," as Adler suggested frequently occurs. Truman grew up a "Mama's boy," loving, enjoying, and respecting women his entire life. Gerald Ford, the adopted stepson, sought to prevent dethroning by becoming the perpetual "Mr. Nice Guy."

By contrast, Johnson and Carter were both "dethroned" and grew up with emotionally neglectful mothers. LBJ responded with attention-seeking—running away when he was a toddler, and demonstrating brash purpose and aggressive ambition as an adult. Carter responded to maternal neglect with striving ambition, but his more humble, conscientious persistence contrasted with LBJ's arrogance and narcissism.

So, was Adler correct in emphasizing the formative influence of family? Without doubt. Birth order, family constellation, inferiority/compensation, striving for power, and social interest are important influences to which Adler directed our attention, but their influences on personality are undoubtedly more complex than Adler suggested. Nonetheless, Adler's emphasis on family-constellation dynamics will probably continue to be a significant force in contemporary thinking as divorce rates remain high and blended families struggle to "blend."

Goals. Among personality theorists of his era, none emphasized goals more than did Adler. He once said "it is not what one has inherited that is important, but what one does with his inheritance" (1929, p. 37). As we have seen illustrated in the lives of American presidents, *goals* are among the most important factors shaping each person's future. Although the presidency "fell" upon Truman's shoulders when FDR died (it is unlikely that HST would have *won* the presidency on his own), most of the other recent candidates set their sights on the White House as a *life goal.* People as widely differing in personality as Johnson, Carter, and Clinton decided early in life to become president.

FACING THE TOUGH TWINS

Is it Testable?

Many of Adler's terms, such as *lifestyle, middle child,* and *inferiority complex* have had such broad appeal that they have become part of everyday language. However, like Freud's psychoanalysis, Adler's Individual Psychology is so broad in scope that many of its constructs are ambiguous and difficult to define or test with precision. Just as in Freud's theory developmental arrests can occur in response to either deprivation or overindulgence, in Adler's theory the concept of the *creative self* allows for almost any outcome in a particular circumstance—as Adler put it, "everything can also be different" (Ansbacher & Ansbacher, 1956, p. 194).

In fact, it was just this sort of "explain-all" quality that led the eminent philosopher of science, Karl Popper, to formulate his ideas regarding the importance of *falsifiability.* Popper recalled discussing a clinical case with Adler in 1919, and being "much impressed" with how Adler explained the child's behavior in terms of inferiority feelings. However, when Popper asked Adler how he could be certain that his explanation was correct, Adler replied "Because of my thousandfold experience" (Popper, 1965, p. 35).

Although impressed at first, upon further reflection Popper concluded that Adler's "thousandfold experience" meant very little:

> . . . since every conceivable case could be interpreted in the light of Adler's theory, or equally Freud's. . . . I could not think of any human behaviour which could not be interpreted in terms of either theory. It was precisely this fact—that

they always fitted, that they were always confirmed—which in the eyes of their admirers constituted the strongest argument in favor of these theories. (Popper, 1965, p. 35)

Indeed, even a brief overview of research carried out on one of Adler's clearest formulations (birth order) appears to illustrate Popper's point regarding how difficult it is to prove or disprove broad formulations.

The heuristic power of birth order. The enduring popularity of Adlerian concepts such as birth order is probably due in part to the fact that "Everyone has a birth order, and it is easy to observe and talk about" (Rodgers and Rowe, 1994, pp. 208–209). Other influences such as genetics, parental influence, and schooling, are less obvious and more complicated to discuss. What is most relevant to our discussion of Adler's theories is the *heuristic power* of his common-sense constructs to generate "remarkable passion, extensive argumentation, and uncountable hours of research" (Rodgers, 2001, p. 505).

Whatever the final outcome of the arguments, this kind of research effort ultimately helps to sharpen concepts and clarify understanding. Some researchers have found significant relationships between birth order and such diverse factors as vocational preferences (Bryant, 1987), self-esteem (Kidwell, 1982), fear of success (Ishiyama, Munson, & Chabassol, 1990), physical health (Elliot, 1992), psychological health (Fullerton, Ursano, Harry, Wetzler & Slusarcick, 1989), toughmindedness (Singh, 1990), and intelligence (Zajonc & Markus, 1975).

Flawed research designs? Steelman (1985, 1986) claims that educational and socioeconomic factors have not been adequately controlled in such studies, and others (e.g., Sulloway, 1996) have reviewed the contradictory research findings and concluded that methodological problems have contributed to more confusion than clarity. Ernst and Angst concluded that birth order research has been so methodologically flawed that it has been "a sheer waste of time and money" (1983, p. xi). Rodgers (2001) and his colleagues argue that there is no relationship between birth order and intelligence, and that when it is found, it is likely the result of cross-sectional research designs that make misleading comparisons, such as "comparing the first-born child in a large middle-class White family in Michigan to the second-born child in a medium-sized affluent Black family in Atlanta to a third-born child in a small low-income Hispanic family in California" (Rodgers, Cleveland, van den Oord, & Rowe, 2000). Rodgers and his colleagues conclude that whatever differences are observed between such children "it is impossible to tell whether they are due to [socioeconomic status], race, region of the country, birth order, family size, or other variables related to these. Yet, that is exactly the type of comparison that arises from cross-sectional [between-family] data" (p. 602).

Pioneer family psychologist. Adler called his theory *Individual Psychology* in order to distinguish it from psychoanalysis, but it might better be described as *family* psychology. Even with the difficulties of studying family constellations, most trends in the research appear to underscore the importance of family. Even while agreeing that much birth order research has been poorly controlled, Sulloway (1996) concluded (based on a massive study of how 3,890 scientists reacted to 28 scientific inventions) that birth order *does* dramatically affect personality development. Regarding firstborns, Sulloway said: "From their ranks have come bold explorers, the iconoclasts, and the heretics of history" (1996, p. xiv). Sulloway found this effect to be independent of family size or socioeconomic level.

Finding your niche in the family constellation. Sulloway formulated an evolutionary model in which he saw siblings competing for resources in a classical Darwinian fashion: "Families are best seen as containing an array of diverse niches, each occupied by a different individual and each presenting different vantage points of life. From these differing perspectives, family members experience the same events differently" (1996, p. 86). So differently do children experience their "niches" in the family constellation that Sulloway states, "Siblings who grow up together are almost as different in their personalities as people plucked randomly from the general population" (1996, p. 352).

Depletion of resources. Downey (2001) studied the relationship between family size and intelligence and noted that, "Across various measures of intellectual skills and educational achievement, individuals with the fewest siblings do the best" (p. 497). According to Downey, it is family *size,* rather than birth order, that is crucial in psychological development. In Downey's "resource depletion model," as the number of children increases, parents' resources of time, energy, and money become correspondingly less available for each subsequent child.

The complex, indirect influence of siblings. Contemporary personality theorists might consider Adler's birth order explanations overly simplistic, but few would question the relevance of the family constellation to psychological development, and interest remains high in dissecting family constellations into researchable portions. For example, Brody, Kim, Murry, and Brown (2003) conducted a four-year longitudinal study in which they found that older siblings who are academically and socially successful contribute to an increase in their mothers' self-esteem and a decrease in depressive symptoms. Not surprisingly, such positive changes in mothers' attitudes promote better parenting practices with younger siblings.

Conversely, Whiteman and Buchanan (2002) found that when parents reported behavior problems with earlier-born children, parental expectations regarding drug usage, rebellious behavior, etc., trickled down to younger siblings. In these and other similar studies, the conclusion has emerged that family constellations are complex systems in which psychological "traffic" moves in many directions simultaneously. At the very least, we need to think not only of how parents influence their children, but also of how children modify their caregivers: "Rather than viewing behavioral influences as flowing in one direction, from parents to children, developmental psychologists now recognize that these influences are reciprocal" (Brody, 2005, p. 145).

Multiple influences. Our biographical examples illustrate, and research appears to support, the notion that a family system contains multiple variables that profoundly shape the lives of growing children. Birth order is but one of a plethora of influences that include race, religion, socioeconomic status, financial and emotional resources, and the influence of parents and siblings. Such variables appear to operate in multiple directions at the same time, making it difficult to investigate Adler's generalizations precisely.

Is It Useful?

The importance of parents, teachers, and friends. Although Adler's concepts have sometimes proved difficult to falsify in the strictest scientific sense, they have been heuristically powerful, stimulating research on a wide variety of topics. Adler's emphasis on such practical issues as parenting, education, and social change didn't win him friends among orthodox Freudians during his lifetime, but they have worn well over the years. For example, Adler's concepts have been the basis for Dinkmeyer & McKay's (1976) STEP: *Systematic Training for Effective Parenting* program. There has been a recent resurgence of Adlerian training institutes and clinics across the United States and Canada, as well as in Western Europe, Scandinavia, Israel, and Japan (Dinkmeyer, 1989). In addition to the many books published by Adlerians, the journal *Individual Psychology: Journal of Adlerian Theory, Research & Practice* serves as a major publication for Adlerian psychologists and has been in existence for over sixty years.

Psychoanalysis for ordinary people. Because he spoke with the homespun charm of "an old grandmother," Adler's ideas have been so completely assimilated by the culture that they fail to remain affiliated with his name, in contrast to the "Freudian slip," for example. Few of us can recall how or when we first heard of Cinderella, the Three Little Pigs, or Jack and the Beanstalk. Similarly, Adler's notions of *birth order, lifestyle, inferiority complex,* and *compensation* so thoroughly permeate our minds, that like Santa Claus and traffic signals, we seldom question their origins and are scarcely aware of their influence. Many of Adler's ideas have been so thoroughly assimilated into our culture that we hardly think of them as psychological theory. While few taxicab drivers could explain Freud's distinction between preconscious and unconscious processes, many might attribute their current struggles to being a "middle child," while others might confess to suffering from an "inferiority complex." This would have pleased Adler, who was fond of saying, with a twinkle in his eye, "I *am* the legitimate father of the Inferiority Complex" (Bottome, 1957, p. 19).

At a time when Freudians emphasized sexuality and unconscious determinism, Adler emphasized the forward-looking conscious mind and its ability to pursue goals in the interest of social betterment. Albert Ellis described Adler as "the first humanistic psychologist," a personality theorist who "stressed holism, goal-seeking, and the enormous importance of values in human thinking, emoting, and acting" (1970, p. 11).

Chapter Summary

We began this chapter with Erich Fromm because he provides a bridge from social psychoanalysts like Horney, Erikson, and Adler to the humanists and existentialists of subsequent chapters. With his rejection of **scientism,** or *a narrow and excessive reliance on the concepts and methods of the "hard" sciences,* Fromm anticipated psychology's third wave—humanism—with its disdain for traditional laboratory methodologies. His discussion of ethics, society, and freedom and, anticipated similar existential concepts elaborated by Rollo May (1981, 1983) and, other existential psychologists (Chapter 12).

Fromm considered the family an important "transmission belt for those values and norms which a society wants to impress on its members" (1962, p. 177). Fromm began his career with a strong belief in the power of family dynamics; however, he ultimately agreed with Marx that society and political systems determine destiny.

Erik Erikson was psychoanalyzed by Anna Freud, and he assimilated her more permissive attitude, moving psychoanalysis in a more social direction; however, Erikson went far beyond what Freud or his daughter might have imagined or sanctioned. Yet, although he pushed the envelope, he never officially left the psychoanalytic fold from which he derived his professional identity.

Although he remained true to Freud's original tripartite *structure* of personality, he expanded psychoanalysis both vertically and horizontally. Erikson applied psychoanalysis across the entire developmental span—from womb to tomb—and by highlighting *mutual regulation* as the primary developmental process, he expanded psychoanalysis from a closed, intrapsychic system to an *interpersonal* social system that includes not only parents and their children, but major cultural institutions as well. In short, Erikson nudged psychoanalysis away from its exclusive focus on the individual psyche in the *Insight Zone* to interpersonal and cultural considerations in the *Social Zone*.

In Erikson's theories the *self* emerged with new clarity and comprehensiveness. In contrast with Freud's *ego*—"sandwiched" between biological impulses and societal expectations—Erikson's *ego* emerged as an *autonomous-yet-social self*. His is an *epigenetic* (integrating past, present, and future stages) and *interpersonal* theory of psychoanalysis that includes *cultural processes*. Erikson viewed ego development as resulting from the mutually regulating interactions between caretaker and child, however, he retained for each participant a clear sense of personal identity. Erikson's life spanned nearly the entire 20th century (1902–1994), and his influence continues to reverberate.

Adler's theory is well summarized by Mosak (1973):

Adler constructed a theory that was holistic, social, teleological, and phenomenological. He perceived man as an actor rather than a victim of drives, instincts, heredity or environment. Man was a "becoming" individual who strived to give meaning both to himself and to life. . . . Adler introduced the concept of the life style, the study of family constellation (which some psychologists erroneously equate with birth order and ordinal position), and the interpretation of early recollections, the "grand-daddy" of projective techniques. . . . A field theorist, Adler felt that man could not be understood except as a social being. . . . The highest ideal was social interest, a multi-dimensional construct which acknowledged that because we live in a social world, we are *responsible* for our fellowman. Man must not merely adjust to society; he is obligated to change it in the interest of the common weal. (p. v)

Points to Remember

1. The suicide of a family acquaintance and the outbreak of World War I caused Erich Fromm to question why people behave as they do. He sought answers at the broadest level, attempting to *synthesize Freud and Marx.*

2. Following Marx's reasoning that members of a high-tech society—working on an assembly line—are separated from the products of their work and the fruits of the earth, Fromm asserted that *basic alienation* is the root cause of all psychopathology.

3. Feeling like an "outsider" in his own family, Erik Erikson experienced an early *identity crisis,* which was repeated in his professional life because of his lack of formal education. Possessing only the equivalent of a high school diploma, Erikson spent his professional career rubbing shoulders with other professionals in such academic meccas as Harvard, Yale, and Berkeley.

4. Although Erikson utilized many of Sigmund Freud's psychoanalytic terms, he infused them with *object-relational, interpersonal,* and *culturally embedded* meanings. Thus his considerable influence, combined with the work of Anna Freud and Melanie Klein, moved classical psychoanalysis away from focusing on the *id* to analyzing the *ego.*

5. In place of Freud's central motivational force, *libido,* Erikson emphasized the interpersonal process of *mutual regulation.* Similarly, he replaced Freud's *psychosexual* stages with his own *psychosocial stages* that emphasized balancing the *dynamic polarities* (e.g., trust versus mistrust) which grew out of interpersonal relationships.

6. Erikson disliked psychoanalysis' emphasis on *origins* as the primary way of understanding development. Instead, he developed an *epigenetic* approach, insisting that each new stage incorporated all the stages preceding it. Thus the adolescent who performs on a gymnastic team or participates in a ballet production *incorporates*—in a refined form—the crawling, walking, running, and jumping of earlier stages.

7. Well ahead of their times, Erik and Joan Erikson mapped development over the *entire lifespan.* Even in very old age (nineties and beyond), they shared an optimistic emphasis on cultivating emerging skills and interests—something Joan termed *gerotranscendance—including play, activity, joy, and song.*

8. Adler believed that *birth order* powerfully shapes personality development. Additionally, he suffered health problems and concluded that everyone suffers from some sort of *organ inferiority* for which they *compensate* by developing a counterbalancing skill and *striving for superiority.*

9. *Fear of death,* brought about by numerous close encounters as a child, influenced Adler's personality development as well as his choice of vocation. Experiencing the horrors of World War I further spurred him to make *social interest* his master

motive in social evolution—analogous to survival-of-the-fittest in the realm of organic evolution.

10. Adler married a Russian wife whose independence and political activism undoubtedly influenced his attempt to *synthesize Darwin, Marx, and Freud.* Adler and Freud parted ways, but ultimately Freud stuck to his *libido-based intrapsychic* model, while Adler moved to a *societal model of the person embedded in a community.*

11. Adler *synthesized structure* and *motivation* into the *law of movement,* and stressed the great importance of *goals.*

12. *Safeguarding tendencies*—interpersonal defense strategies—come into play whenever we feel threatened by *physical* dangers or *social* threats, or in *how we view ourselves.*

13. *Family* is of primary importance in the Adlerian scheme of development. Psychological health is influenced not only by *birth order,* but by whether parents treat their children with *love and tenderness* and whether they *spoil or pamper* their offspring.

14. Adler described four personality styles: *ruler, getting type, avoiding type,* and *socially useful.*

15. Although Adler's theories have not been easy to rigorously evaluate, they have generated considerable interest among researchers, clinicians, and even philosophers of science. Karl Popper was so impressed by the broadness of Adler's claims that he articulated how concepts must be rigorous enough to be *falsifiable.* Considering family constellations of recent American presidents, it seems fair to conclude that many variables besides birth order exert significant influences.

Key Terms

Affiliation (284)

Aggression (298)

Anxiety (298)

Authenticity (282)

Avoiding Types (301)

Birth Order (290)

Codependency (300)

Compensate (289)

Creative Power (297)

Creative Self (300)

Distance Seeking (298)

Earliest Memory (302)

Ego (277)

Elan Vital (295)

Elitism (284)

Epigenetic Principle (279)

Exclusion Tendency (298)

Excuses (298)

Fictional Final Goal (295)

Formalism (283)

From Minus to Plus (300)

Formality (283)

Generativity (284)

Gerotranscendance (286)

Getting Types (301)

Id (276)

Identity (283)

Ideology (284)

Impersonation (282)

Individual Psychology (292)

Inferiority Complex (294)

Integralism (285)

Judicious (282)

Law of Movement (294)

Legalism (282)

Life Goal (290)

Lifestyle   (299)

Masculine Protest   (297)

Mutual Regulation   (277)

Necrophilous Character   (xxx)

Neurotic Behavior   (297)

Numinous Presence (of the mother)   (281)

Organ Dialect   (294)

Organ Inferiority   (289)

Originology   (279)

Polarities   (278)

Ritualizations   (279)

Rulers   (301)

Safeguarding Tendencies   (298)

Sapientism   (285)

Scientism   (308)

Social Character   (274)

Social Interest   (289)

Socially Useful   (301)

Spoiling and Pampering   (300)

Style of Life/Lifestyle   (295)

Superego   (277)

Superiority Complex   (297)

Symptoms   (298)

Totalism   (284)

Will To Power   (296)

Web Sites

Adler

www.alfredadler.org/. The North American Society of Adlerian Psychology.
This cyber-monument to Alfred Adler contains information on conferences, classes for professional development, and an "Adlerians in action" newsletter.

www.utexas.edu/utpress/journals/jip.html. The Journal of Individual Psychology. It contains a journal archive, PDF files of journal abstracts, and submission guidelines for contributors.

http://ourworld.compuserve.com/homepages/hstein. The Alfred Adler Institutes. Students looking to research Adler and the outcroppings of his theory hit a virtual gold mine in this fully loaded site. There are also interviews, audio/video clips, and biographies written from various perspectives.

Fromm

www.erich-fromm.de/e/index.htm. The International Erich Fromm Society.
Read quotes from Fromm about his personal life and other theorists who influenced him, view pictures, see a timeline of his life, and read about society. But watch out, unless you're fluent in German, be sure to select the English version!

http://en2.wikipedia.org/wiki/Erich_Fromm. Wikipedia. This long biography on Erich Fromm has an interesting perspective on the development of his theory.

www.nypl.org/research/chss/spe/rbk/faids/Fromm. The New York Public Library. A serious research site. This website explains how to get access to Erich Fromm's papers, with information on the content and scope of each work.

Learning on the Lighter Side

Recall that McAdams and de St. Aubin (1992) developed a scale to measure *generativity*. How many of the following activities or beliefs do you engage in (or plan, in the near future, to engage in)?

- Being committed to other people, groups, and activities
- Having children or adopting them
- Teaching important skills to others
- Volunteering to work for a charity
- Assuming responsibility for others who are less fortunate
- Feeling needed by others
- Trying to be creative in your activities
- Believing your contributions will survive after death
- Providing advice to others

The more of these you answered "yes," the more *generative* you are, and, according to Erikson, the more fulfilled your life will be.

The movie *Antwone Fisher*—based on a true story—chronicles the life of a young sailor who is in trouble for fighting. Ordered to see a navy psychiatrist, he at first refuses to talk. The psychiatrist (in psychoanalytic style) waits him out, and Antwone finally shares the closely guarded secrets of his past family life. I think Erikson, Adler, and Fromm would all have enjoyed this film, because it captures the importance of family and culture in the formation of personality, and the power of insight-oriented psychotherapy to facilitate healing. I think you might like it too.

Looking Ahead

In the next chapter we will consider the theories of Harry Stack Sullivan, Eric Berne, Jean Baker Miller, Nancy Chodorow, and other theorists who were not interested in merely *modifying* psychoanalysis into a more ego-oriented, object-relational, or culturally sensitive emphasis, but who insisted that the most basic unit of analysis for the study of personality is the **dyad,** *the two-person couple.* This was not "old wine in new wineskins," it represented a drastic departure from Freud's intrapsychic closed-system model of mind and even from object-relational perspectives. Beginning with Sullivan ("For all I know every human being has as many personalities as he has interpersonal relations" [Sullivan, 1964, p. 221]), the genie of personality escaped the bottle of intrapsychic confinement, never to be enclosed again.

chapter 9

From Object-Relations to Dyadic Theories of Personality

Harry Stack Sullivan, Eric Berne, Jean Baker Miller, Nancy Chodorow, and the Stone Center Group

IN THIS CHAPTER YOU CAN

1. Discover Harry Stack Sullivan's *interpersonal theory of psychiatry,* which shifted the focus of psychoanalysis from the *intrapsychic* mind to the *two-person dyad.*

2. Learn that *dynamisms (recurrent patterns of energy)* are Sullivan's primary constructs for building a theory of personality. These range from *subdynamisms* at the *cellular* level, to *interpersonal dynamisms* of social relationships.

3. Realize that *personifications* are the "lenses" through which, based on our past interpersonal relationship, we view the world. They include: *"Good Me," "Bad Me," "Not Me," "Good Mother,"* and *"Bad Mother."*

4. Learn how we *integrate* or "make sense" of interpersonal situations by engaging in *security operations,* or activities designed to avoid or reduce anxiety.

5. View infants and children as passing through the *prototaxic* (stream of consciousness), *parataxic* (loosely ordered events), and *syntaxic* (logically connected events) modes of development.

6. Discover Sullivan's seven *integrating forces* that include such things as *tenderness, acceptance,* and *intimacy.*

7. Encounter Eric Berne's *Transactional Analysis (TA),* which began as a popular version of Sullivan's *interpersonal* focus.

8. Learn how *strokes* combine to form *transactions* of several varieties: *complementary* (compatible), *crossed* (tending toward breakdown of relationship), or *ulterior* (deceptive and "gamey").

9. Notice how Berne—like Sullivan—focuses on the *dyad* as the smallest meaningful unit of analysis.

10. Understand Timothy Leary's *interpersonal circumplex,* a circular map on which emotionally opposite styles of relating are plotted opposite one another like the points of a compass.

11. Learn how the women of the Stone Center Group describe the *self* as both *dyadic* and *differentiated* in the context of *connected relationships.*

A PERSONAL PERSPECTIVE

> "Oh, God, may I be alive when I die."

A playful psychiatrist. Donald Winnicott (Chapter 7) lived his life with a playfulness captured in his own words: "we are poor indeed if we are only sane" (Winnicott, 1945, p. 150). His legendary ability to communicate with babies and children grew out of his own lifelong playfulness. Using Eric Berne's terminology (later in this chapter), we could say that Winnicott remained in touch with his *Natural Child.* Clare Winnicott reminisced about her husband's playfulness:

> . . . somebody came to our house one day—stayed a weekend in our house—and said to me, "You and Donald play, don't you?"
>
> So I said, "Do we? I have not thought of it in that way."
>
> He said, "Oh, yes you do. You play with me. You play with all kinds of things. My wife and I, we don't play."
>
> And I thought a lot about it, and I could see what he meant. We did play with arranging our furniture . . . with books, with reading with—and going out. We had our Saturdays always for play. No work was done by either of us on Saturdays, except enjoying ourselves and thinking what to do . . .
>
> But then he'd had about six coronaries and recovered from them and kept himself going. And didn't stop himself doing a thing. When he went down to his home in Devon, he'd be up at the top of a tree, in the last year of his life. A few months before he died. He was at the top of a tree cutting the top off. I said, "What the hell are you doing up there?"
>
> He said, "Well, I've always wanted the top of this tree off. It spoils the view from our window." Which it did. And he got it off.
>
> And I thought, "I must get him down. He's absolutely crazy." And I thought, "No, it's his life and he's got to live it. If he dies after this, he dies. . . ."
>
> And riding his bicycle. You know, with his feet on the handlebars. Till very late in life. And a policeman stopped him and said, "Fancy an old man like you setting an example to everybody." Coming down Haverstock Hill with his feet on the handlebars.
>
> And also, I've known him to drive his car, sitting with his head through the roof and a walking stick on the accelerator. Oh, I've really driven with him like that. He'd try anything. . . . He was the most spontaneous thing that ever lived. . . .
>
> But this was him. He wanted to live. He had started his autobiography. It was going to be called *Not Less Than Everything.* . . . And then he's put at the bottom: "Prayer: Oh, God, may I be alive when I die."
>
> And he was, really. We'd looked at a film. It was a very comic film of old cars, a very amusing film. . . . I said, "I think you'll like this." We looked at this, and he said, "What a happy-making film!" and went to sleep. And I woke up on the floor, and he was already dead on the floor. . . . We always liked the floor. . . . Yes, we always sat on the floor—him on one side, me on the other. We all had—we had our places. We had a rug that we sat on (1983, pp. 182, 192–193).

Commentary

Winnicott's playful approach to life was also evident in his playful clinical consultations where he typically began by drawing "squiggles" on paper and encouraging the child to complete the picture, thus providing a projective sampling of personality. Winnicott's playfully creative ideas provide a conceptual bridge from the dark, menacing theories of Melanie Klein to the commonsense notions of Harry Stack Sullivan, the transactional games of Eric Berne, and the connectedness of Chodorow, Miller, and the Stone Center Group.

There are important differences, however. Winnicott was an object-relations theorist, emphasizing that the infant *begins* life as part of a *mother–infant couple,* but eventually *differentiates* out of the maternal *dyad.* By contrast, the theorists of our current chapter view the self as remaining mostly *dyadic* across the entire life span.

From intrapsychic or object-relational self to the *dyadic* self. Shifting our view of the *self* from *intrapsychic* to *dyadic* is profound—like the transition from crawling to walking. From an *intrapsychic* perspective, the *self* resides somewhere inside oneself— somewhere within the mind, where it functions as the center of one's personality. By contrast, from a *dyadic* perspective the *self* exists as half of a couple, or a "piece" of a family. Here the *self* never completely differentiates itself out of the relational processes of the *Social Zone.* Correspondingly, our level of analysis broadens and moves to the right—away from the *individual*—to focus primarily on the *dyad* or *couple* as the most elementary unit of analysis. Now the term *"personality"* expands beyond its traditional within-the-skin boundaries to include *a series of interpersonal relationships that characterize a person over time.*

Personality psychologists of this chapter share the conviction that *from the very beginning, the self is dyadic—and remains so throughout life.* Personality is revealed in the successive series of *dyadic relationships* a person participates in throughout the lifespan. This differs markedly from intrapsychic and object-relations viewpoints where the *self* is seen to evolve and emerge out of *mother,* and to differentiate itself into an autonomously functioning center of personality. For Mahler, Winnicott, and other object-relations theorists, the *dyadic self* begins as a transitional state *on the way to* maturity. However, the real mark of maturity is a *differentiated self*—a self that is not enmeshed, entangled, or coupled with another, but is *differentiated* into a relatively *autonomous self.* In contrast, the theorists of this chapter see the *self* functioning primarily in a *dyadic* way from birth to death.

Harry Stack Sullivan—the pioneer dyadic theorist—even referred to the "illusion of personal individuality," suggesting that each person "... has as many personalities as he has interpersonal relations" (Sullivan, 1964, p. 221). Sullivan's ideas have been further investigated by researchers such as Leary, Kiesler, and others who believe that *"I"* can best be understood in relationship to another person—*"You."*

Eric Berne was trained as a traditional analyst. He was personally analyzed by Erik Erikson and spent most of his career focusing on *dyadic* exchanges, which he termed *transactions.* He described the fully developed, mature personality in *dyadic* relationship— "I'm OK, you're OK."

Writing from their perspective as feminists and psychoanalysts, Jean Baker Miller and Irene Pierce Stiver are convinced that *self* is best known and experienced in *interpersonal processes:* "Except perhaps for certain hermits, people are always *in* relationships—in schools, workplaces, and organizations, as well as in families . . ." (Miller & Stiver, 1997, p. 57). They shift focus from a psychology of "entities" to a psychology of "movement and dialogue."

HARRY STACK SULLIVAN'S INTERPERSONAL THEORY OF PSYCHIATRY

Harry Stack Sullivan is one of the most underrated personality theorists of the twentieth century. Although he is sometimes mistakenly portrayed as "neo-Freudian," he was scarcely touched by the psychoanalytic establishment. Instead, out of the starting gate he formulated an original theory that was thoroughly *interpersonal*. He saw all human relationships as based on the *two-person dyad,* and coined one of today's popular buzzwords, *codependency,* to remind us that even alcoholics—seemingly addicted to a chemical substance—typically maintain their lifestyles with the "assistance" of a partner.

Anna Freud, Melanie Klein, and Erik Erikson all shifted focus from the *id* to the *ego,* but theirs was a shift in *emphasis,* even while the *structure* of personality remained traditionally Freudian. Sullivan, by contrast, brought about a *paradigm shift* by suggesting that the psychiatrist is not an "objective" or "scientific" observer, but functions instead as a **participant observer** who is *an actively participating member of the dyad.* This was a revolutionary notion in a psychiatric world dominated by Freud's intrapsychic ***behind-the-couch*** model. Sullivan anticipated our postmodern understanding of science by recognizing that one can never observe "pure" data untouched by the perceptions and predispositions of the observer. As he put it: ". . . the psychiatrist cannot stand off to one side and apply his sense organs . . . to noticing what someone else does, without becoming personally implicated in the operation" (Sullivan, 1954, p. 3).

Background Check

A "coat rack" for his mother's bitterness. Harry Stack Sullivan (1892–1949) grew up lonely and emotionally isolated in the small town of Norwich, New York. The third child of Irish Catholic parents whose parents had emigrated from Ireland after the potato crop failure in the late 1840s, Harry had two older siblings who both died in early infancy, leaving him as the only child of an emotionally withdrawn father and a whining, semi-invalid mother. Harry bore the brunt of his mother's displaced bitterness toward her husband, and he furnished her an audience for her tales regarding the prominence and prosperity of the Stack family in Old Ireland. This led Sullivan to caustically comment that his mother had never taken the trouble to really know him, using him only as "a coat rack on which to hang an elaborate pattern of illusions" (Chapman, 1976, p. 20).

Probably sexually abused. Sullivan was eight and a half years of age when he formed a close friendship with a thirteen-year-old boy from an adjacent farm. It appears that this relationship was sexual in nature. Years later, Sullivan stated that when an early adolescent forms a close relationship with a lonely, younger child, homosexual exploitation of the younger partner usually occurs. Neither Sullivan nor this neighbor boy ever married or established heterosexual relationships. Both became psychiatrists.

From valedictorian to dropout. Sullivan was a superior student, graduating as valedictorian of his high school class and winning a scholarship to Cornell, where he enrolled in the science curriculum. His first-term grades in chemistry, physics, mathematics, and mechanical drawing were above average, but they fell substantially during his second semester, and by the end of that term he was suspended for failing all his subjects. Whatever the reasons, Sullivan's university education was limited to one successful semester, followed by a failed semester, after which he never to returned to college.

Fly-by-night medical school. In those days it was possible to enroll in marginal medical schools directly out of high school. Instruction was rudimentary and graduation depended more upon paying tuition than demonstrating scholastic or clinical competence. So, two years after dropping out of college, Sullivan enrolled in a fly-by-night, run-for-profit medical school that was housed in an old building in a poor section of Chicago. With no hospital or clinical affiliations, this school was accurately described by Sullivan as a "diploma mill," but it was probably Sullivan's only hope to better himself after failing at Cornell.

Little is known about Sullivan's life during these years, except that he lived in poverty and spent most of his time working to pay his school bills. He labored at various jobs, including working as a conductor on the Chicago elevated trains. In 1915, he finally received his diploma, but it was another seven years before he stumbled into psychiatry when he found employment at St. Elizabeth's Hospital in Washington, D.C., a huge government psychiatric hospital where many psychiatrically disabled veterans were housed. Sullivan learned psychiatry by working directly with schizophrenic patients and by attending lectures and seminars.

Following a different drummer. Sullivan's lack of systematic psychiatric training shows itself in various ways throughout his work. His knowledge of many mental disorders frequently appears fragmentary and deficient, and his eccentric and inaccurate use of psychiatric terminology often leaves readers baffled and confused. Nonetheless, it is likely that Sullivan's lack of traditional psychiatric training also contributed to his creativity. One biographer described it well:

> He did not adopt the ideas of any particular school of psychiatric thought.
> He did not acquire the prejudices that extensive formal training would have
> instilled in him, and which might later have hindered him in evolving his own
> unique system of psychiatry. . . . By default Sullivan learned psychiatry from
> the most reliable of teachers, the patients. . . . Sullivan had another important
> source of psychiatric education—his own personality problems which dogged
> him all his life. He was acutely aware of the ways in which his early emotional
> traumas had made him inept in many interpersonal areas, and his homosexual
> urges jabbed him intermittently. . . . (Chapman, 1976, pp. 37–38)

Sullivan did not work well with female patients; they apparently made him uncomfortable. After leaving St. Elizabeth's, Sullivan worked at Sheppard and Enoch Pratt Hospital, a well-known private psychiatric facility in the suburbs of Baltimore. There he organized a six-bed ward for young male schizophrenics and carefully instructed six male aides on how to act and talk around these patients. Sullivan himself conducted daily interviews with each of the patients—often with an aide present, in order to give it a group atmosphere.

It was out of these experiences that Sullivan formulated his interpersonal theories. Unlike his Freudian colleagues who focused on their patients' past lives, Sullivan tried to create an interpersonal environment in which healthy interactions with hospital staff could gradually revise unhealthy patterns of thinking and feeling. The extent of his involvement with patients is illustrated by the fact that in 1927 he adopted a fifteen-year-old boy—a former patient—as his son. This young man remained with Sullivan the rest of his life—running his household, caring for him, and managing his financial affairs.

Shy, creative, and combative. During the 1930s, as Sullivan matured professionally and formulated his ideas more explicitly, the differences between his interpersonal approach and the prevailing physiological, biochemical, or psychoanalytic paradigms became increasingly apparent. Although he was socially shy, Sullivan could be professionally antagonistic. His friends described him as witty and brilliant, but opponents experienced him as cutting and vituperative. Bitter quarrels between Sullivan and the Freudians became more frequent, increasing his loneliness and isolation. Additionally, Sullivan's last years were marred by poor health. His adopted son and close friends nursed him through four serious cardiac illnesses.

Zeitgeist

An "American" psychology. A prominent personality theorist described Sullivan's theory as . . . "a kind of Yankee, cracker-barrel, no-nonsense approach to therapy in which practical, achievable goals were set and carried out . . ." (Rychlak, 1981, p. 369). One of Sullivan's editors described his work as being "as American as Mark Twain," noting that "There was a restlessness about Sullivan, a drive toward the pragmatic, which is curiously American" (Perry, 1962, pp. xxv–xxvi).

Sullivan's theory is "American" because it is *observable,* and Americans prefer the palpable. Whereas psychoanalysts tried to remain *neutral* and *analytic,* Sullivanians *observed* and *participated* in the world of the other. In contrast to Freud, who saw the psychoanalyst as an "opaque screen," Sullivan viewed the psychiatrist as a *participant observer.*

It's safe to conclude that Sullivan was scarcely touched by the psychoanalytic *zeitgeist*—as he might have been had he been successful at Cornell. The first psychoanalysts didn't arrive in Chicago until the early 1920s, so we can be certain that psychoanalysis was not part of Sullivan's marginal medical education. Instead, he stumbled in psychiatry's back door, working with hospitalized schizophrenics and developing his own unique interpersonal theory.

Analogously, in an academic setting, Timothy Leary (later this chapter) moved outside the traditional factor-analytic study of *individuals' traits* to formulate his **interpersonal circumplex,** which is *a circular map that plots personality in terms of interpersonal relationships.* Both Sullivan and Leary failed to receive the respect they deserved partly because their theories were out of synch with the more popular paradigms of their times, and perhaps because their personal lives were also out of synch with the times. Sullivan was suspected of being gay during an era when homosexuality was officially considered a mental illness, and Timothy Leary advocated using LSD to expand one's mind during an era when most professionals considered LSD more likely to "fry" one's brain than to expand it. Fortunately, the spirit of these interpersonal innovators lives on in the subsequent work of Berne (1961, 1964, 1973, 1978), Kiesler (1983, 1996), Wiggins (1982), and others.

ASKING THE BIG FOUR QUESTIONS

For Freud and other Europeans, constructs such as "id," "ego," and "psyche" functioned as *intrapsychic* entities, which could never be *seen or touched.* By contrast, Sullivan formulated a theory of personality that could be *directly observed* in *interpersonal relationships*. Anxiety, according to Sullivan, was always *interpersonal,* and always arose from unhealthy relationships between people that could be observed. *Security operations,* Sullivan's term for behavioral maneuvers designed to avoid anxiety, were also *observably interpersonal* in nature.

What Are the Parts?

Although Sullivan used familiar constructs like self, anxiety, or personality, he used them in an *interpersonal* rather than an *intrapsychic* sense. For example, Sullivan defined **personality** as *"the relatively enduring pattern of recurrent interpersonal situations which characterize a human life"* (1953, p. 111, emphasis in the original). In another

TABLE 9.1A

Sullivan at a Glance

MODEL OF PERSONALITY	DESCRIPTION	DYNAMICS
What Are the Parts?	**Self:** the conscious portion of a person's experiential field that is a dynamic state of interpersonal flux. **Pattern:** an envelope of insignificant differences. **Dynamism:** enduring patterns of energy transformation that characterize a living organism's interactions. **Subdynamism:** patterns at lower levels of analysis (e.g., salivary gland activity vs. digestion as a whole). **Zonal dynamism:** energy expenditures associated with bodily activities. **Interpersonal dynamism:** energy exchanges among individuals, dyads, or larger groups.	Dynamism describes patterns from cellular biology to international relations. Although Sullivan thought of the self in constant fluctuation with regard to interpersonal and zonal dynamisms, he felt that there was an overall pattern of stable energy transformation in these areas.
What Makes a Person Go?	**Integrating tendency:** a person's attempt at making sense of new situations by referencing past situations and looking forward. **Euphoria and tension:** euphoria is considered a state of equilibrium or utter well-being; tension is the opposite of euphoria. **Anxiety:** results of a disturbance in a relationship with a significant other. **Security operations:** activities designed to reduce or avoid anxiety. **Selective inattention:** a way to avoid embarrassment by keeping thoughts unconscious.	Anxiety about the status of relationships is the key motivating factor in Sullivan's model, making the energy between people the fuel for personality. *Security operations* and *selective inattention* keep anxiety from becoming overwhelming. Sullivan postulated an *integrating tendency* that includes present and past interpersonal experiences while propelling humans towards the future.

TABLE 9.1A *(continued)*

Sullivan at a Glance

MODEL OF PERSONALITY	DESCRIPTION	DYNAMICS
What Makes a Person Grow?	Sullivan outlined *Five developmental stages:* Infancy (Birth to 18 months), Childhood (18 months–4 years), Juvenile period (4 years–9 years), Preadolescence (9 years–12 years), and Adolescence (12 years–early 20s). He proposed *three language processing/ thinking styles:* Protaxic mode (birth–8 months), Parataxic mode (8–18 months), and Syntaxic mode (18–48 months).	Sullivan's developmental focus is on how interpresonal situations arise, mature, and become integrated into personality. The states delineated are based on the working out of interpersonal interactions beginning with the parents and opening wider to include friends, society, etc. For a more in-depth look at these periods refer to Table 8.2.
What Makes a Person Unique?	In addition to the five developmental stages and three cognitive processing styles, Sullivan suggested *ten typical personality styles:* lack of duration, self-absorbed, incorrigible, negativistic, stammerer, ambition-ridden, asocial inadequate, homosexual, and chronically adolescent.	Sullivan's emphasis was on the similarities of human personality, however he made provision for uniqueness in the various combinations that might occur among developmental stages, cognitive/language styles, and personality styles.

place Sullivan said that "Personality is the relatively enduring configuration of life-processes characterizing all of the person's total activity pertaining to such other persons, real or fantastic, as become from time to time relevant factors in his total situation" (1972, p. 47). The common theme in Sullivan's meandering definitions of personality is the *interpersonal* emphasis. Personality contains the *patterns of interactions* with other human beings.

Dyadic self. Sullivan's **dyadic self** *is a self that exists only in relationship to another.* The *dyadic self* is not a developmental achievement (as is the *autonomous self* for object-relations theorists). The *dyadic self* is present throughout the life span—in the newborn, in the toddler, in the adolescent, and in the fully mature adult. As Sullivan saw it, we all begin life as a part of an infant–mother dyad and we *continue* to live out our lives in a subsequent series of dyadic relationships with others. We might picture Sullivan's dyadic self as similar to a two-pound, hand-held weight used for aerobic workouts: two spherical ends ("me-you") connected by a thick handle—with almost as much of the mass residing in the dumbbell's handle as in the spherical ends. Similarly, for Sullivan the *self* is always *dyadically coupled,* with nearly as much personality "mass" residing in the relationship as in the separate individuals making up the dyad.

Sullivan described this *dyadic self* as a conscious portion of a person's awareness: "*The self is the content of consciousness at all times when one is thoroughly comfortable about one's self-respect, the prestige that one enjoys among one's fellows . . . "* (Sullivan, 1964, p. 217, emphasis in original).

Notice how Sullivan moves beyond *intrapsychic* definitions to describe the *self* as part of an *interpersonal flux ("among one's fellows")*. For Sullivan, *self* is not simply a component of individual awareness or some sort of within-the-head agent steering the person in one direction or another. Nor is the *self* some sort of inner mirror (like Horney's "Idealized Self") against which an individual measures his or her behavior. Like all of Sullivan's personality parts, the *dyadic* self is *interpersonal* in nature, incorporating the attitudes and behaviors that significant others have manifested toward the infant and child: "The self may be said to be made up of reflected appraisals" (Sullivan, 1940, p. 22).

Considered apart from relationships, Sullivan felt that the term *self* was not very useful: "The self is an entity that is of little service as a general explanatory principle in the study of interpersonal relations" (1964, p. 31). This is probably why he frequently referred to the *dyadic* self as a *self-system* so as to emphasize that *self* is always manifested in an *interpersonal/relational* context.

Self-system as soothing agent. For Sullivan, his own personal *anxiety* was apparently an ever present threat, and he believed that "very few people have the foggiest notion of what a vast part of their life is influenced by anxiety" (1964, p. 216). In an interpersonal world saturated with anxiety, Sullivan saw the **self-system** as an "anti-anxiety system" (1953, p. 108) engaged in maintaining a sense of interpersonal security. Continually concerned with protecting self-esteem, the *self-system* functions as a kind of psychological Valium—calming the nerves, soothing the psyche, keeping distress at bay. It accomplishes this through security operations: *"maintaining a feeling of safety in the esteem reflected to one from the other person concerned"* (1953, p. 373, emphasis added). We will discuss *security operations* further in our "What-Makes-a-Person-Go?" discussion.

Three terms—similar meanings. Sullivan used the terms *self, self-dynamism,* and *self-system* interchangeably. It was only during the last two years of his life that he settled exclusively on *self-system* as his preferred term. Sullivan saw the *self-system* as comprised of the *interpersonal* strategies that a person utilizes in maintaining emotional comfort and being protected from emotional distress. One might think of the self-system as operating like the Secret Service functions to protect the president—always present, always watching, always alert to any potential danger that might harm the commander-in-chief.

Dynamisms in place of mechanisms—embracing Einstein, transcending Freud. Sullivan defined **dynamism** as *"the relatively enduring pattern of energy transformations which recurrently characterize the organism in its duration as a living organism"* (1953, p. 103, emphasis in original). Dynamisms are Sullivan's most important *patterns,* forming the structural foundation of his entire theory. He viewed the universe—and everything in it—from an Einsteinian perspective that: ". . . the ultimate reality in the universe is energy" (1953, p. 102). For Sullivan all material objects and all human activity represent either a dynamic or kinetic form of energy. Thus he uses the term *dynamism* to incorporate Einstein's vibrant view of reality and to escape Freud's quasi-mechanical metaphors involving cathexis or "flow" of libido. The term "mechanism" reminded Sullivan of a diesel engine, "And the one thing we are sure of in interpersonal relations is that there are processes which are dynamic; they are not static, mechanical entities" (1953, p. 5).

A contemporary biologist echoes Sullivan's words: "The things that we see around us, and which we think of as needing explanation—rocks, galaxies, ocean waves—are all, to a greater or lesser extent, stable patterns of atoms" (Dawkins, 1989, p. 12).

Subdynamism. Sullivan's dynamism constructs were elastic enough to include nearly everything in the universe, from the molecular to the cosmic. In the *Physiological Zone,* he ranged from the molecular to the whole person, describing **subdynamisms** *as ranging from individual cells to organs such as kidneys, lungs, and the heart.* Such systems of subdynamisms, in turn, were integrated into the total dynamism of the person.

Still in the *Physiological Zone,* at a higher level of analysis, Sullivan spoke of **zonal dynamisms,** or *energy transformations associated with bodily activities such as eating, drinking, excretion, or sexual intercourse.* Simply stated, *zonal dynamisms* are physiological processes associated with a particular *zone* of the body. Thus eating involves the mouth and alimentary zones, whereas breathing utilizes the nose and lungs.

Interpersonal dynamisms. In the *Social Zone,* Sullivan described recurrent social interactions as **interpersonal dynamisms,** which are *relatively enduring patterns of interaction that characterize interpersonal relations.* These interpersonal dynamisms (patterns) might be so broad as to occur within families, communities, or even nations: "Nations are particular dynamisms which are the locus of unnumbered other sub- or intra-national dynamisms . . ." (Sullivan, 1964, p. 325).

Personifications. Among the earliest *interpersonal dynamisms* are **personifications,** *the cognitive representation of past interpersonal experiences.* These internalized perceptions and fantasies about self and others powerfully shape how we view our interpersonal world. The two broad classes of personifications include personifications of ourselves (e.g., good me, bad me, and not me) and personifications of *others* (e.g., good mother, bad mother, good father, bad father).

Good mother vs. bad mother. Sullivan described the early roots of the *good-mother personification* as growing out of the *dyadic* exchange between infant and caretaker. He believed that the nipple-in-lips was one of the first interpersonal dynamisms that translated into a *personification* on the part of the infant: "Now this personification is not the 'real' mother. . . . It is an elaborate organization of the infant's experience" (Sullivan, 1953, p. 112).

Just as the *good mother* is associated with pleasure and satisfaction, the *bad mother* is associated with anxiety: "To the infant . . . good mother is the symbol of forthcoming satisfaction; and . . . bad mother is the symbol of anxiety and increasing distress" (1953, p. 89). We will discuss this more fully when we consider Sullivan's states of development.

Transference and personifications. Sullivan's personifying process bears some resemblance to Freud's concept of transference, because although personifications are assembled from a mosaic of real experiences, they exist primarily in the mind of the beholder, sometimes only vaguely resembling the real object. According to Sullivan, our *personified "Mother"* is comprised of a *good mother, bad mother, punishing mother, praising mother, etc.,* all melded into a single complex portrait.

Some personifications, such as Santa Claus, might be entirely fantastic yet consistent with what a child experienced in relation to a doting grandfather or a kind uncle. Personifications like Mickey Mouse might have personal associations (such as

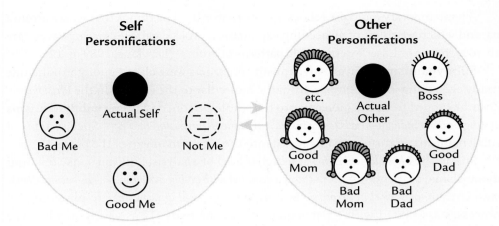

Figure 9.1 ■ *Sullivan's System for Integrating Interpersonal Situations*

membership in the Mickey Mouse Club), while others (e.g., "Uncle Sam" or the Queen of England) could carry a broad national identity with a wide array of associations.

With such an array of dynamisms and personifications—ranging in scope from the single cell to the entire universe—Sullivan's theory is well equipped to analyze the nuances of interpersonal relationships. When we consider how each of us (with our uniquely tinted portraits of self and others) interacts with other people (each with their own unique arrays of personifications for viewing self and others), it comes as no surprise that we sometimes misunderstand others or feel misunderstood by them.

Summary of Sullivan's personality parts. Sullivan's view of personality differs radically from traditional, *intrapsychic* definitions. Personality is *dyadically experienced* and colored by multiple layers of *personifications* by both members of the dyad. Sullivan explains this in his rambling yet profound style: "For all I know every human being has as many personalities as he has interpersonal relations," adding that "a great many of our interpersonal relations are actual operations with imaginary people . . . " (1964, p. 221).

Sullivan's ideas about relationships with "imaginary people" seem particularly relevant in an era when many television viewers and moviegoers form "relationships" with actors. For example, hundreds of thousands of viewers felt they had really become "friends" with their television *Friends*—had really "gotten to know them"—and experienced genuine emotional loss when the series concluded. Previous generations experienced similar losses when such long-running series as *Lucille Ball and Desi Arnez, Gunsmoke, The Mary Tyler Moore Show, Mission Impossible, M.A.S.H.,* or *Cheers* concluded. The tearful gathering of fans to watch the final episodes is consistent with Sullivan's observation that "imaginary" relationships "may have the same or greater validity and importance in life as have our operations with . . . people like the clerks in the corner store . . . " (1964, p. 221).

What Makes a Person Go?

Integrating tendency. Sullivan's core motivational construct is the **integrating tendency,** *a person's attempt to "make sense" of each new situation by relating it to past situations and projecting it into the future—evaluating what it means to the self.*

This *integrating tendency* provides both motivational fuel and integrating glue, energizing our personality components as well as binding them together into a coherent whole that integrates our current experiences responses with past, present, and future experiences. As Sullivan put it, ". . . everything that happens to us that gets any sort of notice from us—conscious or unconscious, witting or unwitting—fits into the theory of the development and refinement of integrating tendencies or interpersonal processes, which characterize us" (1956, pp. 69–70).

Biological integration. Just as Sullivan conceived *dynamisms* to operate in both the *Physiological* and *Social Zones,* he believed integrating tendencies operated at both levels as well: "Integrating tendencies are conceived to be the psychobiological substrata of corresponding integrated interpersonal situations" (Sullivan, 1964, p. 71). Sullivan was interested in integration at all levels of biological complexity, but for him the *interpersonal* aspects of integration mattered most. He saw biological factors as subservient to interpersonal issues.

Interpersonal integration—what to do when hit by a ripe tomato. Sullivan illustrates *interpersonal integration* by beginning at the physiological level and moving to the interpersonal level:

> Let us say, for example, that I have been hit with a ripe tomato, which means that a great many things are impinging on the distance receptors, and so on, with lots of reference to past experiences in terms of color sense, consistencies, splash, and all sorts of things. . . . "How come this tomato? Has it fallen on me by accident or did somebody throw it at me? And if the latter is the case, am I the natural target? Was I intended to be hit? Or am I just an innocent bystander, and someone whose aim is bad has hit me instead of the person he was throwing at?" All these questions are almost automatically asked. . . . because, almost from the cradle to the grave, it is extremely important for us to know whether people are expressing contempt, praise, dislike, like, or what not for us. This is the source of our security and of our insecurity; and the self-system was invented for that business. (1956, p. 67)

Continuing his "ripe-tomato" illustration, Sullivan states that although one has to think about changing clothing, the most important issues involve *integrating* the *interpersonal* implications:

> . . . it calls for changing your clothes as quickly as possible. . . . But this is not the primary activity of the self; the self is primarily concerned with what you do about the impulse that broke loose in the person who hurled the tomato at you. How is that to be dealt with? How is one to avoid such gross, offensive attacks on one's dignity and propriety? (Sullivan, 1956, p. 68)

Sullivan's own skill at integrating interpersonal relationships was illustrated on one occasion when a very disturbed patient struck him. Sullivan smiled slightly and asked, "Feeling better now?" (Chapman, 1976, p. 47).

Coping with tension in the Physiological Zone. In the *Physiological Zone,* Sullivan's motivational polarities are *tension* and *euphoria,* but he doesn't use the term *euphoria* in the usual way to mean ecstasy, joy, or exhilaration; rather, **euphoria** *is a state of equilibrium or quiescence.* Sullivan describes euphoria ". . . as a state of utter well-being. The nearest approach to anything like it . . . might occur when a very young infant is in a state of deep sleep" (1953, p. 34).

Sullivan defines **tension** *as the opposite of euphoria.* For Sullivan, euphoria and tension are in direct, reciprocal relationship: ". . . the level of euphoria varies inversely with the level of tension. . . . The nearest approach to absolute tension that one observes is the . . . state of terror" (Sullivan, 1953, p. 35).

Coping with anxiety at the interpersonal level. Just as euphoria and tension balance each other in the *Physiological Zone,* anxiety and *security* balance each other in the *Social Zone.* For Sullivan, **anxiety** *is a disturbance in the relationship with a significant other.* The first significant other is usually the mother: *"The tension of anxiety, when present in the mothering one, induces anxiety in the infant"* (Sullivan, 1953, p. 41, emphasis in original). For Sullivan, anxiety was always *interpersonal* in nature, as was its balancing counterpart, **security:** "the relaxation of the tension of anxiety . . . is the experience . . . of interpersonal *security"* (1953, p. 42).

Anxiety—the ever-present motivational trigger. Sullivan considered interpersonal anxiety to be the motivational trigger for a wide array of coping maneuvers designed to maintain self-esteem. He believed the source of anxiety was always other people's dissatisfaction: "disapproving attitudes on the part of others, with other people not being satisfied with our performances" (1964, p. 216). After a while, this interpersonal anxiety occurs so easily and operates so smoothly that most people are hardly aware of its presence.

Security operations. Anytime a person faces a new interpersonal situation, anxiety will be part of the mix, calling into action **security operations,** or *activities designed to relieve anxiety.* According to Sullivan, *security operations* are concerned with ". . . maintaining a feeling of safety in the esteem reflected to one from the other person concerned . . ." (1953, p. 373).

Selective inattention. One example of a security operation is **selective inattention,** which *allows one to avoid embarrassment by keeping thoughts unconscious:* "You don't hear, you don't see, you don't feel, you don't observe, you don't think . . . all by the very suave manipulation of the contents of consciousness by anxiety" (Sullivan, 1964, pp. 216–217).

In the above quotation *selective inattention* appears to function much as *resistance* does in the process of psychoanalysis—an attempt to remain outside the reach of helpers who might prove beneficial. However, Sullivan also saw a positive role for selective inattention as a coping mechanism that promotes efficiency by focusing on core issues and ignoring irrelevant details when faced with a complex task such as planning a family reunion or flying a helicopter: *"The thing that determines whether this is done well or ill, from the standpoint of long-range results for the person, is how smoothly the control of awareness excludes the irrelevant and includes the relevant"* (Sullivan, 1956, pp. 42–43, emphasis in original).

Summary of Sullivan's motivational constructs. For Sullivan, it is not libido, reinforcement, or self-actualization that energizes the engine of personality, it is *anxiety* about the moment-by-moment status of interpersonal relationships that fuels the *integrating tendency.* Sullivan does not see energy spouting volcano-like from deep within, nor does he locate motivational forces in an external situation that is dense with reinforcers but depleted of people; instead, Sullivan locates the primary source of motivational power in the *dyad,* where anxieties about how "You" perceive "Me" generate motivational nuclear fission. Perhaps because Sullivan himself was lonely, isolated, and socially anxious, he developed an exquisite sensitivity for the characteristics of interpersonal relationships. His theory frequently blurs distinctions of structure, motivation, and development, pouring them into the stream of dyadic relationships.

What Makes a Person Grow?

TABLE 9.1B

Sullivan's Developmental Epochs*

DEVELOPMENTAL ERA	CHARACTERISTICS OF ERA	ACHIEVEMENTS	FAILURES
Infancy (0–18 mos.)	Primacy of oral zonal dynamisms; earliest development of linguistic and cognitive skills; high sensitivity to caretakers' emotions	Prototaxic or egocentric language; body experience that is primarily of oral/anal zonal dynamisms; Good, Bad, & Not Me personifications	Maternally induced anxiety; defensive avoidance or apathy; preponderance of Bad or Not Me personifications
Childhood (18 mos.–4 years)	Magical/experiential use of language; need for playmates	Parataxic logical "connections" in thinking; coherent sense of "Me"; interpersonal dynamisms that begin to include social relations beyond the family	Dissociative thinking; malevolent personality transformations of feeling unloved; "uncanny" anxiety-ridden emotions
Juvenile Era (4–9 years)	Entering school; significant expansion of social world beyond immediate family	Parataxic & syntaxic reality; consolidation of social skills; correct parataxic distortions	Lack of playmates; failure to develop intimacy with same-gender "chum;" ostracism, withdrawal, loneliness

(continued)

TABLE 9.1B *(continued)*

Sullivan's Developmental Epochs*

DEVELOPMENTAL ERA	CHARACTERISTICS OF ERA	ACHIEVEMENTS	FAILURES
Preadolescence (9–12 years)	Beginning puberty; intimate friendships with members of same gender—"chums"	Mostly syntaxic reality; mostly same-gender "chums"	Discomfort with same and opposite gender persons; social isolation and withdrawal
Early Adolescence (12–16 years)	Puberty; intense interest in opposite gender	Syntaxic reality; intense lust dynamism; opposite-gender partner(s) to facilitate sexual integration	Failure to integrate various selves; conflict between lust and intimacy needs
Late Adolescence (17–maturity)	Heterosexual activity; adult interpersonal relationships	Syntaxic reality; vocational choices; need for life partner of opposite gender; wide range of mature interpersonal relationships	Lack of a significant other; few friends; no clear vocational direction

*based on Sullivan (1953).

Developmental Modes of Experience: Prototaxic, Parataxic, Syntaxic

Sullivan describes how we develop increasingly complex ways of relating to the world, beginning with the *prototaxic* way of experiencing the world and moving on to *parataxic* and *syntaxic*.

Infancy (birth–18 months). During the earliest months of life, the infant functions in what Sullivan called the **prototaxic mode (experiencing events serially):** *the infant perceives the world as a steady stream of raw sensory experiences out of which it is impossible to create order or consistency.* Sullivan referred to this serial chain of sensory stimuli as "the crude stuff of perception" (1953, p. 108). The *prototaxic mode* is based primarily on zonal dynamisms, reminding us of Freud's *oral* stage, where bodily experiences predominate and the sucking reflex is king. The *prototaxic mode* also bears some likeness to Erikson's first psychosocial stage, where the infant's earliest *interpersonal* encounters lay the groundwork for a lifetime of *trust* or *mistrust*.

Sullivan described the *prototaxic mode* as "the crudest . . . the simplest, the earliest, and possibly the most abundant mode of experience" (1953, p. 29). Sullivan included such biological "basics" as breathing and maintaining body temperature among the newborn's earliest prototaxic experiences; however, it was the *interpersonal* aspects of nursing that interested him most. He said that personhood essentially begins ". . . as a function of the first nursing" (Sullivan, 1953, p. 122). The extraphysiological factors—psychological and interpersonal—present in the nursing situation contribute to a growing *personification* of the *good mother* by the infant.

Anxious mother—bad nipple. Conversely, Sullivan believed that even basic physiological processes such as feeding can easily become permeated with anxiety. Then, instead of a gratifying experience with a "good nipple," the baby experiences anxiety in relationship to a "bad nipple," which becomes personified as a "bad mother." For Sullivan, the "bad nipple" is not a result of the infant's introjections and projections (as in Melanie Klein's theory), but results primarily from *anxiety*, which always lurks around the corridors of interpersonal relationships and is easily transmitted from mother to infant. Anxious or depressed parents are—as Sullivan knew from personal experience—difficult emotional hazards for the infant or young child to negotiate.

Zonal dynamism of infancy. The **oral zonal dynamism** *includes thumb sucking and other early oral behaviors:* "Thus thumbs, fingers, toes, and all manner of portable objects have been explored and exploited by the mouth" (1953, p. 136). As a result of such oral-manual manipulations the infant begins to differentiate his or her body from everything else in the environment. The experience of thumb sucking provides the infant with reliable comfort and delineates some of the parameters of "my body."

During Sullivan's era, mothers were warned that thumb sucking could lead to dental problems, and consequently it became important to many mothers to modify what Sullivan described as ". . . the infant's initial venture in self sufficiency-thumbsucking" (Sullivan, 1953, p. 142). Consequently a degree of anxiety frequently interfered with the infant's discovery that his body was dependable and reliable.

Childhood (18 months–approximately 4 years). Sullivan did not specify exact developmental timetables, but he used the term *childhood* to designate the period that begins with the first articulate speech and ends with the need for associating with same-aged children outside the family.

Parataxic mode (8–18 months). Operating in the **parataxic mode (experiencing events side by side without clear causal connections),** *infants begin to make temporal connections between experiences by anticipating familiar sequences.* Here the baby develops its first rudimentary notions of *causality,* assuming that what immediately preceded an event *caused* it to happen. The *prototaxic mode* begins when the infant first begins "baby talk," and concludes when the child begins using language in a genuinely syntaxical manner, about the middle of the second year.

Signs. Sullivan described the parataxic mode in terms of *signs* and *symbols*. **Signs** *are the infant's earliest, simplest signals that yield information about the environment.* The mother's voice, her rhythms, her responsiveness in feeding and diapering—all function as *signs* to the infant.

Symbols. As development proceeds, elemental signs or signals become organized into **symbols,** "categories of signs" or "signs of signs" (1953, p. 87). The use of language symbols represents a giant developmental step forward because it is the use of language that moves the child from the *prototaxic* to the *parataxic* mode. Even the earliest, floundering uses of language begin to free the newborn from the prison of wordlessness. No longer handcuffed to immediate bodily experiences, the baby begins to symbolize and contextualize experiences in terms of events occuring in the past, the present, and the near future.

During the parataxic phase, the child forms links among the various fragments of experience, but such connections are haphazard and disjointed because they do not follow rules of logic. Since language has not yet developed into a syntactical system, we might say the child fails to "connect the dots" of experience to form a larger portrait of self and others.

Gestures. Sullivan emphasized the communicational importance of gestures as well as verbal language. He used the term **gesture** *to mean subtle nonverbal signals that enhance verbal communication.* Speaking of an eleven-month-old, Sullivan noticed that beneath the adult conversation present in the room, the infant appeared to be engaging in a conversation of his own: ". . . what caught my attention was the beautiful tonal pattern . . . so startlingly like speech that I could distinguish it only by careful listening . . ." (Sullivan, 1953, pp. 178–179).

The parataxic infant picks up "more and more of the nonverbal, but nonetheless communicative aspects of speech" (Sullivan, 1953, p. 179). Yet, although symbols and words begin to emerge, life is not logically connected, so experience occurs as momentary, disconnected states of being.

Lust and intimacy. Closely connected to the parataxic mode, Sullivan's **lust dynamism** *involves another person with whom a lustful situation might be integrated.* As with other aspects of parataxic functioning, lust is not verbally well labeled. Culture and anxiety conspire to make certain that lust remains, as Sullivan put it, *"unrepresented in focal awareness"* (1953, p. 288, emphasis in original).

Developing alongside the lust dynamism, **intimacy** *begins in the prototaxic stage as a need for* <u>contact</u>, *and manifests itself during the parataxic stage as a need for* <u>tenderness</u>. During early adolescence, this becomes a need for *friendship, acceptance,* and *intimacy,* and during late adolescence, it is consolidated as the need for *lust* and *intimacy,* which characterizes all of adult life. Only then do these two powerful tendencies become fully integrated.

Three become one. Three of our earliest personifications—*Good-Me, Bad-Me,* and *Not-Me*—gradually integrate into one coherent *Me.* Although the rudiments of these personifications may be present during the prototaxic months of life, it is during the parataxic phase of development that they begin to differentiate more clearly.

Good-Me (emotionally comfortable me). **Good-Me** *is the earliest personification that organizes experiences that have been rewarded by tenderness from a pleased parent.* As the child matures this becomes a summation of the attitudes and feelings that significant others have demonstrated in their treatment of her. The child who has been treated with anxiety-free tenderness and respect will come to view herself as a worthwhile person. These are powerful influences, because until the infant is well into childhood she has little information about the kind of person she is, except as provided by people close to her. As she begins to venture into the neighborhood, school, and society, she will receive evaluations of her *self* from a wider array of people; but nothing is more powerful than those early impressions conveyed by significant others. This is similar to Erickson's *trust versus mistrust* struggle, which is resolved in the direction of *trust* and *hope* when caretakers treat newborns with appropriate kindness and empathy.

Bad-Me (anxiety-ridden me). **Bad-Me** *is the earliest personification of experiences that were associated with increases in tension and anxiety on the part of the parenting one.* If an infant is reared in an anxious, hostile, or rejecting environment, he will perceive himself as worthless, inadequate, or troublesome, and will develop a constellation of painful emotions that will include guilt, shame, inferiority, anxiety, and self-loathing.

Not-Me (panic-ridden me). **Not-Me** *personifications evolve when an infant is treated with extreme anxiety, hostility, or rejection.* The panic-ridden child is plagued with a variety of what Sullivan called **uncanny emotions:** *dread, horror, or loathing.* He described these emotions as having "a sort of shuddery, not-of-this-earth component . . . you may talk about your skin crawling, or this or that" (1953, p. 10). This third personification may be induced very early in the child's life by sudden outbursts of extremely unpleasant emotions by a significant other, causing the helpless infant or young child to experience "sudden attacks of all-paralyzing anxiety" (Sullivan, 1953, p. 316). Such emotions, later in life, are typically accompanied by a desire to vomit or by diarrhea.

The child who is consistently repulsed or humiliated whenever he shows a need for tenderness or friendly cooperation is in danger of developing what Sullivan termed a **malevolent transformation of personality** *in which she believes herself to be unlikable and unattractive, and expects unkindness and trouble from others.*

The *good-me* and *bad-me* personifications remain a lifelong part of consciousness, providing a degree of coherence and consistency in our self-portraits, and a measure of contrast between the satisfactory attributes we like to parade in public and the unsatisfactory parts of our selves we endeavor to conceal or rationalize. The *not-me,* by contrast, tends to be *excluded* from everyday consciousness, returning only in severe states of disorder such as seen in the dissociations of schizophrenia.

Syntaxic mode (18–48 months). The **syntaxic mode (experiencing events as logically connected)** *is the beginning childhood precursor of adult, logical thought, utilizing symbolic language to make sense of experience. Syntaxic experience* emerges during childhood and is characterized by the use of *consensually validated* language—language that both the infant and mother use in approximately the same way. During this stage, a consensus forms between mother and infant so that a word comes to mean the same thing both to the mother and the infant.

What Sullivan had in mind was not simply language, but the consensual validation of *experience,* broadly defined. Thus the young child begins to arrive at a healthy *consensus* about feelings, attitudes, and behaviors—not only word usage. Consensual validation becomes dominant during the third and fourth years of life and continues into adulthood. It is upon the broad foundation of consensual validation that syntaxic thinking is based.

Summary of Sullivan's developmental theories—from birth to early childhood. Imagine yourself a newborn, lying in your crib *prototaxically* experiencing your surroundings as a stream of consciousness that William James famously described as a "blooming, buzzing, confusion." As you *parataxically* develop, you begin to notice time. You become accustomed to affectionate care whenever you cry because you're hungry, cold, or wet. Recently, however, you have begun to notice that late in the afternoon Mama disappears for about an hour and it requires a lot of crying to get her to return if you're hungry or have soiled your diaper. You vaguely realize that this guy with the booming voice ("Da Da") is also at home during the hour that Mama disappears. You find you don't like this "Da Da" guy, and if you could label your feelings—which you can't—they would be some combination of fear and hostility.

You vaguely realize that whenever Da Da returns home from work, he and Mama like to sit around in the family room and sip cold drinks while they exchange news about their daily experiences. *The hostility and fear you feel as an infant—the feeling that your "Da Da" maliciously competes with you for Mama's attention*—would be termed a **parataxic distortion** by Sullivan.

Later in your development—mainly during the *syntaxic mode*—you begin to "make sense" out of this pattern, realizing that Da Da isn't actually competing with you, and that Mama has just as much love to give you after she's been with Da Da. This will become especially obvious if you experience the same kinds of healthy, affectionate relations with Da Da as you have with Mama. Then the feelings of fear and hostility will be resolved through *syntaxic* thinking and experience, and the *parataxic distortion* will not persist into later life. (Sullivan believed that schizophrenic thought in adult life was characterized by *parataxic distortions* of logic and reason.)

In this way, the psychologically successful child learns how to eat, dress, and play. She acquires language skills and learns to interact successfully with parents, siblings, and playmates. The self-system becomes increasingly dominated by the emotionally comfortable *Good-Me,* less permeated by the anxiety-ridden *Bad-me,* and rarely penetrated by the panic-stricken *Not-Me.*

Everything tilts toward the emotional center of gravity—the interpersonal relationship. A child learns to *eat* successfully, because a youngster who slops food all over everyone will be sent from the table to eat alone—over the kitchen sink. The child who cannot play successfully will soon be excluded from playground games. This sort of interpersonal bankruptcy leads to feelings of ostracism and loneliness—emotions that Sullivan understood well, having experienced them in his own life.

Juvenile period: from playmates to isophilic intimacy (4–9 years). Sullivan diverged most noticeably from psychoanalytic thought in the importance he assigned to the *juvenile period.* In Freudian theory, the resolution of oedipal conflicts at around five or six years of age is followed by the *latency period.* As the term *latency* implies, for classical Freudians not much is happening during this period. In Sullivan's theory, quite a different picture is painted. As the child ventures into the neighborhood, Sunday school, and kindergarten, her interpersonal world expands enormously. In place of the two to five people she encounters at home, her interpersonal world might now include twenty, thirty, fifty, or more people. This offers the child extensive opportunities to correct earlier parataxic distortions and to consolidate social skills through consensual validation. Children who emerge from mildly dysfunctional families into this larger environment frequently find it therapeutic. However, children who experience severe interpersonal difficulties in their earlier years frequently enter the juvenile period ill equipped to cope successfully with peers. They suffer the vicious circle of ostracism, withdrawal, and loneliness, followed by more ostracism, withdrawal, and loneliness.

Preadolescence: late juvenile period (9–12 years). Sullivan designated the last year or two of the juvenile period as the *preadolescent period.* Not everyone agrees that such a distinction can be made, and some feel that this "era" represents an intrusion of Sullivan's own personal issues into his theory. During this period, the child experiences **isophilic intimacy,** *an exceptionally close relationship with another member of the same gender—a "chum."* According to Sullivan, *isophilic intimacy* provides the foundation for **heterophilic intimacy,** the *forming of intimate relationships with persons of the opposite sex.*

While the concept of a "chum" and the accompanying distinctions between isophilic and heterophilic intimacy seem to have some value, there is little research or clinical evidence for preadolescence as a distinct developmental phase. In fact developmental studies seem to indicate that very few people form this sort of intense same-gender relationship, and those that do tend to prefer homosexual relationships in adult life (Chapman, 1976, p. 181). These findings, combined with the details regarding Sullivan's own disastrous "chum" relationship, would seem to indicate that this is one of the least trustworthy of Sullivan's formulations.

Adolescence: from genital lust to adulthood (12–early 20s). Sullivan divided adolescence into two periods—split at about year sixteen.

Early Adolescence (12–16). Just as the juvenile had a need for intimacy, the early adolescent experiences a need for lustful gratification. Sometimes—especially during late preadolescence, when the lust dynamism is strong—transitory homosexual behavior occurs between "chums." Sullivan didn't think this was ordinarily something about which to be concerned, suggesting that it could provide an experience in which both participants could learn something about themselves in a shared context, especially if such relationships were ". . . intense enough for each of the two chums literally to get to know practically everything about the other one that could possibly be exposed in an intimate relationship" (1953, p. 256).

Sullivan's theories regarding preadolescence appear so intertwined with his own personal history that many professionals have serious questions about the validity of preadolescence as a stage. Nonetheless, Sullivan viewed adolescence in general as a time of sexual integration.

Late adolescence (17–maturity). Sullivan saw **late adolescence** as the final opportunity for ". . . *the establishment of a fully human or mature repertory of interpersonal relations, as permitted by available opportunity, personal and cultural*" (1953, p. 297, emphasis in original). Sullivan's developmental theory essentially ends with *late adolescence.* Adulthood is seen as a continuation of successful late adolescence: "Insofar as the long stretch of late adolescence is successful, there is a great growth of experience in the syntaxic mode" (1953, p. 298).

Making the most of our luck. More than most personality theorists of his time, Sullivan believed that *chance* and *culture* played a crucial role in life. He believed that whether one continues to be an adolescent throughout life or moves forward to adult maturity ". . . is often no particular reflection on anything more than one's socioeconomic status and the like" (1953, pp. 297–298).

Behind the mask. Sullivan believed that the healthiest adults were those who successfully integrate the interpersonal experiences of infancy, childhood, and the juvenile years into a stable sense of self. They avoid living "behind a mask" or reconstructing the self to accommodate each and every new situation or expectation: "The adolescent may begin the 'life behind a mask'. . . . The mask, however, requires so much energy for its successful maintenance that personality growth is apt to end with its successful construction" (Sullivan, 1972, p. 201).

What Makes a Person Unique?

Our discussion will be relatively brief because Sullivan's focus was not on the uniqueness of the individual so much as it was on the commonalities of interpersonal encounters. Early in his career, Sullivan stated his famous **one-genus postulate:** "We shall assume that *everyone is much more simply human than otherwise*" (1953, p. 32, emphasis in original), clearly setting the tone for his emphasis on *similarities* instead of differences. In the same work he stated that over the years he had seen a great need for a discipline that studied not individual person, but ". . . interpersonal situations through which persons manifest mental health or mental disorder" (1953, p. 18).

Birds of a feather. Sullivan saw personality not as an agentic *cause* of behavior, but rather as an envelope containing the accumulated *effects* of past interpersonal encounters. Consistent with his *one-genus* premise, Sullivan did not focus on individual differences or personal identities, preferring, instead, to study the patterns of those characteristics he assumed to be ubiquitously human" (1953, p. 33).

For him, uniqueness resided not within the individual person, but in the distinctive history of interpersonal relationships a person had experienced in the past and might encounter in the future. Thus, although personality was seen as open ended and ever changing, individuals tended to gravitate toward particular kinds of interpersonal encounters. Although personality patterns are never engraved in stone, each person can be characterized by the cadre of companions with whom he maintains interpersonal relationships—a "birds-of-a-feather" way of defining personality.

Ten Typical Personality Styles: In one of his first books (*Conceptions of Modern Psychiatry*, 1940), Sullivan sketched ten typical personality patterns that appear similar to the sorts of typologies other personologists were presenting in the mid-twentieth century. Sullivan's ten styles included those characterized by a (1) lack of duration, (2) the self-absorbed, (3) the incorrigible, (4) the negativistic, (5) the stammerer, (6) the ambition-ridden, (7) the asocial, (8) the inadequate, (9) the homosexual, and (10) the chronically adolescent. These ten styles are as close as Sullivan comes to dealing with the uniqueness of individuals.

Still, Sullivan does not see the person as simply a set of genes, nor does he envision the individual as caught in the behavioristic crosshairs of reinforcement and punishment, helplessly conditioned by circumstances. Although Sullivan's portrait of the person lacks some of the intrapsychic individuality seen by Freud, Erikson, Rogers, and others, this is replaced by the interpersonal *dyad* in which each person participates more or less as an equal player. Even in the seemingly skewed dyad of the mother and the "helpless" newborn, the baby is supplied with crying behavior, which, as every parent can testify, powerfully invites—or coerces if necessary—the mothering one to respond to the biological needs of the neonate. Only in rare instances does the newborn fail to *integrate* the situation to fulfill his or her needs. In every interpersonal encounter, Sullivan saw two *distinct* individuals attempting to negotiate a settlement (*integration*) that worked to achieve for each of them satisfaction within the dyad.

FACING THE TOUGH TWINS

Because Sullivan's interpersonal perspective is so closely related to the theories of Eric Berne, we will face the "tough twins" after we explore Berne's Transactional Analysis in more detail.

SUMMARY OF SULLIVAN

Sullivan's seven. A brief description of Sullivan's **seven integrating forces** provides a good summary of Sullivan's theory of personality development:

1. The infant's need for *contact with another person* is the first great integrating force, drawing infant and mother together in an interpersonal relationship that secures for the baby the biological requirements for living (air, food, water, warmth, cleanliness, etc.).

2. The infant's need for *tenderness,* which in turn evokes tenderness in the mothering one, becomes a persistent force throughout infancy and much of childhood.

3. The need for *collaborative interaction* with adults enables the child to gradually learn to walk, talk, feed herself, master toilet training, and perform the countless tasks required for interactional living.

4. Subsequently the child develops a need for *relationships with nonfamilial children* of her own general age, thereby consensually validating, modifying, or extending current personality characteristics.

5. Simultaneously there is the need for *acceptance by nonfamilial children and adults* as an adequate and esteemed person.

6. Sullivan originally believed that during late childhood ("preadolescence") there is a need for an intense, close relationship with a *"chum."* Many believe this was an intrusion of his own unresolved personal issues into his theory, and in his final formulation this was not prominent.

7. Adolescence brings the final integrating tendency in the form of *lust,* which pulls people into close relationships with members of the opposite sex. In optimal development, *lust* and *intimacy* are united in this final integrating tendency, setting the stage for family life during adulthood.

Sullivan paints a developmental portrait that details how the newborn enters the world as a helpless biological animal, and through the transforming power of interpersonal relationships becomes a fully functioning human being.

ERIC BERNE'S TRANSACTIONAL ANALYSIS (TA)—DYADIC INTERACTIONS BETWEEN ORDINARY PEOPLE

Harry Stack Sullivan was the undisputed founder of interpersonal psychiatry; however, since he worked primarily with male schizophrenics confined to the locked wards of psychiatric hospitals, his theories were known mainly to other mental health professionals. Many rejected his ideas since they were outside the Freudian mainstream. By contrast, Eric Berne brought a user-friendly variety of interpersonal psychiatry known as *transactional analysis* to America's showcase state—California.

Transactional analysis (TA) *focuses on how internal ego states influence interpersonal transactions.* Although Berne never acknowledged his debt to Sullivan (few ever did!), much of TA is Sullivan's interpersonal psychiatry in populist packaging. When TA first became part of this country's collective consciousness as a result of Berne's 1964 best seller, *Games People Play,* a journalist cleverly dubbed TA as "Berned over Freud." It would have been more accurately described as "Berned over Sullivan."

Background Check

Eric Berne (1910–1970) emigrated to the United States from Canada after graduating from McGill University's medical school. He studied at the New York Psychoanalytic Institute, where Erik Erikson was his training analyst. At first, Berne practiced Erikson's variety of ego analysis; however, the California *zeitgeist* of the sixties transformed Berne from a somewhat intellectual, Canadian-born psychoanalyst into a much more "groovy, groupy, popular" therapist than he might have been had he been practicing elsewhere in the United States or Europe.

From staid analyst to California guru. In 1964, Berne wrote *Games People Play,* in which he described several varieties of *recurring dyadic interactions* that he labeled *games:* marital games, party games, sexual games, underworld games, consulting room games, intellectual games—all sorts of "games" that resonated with the average person. The book became a runaway best seller, and Berne became the leading advocate of a popularized version of *interpersonal* psychiatry. What, twenty years earlier, Sullivan had described as *dyads,* or *interpersonal dynamisms,* Berne now popularized as transactions—*chains of dyadic interactions between two persons.*

ASKING THE BIG FOUR QUESTIONS

What Are the Parts?

Ego states (Parent, Adult, Child). Berne's most basic unit of analysis was the **ego state,** *a person's deeply etched memories of previous dyadic transactions with significant others;* in Berne's words, *"a consistent pattern of feeling and experience directly related to a corresponding consistent pattern of behavior"* (1966, p. 364, emphasis added). Berne was deeply impressed with Penfield and Jasper's (1954) discovery that when certain areas of the human brain are electrically stimulated, a person *reexperiences* (not merely remembers) a *total situation:* "Penfield and his co-workers speculated the brain functions much like a tape recorder [*video recorder* in today's terminology] in preserving *complete experiences* in serial sequences" (1973, p. 17). It was these total experiences that Berne described as ego states. Notice that for Berne these are not primarily *intrapsychic* experiences, because these *ego states* emerge during transactional experiences. Since transactions necessarily involve other *persons,* such experiences tend to be *dyadic* in nature.

Overview of Parent, Adult, and Child ego states. Berne believed that when a person is involved in a *dyadic transaction,* she tends to experience one of three major ego states. When transacting from the *Parent* ego state, a person "feels, thinks, acts, talks, and responds just as one of his parents did when he was little" (1978, pp. 11–12). This parent also influences how a person raises his own children, functioning as a conscience. A person transacting out of the *Adult* ego state operates much like a computer, objectively evaluating the environment and calculating various alternatives and probabilities based on past experience. Finally, each of us carries within ourselves an inner *Child* who thinks, talks, acts, and feels much as we did when we were children.

Replaying the actual past. According to Berne, accessing a particular ego state is much like punching a button on a jukebox or replaying a video recording of an actual artist, deceased or living—Nat King Cole, Frank Sinatra, or Shania Twain. Like Sullivan, Berne believed that his constructs were grounded in *interpersonal encounters between real people*—not merely generated as psychological projections or theoretical constructs: "Parent, Adult, and Child are not concepts, like Superego, Ego, and Id . . . but phenomenological realities . . . " (1973, pp. 3–4).

Parent ego state. The **Parent ego state** *includes attitudes and behavior from any or all of the emotionally significant "parents" we have interacted with in our lives.* Under the general heading of *Parent,* Berne and his followers included the Nurturing Parent and the Critical (Prejudicial) Parent as two major categories of parent types.

Nurturing Parents. According to Berne, **Nurturing Parents** *are nurturing, protective, sympathetic, and reassuring not only to their own children, but to people in general.* They can be heard saying things like "You look tired, let me do the dishes tonight" to a spouse, or "Here, let me kiss your knee where you scraped it" to a child. The surgeon who reassures her patient, "Don't worry, I've done this operation many times, and it's going to be just fine," is transacting from her Nurturing Parent ego state.

Critical or Prejudicial Parent. The **Critical** or **Prejudicial Parent** *displays a know-it-all, authoritarian attitude toward his children and others, and is bubbling with opinions—the right opinions—about politics, gender role expectations, proper dress, appropriate speech, and virtually all facets of life.* Critical Parents are regularly heard saying things like "Women drivers! They'll mess you up every time!" Or, "I can't believe someone with a college degree would do something so dumb!" Within the family, their criticisms are sometimes like heat-seeking missiles, finding the person's most vulnerable spot to attack: "Are you eating again?—no wonder you don't have any dates." Or "If you studied like your sister does, you might get on the honor roll too."

The Parent ego state begins forming during the baby's first encounters with significant others. Since during those early preverbal months of life much that is incorporated is "caught not taught," much of the Parent ego state remains unexamined and contains numerous built-in conflicts:

> In the beginning was I, and I was good. Then came in other I. Outside authority. This was confusing. . . . because there were so many outside authorities. Sit nicely. Leave the room to blow your nose. Don't do that, that's silly. . . . Flush the toilet at night because if you don't it makes it harder to clean. DON'T FLUSH THE TOILET AT NIGHT—you wake people up! Always be nice to people. Even if you don't like them, you mustn't hurt their feelings. Be frank and honest. If you don't tell people what you think of them, that's cowardly. . . . The most important thing is to have a career. The most important thing is to get married. . . . The most important thing is to be clean. The most important thing is to always pay your debts. . . . The most important thing is to see that your children behave well. The most important thing is to go to the right plays and read the right books. The most important thing is to do what others say. And others say all these things. (Stevens, 1967, pp. 1–2)

Adult ego state. The **Adult ego state** *functions like an on-board computer, allowing one to organize, test, and evaluate reality.* The *Adult* is similar to what George Kelly (Chapter 10) had in mind when he said each person is a scientist. Berne described the Adult ego state as being "concerned with the autonomous collecting and processing of data and estimating the probabilities as a basis for action" (1966, p. 220). In another place Berne described the Adult as "organized, adaptable, and intelligent, . . . experienced as an objective relationship with the external environment based on autonomous reality testing" (1961, p. 77).

This is not to suggest that a person transacting in the Adult ego state is always accurate and objective, but it means that in the Adult ego state logical, reality-based thinking is utilized in arriving at optimal solutions—less influenced by parental messages or emotional feelings. During your parents' or grandparents' generation the Adult ego state was perhaps best epitomized by Sgt. Joe Friday of *Dragnet,* interrupting an emotional witness with his famous phrase: *"The facts, Ma'am, just the facts."* For Trekkies, Spock is the consummate Adult, consistently operating on the basis of logic.

Child ego state. The **Child ego state** *contains the impulses and feelings that were experienced during infancy and childhood.* It is comprised of "video recordings" of early encounters with others and how these turned out. Berne suggested that the Child is exhibited in two forms: the *adapted child* and the *natural child.*

Adapted Child. The **Adapted Child** *"is the one who modifies his behavior under the Parental influence. He behaves as father (or mother) wanted him to behave: compliantly or precociously, for example. Or he adapts himself by withdrawing or whining"* (Berne, 1964, p. 26, emphasis added).

Natural Child. By contrast, the **Natural Child** *is spontaneous, creative, and rebellious.* As Berne put it, "In the Child reside intuition, creativity and spontaneous drive and enjoyment" (1964, p. 27). Others have described the *Child ego state* as "inquisitive, affectionate, selfish, mean, playful, whining, manipulative. . . . like a self-centered, pleasure-loving baby responding with cozy affection when his needs are met or with angry rebellion when they are not met" (James & Jongeward, 1971, pp. 127–128).

Little Professor. Some of Berne's students have described another Child ego state, the **Little Professor,** which contains *"the unschooled wisdom of a child . . . that is intuitive, responding to nonverbal messages and playing hunches. With it, a child figures things out, things such as when to cry, when to be quiet, and how to manipulate Mama into smiling"* (James & Jongeward, 1971, p. 128, emphasis added).

Which ego state is best? According to Berne, a person can see, feel, smell, touch, listen, look, or act from *any* of these ego states—there is not a *right* or *wrong* ego state. What determines good adjustment is how flexibly a person shifts to the ego state that deals most effectively with the transaction at hand.

Self. According to Berne, the **Self** *is comprised of whichever ego state is being activated at a given moment:*

> The Self is experienced as that ego state in which the free energy resides at a given time. At the moment the person is expressing Parental anger, he feels "This is really me. . . . " If he sulks just like the little boy he once actually was, he feels that at that moment "It is 'really me' who is sulking." (Berne, 1966, pp. 306–307)

Whereas Freud emphasized the deterministic power of libidinal instincts, Berne put a more agentic *self* in the driver's seat, which is choosing among alternative ego states instead of being pushed around by libido:

> The transactional patient learns to control his free energy to a considerable extent, so that he can shift his "real Self" from one ego state to another by an act of will: shift from Parental anger to attend to his Adult business, or from a Child's sulk to give Parental tenderness to a sick spouse or offspring. (1966, p. 307)

Summary of Parts in TA. We conclude our parts discussion by illustrating how persons transacting from different ego states might respond to various real-life situations.

▪ *To the smell of steaming brussels sprouts*:
  Parent: You should eat your brussels sprouts—they keep you healthy!
  Adult: Brussels sprouts are high in vitamins and help prevent cancer.
  Child: I ain't gonna eat that stinky stuff!
▪ *At the scene of a "fender bender"*:
  Parent: "Why didn't you signal your turn?"
  Adult: "I'll call the police on my cell phone. We'll need an accident report for the insurance companies."
  Child: "Did you get your driver's license in a Wheaties box? What the hell were you thinking—turning in front of me like that!"

What Makes a Person Go?

Different strokes for different folks. Berne's motivational theory describes how *feedback from other people* shapes responding. He begins with a simple, one-on-one dyadic interaction, but extends his analysis to include *chains* of typical transactions that characterize particular dyads. These longer chains, which we will discuss shortly, he describes as *pastimes, games,* and *scripts.*

Strokes—dyadic reinforcers or punishers. In TA, a **stroke** *occurs anytime one person acknowledges another with a smile, a frown, a nod, a body gesture, or a verbal greeting.* *Strokes* are to TA what reinforcement and punishment are to behaviorism—*consequences that shape behaviors.* However, in the *Social Zone* strokes do not usually take the form of food, water, or electric shocks as with conditioned animals in the *Behavioral Zone;* instead, they occur as *dyadic feedback*—sometimes almost imperceptibly as a grin or a sigh. A stroke might be contained in a handwritten note or an e-mail, but most stroking occurs as immediate dyadic feedback. Berne described stroking in this way:

> "Stroking" may be used as a general term for intimate physical contact; in practice it may take various forms. Some people literally stroke an infant; others hug or pat it, while some people pinch it playfully or flip it with a fingertip. These all have their analogues in conversation, so that it seems one might predict how an individual would handle a baby by listening to him talk. By an extension of meaning, "stroking" may be employed colloquially to denote any act implying recognition of another's presence. Hence a *stroke* may be used as the fundamental unit of social action. An exchange of strokes constitutes a *transaction,* which is the unit of social intercourse. (Berne, 1964, p. 15)

Positive strokes. Berne defined a **positive stroke** as *"the unit of recognition; e.g., 'Hello'"* (1966, p. 368). *Positive strokes* range from surface encounters such as greetings exchanged while passing on the sidewalk to intimate encounters with a lover. Positive strokes include compliments ("You really play golf well!" or "I like the way you look in that jacket"); expressions of affection ("You're fun to dance with" or "I've really missed seeing you while you were out of town"); or information about skills and competencies ("You're excellent in math, you could be a scientist if you wanted") or ("You may not have the best ear for pitch, but your rhythm is excellent; maybe you can play drums"). *Positive strokes* promote growth by communicating "You're OK."

Negative strokes/discounts. A **negative stroke** or **discount** *is a lack of attention (neglect), or attention that hurts psychologically or physically.* Negative strokes hurt, humiliate, shame, or discount others. Whenever a person is ignored, teased, physically abused or degraded, laughed at, or in some way treated as insignificant, they get the message "You're not OK." Sometimes discounting is direct ("I can't believe you would be so stupid!") and sometimes it is subtle, carrying a hidden put-down. For example when a wife asks her husband what time he'll be home from work and he answers, "when you see my car in the driveway," he might be discounting the importance of her time and her significance as a person.

A **transaction** *occurs whenever two or more strokes are exchanged.* Thus, a "Hi"-"Hi" exchange of greetings while passing on the sidewalk would be a two-stroke transaction, whereas a seven-stroke transaction might look like this:

"Hi, how's your wife doing?" (2 strokes)
"OK, thanks for asking." (2 strokes)
"I'll see you around." (1 stroke)
"OK, take care." (2 strokes)

Transactions (complementary, crossed, or ulterior).
Moving to a broader level of analysis, Berne defines **transaction:**

> If two or more people encounter each other in a social aggregation, sooner or later one of them will speak, or give some other indication of acknowledging the presence of the others. This is called the *transactional stimulus.* Another person will then say or do something which is in some way related to this stimulus, and that is called the *transactional response.* (1964, p. 29)

Complementary transaction. A transaction is considered a **complementary transaction** when the transactional response is *"appropriate and expected and follows the natural order of healthy human relationships"* (Berne, 1964, p. 29, emphasis added). Thus when a sick child asks for a drink of water and a nurturing parent brings it, we have a *complementary* transaction. Complementary transactions can be Child–Parent, as in the preceding example, or they can occur between any two ego states. Two "soccer moms" driving home from a game are transacting Parent–Parent when they discuss whether the officials were biased in making their calls, and their children are transacting Child–Child when they recount some of the plays. A tired woman is transacting from her Child to her husband's (nurturing) Parent when she tells him about her tough day at the office. If he responds with "Why don't you soak in the hot tub while I fix supper," they have engaged in a *complementary* transaction. The defining characteristic of the complementary transaction is that the transactional stimulus, directed toward a specific ego state, elicits the expected transactional response from that ego state. Such transactions tend to run smoothly, and communication between the two persons can proceed indefinitely.

This does not mean that all complementary transactions are "healthy," but merely that they tend to be stable. Thus a Parental husband, speaking to his Child-like wife, expects a Child-like response from her, and so long as it is forthcoming, their transactions will continue to function smoothly and communication will continue.

Crossed transaction. A transaction is considered a **crossed transaction** *when an unexpected response is made to the transactional stimulus.* Crossed transactions typically result in a breakdown of communications. Thus, if the husband in the preceding example responds to his exhausted wife with "Well my day was no picnic either! First I had to get out a long report, then my boss said he was concerned about my production, and just before I left for home, we got a memo saying we would have to pay a higher portion of our health insurance!" this would be a *crossed* transaction, in which each partner, transacting from his or her tired Child, was seeking a nurturing Parent. If both insisted on being cared for, and neither switched to the Parent ego state, a crossed transaction would remain, and communication would likely be broken off.

Ulterior transaction. **Ulterior transactions** *occur beneath the surface of socially acceptable transactions.* When the car salesman, in an allegedly Adult-to-Adult transaction, tells the customer "this car is probably too expensive for you," the disguised message to the customer's Child is "You wouldn't look like a loser if you owned this car." Telling another prospective buyer, "This is our hottest sports car—probably too

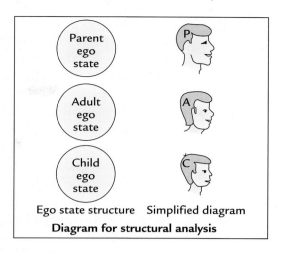

Figure 9.2 ■ *An Overview of Transactional Analysis Diagrams*

fast for someone your age," is designed to hook the Child in the aging adult to respond "Who says I'm getting old? I'll take it!"

Games. Following the phenomenal success of *Games People Play,* Berne's focus turned increasingly to the analysis of **games,** or *complementary ulterior transactions with a predictable "payoff" that reveals the ulterior motives underlying the transactions.* On the surface, games appear to be a series of straightforward transactions; however, the **payoff**—*the real purpose behind the game (e.g., getting rich, getting even, having fun etc.)— usually reveals that the transactions are manipulative maneuvers rather than honest, straightforward exchanges.* Thus, the insurance salesman at a cocktail party may *appear* to be pastiming, when in fact he is skillfully maneuvering to obtain the sorts of information that will enable him to later sell insurance policies to the people in attendance.

Analyzing a typical game: If It Weren't For You (IWFY). In his best seller, Berne states "The most common game played between spouses is colloquially called "If It Weren't For You" (1964, p. 50). Berne demonstrates game analysis using IWFY. He sequentially analyzes the game's *thesis, aim, roles, dynamics, examples, social paradigm, psychological paradigm, moves,* and *advantages.*

Thesis: Mrs. White grumbled that she never learned to dance because her husband restricted her social life. "If it weren't for you," she complained, "I could have done a lot of things." However, when her husband became more tolerant, allowing Mrs. White to sign up for dancing lessons, she became morbidly afraid of dance floors and had to give up her lessons. It thus became apparent that her husband had been providing a service by "restricting" her, thereby saving her from having to admit that she was afraid.

Aim: In IWFY the aim may be stated as either vindication ("He held me back") or reassurance ("It's not that I'm afraid, it's because he won't let me").

Roles: IWFY requires both a restricted and a domineering spouse.

Advantages/payoff: Among the advantages of playing IWFY, Berne lists the *biological* gains derived from this "distressing but apparently effective way" of using belligerence–petulance exchanges to stimulate physiological reactions. The *psychological* advantage is in the form of confirming the wife's position that "All men are tyrants," while simultaneously allowing her to avoid crowds.

This example illustrates how Berne employs the somewhat "cutesy" metaphor of cleverly named "games" to carry out serious analyses at various levels of abstraction. Other games include: Kick Me, Now I've Got You, You Son of a Bitch, See What You Made Me Do, Cops and Robbers, Wooden Leg, and a host of other games with homey, earthy, descriptive titles.

Script analysis. A psychological **script** *is a life plan, defining how a person will live,* in much the same way a stage script determines how actors will perform in a drama. Each script has a cast of characters, dialog, plot, scenes, and props. Berne described his widest scope of analysis—tracing an individual's "life plan" much as Adler used the term. According to Berne, scripting occurs in families, with various family members being assigned certain parts to play. Scripts are usually "written" into the Child ego state through the numerous transactions that occur between parents and children during the early years.

"Scripting" begins during infancy, when babies begin picking up nonverbal messages about themselves and their worth from how they are bathed, fed, handled, spoken to, and interacted with in various ways. Fortunate are the infants who are cuddled, affectionately played with, and generally responded to in loving, caring ways. From their earliest days they begin to "catch" the notion that they are "OK." On the other hand, children (such as Harry Stack Sullivan) who are handled with anxiety, hostility, or indifference learn that they are "Not OK." These early feelings form the basis for life scripts which range from extremely negative ("You'll never amount to anything" or "You're going to end up in prison, just like your Uncle Jim") to affirming and positive ("Someday you might be President!" or "The way you throw a ball, you'll probably pitch for the Yankees!").

Scripts with a curse. The case of twenty-five-year-old Ronald, who hanged himself, illustrates the power of negative scripts. In discussing her son's suicide, Ronald's mother said:

> I'm not really surprised. It was inevitable. We've had several suicides in our family over the years. In fact, my brother slit his own throat. I warned Ronnie many times he might kill himself. Even his sister wouldn't take her medicine. No wonder she died so young. (James & Jongeward, 1971, p. 89)

Summary of TA's motivational constructs. Eric Berne's genius was in translating much of Sullivan's interpersonal psychoanalysis into user-friendly terms. Instead of illustrating psychological dynamics with Greek myths in the style of Freud, or writing in the meandering manner of Sullivan, Berne translated his ideas into the sparkling prose of ordinary persons. Instead of picturing Atlas—doomed by Zeus to carry the weight of the world on his back and the heaviness of the heavens on his shoulders—Berne created modern-day Atlas-like scripts with themes like *Carrying my cross, Bearing the weight of the world, Trying hard, Poor me,* and *Ain't it awful?*

What Makes a Person Grow?

Developing one's own scripts. Berne did not describe clear developmental stages; instead TA is permeated with developmentally evolving ego states, games, and scripts. According to Berne, "Games are passed on from generation to generation. . . . 'Raising' children is primarily a matter of teaching them what games to play. . . . Parents, deliberately or unaware, teach their children from birth how to behave, think, feel and perceive. Liberation from these influences is no easy matter" (1964, pp. 171, 182).

Baby knows best. Berne appears to distrust parents, preferring to rely on the essential goodness of human nature. On the issue of human nature, Berne disagreed with Freud's emphasis on aggression and the dark sides of human nature, aligning himself, instead, with humanists (e.g., Rogers and Maslow—see Chapter 11) who emphasized the essential goodness of human nature. As Berne saw it, "unless and until they are corrupted, most infants seem to be loving . . ." (Berne, 1964, p. 181). The therapeutic focus is on increasing awareness regarding how games and scripts are laid down during infancy and early childhood, thereby empowering the client to consciously discard "old scripts" and to actively steer his or her life in new directions:

> . . . games are quite deliberately initiated by young children. After they become fixed patterns of stimulus and response, their origins become lost in the mists of time and their ulterior nature becomes obscured by social fogs. Both can be brought into awareness only by appropriate procedures. . . . (Berne, 1964, p. 60)

Thus, even in Berne's catchy, colloquial terminology, one can hear the echo of Freud's famous dictum, "Where id was, there ego shall be."

Birth position. Without crediting Adler, Berne emphasized the importance of **birth position,** *one's location in the family constellation,* for influencing one's personal script:

> If the speaker comes into a world which is already occupied by a sister or a brother, it will make a considerable difference in his script decisions whether that sibling is older by eleven months, thirty-six months, eleven years, or twenty years. This difference will depend not only on his relationship with that sibling, but also on his parents' attitude toward that particular spacing of children." (1978, p. 76)

Summarizing TA's Developmental Perspective. The script checklist (see Table 8.3) provides a good summary of Berne's developmental perspective.

TABLE 9.2

Script Checklist
(Adapted from *What Do You Say After You Say Hello?*)

Prenatal Influences
What kind of lives did your grandparents lead?
Were you wanted?
Whom were you named after?

Early Childhood
What does your mother say when she is feeding a baby?
How did the world look to you when you were little?
Are you a winner or a loser? When did you decide that?

Middle Childhood
What was your parents' favorite slogan?
What did they forbid you to do?
If your family were put on the stage, what kind of a play would it be?

Later Childhood
What was your favorite fairy tale as a child?
What kind of feelings bother you the most?
What kind of feelings do you like best?

Adolescence
Who is your hero nowadays?
What is your favorite animal?
What is your life slogan?

Maturity
How many children do you expect to have?
Have you ever attempted suicide?
What will you do in your old age?

Death
How long are you going to live?
How did you pick that age?
What will you put on your tombstone?

What Makes a Person Unique?

Berne captures the uniqueness of personality in the variety of Child, Adult, and Parent ego states that a person experiences in the *Insight Zone* during everyday living. Each individual's uniqueness is also seen in the *Social Zone,* in which each person utilizes a distinctive blend of rituals, pastimes, games, and scripts in transacting with others. Berne broadly summarized these as transactional *positions.*

Four basic transactional positions. Berne did not describe personality *types* in a way that resembled classical *intrapsychic* Freudian formulations such as the "oral" or "anal" personality. Instead, he outlined four broad *interpersonal orientations* that echoed Melanie Klein's notion of *position* as well as Karen Horney's coping strategies of moving *toward, away from,* or *against* others. According to Berne, "Every game, script, and destiny, is based on one of these four basic positions" (1966, p. 270).

First Position: "I'm OK, You're OK." This is the position of optimal psychological health, where people like themselves and others, and trust the world as a safe and predictable place.

Second Position (also referred to as the projective position): "I'm OK, You're Not-OK." Notice how similar this is to Klein's paranoid position where people feel victimized or persecuted, so they in turn feel entitled to victimize and persecute others.

Third Position: "I'm Not-OK, You're OK." This is the stance of persons who feel powerless when compared with others. Such individuals tend to be withdrawn, depressed, and sometimes suicidal.

Fourth Position: "I'm Not-OK, You're Not-OK." This is a position of futility. People in this position frequently lose interest in living and withdraw, or in extreme cases commit suicide or homicide. Whereas people in the first position tend to find life meaningful and socially rewarding, people in the fourth position frequently feel inferior, isolated, and bitter.

Summarizing uniqueness. In TA, a person's *uniqueness* can be expressed in many different possible transactions: ". . . this includes nine types of complementary transactions, 72 types of crossed transactions (theoretically, 6,480 types of duplex transactions, plus all the possible types of angular ones)" (Berne, 1966, p. 300).

So there you have it! No limit on uniqueness. Just as out of a nearly-infinite number of lines, whorls, and swirls your fingers display one-of-a-kind fingerprints, similarly out of the nearly countless interpersonal transactions that are possible, you tend to settle into a comparatively small number of transactions that uniquely characterize who *you* are. Berne uses ego states, games, and scripts to condense your countless possibilities into a working portrait of your personality (or typical transacting style). However, instead of losing your individuality or identity in the vast ocean of interpersonal opportunities, TA clarifies how you *usually* transact social relationships. Your TA therapist helps you to sift out from the nearly countless number of *all possible* transactions, those particular games you are playing at the moment.

Ultimately, TA is more client-centered than Freudian. It is the client who has the final word on who he is. When TA is successful, the client "learns to appraise his own authenticity: is it *really* his real Self who is being Parentally tender, Adultly candid, or freely imaginative, or are these spurious acts of compliance, rebellion, or hypocrisy?" (Berne, 1966, p. 307).

SUMMARY OF TRANSACTIONAL ANALYSIS

Influenced by Erik Erikson's variety of ego analysis, Berne developed a theory of interpersonal psychiatry which, like Sullivan's, emphasized the *interactional dyad* as the primary unit of analysis. Although Berne was not as thoroughly interactional as Sullivan out of the starting gate, after the publication of *Games People Play* he shifted almost exclusively to analyzing interpersonal *games* and *scripts*. He creatively integrated Erikson and Sullivan to portray how personality shapes the lives of ordinary people. For Berne, as for Shakespeare, "All the world's a stage," and each person is an actor—following a script, playing a game. This completes our study of the work of two prominent interpersonal *clinicians*; next, we will briefly consider how interpersonal theories have fared when scrutinized in the research laboratory.

FACING THE TOUGH TWINS

Is It Testable?

Testing interpersonal theory in the laboratory—the Kaiser Permanente Research Project. Because Sullivan practiced psychiatry in a large hospital during a time when psychoanalysis was the dominant force, research was not on the front burners of his mind. However, his ideas were heuristically powerful, stimulating others to investigate personality from an interpersonal perspective. Foremost among these was Timothy Leary, who served as Director of Psychology Research at the Kaiser Foundation Hospital in Oakland, California from 1954 to 1956—the final two years of a six-year study of psychotherapy.

Leary was one of the few psychologists who acknowledged Sullivan as his inspiration, pointing out that although "Sullivan provides an attitude (humility) and an approach (participant observation). . . . His formal structure is disappointingly disorganized and incomplete" (Leary, 1957, pp. 8–10). Leary & Coffey described their research goal as "developing a methodology of investigation which is consistent with Sullivan's theory and gives it some operational meaning" (1955, p. 111). It was a monumental project: "In the development of the interpersonal system more than 5,000 cases (psychiatric, medical, and normal controls) have been studied and diagnosed" (Leary, 1957, p. vi).

A levels-of-analysis, interpersonal perspective. Summarizing the Kaiser research project, Leary stated that *"Personality is the multilevel pattern of interpersonal responses (overt, conscious, or private) expressed by the individual"* (Leary, 1957, p. 15). Consistent with the levels orientation of our text, Leary defined personality as "the durable, multiple-level pattern of interpersonal tendencies organized into stable or unstable equilibria" (1957, p. 25). He and his team of researchers carefully investigated how personality functions at various levels of analysis.

Leary's levels of analysis. At *Level I (Public Communication),* Leary's research team utilized psychometric tests, ratings of moment-by-moment behavior in social situations, as well as sociometric ratings by peers or trained observers in order to examine the interpersonal behavior patterns of people. At *Level II (Conscious*

Communication) they investigated conscious verbal reports. At **Level III** (*Private Perceptions and Symbols*), they studied the individual's dreams and interpersonal fantasies. Leary said: "It is very well known that all individuals have a set of private perceptions, private opinions, and private reactions which often contrast with statements of conscious report" (1957, p. 162).

Level IV (*Unexpressed/Significant Omissions*) is comprised of interpersonal themes that are *avoided* or *omitted*. Leary described Level IV much as Freud viewed the unconscious:

> "This is called the level of the unexpressed. It comprises those interpersonal themes which the patient consistently, significantly, and specifically omits in the three other levels. (1957, p. 192)"

Level V (*Values*) included what Freud referred to as the **superego,** but this was defined by Leary in interpersonal terms: "the interpersonal traits and actions that the subject holds to be 'good,' proper, and 'right'—his picture of how he should be and would like to be" (1957, p. 80).

Bidirectional, circular causality. Following Sullivan's clinical observations, operationalized and refined by the Kaiser research group, subsequent interpersonal theorists have endorsed *circular* rather than linear causality. Behavior is no longer seen as driven *either* by situational factors *or* intrapsychic motivations. "Rather, the client's relationships (including those with the therapist) are framed as two-person groups in which members exert mutual influence (bidirectional causality)" (Kiesler, 1996, p. 3).

Thus, the *level of analysis* shifts (from intrapsychic to dyadic) and the *direction of causality* changes (from linear to circular). Not only does a person *respond* to others, she *elicits* particular reactions from others: "Interpersonal study focuses on human transactions, not on the behavior of individuals" (Kiesler, 1982, p. 5).

Humors, libido, and circles. Leary summarized his extensive research findings in the form of an interpersonal circle, which he related both to Hippocrates and to Freud:

> The four "blended" quadrants fit rather closely the classical humors theory of Hippocrates. The upper left quadrant (hostile strength) equates with the choleric temperament, the lower left (hostile weakness) with the melancholic, the lower right (friendly weakness) with the phlegmatic, the upper right (friendly strength) with the sanguine. (Leary, 1957, p. 71)

Leary adds that "The same fourfold classification reappears in Freudian thought. Freud's treatment of the individual stresses two basic motives—love and hate. His theories of social phenomena and group interaction, on the other hand, emphasize domination, power, and the interaction of the weak versus the strong" (1957, p. 71).

The circumplex as a visual map. Thus we again find personality psychologists grappling with the timeless themes of human existence—love and hate, strength and weakness—but instead of seeking to understand them from a compositional or intrapsychic perspective, interpersonal theorists employ a variety of *interpersonal circumplexes* to provide visual maps of personal relationships. The interpersonal circle represents interpersonal transaction as vectors mapped on a two-dimensional circular space with love-hate and dominance-submission as the coordinates. Leary's quadrants were subsequently followed by a series of circumplexes: Leary (1957), Lorr and McNair (1965), Wiggins (1979, 1981), and Kiesler (1983, 1985). Figure 9.3 pictures Kiesler's most recent reconstruction of Leary's circle.

Perhaps the clearest definition of the circumplex comes from Wiggins, Phillips, and Trapnell: "Interpersonal diagnosis involves the assignment of subjects to typological categories defined by the average directional tendencies of their interpersonal behavior with reference to the coordinates of dominance and love" (1989, p. 303).

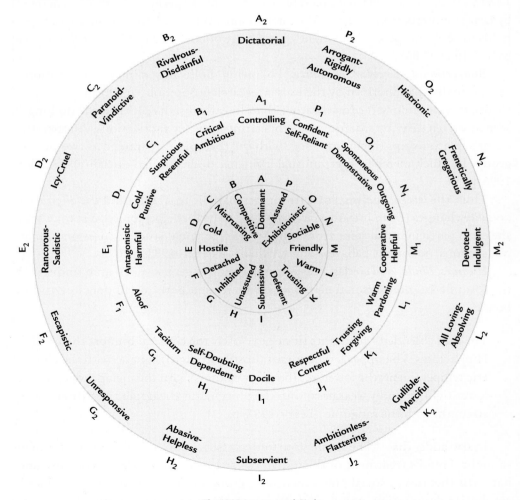

The 1982 Interpersonal Circle.

Figure 9.3 ■ *The Interpersonal Circle*

Researching couples in conflict. Research focusing on *long-term dyads* known as "marriage" offers another contemporary window on interactional psychology. In the past, family psychologists have focused primarily on the deleterious effects of marital conflict on *family systems,* but recent research has provided a more textured portrait by examining the relationship of conflict to numerous other variables within the family. These findings can be summarized in terms of a simple ratio: *for happy couples the ratio of agreements to disagreements is greater than 1, for unhappy couples it is less than 1* (Fincham, 2005, p. 151).

While marital conflict remains a central concern, research (e.g., Karney & Bradbury, 1995) now shows that conflict per se accounts for a relatively small portion of variability in marriage outcomes. For example, Howard & Dawes (1976) and Thornton (1977) found that it was the *ratio* of sexual intercourse to arguments, rather than *base rates* that predicted marital satisfaction. Instead of focusing only on feuding couples, researchers are investigating how personality variables (e.g., attachment, ambivalence, and the disposition to forgive) relate to conflict resolution within families. Even more broadly, it is known that economic stress is associated with marital conflict, and Bradbury, Rogge, and Lawrence (2001) have suggested that it may be "at least as important to examine the struggle that exists between the couple . . . and the environment they inhabit as it is to examine the interpersonal struggles . . . " (p. 76).

Self as *sociometer.* Consistent with Sullivan's view of the *self-system* as an "antianxiety system" involved in assessing how others perceive oneself and attempting to maintain a sense of interpersonal security, some current researchers (e.g., Leary, 1999; Leary & Downs, 1995; Leary, 2005) view the self as a *sociometer,* constantly monitoring the quality of people's relationships with others. Researchers have found that the proposed relationship between low self-esteem and psychological problems has been overstated—the relationships are weaker and more scattered than usually assumed (Mecca, Smelsler, & Vasconcellos, 1989). Instead, self-as-sociometer theory (consistent with Sullivan's view) sees the self as a subjective gauge of interpersonal relations. Thus, the self tracks but does not necessarily cause emotional problems. Thus, although self-esteem is intricately involved with emotional adjustment, Leary (2005) suggests that it functions more as a monitor and historian of interpersonal relationships rather than as a cause.

Is It Useful?

Very useful. Eric Berne's Transactional Analysis has been widely used not only in clinical and counseling settings, but in schools and industry as well. Tim Leary and Don Kiesler have applied Sullivan's ideas in academic and corporate settings as well.

We will conclude our chapter by briefly considering the work of several contemporary theorists who—like Berne—began their clinical careers in the intrapsychic world of psychoanalysis, but ended up in the *dyadic interpersonal* world of Sullivan.

NANCY CHODOROW, JEAN BAKER MILLER, AND THE STONE CENTER GROUP—*SELF IN CONNECTION*

The perspectives of Nancy Chodorow. Trained as both a sociologist and a practicing psychoanalyst, **Nancy Chodrow** (1944–) has explored the significance of object relations and feminist social theory. In such works as *The Reproduction of Mothering* (1978) and *Femininities, Masculinities, Sexualities: Freud and Beyond* (1994), she has depicted the **reproduction of mothering cycle** *as a cyclic process producing daughters with mothering capacities and sons with repressed relational needs.* Although she expressed concerns about Freud's attempts to posit cultural universals in the form of psychosexual stages or oedipal triangles, she recognized that Freud tried to give normative status to heterosexuality in a culture that was male-dominated: "he condemned the conditions that lead to repression and hysteria in women" (Chodorow, 1991). Moving from her earlier emphasis on social determinism, Chodorow has come to more of a here-and-now emphasis that takes into account each persons's subjectivity. Gender, she says, is a *fusion* of cultural and personal meanings that are continually reconstructed (1995).

Dyadic or intrapsychic self? Chodorow describes her theoretical journey from the *Social Zone* to the *Insight Zone,* and back to a Sullivanian *dyadic balancing* of *self* and *other:*

> . . . my early feminist writings have a distinctly social-determinist flavor . . . I [next] responded to what I have elsewhere (1989) called a passion for psychoanalysis. . . . I focused my attention exclusively on the. . . . inner more than the outer. . . . This book [*The Power of Feeling*] represents another swing or shift of the pendulum, back toward outer from inner. More precisely, I attempt to situate myself right on the cusp where both exist together and neither can be thought or experienced without the other. (1999, pp. 7, 8)

Chodorow agrees with Erikson that *individuation* is not "a one-sided separation from the mother" but includes "a kind of internalization of a maternal function" (1999, p. 257). She agrees with Winnicott that there is "no such thing as a baby" and asserts that "The infant as an infant, and the mother as a mother, can be created only in the in-between space of their interaction" (1999, p. 265).

However, as much as Chodorow appears to resonate with Erikson and Winnicott on the *dyadic* beginnings of the self, she worries that "two-person or relational psychologies seem sometimes to flatten and oversimplify inner life" (1999, p. 263), and she concludes by saying that she is "drawn to what must still be called one-person psychologies, where the central role of the other is played out in intrapsychic rather than intersubjective life (1999, p. 263). So, although Chodorow begins her book by locating herself "on the cusp"—where inner and outer life meet—she concludes with an intrapsychic tilt.

Jean Baker Miller and the Stone Center Group. Jean Baker Miller (1973, 1984, 1991) and her colleagues (Irene Stiver, Judith Jordan, Janet Surrey, and others), at the Stone Center for Developmental Services and Studies at Wellesley College in Massachusetts, have also shifted their paradigm for the development of *self.* In place of traditional destinations for the *self* that emphasize *differentiation, autonomy,* and *independence,* they see the self in *connection.* Miller and her colleagues note that against the traditional developmental backdrop (emphasizing self-sufficiency and independence), women's strengths in relating and connecting have frequently been seen as weaknesses.

A fresh view of empathy. From this perspective, *empathy* is seen as a kind of mutual relating in which one's self is not lost in merging with another or blurred beyond recognition in some sort of *dyadic homogenization.* Instead, empathy entails experiencing the emotions and thoughts of another while simultaneously knowing one's own unique thoughts and feelings. Like a well-sung duet, one hears *both* the tenor and alto voices—blended, not blurred. Miller and Stiver propose

> a shift from a psychology of "entities" to a psychology of movement and dialogue. . . . in the ideal pattern of development, we move toward participation in relational growth rather than toward simple attainment of personal gratification. . . . In fact, self, other, and the relationship are no longer clearly separated entities in this perspective but are seen as *mutually forming processes.* (1997, p. 56, emphasis in original)

Self in connection—dyadic <u>and</u> differentiated. What emerges from the work of the Stone Center theorists is a view of the self that is both dyadic and differentiated. They replace traditional intrapsychic views of the self with a more dyadic portrait that resonates with Sullivan's characterization of the psychiatrist as a *participant observer:*

> We do not think in terms of the individual versus the relationship, nor of the individual emerging out of relationships, underlying notions that are often at the root of even other relational theorists' thinking. Nor do we think of being in relationship as anything like "dependency" as that word is usually used. Even the word "interdependent" does not capture our meaning; derived as it is from "dependent," it does not convey the *active* participation necessary in creating growth-fostering interplay. (Baker Miller & Pierce Stiver, 1999, p. 57)

In short, Jean Baker Miller and her colleagues have expanded our options when it comes to viewing the *self.* In place of the *intrapsychic self* of classical psychoanalysis, we are not left with Sullivan's *series of dyadically merged selves,* which led him to famously remark: "For all I know every human being has as many personalities as he has interpersonal relations" (Sullivan, 1964, p. 221). Rather, the self-in-relationship, as described by the Stone Center Group, is a self that *participates* in *dyadic connection* while still retaining its unique identity.

Thus, I grow to understand you by "walking two miles in your moccasins," but I do not become you by walking in your shoes. Rather, I retain the awareness that I am I, and you are you—in connection.

Chapter Summary

In this chapter we learned how a number of personality theorists made the quantum leap from *intrapsychic* to *dyadic.* Donald Winnicott carefully observed infants *and* their caretakers—the "nursing couple," as he picturesquely phrased it. He reassured an entire generation of mothers that they were *good enough* and provided a sunlit bridge from the dark recesses of Kleinian object relations to the *dyadically based* theories of this chapter.

Harry Stack Sullivan was the great pioneer of *interpersonal* relations. With few mentors, few friends, and no deeply engraved theoretical loyalties, Sullivan was free to create his own ingenious theory of interpersonal relations. His theories inspired subsequent researchers such as Leary and Kiesler to carefully investigate his ideas in the laboratory. The *interpersonal circumplex* is an empirically derived tribute to Sullivan's creativity.

Eric Berne, by contrast, began his career as an establishment psychoanalyst—although, with Erikson as his training analyst, he was more socially oriented. However, that all changed when, thanks to the 1960s California zeitgeist, Berne's book *Games People Play* became a runaway best seller, transforming him into something of a folk hero among therapists. Soon TA slogans such as "I'm OK, You're OK" began appearing as California bumper stickers, and this celebrity status irretrievably catapulted Berne from his classical intrapsychic launching pad into the *Social Zone,* where *dyadic* transactions, games, and scripts characterized his work for the remainder of his professional career.

We concluded with a brief discussion of the refreshing work of Nancy Chodorow, Jean Baker Miller, and colleagues at the Stone Center Group. Their writings emphasize that the *self* can become *differentiated* while still remaining *connected*.

Points to Remember

1. Harry Stack Sullivan was a shy, lonely child who excelled in elementary and high school but failed in college. He later graduated from a fly-by-night medical school and went on to formulate his *interpersonal theory of psychiatry*—shifting focus from the individual to the *dyad* as the unit of analysis, and changing the psychoanalyst from a behind-the-couch Buddah to a *participant observer*.

2. Sullivan builds his theory of personality on *dynamisms*—recurrent patterns of energy that range from individual physiological cycles, to interpersonal social patterns, and even to national and international patterns of diplomacy, war, etc.

3. *Personifications* are among the earliest and most important interpersonal dynamisms. They are the psychological "lenses" through which we see the world based on our past interpersonal experiences. The most important personifications of self are *"Good Me," "Bad Me,"* and *"Not-Me";* the most important personification of others is "Good Mother" vs. "Bad Mother."

4. We engage interpersonal relationships by *integrating* or "making sense" of situations. *Security operations* are activities we perform in order to avoid or reduce anxiety regarding how others treat us or how we are coming across in social situations.

5. From birth to eight months, the infant operates in the *prototaxic mode*, perceiving the world as a raw stream of sensory experiences. During the *parataxic mode* (8–18 months) the infant experiences life as a loosely connected sequence of events. During the *syntaxic mode* (18–48 months), the child, assisted by language, begins to make logical connections between events.

6. *Infancy* (birth–8 months) is followed by *childhood* (8 months–about 4 years) as a time that begins with articulate speech and ends with the need for same-aged friends. During the *juvenile period* (4–about 9 years), the child ventures out into the larger social world of school and church, attempting to consolidate social skills. *Preadolescence* (9–12) is Sullivan's most controversial stage—a time when he claimed everyone needs a "chum" or intimate friend of the same sex. *Adolescence* (12–early 20s) is a time when *lust* for the opposite sex is integrated with *intimacy* to establish a significant relationship with a member of the opposite sex.

7. *Seven integrating forces* emerge during development, nudging the person to "work out" interpersonal relationships. The infant needs *contact with another* person as well as *tenderness*. The young child learns through *collaborative interaction* with adults, but also needs *relationships with,* and *acceptance by, nonfamilial children*. Sullivan thought everyone needs a *"chum"* or *intimate same-sexed friend* during "preadolescence." During adolescence and early adulthood, *lust* and *intimacy* coalesce, setting the stage for family life.

8. Eric Berne began his career analyzing the *(Parent, Adult, or Child) ego states* within the personality of an individual, much as other ego-oriented psychoanalysts might do. Soon however, he shifted almost exclusively to the study of *transactions between persons,* developing his own brand of interpersonal psychoanalysis known as *Transactional Analysis (TA)*.

9. *Strokes* are the basic units of social interaction in TA, and can be *positive, negative,* or *maintenance*. In TA, anytime one person acknowledges another a stroke is exchanged; e.g., "Hi" = 1 stroke, and "Hi, what have you been doing lately?" = 2 strokes.

10. *Transactions* occur in three major varieties: *complementary* (when appropriate and expected strokes are exchanged), *crossed* (when an unexpected response occurs), and *ulterior* (when a hidden message occurs under the guise of an ordinary communication). *Games* are comprised of a series of *ulterior transactions* that include a *hidden agenda,* and a *payoff*—the real purpose behind the game. Games are basically dishonest.

11. A *script* is a life plan, strongly influencing the course of a person's transactions. Berne believed that the most important task of TA was *script analysis*. The goal of the TA therapist is to liberate people for "game-free relationships" so that they can transact relationships from a *healthy* ("I'm OK, You're OK") position rather than from a position of *paranoia* ("I'm OK, You're Not-OK"), *powerlessness* ("I'm Not-OK, You're OK"), or *futility* ("I'm Not-OK, You're Not-OK")

12. Berne rendered psychoanalysis more user-friendly. He illustrated his ideas with stories of Little Red Riding Hood or Cinderella, instead of Freud's favorite Greek heroes like Oedipus or Narcissus. But his most important contribution was reinforcing Sullivan's insistence that the *transaction* was the smallest meaningful unit of analysis.

13. Whereas Berne's *Transactional Analysis* did much to popularize Sullivan's ideas for clinicians, Timothy Leary operationalized Sullivan for academic researchers by devising the first *interpersonal circumplex:* a mapping of interpersonal tendencies onto a two-dimensional circle that had *love-hate* and *dominance-submission* as its major axes.

14. Nancy Chodorow, Jean Baker Miller, and the women of the Stone Center Group described a *self* that is both *dyadic* and *differentiated,* and that functions in the context of *connected relationships.*

Key Terms

Adapted Child   (338)

Adult Ego State   (338)

Anxiety   (326)

Bad-Me   (331)

Birth Position   (334)

Child Ego State   (338)

Complementary Transaction   (341)

Critical Parent   (337)

Crossed Transaction   (341)

Discount   (340)

Dyadic Self   (321)

Dynamism   (322)

Ego State   (336)

Euphoria   (326)

Games   (342)

Gesture   (330)

Good-Me   (330)

Heterophilic Intimacy   (333)

Integrating Tendency   (324)

Interpersonal Circumplex   (319)

Interpersonal Dynamisms   (323)

Intimacy   (330)

Isophilic Intimacy   (333)

Late Adolescence   (333)

Little Professor   (339)

Lust Dynamism   (330)

Malevolent Transformation of Personality   (331)

Natural Child   (338)

Negative Stroke   (340)

Not-Me   (331)

Nurturing Parents   (337)

One-Genus Postulate   (334)

Oral Zonal Dynamism   (329)

Parataxic Mode   (332)

Parent Ego State   (337)

Participant Observer   (317)

Payoff   (342)

Personality   (320)

Personifications   (323)

Positive Stroke   (340)

Prejudicial Parent   (337)

Prototaxic Mode   (328)

Reproduction of Mothering Cycle (350)

Script   (342)

Security   (326)

Security Operations   (326)

Selective Inattention   (326)

Self   (339)

Self-System   (322)

Seven Integrating Forces   (335)

Signs   (329)

Stroke   (340)

Subdynamisms   (323)

Superego   (347)

Symbols   (329)

Syntaxic Mode   (331)

Tension   (326)

Transaction   (340)

Transactional Analysis   (336)

Ulterior Transaction   (341)

Uncanny Emotions   (331)

Zonal Dynamisms   (323)

Web Sites

Harry Stack Sullivan

www.haverford.edu/psych/ddavis/sullivan.sx.html. A very brief but interesting excerpt of Harry Stack Sullivan's writing about his work with schizophrenic patients.

Eric Berne

http://frogsandprinces.dawntreader.net/appendixa.html. This is a collection of appendixes that give short descriptions of some of Berne's social games and apply Transactional Analysis to different relationships.

Jean Baker Miller & Stone Center Group

www.wellesley.edu/JBMTI/index.html. The Jean Baker Miller Training Institute and Stone Center. Read about this amazing woman and explore the institute names in her honor. Visit the list of related Web sites or even take a home-study course from the institute!

Nancy Chodorow

http://en.wikipedia.org/wiki/Category:Feminist_scholars. Wikipedia. Follow this link to see a large list of feminist researchers, in which Chodorow is included.

Learning on the Lighter Side

Try putting TA to work for you. For the next twenty-four hours, pay special attention to how people transact with one other. Notice what ego state the first speaker comes from, then see if you can tell what ego state she "hooked" in the other person. Was the transaction complementary or crossed? What ego state "gets you going"? If someone comes from their Parent telling you what you *should* do, or how you *ought* to act, do you immediately revert to your resentful child? Which ego states "pull" the nurturant parent from you? What kinds of people bring out the "bossy" side of you?

Take some time to focus on this and you'll learn much about yourself and others. Do a "two-step" dance with every transaction you encounter: (1) What is my ego state? (2) What is their ego state?

Looking Ahead

Entering a construction zone. In Chapter 10, we will learn how the *constructivist* theories of Jean Piaget, George Kelly, and Albert Ellis provide a bridge from the deterministic constraints of *behaviorism* and *psychoanalysis* to the choice-oriented, meaning-making theories of *humanistic* psychology. By directing our attention to how individuals actively *construct* their own psychological realities, Piaget, Kelly, and Ellis endow the person with agency, choice, and responsibility—crucial ingredients for the humanistic, existential, and spiritually oriented theories that occupy the subsequent chapters of our text at the highest levels of abstraction.

Chapter 10 will involve such a pivotal paradigm shift that we could, perhaps, think of it as the "Continental Divide" of our text. The level of analysis does not become broader—you can't get much broader than Adler's social evolution or Fromm's Marxist synthesis of Freud—instead, we will experience a monumental shift to the left (emphasizing agency and person-as-center). In previous chapters (at lower levels of analysis) the person was seen as "composite" of biochemical elements, the "animal" to be trained, the "computer" to programmed, or the "analysand" to be analyzed. In those theories the person was acted upon, buffeted about, shaped by the situation, or analyzed by the expert. In our current chapter we saw this situational emphasis soften as the *person* became a *participant* in a *dyadic coupling* with parents and other caretakers. However, even as part of a "nursing couple," the newborn is more of a dance partner than a creator.

In our upcoming chapter, the constructivists will invite us to consider the person as a "creator." This will open the gateway for the humanists to urge us to transcend "scientific," "objective" analyses and appreciate the innate power of the *self* to *actualize*. The existentialists will urge us not only to analyze meaning, but to *create* meaning.

In the remainder of our text we will see the *self* as an active agent—the *subject* rather than the *object,* the *pilot* rather than the *passenger.* Whereas at lower levels of analysis, *personal agency* has frequently been subverted by the biochemical determinism of the compositionists, sabotaged by the situational emphasis of the behaviorists, diffused by the dispositional focus of the trait theorists, and diluted into dyads by the interpersonalists, this all changes in Chapter 10.

Placing *agency* at the center of personality is a caterpillar-to-butterfly transformation that irrevocably changes the face of personality. *Constructivists* view the person as more an agent than a subject, more a person than an animal, more an artist than a computer, more a philosopher than a technician. They provide us with a theoretical overpass by which we can journey from the laboratory-based or clinically derived theories of person-as-object or person-as-patient to the humanistic, existential, and spiritual perspectives of person-as-creator.

chapter 10

Self as Constructor

The Constructivist Bridge from Behaviorism and Psychoanalysis to Humanism and Existentialism

Jean Piaget, George Kelly, and Albert Ellis

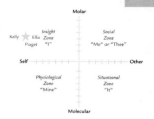

IN THIS CHAPTER YOU CAN

1. Understand how *constructivism* portrays humans as *meaning-making* creatures, actively involved in constructing their experiences.

2. Learn how Jean Piaget retained a lifelong interest in the biological foundations of intelligence and in understanding how *patterns function as part of a larger whole.*

3. Understand Piaget's twin processes of development: *assimilation* (taking in) and *accommodation* (modification as a result of experience).

4. Discover that Piaget described infant development as a series of *circular reactions*—simple, recurrent actions, such as sucking one's thumb or shaking a rattle, that are repeated over and over because they are pleasurable.

5. Learn that for Piaget *construction is destiny;* development consists of constructing one's own personality

and thereby determining one's destiny. Piaget's constructivism has profoundly influenced how we think about children (as little thinkers rather than conditioned animals).

6. Appreciate how George Kelly saw each person as a "scientist" attempting to make sense of the world—deriving *meaning* from life by how she *anticipates* events and using *personal constructs* for viewing the world in terms of *similarities* and *differences.*

7. Discover that *constructivists* view the person as an active, conscious *meaning-maker,* thereby providing a theoretical bridge from behaviorism, psychoanalysis, and object relations to humanism and existentialism.

8. Be surprised to find out that Albert Ellis—usually regarded as a cognitive learning psychologist—is really a *constructivist* at the core.

A PERSONAL PERSPECTIVE

A profane and pragmatic constructivist. Albert Ellis was famous for his in-your-face, peppered-with-profanities style of debate. Ellis was the "bad boy" of academic psychology, dramatically deposing contrary ideas as "horse #*!§ (expletive deleted) or diagnosing differing opinions (on the part of clients or academic opponents) as "nutty beliefs." Something of a stand-up comedian, Ellis never failed to draw a crowd, and when he participated in a symposium it usually becomes standing room only. I once heard him describe the successful outcome of a sex therapy case: "By the time we were finished, they were f__king like rabbits!" On another occasion I heard Ellis "refine" his famous "horse #*!§" rebuttal by telling his opponent that there exists bull #*!&, horse #*!&, and elephant #*!&, hastening to add that his opponent's arguments were elephant#*!&.

Commentary. Although such shenanigans delighted audiences for decades, there is danger that Ellis's earthy showmanship and ribald retorts distract us from realizing that his substantial agenda was always to *reconstruct* people's philosophy of life—from irrational to rational (or, critics might observe: from *theirs* to *his*). He stated that "Rationalism is a tenable philosophic position insofar as the term means opposition to all forms of supernaturalism, spiritualism, mysticism, revelation, dogmatism, authoritarianism, and antiscientism" (Ellis, 1962, p. 124). With respect to the nitty-gritty of daily living, Ellis was a cognitive constructivist—enthusiastically confident that with a bit of help from the sidelines, each of us can leave the irrationalities of childhood behind and live our lives as clear-thinking adults.

"Alien" forces. Behaviorism and psychoanalysis both share the premise that humans are pushed around by alien forces. These "alien forces" are not creatures from another planet, but urges from within or effects from outside. Behaviorists emphasize the importance of outside effects—the *situational consequences* of daily life that shape our personalities. Such effects include the milk-and-cookies gratifications, the smile-and-praise encouragements that sweeten and shape our daily experiences, as well as life's ubiquitous punishers: frowns or stares, scoldings or spankings, accidental slips on the ice.

Freudian "alien forces" occur not as slips on the ice, but as slips of the tongue or slips of the pen. Like the eyes and nostrils of a crocodile or hippopotamus appearing as little blurbs on a serene surface of water, Freudian "slips" are seen as the surface manifestations of forbidden leviathans of libido lurking beneath the surface of conscious awareness.

Regardless of the differences—whether external or internal, conscious or unconscious, friendly or hostile—such forces remain *ego-alien*. Whether we experience them as emotional volcanoes within ourselves or feel them sweep over us like floodwaters from the outside, we feel "pushed around" by forces we can't seem to control. We experience ourselves as less agentic, less human. Neither Skinner's conditioned animal nor Freud's semiconscious person is truly free to choose.

Constructivists, on the other hand, believe that we actively *construct* our reality. This is why we locate constructivist theories farthest to the left of any theories in the *Insight Zone;* they see the *agentic self* as guiding one's destiny—not only by *choosing* the direction of one's life, but by actively *constructing* reality to make it happen.

"Bootstrapping" from alien forces to agency. Constructivism *emphasizes the active participation of each person in the development, construction, and organization of personality.* Constructivists see *meaning-making* as one of the primary purposes of human existence, and view people as actively constructing their inner worlds. Persons are seen as most splendidly human when making difficult choices and accepting responsibility for their choices. In times of crisis (e.g., the terrorist attacks of 9/11) humans—and only humans—are capable of creating existential meaning and finding spiritual purpose.

Only with an *agentic self* in the driver's seat are we genuinely free to choose. When such a self is constructed from within and is "owned" by the constructor, it carries both a sense of responsibility and a feeling of freedom. Frank Sinatra's ballad, "*I Did It My Way,*" is a song that arises from the heart of a constructivist. In this chapter we will learn how Piaget, Kelly, and Ellis bridge the path from the external forces of the *Situational Zone* and the internal impulses of the *Physiological Zone*, to construct *agentic* choices in the *Insight Zone*.

From molecules to meaning-making. Viewing the person as a *constructor* instead of an *object* moves us significantly above the *Physiological* and *Situational Zones* on the vertical axis. Constructivists view the person as an *active agent* instead of a biological bag of chemicals, a collection of traits, or a cauldron of conflicting forces. In the world of constructivism, persons make choices, take risks, and assume responsibility for those choices and risks. The move from *reactor* to *initiator* takes us diagonally upward and to the left in our continuing climb from molecules to meaning-making.

The *agentic self* sprouts in the soil of Piaget's biological constructivism, grows in Kelly's cognitive constructivism, and blossoms even more fully in Ellis's world of cognitive new beginnings. Thus constructed, we emerge with the potential to become the *self-actualizing person* envisioned by the humanists; the *courageous person* pictured by the existentialists; even possibly the *transcendent, spiritual seer* envisioned by transpersonal psychologists.

THE BIOLOGICAL CONSTRUCTIVISM OF JEAN PIAGET

Piaget constructed personality out of biological rhythms and reflexes. His basic building blocks were **circular reactions,** or *simple pleasurable behaviors that infants repeat over and over, such as sucking their thumbs, shaking rattles, or repeating simple sounds.* Piaget believed that *circular reactions* are essential for establishing a foundation of predictability during infancy.

Subsequently, young children develop early forms of "prelogical" thinking—replacing the manipulation of physical objects with the maneuvering of verbal symbols and cognitive ideas. Piaget sees the mature adult as a logic machine—constructing a meaningful subjective world out of the raw materials of bodily sensations and external stimuli.

Background Check

From Mama to mollusks. Jean Piaget (1896–1980) was a child prodigy whose early interest in science was driven by a desire to identify with his father and escape his mother. Piaget described his father as "a man of a painstaking and critical mind . . . he taught me the value of systematic work, even in small matters" (1952a, p. 237). He remembered his mother as "very intelligent, energetic, and fundamentally a very kind person"; he confessed, however, that "her rather neurotic temperament, however, made our family life somewhat troublesome" (1952a, pp. 237–238).

Piaget is candid in connecting his developmental dots: "One of the direct consequences of this situation was that I started to forgo playing for serious work very early; this I obviously did as much to imitate my father. . . . an attitude which I relate to . . . my mother's poor mental health . . ." (Piaget, 1952a, p. 238). Piaget distanced himself from his mother's "neurotic temperament" by reading science books and spending long hours collecting biological specimens—mostly mollusks. It comes as no surprise that his theory of personality lacks the lust for Mom and fear of Dad so central in Freud's thinking.

Parts–whole perspective. In a manner similar to the levels-of-analysis style of our text, Piaget approached his early scientific studies in a bottom-up, hierarchical style that would characterize all his subsequent work: "I suddenly understood that at all levels (*viz.,* that of the living cell, organism, species, society, etc., but also with reference to states of conscience, to concepts, to logical principles, etc.) one finds the same problem of relationship between the parts and the whole . . ." (Piaget, 1952a, pp. 241–242).

Piaget applied this parts–whole perspective to his study of children's cognitive development, noticing "with amazement" that when eleven- or twelve-year-olds were given simple reasoning tasks involving the inclusion of a part in the whole, they met with "difficulties unsuspected by the adult" (1952a, p. 244).

Zeitgeist

It was during this period that Piaget discovered **Gestalt psychology,** *a perspective that emphasizes patterns, configurations, and wholeness, as opposed to a reductionistic focus on basic elements or essential ingredients.* Gestalt psychology's famous assertion "The whole is greater than the sum of its parts" struck a responsive chord with Piaget's own notions concerning structures-of-the-whole.

One big idea: parts embedded in wholes. During the 1930s Piaget studied cognitive processes in children, discovering "the operative structures-of-the-whole that I had been seeking so long" (Piaget, 1952a, p. 252). During the 1940s he continued to expand and evolve his ideas regarding the relationships between parts and wholes: "My one idea, developed under various aspects in (alas!) twenty-two volumes, has been that intellectual operations proceed in terms of structures-of-the-whole" (Piaget, 1952a, p. 256).

ASKING THE BIG FOUR QUESTIONS

What Are the Parts?

The disappearing fist. There is perhaps no better way to begin our study of Piaget in particular, and construcivists in general, than performing the "magic" trick suggested by Alan Watts (1936) of making a fist. Go ahead—don't be bashful!—make a fist. Now, take a moment to analyze what you have created. Is this fist a genuine "part" of who you are? Of course it is. Did *you* construct it? Of course you did.

Now, open your hand. See?—like magic—the fist is gone! This so-called fist can be made to disappear because it's not only a *thing,* expressed as a noun—it's also a *process,* expressed as a verb (closing your hand). Western language tends to separate entities and processes as if such distinctions were reality. Eastern cultures tend to be more dialectical—less dichotomous—and see the world as made up of *processes* as much as of *entities.* Constructivists—like Zen masters—blend being and doing; they see persons as actively engaged in the process of *being.* Piaget's *scheme,* which we are about to study, is a process more than a structure. That's true of most personality *constructs;* they are processes more than palpable "parts." Still, just because a trait isn't as touchable as a fist, it refers to a real process. We can be reasonably certain that a man who angrily curls his fingers into a fist whenever someone disagree with his opinions, likely carries the unseen-but-real *trait* for aggressiveness.

Scheme. Piaget defines a **scheme** as *"what there is in common among several different and analogous actions"* (Evans, 1973, p. 18, emphasis added). For example, whether a child reaches for a toy, walks toward the dinner table, or approaches a playmate, all these *schemes* share in common the behavior of *moving toward* something or someone. The earliest schemes are what Piaget termed "sensorimotor"—taking place primarily in the *Physiological Zone*—including such things as rooting, sucking, grasping, etc.

Pattern. Building upon this action-oriented foundation, the toddler or young child combines these early sensorimotor schemes into **complex patterns**—*combinations of simple patterns*—such as approaching a table and sitting down. This new sequence is not simply additive (move + rest) but involves a new configuration (or *pattern*) of relationships. Next, the young child combines complex patterns into structure.

Structure. Piaget's use of *structure* shares much in common with the Gestalt notion that the whole is more than the sum of the parts. **Structure** is *a distinctive pattern that "presents the laws or properties of a totality seen as a system"* (Piaget, 1967, p. 143). In other words, when you see the *structure* of something, you understand the "big picture." Piaget's use of the term *structure* makes it clear that he was neither a behaviorist nor a nativist, but a *constructivist*. Whereas behaviorists see the newborn's mind as a *tabula rasa*, and nativists believe in certain "innate categories" of knowledge, Piaget sees the acquisition of patterns of knowledge *(structure)* as a long, slow process of constructing stable meanings by relating new activities and ideas to earlier ones. The child isn't a passive receiver—like a strip of film being exposed to the environment, or a copying machine—simply scanning the surroundings; rather, he seeks out and organizes information, *constructing* it into manageable patterns and assimilating it into previous knowledge.

System. Finally, at the highest level of the "big picture" we discover a **system,** or *an interdependent group of schemes and structures, forming a unified whole.* Since *systems* emerge at high levels of abstraction, they are able to undergo changes or transformations without losing their basic identity. Thus, a mathematical system such as $2 + 2 = 4$ can be *transformed* into $(1 + 1) + (1 + 1) = 4$ without losing its *identity.* Furthermore, whether you're counting kumquats or kookaburras, $2 + 2$ still equals 4. And, if you don't know what a kookaburra is and you're not curious enough to look it up, that doesn't matter either! If you hold two kookaburras in each hand you'll still have a total of four.

Bottom-up, biologically based cognitive construction. As we might expect from the kid who collected mollusks, personality structures are *biologically based (Physiological Zone)* and *cognitively constructed (Insight Zone)* from the bottom up: "a structure would lose all truth value if it did not have a direct connection with the [physical] facts" (Piaget, 1970a, pp. 118–119). Piaget sees all higher-order patterns of thinking and logic—even abstract mathematics—emerging from the interplay of real physical events occurring at lower levels of analysis *(Physiological Zone)*: "There is no structure apart from construction, either abstract or genetic" (Piaget, 1970a, p. 140).

Personality. According to Piaget, *schemes* combine to form *patterns,* which combine to form *structures,* which combine to form *systems,* which combine to form **personality,** which is *the totality of interlacing schemes, patterns, structures, and systems.* Piaget strongly disagreed with psychoanalysts and others who assert that before action occurs there is some sort of internal image. Piaget reversed this, arguing that *first* we act, *then* we form images.

Piaget saw no conflict between lower and higher levels of construction—between the component physiological "parts" and the higher, cognitive "whole." For Piaget, all higher structure is constructed of both organic and cognitive component with which the person actively constructs new structures and evolves new systems. Like Rogers (Chapter 11) and other **phenomenologists:** *psychologists who derive their understanding of human experience from people's private, experiential reports—"walking in their moccasins,"* Piaget sought to understand children from the inside out. However, he differed from most humanists and existentialists by insisting that we must first understand the biological bases of children's constructions.

From body to mind. Piaget was not a biological reductionist who tried to *reduce* the mind to chemical substrates; rather, he sought to remind phenomenologists and others that cognitive conceptions are not innate givens, that they emerge from biological foundations. For Piaget, the direction of development always moved from body to mind, not vice versa. This occurs as a series of smooth transformations, with biological *structures* gradually creating higher-order *patterns,* which in turn transform themselves into higher-order *systems.*

For Piaget, *mind* and *personality* result from constructive activities low in the *Physiological Zone*—beginning with *primary circular reactions* (we'll discuss these in detail shortly) and gradually evolving into higher-order cognitive patterns, groupings, and systems. Construction is not simple copying or internalization, corresponding to *imitation* in social learning theory or *introjection* in psychoanalysis. For Piaget, **construction** means *macro-level cognitive syntheses and reconstruction of micro-level biological rhythms and reactions.*

Mind: conscious or unconscious? For Piaget, **mind** *results from a continuous process of self-constructive activity that is both conscious and unconscious:*

> When in play a child assimilates one object to another, it can usually be said that this assimilation is conscious. . . . But in many games we find symbols whose significance is not understood by the child himself. . . . we shall call a case of this kind secondary or unconscious symbolism. (Piaget, 1962, p.171)

Piaget did not wish to draw the conscious–unconscious distinction too sharply, because he believed that "even the most rational, is both conscious and unconscious" (1962, p. 171).

Constructing the mind. According to Piaget, the mind develops by internalizing and exploring the structures of the body, thereby establishing the biological roots of thought. He stated that his aim was to "uncover the psychogenetic and biological roots of thought" (Piaget, 1970b, p. 53). However, alongside his strong biological emphasis, Piaget saw the person as an *agent* who interacts with the environment. He believed that the mind actively constructs itself—primitively at first, but becoming progressively more sophisticated and stable. As a result of the baby's actions upon the environment and the resulting feedback, the mind is constructed in much the same way a sculptor shapes a statue from clay. The clay is molded, modified, and continually reworked, until a satisfactory likeness emerges. Then it is baked into a semipermanent model, and finally cast in bronze.

Next, we will study the two complementary processes that form the core of Piaget's motivational theory: assimilation and accommodation.

What Makes a Person Go?

Assimilation and accommodation. For Piaget, personality is powered by two reciprocal processes. The first of these is **assimilation,** or *"taking-in" the surrounding environment.* The complementary process is **accommodation,** which is *"remodification of the behavior as a result of the experience"* (Piaget, 1967, p. 18, emphasis added). During normal development, a child progressively *assimilates* more and more of the surrounding environment. But assimilation of the outside world cannot proceed without internal *accommodation* or adaptation by the organism. For instance, when the baby learns to suck her thumb she *assimilates* this appendage into the oral action schemes already built up around sucking Mother's breast. However, since Baby's thumb differs from Mother's nipple in size, texture, and milk-producing ability, Baby must make certain *accommodations* when sucking her thumb. Each new *assimilation,* or "taking-in" of the external environment, must be accompanied by an appropriate *accommodation.*

Thus, the baby reshapes her mouth when sucking her thumb in order to *accommodate* the novel size and shape—as she will when subsequently assimilating and accommodating a host of new "suckables": pacifiers, crayons, lollipops, ice-cream cones, drinking straws, oranges, and ballpoint pens.

What Freud termed the oral stage was for Piaget only the opening steps of a lifelong dance between assimilation and accommodation. This begins with the neonate's infatuation with sucking, but soon spreads to a host of other locations and modalities. Thus, instead of narrowly defining this as the "oral stage," Piaget assigned it the more generic term *sensorimotor stage,* which we shall study in detail shortly. In the current discussion, it is important only to note that whereas Freud's designation of *oral stage* emphasized anatomy, Piaget's *sensorimotor stage* highlighted *constructive process.*

Equilibration. Piaget described this developmental "dance" as **equilibration,** *the process by which assimilation and accommodation balance each other to achieve a steady state.* Imagine *assimilation* and *accommodation* as your two legs, and *equilibration* as the "dance." Just as successively shifting your body weight back and forth, from leg to leg, allows you to walk or dance, so alternating between assimilation and accommodation allows you to equilibrate.

Thus, *equilibrium* is a kind of "steady state" that occurs within a system of shifting coordinates and changing balances, while the organism "dances" the developmental journey of life. In the beginning, *equilibrium* takes place at the simplest sensorimotor levels (e.g., thumb sucking is a primary circular reaction); however, it subsequently comes to include both physical and psychological aspects of life. It is through our many and varied equilibrations with our surroundings that we construct our own unique personalities: "A pebble may be in states of stable, unstable, indifferent equilibrium with respect to its surroundings and this makes no difference to its nature. By contrast, an organism [a living being] presents, with respect to its milieu, multiple forms of equilibrium . . ." (Piaget, 1967, p. 102).

From Freud to feedback loops. Whenever **disequilibrium,** *an imbalance between assimilation and accommodation,* occurs, the organism is motivated to rectify the disturbance by adjusting or recalibrating. Here Piaget further distanced himself from

Freud's opposing forces (e.g., cathexis versus anticathexis) by viewing equilibration as similar to cybernetic *feedback loops:*

> Now I did not use cybernetic terminology when I began talking of this factor [equilibration], but nonetheless since the beginning I have insisted that it was not a balance of opposing forces, a simple case of physical equilibrium but that it was a self-regulation. And of course today cybernetics is precisely that, the study of self-regulating models. (Evans, 1973, pp. 45–46)

Adaptation. Piaget disagreed with biologists who defined *adaptation* "simply as preservation and survival . . ." (Piaget, 1952b, p. 5). Instead, Piaget defined **adaptation** as *equilibration (balancing) of assimilation and accommodation:*

> This definition applies to intelligence as well. Intelligence is *assimilation* to the extent that it incorporates all the given data of experience within its framework. . . . There can be no doubt either, that mental life is also *accommodation* to the environment. . . . In short, intellectual adaptation, like every other kind, consists of putting an assimilatory mechanism and a complementary accommodation into progressive equilibrium. . . . (Piaget, 1952b, pp. 6–7)

Teleonomic (goal-oriented) behaviors. Like Adler, Piaget believed that humans are goal-oriented creatures, and he coined the term **teleonomic** to describe the *goal-oriented nature of development.* He believed that during the earliest sensorimotor development, equilibrating behaviors consist of simple reflexes; but as behavior becomes more highly developed, motives and goals become evident.

Cognitions trump emotions. Piaget recognized that emotions and cognitions both participate in our construction of reality; however, he felt that *cognitions* were of paramount importance:

> Affectivity is the motor of any conduct. But affectivity does not modify the cognitive structure. Take two school children for example. One who loves mathematics, who is interested and enthusiastic . . . and the other who has feelings of inferiority, dislikes the teacher, and so forth. . . . but for both of them two and two makes four in the end. It doesn't make three for the one who doesn't like it and five for the one who does. Two and two are still four. (Evans, 1973, p. 7)

Thus, although emotions energize behavior, Piaget saw feelings as operating in concert with—not separate from—cognitions:

> There is never a purely intellectual action, and numerous emotions, interests, values, impressions of harmony, etc., intervene—for example in the solving of a mathematical problem. Likewise, there is never a purely affective act, e.g., love presupposes comprehension. (Piaget, 1967, pp. 33–44)

What Makes a Person Grow?

Never one to shrink from details or classification, Piaget divided development into *four major periods,* some of which were further divided into stages. A brief description of each developmental period furnishes a flavor of his work.

TABLE 10.1

Piaget's Developmental Stages

I. Infancy—Sensorimotor Period (birth–2 years)

(1) **Ready-made reflexes** (birth–1 month) Sucking, grasping, visual tracking

(2) **Primary circular reactions** (1–4 mos.) Sucking thumb, other simple motor movements

(3) **Secondary circular reactions** (4–8 mos.) Shaking rattle, rhythmically banging utensils or toys on high-chair tray or table

(4) **Coordinating schemes** (8–12 mos.) Looking, grasping, or moving to achieve goals

(5) **Tertiary circular reactions** (12–18 mos.) Acting on schemes or objects to bring about novel effects

(6) **Mental/symbolic play and exploration** (18 mos.–2 years) Mental representation using "make believe" people or toys

II. Early Childhood—Preoperational Period (2–7 years)

(1) **Preconceptual** (2–4 years) Magical/animistic thinking: "The car runs because it is alive"

(2) **Prelogical** (4–7 years) Perception-bound: believing things are exactly as they appear

III. Late Childhood—Concrete Operations (7–11 years)

Understanding the changeless nature of matter, classifying, ordering objects serially, and reasoning more logically; beginning to develop a sense of self

IV. Adolescence—Formal Operations (11 years–adulthood)

Developing capacity for abstract reasoning using words and symbols not necessarily tied to objects in the real world; self-consciousness peaks during this period

I. Infancy—the sensorimotor period (birth–2 years). The earliest developmental period is the **sensorimotor stage** *when infants "think" by exploring the world around them with their mouths, eyes, ears, hands, and other sensory equipment.* By sucking, seeing, hearing, touching, holding, and otherwise manipulating the surrounding world, babies begin to develop minds, or what Piaget called *sensorimotor intelligence.*

Stage 1—Reflexive schemes (birth to 1 month). The reflexes of the neonate provide the building blocks of sensorimotor intelligence. During this stage, newborns indiscriminately suck almost anything, orally assimilating the world around them. The neonate's experiences are "locked in egocentrism" with no awareness of self or any distinction between self and external world. The baby's **egocentrism** *is not "selfishness" in the common sense, but rather a lack of differentiation between self and the environment.*

Stage 2—Primary circular reactions (1–4 months). The newborn begins to acquire some voluntary control over behavior, and begins to repeat those accidentally-stumbled-upon behaviors that prolong satisfaction. Piaget called them **primary circular reactions,** *or simple motor habits, such as sucking one's thumb, or repetitively opening and closing one's fist.* These simple repetitive behaviors are pleasurable and are centered on the infant's own body (since, of course, Baby is not out riding her tricycle around the neighborhood).

Stage 3—Secondary circular reactions (4–8 months). Now, as the baby develops the ability to sit up, he becomes more skilled in grasping and manipulating objects that are not part of his own body. This is the stage of **secondary circular reactions,** or *repeatedly generating and enjoying interesting effects in the surrounding world, such as shaking a rattle or banging one's spoon on the high-chair tray.* During this stage the infant becomes more interested in others (imitating familiar behaviors) and in the surrounding world, but he still lacks **object permanence,** which is *the ability to retain a mental image of an object when it is not directly in one's vision*—without object permanence, "out of sight *is* out of mind."

Stage 4—Coordination of secondary circular reactions (8–12 months). During the latter part of the first year, goal-directed, intentional behavior emerges. With the achievement of *object permanence,* improved anticipation of events, and the ability to imitate behaviors slightly different from those familiar to the infant, the baby creates a more complex, yet predictable subjective world. Piaget devised an object-hiding task in which an attractive toy was hidden under a blanket or behind a barrier. At this stage, most babies can combine two schemes "pushing" aside the obstacle, and "grasping" the hidden toy, which they know is there because of having achieved object permanence.

Stage 5—Tertiary circular reactions (12–18 months). During the first half of the second year, the toddler engages in **tertiary circular reactions,** *exploring objects by acting on them and repeating behaviors with slight variations that bring about novel effects.* The toddler who throws toys out of his playpen one by one to see which ones bounce, break, thud, or crash with a loud noise, is engaging in *tertiary circular reactions.* Object permanence is now well established, allowing the toddler to follow visual displacements of an object being hidden, and to search where it was last seen. She recognizes pictures of familiar persons and can follow simple verbal instructions.

Stage 6—Mental combinations (18 months–2 years). Internal representation of objects, and the ability for deferred imitation, greatly expand the toddler's world. Now, instead of being limited to **functional play** *with real toys and real people,* the young child is able to engage in **make-believe** or **symbolic play,** *utilizing pretend people or imaginary toys, and manipulating mental combinations.* This greatly expands psychological development, marking the transition from sensorimotor activity to representational activity. The child now shows intention, purpose, and the beginnings of deductive reasoning, as well as a rudimentary understanding of time, space, and causality. The toddler is leaving the palpable world of *sensorimotor experience* to enter the higher spheres of *symbolic representation.*

II. Early childhood—the preoperational period (2–7 years). Preschoolers begin using symbols to represent and replace their earlier sensorimotor discoveries. Symbolic representation is seen in dreams, drawings, language development, and make-believe play. Language development is explosive during this stage, with the child adding new words on a daily basis. By allowing the child to separate thought from action, language permits cognition to be far more efficient.

Preconceptual stage (2–4 years). At this stage, a child's thinking still lacks the logical qualities present in older children. Although the three-year-old can now manage quite realistically in the physical world, her thinking is compromised by egocentrism as well as *magical* and *animistic* thinking. **Magical thinking** *is based on the illusion that one can control natural events through thoughts, gestures, or rituals.* Thus, for the toddler, *wishing* someone were dead might *cause* them to die. **Animistic thinking** *assumes that all natural objects are alive and have feelings just as the child does: "The moon is happy to see us," or "The car is alive, because it runs."*

Prelogical or intuitive stage (4–7 years). The prelogical child tends to be **perception-bound,** *believing things are exactly as they appear.* For a five-year-old, half a cup of juice that fills a small glass is more than half a cup that fails to fill a larger glass. Such abilities as hierarchical classification have not yet developed, and language is used in an egocentric way, based on the child's limited experience.

Development of the self. It is only toward the end of early childhood that children begin to engage in *self-evaluation.* Prior to this time, the child has no real sense of self. Piaget refers to the parents as *ego ideals* for the child because since the young child lacks self-awareness, early childhood is characterized by egocentrism. Now, however, the child becomes more aware of self and begins to master challenges of both a social and impersonal nature. In addition to getting along with peers, children of this age begin to feel competent to dress themselves, handle eating utensils, mark with a pencil, color with crayons, etc. Such personal skills, along with favorable evaluations by significant others, provide the foundations for mental health.

Will power. During the middle years of childhood, Piaget sees the appearance of **will power,** *which functions to bolster correct thinking and to steer personality to transcend the mere gratification of biological impulses. Will power* represents a stable equilibrium of organized emotions, somewhat similar to the neo-Freudian notion of "ego strength"—the ego's capacity to mediate emotional conflict and postpone instinctual gratification. According to Piaget, when a conflict arises between two disparate emotions, *will power* comes to the rescue, reinforcing "the superior but weaker tendency so as to make it triumph" (Piaget, 1967, p. 59). In this way *will power* exerts a steering function on personality, e.g., assisting a person to stay on a diet, even when tempted by the sight of chocolate cake.

III. Late childhood—the period of concrete operations (7–11 years). During the early school years, the child's reasoning becomes more logical. Children of this age achieve what Piaget considered one of the most important cognitive accomplishments of childhood, known as **conservation,** or *the ability to appreciate the changeless nature of matter.* Children of this age learn that a certain amount of Play Doh™ or lemonade remains the same regardless of appearances. Whether Play Doh™ is formed into a single large ball or made into a dozen smaller pieces, the amount does not change. Whether a half pitcher of lemonade is poured into six large tumblers, or twelve small cups, it still remains the same amount of liquid.

Another important achievement of this period is **reversibility,** or *the ability to think forward and backward in time. Reversibility* speeds up logical thinking, allowing the child to make deductions, such as, If adding 2 to 2 gives you 4, then "taking back" 2 from 4 again leaves you with 2. Cognitive development during this stage spirals upward to higher and more abstract levels. New cognitive skills, such as **classification** *(a ten-year-old boy sorts his baseball cards by various categories—e.g., teams, batting averages, playing positions);* **spatial reasoning** *(most 9-year-olds can give clear directions how to get from place to place based on their own "mental walk");* and **seriation** *(the ability to order* *items by increasing or decreasing dimensions such as height, weight, or length)* help move the child in the direction of adult logical thinking. Still, according to Piaget, the child's capacity for logical thought is incomplete.

IV. Adolescence—the period of formal operations (11 years–adulthood). The capacity for **abstraction,** or *reasoning with words or symbols that do not necessarily refer to objects in the real world,* allows adolescents and adults to do math, think up poems, and mentally "try out" various solutions to problems, without having to actually engage in the behaviors.

Piaget's last and most highly developed cognitive achievement is **propositional reasoning,** which is *the ability to reason using propositions (verbal statements) in place of concrete objects—e.g., doing addition "in one's head" instead of counting poker chips. Propositional reasoning* makes possible argumentativeness, idealism, and criticism. The cognitive achievements of this period allow adolescents to grasp the essentials of scientific thinking much better than they could at earlier ages.

Adolescents frequently hone these new skills to a fine edge by arguing with parents and other authority figures. The formerly compliant school-age child evolves into the argumentative teen who can marshal facts and ideas to make a case. Because abstract thinking allows adolescents to go beyond the real world, it sometimes tilts them toward idealism and perfection. Teenagers are adept at imagining "superior" alternatives in religion, politics, and moral systems, leading them to construct grand visions of a perfect world—a world without hunger, poverty, or war.

Self-consciousness reaches exquisitely sensitive proportions during this era. Now, adolescents experience a more advanced version of childhood egocentrism, becoming wrapped up in their own thoughts, appearance, and behavior. According to Piaget, two distorted images of the relationship between self and others appear. The first he called the **imaginary audience** (Elkind & Bowen, 1979), *which involves the feeling that one is always on stage—the focus of everyone's attention.* The second distortion is the **personal fable,** *a sense of specialness and importance that accompanies the feeling of always being on stage.* Adolescents frequently develop an inflated sense of their own importance (Elkind, 1994).

Work. Like Erikson, Piaget sees a major role for work, not so much as an opportunity to find one's identity, as in Erikson's model, but to anchor the idealism of adolescence in the real, workaday world. With the dawning of adolescence, personality flowers more fully, because the teenager can now think beyond the present to build ideologies and political systems that transcend contemporary systems. Indeed, the adolescent might risk becoming so idealistic as to lose touch with the concrete realities of everyday life, so Piaget's antidote for excessive adolescent idealism was *work.* "Effective enduring work, undertaken in concrete and well-defined situations," said Piaget, "cures all dreams. . . . One should not be disquieted by the extravagance and disequilibrium of the better part of adolescence. . . . True adaptation to society comes automatically when the adolescent reformer attempts to put his ideas to work" (Piaget, 1967, pp. 68–69).

Summary of Piaget's theories. It's not difficult to see why Piaget is remembered more as a developmental psychologist than as a personality theorist. However, his stages of *cognitive* development complement Freud's stages of *sexual* development, giving a more complete picture of a child's maturation. In our text, Piaget, perhaps more than any other personality psychologist, illustrates levels of analysis. Beginning the self-construction of personality in the *Physiological Zone* during the sensorimotor period, Piaget systematically works his way up to higher and more abstract levels of analysis and construction in the *Insight Zone.*

Although Piaget began his work in the early 1930s, it remained in obscurity for decades, because his ideas were eclipsed by the prevailing behaviorism of the mid-twentieth century, and his *idiographic* (see Allport, Chapter 4) clinical approach was discordant with the statistically based experimental approaches so popular in research universities. So it has been relatively recently that interest in Piaget's work has broadened, and his idiographic approach to studying and educating children has become more popular.

During the 1960s and early 1970s, Piaget's insistence that young children learn mainly through acting on the environment—not through language-based curricula—led many teachers to endorse **open classrooms** *where children are viewed as active agents in their own development.* Like so many trends in American education, however, the pendulum soon swung back. As high school students' SAT scores declined during the 1970s, a "back to basics" movement arose and now, with federal "No Child Left Behind" initiatives, classrooms have returned to more traditional teacher-directed learning.

What Makes a Person Unique?

Since Piaget saw the ego as self-centered, he viewed the mature personality as a kind of "decentered ego." Piaget saw the young child as egocentric, with limited ability to understand, cooperate with, or relate to others, so it is hardly surprising that the mature personality does not emerge until adolescence. Even then, Piaget says relatively little about the *self* or about the uniqueness of each individual's *personality.* What he did write about emotional life appears in scattered paragraphs or short chapters here or there. Compared with most modern theories of personality, Piaget's might appear inferior; however, it is somewhat unfair to measure his work against other personality theories because his lifelong interest was *not* in personality. After he quit searching for mollusks, his prime interest was in searching for the universal foundations of intelligence. He spent comparatively little time thinking about personality per se.

SUMMARY OF PIAGET

Construction is destiny. In contrast to Freud's anatomy-is-destiny theories, Piaget emphasized self-construction. He minimized many of the individual-differences factors (e.g., language systems, societal norms) by which other personality theorists build uniqueness into their models. Piaget relied primarily on built-in biological variation to explain the wide diversities that we observe in babies and young children, because he believed that language and socialization are minor players during the crucial early months when the rudiments of mental life are beginning to form: "prior to any language, more or less complex systems of representation can be formed" (Piaget, 1962, p. 69).

Piaget's bottom line is that mind and personality are only mildly affected by social or cultural influences. All learning (including personality development) is *constructed* from biologically based sensorimotor *actions*. Nonetheless, we remain unique—like snowflakes and flowers—because our biological makeup is one-of-a-kind (unless, of course, we have an identical twin). That's the biological part. Additionally, each of us combines unique *schemes,* particular *patterns,* distinctive *structures,* and idiosyncratic *systems* to construct a one-of-a-kind *personality* that reflects our unique biological heritage as well as our own specific circumstances.

In the final analysis, Piaget remains a *constructive interactionist* because he believes we *construct* our experience—it isn't stamped into us, as behaviorists might imply; nor is it preexistent, as nativists might argue. For Piaget, anatomy is *not* destiny—construction is. Mother Nature drops off the bricks and boards at our construction site, but we have to pound the nails and mix the mortar as we construct our psychological dwelling place.

FACING THE TOUGH TWINS

Is It Testable?

Piaget utilized a few basic constructs (e.g., assimilation, accommodation, and equilibration) across many levels of analysis, leaving himself open to the criticism that he overgeneralized—deriving an elaborate theory of mind from a few biologically based circular reactions.

A few big ideas. Piaget developed most of his theoretical ideas by carefully observing and recording his own children as they matured from infancy through childhood. This resulted in hundreds of pages of handwritten notes that combine a father's love with a mollusk-collector's attention to detail. His "findings" read like a court reporter's transcription of a three-year trial—you feel like you're drowning in details.

Out of this quagmire of minutiae Piaget successfully extracted a few foundational concepts such as *circular reactions, assimilation, accommodation,* and *equilibration.* Using these, he "bootstrapped" his way to a theory of cognitive development that was broadly applicable: "He tries to show that equilibrium structures . . . are applicable to the field of logical, moral, and legal behaviour" (Mays, 1982, p. 49). One admirer wrote that "Einstein is reputed to have said of Piaget's theory, 'It's so simple that only a genius could have thought of it'" (Pulaski, 1980, p. 217). However, anyone who has read Piaget's notes in the original might add, "It takes an Einstein to find simplicity in Piaget."

Piaget has not been without his critics. In a wryly titled article "The Garden Path to the Understanding of Cognitive Development: Has Piaget Led Us into the Poison Ivy?" the authors contend that many aspects of Piaget's theory have not been empirically supported: "Piaget has generated the most significant theory in the field of cognitive development. . . . There are, however, problems with Piagetian methodology and interpretation . . ." (Siegel & Hodkin, 1982, p. 78).

Next, we will consider some contemporary research that bears on Piaget's work so that you can decide for yourself.

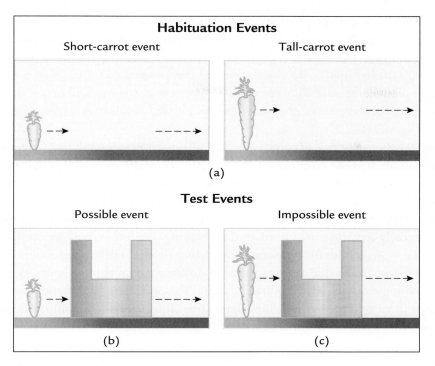

Figure 10.1 ■ *Habituation Events*

Idiographic versus experimental studies. Investigating Piaget's theories using modern experimental methods illustrates the limitations of idiographic or case-study methods in personality research.

Object permanence. Recall that by hiding toys under a blanket or behind a barrier, Piaget concluded that *object permanence* was established between 8 and 12 months of age. However, Baillargeon & DeVos (1991) found evidence for object permanence as early as 3½; months, using the **habituation–dishabituation response:** *infants are shown a stimulus until they "habituate"—no longer respond with eye contact and accompanying signs of curiosity or excitement.* In the first phase of this experiment, infants were *habituated* to a tall carrot and a short carrot passing behind a screen (see Figure 10.1). In the second phase, the screen contained a "window," and in the "possible" event the short carrot passed behind the screen (under the bottom ledge of the window) and reappeared on the other side. In the "impossible" event the tall carrot did not appear in the window, but emerged (as did the short carrot) on the other side. Infants as young as 3½ months *dishabituated* (looked longer, with renewed interest) at the "impossible" tall-carrot event, suggesting that they understood *object permanence.*

These sophisticated research techniques allow researchers to discover what an infant *knows* that may not yet be evident in its searching behavior. Apparently babies *understand* far more than they are able to communicate by their searching behaviors. Supporting this notion is a study (Goubet & Clifton, 1998) that showed that when the searching aspect of a task is simplified to one action (reaching directly toward an object—not having to push aside a barrier or uncover a toy), even 6½-month-olds can easily retrieve an object.

Animistic and magical thinking. Piaget apparently overestimated children's *animistic beliefs* because he questioned his subjects about objects with which they had little familiarity (e.g., the sun, moon, and clouds). Whereas Piaget believed that many four-year-olds think animistically, recent research (e.g., Massey & Gelman, 1988; Poulin-Dubois & Heroux, 1994) reveals that children as young as three seldom think that familiar inanimate objects such as crayons and rocks are alive. Similarly, although most three- and four-year-olds still believe in the magical power of fairies and other mystical creatures, they deny that magic plays a role in everyday experiences (Subbotsky, 1994).

Conservation—the role of culture. Finally, although Piaget paid little attention to cultural variables, more recent research (e.g., Fahrmeier, 1978) indicates that in tribal societies where children rarely attend school, even the most basic conservation tasks—involving length and numbers—are not understood until age 11 or later. This suggests that in order to master conservation and other Piagetian concepts, children must participate in daily activities that promote such thinking (Light & Perret-Clermont, 1989).

With my own children, for example, dividing things "fairly" (in equal portions) became a finely honed skill as they practiced dividing candy, cookies, crayons, and almost anything else they were required to share. This was done with meticulous care—especially in view of the "house rule" that if one child divides the cookie in two, the other gets to choose which piece to take.

Summary of Research on Piaget's theories

Sophisticated research strategies have revealed that when cognitive tasks are scaled down in difficulty, young children appear to understand in ways that are closer to older children and adults than Piaget believed. Furthermore, many developmental researchers fail to find "stages," and view development as a gradual and continuous process. Nonetheless, Piaget's *constructivism* has revolutionized how we understand children's development, and has led to educational practices that emphasize discovery learning through direct contact with the environment.

In the field of personality, Piaget's influence has been indirect but profound. During an era when behaviorism was the dominant force in American psychology, Piaget provided a *constructivist* "base camp" from which the *self* could again climb to ascendency in the humanistic and cognitive revolutions that were to follow.

Is It Useful?

Understanding kids from the inside out. It's safe to say that no theorist has had a greater *heuristic* influence on developmental psychology than has Jean Piaget. He created a theory of development from the inside out—observing, questioning, and analyzing the inner workings of the child's mind. Using his skills as an interviewer, his patience as a parent, and his own children as subjects, Piaget gained entrance to the inner world of the child's mind and then formulated his theories with the aid of concepts drawn from such diverse fields as biology, mathematics, psychology, and philosophy. Piaget's portrait of the inside of a child's evolving mind remains his lasting legacy. The following story illustrates the profundity of his insights:

> One day a mother of two was at the end of her rope with her sons' constant bickering. The current squabble was over the allocation of a dessert pastry. The mother had given two of the small squares to her ten-year-old and one to her

four-year-old. She had explained to her aggrieved younger son that he had received only one because he was smaller, that when he was bigger he could have two. He was quite unappeased by this logic, as you can imagine, and he continued to bemoan his fate. The mother lost her patience, and in a fit of sarcasm she swept down on his plate with a knife saying, "You want two pieces? Okay, I'll give you two pieces. Here!"—whereupon she neatly cut the younger boy's pastry in half. Immediately, all the tension went out of him; he thanked his mother sincerely, and contentedly set upon his dessert. (Kegan, 1982, pp. 27–28)

It was the genius of Piaget to recognize that the world of the four-year-old is not a dim, underdeveloped version of reality-as-seen-by-adults; rather, it is a unique world where the child employs "logic" that appears erroneous when judged by the yardstick of adult thought, but which is consistent and coherent for the child's purposes of making sense of the world.

THE COGNITIVE CONSTRUCTIVISM OF GEORGE KELLY

Like Piaget, George Kelly replaced Freud's "seething cauldron" of untamed emotions with a mind that constructs a personality shaped by choices. Kelly's theory of personality is not as biologically based as Piaget's, nor as conflict-ridden as Freud's (the ego subduing the id or kowtowing to the superego). Instead, people are seen as choosing among alternative "templates" for viewing the world. According to Kelly, everyone is a "scientist"—analyzing, constructing, and shaping his or her own experience of the world.

Each person selects from among a vast array of cognitive, emotional, and behavioral alternatives, endowing some options with great meaning and significance, while simultaneously devaluing others; hence, Kelly's term "constructive alternativism." Here Kelly achieves his stature as a humanist as well as a cognitive psychologist, because only in a milieu of genuine choices can humans authentically actualize themselves. Anything less is determinism, by whatever alias it travels.

Background Check

Early life and education. George Alexander Kelly (1905–1970) was born on a farm near Perth, Kansas. As an only child, Kelly received a lot of caring, but his family frowned on drinking, dancing, card playing, and other such amusements, emphasizing instead the virtues of hard work. Embarking on his educational journey in a one-room school on the Kansas prairie, Kelly had eclectic interests. In college, in addition to enrolling in science and math courses, he was active in music and debate.

Graduating with a B.A. in math and physics, Kelly was originally attracted to aeronautical engineering. However, after working in the field for a short time, he became increasingly interested in social problems, so he enrolled in a master's program at the University of Kansas, majoring in educational sociology and minoring in labor relations. In 1929, he was awarded an exchange scholarship to the University of Edinburgh, and while in Scotland, he studied with the distinguished statistician and educator, Sir Godfrey Thompson, who sparked his interest in psychology. By the time Kelly received his Ph.D. in 1931, he had studied mathematics, physics, education, sociology, cultural anthropology, labor relations, economics, speech pathology, and biometrics.

Pragmatic clinician. Beginning his professional career during the Great Depression, Kelly quickly discovered that his graduate training in physiological psychology was not in demand. People were confused and desperate, their lives in upheaval, and they were in great need of clinical and counseling services. So, Kelly—ever the pragmatist—switched his focus to clinical psychology. Because Kelly had not been formally trained in any particular "school" of therapy, he felt free to try "whatever worked." During his thirteen-year career at Fort Hays, Kelly achieved two great insights, both of which figured prominently in his subsequent theory of personality.

Early constructivist insights. During graduate school, Kelly had been put off by psychoanalytic theory, but, he now discovered that when he offered Freudian insights to his clients, many were profoundly helped. He wondered if these insights were effective because they were true, or mostly because clients *believed* them to be true. Kelly concluded that it was the *perceptual reframing* of the problem that was most helpful, so he experimented with offering clients a variety of different interpretations:

> I began fabricating "insights." I deliberately offered "preposterous interpretations" to my clients. Some of them were about as un-Freudian as I could make them— first proposed somewhat cautiously, of course, and then, as I began to see what was happening, more boldly. My only criteria were that the explanation account for the crucial facts as the client saw them, and that it carry implications for approaching the future in a different way. (1969, p. 52)

Secondly, Kelly (who developed the first traveling psychology clinics to serve public schools in Kansas) noticed that a teacher's complaint usually said more about the teacher than about the student. He came to believe that *the way a teacher saw things*— rather than objective reality—profoundly influenced the nature of the presenting "problem." Both of these *constructivist* insights played pivotal roles in Kelly's subsequent theory of personality.

The kid from Kansas plows a straight furrow. George A. Kelly grew up on a farm, and when you grow up on a farm, you learn the importance of plowing a straight first furrow. If you don't, your plowed field will have a "wavy" look. Although you might get away with that in the rolling hills of West Virginia, that's not acceptable on the prairies of Kansas, where farmers take pride in straight fences, straight furrows, and straight corn rows.

Having been a farm boy myself, I learned the secret of a straight furrow and it's this: pick your target and never look back—not even once! You drive your tractor to one end of the field, pick a fence post, a tree, or some other "target" at the far end of the field, drop your plow, look straight ahead, start driving, and *never, ever* take your eyes off the target until you've reached the end of the field. If you do that, you'll have a straight first furrow—guaranteed. But if you look behind to see how things are coming along, if you look sideways to wave at a passing neighbor, if you swat at mosquitoes or drink from your thermos, your first furrow will map each "blip" with the accuracy of a seismograph, and the neighbors will secretly say "That guy's no farmer." That's why a farmer plows the first furrow with as much intensity and focus as a brain surgeon making her opening incision.

What has plowing got to do with Kelly's theory of personality? If you read his books, you can almost picture this farm kid from Kansas chugging along on his tractor, glancing neither right nor left—and certainly not back!—totally concentrated, totally focused on that tree or fence post at the opposite end of the field. His theory of personality has that same look-neither-to-the-right-nor-to-the-left, care-not-what-others-think-or-say quality. Kelly introduces his theory by saying that the term *learning,* which permeates most psychology textbooks, hardly appears at all; that he is intentionally "throwing it overboard altogether" (1955, p. x). He goes on to jettison a number of such time-honored constructs as *reinforcement, drives,* and the *unconscious,* replacing them with his own new terms such as *constructive alternativism, preemption, fixed-role therapy, creativity cycle,* and the like.

Person-as-scientist: the tree at the end of the field. Kelly's focus is unmistakable: he views every person as a scientist trying to make sense of the world. "Let us then, instead of occupying ourselves with *man-the-biological-organism* or *man-the-lucky-guy,* have a look at *man-the-scientist*" (Kelly, 1955, p. 4, emphasis in original). Thus, Kelly constructs a personality theory based on his view of the ordinary person functioning as a *constructing* "scientist." In the *Insight Zone,* Kelly is located a bit above and to the right of Piaget. He is less biologically oriented than Piaget and—especially when it comes to his fixed-role therapy (which we will discuss later)—more interactional in orientation.

Zeitgeist

During his years at Fort Hayes, Kelly experimented with a variety of clinical approaches, using his prairie-grown pragmatism to implement whatever worked and to discard what didn't. During this period he developed his own unique personality theory that he called **constructive alternativism:** *the idea that no one need be hemmed in by circumstances—alternative choices can always be found.* And, as we learned earlier, Kelly concluded that it didn't matter whether a clinical formulation was "correct," so long as it provided the client an alternative way of construing the world.

In summary, the prevailing zeitgeist of psychoanalysis in Europe and behaviorism in America was not a rich source of ideas for Kelly. He was more influenced by the farm in Kansas, the Great Depression, and World War II than he was by the books in his library. The chronic confusion that people experienced as a consequence of the Depression and WW II kindled in Kelly the conviction that ordinary folks—like scientists—seek to understand and control the circumstances of their private worlds.

ASKING THE BIG FOUR QUESTIONS

Person in the driver's seat. Kelly places the person in the driver's seat, actively construing his or her surroundings. Since each person construes the universe in different ways, constructive alternatives are always possible. According to Kelly, no one needs to be "the absolute victim" of past history or present circumstances (1955, p. 43).

There, in a couple of sentences, Kelly summarizes the core of his personality theory: *you* in the driver's seat *continuously construing and constructing* your world. Having survived The Great Depression and a world war, Kelly was in no mood to facilitate victimhood or become an enabler. In his no-nonsense theory, *you*—not your anatomy, parents, or conditioning history—are responsible for creating your experience. Since you are free to choose among many possible alternatives, Kelly would advise you to quit whining, grab the steering wheel, get your life in gear, and *drive!*

We will discover that Kelly answers all of the "Big Four" questions by referring back to his **fundamental postulate:** "A PERSON'S PROCESSES ARE PSYCHOLOG-ICALLY CHANNELIZED BY THE WAYS IN WHICH HE ANTICIPATES EVENTS" (Kelly, 1955, p. 46, capitalization in the original).

A key word here is *anticipates.* Kelly's theory is tilted toward the future, but his forward-leaning stance is more than motivational; it involves far more than the "carrot-out-front" incentives of future rewards. According to Kelly, how you *construe* your future profoundly shapes your present experience. He elaborated his fundamental postulate with eleven *corollaries,* which we will consider in more detail in the context of our "Big Four" questions.

What Are the Parts?

The mind–body problem—"No problem!" To comprehend Kelly, we need to realize that everything follows from his main premise: *people ceaselessly and uniquely construe experience.* Kelly explains learning, motivation, development, and uniqueness as specific manifestations of the overarching process of *construing.*

He dispenses with Decartes's dualism by suggesting that a single event can simultaneously be *construed* from the perspective of various disciplines—"physiology, political science, or psychology" (Kelly, 1955, p. 10). This is consistent with our zonal perspective of viewing scientists as working at different levels of abstraction. Accordingly, Kelly views all of us as "scientists" who utilize *personal constructs* to create our own realities by *choosing* from among chemical, biological, existential, or spiritual construct—those particular "templates" that make the most sense to us.

Personal constructs—cognitive templates for viewing the world. The "engine" of Kelly's theory is the **personal construct,** *a bipolar, cognitive template that a person "tries on for size" when construing (interpreting, explaining, or making sense of) experience.* Kelly emphasized that all interpretations of the universe are tentative and open to revision ". . . *[our theory] emphasizes the creative capacity of the living thing to represent the environment, not merely to respond to it*" (Kelly, 1955, p. 8, emphasis in original).

Simple and straightforward, Kelly's two-sided constructs are pivotal to his theory of personality. Compared with the complex constructs of psychoanalysis or the intricacies of Piaget's ideas, Kelly's personal constructs are straightforward and reliable, sharing much in common with those trusty, two-stroke John Deere tractors that farmers used to plow the Kansas prairies. With only a few moving parts, those tractors faithfully chugged along year after year, requiring few repairs, giving their owners little grief.

Dichotomy corollary. *We tend to compare things in terms of their opposites and their similarities.* In Kelly's words, "a person's construction system is composed of a finite number of dichotomous constructs" (1955, p. 59). Like Freud, Kelly loved opposites; however, these were not Freudian forces, colliding with one another in the style of cathexis versus anticathexis or eros versus thanatos. Instead, Kelly used opposites to delineate the dimensions of cognitive constructs—much as a head and a tail define a coin. All constructs have a **similarity pole,** that is, *how two things are alike—"Rachel and Deborah are gentle"*—and a **contrast pole,** *how two similar things differ from a third—* "Stephanie is harsh." As Kelly put it, "One does not understand a personal construct simply by apprehending some basis of *similarity* between objects; he must understand the basis of *distinction* as well. Both similarity and contrast are involved . . ." (Kelly, 1969, p. 169).

A **superordinate construct** *is a high-order, general construct that includes other lower-level constructs.* "Honesty," for example, is a construct that might include finances, feelings, and communications (verbal, written, or body language). A superordinate construct such as "patriot," "environmentalist," or "pro-lifer" includes numerous other constructs, coloring their meanings and shaping their directions. A **subordinate construct** *is a construct that is subsumed under a more abstract construct.* For example, a *superordinate* construct like "loyalty" might include more specific, *subordinate* constructs like "toiling unselfishly" for the good of the company, "refusing to gossip or spread false rumors about administration," etc.

Range corollary. *Each construct is useful for anticipating experiences within a limited range.* Thus, the construct *tall versus short* might be useful for describing horses, houses, people, or trees as variously short or tall, but it has little value for construing weather, which falls outside its range, and could better be described in terms of *stormy versus calm,* or *cloudy versus bright.*

According to Kelly, constructs vary in how broadly or narrowly they are defined. A **loose construct** *("women drivers" or "workaholic husbands") is a construct that covers such a broad range of meanings that it tends to become blurry or indistinct.* On the positive side, loose constructs encourage creativity by applying a "rubber-sheet template" (Kelly, 1955, p. 1031) to experience. We might say that Will Rogers had a *loose construct* for choosing friends ("I never met a man I didn't like").

A **tight construct** *will be highly discriminating.* No Will Rogers here—my "friends" might include only half a dozen persons: my wife, my kids, the best man at my wedding, my racquetball partner, and my fishing buddy. If a construct is too *tight* (e.g., redheads have hot tempers) it can become frozen into rigid, inflexible definitions. For example, if my construct for *chair* is too tight, I will think of it as *only* "something used for sitting" and fail to see its potential uses as a ladder, table, barricade, or TV tray. Contrasting loose and tight constructs, we could say that a "wino" has a loose construct for choosing which wine to drink, whereas the wine taster—employed by the winery to oversee quality control—would have an extremely tight construct for wine flavors. *Artistic talent* is a loose construct, allowing for great variation in what people consider "outstanding." *Pregnancy* is quintessentially "tight"—either you're pregnant or you're not.

Constructs are meaning-making devices. If Kelly's constructs and corollaries sound exceedingly cerebral or abstract, don't be mistaken, Kelly viewed constructs as cognitive processes for making sense of everyday life. Without patterns the world would appear homogenous and undifferentiated. "Even a poor fit is more helpful . . . than nothing at all" (Kelly, 1955, p. 9). "Personal constructs are not abstractions that float around in thin air," he insisted. They represent the ways we deal with things" (Kelly, 1969, p. 172).

The "unconscious" mind (preverbal, submerged, and suspended constructs). In contrast to Freud, who placed so much emphasis on unconscious motivation, Kelly mentioned the unconscious only briefly, and almost with reluctance: "We do not use the conscious–unconscious dichotomy, but we do recognize that some of the personal constructs a person seeks to subsume within his system prove to be fleeting or elusive" (Kelly, 1969, p. 92). Still, although Kelly found Freud's "unconscious" distasteful to his own Kansas prairie pragmatism, he could not completely escape it, so he dealt with the "unconscious" through less-than-aware constructs that called *preverbal, submerged,* or *suspended.*

Preverbal construct. Long before verbal fluency is possible, the newborn begins to construe his or her world. Since humans are *construing* organisms from the moment of birth, Kelly believed that babies construe their experience using nonverbal symbols—beginning with Mother: "Thus one's mother become a symbol for the services upon which one sees himself as being dependent for life and sustenance" (1955, p. 459).

Submerged and suspended constructs. Since all constructs have two poles, Kelly sometimes referred to the less-aware pole as the "unconscious" or "submerged" end. Another way Kelly dealt with low awareness was with the notion of *suspension.* Kelly admitted that sometimes a particular construction is incompatible with a person's overall system, so it must be held in abeyance or suspended until a construct system is created that can assimilate or utilize it. The sort of "forgetting" that occurs when incompatible structures are present is similar to "repression" in other theories. Kelly preferred his own term: he called it *"suspension"* (1955, p. 473, emphasis in original).

Defense mechanisms. It comes as no surprise that, having largely dispensed with unconscious motivation, Kelly did not favor a defense-mechanism analysis of behavior. Instead, he redefined classical Freudian defense mechanisms in Personal-Construct terms. As we just learned, Kelly saw *repression* as a *suspension* of the construing process. Similarly, other Freudian defense mechanisms were redefined in Kelly's cognitive format. *Identification* and *introjection* referred to taking over constructs from other family members or acquaintances (Kelly, 1955, p. 768). *Regression* referred to the use of preverbal or very immature constructs (Kelly, 1955, p. 997). Kelly saw *reaction-formation* as the attempt to put the opposite construct pole into effect in spite of the fact that it was the other pole that carried significance for the person.

"Self" as a role construct. Kelly was *not* a self theorist, and he didn't think of the *self* as an agentic entity. Instead (like Sullivan) he saw clusters of self experiences in which a person *compares himself to others* as a way of socially gauging behavior: "Thus, much of his social life is controlled by the comparisons he has come to see between himself and others" (Kelly, 1955, p. 131).

Names, nicknames, and curses as constructs. According to Kelly, even a person's name or nickname can be understood as a personal construct. As he picturesquely put it: "One cannot call another person a bastard without making bastardy a dimension of his own life also" (Kelly, 1955, p. 133). Never tiring of reminding his reader of the bipolar nature of constructs, Kelly pointed out that calling another person a bastard may be a way of seeing oneself as definitely *not* a bastard. Similarly, when we nickname someone "Baldy," "Fatso," or "Sawed-off," it might mean that hair, weight, or height are important dimensions in our own lives. To put it more positively, when we refer to another as "Sugar," "Little Professor," or "Lover" it suggests we value sweetness, intelligence, or sexuality as important personality dimensions in our own lives.

Role constructs—seeing things from another person's perspective. Kelly used the term **role construct** for constructions that: ". . . provide the person with some notion of how matters appear to the other person, then we give them a special name, *role constructs*" (Kelly, 1969, p. 178).

What Makes a Person Go?

Hitting the ground with your feet running. In spite of his strong disclaimers to the contrary ["personal construct theory completely abandons the notion of motivation" (1969, p. 169)], Kelly did not so much abandon motivation as redefine it: ". . . we accept the view that the organism is already in motion simply by virtue of its being alive . . ." (Kelly, 1969, p. 81).

For Kelly, the person is not a caboose, passively pulled along a predetermined track by a train of incentives; nor is a person pushed around by the undercurrents of unconscious motivation: "For our purposes, the person is not an object which is temporarily in a moving state but is himself a form of motion" (Kelly, 1955, p. 48). Echoing Adler, Kelly saw all such "motion" as anticipatory and future-oriented: *"A person lives his life by reaching out for what comes next and the only channels he has for reaching are the personal constructions he is able to place upon what may actually be happening"* (Kelly, 1969, p. 228).

Construing and reconstruing. For Kelly, **construing** *is interpreting or "making sense" of one's experiences.* This is the motivational fuel that powers the engine of personality. The activity of construing involves constant experimentation, validation, and **reconstruing,** or *reinterpreting and revising one's expectations or hypotheses.* In this way each person's experience "undergoes a progressive evolution. The person reconstrues" (Kelly, 1955, p. 72).

Construction corollary. *We anticipate events by noticing recurrent themes.* As Kelly phrased it, "A person anticipates events by construing their replications" (1955, p. 50). The term **construe** means *to make an interpretation—to explain or try to make sense of an experience.* When a person *construes* an experience, she notices which elements in a series are similar and which are dissimilar. Or, as Kelly picturesquely put it, "To construe is to hear the whisper of recurrent themes in the events that reverberate around us" (1955, p. 76).

Regularity runs through our lives like a river, and although philosophers assert that a person can't "step into the same river twice," Kelly asserted that the regularity of recurring events allows us to anticipate and make predictions. So, although each day is a unique segment of the incessant stream of time—a stream we can never step into twice in precisely the same place—Kelly believed that we could still find recurrent themes in the stream of time, for example, "the rising and the setting of the sun" (1955, p. 53).

Choice corollary. *When we come to a fork in the road, we choose the most promising path.* Kelly said that people choose alternatives that "make more and more of life's experiences meaningful" (1955, p. 66).

Sociality corollary. *To the extent that we can anticipate and understand someone else's thinking processes, we can interact socially with him.* In his *sociality corollary* Kelly defined the term **role** to mean *understanding the expectations of others so well that instructions aren't necessary.* As Kelly put it, "a role is a position that one can play on a certain team without even waiting for the signals" (1955, p. 98). Thus, "playing a role" for Kelly does *not* mean being phony or faking it; to the contrary, it means becoming socially involved with others. However, in order to be involved one must first understand where the other person is coming from—how *she* see things. Thus to say "I'll play shortstop," or "I'll pitch," one must understand how others *construe* those positions.

This corollary contains Kelly's major statement on social relationships, and locates this part of his theory in the *Social Zone.* He believed that in order to successfully interact with others, we must first take their perceptions into account. He cited the "extremely complex, and precise weaving of traffic" as an example of how we "stake our lives" on our ability to predict what the drivers of cars we are meeting will do (1955, p. 95).

What Makes a Person Grow?

Kelly didn't formulate developmental stages as did Freud, Erikson, or the object-relations theorists. He didn't delve into biological beginnings or circular reactions as did Piaget. In place of *stages,* Kelly described two major *cycles* of change: the *Creativity Cycle* (cultivating creativity) and the *C-P-C Cycle* (promoting decision making). We will consider these in more detail at the end of this section.

Construing preverbal development. With his emphasis on *present* and *future* behavior, it is perhaps not surprising that Kelly formulated few developmental constructs. Nonetheless, like most personality theorists Kelly could not sidestep completely the importance of early development, so he formulated a **dependency construct:** *a tendency to use people as symbols for constructs.* Previously, we discussed how *preverbal* and *submerged* constructs form during the earliest weeks of life as newborns use their caretakers as construct surrogates.

Construing early caretakers. Kelly's developmental psychology isn't anything like that of the object-relations theorists for whom the maternal breast was the fount of all good things. He describes the mother as a point of intersection of the child's earliest constructs. Since the baby has little verbal capacity, Mother "represents the intersect of certain personal construct dimensions . . . their point of intersection becomes, in the child's eyes, the Mother figure" (Kelly, 1955, p. 297).

Construing social development. Kelly described a **commonality corollary:** *When we feel as if we're on "the same wavelength" as someone else, it is because our construction of events—not necessarily the events themselves—is similar.* This corollary highlights Kelly's conviction that how we subjectively construe our experience matters most. Two people may have identical experiences but construe them differently; or, they may have distinctly different experiences, yet construe them similarly. It's all in the construction.

Construing language development. Kelly was fascinated by the potential of language to create what he termed an **invitational mood,** *a "Let's-pretend" way of creatively considering new ways to construe experience.* Thus, instead of simply saying "The floor *is* hard," Kelly suggested that an *invitational* use of language might lead one to wonder "What if the floor were made of foam rubber? . . . plastic? . . . jello?" Such questions, suggested Kelly, "invite the listener to cope with his circumstances—in this case, the floor—in new ways" (Kelly, 1969, p. 149). Like Adler, Kelly was intrigued by Vaihinger's "as if" philosophy (Vaihinger, 1911), finding it compatible with his own construing approach.

Summary of developmental cycles. In Kelly's theory, maturity does not result from weaning, solving oedipal conflicts, compensating for organ inferiority, or learning to manage interpersonal anxiety; rather, it results from *continuous cycles of construing experience.* We will conclude this section by considering Kelly's two major cycles of change: the Creativity Cycle and the C-P-C Cycle. Kelly saw these two cycles as complementary.

Creativity Cycle. Kelly said: "Creativity always arises out of preposterous thinking." He defined the **Creativity Cycle** in the following words: *"The Creativity Cycle is one which starts with loosened construction and terminates with tightened and validated construction"* (Kelly, 1955, p. 528, emphasis in original). Such "loosened construction" allows additional elements to be added to a personal construct. At the beginning stages of treatment, a Kellyian psychotherapist encourages "loosening" of all constructs. *Loosening* increases the client's tolerance for ambiguity, resulting in more freedom to construe problems in creative ways. Kelly characterized therapy as "a series of Creativity Cycles. . . . The therapist tries to help the client release his imagination and then harness it" (1955, p. 529).

Loosening of personal constructs might be seen as similar to the psychoanalytic processes of free association—encouraging the client to "Say whatever comes to mind—even if it doesn't make sense." However, Kelly did not see the contents of such free associations as "true thoughts" or "deep insights"; rather, he viewed them as "new hypotheses which must still be tightened up and tested before they are to be accepted as useful" (1955, p. 530). Instead of seeing this process as plumbing the depths of the unconscious, Kelly believed loosened constructs allowed new constructs to take shape "within the vague mass" of newly loosened constructs.

He warned that a balance must be struck between loosening and tightening, because if one's constructions were too "tight" creativity would be stifled; however, too-loose constructions would also hinder creativity because such a person "would never get around to setting up a hypothesis for crucial testing" (Kelly, 1955, p. 529). Kelly viewed psychotherapy as a creative process in which the therapist facilitates the client's movement through a series of Creativity Cycles, much as one might conduct a series of scientific experiments.

C-P-C Cycle. Running alongside the *Creativity Cycle* is the **C-P-C Cycle,** *"a sequence of construction involving, in succession, circumspection, preemption, and control and leading to a choice which precipitates the person into a particular situation"* (Kelly, 1955, p. 515). Kelly believed that the C-P-C cycle can be used not only in psychotherapy but in everyday life, to facilitate change.

The first **C** stands for **circumspection,** in which *a person mulls over various possibilities, tentatively construing a problem from many different angles, remaining open to alternative hypotheses.* In this phase, "Any roundish mass . . . may be considered . . . a ball" (Kelly, 1955, p. 155).

The **P** stands for **preemption:** *the elements of a construct are preempted for exclusive membership within a construct.* Thus, having decided that "a chair is a chair," *preemption* implies that it is nothing but a chair, and cannot be subsumed under any other construct (e.g., ladder, table, barricade). Whereas *circumspection* considers adding further elements, *preemption* rules them out: "Preemption commits one to handling a given situation at a given time in one way and in one way only" (Kelly, 1955, p. 520). If "ball" is your preemptive construct, you can rule out other roundish "nonball" items such as marshmallows, balloons, or BBs.

Preemptive constructs can be negative, as in the case of gender-biased or racist constructs. A man who says "Well, what did you expect from a woman driver?" implies that *all* females hesitate for too long at intersections, or lack essential driving skills that males are genetically endowed with. On the other hand, preemptive constructs can be positive as well, by eliminating numerous alternatives in order to take specific action. Because one cannot "mount a horse and ride off in all directions," it is necessary in life to finally make a decision. Shakespeare's Hamlet knew he could not spend his life *circumspectly* pondering whether "To be, or not to be," so he *preemptively* decided to kill Claudio. And so it is with all of us: not only in love and war, but in ordinary life, "he who hesitates (for too long) loses."

The final **C** *stands for both choice and control.* At this point, a person *chooses* a construct from among the alternatives—a construct that promises greater fulfillment and extension of his or her system. *Control* results from the preemptive *choice* of an alternative, because in order to achieve control of self or situation, a person must preemptively choose a course of action and then (as the Nike ads put it) "Just do it!"

According to Kelly, the *self-controlled* person tends to construe himself in one way, and one way only: "For example, in combat, the soldier usually performs most effectively if he construes himself as a soldier and as nothing else" (Kelly, 1955, p. 521). If he thinks of himself as a husband, father, friend, teacher, or member of the Rotary club, he may find it difficult to "climb out of his foxhole at zero hour" (1955, p. 521).

Thus, in the end, creativity (as delineated in the *Creativity Cycle*) and control (as outlined in the *C-P-C Cycle*) operate in tandem, counterbalancing each other much as looseness and tightness of constructs balance one another. Control and prediction emerge from this balance. Loose constructs, such as "tomorrow's weather" or "variables influencing the stock market" allow for plausible or probabilistic predictions; tight constructs, such as pregnancy, death, or taxes allow for absolute predictions. In this way Kelly's developmental process is reminiscent of Piaget's *assimilation–accommodation* process or Erik Erikson's *mutual regulation.*

What Makes a Person Unique?

Individual variation and uniqueness is built into Kelly's system at the very core—at the point of *personal* constructs—each person construes experience in a characteristically distinctive way. *All* personal constructs are *subjective* "templates" for making sense of the world, and since all of these "templates" interact with one another—much as individual instruments in an orchestra intermingle their sounds—the possibilities for unique, one-of-a-kind individuality to emerge are almost limitless. We conclude by considering some corollaries that particularly focus on distinctiveness.

Individuality corollary. *Each of us construes our experiences differently.* This corollary emphasizes Kelly's conviction that it is the *subjective interpretation* of an experience that counts most. For Kelly, not only does beauty reside "in the eye of the beholder," *everything* does!

Modulation corollary. *Our personal constructs are open to change and alteration, limited primarily by their permeability, or the ease with which they can assimilate new experiences.*

Persons vary considerably in how *permeable* their constructs are, and this variation contributes to the individual differences we see among people.

Some people's constructs are more **permeable,** that is *open to experience,* than others'. *Permeable constructs* have the capacity to include new elements. "Loyalty" might be permeable enough to include not only one's immediate family and friends, but new work associates, a new baseball franchise, or a new employer. If, for example, a certain person's "family" construct were relatively **impermeable** *(one that does not easily add new elements)*, she might have difficulty "accepting" a new daughter-in-law or relating to a stepchild.

Roles and social interactions. From what we've discovered up to this point, you might have guessed that psychotherapy with Kelly as your therapist would be a highly cognitive, private, analyze-your-constructs sort of process. Wrong! Surprisingly, when it came to therapy, Kelly was far more interpersonal than we might have expected— far more Sullivanian than Freudian or cognitive.

In Kellyan psychotherapy both the clinician and the client play specific *roles*. However, Kelly strongly emphasized that *playing a role* is *not* to be confused with some sort of phony social posturing; rather it refers to the ongoing process of seeking to understand someone else's construct system in order to mesh more comfortably with them. This sort of understanding is not to be confused with *empathy*, which implies a reciprocal sharing of understanding or feelings. Playing one's role (position on the team) doesn't mean someone else will necessarily be in the same space (you don't need two shortstops on a team), only that you will understand what others expect of you in a particular position. Kelly thought of the management of transference and countertransference in psychoanalysis as an example of the development of *roles* for both the patient and the analyst.

The Role Construct Repertory Test (Rep Test). The **Rep Test** *asks the responder to compare more than twenty different people (e.g., the most interesting, intelligent, or successful people you know, as well as people who appear to dislike you, neighbors you find you hard to understand, etc.) as to differences and similarities.*

The person taking the *Rep Test* considers twenty-two different social roles: father, mother, sister, spouse, brother, boss, minister, friend, etc. The responder is asked to consider a specific triad (e.g., mother, boss, friend) and write down how two of these people are alike, yet different from a third. Then another combination of three is given, and the respondent again lists similarities and differences. This procedure is repeated a dozen or two dozen times—sometimes more.

By thus mapping each person's distinctive configuration of personal constructs, Kelly hoped to delineate not only the "point of intersection" of how a child viewed her mother, but also of how she viewed herself and significant others as well. By identifying the unique constructions people make for themselves, Kelly hoped to grasp each person's own singular slant on life, and to avoid pigeonholing or labeling.

Fixed-Role therapy—"fake it till you make it." Kelly believed that you *are* what you construe yourself to be. It's not surprising that he developed a style of therapy called **Fixed-role therapy,** *a process in which you "try on" a new identity, behave in unprecedented ways, and ultimately free yourself to become a different person. Fixed-role therapy* was not designed to be therapy or healing so much as it was meant to be an exercise in self-experimentation. Kelly believed that no one needed to be trapped by their life histories or their conflicted drives, and *fixed-role therapy* was his device for freeing people for new beginnings: "Any attempt to make it a *repair* process rather than a *creative* process seems to result in some measure of failure" (Kelly, 1955, p. 380, emphasis in the original).

After a client had been in therapy for a few sessions, Kelly might ask him or her to write down a self-character sketch, describing himself as if he were the principal actor in a play. Then Kelly and his associates would write out a **fixed role,** *a role that contrasted with the client's self-characterization.*

From "Ronald Barrett" to "Kenneth Norton." Kelly reported the self-characterization of one of his patients, "Ronald Barrett," who described himself as frequently arguing with people and trying to prove his point. By contrast, Kelly and his panel of clinicians wrote a script for Ronald—changing his name to "Kenneth Norton"—that portrayed a person characterized "by the understanding way in which he listens" and who became completely absorbed "in the thoughts of the people with whom he holds conversations" (1955a, p. 374).

"Ronald Barrett" was instructed to *pretend* for two weeks that he was "Kenneth Norton." This was followed by several sessions that involved *rehearsing* how "Kenneth Norton" might act at work, in social relations with other males, in social situations involving a spouse or females, in situations with parents, and in situations involving life plans. According to Kelly's account, after a period of time "Ronald Barrett" was able to construe himself in a more open and friendly way with others by adopting aspects of "Kenneth Norton" into his own life.

FACING THE TOUGH TWINS

Is It Testable?

Cognitive complexity. One of Kelly's students (Bieri, 1955) used the Rep Test to distinguish between cognitively complex and cognitively simple persons, and found (consistent with Kelly's theory) that cognitively complex persons were significantly better at predicting how others would behave. Subsequently, a whole array of variables have been shown to be related to cognitive complexity, including *age* (Vacc & Greenleaf, 1975), *vocational choice* (Bodden, 1970; Neimeyer, 1992), *marital satisfaction* (Neimeyer, 1984), *the ability to cope with stress* (Smith & Cohen, 1993), and even *decisions of Supreme Court justices* (Gruenfeld, 1995).

Built-in diversity—international appeal. The color-blind, gender-neutral individuality of personal construct theory has undoubtedly contributed to its rising popularity in the international community. Neimeyer and Jackson (1997) describe an international network of research centers involved in investigating personal construct theory:

> The outpouring of nearly 3,000 conceptual, clinical, and empirical publications generated by this international community (the majority in the last decade) demonstrates that interest in personal construct theory continues to burgeon; there is no indication that interest in the theory has peaked or entered a period of decline across its 35-year history. (p. 370)

The relationship between traits and Kelly's personal constructs. Recent research (Robinson & Clore, 2002; Robinson, Solberg, Vargas, & Tamir, 2003) has generally supported Kelly's notion that personal constructs (categorization tendencies) are predictive of emotional states. However, this research has shown that emotional outcomes also depend on a person's traits. Thus, the most current thinking is that traits and personal constructs *interactively* determine emotional states.

Is It Useful?

The Rep Test. Although many aspects of Kelly's theory have received research attention, the *Rep Test* has been most widely investigated—especially in industrial–organizational settings (Bannister & Fransella, 1971). Since market researchers are interested in how consumers might perceive a product, the Rep Test has been used to determine how consumers construe various products. Stewart & Stewart (1982) cite numerous examples where the Rep Test has been applied to business. In one study, for example, the Rep Test was used to explore what "constructs" consumers used in evaluating various cosmetics and perfumes. Since consumers make purchasing decisions based on such constructs, advertisers can use such information to appeal to potential buyers. In training management personnel, variations of the personal construct grid have proved useful in facilitating the transmission of corporate philosophy to incoming junior executives (Eden & Sims, 1981). In the area of product quality control, repertory grid techniques have been utilized in assessing which constructs experienced inspectors use in judging the quality of merchandise.

Using grid assessment techniques, researchers found that quality-control inspectors of Teddy Bears judged the toys to be defective if the distance between the eyes and nose was not equal to the distance between the nose and mouth, or the dark material used for the pupil of the eye was not in the center of the white. Prior to assessment, inspectors intuitively referred to "feelings of rightness" but could not specify how they reached their judgments. Grid-based information allowed the company to train future Teddy Bear inspectors to inspect with more ease and consistency (Stewart & Stewart, 1982). Other business applications have included utilizing Personal Construct theory to develop employee training programs (Easterby-Smith, 1980), and to assess how bank officers judged loan applicants (Jankowicz & Hisrich, 1987).

Fixed-role psychotherapy. We discussed earlier how Kelly and his students liked to enliven their therapy sessions with *role-playing* situations. Kelly saw role playing as a way to help clients develop their social skills for interacting with others. Role reversals might occupy no more than a few minutes during therapy, but Kelly believed they were crucial in helping people to approach life with an "as-if" perspective, testing how various personal constructs functioned in the real world. Clearly, when it came to therapy, Kelly was very *interpersonal*.

SUMMARY OF KELLY

A "jackass" theory of personality. For Kelly, "person as scientist" meant that the person was an active *constructor* rather than a passive *reactor*. Describing his own theory as a "jackass" theory captured Kelly's Kansas–farm boy resistance to the popular dogmas of his day:

> Motivational theories can be divided into two types, push theories and pull theories. . . . In terms of a well-known metaphor, these are the pitchfork theories on the one hand and the carrot theories on the other. But our theory is neither

of these. Since we prefer to look to the nature of the animal himself, ours is probably best called a jackass theory. (Kelly, 1958, p. 50)

In this context, Kelly uses "jackass" not to convey stupidity or ignorance, but rather to portray humans as stubbornly unique—unyieldingly resistant to simply falling into line. Instead of viewing the person as a Pavlovian dog under harness, passively salivating in response to programmed stimuli, Kelly saw people as more similar to farm mules—practical but self-directed, actively resisting attempts at being harnessed into conformity.

"Stubborn" humanist. Kelly was one of the presenters at the Old Saybrook Conference, where humanistic psychology was founded (Fadiman & Frager, 2002). It was Kelly's insistence that people are able to reinvent and renew themselves that won him a place in the humanists' hall of fame—alongside Rogers, Maslow, May, and others.

Interpersonal constructivist. Kelly's theory might appear *intrapsychic* in portraying personality as a composite of personal constructs; however, when it comes to *changing* (oneself or others) the focus is clearly *interpersonal.* The Rep Test, for example, was designed to assess not only how respondents formed personal constructs, but how they perceived the constructs of socially significant others. Many of Kelly's therapeutic techniques are highly interpersonal in nature, consistent with his notion that interpersonal roles are the bread and butter of everyday life.

Pioneer postmodernist. Using the fulcrum of constructivism, Kelly pried psychology loose from the grip of behaviorism and scientism, and in so doing anticipated postmodernism's cynicism regarding our ability to receive "truth" from "authorities." Kelly said, "One need not assume he has possession of any shiny bits of 'revealed truth,' picked up either on Mt. Sinai or in a psychological laboratory" (Kelly, 1977, pp. 1–19).

Responsible existentialist. Although Kelly shared much of postmodernism's cynicism regarding certainty and authority, he was in sharp disagreement regarding personal responsibility. Here he was aligned with existentialists and others who assert that humans are conscious, self-determining, and *responsible!* He left no doubt here: "So one's construction of a situation, for which he must always take full personal responsibility—whether he can put it into words or not—provides the initial grounds for seeking experience with events" (1977, pp. 1–19).

There is little doubt that Kelly would have taken issue with postmodernism's attempt to "delegitimate all mastercodes" (Hassan, 1987, p. 169). Reduction of the world's great religions to the same status as Stalinism, witchcraft, or astrology would doubtless have drawn fire from Kelly, who was a practicing Christian his entire life. He would have strongly disagreed with postmodernism's attempt to reduce "Marxism, Christianity, Fascism, Stalinism, capitalism, liberal democracy, secular humanism, feminism, Islam, and modern science to the same order," dismissing them all as "logocentric, transcendental totalizing meta-narratives that anticipate all questions and provide predetermined answers" (Rosenau, 1992, p. 6). And he would most certainly have challenged Schweder's (1986, p. 11) assertion that all such systems of thought rest on assumptions no more or less certain than those of witchcraft, astrology, or primitive cults.

Never one to argue for absolute certainty or unequivocal truth, Kelly nonetheless believed that some constructions were better than others: ". . . it is important to appreciate the fact that there have been some mighty ingenious approximations of truth, and some can be shown to be a lot better than others. Still, ingenious as these approximations are, one may live in the *faith* that better ones can be contrived . . ." (1977, pp. 1–19).

ALBERT ELLIS—ECLECTIC CONSTRUCTIVIST

Many might think Ellis misplaced in this chapter, as he is most often perceived to be a *cognitive behaviorist*. However, from a zonal perspective, he appears to be an inside-out *constructivist* rather than an outside-in *situationist*. Although Ellis focuses on changing *behaviors,* he does this by first changing *internal cognitions* much as Kelly might try to "loosen" or "tighten" constructs. Whereas behaviorists manipulate the situational variables in order to shape personality (outside-in), constructivists recon-figure internal meanings or personal constructs as a way of facilitating behavioral changes (inside-out). By challenging a person's maladaptive thinking ("nutty beliefs" as Ellis likes to call them) from the inside, Ellis seeks to change overt behaviors. That is not how behaviorists operate.

Still others might question Ellis's appearing as a personality psychologist, since most of his work was in the clinical arena, operating as a cognitive learning theorist. Nevertheless, as we said earlier, any psychologist who attempts to alter behavior in a practical setting must become—at least temporarily—a personality psychologist, ask-ing, What are the parts—how is this person wired? What makes her go—what makes her tick? In this sense, Ellis passes muster. He clearly and repeatedly stated his convic-tion that all of life revolves around how you *construct* your belief systems. Our discus-sion will be relatively brief, because his work is well known, and references abound.

The eclectic constructivism of Albert Ellis. Albert Ellis's theory of personal-ity was developed around his theory of **Rational–Emotive Behavior Therapy (REBT),** *a form of therapy in which "irrational" beliefs (e.g., "I must be loved by everyone") existing in the form of "self talk" are challenged by direct confrontation.* First outlined in journal articles (Ellis, 1955, 1958) and subsequently detailed in books (Ellis, 1962, 1978, 1991; Ellis & Harper, 1975; Ellis & Becker, 1982), REBT has been widely uti-lized, and is usually described as a form of cognitive-behavioral therapy. Subse-quently, Ellis continued to modify and expand his therapy techniques (e.g., Ellis & Becker, 1982; Ellis & Harper, 1975; Ellis, 1991), expanding the techniques—and even the name—from Rational Therapy (RT) to Rational Emotive Therapy (RET) to Rational Emotive Behavior Therapy (REBT) to reflect the behavioral component that has always been present.

Background Check

A neglected child. Albert Ellis (1913–) felt neglected as a child, describing himself as a "semi-orphan," since his father traveled a great deal and spent little time with his chil-dren. His mother, states Ellis, was totally unprepared to raise children, so "I was almost as instrumental in raising my mother (and, to an even greater degree my younger brother and sister) as she was in raising me" (Engler, 1999, p. 420). Neglected by both parents, Ellis was frequently ill and suffered from nephritis, which necessitated frequent hospitalizations. He was not allowed to engage in active play, so—like Adler—Ellis grew up introverted and shy, readily outshone by his extraverted brother.

He attended the High School of Commerce in New York with the dream of becoming a millionaire, but since his graduation coincided with the beginning of the Great Depression, he had to give up that dream. Enrolling in City College, he majored in English (as did B. F. Skinner). After graduation he spent a great deal of time writing, but he could not get any of his six novels published (an experience similar to Skinner's), so he began writing about sexual issues, and friends began to seek his advice. Since he enjoyed counseling, he decided to pursue graduate study in psychology, and received his Ph.D. from Teachers College of Columbia University.

Inferiorities and compensation. Ellis appears as yet another example of Adler's notion of inferiorities and compensation. The shy, none-too-attractive introvert launched his career in clinical psychology by writing about—what else?—sex. After his books on sex became popular, he devoted the rest of his long career to helping people overcome their various hangups—which turned out to be pretty much whatever Ellis thought were "nutty beliefs." Equally impressive was his compensation in the area of physical inferiorities. The physical problems of childhood continued to plague him as an adult. He suffered his entire life from a variety of physical ailments (diabetes, poor hearing, weak eyesight, and other handicaps) that would have sidelined the less resilient. Even in his nineties, Ellis practiced psychotherapy, wrote articles, engaged in symposia discussions, and made professional presentations. Although his critics might argue (with some validity) that Ellis simply rephrased his same basic idea several hundred times, his prodigious output of publications assured him a permanent place among the great names of psychology. Knowing of his diabetes and other physical problems, it was inspiring to all but the most cynical to see this feisty, ninety-year-old man at psychology conventions, making presentations, reiterating his theories, and peppering his opponents with profanities.

Zeitgeist

Describing his clinical career, Ellis said, "I was a good young psychoanalyst at this time. . . . And my therapeutic results were, so far as I could see, as good as those of other New York analysts" (Ellis, 1962, p. 4). However, he soon became impatient with what he deemed an inefficient process:

> Long, unhelpful silences (sometimes for practically the entire analytic session) would frequently occur, while I (in accordance with classical technique) sat idly by with a limply held pencil. Quite consistently, although I did my best to hold them with their backs rooted to the sofa, patients would want to jump up and pace across the room, or sit up and look at me, or do everything but stare reflectively at the ceiling. Ever so often, they would bitterly turn on me, complain that I wasn't doing anything to help them, and say that that was just about all they could stand of this kind of nonsense. (Ellis, 1962, p. 5)

Verbal reinfection. Ellis came to believe that a much more active approach was needed in order to keep people from verbally "reinfecting" themselves. He concluded that people

> ". . . actively-directively *kept* reindoctrinating themselves with the original hogwash, over and over again, and thereby creatively *made* it live on and on and

become an integral part of their basic philosophies of life." (Ellis, 1962, pp. 20–21, emphasis in original)

The fact that humans talk to themselves and others "enabled them to abuse this facility by talking utter nonsense to themselves: to *define* things as terrible when, at worst, these things were inconvenient and annoying" (1962, pp. 20–21).

A new philosophical slant—therapist as counter-propagandist (counter-constructivist). Armed with this insight, Ellis's work with patients "took on a radically new slant . . . I had been stressing psychodynamic rather than philosophical causation, and had been emphasizing what to undo rather than what to un*say* and un*think*" (1962, p. 22). Ellis concluded that the therapist must function as a "frank counter-propagandist who directly contradicts and denies self-defeating propaganda and superstitions which the patient has originally learned and which he is now self-instilling" (1962, p. 95). Ellis believe that it was usually necessary to convince the patient to actually *do* something different as well:

> The rational–emotive behavior therapist encourages, persuades, cajoles, and occasionally even insists that the patient engage in some activity (such as doing something he is afraid of doing) which itself will serve as a forceful counter-propaganda agency against the nonsense he believes. (1962, p. 95)

"Nutty beliefs" and "musterbation." The pivotal concept of Ellis's entire system is the **irrational ("nutty") belief,** which is *an illogical idealization or catastrophic exaggeration that frequently includes a "must" or a "should" (e.g., "Since I treat others with consideration, they <u>must</u>, in turn, treat me with respect." "I <u>must</u> pass this exam, or I'm an <u>awful</u> person!" "If <u>everyone</u> doesn't approve of me, It's <u>awful!</u>").*

"Nutty beliefs" (Ellis's term for illogical thinking) include absolutistic demands for perfection, frequently accompanied by an exaggerated sense of disaster or unworthiness when one is less than perfect (as, in daily life, is usually the case). Such a person is caught in cognitive conflict between irrational or exaggerated expectations for performance ("I *must* be perfect!") and an exaggerated fear of consequences ("I *must* get everyone to like me, or I'm a *total loser!*").

Over and over again. Ellis's treatment consists of pointing out to the client the illogical nature of his or her beliefs (expectations) for self and others. Consistent with his own personality style of repeating and rephrasing his ideas again and again (Ellis published several hundred articles, and numerous books in which he repeated the same ideas like a mantra), Ellis advised therapists to ". . . keep pounding away, time and time again at the illogical ideas which underlie that patient's fears and hostilities" (1962, p. 96).

ASKING THE BIG FOUR QUESTIONS

What Are the Parts?

Ellis was primarily interested in techniques of psychotherapy; consequently in his writing and work, therapy has always been the tail that wagged the personality dog. For Ellis, personality is important only as it relates to therapy. In what follows we will discuss personality from the perspective of therapy, because that's how Ellis presented it.

TABLE 10.2

Ellis's A–B–C Theory of Motivation

A

B

C

According to Ellis's A–B–C theory of motivation, a person typically believes that an emotionally charged situation **(C)** is the result of an activating event **(A)**. However, Ellis insisted that emotional states are the result of personal expectations/beliefs **(B)**. Ellis was famous for saying "A never leads to C, it always leads to B." He dubbed many such personal beliefs as "irrational" or "nutty."

The ABC's of Ellis's theory of personality. Ellis's A–B–C theory of personality *asserts that cognitive beliefs—not actual events—cause emotional responses.* For example, even when it appears that an *activating event A* (such as being chased by a dog) causes an intense *emotional response C* (extreme fear), the *real reason* for emotional consequences is *B (the belief system)* that "All dogs are dangerous." Ellis was fond of saying, "A never leads to C! A always leads to B." By this he emphasized the central role of beliefs (cognitions) in causing emotional reactions. I remember Ellis using the following illustration during one of his workshops I attended some years ago:

> Imagine you're sitting on a crowded bus and this big, clumsy person comes ambling down the aisle and steps on your toe **(A)** as he walks by your seat. That makes you angry **(C)**, and you think to yourself "Watch where you're going. Idiot! But, Ellis reminded us, "**A** (pain in my toe) never leads to **C** (anger); what leads to anger is my **B** (belief) "That idiot *should* watch where he's going!" "Imagine," said Ellis, "that as you're getting ready to give this guy a sharp elbow in the side you notice he's carrying a white cane and wearing dark glasses. *Instantly* your anger vanishes. Why? Because you have a different set of **B** (beliefs) for blind people. Your toe still hurts **(A)**, but instead of seething with *rage* you're feeling **(C)** *chagrined,* thinking 'I almost clobbered a blind person!'"

Then, with a grin on his face, in his slightly whiney voice Ellis reminded us *again* (he was *not* reluctant to repeat himself!) *"A never leads to C, A always leads to B."* Lesson learned!

However, since the sum of one's beliefs constitute a person's philosophy of life, and since this is precisely what Ellis strived to change, REBT is ultimately a constructivist existential treatment. Ellis tried construct new thoughts—a new philosophy of life—which he believed would result in changes in emotions and in behavior.

What Makes a Person Go?

Motives and emotions are learned. Reacting against the view that people are hopelessly enslaved by their sinful natures or by unconscious motives, Ellis stated that

> . . . so-called emotions or motivations of adult human beings . . . largely consist of attitudes, perceptual biases, beliefs, assumptions, and ideas which are acquired by biosocial learning and which therefore can be reviewed, questioned, challenged, reconstructed, and changed with sufficient effort and practice on the part of the emoting individual. (1962, p. 125)

Unlike Freud and others whose primary concern was the underlying *motives* of patients, Ellis relegates motives to a taken-for-granted status, and assumes that people have the power to choose and to change. Sounding very much like an existentialist, Ellis contended that the power of choice is accompanied with personal responsibility:

> RT [Rational Therapy], then, gives the individual a fully realistic view of marriage and the fact that he'd better stop blaming his fiancee or wife and buckle down to cultivating his *own* marital garden in a more efficient manner. But it also gives him the "idealistic" philosophy that, win or lose, he is still largely the master of his own fate and the captain of his own soul. . . . It encourages him. . . . to assume full responsibility for his own actions and reactions. . . . (Ellis, 1962, p. 230)

Thus, for Ellis, feelings and emotions do not "well up inside" to energize behavior; motives are not derived from Freud's "seething cauldron" of impulses; rather, it is our *learned* beliefs and expectations that motivationally push us around. The good news, according to Ellis, was that we could *relearn* new beliefs and outfit ourselves with new motives.

What Makes a Person Grow?

Ellis viewed children as impulsive, irrational, impressionable, and limited in their ability to think logically. His developmental theory could succinctly be summarized as "Grow up!"

Children are naturally irrational. Children, according to Ellis, cannot help themselves—they are intrinsically irrational:

> I have personally believed for many years that man inherits a predisposition to think unclearly during his childhood and that it is very easy, and entirely statistically normal, for him to continue unthinkingly to accept and act upon, during his adulthood, the most ridiculous, unsensible, and often insane assumptions and conceptions. (1962, p. 347).

When carried into adult life—as they frequently are—numerous childhood thinking patterns contribute to a life of neurotic irrationality. Ellis contends that children are shortsighted, highly suggestible, and naturally irrational.

Ellis didn't see childhood (as did Piaget) as a time of great creativity and evolving capacities. Rather, he viewed it as a time when the child is particularly vulnerable to the irrationalities of society and particularly prone to incorporate these as a working set of ("irrational") rules for dealing with life.

What Makes a Person Unique?

Ellis believed that a person's uniqueness resulted from the distinctive configuration of cognitions and "rules" that were learned during childhood and are carried into adult life. However, for Ellis the person is much more than a Watsonian "blank slate" upon which the environment writes a unique history:

> A man's existing or being, as the Existentialists point out, is never a static thing, but includes the possibility of his *becoming*—of his creatively making himself into something different from what he is at any given moment. . . . As long as he is *alive,* he can still remain in process, have a future, change himself to a better or more satisfying state. (1962, pp. 152–153)

FACING THE TOUGH TWINS

Is It Testable?

Ellis was an equal-opportunity eclectic constructivist, incorporating useful ideas from many areas of psychology. Even the name changes (Rational Therapy —›Rational Emotive Therapy —›Rational Emotive Behavior Therapy) reflect Ellis's incorporation of "what works" from a wide spectrum of ideas. Ellis & Dryden (1987) pointed out that this sort of pluralism was nothing new to REBT. Accompanying his willingness to utilize ideas from many different sources was Ellis's (1996) recognition that ongoing empirical research is essential for maintaining and enhancing the effectiveness of REBT.

Do changed *beliefs* result in changed *behaviors*? According to Ellis, "Yes." However, research results are mixed. Gossette and O'Brien (1992) carefully analyzed 107 studies of RET that focused solely on therapists' attempts to change irrational beliefs and were *not* accompanied by other interventions (such as behavioral rehearsal, reinforced practice, etc.). They measured irrational thoughts, emotional distress, and behavioral improvements. Compared with other treatments, RET was more successful in changing clients' irrational self-talk in 46 percent of the cases, but when it came to reducing emotional distress RET was more effective in only 27 percent of the cases. Finally, RET had *no measurable effect* on behavioral outcomes such as approaching a feared object. This review suggests that RET therapists may achieve most of their success through various "homework" assignments (e.g., "Practice talking to seat mates on your commuter ride, to lessen your shyness"), rather than by disabusing people of their irrational beliefs.

In another study, Sweet & Loizeaux (1991) compared purely behavioral therapies with the same methods plus an added cognitive component. They found that 83 percent of the studies showed no added benefits when cognitive-restructuring components were added. Only in cases of social anxiety did a cognitive component appear to enhance improvement.

Rational thoughts or rule-governed behavior? These findings suggest that when RET works, it might be because it clarifies *rules that govern behavior*. A **rule** *describes a three-term relationship (antecedents-behavior-consequences)*. As a children, our lives were shaped by *rules:* during supper (antecedent), if you eat your broccoli (behavior), you'll get dessert (consequence). After breakfast (antecedent), if you don't hurry (behavior), you'll miss the school bus (consequence). Adults still follow rules, although often only one term is stated, while the rest are implied. For example, the sign **SCHOOL ZONE** states the *antecedent*, while the *expected behaviors* (slow down) and *consequences* (or you'll get a speeding ticket) are implied.

By clarifying the relationship of behavior to consequences, RET may help clients function more effectively. Thus if you told your RET therapist, "It's *awful,* I just lost my job," she might typically respond, "Just because you lost your job it doesn't make you a rotten person." The research suggests that in such a circumstance, the therapist might be more helpful by suggesting some *rules* (e.g., "If you check the want ads . . ." or "There's an employment agency downtown . . .") that lead to effective action that will be reinforced by the natural environment. Thus, some attempts at cognitive restructuring may prove ineffective because they do not identify specific behaviors or situations that lead to reinforcing consequences.

Is It Useful?

Even the titles of Ellis's books ooze with "how-to" pragmatism: *How to Live with a Neurotic* (1957); *The Art and Science of Love (1960); How to Stubbornly Refuse to Make Yourself Miserable about Anything—Yes Anything* (1988). A good overview of the breadth of Ellis's system can be sampled in his *The Handbook of Rational-Emotive Therapy* (1986);

Ellis & Dryden's *The Practice of Rational Emotive Therapy* (1987); Ellis & Greiger's *Handbook of Rational Emotive Therapy* (1987); and Bernard's (1986) *Staying Alive in an Irrational World: The Psychology of Albert Ellis.*

There can be little doubt that Ellis's theory has proved itself heuristic in a variety of settings with normal as well as dysfunctional personality styles. And although Ellis himself was prone to "pound away" on the merits of REBT, few would question its usefulness for at least some people. Some feminists (e.g., Kantrowitz & Ballou, 1992) have raised concerns that REBT may not be appropriate for Asians, who tend to emphasize emotional harmony with cultural norms, or for women, who might find strength in affiliation rather than in independence.

CONCLUDING COMMENTS REGARDING ELLIS

Constructive existentialism. Ellis viewed people as having the ability to existentially transcend the confines of their surroundings by changing their thoughts. We will consider existential philosophy in more detail in the next chapter; here we simply notice that in the crucible of psychotherapy, where philosophies and theories are smelted into the molten motives that drive daily living, existentialism emerges as Ellis's guiding philosophy:

> Philosophically, the rational–emotive therapist is also quite in sympathy with most of the goals for living of the modern existentialists, such as Buber (1955), Sartre (1957), and Tillich (1953). An excellent list of the main existentialist themes for living has recently been made by Braaten (1961); and, with some relatively minor modifications, these main themes are also dear to the heart of the psychotherapist who practices rational analysis. They include: "(1) Man, you are free, define yourself; (2) Cultivate your own individuality; (3) Live in dialogue with your fellow man; (4) Your own experiencing is the highest authority; (5) Be fully present in the immediacy of the moment; (6) There is no truth except in action; (7) You can transcend yourself in spurts; (8) Live your potentialities creatively; (9) In choosing yourself, you choose man; and (10) You must learn to accept certain limits in life." (Ellis, 1962, pp. 124–125)

Philosophical laundromat. We have seen that for Albert Ellis, rational–emotive therapy functioned somewhat as a philosophical laundromat, allowing neurotics to purge themselves of the "irrational" philosophies that underlie the dysfunctional relationships they maintain with themselves and others. But, we might wonder, how does one arrive at the correct counter-propaganda? Who decides which philosophies are "rational" and which are not? The somewhat snide answer might be: *"Albert Ellis does!"* And critics might charge that Ellis's "laundromat" specializes in *brainwashing!* To which Ellis would reply:

> . . . it is not the *patient* but his *ideas* which are forcefully attacked by the therapist. In political–economic brain-washing, the individual is *himself* attacked. . . . This therapeutic motivation is exactly the opposite of that of the political–economic brain-washer, who obviously does not care for the rights or

well-being of the individual but only for those of the state or system he, the brain-washer, upholds. (1962, p. 369)

It is widely recognized today that all therapists have their own private value systems that cannot be totally kept out of the treatment situation. Most experts agree that therapists ought to be conscious of their own values and communicate something of their general orientation to prospective clients, so that people can "shop" intelligently for a therapist. Ellis said as much over four decades ago:

> . . . the therapist has every right to let his own values be known in the course of the therapeutic sessions . . . since he will consciously or unconsciously tend to communicate his values to his patients, it is better that he do so overtly rather than covertly, with full consciousness of what he is doing. (Ellis, 1962, p. 367)

Similarities of rational–emotive therapists and existential therapists. In conclusion, we have discovered that although Ellis uses the vocabulary of learning theory, his core ideas include constructivist as well as existential (see Chapter 12) elements. Ellis, himself, recognized this:

> . . . the main aims of Existentialist therapists are to help their patients define their own freedom, cultivate their own individuality, live in dialogue with their fellow men, accept their own experiencing as the highest authority, be fully present in the immediacy of the moment, find truth through their own actions, and learn to accept certain limits in life (Braaten, 1961; May, 1961; Royce, 1962). RT practitioners largely accept these views, though they may use somewhat different terminology and emphasis. (Ellis, 1962, pp. 325–326)

CONSTRUCTION OF THE *SELF* IN CONTEMPORARY PERSONALITY PSYCHOLOGY

Before concluding our chapter, we will briefly consider how the construction of *self* has fared among contemporary constructivists.

The person-as-agent in constructivist theories. We have just discovered that in spite of great diversity among them, constructivists view the *person* as the epicenter of meaning making. The *self* or the *person*—not the environment or the unconscious mind—is the constructing, meaning-making nucleus of personality. Focus shifts away from situational stimuli to the *agentic self* (centered within the person and actively *constructing* the situation rather than merely *responding* to it). This changes how we view the *self* in our postmodern world.

Self as architect. An energetic debate is currently under way among personality psychologists regarding the role of the *self* in a postmodern world. On one side of this debate are those (e.g., Greenberg & Pascual-Leone, 1999; Kelly, 1955; Kegan, 1982; Mahoney, 1991; and Rychlak, 1990) who assert that whenever a person interfaces with the real world, the *self* emerges as an experiencing and organizing force. From this perspective, the *self* not only interprets incoming data from the surrounding world, but also acts as its own *architect*.

Self as sponge. On the other side of this debate, postmodernists (e.g., Gergen, 1985; Goncalves, 1995; Lather, 1992; Sampson, 1989; Sass, 1992) argue that *self* can only be defined as part of the interplay between the individual and his or her culture. They refer to the "death of the self," declaring that the individually contained self is an illusion—that the person is inseparable from the "project" he actualizes.

In Gergen's view, the *self* acts as a sponge absorbing its surroundings: "Emerging technologies saturate us with the voices of humankind—both harmonious and alien. As we absorb their varied rhythms and reasons, they become part of us and we of them" (1991a, p. 6). This sounds reminiscent of the "absorbent self" we encountered in object–relations theory, but there is a major difference. You will recall that for Mahler, Kohut, and other object–relations theorists the self forms by absorbing many of the qualities of the mother (caretaker). Soon, however, the self *differentiates* and becomes separate from the mother, maturing into an *autonomous* self. By contrast, the "spongy" self of postmodernism becomes increasingly indistinguishable from its surroundings: "Indeed, in postmodern times, the reality of the single individual, possessing his/her own values, emotions, reasoning capacities, intentions and the like, becomes implausible . . . " (Gergen, 1991b, p. 28). Or, as Sass put it: "we enter into a universe devoid both of objects and selves: where there is only a swarming of 'selfobjects,' images and simulacra filling us without resistance" (Sass, 1992, p. 176).

It's probably fair to say that postmodern deconstructionists have threatened the status of the self as the center of personality. If we were to accept the "death of the self" proposed by radical postmodernists, it would demolish much of the *constructivist* bridge for moving from the situation-focused world of behaviorism or the unconscious forces of psychoanalysis to the agentic worlds of humanism and existentialism.

Self as construction foreman. Constructivist theorists see the person as an *agent,* possessing the power to transcend proximal situational stimuli in favor of long-range goals and inner directives. Kelly places the person-as-scientist in the driver's seat. From the earliest moments of life, the neonate begins assembling a network of personal constructs, which will eventually be as unique as her fingerprints. All of this is done from the inside out, with Mother Nature functioning as a permissive parent, allowing the child almost unlimited personal freedom in construing experience. Ellis replaces the irrationalities and illusions of childhood and the "nutty beliefs" of past conditioning with the sense and sanity of rational adult thinking. In the countryside of constructivism, the *self* is no longer caught in the brambles of behaviorism or the thickets of psychoanalytic conflict. Personal freedom is in full flower in the *construction zone.*

Chapter Summary

From conflict and conditioning, to *constructivism.* In this chapter we've learned how constructivists shifted attention away from the behaviorist focus on *conditioning* in the *Situational Zone* or the Freudian analysis of *intrapsychic conflict* in the *Insight Zone* to *agency* and *meaning making.* According to constructivists, humans continually strive to "make sense" of their lives, and this trumps all other considerations.

Piaget saw children operating like little Swiss logicians, deftly oscillating between assimilation and accommodation as they constructed cognitive schemas from the raw materials of biological reflexes and rhythms. Kelly "scientists" were equally remarkable, creating networks of personal constructs that enabled them to analyze, predict, construe, and control events in their surrounding worlds. Kelly was far less biological than Piaget, emphasizing the *creation* of constructs rather than their preexistence. When it came to the *alteration* of personality, Kelly shifted from an *intrapsychic* focus to the *Social Zone.* His Fixed-Role therapy, for example, is a thoroughly social–psychological model, in which he no longer confines himself to understanding the personal constructs of the individual, but utilizes role relationships to catalyze the development of new interpersonal relationships.

Ellis's clear-thinking adults left behind their childish confusions and absurdities to construct a rational world for themselves—an environment where healthy *relationships* can flourish.

Constructivism provides a conceptual "base camp" on our hierarchal climb from the bedrock of biochemical composition, behaviorism, and psychoanalysis (Chapters 2–9) to the broader analyses of humanism, existentialism, transpersonalism, and spirituality (Chapters 11–14). Constructivism strengthens the theoretical foundations for *agency* and *responsibility*—crucial ingredients of the humanistic, existential, and transpersonal paradigms.

Points to Remember

1. *Constructivist* psychologists emphasize the active role humans play in constructing their experienced realities. Theories differ in their emphases, but all constructivists highlight the active participation of each person in his or her own psychological experience.

2. Jean Piaget had a strong, early interest in biology, publishing his first scientific paper at the age of ten. After completing his doctoral dissertation on the topic of mollusks, he spent the remainder of his career studying the biological foundations of intelligence and developing his "one big idea"—that *patterns are always embedded in a larger whole.*

3. For Piaget, personality is comprised of the *totality of interlacing patterns, structures, and systems.*

4. According to Piaget, all development—physical or intellectual—proceeds through the twin processes of *assimilation* (taking in) and *accommodation* (modification as a result of experience), which reach a "steady state" through the process of *equilibration.*

5. Piaget described early development in terms of *circular reactions* (simple behaviors such as sucking one's thumb or shaking a rattle) that were repeated because they were pleasurable.

6. Building on these early biological foundations, the child evolves from a perception-bound five-year-old (to whom things *are* as they appear) to an adolescent or adult who is able to *reason logically using verbal statements and other symbols* in place of concrete objects.

7. *Construction is destiny.* In place of Freud's "anatomy is destiny" emphasis, or the behaviorists' highlighting of environmental forces, Piaget sees people as assembling and constructing their own personalities. This is a conscious, logical process.

8. Research has shown that Piaget underestimated the competencies of infants and preschoolers, and that his various "stages" are not as clearly defined as he suggested. Nonetheless, his constructivist theories have revolutionized our understanding of children and have stood the test of time.

9. Kelly's *constructive alternativism* is less biologically based than Piaget's developmental theories, presenting each person as a "scientist" making sense of the world.

10. Kelly said that people's psychological processes are *channelized* by the ways in which they *anticipate* events. Combining this carrot-out-front focus on anticipated rewards with the cognitive constructive activities of the person, Kelly formulated a theory that is experiencing a postmodern resurgence.

11. The engine of Kelly's theory is the *personal construct*, a bipolar conceptual template for viewing the world in terms of similarities and differences: e.g., apples and pears are easy to slice and crisp to chew, unlike raspberries, which are mushy to chew and nearly impossible to slice.

12. Kelly did not formulate a theory of motivation, stating simply that people are born *already in motion.*

13. Kelly explained psychological development in terms of two cycles: the *creativity cycle* (a three-step cycle of *loosening, retightening,* and *reevaluating* personal constructs), and the *C-P-C Cycle* (a three-step cycle of *circumspection, preemption,* and *control*).

14. Although Kelly's early focus was cognitive and *intrapsychic,* he shifted toward *interpersonal* assessment with his *Role Constructs Repertory Test (Rep Test)* designed to ascertain how people construed the significant others in their lives.

15. *Constructivism* provides a theoretical bridge from behaviorism and psychoanalysis to humanism and existentialism. Varieties range from *classical constructivism* (emphasizing preexistent categories) to *dialectical constructivism* (focusing on the creative synthesis of conflicts), but all varieties emphasize the importance of the person as a meaning-making creature.

16. Radical postmodernists have attempted to *deconstruct* the *self* as nothing more than *part of the interplay between the person and his or her culture.* More moderate *dialectical constructivists* have argued that when a person connects with the real world, the *self* functions to organize and make meaning of experience. The deconstructing threats of postmodernism have stimulated constructivists to clearly articulate and defend their positions.

17. Albert Ellis is usually regarded as a cognitive learning psychologist, but a careful study of his theory reveals him to be a *constructivist* at the core. Ellis uses learning techniques as *tools* to bring about changes in a person's *philosophy of life*.

18. Ellis encourages clients to critically examine the private beliefs (expectations) they hold regarding how they and others ought to act in the world. When such beliefs are irrational (such as the belief that one must be "nice to everyone") they result in dysfunctional behavior.

Key Terms

Abstraction   (368)

Accommodation   (363)

Adaptation   (364)

Animistic Thinking   (367)

Assimilation   (363)

Circular Reactions   (359)

Circumspection   (381)

Classification   (367)

Commonality Corollary   (380)

Complex Patterns   (361)

Conservation   (367)

Construction   (362)

Constructive Alternativism   (375)

Constructivism   (358)

Construing   (379)

Contrast Pole   (377)

C-P-C Cycle   (381)

Creativity Cycle   (381)

Dependency Construct   (380)

Dichotomy Corollary   (376)

Disequilibrium   (363)

Egocentrism   (365)

Equilibration   (363)

Fixed Role   (384)

Fixed-Role Therapy   (383)

Functional Play   (366)

Fundamental Postulate   (376)

Gestalt Psychology   (360)

Habituation–Dishabituation Response   (371)

Imaginary Audience   (368)

Impermeable   (383)

Individuality Corollory   (382)

Invitational Mood   (380)

Irrational ("Nutty") Belief   (389)

Loose Construct   (377)

Make-believe   (366)

Magical Thinking   (366)

Mind   (362)

Modulation Corollory   (382)

Object Permanence   (366)

Open Classrooms   (369)

Perception-Bound   (367)

Permeable   (383)

Personal Construct   (376)

Personal Fable   (368)

Personality   (361)

Phenomenologists   (362)

Preemption   (381)

Preverbal Construct   (378)

Primary Circular Reactions   (365)

Propositional Reasoning   (368)

Rational–Emotive Behavior Therapy (REBT)   (387)

Reconstruing   (379)

Rep Test   (383)

Reversibility   (367)

Role   (380)

Role Construct   (379)

Rule   (393)

Scheme   (361)

Secondary Circular Reactions   (365)

Sensorimotor Stage   (365)

Seriation   (367)

Similarity Pole   (377)

Spatial Reasoning   (361)

Structure   (361)

Submerged and Suspended Constructs   (378)

Subordinate Construct   (377)

Web Sites

Piaget

http://carbon.cudenver.edu/~mryder/. The Web site of Martin Ryder at the Univ. of Colorado, Denver. He has pulled together an amazing collection of links and resources for many fields of knowledge. Follow the link to Constructivism or check out the index for much more.

www.piaget.org/index.html. The Jean Piaget Society. Check out the links page, current research, and resources for students.

Kelly

www.repgrid.com/RepIV/. The Center for Person–Computer Studies. Download a free Rep Test to your Mac or PC.

Learning on the Lighter Side

The *Matrix* trilogy (*The Matrix*, 1999; *The Matrix Reloaded*, 2003; and *The Matrix Revolutions*, 2003) provides sci-fi movie fans an opportunity to enter a universe where reality is seldom what it appears to be on the surface. It also illustrates the centrality of Kelly's *personal constructs*. Everyone has constructs: you have constructs, your great great grandparents had constructs, your great great grandchildren will have constructs, Asian college students studying on the opposite side of our planet have constructs, modern scientists have constructs, and the mentally ill have constructs. How *you* see reality, how *I* see reality, and how reality *really is* depends mightily upon our constructs. Viewing *Matrix* movies is one way to remind ourselves of this; another might be to ask a friend if a woman would make a good president.

Having said that, we should note that even Kelly would insist that some constructions are better than others. My physician's construction of my illness is better—I trust—than that of the village witch doctor. My pastor's construction of the spiritual meaning of my illness may not be better or worse—simply different—if carried out in the *Transpersonal Zone*, instead of the *Physiological Zone*.

Check out the Web site **http://webspace.ship.edu/cgboer/kelly.html** for more discussion of Kelly and the opportunity to try out the *rep grid*. You can choose half a dozen of the most significant people in your life and compare them in terms of similarities and contrasts. This will enable you to more clearly understand which constructs are most important to you when relating to others.

Finally, you might like to read *The Enlightened Bracketologist: The Final Four of Everything* written by Mark Reiter and Richard Sandomir (2007). Reminiscent of Kelly's dichotomy corollary, Bracketology is the practice of parsing people, places, and things into one-on-one matchups. For years, a crude form of Bracketology has been how a committee, meeting secretly each March, has decided which college basketball teams would advance to the "Final Four," also known as "March Madness." These authors—like Kelly—insist that all of reality can be "bracketed" into dichotomous opposites, enabling people to make cleaner and clearer decisions about what is good, better, or best in the universe. Even such mundane decisions as whether to have a ham sandwich or a hot dog for lunch can benefit from bracketizing. Check it out. See what you think.

Looking Ahead

The third wave. In the next chapter, two of the best-known psychologists of the twentieth century—Carl Rogers and Abraham Maslow—guide our journey to the loftier peaks of human experience. Although Rogers is known as one of the founders of "third-wave" humanistic psychology, we will learn that when it comes to the *structure* of personality, he formulated a conflict model that has much in common with psychoanalysis. He differed most from Freud in his positive view of human nature.

Freud saw the id as a seething cauldron of dark and dangerous impulses—in need of repression by the ego or constraint by the culture. For Freud the best possible outcome would be when such earthy, forbidden, sexual, or aggressive impulses were sublimated to serve the higher cultural good. Adjustment was a lifelong balancing act, with the forces of the id pushing for expression on one side, the culture (superego) suppressing such raw emotions, and the ego in the middle, seeking to forge an acceptable compromise (sublimation).

Rogers, by contrast, saw a person's biological, animal side not as something in need of repression or constraint, but as providing the basis for the *organismic valuing process* (Rogers's biologically based construct, which we will discuss in detail in the next chapter). Rogers differed drastically from Freud in how he viewed the "organic" side of personality. For Freud the body was the primary source of unacceptable urges, for Rogers it was the source of values. Rogers stood psychoanalysis on its head, insisting that the final arbiter of values should be one's gut, not one's culture. Whereas both Sigmund and Anna Freud believed one's gut should be refined and redirected into higher cultural pursuits (sublimation), Rogers suggested that it was interference with one's "organic" or "natural" side that lay at the root of neurosis. What the Freudians distrusted most, Rogers sought to free. In Freud's formulation the organic, visceral side of personality is often handcuffed, sometimes imprisoned, but always under scrutiny—on parole, at best. In Rogers's system, viscera are appointed a Supreme Court justice, becoming the most reliable basis for determining whether something is right or wrong. According to Rogers, our behavior ought to be guided not by some culturally based set of ethics, but by the feeling in one's gut. If it feels *right*, it must *be* right.

chapter 11

Humanistic Psychology (The Third Force)

Carl Rogers and Abraham Maslow

IN THIS CHAPTER YOU CAN

1. Discover that Carl Rogers and Abraham Maslow *co-founded humanistic psychology.*

2. Understand that humanistic psychologists affirm human nature to be *essentially good* and believe that persons are *naturally inclined toward growth, creativity, and meaningful values.*

3. Learn about Rogers's unique treatment approach, called *client-centered therapy.*

4. Realize that *Self* (the conscious portion of the *experiential field*) is the centerpiece of Rogers's theory.

5. Find out that Rogers—like Freud—saw people as *caught in conflict* between the *self* and the *organism.* However, Rogers replaced the "father-knows-best" attitude of psychoanalysis with his "baby-knows-best" version of humanism.

6. Discover that in place of *conditions of worth* put on children by their parents, Rogers advocated *empathy, unconditional positive regard,* and *genuineness* as the major healing processes both in therapy and in life.

7. Remember Maslow as most famous for describing a *hierarchy of needs:* a model that ranks needs from lower *physiological* needs to higher *being (growth-oriented)* motives.

8. Discover that in place of lower *deficiency needs (e.g., hunger, thirst, etc.), self-actualized* people operate primarily on the basis of higher *Being-Values (B-Values)* such as *truth, goodness, beauty, playfulness, etc.*

A PERSONAL PERSPECTIVE

"If life gives you lemons"

Little Abe's father was a whiskey-loving, woman-chasing, cantankerous man who thought his son was ugly and stupid, and made no effort to hide his feelings: "Isn't Abe the ugliest kid you've ever seen?" (Hoffman, 1988, p. 6), he would ask from time to time, much as one might casually inquire "Isn't this weather something?" Not surprisingly, young Abe became so convinced of his personal ugliness that for a time he tried to ride in empty subway cars so others would not have to look at him.

But if Dad was discounting, Mom was malignant. She kept a bolted lock on the refrigerator, unlocking it only when she was in the mood to serve food, being especially careful to keep the refrigerator bolted when Abe had a friend over. Her miserliness was not born of necessity, as Abe's father, a barrel maker by trade, was earning a good living at the time. It was, rather, an expression of a malignant stinginess that would scar her son for life. Small wonder that he would subsequently center his entire professional life around physical and psychological *needs*.

When he was a youngster, Abe found two abandoned baby kittens in the street, quietly carried them home, and took them down to the basement to care for them. When his mother came home and heard the kittens' meows, she ran down the basement steps and discovered Abe feeding the kittens from a dish of milk. "Doubly enraged that he had brought stray kittens into her house and then used her dishes to feed them, she seized the kittens. Before his horrified eyes, Rose smashed each one's head against the basement wall until it was dead" (Hoffman, 1988, p. 8).

Commentary

It's hardly surprising that Abraham Maslow hated his mother, even refusing to attend her funeral. He described her as ignorant, cruel, and hostile—so unloving as to nearly induce madness in her children. Although Maslow eventually made peace with his father and spoke kindly of him, he hated his mother until the day he died. Freud, the favorite son in his family, might have been in love with his mother, but Maslow definitely was *not!*

From hatred to humanism—"If life gives you lemons . . ." It seems ironic that someone growing up amid such parental callousness and animosity would formulate a gentle, affirmative, utopian view of humankind. However, Maslow's reaction to his mother illustrates the kind of coping mechanism Freud called *sublimation* and Adler labeled *compensation*. Maslow experienced his mother as totally selfish, and confessed that he hated not only her physical appearance but also

> . . . her values and world view, her stinginess, her total selfishness, her lack of love for anyone else in the world, even her own husband and children . . . her lack of concern for her grandchildren, her lack of friends, her sloppiness and dirtiness, her lack of family feeling for her own parents and siblings. (Lowry, 1979, p. 958)

Shortly before he died, Maslow wrote in his personal journal:

> I've always wondered where my Utopianism, ethical stress, humanism, stress on kindness, love, friendship, and all the rest came from. I know certainly of the direct consequences of having no mother-love. But the whole thrust of my life-philosophy and all my research and theorizing also has its roots in a hatred for and revulsion against everything she stood for. (Lowry, 1979, p. 958)

A kind uncle. Confessing that during his first twenty years he was "extremely neurotic . . . depressed, terribly unhappy, lonely, isolated, self-rejecting, and so on," Maslow said that in later years, he was "awfully curious" to find out why he hadn't gone insane.

> And so I traced it back and found that my mother's brother—my maternal uncle—who's a very kind and good man to this day, and who lived nearby—took care of me. . . . He liked babies and children, and simply took care of us whenever my mother got herself a new baby. He may have saved my life, psychically. . . ." (Wilson, 1972, p. 131)

Maslow, more than most, understood the meaning of the aphorism "If life gives you lemons, make lemonade." With the help of his caring uncle, Maslow splendidly sublimated the sour sarcasms of his parents into the sparkling lemonade of humanistic psychology.

In this chapter we will consider the work of Abraham Maslow and Carl Rogers, two of the most influential humanistic psychologists of the twentieth century. They challenged the dominant theories of behaviorism and psychoanalysis as inadequate for portraying the complexities of human functioning; behaviorism was too simplistic, they said, psychoanalysis too pessimistic. In terms of our grid, Rogers and Maslow are at about the same vertical level as the constructivists but located more to the right because of Rogers's emphasis on the *dyadic* influence of parents (who place *conditions of worth*). It is not so much on the *structure* of personality as on the nature of *human nature* that humanists differ most drastically from psychoanalysts and other theorists. More about that in a moment.

What is Humanistic ("Third Force") Psychology?

Humanistic psychology has frequently been defined by what it is *not*—it is *not* psychoanalysis, *not* behaviorism—rather a "third-force"alternative to the two dominant forces that shaped American psychology during much of the twentieth century. However, as Kelly reminded us in the previous chapter, understanding something requires that we comprehend both how it is *different* from, and *similar* to, other things. So before proceeding further, we will contrast and compare humanism with psychoanalysis and behaviorism.

Human nature is intrinsically good. It is in defining human nature that humanists differ most drastically from behaviorists, and psychoanalysts. Although Maslow believed that psychoanalysis was an excellent system for understanding and treating psychopathology, he believed it was inadequate for understanding humans in the broadest sense:

> The picture of man it [psychoanalysis] presents is a lopsided, distorted puffing up of his weaknesses and shortcomings. . . . Practically all the activities that man prides himself on, and that give meaning, richness, and value to his life, are either omitted or pathologized by Freud. (Maslow in Goble, 1971, p. 244)

Much the same view was expressed by Rogers:

> I have little sympathy with the rather prevalent concept that man is basically irrational, and thus his impulses, if not controlled, would lead to destruction of others and self. Man's behavior is exquisitely rational, moving with subtle and ordered complexity toward the goals his organism is endeavoring to achieve. (1969, p. 29)

Humanistic psychologists view human nature as predominantly positive. They challenge the reductionism of behaviorism by asserting (in Gestalt fashion) that humans cannot be reduced to basic components. They counter Freud's emphasis on unconscious determinism by insisting that "Human beings are aware and aware of being aware—i.e., they are conscious" (Greening, 2001, p. 3). Humanists agree with Adler in stressing the importance of *goals,* and they concur with constructivists such as Kelly in emphasizing *self-direction* and the search for *meaning:* "Human beings are intentional, aim at goals, are aware that they cause future events, and ⸱⸱ ⸱ meaning, value, and creativity" (Greening, 2001, p. 3).

Maslow didn't believe that psychoanalysis was *wrong* so much as it was *incomplete:* "Freud supplied us the sick half of psychology and we must now fill it out with the healthy half" (Maslow, 1968, p. 5). What Maslow, Rogers, and other humanistic psychologists attempted to portray was a more holistic and optimistic view of human nature and human functioning.

Humanistic therapy techniques. Since humanists believe that people are innately good and naturally evolve toward higher levels of caring, creativity, insight, and self-fulfillment, the **humanistic therapist** *partners with the person to facilitate and enhance inherent growth tendencies.* Instead of trying to recondition maladaptive behaviors as do the behaviorists, or analyze and heal "patients" as do the psychoanalysts, humanistic therapists seek to cultivate the inherent growth tendencies that they believe are common to all humankind. In place of the *maladaptive behaviors* seen by behaviorists or the *intrapsychic conflict* envisioned by psychoanalysts, humanistic psychologists view **neurosis** as *a blockage of the innate tendency toward self-actualization.*

Exploring the "attic" with Rogers and Maslow. Humanistic psychologists see people as naturally inclined to laugh, sing, paint pictures, compose music, invent games, make love, and engage in a host of other self-actualizing activities. Still, although Rogers and Maslow painted their portraits of people in bright splashing colors with sweeping brushstrokes, they preferred to "stay on the canvas" of scientific methodology. Both obtained their doctorates from academic institutions where scientific methodology was held in high esteem, so their humanism retained a data-based focus. Instead of embracing the cosmic constructs of the *existentialists* (Chapter 12) or joining the beyond-data safaris of the *spiritual seekers* and *transpersonalists* (Chapter 13), Rogers and Maslow attempted to anchor their humanistic constructs in the empirically verifiable world of science.

Rogers was the first therapist ever to tape record and analyze his counseling sessions, and Maslow's famous hierarchy of needs was inspired by his research with primates. The fact that each man served a term as president of the American Psychological Association suggests that their brand of humanism was not repugnant to their colleagues in the scientific community. The paradigms they proposed were not considered on the "fringe" so much as they were seen as *holistic.* One biographer put it in the following way: "Maslow was the first person to create a truly comprehensive psychology stretching, so to speak, from the basement to the attic" (Wilson, 1972, p. 181).

CARL RANSOM ROGERS (1902–1987)

Actualizing self. Carl Rogers, one of the founders of humanistic psychology, developed a *self-in-conflict* model of personality that *structurally* resembled Freud's intrapsychic closed system. However, instead of leaving the ego trapped—as Freud did—between biological determinism and societal constraints, Rogers arranged an escape. Convinced of the innate goodness of human nature, Rogers fully trusted a person's (biologically based) *organismic valuing process* to unfold values that allow both biological impulses and the "higher" values of humanity to live alongside one another in harmony, or *congruence* as he termed it.

Rogers's notion of *incongruence* between *self* and *experience* echoes Horney's core neurotic conflict (alienation between the *real self* and the *idealized self*). Horney's remedy for this disparity was much like the *self-actualizing* solutions proposed by the humanists: "You need not, in fact cannot, teach an acorn to grow into an oak tree . . ." wrote Horney (1950, p. 17). Horney saw the self caught in *interpersonal conflicts* that become internalized as contradictory attitudes toward one's self. This was a move away from Freud's biological determinism, but when compared with the *self-actualizing self* of the humanists, Horney's self remained more a *reactor* than a *constructor*.

Although we could accurately designate Horney a "pioneer humanist," it remained for Rogers and Maslow, with their irrepressible optimism regarding human nature, to fully transfer the center of gravity from the *entrapped self* to the *constructive self*. In their brand of humanism, the self no longer remained sandwiched between the powerful, biologically based forces of the *id* and the censoring eyes of the *superego*. Although the *organismic valuing process* is biologically based, it is a facilitator more than a force. Rogers replaced the eighteen-wheeler momentum that biological instincts pack in Freud's psychoanalysis with a more gentle, self-actualizing growth potential.

Background Check

A rather sickly child. Born on January 8, 1902, Carl Rogers was described by one biographer as "a rather sickly child—slight, shy, prone to tears, often the target of jokes and teasing by his older brothers" (Kirschenbaum, 1979, p. 2). His father was an engineer who supervised the construction of railroad bridges and tunnels. He was absent from home much of the time, so little Carl developed warmer feelings for his mother. As "baby" of the family for more than five years, he received substantial attention from Mom as well as from the older children who taught him to read (Bible-story books) at about four years of age. However, he also recalled that family members teased one another incessantly, and that the humor frequently had a "cutting and biting edge on it" (Rogers, 1967, p. 344).

Church attendance, family worship, few amusements, lots of chores. The Rogers household was strongly religious. Breakfasts were always followed by morning worship—seven days a week—when the family would sit in a circle, taking turns reading portions of scripture, before kneeling for prayer.

Even as a child, Carl had responsibilities. He cared for the chickens, sold eggs to neighbors, and kept careful records. During high school, he arose at five o'clock or earlier to milk a dozen cows before going to school. His parents' plan to keep the children so busy with chores and responsibilities that they had no time for dancing, drinking, movies, and other "evil influences" that tantalized most high schoolers apparently worked quite well; Rogers was socially isolated from his peers—he had only one date in high school. Carl remembered "the agony I went through in inviting an auburn-haired lass whom I had admired from a distance" (Rogers, 1967, p. 348).

Relying on self. Graduating from the University of Wisconsin with a bachelor's degree in history (he had taken only one psychology course—by correspondence), Rogers married Helen Elliott, a childhood playmate who became his first date in college because he was too shy to date a stranger. They immediately headed for New York, where Rogers enrolled at Union Theological Seminary. His father had offered to pay all expenses if Carl would enroll at Princeton Seminary, which was, at that time, a center of **fundamentalism,** *a branch of Protestantism that emphasizes the literal interpretation of the Bible as* fundamental *to the Christian life.* However, Rogers was seeking to *escape*, rather than reinforce, the religious fundamentalism of his childhood, so he chose to pay his own way at Union "because it was the most liberal in the country" (Rogers, 1967, p. 353). As part of his seminary training, Rogers pastored a small rural church for a few months, but scarcely a year later, he decided to leave Union Theological Seminary to pursue graduate studies in psychology. This decision was typical of Rogers's lifelong autonomy and continual distancing from the rigid religiosity of his mother. It is clear from his autobiography that it was not *spirituality* Rogers was rejecting, so much as it was *fundamentalism.* He continued to be engaged by the "big" philosophical questions regarding the meaning of life, but he chafed at the idea of having to follow prescribed religious doctrines.

> It seemed to me that it would be a horrible thing to have to profess a set of beliefs in order to remain in one's profession. I wanted to find a field in which I could be sure my freedom of thought would not be limited. (Rogers, 1967, pp. 354–355)

Zeitgeist

You might be surprised to learn that Carl Rogers did not invent the concept of *self-actualization.* In the early 1900s academic psychology was coming into its own on two fronts—assessment of humans and experimental work with animals—and clinical psychology was treating people in ways that were profoundly different from the organic-etiology models characteristic of late-1800s psychiatry. Freud's revolution had crossed the Atlantic, and although his followers in America frequently modified his theories, psychoanalysis and psychotherapy were beginning to establish a foothold in New York and several other cities along the eastern seaboard.

Alongside psychoanalysis, **Gestalt psychology,** *an approach that focuses on understanding experience in terms of configurations or patterns instead of single "parts,"* was gaining momentum. Based on his work with brain-damaged patients, Kurt Goldstein (1939) concluded that one had to assume only a single drive—the drive of *self-actualization.*

However, during the 1940s, 1950s, and 1960s, when behaviorism was dominant in American academia and psychoanalysis ruled professional practice, it was Carl Rogers who brought the *organismic perspective* into the mainstream:

> There is one central source of energy in the human organism; that is a function of the whole organism rather than some portion of it; and it is perhaps best conceptualized as a tendency toward fulfillment, toward actualization, toward the maintenance and enhancement of the organism. (Rogers, 1963, p. 6)

"Freud" was a dirty word. When Rogers was completing his doctoral training at Teachers College, the emphasis was on measurement and statistics; "Freud was a dirty word," he recalled (1967, p. 356). However, when he began his internship at the Institute for Child Guidance, in Rochester, New York, Rogers was exposed to "different shades of psychoanalytic thinking and other psychiatric and psychological views" (Rogers, 1967, p. 357) presented by such prominent psychoanalytic dissenters as Alfred Adler and Otto Rank. Apparently, however, Rogers remained skeptical, as indicated by his comments about working with his first client—a young boy: "I made real progress in helping him, though I was full of the psychoanalytic theories which I was trying out at the time" (Rogers, 1967, p. 357). Apparently Rogers believed that it was *in spite of,* not *because of,* psychoanalytic theories that he was able to help the child.

The client knows best. While at Rochester, Rogers concluded that clients usually know more about their own needs than do their therapists. He recalled working with a "highly intelligent mother whose boy was something of a hellion" (1967, p. 359). Although Rogers believed that much of the problem stemmed from the mother's early rejection of the boy, he had not been able to bring the mother to accept that insight and he had given up on treatment. During what was to have been their closing session, Rogers told the mother that it appeared they had both tried but had failed, so they might as well give up. Concluding the interview, he shook hands with the mother, and as they began walking toward the door the mother turned and asked, "Do you ever take adults for counseling here?" When Rogers answered affirmatively, she said, "Well then, I would like some help."

The mother returned to the chair she had just left and began pouring out her despair about her marriage, her sense of confusion, and her feelings of failure. "Real therapy began then," said Rogers, "and ultimately it was highly successful—for her and for her son" (Rogers, 1967, p. 359).

Freud's influence on Rogers—via the "startled bird" of psychoanalysis. Freud may have been a "dirty word" at Teacher's College, but his influence on Rogers was significant, albeit indirect—mediated by one of Freud's earliest and most faithful disciples, Otto Rank (1884–1939). Rank wasn't the kind of person who made a powerful first impression. According to his biographer, "His short, slender stature, beady eyes, prominent ears, and upright crown of hair made him look like a startled bird" (Lieberman, 1985, p. 122). One of Freud's closest disciples, Rank faithfully served the "master" for over twenty years—one of the few males who was able to maintain a long-term relationship with Freud. It is a tribute to Rank's diplomacy—some might say "sycophancy"—that he was Freud's close confidant for some twenty years before he (like so many others) was sent packing over ideological issues.

The "little frog on a leaf" who impressed a youthful Carl Rogers. After his falling out with Freud, Rank joined the faculty of the Pennsylvania School of Social Work. While at Pennsylvania, he presented a three-day series of lectures at the Rochester Institute for Child Guidance. One of the students in attendance remembered Rank as a small man who "sat up there like a little frog on a leaf. He had a lot of personality, spoke clear as a bell" (Lieberman, 1985, p. 365). Rank's lectures favorably impressed one of his listeners, a young psychologist named Carl Rogers.

Relationship trumps insight. For Rank, *relationship* took precedence over Freud's focus on *insight,* and the therapeutic hour was seen as a microcosm of life in the real world. Rank's emphasis on constructing one's *self,* and his view that the therapeutic relationship can be a prime facilitator of such growth, was echoed in Rogers's client-centered approach. In this way Freud's erstwhile disciple came to have a significant impact on the emerging new "third force" of humanistic psychology.

Staying "in the now." Rank was not very precise in describing how he actually conducted therapy, stating that he followed no technique except to utilize his experience and understanding to form a straightforward, respectful, and honest "conversational partnership" with patients. It was Rank's *attitude* toward patients, more than specific techniques, that impressed young Rogers. Unlike the classical psychoanalysts, who lingered in the shadows of the analytic couch, Rank involved himself in the here-and-now of the therapeutic encounter, celebrating the creative potential of the "real relationship."

In words that would be echoed by Carl Rogers, Rank said: "The therapist may do whatever he believes is pertinent to the process and *moment of therapy* with a particular individual as long as he takes responsibility for and deals helpfully with what he precipitates in the patient" (Leiberman, 1985, p. xxxvii).

From midwestern research to California encounters. In 1940, Rogers accepted a faculty position at Ohio State University, where he began formulating his own approach to psychotherapy. In 1945 Rogers moved to the University of Chicago, where he pioneered the use of electronic recordings to study the process of psychotherapy. In 1957 he moved to the University of Wisconsin, but eventually became discouraged with what he felt was an overly competitive atmosphere, and in 1967 he joined the Western Behavioral Sciences Institute in La Jolla, California. Subsequently, Rogers became deeply involved with the encounter group movement, facilitating dozens of groups lasting from one to eight days. However, since most of Rogers's personality theory was formed during his earlier work with individuals—not encounter groups—he is remembered for client-centered therapy, and our discussion will deal primarily with his early work.

TABLE 11.1

Rogers at a Glance

MODEL OF PERSONALITY	DESCRIPTION	DYNAMICS
What Are the Parts?	***Experiential/Phenomenal field:*** all mental and physical experiences (conscious, unconscious, and preconscious) ***Meaning of experience:*** includes the psychological meaning of physical and emotional experiences, both conscious and unconscious ***Self:*** conscious, organized, conceptual gestalt related to "I" or "me" ***Ideal Self:*** the kind of person one wishes to become	The broad construct of the *experiential/phenomenal field* is the ballpark for Rogers's main player, *experience*. The *self* is primarily conscious, but unconscious and preconscious experiences are also contained within it (*subceived* but *unsymbolized*). The *ideal self* has a futuristic tilt, working toward goals that promise to fulfill one's wish to become an exemplary person.

TABLE 11.1 *(continued)*

Rogers at a Glance

MODEL OF PERSONALITY	DESCRIPTION	DYNAMICS
What Makes a Person Go?	***Organismic enhancement/Actualizing tendency:*** the "master motive"—the one basic tendency of the organism—is to actualize, maintain, and enhance experiencing organism. *Self-actualization* is a subdivision of this larger *actualizing tendency.* ***Incongruence:*** arises when organismic experiences are inconsistent with one's perceived self, and self-needs are out of synch with organismic needs ***Goals:*** Rogers's causality was forward-looking and goal-oriented, pulled by the future	Rogers saw all organisms as having the inherent drive toward *organismic enhancement,* and since human nature is innately good, development proceeds in the direction of enhancement. In this area Rogers saw *organismic experience* as taking precedence over all other forms of truth. Rogers believed that incongruence between *self* and the *organism* caused conflict, but that in this sort of showdown, persons should trust their "viscera" over their "heads."
What Makes a Person Grow?	***Unconditional Positive Regard:*** "prizing" another person for who they are—with minimal regard for performance ***Organismic Valuing Process:*** earliest, *biologically based* regulatory feedback system ***Conditions of Worth:*** Self-experiences begin to be discriminated as worthy or unworthy by others. ***Anxiety, Threat, Defense, and Breakdown:*** If a person continues to live in a state of incongruence, this chain of events begins and ends with destructive consequences.	For Rogers the emergence of self gives rise to a need for positive self-regard. These work as part of the organismic valuing process or feedback systems, giving infants info about how society values them and how they value themselves. When parents or society begin to put *conditions of worth* on the infant, instead of showing unconditional positive regard, incongruence can occur. If such incongruence is persistent, anxiety and breakdown may result.
What Makes a Person Unique?	***Phenomenological reality:*** immediate, ongoing experience that can never be fully known by anyone else, but can be empathically perceived by another person who is *congruent* with one's experiential field	Rogers saw each individual as living in his or her own subjective phenomenal field or reality. He believed that each human constructs his or her own personal world, with no two being alike.

ASKING THE BIG FOUR QUESTIONS

What Are the Parts?

Experience. A key concept for Rogers is *experience*. Although Rogers had little patience with reductionistic physiological explanations of behavior, he wanted to stay *experientially* in touch with his physical roots. To that end, Rogers distinguished between **awareness:** *as symbolized experience,* and **unawareness:** *as unsymbolized experience,* in a way that strongly echoes Freud's use of conscious and unconscious mental processes. The following passage could have been written by either Freud or Rogers:

> There are many of the impulses which I feel, or the sensations which I experience, which I can permit into consciousness only under certain conditions. Hence my actual awareness of and knowledge of my total phenomenal field is limited. (Rogers, 1951, p. 484)

Reducing intrapsychic conflict. Echoing the psychoanalytic goal of reducing intrapsychic conflict by bringing the unconscious into awareness, Rogers emphasized the importance of accurate symbolization:

> As experiences occur in the life of the individual, they are either (a) symbolized, perceived, and organized into some relationship to the self, (b) ignored because there is no perceived relationship to the self-structure, (c) denied symbolization or given a distorted symbolization because the experience is inconsistent with the structure of the self. (Rogers, 1951, p. 503)

Experiential field—Rogers's answer to mind–body dualism. Like Freud, Rogers formulated a dualistic structure for personality, but instead of using *instinct* to bridge mind and body, Rogers circumvented Descartes's dualistic split by having both mental and physical processes funnel into what he designated the *experiential field* or *phenomenal field.* The **experiential/phenomenal field** *contains all mental and physical experiences—conscious, preconscious, and unconscious.* In a definition reminiscent of Freud's distinction between conscious and unconscious thought, Rogers states: "only a portion of that experience, and probably a very small portion, is *consciously* experienced. Many of our sensory and visceral sensations are not symbolized" (Rogers, 1951, p. 483).

Although Rogers recognized the biological foundations necessary for emergent awareness, he deemed reductionistic, physiological theories as useless for understanding human personality because they are so experience-distant. He once described the work of laboratory-based, learning-theory psychologists as "a pompous investigation of the trivial" (Rogers, 1967, p. 377).

Symbolized (conscious) portions of the experiential field. Symbolized portions of the

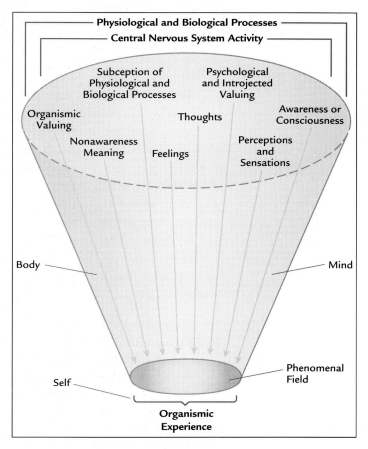

Figure 11.1 ■ *Rogerian Synthesis of Mind & Body in the Phenomenal Field*

phenomenal field include highly emotional areas such as sexual expression, but they also include such ordinary processes as *symbolizing* a hardware store:

> I walk down a street a dozen times, ignoring most of the sensations which I experience. Yet today I have need of a hardware store. I recall that I have seen a hardware store on the street, although I have never "noticed" it. Now that this experience meets a need of the self it can be drawn from ground into figure. (Rogers, 1951, pp. 503–504)

Unsymbolized (unconscious) portions of the experiential field. Some aspects of the phenomenal field remain unsymbolized (outside conscious awareness) because the person **subceives,** that is, *dimly perceives* that such an experience would be *incongruous* with the *self* structure. In such cases the person reacts with denial of awareness or distortion of symbolization. The *subception* process functions similarly to the unconscious portion of Freud's superego—as a silent censor, outside conscious awareness: "There is at least a process of 'subception,' a discriminating evaluative physiological organismic response to experience, which may precede the conscious perception of such experience" (Rogers, 1951, p. 507).

Some portions of the experiential field remain unsymbolized because of irrelevance. According to Rogers, not all unsymbolized experiences are a result of defensiveness; a portion of the phenomenal field is similar to Freud's preconscious as illustrated in the "hardware store" example just cited. As Rogers saw it: "the great majority of our sensory experiences are thus ignored . . . without ever having been related in any way to the organized concept of the self or to the concept of the self in relation to the environment" (Rogers, 1951, p. 504).

Self—the conscious portion of the experiential field. The "North Pole" around which Rogers organizes personality is the **self,** *an organized, fluid, but consistent conceptual pattern of perceptions of characteristics and relationships of the "I" or the "me," together with the values attached to these concepts* (Rogers, 1951, p. 498, emphasis in original). Although Rogers's *self* appears to include functions similar to those of Freud's ego and superego, the *self* is *completely* conscious or preconscious, "available to awareness though not necessarily in awareness" (Rogers, 1959, p. 200). By comparison, portions of Freud's ego and superego remain unconscious.

Rogers's *self* performs the work of *both* the ego and superego, including among its duties the superego's censoring activities. For example, Rogers cited the example of a woman, who, having been raised in a very strict, religious home (as was Rogers), experienced strong biological cravings for sex, but was conflicted about their expression:

> To symbolize these, to permit them to appear in consciousness, would provide a traumatic contradiction to her concept of self. The organic experience is something which occurs and is an organic fact. But the symbolization of these desires, so that they become part of conscious awareness, is something which the conscious self can and does prevent. (Rogers, 1951, p. 505)

Finally, we need to note that Rogers's *self* is a much more *interpersonal* self than arises out of intrapsychic conflicts. This locates him farther toward the *Social Zone* than psychoanalysts, object-relations theorists, or other constructivists. From the very beginning (even before he became a California facilitator), Rogers saw the *self* as emerging out of *interpersonal interactions,* i.e., his level of analysis was similar to what we saw with Sullivan, Leary, and Berne: *"As a result of interaction with the environment, and particularly as a result of evaluational interaction with others, the structure of self is formed . . ."* (Rogers, 1951, p. 498).

Ideal self. Rogers uses this structural construct to designate a kind of "older-sister-on-a-pedestal" to the self. The **ideal self** is *the self that a person would most like to be, the kind of person one would like to become.* It seems similar to the *ego ideal* portion of Freud's *superego* and also echoes Horney's *ideal self.* William Stephenson, one of Rogers's colleagues at the University of Chicago, experimentally studied the *ideal self,* using the **Q-sort technique:** *100 cards containing self statements that can be sorted to describe one's real self or one's ideal self.* We will discuss the Q-sort technique in greater detail later.

What Makes a Person Go?

Organismic enhancement—the master motive. Rather than postulate a number of different needs and motives, Rogers believed it was possible to describe all organic and psychological needs as different aspects of one fundamental need, an **organismic enhancement** or **actualizing tendency,** *the master motive that includes the inherent tendency of the whole organism to enhance itself by fully developing not only the self, but the* entire *organism.* Rogers described it as the organism's *"tendency and striving—to actualize, maintain, and enhance the experiencing organism"* (Rogers, 1951, p. 487).

Organismic refers to *the patterned, hierarchically ordered, holistic responses of the entire organism.* It will become clear as we study further, that self-actualization can be warped or unhealthy if the self-concept lacks *congruence* with the organismic valuing process. More about that shortly.

Experience, the highest authority—if it *feels* good, do it. Rogers stood psychoanalytic theory on its head by reversing Freud's view of intellectual processes as superior to biological impulses ("where id was, there ego shall be"). Consistent with his belief in the innate goodness of persons, Rogers trusted his viscera more than his mind: "I have learned that my total organismic sensing of a situation is more trustworthy than my intellect" (Rogers, 1961, pp. 22–24).

Then, leaving little doubt regarding what he meant, Rogers said:

> I have never regretted moving in directions which "felt right," even though
> I have often felt lonely or foolish at the time. . . . *Experience is for me the highest
> authority.* . . . Neither the Bible nor the prophets—neither Freud nor research—
> neither the revelations of God nor man—can take precedence over my own
> experience. (Rogers, 1961, pp. 22–24, emphasis in original)

Emotions over mind. Whenever Rogers compared thoughts with feelings, he came down on the side of *feelings* as the more reliable guide. His "matter-over-mind" perspective permeated his writings even before he moved west and became involved with the touchy–feely encounter group movement:

> Just as the infant places an assured value upon an experience, relying on the evidence of his own senses . . . so too the client finds that it is his own organism which supplies the evidence upon which value judgements may be made. He discovers that his own senses, his own physiological equipment, can provide the data for making value judgements and for continuously revising them. . . . (1951, pp. 523–524)

Incongruence—conflict between the self and the organism. Rogers defined **incongruence** *as arising when organismic experiences are inconsistent with one's perceived self—when the needs of the organism are "out of synch" with the needs of the self.* Since most values are taught to children by adult authorities—received "second hand"—Rogers believed that what we *experience* viscerally is frequently at odds with what we *think* consciously: "In order to hold the love of a parent, the child introjects as his own, values and perceptions which he does not actually experience" (Rogers, 1966, p. 192).

According to Rogers, such introjected values are frequently divorced from a child's "organismic functioning":

> The primary sensory and visceral reactions are ignored, or not permitted into consciousness, except in distorted form. The values which might be built upon them cannot be admitted to awareness. (Rogers, 1951, p. 501)

In all conflicts between biological sensations and intellectual values, Rogers advised trusting your gut instead of your head.

Goals versus conditioning. Before leaving our discussion of motivation, we should note that for Rogers causality was in the present: "Behavior is not 'caused' by something which occurred in the past. Present tensions and present needs are the only ones which the organism endeavors to reduce or satisfy . . . there is no behavior except to meet a present need" (Rogers, 1951, p. 492).

What Makes a Person Grow?

Rogers did not formulate a detailed stage-theory of development linking personality traits or intellectual skills to specific developmental eras (in the style of Freud, Erikson, Sullivan, or Piaget). Instead, he focused on how the *self* developed out of the larger organismic experiences along lines that would be consistent with the infant's *organismic valuing process.*

Gas masks and flower children—the nature of human nature. Alongside his broad organismic perspective, Rogers also maintained an ebullient optimism regarding the intrinsic goodness of human nature:

> I have little sympathy with the rather prevalent concept that man is basically irrational, and that his impulses, if not controlled, will lead to the destruction of others and self. Man's behavior is exquisitely rational, moving with subtle and ordered complexity toward goals his organism is endeavoring to achieve. (Rogers, 1961, pp. 194–195)

Rogers believed that when humans are offered a safe and nonthreatening (client-centered) relationship, they might at first express bitterness, abnormal impulses, antisocial desires, bizarre or murderous feelings; but if allowed to live in such a relationship, they will *naturally* evolve toward greater degrees of harmony and self-regulation, which in turn will enhance the person and the species. Rogers described humans as

> one of the most widely sensitive, responsive, creative, and adaptive creatures on this planet. . . . So when a Freudian such as Karl Menninger tells me (as he has, in a discussion of this issue) that he perceives man as "innately evil," or more precisely, "innately destructive," I can only shake my head in wonderment. (Kirschenbaum, 1979, p. 250)

We might wonder how much of Rogers's glowing optimism regarding human nature was a function of growing up the son of a gentleman farmer and a devout Christian mother. Although he was taught the fundamentalist doctrine of the innate evilness of humans, his *experience* was primarily framed in goodness and light. Unlike Freud, who experienced his life sandwiched between the Italian Fascists and German Nazis, and who finally fled to England for safety, Rogers lived a comparatively charmed life.

Melanie Klein, in her notes regarding her psychoanalysis of a ten-year-old boy in 1939, included the following sketch: **"Then he [Richard] put on his gas-mask (which he carried when traveling) and said that some people made a fuss about it. He quite liked it, and also the rubber smell . . ."** (Klein, 1961, pp. 330–331). Conducting psychoanalysis in 1939 (on Hitler's doorstep, under the ominous shadow of the growing Nazi threat) must have differed drastically from facilitating encounter groups in sunny California, where Rogers worked out his increasingly optimistic view of human nature.

Organismic valuing process. According to Rogers, infants are born with an **organismic valuing process:** *a biologically based regulatory "feedback" system.* It is this organismic valuing process that keeps the infant "on the beam of satisfying his emotional needs" (1959, p. 222).

Need for positive regard (from others). Sometime during early infancy (Rogers does not delineate developmental mileposts) the *self* emerges, as the conscious portion of experience, accompanied by the **need for positive regard,** that is, *positive social feedback regarding various aspects of one's personality.* Rogers believed that the need for positive regard "is universal in human beings, and in the individual, is pervasive and persistent" (1959, p. 223). This is the social side of personality, dependent on feedback from others. Since the person can only *infer* how others evaluate him or her, this feedback sometimes becomes blurred. Nonetheless, Rogers considered this to be one of the most potent needs—even frequently overriding the organismic valuing process.

Need for self-regard. In addition to the importance of feedback coming from significant others, each person has a **need for self-regard,** or *self-appraisal that is relatively independent of how others see the individual.* In this realm the person functions as his or her own significant social other.

Unconditional positive regard—"prizing" another. Rogers defined one of the key developmental constructs of his theory as **unconditional positive regard,** or

"*Your mother and I have seen your report card, and we've decided to distance ourselves from you.*"

"prizing" another person, regardless of how we might value his or her specific behaviors:

> . . . to feel unconditional positive regard toward another is to "prize" him. . . . This means to value the person, irrespective of the differential values which one might place on his specific behaviors. A parent "prizes" his child, even though he may not value equally all of his behaviors. (Rogers, 1959, p. 208)

Conditions of worth. According to Rogers, **conditions of worth** *develop when a child's self-experiences begin to be discriminated by significant others as either worthy or unworthy. The child then begins to perceive— however dimly—that only under certain conditions is she positively valued.* Such a child is likely to develop incongruence: *disparity between the self structure and organismic experience,* because in attempting to please others, the child becomes less attuned to his or her feelings—by denying or distorting organic experiences. Subsequently, the child begins to *selectively perceive* his or her self experiences, evaluating them in terms of these internalized *conditions of worth.* This ultimately leads to *incongruence* or a lack of integration:

> It is thus because of the distorted perceptions arising from the conditions of worth that the individual departs from the integration which characterizes his infant state. From this point on, his concept of self includes distorted perceptions which do not accurately represent his experience, and his experience includes elements which are not included in the picture he has of himself. Thus he can no longer live as a unified whole person. (Rogers, 1959, p. 226)

Imaginary playmates—the antidote to "conditions of worth"? It appears that "evaluational interactions" with others and with one's *ideal self* powerfully shape how we see ourselves. Rogers viewed *conditions of worth* quite negatively, and much of what he outlined as his theory of therapy involved *"prizing" (instead of evaluating)* the client. Perhaps this dynamic sometimes accounts for the invention of an "imaginary playmate" (a relatively common occurrence among younger children). Your "friend" provides a psychologically safe sidekick. Now, instead of being compared by your parents or teachers to an older sibling who gets better grades in school or is more polite to company, you create a "playmate" whom you can easily surpass whenever necessary—a "friend" who always likes to play the same games you do and enjoys exactly the role you've assigned—someone who definitely does *not* do her homework regularly or practice the piano more faithfully.

I recall working with a family where the *mother* had created an imaginary sibling ["Peter"] for her only child. Thus, even though there wasn't an older brother on the honor role, this young boy faced comments like "I don't think Peter would have done that," or "Do you think Peter would argue with his Mommy like that?" Now, *that's* conditions of worth!

Baby knows best. Rogers appeared to distrust parents as reliable guides for their children, suggesting that they usually create *conditions of worth* by specifying the circumstances under which they will value (or devalue) their children. Instead of viewing this as a positive part of socialization, Rogers believed that conditions of worth became permanently attached to the child's self-structure. Subsequently, instead of being guided by their own organismic valuing processes, children attempted to act in accordance with parentally inspired conditions of worth.

"Editing" awareness. Instead of listening to his or her own inner voices, the young child tries to behave in a way that pleases parents or teachers. But since this is frequently not congruent with the real self, she has to edit awareness: "Selective perception creates an incongruence between the self and experience because certain experiences that may be conducive to positive growth may be distorted or denied. Once this incongruence between self and experience exists, people are vulnerable, and psychological maladjustment may result . . ."(Rogers 1959, pp. 226–227).

Anxiety, threat, defense, and breakdown. According to Rogers, if a person continues to live in a state of incongruence between organismic experience and the self, she becomes vulnerable to a chain of destructive consequences that can proceed from *anxiety* and *threat* to *defense,* and finally *breakdown.* **Anxiety** *is* <u>subjectively</u> *experienced as a state of uneasiness whose cause is indefinite or unknown.* **Threat** *is the* <u>external</u> *aspect of what the person experiences as anxiety,* and **defense** *is the* <u>perceptual distortion</u> *seeking to reduce the anxiety and threat of incongruence.* If such conditions persist, they lead to **breakdown,** *a state of disorganization that results from experiences becoming conscious that are at variance with the self-structure.* In such a condition behavior frequently becomes erratic and inconsistent.

That's about as bad as it gets for a Rogerian client—none of the murder and mayhem Klein found, little of the incest and castration anxieties of Freud's patients—just disorganizing incongruence between *organismic experience* and the *self.* For the (few) persons who have unconditionally positive parents, or for those (fortunate) clients who experience an empathic, unconditionally positive therapist, Rogers believed this slide toward breakdown and disorganization could be avoided or reversed.

Life experiences as therapy. If we view life through such wide-angle-lens constructs as the *experiential field, organismic enhancement,* or *unconditional positive regard,* it is hardly surprising that boundaries between traditional disciplines such as psychotherapy, psychiatry, social work, education, ministry, etc. become less distinct as focus shifts to an ever-widening "big picture." For example, Rogers wrote: "To my mind, the 'best' of education would produce a person very similar to the one produced by the 'best' of therapy" (1969, p. 279). In this sense, Rogers saw almost everyone—parents, teachers, and friends—as potential "therapists."

Healing through reintegration. According to Rogers, **reintegration** *occurs when unconditional positive regard is present and conditions of worth are minimal.* Then healing can take place and the negative processes associated with incongruence are reduced or removed. This healing is facilitated by **empathy,** *the ability to perceive someone else's internal experience as if it were one's own—but without losing the "as if" quality.* For Rogers, *empathic listening* was central to therapy and to life itself, but he believed it was rare: "We think we listen, but very rarely do we listen with real understanding, true empathy. Yet listening, of this very special kind, is one of the most potent forces for change that I know" (Rogers, 1980, pp. 115–116).

The importance of empathy. For Rogers, *empathy* encompassed far more than passive listening. In one of his most concise descriptions of *empathy,* Rogers said it "means temporarily living in the other's life, moving about in it delicately without making judgements" (1980, p. 142). Like Sullivan's "participant observer," Rogers's *empathic listener* seeks to actively enter into the experience of another: "You have to really understand what it feels like to be this person in this situation. . . . To really let oneself go into the inner world of this other person is one of the most active, difficult, and demanding things I know" (Rogers, 1987, p. 45).

These conditions—seen by Rogers as forming the foundations of the therapeutic process—were also the kinds of affirming experiences he recommended that parents, teachers, and friends ought to provide for children and peers. It didn't matter to Rogers whether the setting was the kitchen, the counseling office, or the classroom; what counted was the psychological atmosphere. Rogers believed that if a child were rooted in the soil of empathic relationships, warmed by the sunshine of unconditional positive regard, and rid of the weeds of conditions of worth, the flower of a fully functioning personality was bound to bloom.

Fully functioning person. Rogers believed that "baby knows best," and he asserted that the **fully functioning person** *functions much like an infant, living according to his or her own organismic valuing process, instead of externally imposed conditions of worth.* For Rogers, the uncontaminated, viscerally based *organismic valuing process* is the truest measure of optimal adjustment. As a person increasingly learns to live in accordance with his or her own organismic valuing process rather than trying to fulfill the conditions of worth imposed by others, she will become more *fully functioning.*

What Makes a Person Unique?

Phenomenological reality. According to Rogers, each of us lives within our own subjective world—inside our own **phenomenological reality:** *the immediate, ongoing experience that can never be fully known by anyone else, but which can only be vicariously or empathically known by another:*

> The only reality I can possibly know is the world as *I* perceive and experience it at this moment. The only reality you can possibly know is the world as *you* perceive and experience it at the moment. The only certainty is that those perceived realities are different. There are as many 'real worlds' as there are people! (Rogers, 1980, p. 102)

It doesn't get more unique than that—snowflakes, flowers, fingerprints, or *personal realities*—no two alike.

FACING THE TOUGH TWINS
Is It Testable?

The first electronic recordings of psychotherapy. Perhaps Rogers's most significant legacy is that he pioneered the scientific investigation of psychotherapy. With the assistance of an electronically adept graduate student, Rogers recorded 800 sides of 78-rpm discs, providing for the first time ever a complete transcript of his counseling sessions with a client. These sessions constituted the last 170 pages of *Counseling and Psychotherapy* (Rogers, 1942), allowing readers to go along for the ride. Rogers encouraged readers to cover up the counselor responses, and ask themselves "How would I have responded at that point?" Almost overnight, the book catapulted Rogers to national fame as the foremost proponent of a new approach to counseling and psychotherapy. Although Rogers stressed the importance of the experiential field of the individual, he did not shrink from scientific investigation of such phenomena, describing himself as a scientist-practitioner:

> Therapy is the experience in which I can let myself go subjectively. Research is the experience in which I can stand off and try to view this rich subjective experience with objectivity, applying all the elegant methods of science to determine whether I have been deceiving myself. (Rogers, 1961, p. 14)

It is ironic (in a positive sense) that Rogers—who insisted the only way to really know a person was by empathically attempting to understand his or her inner, private world—was also the researcher who initiated the scientific study of psychotherapy through the use of electronic recordings.

The Q-sort technique. The *Q-sort technique,* developed by Stephenson (1953) and refined by Block (1961), is used by Rogerian therapists to assess discrepancies between a person's ideal and real selves. The client is instructed to sort the statement cards (e.g., I am intelligent, I express my emotions freely, I despise myself, etc.) into nine piles according to how well the statements reflect the client. At one extreme are piles that are *least* like the client, at the other end are those *most* like the client, and in the middle are those statements about which the client is *neutral or undecided.* During the **self-sort,** the client is asked to sort statements into piles that best *describe the way he or she is,* and during the **ideal-sort,** into piles *describing the person he or she would most like to be.* This allows the researcher to more objectively assess subjectively experienced phenomena such as *congruence* (or *incongruence*) between one's *real self* and *ideal self.* Such measurements can be carried out before, during, and after psychotherapy, allowing the researcher to assess the effectiveness of psychotherapy in bringing about *subjectively experienced* change.

More recently, Higgins (1987) reviewed a number of studies and outlined a self-discrepancy theory that included, but went beyond, Rogers's focus on the incongruence between *actual* and *ideal* selves. Specifically, Higgins also studied discrepancies between the *actual* and *ought* selves. He predicted that different sorts of negative emotions would be generated by different kinds of self-discrepancies. A number of studies showed that *actual–ideal* (Rogerian) self-discrepancies typically lead to emotions of disappointment, dissatisfaction, and sadness; whereas *actual–ought* self-discrepancies are associated with agitation, fear, and restlessness. Higgins's theory represents not so much a contradiction of Rogers as an expansion of his ideas. We might see it as providing a synthesizing framework for addressing Rogerian therapists' concerns regarding *incongruence* and *conditions of worth* in their clients, and REBT therapists' concerns with *"musterbation."* Higgins's work is a nice illustration of how the *heuristic* aspects of theories (client centered, rational-emotive) lead to further investigations and refinements.

Is It Useful?

The "big three"—empathy, unconditional positive regard, and genuineness. Research has generally confirmed that Rogers's "big three" conditions are effective in a wide variety of settings. Although Rogers is best known among psychologists, he has also had a significant influence in corporate and educational settings, as well as in the general population.

Clinical or counseling settings. Truax & Mitchell (1971) found that to the extent that empathy, unconditional positive regard, and genuineness characterized the therapy process, to that extent it was successful. Gurman (1977) reviewed twenty-two studies and found that clients who perceived their therapists as empathic, genuine, and exhibiting unconditional positive regard also perceived their therapy as effective.

However, other researchers (e.g., Sexton & Whiston, 1994) have suggested that Rogers's "big three" are not *sufficient* for effective therapy. It appears that clients *differentially* respond to the "big three"—i.e., some personality types benefit more than do others.

Encounter groups. Rogers was active in creating and facilitating **encounter groups,** or *small groups designed to develop communication skills and social sensitivity.* Sometimes known as *sensitivity groups or T-groups,* such groups have been widely used in corporate settings to "sensitize" executives, middle-managers, and other administrators to the importance of human relationships in a corporate setting. They have also been widely used for therapeutic purposes with the general public.

Classrooms. Rogers was influential both in modeling and writing about a student-oriented approach to education that was analogous to his client-centered approach to therapy. Just as Piaget's influence shifted educational practices in a discovery-learning direction, Rogers's influence brought about an attitudinal shift toward less authoritarian, more user-friendly educational practices.

Emphasizing personal experience over curriculum. From the beginning of his teaching career at Ohio State University, Rogers tried to make classroom learning *experiential.* His teaching methods were characterized by the same kind of unstructured empathic listening (with very few guidelines) that characterized his therapy. Gradually he evolved a style of "nondirective teaching" which he summarized in the following sentence: *"We cannot teach another person directly; we can only facilitate his learning"* (Rogers, 1951, p. 389). A related proposition sounded much like his approach to therapy: *"A person learns significantly only those things which he perceives as being involved in the maintenance of, or enhancement of, the structure of self"* (1951, p. 389).

Encounter group–flavored education. During the late sixties and early seventies, encounter groups were something of a fad in California where Rogers lived; not surprisingly, he combined his interest in encounter groups with educational reform.

At Alma College, a center for training Jesuits, Rogers and nine of his associates conducted a weekend of encounter groups, which resulted in the kind of educational upheaval that delighted Rogers:

> In the dining room, where faculty, students and lay brothers used to sit at separate tables, all now eat together. In some classrooms where dry lectures had been customary, small groups now engage in lively discussion. One professor scrapped the notes for an entire course soon after the weekend and asked his students to draw up personal study plans. A few students left the order for civil life. One, who was inspired to explore himself and world beyond sanctioned boundaries, was dismissed. (Kirschenbaum, 1979, p. 381)

This illustrates how Rogers's educational ideas worked out: at the higher levels of education—in college and university settings—his "student-centered" reforms met with mixed reviews, but were sometimes avenues for creative change. At the elementary level, however, as experienced teachers well know, lack of structure invites chaos. Permissive teaching, like permissive parenting—however well intentioned—usually doesn't work.

Research confirmation for emotional engagement. However, if Rogers's ideas for loosely structured classrooms and experientially based curricula frequently met with disillusionment, his emphasis on engaging students' emotions proved more useful. Researchers have confirmed that Rogers's "big three" facilitate favorable outcomes in the classroom. Aspy & Roebuck (1974) collected audiotapes of over 3,500 hours of teacher–student interactions from elementary and secondary schools in various parts of this country and abroad. They found that the most important variable in producing favorable educational outcomes was teacher empathy. Genuineness and unconditional positive regard were also significant, and taken together these three produced a powerful effect.

Rogers's nondirective style was in evidence when he delivered the Sonoma State College commencement address on June 7, 1969. He began by stating that as an undergraduate student, he had majored in medieval history, and had great respect for the scholars of the Middle Ages. He then continued: "But I want to speak to you as Carl Rogers, in 1969, not as a medieval symbol. So I hope I will not offend you if I remove these medieval trappings—this nonfunctional cap, this handsome but useless hood, and this robe, designed to keep one warm even in the rigors of an European winter" (Kirschenbaum, 1979, p. 395). Then the 67-year-old Rogers began discussing the "person of tomorrow"—that was vintage Rogers.

SUMMARY OF ROGERS

Rogers painted an optimistic portrait of human nature—quite different from the dark depictions of Freud and Klein. However, conflict or *incongruence* remained a powerful driving force in client-centered theory. Rogers stood psychoanalysis on its head with respect to human nature (perceiving innate goodness where Freud saw untamed aggression and sexuality, and trusting one's own biology over cultural values). Still, for both Rogers and Freud, conflict or incongruence usually results from a clash between biological urges and the values of the self.

Rogers's *fully functioning person* provides a personification of Rogers's entire theory. Such a person is at peace within herself because her values are based upon her own organic sense of what she needs. Since human nature is basically good, when people are congruent with their deepest physiological needs (absent externally imposed "conditions of worth"), they develop into sensitive, caring, fully functioning individuals. However, this is a somewhat rare occurrence, given the fact that so much parenting, teaching, and socialization is directed toward inculcating societal and parental values into a child's personality.

Here Rogers differs most drastically from the psychoanalysts. His description of fully functioning persons, operating congruently with their organismic valuing processes, appears opposite to a person using the Freudian process of *sublimation* to tame primitive biological impulses and redirect them into more societally approved forms of expression. Rogers's description of how to handle a toddler who hits his brother, or defecates on the carpet, captures the client-centered approach to child rearing and illustrates profound differences with more traditional approaches:

> I can understand how satisfying it feels to you to hit your baby brother (or to defecate when and where you please, or to destroy things) and I love you and am quite willing for you to have those feelings. But I am quite willing for me to have my feelings, too, and I feel very distressed when your brother is hurt, (or annoyed or sad at other behaviors), and so I do not let you hit him. Both your feelings and my feelings are important, and each of us can freely have his own. (Rogers, 1959, p. 223)

While experienced parents and teachers might applaud Rogers's positiveness and his emphasis on prevention, they might question the value of such a permissive approach in the real world. How would one handle a situation where a child had *already* pummeled his little sister? What to do with the playground bully who terrorizes smaller children at every opportunity? Would unconditional positive regard suffice to bring aggressive behavior within socially acceptable (to most people) boundaries?

Finally, there is the basic problem of how to provide unconditional acceptance in the face of aggression or danger. Although Molly, my Black Lab, probably provides more unconditional positive regard than many humans (happily wagging her tail whether greeting family or strangers alike), we are left to wonder just how one could muster acceptance—to say nothing of "positive regard"—in the face of aggression directed toward oneself or one's family. Can I "positively regard" a child whose muddy footprints have stained my freshly cleaned beige carpet? Maybe. Can I empathically relate to a psychotic patient who smeared feces on the hospital wall? Probably. But intentionally hurt or molest my child? I busta ya face!

ABRAHAM HAROLD MASLOW (1908–1970)

Introduction

Unlike Carl Rogers, who spent much of his career engaged in counseling and therapy, Abraham Maslow spent most of his career in academia, teaching and formulating a theory of "higher" human functioning. He was profoundly influenced by Max Wertheimer and Kurt Koffka, founders of Gestalt psychology, and by Ruth Benedict, the brilliant cultural anthropologist. He described them as "very, very wonderful people" whom he "loved, adored, and admired." He held them in such high regard that it seemed to him "as if they were not quite people but something more than people" (Maslow, 1971, pp. 40–41). It was Wertheimer and Benedict who inspired Maslow's first investigations of *self-actualization:*

> When I tried to understand them, think about them, and write about them in my journal and my notes, I realized in one wonderful moment that their two patterns could be generalized. There was wonderful excitement in that. I tried to see whether this pattern could be found elsewhere, and I did find it elsewhere, in one person after another. (Maslow, 1971, pp. 40–41)

Maslow earned his Ph.D. at the University of Wisconsin, where he obtained a solid background in scientific methodology and behaviorist psychology. However, even as a behaviorist graduate student, Maslow was convinced that Freud's emphasis on sexuality was essentially correct. Consequently, for his doctoral research he studied the relationship between sexuality and dominance among primates. Almost immediately upon graduating, he became interested in the "higher" needs, cognitions, and motives of humans, and spent his entire career endeavoring to understand them. However, Maslow always appeared conflicted about the lack of rigor in his studies of self-actualization: "By ordinary standards of laboratory research, i.e., rigorous and controlled research, this simply was not research at all" (1971, pp. 40–41).

After obtaining his doctorate, Maslow conducted very little scientific research. Instead, he spent most of his academic career elaborating the *hierarchy of needs* for which he is remembered, which provided the foundation for his version of humanistic psychology.

Background Check

Jewish kid in a gentile neighborhood. Born of poor, uneducated Russian immigrant parents in a slum district of Brooklyn, New York, Abe Maslow was shy, lonely, and unhappy. He compared growing up Jewish in a non-Jewish neighborhood to being the only Black person enrolled in an all-white school: "I was isolated and unhappy. I grew up in libraries and among books, without friends" (Hall, 1968, p. 37). However, it probably wasn't the feeling of being different from his peers that was most damaging to Maslow's view of himself; as we learned earlier it was his parents who inflicted his deepest emotional wounds.

Urinating with "angels." Maslow experienced most of his college and graduate school professors as radiant contrasts to his dismal, disparaging parents. So great was Maslow's regard for his professors that it bordered on worship. He recalled his amazement and awe to find himself in a men's room alongside his philosophy professor, Eliseo Vivas, who was using the adjoining urinal. "How did I think that professors urinated? Didn't I know they had kidneys?" Maslow relates that seeing his professor urinating next to him "like any normal mortal" was so stunning that "it took hours, or even weeks for me to assimilate the fact that a professor was a human being and that he was constructed with the same plumbing that everyone else had" (quoted in Wilson, 1972, p. 138).

Dropping out of medical school—with a plop. After successfully completing his Ph.D. in 1934, in the midst of the Great Depression, Maslow discovered that jobs for academic psychologists were not plentiful, and for a Jew, almost nonexistent. So although his heart remained in psychology, out of financial concern, he enrolled in the University of Wisconsin's medical school. However, he found the rote memorization boring and the professors' attitudes toward pain and suffering flippant and insensitive. The deciding event was a mastectomy which ended with the surgeon cutting off the breast and flipping it through air where it landed on a marble counter with a plop:

> I have remembered that plop for thirty years. It [the breast] had changed from a sacred object into a lump of fat, garbage, to be tossed into a pail. . . . this was handled in a purely technological fashion: the expert was emotionless, cool, calm, with even a slight tinge of swagger. (quoted in Hoffman, 1988, pp. 66–67)

After dropping out of medical school, Maslow received an offer to return to New York as a postdoctoral fellow to assist the eminent learning theorist, Edward Thorndike, at Columbia University. At one point in their friendship, Thorndike revealed to Maslow that he had scored an astounding 195 on one of his intelligence tests. This made a profound impression: "He [Thorndike] made me feel important. Thereafter, if I retreated in the face of opposition, I'd wake up in the middle of the night and say, 'But dammit, I'm smarter than he is. Why should I feel that he's right and I wrong?'" (quoted in Hoffman, 1988, p. 80).

Compensating for the scars of childhood inferiority. In what appears as yet another Adlerian *compensation* for his father's describing him as "ugly and stupid," Maslow used his IQ score to reassure himself and his colleagues of his value:

> At parties and social gatherings, he liked to spark conversation by casually inquiring into someone's IQ and then volunteering his own. He once asked his Brandeis colleague Max Lerner, the well-known political analyst, "Do you know what your IQ is?" "No, I don't think so," replied Lerner. "Don't worry," Maslow assured him, "it's probably almost as high as mine." Few in Maslow's circle of acquaintances did not hear about his IQ score. (Hoffman, 1988, p. 74)

Zeitgeist

From behaviorism to a baby girl. Abraham Maslow, sometimes referred to as the "spiritual father of humanistic psychology," began his psychology career as a behaviorist. He first fell in love with psychology when, as an undergraduate student at City College of New York, he discovered the work of Watson: "I was sold on behaviorism, I was so excited about Watson's program. It was beautiful" (Hall, 1968, p. 37).

However, the birth of Maslow's baby girl changed all that:

> It made the behaviorism I had been so enthusiastic about look so foolish I could not stomach it anymore. . . . I felt small and weak and feeble before all this. I'd say anyone who had a baby couldn't be a behaviorist. (Hall, 1968, p. 55)

Late in life, Maslow repeated this same critique of behaviorism, stating that although behaviorism works well in the laboratory, "It's useless at home with your kids & wife & friends. It does not generate an image of man, a philosophy of life, a conception of human nature" (Lowry, 1982, p. 267).

Positively influenced by Freud. Maslow was never "anti-Freudian." In fact, late in his life, Maslow underwent psychoanalysis, describing it as a profound learning experience that he valued "more highly than any particular course or any degree" (Maslow, 1971, p. 170). Less than two years before he died, Maslow wrote: "It [psychoanalysis] was *so* successful, so meaningful, so crucially important to me, & changed me so much that I don't care about 100 experiments that fail to prove psychoanalysis has any effects" (Lowry, 1982, p. 271).

Maslow felt that Freud was not wrong so much as incomplete, and he saw himself as differing from Rogers on that issue: "I accept basic Freudian concepts & he [Rogers] doesn't. Viz.: repression; defense & defense mechanisms; resistance; transference; dream analysis; neurosis as a compromise between fear & persistent desire getting *some* gratification in a sneaky way, under cover . . ." (Lowry, 1982, p. 52).

Inspired by Wertheimer. Maslow was also a serious student of *Gestalt psychology* ("the whole is more than the sum of the parts"), greatly admiring the work of Max Wertheimer, whose writings on cognition undoubtedly inspired Maslow's work on creativity. Kurt Goldstein, a neurophysiologist who emphasized the unity of the organism (what happens in one part affects the entire system), was another important influence on Maslow's thinking. So important was Goldstein's influence that Maslow dedicated *Toward a Psychology of Being* (1968) to him:

> If I had to express in a single sentence what Humanistic Psychology has meant for me, I would say that it is the integration of Goldstein (and Gestalt Psychology) with Freud (and the various psychodynamic psychologies), the whole joined with the scientific spirit I was taught by my teachers at the University of Wisconsin" (1968, p. v).

Scientific humanism. These words of dedication summarize how Maslow tried to synthesize the *zeitgeist* of his era with the experiences of his childhood to formulate a more complete model of human functioning—a model that brought the positive as well as the negative aspects of human nature into focus, and assimilated a broad spectrum of disciplines, including behaviorism, psychoanalysis, Gestalt psychology, and social anthropology. Throughout his career, Maslow struggled to envision a humanism that was broad in scope, yet based on scientific foundations.

ASKING THE BIG FOUR QUESTIONS

Maslow would likely have approved of the levels-of-analysis perspective we have followed in moving from biochemical, conditioning, and processing paradigms to the higher-order perspectives of psychoanalysis, humanism, existentialism, transpersonalism, and spiritual psychology. In his last book, he described his own levels-of-analysis orientation: "I am Freudian and I am behavioristic and I am humanistic, and as a matter of fact I am developing what might be called a fourth psychology of transcendence as well" (1971, p. 4).

TABLE 11.2

Maslow at a Glance

MODEL OF PERSONALITY	DESCRIPTION	DYNAMICS
What Are the Parts?	*Self:* a person's biologically based inner core, which refers not so much to a "part" of personality as to the whole person *Real Self:* authentic inner voice	Maslow is not very clear on how the *real self* relates to the person as a whole. He prefers not to fractionate the person, generally speaking of the whole individual.
What Makes a Person Go?	*Physiological needs (also known as D-needs or Deficiency needs):* include oxygen, water, food, sleep, and sex *Safety, belonging, and love needs:* Once basic physiological needs are met, other needs—higher in the hierarchy, such as belonging and love—become dominant. *Metaneeds (Being-Values):* include seeking for truth, beauty, goodness, justice, and the like	One of the most famous constructs in psychology; every introductory psychology student has heard of the *hierarchy of needs*. Unlike some of psychology's more abstract concepts, this one "makes sense" at a very personal level. Hold your breath or swim under water for 45 seconds and it's difficult to think of anything (truth or beauty—even food or sex) except *oxygen!*
What Makes a Person Grow?	*Hierarchical growth:* Development occurs not in "stages," as in other theories, but in moving up the hierarchy of needs from *Deficiency-needs* such as oxygen and water, to seeking to fulfill *Being needs and values* that include beauty, love, playfulness, curiosity, and other such "higher" values.	Development is not chronologically tracked; rather, it occurs in *shifts* to higher needs and aspirations. As they grow, persons learn to meet their biological needs in a taken-for-granted sort of way, and become free to seek to actualize themselves at the highest levels of psychological functioning, which include spiritual, esthetic, and playful dimensions.
What Makes a Person Unique?	Uniqueness is "built in" to humanistic psychology. Humanists reject the notion that people can be understood *en masse,* and insist on the uniqueness of the human species.	Each person seeks to actualize his or her own *singularly distinct* self.

What Are the Parts?

Self. One might expect that since *self-actualization* is perched atop Maslow's *hierarchy of needs* as the ultimate personal achievement, Maslow would have carefully defined what he meant by the *self.* But alas, one searches his writings in vain for a clear definition of self. One writer described Maslow's prose as "a flow of words full of fresh idioms and playful constructions that bounce about until his exact meaning is served" (Lowry, 1982, back cover). Indeed, Maslow "bounces about" in defining self as *a person's inherent nature* or *biologically based inner core that includes tastes, values, interests, and goals.* But he does not describe the self as a specific "part" of personality—for Maslow, *self* means *total person*. What Maslow designated as *self*-actualization could more accurately be described as *person*-actualization. Writing in his journal approximately five years before his death, Maslow reflected that to be *self-actualized* was to be *whole: "give up being a split, dissociated, multiple personality with different levels or selves in conflict, with impulses warring with repressive controls . . . get unified, organized, harmonious; pull yourself together; get your selves together; become One"* (Lowry, 1982, pp. 126–127). Then, he defined self in the following words: "Self *equals* these thousands of little real experiences which add up to 'I am this kind of guy' = self-knowledge" (Lowry, 1982, p. 127).

Real self. In another place, Maslow portrays the **real self** as *an authentic inner voice* in much the same way as Karen Horney used the term *real self* or Transactional Analysts referred to the *Little Professor.* Maslow speaks of "differentiating the inner voice of neurosis from the voice of the authentic, real self of Little Abraham from Dr. Maslow," adding that listening to the *real self* is not easy: "I must say candidly that this is extremely difficult, because ultimately the differentiation has to be phenomenological. . . . In the very moment of listening to one's inner voices & deciding on which to act & on which *not* to act, one must know which to trust" (Lowry, 1982, pp. 175–176).

Maslow suggests that one can distinguish the *real self* from other counterfeits because the *real ("biologically sound") self* seems to fit. This chose Rogers's trust of his viscera:

> The biologically sound voices seem to fit, to suit, to sit well, to have a rightness & a suitability & belongingness. The feeling is of recognition: this is *it*. This is for me. *This* is what I've been missing. . . . Like trying on dozens of shoes & then one is just right. . . . There is always some feeling of *certainty*. . . . The false voice phenomenologically lacks this same sense of settling the problem of just-rightness, of certainty, of finality, of suitability. . . . (Lowry, 1982, pp. 176–177)

Notice, however, that whether Maslow is referring to the *self,* the *real self,* or some sort of *counterfeit self,* the meaning would remain the same if the word *person* were substituted for *"self,"* because what he is referring to is the entire organism, not a subpart of personality. Thus although Maslow is sometimes portrayed as a *self* theorist, a close study of his work shows him to be focused not so much on the self, as on the person as a whole.

What Makes a Person Go?

Needs and metaneeds. Just as psychoanalysts see people as driven by libido, Maslow views people as driven by their needs—"perpetually wanting" (1943, p. 172). **Perpetually wanting** means that *when "lower" urges are satisfied, "higher" needs emerge to dominate consciousness.* Thus, one can never be fully satisfied but can only move among various kinds of needs, satisfying "higher" needs, but continuing to be "perpetually wanting." As Maslow saw it:

> It is quite true that man lives by bread alone—when there is no bread. But what happens to man's desires when there is plenty of bread and when his belly is chronically filled? *At once other (and higher) needs emerge,* and these, rather than

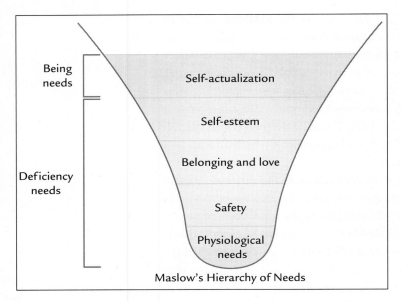

Being needs

Deficiency needs

Self-actualization

Self-esteem

Belonging and love

Safety

Physiological needs

Maslow's Hierarchy of Needs

Figure 11.2 ■ *Needs Hierarchy*

physiological hungers, dominate their organism. And when these in turn are satisfied, again new (and still higher) needs emerge, and so on. This is what we mean by saying that the basic human needs are organized into a hierarchy of relative prepotency. (Maslow, 1987, p. 17)

Hierarchy of needs. Maslow blended parts and motives in his famous **hierarchy of needs,** *a motivational model in which needs are ranked hierarchically.* First, the *physiological needs* for air, water, and food must be satisfied. Next, the *psychological needs* for safety, love, and esteem emerge. Finally, *metaneeds (e.g., truth, beauty, justice, etc.)* appear at the highest levels of psychological functioning in the process of *self-actualization.*

Maslow's *hierarchy of needs* is not comprised of precisely defined parts, nor is it a model that specifically describes how various needs are met. Rather, it is a *hierarchical mapping* of how multiple psychological factors influence a person's behavior. Maslow's model shares much in common with Freud's id, ego, and superego dynamics, but is less anchored to biology. Whereas Freud anchors most adult behaviors to early biological experiences, Maslow easily discusses such "metaneeds" as justice, playfulness, meaningfulness, and beauty, without attempting to anchor these to biological bedrock or to earlier developmental stages.

Maslow saw his hierarchy as more rubbery than rigid. Instead of needs emerging and being satisfied in a preordered, predetermined, bottom-to-top sequence (much as one *must* satisfy the need for oxygen before attempting other goals), Maslow believed that needs might emerge simultaneously, or even "top-down":

> We have spoken so far as if this hierarchy were a fixed order but actually it is not nearly as rigid as we may have implied. . . . There are some people in whom, for instance, self-esteem seems to be more important than love. . . . There are other, apparently creative people in whom the drive to creativeness seems to be more than any other counter-determinant. (Maslow, 1943, pp. 165–166)

Maslow believed that people are motivated by multiple influences—sometimes acting in concert, sometimes producing conflict: "These needs must be understood *not* to be *exclusive* or single determiners of certain kinds of behavior. . . . Or to say it in another way, most behavior is multi-motivated" (Maslow, 1943, p. 168).

Basic (instinctoid) needs. Maslow referred to psychological needs as *instinctoid* because he believed that humans are born with tendencies for compassion, altruism, and the like. In his hierarchy these *inborn* or *instinctoid needs* and *metaneeds* range from *physiological* needs at the lower end to *esteem* needs at the top.

Physiological needs. Included among **physiological needs** are *oxygen, water, food, sleep,* and *sex.* Maslow stated that *physiological needs* dominate the organism when *most* other needs are unsatisfied. For a choking person the need for oxygen becomes overwhelming, but if one isn't choking, one might be motivated to find food or get a drink of water. And if one is well fed and not thirsty, shopping for a new pair of shoes or calling a friend for a date might emerge as a need. In our culture, where many of our basic needs are easily met (for example, large cities supply uncontaminated drinking water to millions of residents), many people find time to pursue higher goals such as enhancing self-esteem or seeking love.

Safety needs. This refers to a person's need to live in a relatively safe and predictable environment. Most of us prefer structure, predictability, and order to chaos and crime. People function best when they are free from fear and anxiety, and in most modern Western countries *safety needs* only become dominant in emergencies such as natural disasters, riots, or epidemics. Normally people take a stable, smoothly running society for granted and feel free to pursue higher needs.

Belonging and love needs. Most of us are motivated to seek love and intimacy with others and to be part of a larger group such as a family, club, or circle of friends. Sometimes in a highly mobile society such as ours, educational and vocational opportunities result in family members' living great distances apart, and even friendships formed in work settings tend to be temporary, as people change jobs much more frequently than did their parents.

Esteem needs. Taking his cue from Adler, Maslow (1987) described two kinds of *esteem needs:* (1) a desire for personal competence and achievement, and (2) respect and recognition from others—status, fame, appreciation, and recognition.

Need for self-actualization. Even when all the lower needs are fulfilled, unless people experience the full use of their creative capacities and the maximum use of their talents, they will still feel frustrated or incomplete and experience various *metapathologies.* Maslow defined **self-actualization** as "*. . . the full use and exploitation of talents, capacities, potentialities, etc. Such people seem to be fulfilling themselves and to be doing the best that they are capable of doing. They are people who have developed or are developing to the full stature of which they are capable*" (1950, p. 12, italics added).

Maslow described *self-actualized* people as relatively free from crippling guilt or shame, with the ability to freshly appreciate their surroundings:

> Thus, for such a person, every sunset is as beautiful as the first one, any flower may be of breath-taking loveliness, even after he has seen a million flowers. The thousandth baby he sees is just as miraculous a product as the first one he saw. . . . For such people even the casual workday, moment-to-moment business of living can be thrilling, exciting, and ecstatic. (Maslow, 1950, pp. 16–25)

Maslow did not see *self-actualization* as a once-for-all-time accomplishment; rather he saw it as an evolving psychological process wherein a person mostly transcends the urgency of basic needs and deficiency-motives, and grows to become fully the person he or she was designed to be:

> Musicians must make music, artists must paint, poets must write if they are to be ultimately at peace with themselves. What humans *can* be they *must* be. They must be true to their nature. This need we may call self-actualization. (1987, p. 22)

Metaneeds (Being-Values), metamotives, and metapathologies. People who have met their basic needs for safety, love, and esteem typically concern themselves with finding fulfillment and meaning in their lives. This process of *self-actualization* is inspired by such **metaneeds (Being-Values)** as *the search for truth, beauty, justice, and the like.* Maslow used the term **metamotivation** to describe *the mobilization of behavior in the service of these "higher" (growth-oriented) values and needs.* Maslow believed that self-esteem, vocational success, and a commitment to values larger than oneself are as essential for one's psychological well-being as food and water are for physical survival. Failing to pursue or find such *B-Values* results in what Maslow termed **metapathologies,** or *spiritual–existential ailments (e.g., cynicism, boredom, drug addiction, delinquency, despair, hopelessness, powerlessness, loss of zest, lack of fulfillment)* that afflict so many in modern times.

It is important to notice that at these higher levels, metaneeds such as *truth, goodness, beauty, meaningfulness, playfulness, justice, uniqueness, etc.* are *not* hierarchically arranged but are more or less simultaneously present. Having reached the level of *self-actualization,* people seek to meet their *metaneeds* in uniquely personal ways.

Maslow believed that *metaneeds* such as playfulness, truth, and beauty are just as real—just as necessary for survival—as biological needs for food and water. We saw an illustration of this in the Great Proletarian Cultural Revolution of China during the 1960s, when Chairman Mao attempted to eradicate beauty as a bourgeois luxury. Red Guards closed flower shops and the Chinese people were ordered to destroy their goldfish. Everyone was compelled to dress alike—in drab, unisex uniforms. What actually took place, it was later discovered, was that beauty went underground: children hid jars of goldfish under their beds and women wore brightly colored blouses under their gray Mao jackets. Over the remaining chapters of our text, we will explore existential, spiritual, and transpersonal theories of psychology, affirming what Maslow believed and what ordinary Chinese recognized—that beauty and truth are as necessary for life as food.

Metagrumbles. Maslow coined the term **metagrumble,** referring to *higher-order concerns, such as a lack of fulfillment in a person's job or lack of appreciation by their superiors, that arise when "lower" needs have been fulfilled.* Thus, when members of a committee to petition the city to plant shade trees and construct a biking path alongside Main Street squabble about details, they are engaging in "metagrumbling"; having taken care of lower physiological and safety needs, they are free to worry about higher needs involving beauty and recreation. As Maslow put it, "To have committees . . . heatedly coming in and complaining that rose gardens in the parks are not sufficiently cared for . . . is in itself a wonderful thing because it indicates the height of life at which the complainers are living" (1965, p. 240).

What Makes a Person Grow?

Hierarchical growth. It is hardly surprising that Maslow saw growth and maturation unfolding hierarchically rather than occurring in developmental "stages." In his last book, *The Farther Reaches of Human Nature* (1971), Maslow outlined his developmental theory in terms of **Being-Psychology:** *a perspective that emphasizes* *positive values such as goodness, truth, and beauty; and appreciates individuals for their uniqueness, wholeness, and aliveness.*

This is humanistic psychology at its best, contrasting markedly with traditional animal-based or psychoanalytic theories of development, which, according to Maslow, were heavily biased toward **deficiency motives, values, and cognitions,** *which cause people to behave on the basis of "deficiencies" of water, food, safety, or sex.* In place of *deficiency motives,* Maslow emphasized "The far goals of 'creative,' 'humanistic,' or 'whole person' education" (1971, p. 139), which included such nonverbal activities as art, dance, music, and the like.

Maslow distinguished between *deficiency* needs or values ("D-Needs" or "D-Values") and *being* needs and values ("B-Needs or "B-Values"). He outlined eight ways in which individuals grow in the direction of *being,* toward the highest goal: self-actualization. Let's briefly explore Maslow's various distinctions between *being* and *deficiency.*

Being-Values. B-Values occur during **peak experiences,** which are *joyous, exciting moments usually inspired by love, nature, or great music.* Maslow described a dozen and a half B-Values, and he didn't hesitate to use values such as rightness and honesty as being part of *both* goodness and beauty. Also, there is no hierarchy intended here—all fifteen were deemed to be of equal importance.

Being love versus deficiency love. D-love *seeks to fulfill a need (e.g., for self-esteem) or avoid loneliness by loving another,* whereas **B-love** is *nonpossessive and appreciates others for whom they are without attempting to change them or interfere with their lives.* For Maslow, *B-love* "becomes so great and so pure (unambivalent) for the object itself that *its* good is what we want, not what it can do for us . . ." (1971, p. 142):

> So we feel half-consciously that the dog improver is not really a dog-lover. The real dog-lover will be enraged by the tail cropping, the ear cropping or shaping, the selective breeding that makes this dog fit a pattern from some magazine, at the cost of making it nervous, sick, sterile, unable to give birth normally, epileptic, etc. . . . (1971, pp. 142–143)

Being motivation versus deficiency motivation. B-motives *seek to satisfy positive goals, such as playfulness and curiosity.* **D-motives** *seek to change the current state of affairs—to lessen or remove frustration or dissatisfaction.* Here again we see that Maslow's motivational system is hierarchically comprehensive. He does not deny that *D-motives* exist, only that they are more relevant to animals than to humans. Maslow felt that animal laboratory–based theories of motivation gave a distorted picture of human functioning because they were based on water- or food-deprivation studies:

> Obviously a good way to obscure the "higher" motivations, and get a lopsided view of human capacities and human nature, is to make the organism extremely and chronically hungry or thirsty. . . . If all the needs are unsatisfied, and the organism is then dominated by the physiological needs, all other needs become simply nonexistent or pushed into the background. . . . (Maslow, 1943, pp. 373–375)

Unless humans are in deprived or emergency circumstances, they usually are able to meet their physiological requirements, and then such D-needs cease to actively motivate behavior. In their place, "higher" B-motives come into play. Maslow

TABLE 11.3

B-Values and Metapathologies

B-VALUE OR METANEED	PATHOGENIC DEPRIVATION	SPECIFIC METAPATHO-LOGIES (MOTIVATION DISEASE)
1. Truth	Dishonesty	Disbelief; mistrust; cynicism
2. Goodness	Evil	Utter selfishness; hatred, reliance only on self; disgust, nihilism
3. Beauty	Ugliness	Vulgarity; loss of taste; tension; fatigue
4. Unity-Wholeness	Chaos, atomism	Disintegration; arbitrariness
4A. Dichotomy-Transcendence	Black/White dichotomies; forced choices	Either/or thinking; seeing everything as dualistic; a simplistic view of life
5. Aliveness; process	Deadness; mechanizing of life	Robotizing; feeling totally determined; loss of zest in life
6. Uniqueness	Sameness; uniformity	Loss of feeling of individuality or being needed
7. Perfection	Imperfection; sloppiness	Discouragement (?); hopelessness
7A. Necessity	Accident; occasionalism; inconsistency	Loss of safety; unpredictability
8. Completion; finality	Incompleteness	Cessation of striving
9. Justice	Injustice	Insecurity; anger; cynicism; mistrust
9A. Order	Lawlessness; chaos	Insecurity; wariness; loss of safety
10. Simplicity	Confusing complexity	Overcomplexity; confusion; loss of orientation
11. Richness; totality	Poverty	Depression; uneasiness; loss of interest
12. Effortlessness	Effortfulness	Fatigue; strain; clumsiness
13. Playfulness	Humorlessness	Grimness; depression; paranoid humorlessness
14. Self-sufficiency	Accident; occasionalism	Dependence upon the perceiver and others
15. Meaningfulness	Meaninglessness	Despair; senselessness of life

did not completely discard animal-based studies of learning and motivation ("Man's higher nature rests upon man's lower nature, needing it as a foundation and collapsing without this foundation" [Maslow, 1968, p. 173]); rather, he disputed the relevance of animal-based research to much of human behavior that seeks goals "higher" than food or water.

What Makes a Person Unique?

Uniqueness was a primary concern for Maslow. Not only did he emphasize personal uniqueness, he underscored the uniqueness of the human species as compared with primates, pigeons, and rodents—the standby animals for experimental studies in most of the leading psychological laboratories of his time. Maslow believed that most animal studies were irrelevant to human concerns: "If one took a course or picked up a book on the psychology of learning, most of it, in my opinion would be beside the point—that is, beside the "humanistic" point . . ." (Maslow, 1971, p. 168).

The paradigm of *humanistic* psychology was founded on the uniqueness of human beings. At the lower end of Maslow's hierarchy, humans share many physiological needs with other animals; however, when we move beyond hunger, thirst, and sex to issues of love, self-esteem, and self-actualization, each person's journey is one-of-a-kind, distinctive, and special. The ultimate expression of uniqueness occurs at the summit of the hierarchy in the process of self-actualization.

Eight pathways to self-actualization. Maslow delineated eight ways in which individuals might facilitate self-actualization. He didn't present these in a logically tight sequence, but coming at the end of his career these suggestions represent the culmination of his thinking on the topic. Although this listing is not strictly hierarchical, Maslow believed that following the first four provided the foundation for the fifth: judgment.

(1) Concentration. Self-actualizing requires total absorption and full concentration—losing oneself in the process. As Maslow put it, "self-actualization means experiencing fully, vividly, selflessly, with full concentration and total absorption" (1971, p. 45).

(2) Growth choices. Life can be seen as a series of choices, and self-actualizers take the risk of making decisions for growth. To choose safety, instead of self-actualization, allows one to remain in familiar territory but avoids growth. To grow, one must choose new challenges even at the risk of failure. According to Maslow, this is a daily process: "To make the growth choice instead of the fear choice a dozen times a day is to move a dozen times a day toward self-actualization. *Self-actualization is an ongoing process . . .*" (1971, p. 45).

(3) Self-awareness. As we progress toward self-actualization, we become more aware of our inner nature and behave accordingly. This, in turn, facilitates further self-actualization in the process of deciding for ourselves what movies we enjoy, what books we prefer, or what music we choose. Maslow suggested that when given a glass of wine we ought *not* to look at the label on the bottle and try to decide if we *should* like this wine; rather we should close our eyes, let the wine swirl about our tongues and then consult the "Supreme Court" inside ourselves.

(4) Honesty. Candor, honesty, and responsibility for our actions are essential elements in self-actualization. Instead of behaving to please or impress others, self-actualizers seek to look within themselves for answers and take responsibility for their responses. Maslow says that "responsibility has been little studied. . . . for who can investigate responsibility in white rats?" He then states that "This is one of the great steps. Each time one takes responsibility, this is an actualizing of the self" (1971, pp. 46–47).

(5) Judgment. Following the first four steps provides a foundation for making better choices about what is "constitutionally right" for each person. Maslow says that "One cannot choose wisely for life unless he dares to listen to himself, *his own self,* at each moment in life, and to say calmly, 'No, I don't like such and such'" (1971, p. 47).

(6) Self-development. Self-actualization is not a *thing* a person possesses, or a *part* of one's personality—it isn't something you either have or don't have. Rather, it is an *ongoing process* of becoming fully oneself. As Maslow described it, "self-actualization is not only an end state but also the process of actualizing one's potentialities at any time, in any amount." (1971, p. 47).

(7) Peak experiences. Maslow defined peak experiences as *"transient moments of self-actualization. They are moments of ecstasy which cannot be bought, cannot be guaranteed, cannot even be sought"* (1971, p. 48). Such moments are what C. S. Lewis (1995) referred to as "surprised by joy." Maslow maintained that nearly everyone has peak experiences, but not everyone recognizes them. He said that one of the jobs of the counselor is "helping people to recognize these little moments of ecstasy" (1971, p. 48).

Pathways to heaven. Maslow said that *music* and *sex* were among the most commonly reported pathways to peak experiences. As he put it: "there are many paths to heaven, and sex is one of them, and music is one of them. These happen to be the easiest ones, the most widespread, and the ones that are easiest to understand" (1971, p. 175). However, Maslow made it clear that peak experiences are not restricted to the throbbing excitements generated by music or sex. Hearing a baby's laughter, coming upon a meadow filled with wildflowers, or viewing a splendid sunset might trigger a peak experience. According to Maslow, almost anything can trigger peak experiences: "It looks as if any experience of real excellence, of real perfection, of any moving toward the perfect justice, or toward perfect values tends to produce a peak experience" (1971, p. 175).

"Mathematics can be just as beautiful, just as peak-producing as music," said Maslow, adding wryly, "of course, there are mathematics teachers who have devoted themselves to preventing this" (1971, pp. 177–178). In addition to *peak experiences,* Maslow described less-intense but equally-meaningful *plateau experiences.*

Plateau experiences. In contrast to peak experiences, which typically last only a few minutes—or a few hours at most—Maslow described the **plateau experience,** *a more steady, enduring experience that involves a fundamental change in attitude affecting one's viewpoint and creating an intensified awareness and appreciation of the world.* According to Maslow, *plateau experiences* are more voluntary than peak experiences, so one can cultivate *plateau experiences* by visiting an art museum, or a meadow, or the oceanside:

> I think you can teach plateau experiences; you could hold classes in miraculousness . . . it's possible to sit and look at something miraculous for an hour and enjoy every second of it. On the other hand, you can't have an hour-long orgasm. In this sense the plateau type of experience is better. It has a great advantage, so to speak over the climactic, the orgasm, the peak. . . . There tends to be more serenity rather than emotionality. . . . However, calmness must also be brought into one's psychology. (Maslow in Krippner, 1972, pp. 112–115)

(8) Becoming less defensive. Reflecting on his late-in-life, positive experience with personal psychoanalysis, Maslow stressed the importance of "finding out who one is, what he is, what he likes, what he doesn't like, what is good for him, and what bad, where he is going and what his mission is . . ." (1971, pp. 48–49). "This is painful," he admits, "because defenses are erected against something which is unpleasant. But giving up the defenses is worthwhile. If the psychoanalytic literature has taught us nothing else, it has taught us that repression is not a good way of solving problems" (1971, p. 49).

Accumulating self-actualization. After describing the eight pathways, Maslow summarized self-actualization in the following words:

> Put all these points together, and we see that self-actualization is not a matter of one great moment. It's not true that on Thursday at four o'clock the trumpet blows and one steps into the pantheon forever and altogether. Self-actualization is a matter of degree, of little accessions accumulated one by one. (1971, p. 50)

FACING THE TOUGH TWINS

Is It Testable?

Studying "saints" instead of cripples. Maslow's formulation of *self-actualization* was based on the study of a small sample of highly successful subjects (approximately a dozen historical figures: e.g., Lincoln, Jefferson, Einstein, Eleanor Roosevelt, Walt Whitman, Henry Thoreau, Beethoven, and Freud, as well as sixteen of Maslow's contemporaries, e.g., G. W. Carver, Albert Schweitzer, and Fritz Kreisler). He reports that out of three thousand college students that he screened for participating in the project, he found only one usable subject. Maslow conceded that choosing subjects from among a few historically famous figures and from among his own personal acquaintances and friends was not a scientific way to acquire a sample, but he published his ideas nonetheless, "with due apologies to those who insist upon conventional reliability, validity, sampling, etc." (Maslow, 1950, pp. 11–12).

Maslow here seems to imply that only scientific fuddy-duddies—those who are overly concerned with trifles—would insist on "reliability, validity, sampling, etc." However, the fact that he found only *one* in *three thousand* college students that he considered to be self-actualized raises serious questions regarding the applicability of his theories to the average person. Although it was Maslow's stated intention to study distinctive and transcendent examples of humanity—not necessarily *average* people— we are left to wonder to what extent *self-actualization* is of practical value. Just as he was convinced that the study of *animals* would not yield useful information about *humans,* he questioned whether studying ordinary people (whom he compared to "cripples") would prove as useful as studying exceptional ones:

> Certainly a visitor from Mars descending upon a colony of birth-injured cripples, dwarfs, [and] hunchbacks . . . could not deduce what they *should* have been. But then let us *not* study cripples, but the closest thing we can get to whole, healthy men. . . . In a certain sense, only the saints *are* mankind. All the rest are cripples. (Quoted in Hoffman, 1988, p. 173)

Although Maslow deliberately studied only those whom he considered to be psychologically superb, he still insisted that his self-actualizers were quite human in many ways:

> *There are no perfect human beings!* Persons can be found who are good, very good indeed, in fact, great. . . . This can certainly give us hope for the future of the species even if they are uncommon and do not come by the dozen. And yet these very same people can at times be boring, irritating, petulant, selfish, angry, or depressed. (Maslow, 1970, p. 176)

Commando raids and guerrilla attacks. Maslow's scientific work was mostly exploratory and inconclusive and he was aware of the limitations of his speculations:

> It's just that I haven't got the time to do careful experiments myself. They take too long, in view of the years that I have left and the extent of what I want to do.
>
> So I myself do only "quick-and-dirty" little pilot explorations, mostly with a few subjects only, inadequate to publish but enough to convince myself that they are probably true and will be confirmed one day. Quick little commando raids, guerilla attacks. (Maslow, quoted in International Study Project, 1972, pp. 66–67)

Bad science, bad dreams? However, try as he might, Maslow could never completely leave his University of Wisconsin graduate training behind. Near the end of his life he confessed that he had "been tense for weeks & weeks—bad sleep, fatigue, preoccupation, etc. Partly due, according to dreams, to getting all wound up & a little awed & scared by tremendous implications of work I'm doing contrasted with very shaky foundations it's all based on. So get scary dreams . . ." (Lowry, 1982, p. 79).

Heuristic inspiration. Although Maslow himself conducted little rigorous research after completing his own doctorate, some of his students were inspired to investigate various aspects of his theories. Shostrom (1963) developed a Personal Orientation Inventory (POI) to measure self-actualization, and other investigators (e.g., Gray, 1986; Rychman, 1985) have conducted research using this instrument. Maslow's concept of peak experiences has also received significant research attention (see Mathes, Zevon, Roter, & Joerger, 1982, for a review of this research). Not surprisingly, most of the studies conducted by his students have tended to confirm the validity of Maslow's theories; yet, his work is not without its critics.

Is self-actualization primarily a Western value? Some have suggested that Maslow's view of the self-actualized person is rooted in American values of individual achievement. Whereas parents in Western societies attempt to develop positive self-esteem in their children, in Japan and China the autonomous self is *not* stressed; rather, children are taught to cooperate and avoid hurting others' feelings by demonstrating their superiority (Kitayama & Markus, 1992). Others (e.g., Chang & Page, 1991) believe that cross-cultural research comparing Maslow, Rogers, Lao Tzu, and Zen Buddhism supports Maslow's assumption that all people have an actualizing tendency toward positive growth.

The psychology of women. Maslow never claimed to understand women; rather, he regarded them with a sense of awe—almost reverence: "Women are really kind of perpetual miracles. They are like flowers. Every person is a mystery to me, but women are more mysterious than men" (Maslow, in Hall, 1968, p. 56).

Lerman (1992) suggests that Maslow failed to address how the environment frequently fails to facilitate the basic needs of women, and Norman, Murphy, & Gilligan (1982) have observed that women's experiences and needs differ from those of men. Betty Friedan refers extensively to Maslow in *The Feminine Mystique* (1977), in which she encourages women toward self-actualization beyond the roles of wife and mother. Yet, when women are viewed from the hierarchy-of-needs perspective, they cannot consistently be characterized by Maslow's highest levels. As Ruth Cox, one of Maslow's admirers, put it: "Although Maslow was attempting to define self-actualization in both sexes, his definition of psychological health does not fundamentally represent the psychology of women" (quoted in Maslow, 1987, p. 261).

Flow—research about optimizing existence. We will conclude our survey of humanistic research by considering the work of Csikszentmihalyi on **flow,** *a pleasurable state of focused consciousness, during which time passes rapidly while a person engages in* <u>autotelic</u> *activity.* The term *autotelic* is derived from the Greek *auto* meaning self, and *telos* meaning goal. This refers to an activity that is done not with the expectation of reward, but because the doing itself is the reward. Over the past two decades Csikszentmihalyi (1990) has examined the experiences of athletes, dancers, writers, and others when they engaged in the *autotelic* activities they enjoyed most, e.g., playing racquetball, performing music, acting on stage, playing Sim City on the computer, snowboarding, or reading an engrossing novel. He found that during *flow,* people experience a loss of self-consciousness and a transformation of time. Although *flow* has similarities with Maslow's *peak experiences,* Csikszentmihalyi incorporates *flow* into everyday life: work as flow, the flow of thought, the body in flow.

Is It Useful?

We have seen that Maslow derived most of his theoretical inspirations and ideas from teachers, friends, personal acquaintances, and historical superstars rather than from the laboratory. Consequently, much of his theory is based on loosely structured interviews and his own personal speculation, making it difficult to evaluate in a rigorous manner. Although his ideas did not win wide acclaim among "hard-nosed" academic researchers of his era, many of his ideas have been subsequently utilized in psychology, education, business, and health care—to name but a few.

Positive psychology. Part of Maslow's legacy is today's **positive psychology,** *a psychological perspective that emphasizes positive traits, positive subjective experience, and positive institutions.* Martin Seligman, a past president of the American Psychological Association with a strong research background, relates how he became turned on to positive psychology:

> The moment took place in my garden while I was weeding with my five-year-old daughter, Nikki. I have to confess that even though I write books about children, I'm really not all that good with children. I am goal oriented and time urgent, and when I'm weeding in the garden, I'm actually trying to get the weeding done. Nikki, however, was throwing weeds into the air, singing, and dancing around. I yelled at her. She walked away, then came back and said,
>
> "Daddy, I want to talk to you."

"Yes, Nikki?"

"Daddy, do you remember my fifth birthday? From the time I was three to the time I was five, I was a whiner. I whined every day. When I turned five, I decided not to whine anymore. That was the hardest thing I've ever done. And if I can stop whining, you can stop being such a grouch." (Seligman & Csikszentmihalyi, 2000, pp. 5–6)

Seligman reports that this incident was an epiphany for him; he recognized that rearing his daughter was not about correcting whining. "Rather," he writes, "I realized that raising Nikki is about taking this marvelous strength she has—I call it 'seeing into the soul'—amplifying it, nurturing it . . . Raising children, I realized is vastly more than fixing what is wrong with them. It is about identifying and nurturing their strongest qualities, what they own and are best at, and helping them find niches in which they can best live out these strengths" (p. 6).

Similarly, the authors emphasize that "psychology is not just the study of pathology, weakness, and damage; it is also the study of strength and virtue. Treatment is not just fixing what is broken; it is nurturing what is best" (p. 7). Although much of this might have seemed like "reinventing the wheel" to Maslow, he would doubtless have been pleased with the conclusions of this lead article in an issue of the *American Psychologist* devoted entirely to positive psychology.

Educational and clinical applications. Maslow didn't think psychotherapy was the most efficient way to change society; it was in schools and work settings that he believed change needed to occur. Schools, he suggested, should help students to look within themselves and from this knowledge develop a set of values.

Needs hierarchy in a school setting. Guest (1985) reports that some school districts have evaluated their programs to determine whether they meet children's *physiological* (e.g., transportation, free lunches, etc.), *safety* (fire drills, abuse reporting), and *love and belonging needs* (friendship groups, class meetings, counseling). Programs aimed at fostering *esteem* and *self-actualization* have included displaying students' work, reinforcing rewards, and participating in school productions and special activities.

Multiple intelligences. Maslow believed that individuals operating at the higher levels of the needs hierarchy are creative in a variety of ways. Gardner (1983) published a theory of multiple intelligences that confirmed Maslow's contention that there are many ways to solve problems and that education should address a student's linguistic, spatial, bodily, kinesthetic, logico-mathematical, musical, and personal intelligences.

Maslow in the marketplace. As a visiting fellow at Non-Linear Systems, a high-tech plant in Del Mar, California, Maslow became infused with the idea of humanizing the workplace: "Individual therapy is useless for the masses," he wrote. "I had thought of education as the best bet for changing society. But now the work situation seems even better" (Lowry, 1979, p. 191). Coining the word *eupsychia* to describe institutions that were moving toward humanistic values, Maslow formulated his **Theory Z,** *a theory that moved beyond classic economic scarcity models to include trust, intimacy, shared decision making, and self-actualization in the work setting.* Some twenty years later, Ouchi published his well-known book on Japanese business practices entitled *Theory Z* (1981). Ouchi makes no reference to Maslow in his book.

The Values and Life (VALS) Project. One of the most successful business applications of Maslow's model was developed at Stanford, where the Values and Life Project (VALS) profiled nine different types of people, based on Maslow's needs hierarchy (Mitchell, 1983, p. 4). These VALS profiles have been successfully utilized in matching employees with jobs, profiling consumer preferences, and numerous other business applications.

Holistic health and personal responsibility. Maslow's influence has been felt in health care settings, where, thanks partly to his *holistic* hierarchy of needs, the practice of *holistic* medicine is no longer associated with herbal remedies, zealots, and fanatics. Closely connected with a nonreductionist approach to health care is the idea that people need to take responsibility for their own wellness. As Leonard (1983) put it, "If anything can solve the crisis of medical depersonalization and rising costs, it is the classically Maslovian shift: more and more people working against a pathogenic environment and society while taking personal responsibility for their own positive good health" (p. 335).

SUMMARY OF MASLOW

Maslow did not specifically formulate a theory of personality; however, his *hierarchy of needs* struck such a responsive chord that this model became the foundation for all his subsequent work. It remains his lasting legacy, his identity badge. Just as we associate Freud with a couch, Pavlov with dogs, and Skinner with pigeons, Maslow has come to mean *hierarchy of needs* to subsequent generations of psychology students.

Maslow's legacy is not in the experiments he conducted or the doctoral dissertations he directed. His scientific studies are relatively few and his students (sometimes referred to as "Abe's groupies" by other members of the Brandeis psychology faculty) did not distinguish themselves by conducting rigorous research to test their mentor's theories. Rather, Maslow will be remembered for shifting the paradigm—for altering the "big picture." He was one of the major "midwives" at the birth of humanistic psychology.

If we were to summarize Maslow's life in a single word, it would be *evolving*. He was a restless and creative person. Entries in his journal reveal frequent sleepless nights with his mind in ferment. He was constantly changing, continually growing, ceaselessly self-actualizing; hence, his untimely death at 62 was especially tragic. Had this pioneer third-force psychologist lived another quarter century, he would likely have been surfing the cusp of yet another wave—the fourth wave.

A Fourth Force. In subsequent chapters we will analyze *transpersonal* and *spiritual* theories in more detail, but here we will simply note Maslow's movement in the direction of those higher levels. Near the end of his life, Maslow believed he could bring all the major religions under the rubric of psychology, and had he lived to 83 as did Freud, or 85 as did Rogers, or 86 as did Skinner, he undoubtedly would have turned his creative mind and considerable energies toward developing a "fourth wave," **transpersonal psychology,** or *looking beyond the individual to grapple with larger issues— the timeless topics (traditionally pursued by theologians, mystics and other "spiritual" types) relating to life and death, good and evil, decay and transcendence.*

Transcending self-actualization. In his final book, Maslow devoted an entire chapter to the topic of *transcendence:* transcendence of one's skin, transcendence of culture, transcendence of one's past, transcendence of self and selfishness, transcendence of the opinions of others, transcendence of one's weakness and dependency. Sounding somewhat like an Eastern guru, Maslow conceptualized **transcendence** *as an emergence from holistic experiences that facilitate a person's moving even beyond self-actualization.* Maslow described this as living at "the very highest and most inclusive or holistic levels of human consciousness, behaving and relating, as ends rather than as means, to oneself, to significant others, to human beings in general, to other species, to nature, and to the cosmos" (Maslow, 1971, p. 279).

Including spirituality. Describing this new "Fourth Force," Maslow emphasized the importance of spirituality:

> The Third Force is like Sweden, Norway, and Denmark, where God died and there *is* no god, where everything is sensible, rational, commonsensical, logical, empirical but not yet transcendent. You can admire and respect Scandinavia, but you can't love it, much less worship it! Everything that a good, mundane, this-worldly, reasonable . . . intelligence could do has been done there. But it's not enough! (Maslow, in Lowry, 1979, p. 283)

Confronting evil. Had he lived longer, Maslow would likely have elaborated his ideas in both directions—exploring evil as well as good. Critics frequently denounce Maslow and Rogers for being *too* positive and castigate them as naive for failing to deal with the dark side of human nature. However, a careful reading of Maslow's later works suggests that he was not unaware of the problems of evil, but that he had not yet found time to explore it in depth:

> It's a psychological puzzle I've been trying to solve for years. Why are people cruel and why are they nice? Evil people are rare, but you find evil behavior in the majority of people. The next thing I want to do with my life is to study evil by understanding it. (Maslow, in Hall, 1968, p. 35)

Nor was he sparing of fellow humanist Carl Rogers:

> Rogers doesn't have enough sin, evil, & psychopathology in his system. He speaks of the only drive as self-actualization, which is to imply there is only a tendency to health. Then where does all the sickness come from? He needs more theory of psychopathogenesis, of fear, of resentment, of countervalues, of hostility. (Lowry, 1971, p. 52)

Postmodernism. Some thirty years ago, Maslow anticipated the postmodern perspective that each individual's personality is an ongoing "project." He would likely have seen postmodernism as an opportunity for holistic synthesis:

> . . . man is in a way his own project and he does make himself. But also there are limits upon what he can make himself into. The "project" is predetermined biologically for all men; it is to become a man. He cannot adopt as his project for himself to become a chimpanzee. Or even a female. Or even a baby. The

right label would have to combine the humanistic, the transpersonal, and the transhuman. Besides, it would have to be experiential (phenomenological), at least in its basing. It would have to be holistic rather than dissecting. (Maslow, 1971, p. 350)

Points to Remember

1. Considered one of the *founders of humanistic psychology,* Carl Rogers was influenced by Otto Rank, one of Freud's closest followers. Rank advocated a much more active role for the therapist than recommended by Freud. Rogers's emphasis on empathy, genuineness, and warmth are in sharp contrast to the psychoanalytic Buddah behind the couch or blank screen.

2. Considered by many to be the *spiritual father of humanistic psychology,* Abraham Maslow was *influenced by the behaviorist theories* of Watson and by his doctoral studies with the eminent primate psychologist, Harry Harlow. Following the birth of his first child, Maslow rejected behaviorism as foolishly simplistic for the task of rearing a child, and began seriously developing his humanist approach.

3. Humanist psychologists believe that human nature is *essentially good* and that persons are *naturally inclined toward growth, creativity, and meaningful values.* Further, humanists tend to emphasize the *conscious* pursuit of self-actualization, as contrasted with the determinist conditioning of the behaviorists or the unconscious motives of psychoanalysis.

4. *Otto Rank,* Freud's faithful lieutenant for two decades, disagreed with the "Master," was unceremoniously dismissed, and emigrated to the United States, where he enjoyed a measure of respectability and renown as a faculty member of the Pennsylvania School of Social Work. It was during a three-day series of invited lectures that Rank *impressed a youthful Carl Rogers with his approach to therapy.*

5. *Carl Rogers grew up in a strict, but loving religious home* where Christian worship and family devotions were faithfully practiced, amusements were shunned, and work was seen as the antidote to evil.

6. In an effort to actualize his religious devotion while simultaneously fleeing his family's religious fundamentalism, Rogers enrolled in the liberal Union Theological Seminary to study for the ministry. However, after two years at Union he moved "across the street" to Columbia, where he completed his doctoral degree in psychology.

7. Describing himself as "too religious for organized religion," Rogers showed a similar Lone-Ranger sort of autonomy in his pursuit of psychology as well. Acknowledging his debt to both Karen Horney and Otto Rank, Rogers *developed his own unique approach* to counseling, which he called *client-centered.*

8. Rogers's core construct, the *phenomenal field,* combines both mental and physical experiences—both conscious and unconscious. The *self,* as the conscious portion of the phenomenal field, *is the centerpiece of Rogers's theory.*

9. According to Rogers, *organismic enhancement* (also known as the actualizing tendency) is the *master motive in human functioning*.

10. Like Freud, Rogers saw people *caught in conflict*. However, instead of the classic id–ego–superego conflicts of Freudian theory, Rogers saw conflicts occurring between the (psychological) *self* and the (biological) *organism*. Unlike Freud, who came down on the side of society (superego) as the ultimate arbiter of values, Rogers *trusted the organismic valuing process over the parentally transmitted values of society*, replacing the "father-knows-best" attitude of psychoanalysis with his "baby-knows-best" version of humanism.

11. In place of *conditions of worth* instilled in children by their parents, Rogers advocated *empathy, unconditional positive regard,* and *genuineness* as the *major healing components* both in therapy and in life.

12. Although later in his career Rogers became caught up in California's encounter group movement, his *early work was solidly experimental* (e.g., he was the first therapist to electronically record sessions).

13. Abraham Maslow grew up *painfully shy* and self-conscious. Raised by a toxic father and a malignant mother, he was the only Jewish boy in his Brooklyn neighborhood. Maslow was bright, did well in school, and studied psychology at the University of Wisconsin as Harry Harlow's first doctoral student.

14. After completing his doctoral research with *monkeys,* he briefly entered medical school, but soon dropped out as he found the studies boring and perceived his professors to be flippant toward pain and suffering. His real interest was in *human psychology,* so he subsequently studied with a number of eminent academicians such as Thorndike, Wertheimer, and Goldstein, as well as with prominent psychotherapists such as Adler, Horney, and Fromm.

15. Like Rogers, Maslow uses the terms *self* and *self-actualization* frequently, but he uses the term *self* primarily as a synonym for the *whole person,* not as a specific "part" of personality.

16. Maslow is most famous for his hierarchy *of needs,* portraying behavior as motivated by an array of needs ranging from the "lower" *physiological* needs to "higher" motives that fuel the *self-actualizing process.* Maslow refers to the "higher" (growth-oriented) values and needs (e.g., self-esteem, job satisfaction, beauty, etc.) as *metaneeds* and *metamotives.* Failure to meet *metaneeds* leads to *metapathologies:* spiritual–existential ailments such as *cynicism, boredom, drug addiction, despair, hopelessness, and the like.* Maslow coined the word *metagrumble* to describe "higher" patterns of complaining (e.g., about such things as poorly landscaped public parks), which occur only *after* people's basic needs for food, shelter, and safety have been met.

17. In place of *deficiency needs (e.g., hunger, thirst, etc.), self-actualized* people operate primarily on the basis of "higher" *Being-Values (B-Values).*

18. *B-Values* occur during *peak experiences: joyous, exciting moments inspired by music, love, nature, and other such sublime experiences.* Maslow described fourteen *B-Values: truth,*

goodness, beauty, wholeness, dichotomy-transcendence, aliveness, uniqueness, perfection, necessity, completion, justice, order, simplicity, richness, effortlessness, playfulness, self-sufficiency.

19. *Eight pathways* to self-actualization include: *(1) concentration, (2) growth choices, (3) self-awareness, (4) honesty, (5) judgment, (6) self-development, (7) peak and plateau experiences, and (8) becoming less defensive.*

20. Critics question whether Maslow's self-reliant, self-actualized person is a *Western idealization,* inappropriate for Oriental cultures or Eastern orientations. Feminists have said that Maslow's description of the self-actualized person does *not* portray the *psychology of women* accurately.

21. Unlike Rogers, Maslow outlined few specific clinical techniques, but his *hierarchy of needs* and his holistic emphasis on "higher" *growth-oriented motives* have significantly influenced mental health professionals, teachers, and businesspersons, as well as the general public.

Key Terms

Actualizing Tendency   (413)

Anxiety   (417)

Awareness   (411)

Being-Psychology   (430)

Being Love (B-Love)   (431)

Being Motives (B-Motives)   (431)

Breakdown   (417)

Conditions of Worth   (416)

Defense   (417)

Deficiency Cognitions (D-Cognitions)   (431)

Deficiency Love (D-Love)   (431)

Deficiency Motives (D-Motives)   (431)

Deficiency Values (D-Values)   (431)

Empathy   (418)

Encounter Groups   (420)

Experiential/Phenomenal Field   (411)

Flow   (437)

Fully Functioning Person   (418)

Fundamentalism   (407)

Gestalt Psychology   (407)

Hierarchy of Needs   (428)

Humanistic Therapist   (405)

Ideal Self   (413)

Ideal-Sort   (419)

Incongruence   (414)

Metagrumble   (430)

Metamotivation   (430)

Metaneeds   (430)

Metapathologies   (430)

Need for Positive Regard   (415)

Need for Self-Regard   (415)

Neurosis   (405)

Organismic   (413)

Organismic Valuing Process   (415)

Peak Experiences   (431)

Perpetually Wanting   (427)

Phenomenological Reality   (418)

Physiological Needs   (428)

Plateau Experience   (434)

Positive Psychology   (437)

Q-Sort Technique   (413)

Real Self   (427)

Reintegration   (417)

Self   (412)

Self-Actualization   (429)

Self-Sort   (419)

Subceives   (412)

Theory Z   (438)

Threat   (417)

Transcendence   (440)

Transpersonal Psychology   (439)

Unawareness   (411)

Unconditional Positive Regard   (415)

Web Sites

Rogers

http://nrogers.com/carlrogers.html. This site offers a great opportunity to learn about Rogers from someone who knew him best—his daughter Natalie Rogers. It has a full Rogers bibliography, biography, life events schedule, and links. Some of the links provide aid for finding his written work and a host of other things!

http://ahpweb.org/index.html. The Association for Humanistic Psychology. Read about humanistic theory, find publications, and find schools that teach Humanistic Psychology.

Maslow

www.maslow.com/. Maslow Publications. A helpful academic site that makes researching Maslow a piece of cake. It lists Maslow's books, in and out of print, all his articles, and audio/visual materials.

www.pbs.org/wgbh/aso/databank/entries/bhmasl.html. PBS. A well-put-together biography and picture of Maslow. The fun feature is a link at the bottom of the page. It is a game called "That's my theory!" You must figure out who the hidden theorist is by the clues in their answers to questions.

Learning on the Lighter Side

Good Will Hunting stars Robin Williams as a psychiatrist who helps Will Hunting (played by Matt Damon) get his life on a more self-actualizing track. Hunting was severely abused as a child and consistently in trouble with the law ever since. In a pretty authentic portrayal of humanistic counseling, Will's therapist helps him to come to terms with the blows life has dealt him.

Looking Ahead

Ascending the hierarchy—from biology to beauty. Maslow's hierarchy-of-needs orientation is consistent with the vertical axis of our grid. Instead of forcing "either–or" choices (e.g., behaviorism *or* trait theory, ego-analysis *or* humanism), we have explored a wide array of theories within a *hierarchical constructivist* framework, viewing each theory as part of a larger whole. As we continue our ascent, exploring the broad concepts of existential and transpersonal theories, we will continue to relate the ideas we discover to the empirical foundations we have established, much as Maslow sought to synthesize "lower" physiological needs with "higher" metaneeds.

In the past, many mainstream psychologists have viewed such theories of personality as "mystical' and "other-worldly," appropriate perhaps for the self-help section of the bookstore alongside tarot cards and astrology books, but hardly the stuff of "real" psychology. However, the issues addressed by existential psychologists in our next chapter—meaning, hope, faith, despair, and death—are topics of concern to ordinary people in their everyday lives. Such topics, addressed by existential and transpersonal theories, deserve careful study. In grappling with "big" issues, we need not revert to solipsism, the *philosophical position that my mind, with its thoughts, is the only thing that really exists;* instead, like Rogers and Maslow, we will seek to synthesize issues at higher and broader levels of analysis without abandoning our empirical foundations. Both biology and beauty are necessary for a complete accounting of human personality.

Out of the attic and onto the roof. Maslow and Rogers invited us up to the "attic" to explore the higher levels of human functioning, and in following them we encountered the "third force." However, it will remain for the existentialists, transpersonalists, and spiritual seekers of Chapters 12–14 to take us from the attic out onto the roof, so that we may gaze into the vast galaxies of the night sky and ask questions that are not empirically answerable—questions about the "fourth force." This promises to be an exciting trek, so fasten your seat belt, and "May the Force be with you!"

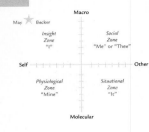

chapter 12

Person as Meaning Maker:

Existential Theories of Personality

Rollo May and Ernest Becker

IN THIS CHAPTER YOU CAN

1. Understand that *existentialists* address the *ultimate concerns* of human beings (e.g., life, death, meaning, and despair).

2. Discover that although some existentialists pessimistically conclude that "life sucks," others find in tragedy a summons to courage, and in death a challenge to make life count.

3. Learn how Rollo May probes existential issues using *Hegelian dialectics*.

4. Comprehend how May existentially reinterprets psychoanalysis, replacing *libido* with *self-consciousness* as the core motivational force.

5. Understand May's six existential themes: *(1) awareness, (2) centeredness, (3) consciousness, (4) courage for self-affirmation, (5) participation with others,* and *(6) anxiety about nothingness.*

6. Comprehend how existentialists view human experience *binocularly*, insisting that while one eye

might focus with the humanists on love, beauty, and goodness; the other must unblinkingly stare evil, ugliness, and death in the face, thus creating "depth" perception.

7. Explore with Ernest Becker how our *terror of death—* rather than *sexual libido—*is the driving force beneath human experience.

8. Try out Becker's idea that *art* is the ultimate synthesis of *life versus death.* By losing oneself in a work of art, the artist achieves the ultimate synthesis of living life fully—at the edge—while remaining aware of his or her mortality.

9. Probably agree that the ultimate existential tragedy is the failure to find a larger cause in which to spend one's life. The *successful artist* is the *quintessential model of "good mental health,"* and the *neurotic* is seen as a *failed artist.*

Finding Existential Meaning in a Concentration Camp

We stumbled on in the darkness, over big stones and through large puddles, along the one road leading from the camp. The accompanying guards kept shouting at us and driving us with the butts of their rifles. Anyone with very sore feet supported himself on his neighbor's arm. Hardly a word was spoken; the icy wind did not encourage talk. Hiding his mouth behind his upturned collar, the man marching next to me whispered suddenly: "If our wives could see us now! I do hope they are better off in their camps and don't know what is happening to us."

That brought thoughts of my own wife to mind. And as we stumbled on for miles, slipping on icy spots, supporting each other time and again, dragging one another up and onward, nothing was said, but we both knew: each of us was thinking of his wife. Occasionally I looked at the sky, where the stars were fading and the pink light of the morning was beginning to spread behind a dark bank of clouds. But my mind clung to my wife's image, imagining it with an uncanny acuteness. I heard her answering me, saw her smile, her frank and encouraging look. Real or not, her look was then more luminous than the sun which was beginning to rise. . . . Then I grasped the meaning of the greatest secret that human poetry and human thought and belief have to impart: *The salvation of man is through love and in love*. . . . (Frankl, 1959, pp. 36–37, emphasis in original)

Commentary

As this brief narrative illustrates, *existentialists* seek to derive meaning from *all experiences*. Such meaning making goes beyond Kelly's constructive alternativism or Maslow's self-actualization to include the most vicious of circumstances. In the example above, Frankl finds a way to distill meaning from the harsh circumstances surrounding an enforced march that, for all he knew, might end on the doorstep of the Nazi incinerators. It is this sort of transcendent meaning making—even in the midst of evil or misfortune—that characterizes much of existential philosophy. Of course, some of the most famous existentialists (e.g., Sartre, Camus) could hardly be described as "optimistic," but whatever their bent, all existentialists focus on the *meaning* of experience, grappling with how each of us matters—or doesn't matter—in the grand scheme of things.

About smoking tires and unicorns. The term *existentialism* comes from the Latin *existere,* which literally means *"to stand out."* Our English translation, *"exist,"* is more passive, failing to capture the active energy of the moment. We might compare psychoanalysis to a father who, returning home in the evening, notices black marks on the driveway and suspects that his son was "hot rodding." Existentialism is more like the father who goes outside to pick up the morning paper moments after his adolescent son "peeled out" of the driveway. In addition to having heard the sounds of a roaring engine and screeching tires only seconds before, he now smells burning rubber and notices small wisps of gray smoke loitering above black tire marks. He existentially *experiences* the event.

Existential psychologists seek to focus our attention on *existence-as-experienced*. They point out that something might be *true,* but *existentially unreal*. Thus, while it is *logically* true that "two unicorns plus two unicorns, equals four unicorns," such a statement doesn't refer to anything real.

Players versus spectators. Active involvement—not armchair philosophizing—is what existential psychologists emphasize. Think of the difference between players and spectators at a football game. Spectators are *somewhat involved* in the game—cheering for their team while the sports "psychoanalysts" in the television booth dissect and analyze the game for viewers back home. Nonetheless, the real "existentialists" are the guys with helmets on their heads and numbers on their jerseys. They're down on the field *actually playing the game*. That's the crucial difference between existentialists and psychoanalysts—existential analysis is not primarily about *observing and analyzing*, it's about *playing the game.*

The wide-angle lens of existentialism. We will briefly summarize the work of several well-known existential philosophers, in order to better understand how some personality psychologists use existential philosophy in their theories. We will notice some similarities with the work of constructivists and humanists. Like humanists, existential psychologists focus on the personal choices and constructive (meaning-making) activities of individual persons, but they do so in *broad and far-reaching ways.* For example, although each of us experiences our own anxiety as a private ordeal, existentialists view each person's anxiety as the firsthand experience of a much broader **existential angst,** *an anguished awareness—shared by all humans—that we are "food for worms," destined to die.*

Similarly, although therapists of various theoretical orientations assist people with crises arising from career changes, financial stresses, or family relationships, existential psychologists see such individual crises as personal "brush fires" compared with the larger "forest fire"—the **existential crisis** *of finding and fulfilling one's purpose for existence in a universe where destined-to-die humans are frequently alienated from themselves and others.*

Personal ultimates. Existential psychologists grapple with many of the same issues that occupy other psychologists, but they tend to reframe them in higher-level *ultimate* terms. Whereas a humanistic psychologist like Maslow might investigate how you find meaning in your social relationships or in your career, an existentialist might wonder whether you experience your life to be of *eternal significance.* A behavior therapist might assist you in coping with your panic attacks by employing relaxation training, whereas an existential therapist might encourage you to *fully experience* your panic or depression as a way of discovering your place in the cosmos—*the ultimate meaning of your existence.*

Existential clinicians deal with psychological problems at a personal level, yet they view such predicaments in the broadest perspective imaginable—ultimate meanings and ultimate outcomes. While they grapple with issues that are intensely *personal,* they focus on the *ultimate* meanings (e.g., freedom, choice, responsibility, meaninglessness, despair, life, and death). Soren Kierkegaard, one of the founders of modern existentialism, expressed both the personal and ultimate nature of this approach when he wrote in his journal, "I must find a truth that is true *for me . . . the idea for which I can live or die"* (Dreyfus, 2001).

Ontology: the study of ultimate concerns. **Ontology** *is a branch of philosophy concerned with the study of ultimate reality and being.* Existential psychologists bring an *ontological perspective* to working with clinical problems. They try to help their clients find *ultimate* meaning in their lives: Where did I come from? Where am I going? What does it matter? Whenever we use the term *ontology* or *ontological analysis* we are employing the broadest perspective possible—examining how people search for meaning not only in their jobs and family relationships but in life itself. Humanists focus on the *human* in <u>human</u> being, whereas existentialists emphasize the *being* aspect of human <u>being</u>. Remember how Rogers and Maslow stressed the intrinsic goodness of *human* nature? They insisted that if left to herself the human infant would self-actualize into a beautiful creature. Existentialists are less optimistic about human nature, viewing people as frequently fickle and sometimes evil; yet, existentialists stress the importance of living responsibly and courageously in the face of the apparent meaninglessness that frequently haunts human existence.

Dealing with the dark side. Exploring the world of existentialism will take us beyond the warm glow of Rogers's unconditional positive regard and the exhilaration of Maslow's "peak experiences." We will explore the shadows that exist alongside the peaks—even to descend to the "valley of the shadow of death." If, as some critics assert, humanistic psychology has been too blissfully optimistic regarding human nature, existentialism provides a dark, brooding counterpoint. Compared with the humanistic portrait of persons evolving into increasingly more loving individuals who congenially coexist with one another, existentialists profile a darker image that includes greed, envy, and hatred as fundamental ingredients of human nature, leaving in their wake angst, absurdity, murder, mayhem, death, and despair. Balancing the humanists' optimism regarding what we might *become,* existentialists urge us to focus on the here-and-now of what *is*—even when it is unpleasant. *Ultimately,* they remind us—self-actualized or not—we are all destined to *die.* Becker bemoans the fact that although a person spends years developing talents and cultivating gifts—transcending the animal condition—it doesn't appear to matter as far as ultimates are concerned: "even with the highest personal development and liberation, the person comes up against the real despair of the human condition. . . . He [or she] "has to go the way of the grasshopper, even though it takes longer" (Becker, 1973, pp. 268–269).

Psychological morticians? With their brooding focus on death and nothingness, we might be tempted to regard existential psychologists as the morticians of personality theory, bidding us to enter a gloomy world in which the twin villains of aging and oxidation reduce all but the sequoia trees to small heaps of dust. However, that is not true. Existential psychologists are not generally macabre or morose, but they consider both life *and* death as inseparable parts of human existence.

When C. S. Lewis (1970, p. 33) was asked which of the world's religions gives its followers the most happiness, he explained that he wasn't religious in order to be happy—a good bottle of wine could do that. Similarly, existentialists seek more than humanistic cheer or the warmth of wine, they seek ultimate meanings—wherever the search might lead.

Life and death—the ultimate paradox. Since death is the ultimate threat to *existence,* it shouldn't surprise us that existentialists discuss death extensively. Neither should we be surprised to find a wide spectrum of ideas regarding death. Pessimistic existentialists like Sartre saw death as the ultimate absurdity in an absurd world, whereas holocaust survivor Viktor Frankl (1959) confessed that his daily encounters with death rendered life more precious.

Frankl was among a group of prisoners being transferred from Auschwitz to Dachau. It was an arduous journey—two days and three nights with prisoners packed so densely that few could sit down. Arriving finally at Dachau, they had to stand in the freezing rain as punishment because someone had fallen asleep and missed roll call. Yet, they were extraordinarily happy, laughing and joking. Why? Because Dachau had no incinerator chimney!

The "Mount Rushmore" of existential philosophy. The faces of four men (Kierkegaard, Nietzsche, Heidegger, and Sartre) are etched into the conceptual granite of existential philosophy—four intellectual giants who provided streams of thought that trickled down in the work of subsequent existentialists. These four took as their starting point the *person as a conscious subject*. They saw a person who sometimes encountered the meaninglessness and nothingness of human existence, consciously experienced anguish and despair, yet courageously lived life in the lurch.

Existence trumps essence. Whereas previous philosophers showed little interest in the effect of their philosophies on the consciousness of the individual, these four philosophers—like all ensuing existentialists—were "psychologizing" philosophers, concerned with the *existence of the person*. Existential analysts do not dissect, divide, or quantify persons in terms of constituents or categories considered "essential" by scientists, politicians, theologians, or other "classifiers" of humankind. Instead, their goal is to understand the *ongoing existence* of a conscious, living, thinking person, rather than to assess biological composition or evaluate psychological traits. In philosophical terms, **existentialism** *gives priority to existence over essence—meaning that how I live is more important than what I'm composed of.* One philosopher summarized it in the following way:

> Existentialism affirms the ultimate significance, the primacy of my existence as this flickering point of consciousness of myself . . . against all efforts to define me, to reduce me to a Platonic essence, or to a Cartesian mental substance . . . or to a scientific neurological mechanism, or to a social security number. (Lavine, 1984, p. 328)

Soren Kierkegaard (1813–1855). Soren Kierkegaard, who is credited with being the first philosopher in modern times to think existentially, lived out his short life in Denmark during the first half of the nineteenth century. Themes of anxiety and despair permeate his work: "Hear the cry of the . . . mother at the hour of giving birth, see the struggle of the dying at the last moment: and say then whether that which begins and that which ends like this can be designed for pleasure" (quoted in Lavine, 1984, pp. 322–323). However, Kierkegaard believed that when despair is fully entered into, it becomes the pathway to faith and meaning, as he put it in *Either/Or* (1944): "In making a choice it is not so much a question of choosing the right as of the energy, the earnestness, the pathos with which one chooses . . ." (p. 141). According to Kierkegaard, the way to overcome depression is to embrace despair—to sink so deeply into despair that you give up all the comforts and satisfactions of life. Then—and only then—can you make the leap of faith to God. For Kierkegaard, the only way to overcome anxiety, despair, and the meaninglessness of existence is through absolute faith and the leap to God.

Friedrich Nietzsche (1844–1900). Friedrich Nietzsche regarded Kierkergaard's "leap to God" as pure nonsense. It was Nietzsche who famously proclaimed that "God is dead." By this he did not mean that God, defined as an eternal being, had died; rather that *belief* in God was dead. Like Freud and Marx, Nietzsche believed that a loss of faith enables humans to shed their infantile dependence on God. Nietzsche recommended that we aspire to become like gods—joyous, independent, hardworking superpersons. He would break the slabs of stone containing the Judeo-Christian moral laws and enjoin us to be powerful, creative, and free. For Nietzsche, the only morality is to affirm life.

Martin Heidegger (1899–1976). Heidegger asserted that we live in an incomprehensible and indifferent world. Humans can never hope to understand why they are here, but according to Heidegger each individual should choose a goal and follow it with passion and conviction—aware of the certainty of death and the meaninglessness of one's life. For Heidegger, death is the most authentic touchstone of reality. Instead of trying to escape death and behaving as if it does not exist, Heidegger suggests that we acknowledge death, face it squarely, and take it into our lives. Only then can we be emancipated from anxiety about death and free to live life fully. Heidegger goes so far as to say that death is a person's most authentic moment.

Jean-Paul Sartre (1905–1980). The French existentialist Jean-Paul Sartre disagreed intensely. Although Sartre saw all of existence as meaningless, shapeless, and lacking purpose, death—far from being one's most authentic moment—was the ultimate *absurdity*. In his philosophical novel, *Nausea* (1964), Sartre's principal character, Antoine Roquentin, is plagued with depression, nausea, and a foreboding feeling that he is slowly losing his grip on reality. Riding the streetcar, Roquentin's nausea increases as he feels surrounded by nameless frightening things. Feeling as if he is suffocating, he jumps off the streetcar, runs to the park, and sits down on a bench. Suddenly, right in front of him, Roquentin discovers the roots of a large chestnut tree protruding from the ground beneath his bench:

> The chestnut tree pressed itself against my eyes. . . . *In the way:* it was the only relationship I could establish between these trees, these gates, these stones. . . . I had found the key to Existence, the key to my Nauseas, to my own life. . . . The moment was extraordinary. I was there, motionless and icy, plunged in a horrible ecstasy; I understood the Nausea, I possessed it. To exist is simply *to be there;* those who exist let themselves be encountered. (Sartre, 1964, pp. 127–131)

One is reminded of Woody Allen's pithy observation that "Ninety percent of life is just being there" (Quoted in Clark, 1977, p. 9). In spite of Sartre's pessimistic view of life as a "futile passion," he insisted that his existentialism was a form of humanism, because he strongly emphasized freedom, choice, and responsibility.

A wide array of "unsystematic" systems. Existentialists appear to delight in being deliberately unsystematic. Since they believe that the crucial existential questions are not accessible to scientific reasoning or linear logic, they employ a patchwork of parables, anecdotes, paradoxes, dialogs, and clinical cases to illustrate their ideas. This can be confusing and disheartening for readers, but it reflects the existentialists' (postmodern) conviction that each reader must design her own project to deal with existential angst. There are no one-size-fits-all, cookie-cutter solutions to the profound paradoxes of human existence.

Our confusion will be considerably lessened if we are aware that certain core existential themes recur again and again, in a variety of contexts. We will also discover that even when illustrations are drawn from daily life or clinical encounters, existentialists tend to frame their conclusions in ultimate, life-or-death terms. It will hardly surprise us, then, to find little agreement about what constitutes optimal existence or what sorts of coping strategies people ought to employ when encountering the inevitable tragedies and absurdities that permeate human existence. For example, in comparing Kierkegaard and Nietzsche, one scholar observes:

> They arrived at positions that were in many respects entirely contrary, for Kierkegaard was deeply committed to the idea of the Christian God while Nietzsche was just as deeply divorced from it; but in other respects they were alike. They shared the same experience of loneliness, anguish, and doubt, and the same profound concern for the fate of the individual person. . . . (Carruth, 1994, p. vii)

Since existentialism is a philosophical attitude for making sense of our lived experience, it cannot easily be corralled by words; nonetheless, important themes recur, and we will briefly examine these.

Six Recurring Themes of Existentialism

(1) Existence trumps essence. Existentialists assert that human beings are conscious, choosing, self-aware subjects, not things to be manipulated, classified, or otherwise pigeon-holed.

(2) Anxiety and anguish are intrinsic to existence. Existentialists believe that a generalized uneasiness—not a fear or dread directed toward any specific object—pervades human consciousness. This anguish is the dread of the nothingness.

(3) Absurdity abounds. The theme of absurdity was, perhaps, most highly developed by Sartre, but it can also be found in the works of Blaise Pascal, a seventeenth-century French mathematician and philosopher:

> When I consider the short duration of my life, swallowed up in the eternity before and after, the little space I fill. . . . I am frightened, and am astonished at being here rather than there, why now rather than then. (quoted in Lavine, 1984, p. 331)

(4) The void of nothingness. If, as an existentialist, I am convinced that no essences define me, and I reject all theories, philosophies, sciences, and religions as failing to accurately reflect my existence; then how will I structure my world? Standing at the edge of the abyss, conscious only of my momentary existence, I stare into the nothingness. I live with angst.

(5) Death—the ultimate "nothingness." Death, hanging over me like the sword of Damocles, is the ultimate nothingness. Although Heidegger viewed death as a person's most authentic moment, few other existentialists contemplate death so cheerily. Sartre, for example, saw death as the ultimate absurdity.

(6) Alienation and estrangement. Since Hegel (1770–1831) and Marx (1818–1883) opened up the theme of *alienation* for the modern world, it has been widely adopted and elaborated by existential philosophers and psychologists. Hegel and Marx viewed alienation in broad societal terms (e.g., alienation between the wealthy and the working classes; alienation of workers from the products of their labors; alienation of workers from other social institutions such as law and government). Contemporary existential philosophers perceive persons as largely alienated from human institutions such as governments, churches, and national religious organizations.

Even more personally, existential clinicians see alienation occurring within families, painfully poisoning relationships among parents and children, husbands and wives. Finally, at the most basic existential level, I experience the alienation between my momentary, conscious self and all else—all "otherness."

These are the themes we find reappearing again and again among the patchwork quilt of existential philosophy. Next, we consider the work of one of the foremost existential psychologists of the twentieth century, Rollo May.

THE EXISTENTIAL PSYCHOLOGY OF ROLLO MAY

Psychoanalysis and existentialism sprouted from similar cultural soil. During the last half of the nineteenth century, some Western industrialists tended to view employees as the sprockets and gears of their corporations. Working on the assembly lines of giant factories, or sewing pockets into pants, workers became separated ("*alienated*") from the products of their labors. Division of labor on the assembly line had its counterpart in division of the self in the inner life. Alienation occurred not only in factories but in personalities as well, where subjective experience was segmented into the pigeonholes of thoughts, feelings, or behaviors, which were further fractionated into categories of conscious, preconscious, or unconscious.

It was Freud's genius that he attempted to restore a measure of wholeness by lifting repression—making the unconscious conscious. He was constrained, however, by his admiration for his mentors, and he never completely shook off the shackles of their biological determinism. Classical psychoanalysis remained *experience-distant,* with Freud's descriptions of personality oscillating between the reductionistic constructs of biology and the literary metaphors of Greek mythology. Psychoanalysis transformed the vibrant immediacy of clinical encounters into complex abstractions that frequently failed to capture the urgency of the *now*. Rollo May combined the genius of Freud's insights with an existential focus on *immediate experience* to forge a broader understanding of human experience.

Background Check

Childhood, education, and travel. Rollo May (1909–1994) grew up in Marine City, Michigan in a family where an anti-intellectual attitude prevailed. May remembers his father commenting on several occasions that Rollo's older sister's "nervous breakdown" was the result of "too much education" (May, 1983). Nonetheless, May attended Oberlin College in Ohio, where he remembered being charmed by the simple but elegant lines of a Greek vase that was on display in one of the classrooms. Upon graduating, he decided to visit Greece, where he remained for three years, teaching during the school year and traveling during the summer. He also traveled to Vienna where he studied briefly with Alfred Adler, whose approach influenced him substantially. May's life abroad had a formative influence on his subsequent theories.

Zeitgeist

Enrolling at Union. After traveling abroad, May experienced American psychology's mechanistic approach as naive and simplistic, so he enrolled at Union Theological

Seminary, where half a dozen years earlier Carl Rogers had matriculated. Unlike Rogers, who had enrolled at Union with the intention of becoming a minister, May had no interest in becoming a preacher; instead, he desired to delve into the difficult questions provoked by experiences of despair, anxiety, or suicide—questions that were largely being ignored by psychologists. He also hoped to understand their positive counterparts, such as joy, courage, and living life fully. While a student at Union, May formed a friendship with the celebrated Protestant theologian Paul Tillich. It blossomed into a lifelong relationship that enriched the writings of both men.

A brush with death. In his early thirties, May came down with tuberculosis—for which there was no medication at the time—and he spent three years in a TB sanitorium not knowing whether he would live or die. During this time he read Freud's *The Problem of Anxiety* and Kierkegaard's *The Concept of Dread.* Although he was impressed with Freud's careful formulations, he felt that Kierkegaard more accurately captured the immediacy of human beings in crisis. During his illness, May came to more deeply appreciate the importance of the existentialist point of view, and his own book *The Meaning of Anxiety* (1977) was one of the first in America to foster a genuine union between philosophy and psychology.

Existential psychoanalysis. Rollo May replaced Freud's intrapsychic metaphors with more interpersonally oriented constructs (he received his psychoanalytic training at the William Alanson White Institute, cofounded by Harry Stack Sullivan). May broadened the horizon even further by portraying human beings as *active agents* seeking to find *existential meaning* in all of life.

From abstractions to actions—existentially redefining terms. We will need to remember that although many of the terms we encounter will appear familiar (e.g., the unconscious), May employed these terms in a uniquely existential way; for example, he redefined Freud's "unconscious" as *existential potentialities* rather than a *place:*

> The "unconscious," then, is not to be thought of as a reservoir of impulses, thoughts, wishes which are culturally unacceptable, I define it rather as *those potentialities for knowing and experiencing which the individual cannot or will not actualize . . .* (May, 1960, p. 178)

In this way, May transformed the third-person *abstractions* of psychoanalysis into the first-person *experiences* of existentialism. The *"unconscious"* becomes not a *place* filled with unacceptable impulses or a *structure* where repressed urges are housed; instead May redefines the unconscious as a *process* engaged in by a *whole person.* From the existential perspective, a person does not *have* dreams, the person *is* a dreamer; a person doesn't *possess* defense mechanisms, s/he *actively defends* against threats; the unconscious is not a *place* containing repressed thoughts, it is a *potential* for knowing what has not yet been actualized.

Before proceeding to our "parts" discussion we will take a brief philosophical side trip to help us understand the roots of Rollo May's thinking. Otherwise, his mixing of psychoanalytic terminology with difficult-to-define existential concepts might bewilder our minds. But don't worry, a brief survey will suffice; we won't have to become Plato or Socrates to understand Rollo May.

Dialectical thought in philosophy and psychology. Plato defined **dialectic** as *the contradictory, oppositional nature of reality.* Dialectic is one of philosophy's oldest concepts, dating to the ancient Greeks who, five hundred years before Socrates, taught that reality is composed of four "essences" that are in perpetual *opposition.* In more recent times, the German philosopher Georg Wilhelm Friedrich Hegel (1770–1831) brought dialectical thinking into the modern world. One scholar depicted Hegel as "the master of dialectic," describing his theory as "the most completely developed, ambitious, and powerful theory of dialectic that has ever been formulated" (Lavine, 1984, p. 210).

Hegel's influence on Freud. Hegel died twenty-five years before Freud was born, but his influence on the founder of psychoanalysis is seen in the many opposites found in psychoanalytic theory. Whereas Freud endeavored to resolve conflicts by *analysis,* Hegel used *synthesis.* Hegel's dialectical reasoning is a three-stage process that begins with a **thesis,** *a foundational idea or concept* that spawns an **antithesis,** *an opposing idea or concept.* **Synthesis** *occurs when a higher-level process (1) cancels the conflict, (2) preserves the elements of truth contained in both the thesis and antithesis, and (3) transcends and sublimates the conflict into a higher truth.* This thesis–antithesis–synthesis formula is sometimes known as *Hegel's dialectical triad.*

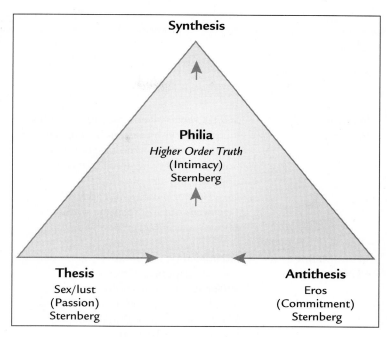

Figure 12.1
SYNTHESIS:
1. Cancels conflict between thesis and antithesis.
2. Preserves the element of truth *within* thesis and antithesis.
3. Transcends the opposition and *sublimates* conflict into higher-order truth.

What Are the Parts (Ontological Categories)?

As we learned earlier, existential personality psychologists view individuals as whole persons—confronting despair and darkness, making sense of absurdity—living life fully even while knowing we all must die. In their attempts to portray the daily dramas of human existence without shrinking them into triviality, existentialists have avoided dissecting personality into parts; instead, they emphasize *process.* For May, the key existential dilemma is, How can I live *my* life, *my* existence in a way that is authentically *me,* over and against the world "out there" with all of its situational demands and circumstantial expectations? How can I be true to *my authentic self* without pandering to the expectations of *others ("out there")?*

Synthesizing self versus other with *consciousness of self.* For May, *subject* versus *object* is *the* pivotal existential dichotomy. Instead of resolving this dichotomy by raising awareness via psychoanalysis ("making the unconscious conscious"), May focuses on what ego psychologists have called the *observing ego* and the *observed self*—meaning the "me" that "I" see when I think about myself. May considers this **consciousness of self,** *the ability to stand outside oneself as an observer,* to be a uniquely human characteristic.

TABLE 12.1

May at a Glance

MODEL OF PERSONALITY	DESCRIPTION	DYNAMICS
What Are the Parts?	*Subject versus object:* May resolves this dichotomy with **consciousness of self** (the human ability to simultaneously be both the observing agent and the observed object). *Umwelt:* our biological world *Eigenwelt:* our intrapsychic world *Mitwelt:* our interpersonal world	*Consciousness of self* is similar to what has been called the *observing ego.* Persons function at three different levels—three different worlds: *Umwelt, Eigenwelt,* and *Mitwelt.*
What Makes a Person Go?	*Intentionality:* imaginatively anticipating and participating in one's future. *Willpower:* the conscious portion of intentionality—the conscious organizing of one's self in a certain direction, moving toward a goal *Destiny:* the "givens" in life—the "cards" we are dealt *Six existential "forces":* include *awareness, centeredness, consciousness, courage for self-affirmation, participation with others, anxiety about nothingness*	Existentialists give *willpower* a crucial role in guiding behavior. *Willpower* gives direction and power to *intentionality,* and allows humans to confront, challenge, and rebel against the limitations *of destiny,* "Motives" are circumvented with *six ontological principles (forces) that serve to focus and clarify existence.*
What Makes a Person Grow?	*Consciousness of self:* emerges in four stages: innocence, rebellion, ordinary self-consciousness, and creative self-consciousness	Avoiding such mundane topics as weaning, walking, or toilet training, existentialists focus on the child's emerging sense of self-consciousness.
What Makes a Person Unique?	*Individual distinctiveness:* is at the core of all existential philosophies. Existentialists care little about the "average person," or "group mentality." They ardently insist that meaning must be individually derived	The heart of existentialism is the *individual person* authentically struggling to "makes sense" of life, courageously striving to find meaning in daily existence.

In a levels-of-analysis sort of way, May recognizes that all humans are grounded in the *Physiological Zone:* "we have our roots in nature . . . the chemistry of our bodies is of essentially the same elements as the air or dirt or grass" (1953, p. 73). However, May recognizes that the *Insight Zone* is uniquely human: "in another respect man is very different from the rest of nature. He possesses consciousness of himself; his sense of personal identity distinguishes him from the rest of the living or nonliving things" (1953, p. 73). According to May, it is this *consciousness of self* that distinguishes humans from other animals, and provides the key to existentially understanding human experience.

May offers the illustration of a friend's dog who waits all morning by the front door, expectantly barking at whoever appears: "My friend holds that the dog is saying in his barking: "here is a dog who has been waiting all morning for someone to come to play with him. Are you the one?" (1953, pp. 84–85). May rejects such "cozy thoughts" as precisely what a dog *cannot* say. Although a dog might show you (by bringing a ball and barking excitedly) that he wants to play, May argues that a dog "cannot stand outside himself and see himself as a dog doing these things. He is not blessed with the consciousness of self" (1953, pp. 84–85).

I agree. Dog lover though I may be, I am quite certain that when Molly excitedly races around my backyard, leaping into the air to catch the Frisbee that I've flipped in her direction, she is completely focused on that Frisbee. When she returns it to me, drops it at my feet, and begins to bark excitedly, I suspect she might be "thinking" *Will he throw it again? Which direction?* At a stretch, she might even be "thinking": *The game isn't over, is it? Won't you throw it one more time?—Please, I'm begging!* But whatever her canine cognitions might be, I'm quite certain they are not *self-reflective,* it's not about Molly. She is *not* thinking *Gee, I've been gaining weight, I need to get more exercise.* Or, *I've only worked out twice this week so I'd better get off my duff and do some retrieving—if I can get this idiot to throw the Frisbee, that is!*

Of course, Molly's lack of *consciousness of self* also means she is not plagued with existential angst about dying, she isn't bogged down with guilt, she doesn't appear to worry. Yet, few of us would trade our humanity for a dog's life. And May uses this *consciousness of self* to synthesize the core existential split between subject and object: ". . . man's consciousness of himself is the source of his highest qualities. It underlies his ability to distinguish between 'I' and the world'" (1953, p. 85).

What Makes A Person Go?

Just as existential psychologists resist fragmenting the wholeness of the person into self versus object, or parts versus motives, they also resist any fine-grained motivational analyses that would parcel motives into "conscious" versus "unconscious," or into "higher" versus "lower." Existential psychologists shun the animal-based, drive-reduction definitions of motivation used by behaviorists, and they appear equally allergic to motivational research carried out by experimental psychologists. Conducting "motivational research"—to determine why consumers prefer certain products over others—would be anathema. Instead they prefer to address "ontological" issues such as anguish, despair, courage, love, sex, life, death, and other *ultimate* concerns that are encountered by existing, meaning-making human beings.

Nevertheless, most of these "ontological" issues are motivational at the core. If these "ontological" concepts are taken beyond the circles of philosophical discussion into the real world where people *exist,* topics such as death and dying have powerful motivational force. As Samuel Johnson famously said: "The prospect of being hanged, focuses the mind wonderfully." In fact, existential psychologists are deeply concerned with "motives," though at a much higher level of analysis than earning water if you're a thirsty pigeon or winning access to food if you're a salivating dog.

Although Sartre might have allowed himself to sink into the despair of absurdity with "no exit" in sight, Tillich, May, and others were keenly concerned with inspiring us to "live life fully" while simultaneously facing tragedy or death with "courage." Surely these are motivational issues, but they are concerned with the pursuit of ultimate meanings rather than with the procurement of food pellets. The central motivational force for May is not drive reduction, libido satisfaction, or self-actualization, but *meaning-making synthesis through intentionality.*

Answering the "big questions" of life with intentionality. Rollo May, like so many other existentialists, places choice at the center of personality. He does this with the construct of **intentionality,** defined as *"our imaginative participation in the coming day's possibilities . . ."* (1969, pp. 223). For May, *intentionality* shapes how we advance into the future and how we perceive the present: "intentions are decisive with respect to how we perceive the world" (1969, p. 224). May uses *intentionality* as a great *synthesizing* force for resolving dialectical opposites at various levels of functioning. He devotes two entire chapters of *Love and Will* (1969) to showing how intentionality *synthesizes* biological polarities and psychological conflicts, as well as integrating the broadest ontological dichotomies at the highest levels of existential experience—the "big potatoes."

Intentionality—an "artesian well" of human experience. From a zonal perspective, we might say that *intentionality* bubbles upward through Maslow's hierarchy and Rollo May's existentialism like an artesian well, synthesizing biological polarities in the *Physiological Zone,* endowing the intrapsychic *Insight Zone* with psychological and spiritual meanings, and ultimately flowing into the interpersonal *Social Zone* to facilitate mutual relationships that include intimacy, trust, hope, caring, and love. That is why May said "Intentionality, in human experience, is what underlies will and decision" (1969, p. 201).

Intentionality synthesizes subject versus object. Sounding much like Hegel or other dialecticians, May states that *intentionality* has the capacity to *synthesize* the *subject* with the *object:* "Intentionality is the bridge. . . . which makes it possible for us, subjects that we are, to see and understand the outside world, objective as it is. In intentionality, the dichotomy between subject and object is partially overcome" (1969, p. 225).

Intentionality synthesizes thinking versus doing. May also uses *intentionality* to *synthesize* the *opposites* of thinking and doing. "In fact," argues Monte (1999), "an intention and its resulting act are one and the same. It is only an artificial separation to assume that one first intends something and then does it. Rather, the act is in the intention, and the intention is in the act. The only difference is time" (p. 599).

Summarizing intentionality: a cabin in the mountains. May might have rephrased the aphorism "Beauty is in the eye of the beholder," to say "Beauty is in the *intention* of the beholder." According to May, *intentionality* is the primary existential process that shapes how we construe the world—even a cabin in the mountains. For example, if May were trying to decide whether friends might want to rent a particular mountain house for the summer, he would pay particular attention to "whether it is sound and well-built, gets enough sun, and other things having the meaning of 'shelter' to me." As a real estate investor, he would ascertain "how easily the house can be fixed up, whether it will bring a price attractively higher than what I shall have to pay for it." If May were visiting friends who owned that particular cottage, he would "look at it with eyes which see it as 'hospitality,'—its open patio and easy chairs will make our afternoon talk more pleasant." If, on the other hand, the house belonged to people who had snubbed him on a previous occasion, May might begin "seeing things that indicate that anyone would prefer my cottage to theirs." Finally, if he were outfitted with his watercolor materials and intent on doing a sketch, May would notice "how the house clings to the side of the mountain, the pattern of the lines of the roof leading up to the peaks above and sweeping away into the valley below." He might even "prefer the house ramshackle and run down for the greater artistic possibilities this gives me" (1969, p. 224).

May concludes by saying (as Kelly or other constructivists might), "In each of these five instances it is the same house that provides the stimulus, and I am the same man responding to it. But in each case, the house and experience have an entirely different meaning" (1969, p. 224)

Using love to synthesize sex and passion. May synthesized the sex versus eros dialectic using the higher-order *philial* and *agape* forms of love. He said that the ability to "make love"—not merely "have sex" with one's partner—is rooted in *philial* and *agape (caring varieties of love).*

May distinguishes among four styles of loving, which he defines dialectically:

1. *Sex or lust* refers to the sexual drive in its most elemental, biological form— a drive for sexual gratification. May believes that in modern times, sex has become depersonalized. We "have sex" or "get laid" rather than "make love." Lust emphasizes *sensation* rather than *passion.* May contends that sex is frequently a flight from eros: "Sex is the handiest drug to blot out our awareness of the anxiety-creating aspects of eros" (1969, p. 65).

2. *Eros* is the drive to *passionately* procreate. May believes that our cultural emphasis on the techniques and sensations of sex masks our alienation from, and repression of, the deeper passions associated with *eros.* He asserts that we have lost our hold on nature and our capacity to give ourselves over to "some primitive and powerful biological process, partake of some deeper pulsations in the cosmos" (1969, pp. 70–71).

3. *Philia* is the basis of friendship and brotherly love.

4. *Agape or Caritas* (Latin root for *care*) refers to the highest, far-reaching kind of love that is concerned with the ultimate well-being of others. May uses these *caring* varieties of love to *synthesize* the dialectical tensions between *eros* and *sex.* Notice how he dialectically sets up his opposites and then synthesizes them with a third process.

Sex versus eros. Entrapped by commercialized, technique-oriented definitions of sex, we paradoxically become more obsessively concerned with procedures and techniques, while at the same time we feel more alienated from our feelings: "We fly to *the sensation of sex in order to avoid the passion of eros*" (May, 1969, p. 65). May described a patient who was concerned that he was a premature ejaculator, even though he

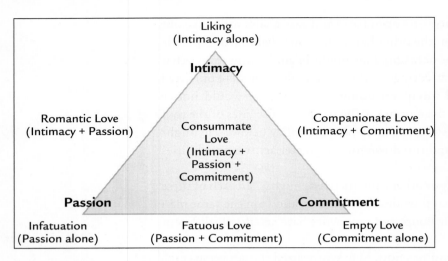

Figure 12.2 ■ *Sternberg's Triangular Model of Love*

frequently experienced penetration for ten minutes or more before ejaculating. Finally, this man obtained a prescription from his family physician that was designed to anesthesize his penis so he could perform longer without ejaculating. As May put it: "Making one's self *feel less* in order to *perform better!* This is a symbol, as macabre as it is vivid, of the vicious circle in which so much of our culture is caught . . ." (1969, p. 55).

Philia and agape (caring)—the great synthesizers. *Philia (interpersonal caring)* and *agape (divine caring)* are May's synthesizers of the dialectical opposites of sex and eros: "Care is a state in which something does *matter;* care is the opposite of apathy. Care is the necessary source of eros, the source of human tenderness" (1969, p. 289).

May's suggested synthesis involves "a new consciousness in which the depth and meaning of personal relationship will occupy a central place" (1969, p. 279). This is echoed in Sternberg's (1988) triangular theory of love: passion and commitment are pictured at the two base corners of the triangle while intimacy is at the top. Sternberg's *passion* and *commitment* bear some resemblance to May's *sex* and *eros,* while *intimacy* appears to contain elements of *philia* and *agape* emphasizes the importance of depth and caring in a love relationship.

Summary of motivational issues. May typically sets up a dialectic between two opposing forces (thesis versus antithesis), which he then synthesizes with a higher-order process. Over and over again we see this dynamic at work throughout his theory of personality. These broad ontological concerns we have encountered are not unique to Rollo May, but are considered pivotal by most existentialists. What is unique about May is how he uses Hegelian dialectical synthesis to reformulate Freud's constructs into an existential theory. May's final theory only remotely resembles classical psychoanalysis and is permeated with existential concepts like *courage, caring,* and *intentionality.* May begins with such classical Freudian concerns as anxiety, sexuality, and guilt, but adds his own existential ingredients and ontological categories.

Six ontological principles. Although existentialists resist defining "motives" in drive-reduction terms, May's six ontological principles are motivational in flavor—not billiard-ball, push–pull motivation, but existentially impelling.

(1) Awareness: At the most basic level of our surrounding environment (in the Physiological Zone) May equates *awareness* with *vigilance.* According to May, the subjective side of *centeredness* is *awareness,* but if we become too aware of our roots in nature—"the fact that the chemistry of our bodies is of essentially the same nature as the air or dirt or grass"—it may become overwhelming. "It takes a strong self," says May, "to relate fully to nature without being swallowed up" (1953, pp. 73–74).

A person might stand on a rocky cliff and contemplate the ocean, which cares not a whit whether we live or die, sink or swim, and would swallow us up with "scarcely an infinitesimal difference being made to the tremendous ongoing, chemical movement of creation" (1953, p. 74). However, that would be an anxiety-provoking experience to many people who would "flee from the threat by shutting off their imagination, by turning their thoughts to the practical and humdrum details of what to have for lunch" (1953, p. 74).

(2) Centeredness: To existentially understand person, we must not view the individual as simply as an aggregate of biological drives and deterministic forces in the *Physiological Zone*. When people are analyzed or dissected in that way, May said, "you have defined for study everything except the one to whom these experiences happen, everything except the existing person himself" (May, 1960, p. 179). The way to understand people, according to May, is to realize that each person loves, hates, lives, and dies *centered in self.*

(3) Consciousness: At the level of *the Insight Zone,* consciousness is the ability to know oneself as the person being threatened. As we learned earlier when we discussed *intentionality,* May, and other existentialists, consider human beings as *unique among animals in their ability to be self-conscious.*

(4) Courage for self-affirmation: Taking a page from Tillich, May defines self-affirmation as the "courage to be" (Tillich, 1952). Notice how Tillich used *courage* to *synthesize* the dialectical opposites of *anxiety* versus *despair:* "Anxiety turns us toward courage, because the other alternative is despair. Courage resists despair by taking anxiety into itself" (Tillich, 1952, p. 66). If we did not understand how dialectical reasoning blends opposites into a higher-order synthesis, then this "courage . . . taking anxiety into itself" might just sound like a lot of philosophical mumbo jumbo. However, we now know that *courage* allows us to synthesize despair and anxiety by directly confronting or "embracing" them.

One of the most successful areas of clinical psychology has been the treatment of phobias through direct confrontation with feared objects. Although most clinicians don't refer to this as "embracing fear," that is essentially what happens. We will discuss some of this research in more detail later in this chapter; here we need only to realize that when existentialists use broad constructs such as *"courage"* they probably have in mind processes that are also used by researchers in other zones—at lower levels of analysis. Cognitive–behavioral therapists might use the existential notion of *"courage to be"* but apply it to specific behavioral goals: the "courage to be" *not depressed,* or the "courage to be" *not afraid.* An existential therapist might inspire a client with "courage to self-actualize" by giving up a lucrative career in law to pursue teaching high school in the inner city.

(5) Participation with others: In the *Social Zone,* May sees the "neurotic" as a person who becomes "so afraid of his own conflicted center that he refuses to go out but holds back in rigidity and lives in narrowed reactions and shrunken world space, his growth and development . . . blocked" (1960, p. 181). The neurotic experiences these inner conflicts as a psychological tug-of-war between *participation and alienation.* May points out that it is possible for a person to become uncentered either by *"overparticipating"* with others (1967, p. 8), or by experiencing **alienation,** *"felt as a loss of the capacity to be intimately* *personal"* (1969, p. 71). In the area of sexuality, for example, May sees *alienation* frequently manifested as a "repetitive pattern of fucking-to-avoid-the-emptiness-of-despair" (1969, p. 71). As we learned earlier, *philial* or *agape caring* provides a healthy *synthesis* to such *overparticipation* versus *alienation* conflicts in sexual relationships.

(6) Anxiety about nothingness: Existential anxiety is not simply worrying about my career, my car payment, or my mortgage. Existential angst *carries the connotations of "dread" and "anguish" and is a deep worry about "losing being."* As Tillich conceptualized it: "The basic anxiety, the anxiety of a finite being about the threat of nonbeing, cannot be eliminated. It belongs to existence itself" (1952, p. 39).

Angst—this far-reaching form of anxiety—is the most *existential*. It isn't about escaping predators in the Situational Zone or finding fulfillment in one's family and friends in the Social Zone; it has to do with our inexorable, inescapable journey toward *nothingness*. May said, "Death is . . . the one fact of my life which is not relative but absolute, and my awareness of this gives my existence and what I do each hour an absolute quality" (May 1958b, pp. 48–49).

Existential expansion of anxiety, guilt, transference, and repression. By now we realize that Freudian anxiety (about unacceptable impulses or behaviors) or the *anxiety* of Sullivan (about maintaining one's self-esteem in interpersonal situations) are not *existential angst* about "big potatoes" issues like *nothingness*. Later in this chapter we will see how contemporary researchers have carefully investigated the illusive concept of "dread of nothingness."

What Makes a Person Grow?

Four stages in the emerging *consciousness of self.* By now, we wouldn't expect anything resembling "developmental stages" from existentialists. Focused on broadly defined ontological issues, existentialists spend little time on such mundane topics as weaning, walking, and toilet training. The closest we come to finding developmental stages occurs in May's description of how *consciousness of the self* emerges in stages.

(1) Innocence. Prior to developing an awareness of self, the infant is assumed to exist in a state of *innocence*. May has little to say about this stage.

(2) Rebellion. This stage is best understood existentially rather than chronologically. *Rebellion* occurs in toddlers, adolescents, or defiant adults; and whenever it takes place, it is seen as a necessary transition to something better: "In a greater or lesser degree rebellion is a necessary transition as one cuts old ties and seeks to make new ones" (May, 1953, pp. 138–139).

(3) Ordinary consciousness of self. According to May, this is the stage when "a person can to some extent see his errors, make some allowances for his prejudices, use his guilt feelings and anxiety as experiences to learn from, and make his decisions with some responsibility. This is what most people mean when they speak of a healthy state of personality" (1953, p. 139).

(4) Creative self-consciousness. This stage is similar to Maslow's peak experiences. May describes **creative self-consciousness** as *"a stage that most of us achieve only at rare intervals; and none of us, except the saints, religious or secular, and the great creative figures, live very much of our lives on this level"* (1953, p. 141). Although this might sound like some mystical, other-worldly experience, May views *creative self-consciousness* as exerting a lasting influence on one's existential experience:

> Many people have experienced this consciousness in some special moment, let us say, in listening to music, or in some new experience of love or friendship which temporarily takes them out of the usual walled-in routine of their lives. It is as though for a moment one stood on a mountain peak, and viewed his life from that wide and unlimited perspective. One gets his sense of direction from his view of the peak and sketches a mental map which guides him for weeks of patient plodding up and down the lesser hills when effort is dull and "inspiration" is conspicuous by its absence. . . . the fact that we have had these glimpses gives a basis of meaning and direction for all of our later actions. (1953, pp. 141–142)

What Makes a Person Unique?

This will be a brief discussion, not because Rollo May was indifferent to individual uniqueness, but rather because uniqueness permeates *all* of existentialism. We could say that the distinctiveness of each person is the yeast that causes the dough of existentialism to rise. Borrowing from May's dialectical tool box, we could set up the thesis-antithesis as *unique person* versus *average representative of humankind*. This is the *idiographic versus nomothetic* distinction that Allport (1937) imported into personality psychology from the philosopher W. Windelband (1894). Instead of studying large numbers of individuals to find average commonalities (nomothetic research), Allport preferred to focus on (idiographic) data provided by the individual.

For example, in his famous (idiographic) study of "Letters from Jenny" (1965), Gordon Allport collected a total of 301 letters written by Jenny from March 1926 to October 1937. He then submitted these letters (along with 198 trait names to describe Jenny) to 36 judges, who rated the content. When synonymous traits were lumped together, it was found that Jenny could be described in terms of eight traits: quarrelsome, self-centered, independent, dramatic, aesthetic-artistic, aggressive, cynical, sentimental. Subsequently, one of Allport's students (Paige, 1966) performed a factor analysis of the letters using a computer and also isolated eight factors.

This sort of intense study of the individual is preferred by existentialists, who would likely find more existential significance in the personal correspondence of one person, than in the averaged scores of fifty people on standardized tests.

FACING THE TOUGH TWINS

Is It Testable?

Sounding much like Rogers or Maslow, May challenged the deterministic and reductionist philosophies that underlay much of the research of their eras. May insisted that until we understand the *symbols* and *myths* underlying what it means to be a human being, our research will render distorted portraits: "Academic psychologists tended . . . to accept the position that as psychologists we were concerned only with what was determined and could be understood in a deterministic framework" (1969, p. 195).

May believed that our failure to understand ourselves is not because we haven't conducted enough experiments or collected enough data. It is rather because we don't have the "courage" to investigate questions that really matter. Imprisoned by our determinist philosophies and our misguided myths about who we are, we fail to distinguish between *knowing ourselves* and *knowing about ourselves.*

Existential hypotheses are potentially researchable. May's own doctoral dissertation, investigating anxiety among unmarried mothers, led to some rich insights regarding the meaning of anxiety. *Intentionality* is one of May's major constructs, and questions regarding how intentionality shapes perception and influences behavior are certainly researchable. *Self-consciousness, apathy, vitality,* and even *courage* can be experimentally studied as well. Even some of the more difficult-to-operationalize existential constructs such as *terror of* death or *"nothingness"* can be experimentally studied, as we will see later in this chapter. Following our discussion of Becker, we will return to the topic of existential terror management to review the considerable research it has generated.

Increasing the courage to face one's fears. Most existentialists would not consider the fear of flying on a par with existential angst about "nothingness." Still, persons suffering from phobias find their existential world severely circumscribed by their fears, and finding the "courage" to face specific fears may provide them with the psychological foundations for facing even larger "ontological" fears about nothingness or dying.

*A **virtual cure.*** The term *cure* is not used widely among psychologists, because many of the problems encountered by clinicians are multidimensional, influenced by multiple variables, and difficult to "cure." Phobias are the exception. Psychologists have achieved remarkable success eliminating phobias by having clients learn to relax (*progressive relaxation*) while gradually approaching the feared object or circumstance. This builds "courage" in the client, lessening fear and frequently eliminating the phobia completely.

Recently, the growth of "courage" has received a high-tech boost in the form of *virtual reality* (Yancy, 2000; Kamphuis, Emmelk, & Krijn, 2002; Winerman, 2005). Instead of having clients merely imagine taking off in an airplane, touching a snake, or holding a spider, clinicians create a *virtual reality* with the help of electronic equipment. Entering the therapist's office, the client dons headgear that appears somewhat like an oversized bicycle helmet with flip-down screen and earphones, and sits in a chair that's on a platform that can vibrate and turn. After some training in progressive muscle relaxation, the flight-phobic client experiences a *virtual takeoff.* Sensors in the helmet pick up any head-turning, and the picture on the screen changes appropriately, so when the client turns her head to the right she might see other passengers across the aisle, when she looks to the left she might be looking out the window. Meanwhile as the platform rumbles and shakes, earphones transmit the sounds of jet engines beginning to rev, flight attendants giving instructions, and the pilot making announcements. The client "knows" it's not a real takeoff, but the simulation incorporates many of the same kinds of stimuli that would be experienced in a real-life takeoff.

Treating social phobia and agoraphobia. **Social phobia** *is a severe and persistent fear of performance or social situations in which embarrassment might occur;* **agoraphobia** *is severe anxiety about being stuck someplace where escape might be difficult or embarrassing (e.g., traveling alone in a bus, car, or plane; riding in an elevator; caught in a crowd of people, etc.).* I once treated an agoraphobic client who was afraid to travel more than a mile or two from home without being accompanied by his wife (so that in the event of an emergency such as a heart attack, *she* would be able to drive him to safety). He felt even safer if his wife's mother was also present in the car as a "backup." After he began to improve, I gently joshed that we had saved him having to purchase a van to transport his support group of wife, mother-in-law, as well as half a dozen relatives or friends for multiple "backups."

Agoraphobia and social phobias are among the most disabling fears, because they are so broad. If you're afraid of spiders, snakes, or flying, you can sometimes organize your life to avoid such situations, but if you must avoid people in general or almost any situation where you might be alone, this becomes a genuine impairment. It is estimated that about 5 million American adults have social phobia, making it the third most prevalent mental disorder, behind depression and alcoholism. The good news is that with cognitive behavior therapy or antidepressant medication 80 percent of social phobics can alleviate their symptoms (Heimberg et al., 1998).

New research directions. Since one of the keys to effective virtual treatment is "presence," therapists are constantly seeking new ways to increase "presence." Researchers have found that sometimes thousands of dollars worth of graphics are not as effective as a $12 fan blowing in your face. Recently, therapists (e.g., Hoffman et al., 2003) reported that having clients touch an artificial, furry tarantula while visually immersed in a virtual "Spider World" is twice as effective as visual exposure alone.

In another recent study (Carlsson et al., 2004) researchers used *f*MRI to study persons who were phobic of either snakes or spiders. They flashed pictures of a snake and a spider, each followed by a neutral picture. When the presentation was so fast that participants were not consciously aware they had seen a spider or a snake, they responded to *both* pictures with increased anxiety. However, when images were presented slowly enough to be perceived in conscious awareness, they responded only to the phobic stimulus (snake-phobics responded to snakes, but *not* to spiders; and vice versa).

These studies illustrates how research can enhance our knowledge across various levels of analysis. In the *Physiological Zone*, the use of *f*MRI allows researchers to track phobic activity in the biological world, as well as studying the differences between unconscious and conscious awareness in the Insight Zone or private world of the person. *Virtual realities* provide other avenues for accessing phobic responses. In the Social Zone or being-with-others world, the successful treatment of *social phobias* and *agoraphobia* illustrates a more existential sort of "courage to be" . . . up in front of people talking, or the "courage" to face the "nothingness" of an elevator alone.

Perhaps such practical applications were not what May and other existentialists had in mind when they discussed "courage," but it illustrates how these concepts can be brought down from the philosophical stratosphere to practical situations.

Is It Useful?

Here we would respond with a resounding "Yes!" As one scholar put it:

> The breadth of May's "theory" is astounding, for it encompasses most of the major philosophical questions and ideas of the last two thousand years of human thought. . . . May wastes no time on "small potatoes." His concepts are grand, philosophical, sometimes ambiguous, sometimes paradoxical, and always intriguing. (Monte, 1999, p. 603)

Another writes:

> For the most part, psychologists have tended to ignore May's theory because they cannot treat it as a scientific hypothesis. Concepts like intentionality and the daimonic are virtually impossible to define operationally and test empirically. . . . May runs a strong risk of being given short shrift by the psychological establishment and having little impact on personality theorizing. This is ironic because in many ways the humility and openness to change characteristic of May's theory are more in keeping with the nature of the scientific enterprise than the attitude of those who seek to limit and confine research. By ignoring May, psychologists deprive themselves of the challenge of reexamining their own philosophical assumptions and, perhaps, reconceiving the goals and methods of their science. (Engler, 1999, p. 395)

May's theory/philosophy has proven valuable both in clinical and academic endeavors. May wasn't an existentialist who abandoned a person to wander in a world of absurdity or face one's inevitable demise alone; instead, he offered a dialectical method to resolve existential conflicts with higher-order syntheses. Transcending his classical training, he synthesized psychoanalysis and existential philosophy into an experience-near system of thought that addressed many of life's major conflicts (e.g., anxiety versus vitality, thinking versus doing, freedom versus fate, sex versus love, life versus death).

Next, we consider Ernest Becker's brilliant resuscitation of Otto Rank's theories. In the previous chapter we learned how Rank influenced Rogers's humanism; here we will discover how Rank also influenced Becker's existentialism.

THE DEATH-DEFYING EXISTENTIALISM OF ERNEST BECKER

Death—a Distinguishing Issue Between Humanism and Existentialism

The humanistic perspective on death. Humanists like Rogers did not loiter long around death's door, choosing instead to focus on *life*—fully lived, self-actualized, and generously sprinkled with peak experiences. Death, when briefly mentioned, served primarily to sharpen the senses and activate one's appreciation for *life*. In a letter written while he was recuperating from a heart attack, Maslow captured this spirit vividly:

> The confrontation with death—and the reprieve from it—makes everything look so precious, so sacred, so beautiful that I feel more strongly than ever that impulse to love it, to embrace it, and to let myself be overwhelmed by it. My

river has never looked so beautiful. . . . Death, and its ever present possibility makes love, passionate love, more possible. I wonder if we could love passionately, if ecstasy would be possible at all, if we knew we'd never die. (quoted in May, 1969, p. 99)

Congenial, contrary correspondence. In the hands of the humanists, death appears almost radiant: "my river has never looked so beautiful." By contrast, existentialists seek to "cheat" death with a gritty sort of inspiration-in-the-face-of-evil, typified by Viktor Frankl's (1959) recollection of clinging to a mental image of his wife even while stumbling through the icy darkness of a concentration camp with guards shouting orders and prodding prisoners with rifle butts. This difference between humanistic and existential perspectives of death was illustrated in some correspondence that took place between Carl Rogers and Rollo May late in their lives:

Dear Carl:
It is difficult to write this letter because of my affection for you and our long friendship. But the problem of evil is so crucial that it is imperative that we see it clearly . . . I am not arguing that we human beings are only evil. I am arguing that we are bundles of both evil and good potentialities. . . . I am pleading for a realistic approach to human evil. . . . The issue of evil—or rather, the issue of not confronting evil—has profound, and to my mind adverse, effects on humanistic psychology. I believe it is the most important error in the humanistic movement. . . .

    I write this letter, dear Carl, with profound respect for you and your contribution in the past to all of us. If I speak strongly, it is because I believe strongly.
      Yours
      Rollo May   (Kirschenbaum & Henderson, 1989, pp. 239–250)

Rogers responded:

Dear Rollo:
Your thoughtful analyses and arguments will provoke a lot of good thinking and I appreciate that. . . . I would like to try to clarify my reasons. I feel that the tendency toward actualization is inherent. In this, man is like all other organisms. I can count on it being present. . . . I have given an example of potatoes in a basement bin, sending their feeble white sprouts upward in a futile effort to reach the light. . . .

    I find in my experience no such innate tendency toward destructiveness, toward evil. I cannot count on the certainty that this individual is striving consciously or unconsciously to fulfill an evil nature. . . . They [African wild dogs] kill, but normally only in the interest of actualizing themselves. I gather that you feel the central tendency in human nature is a dual one, aiming both toward creative growth and destructive evil. . . . I don't find that describes animal behavior, or plant behavior, or human behavior. If the elements making for growth are present, the actualizing tendency develops in positive ways.

    Rollo, you have raised many profound points and this is, I am well aware, a hasty and inadequate reply. Yet I hope that between the two documents people will be stirred to constructive thought. As I said in my earlier published remarks about you, you have been a great contributor to humanistic psychology and I value you very much for that. I hold you in affectionate regard.

Sincerely,

Carl Rogers   (Kirschenbaum & Henderson, 1989, pp. 251–255)

Although these letters are a model of respectful communication (especially in an era when Jerry Springer's style of in-your-face confrontation seems to be the order of day), they leave unresolved the profound differences between the humanistic and existential perspectives on death.

As the truism puts it, "Only death and taxes are certain." Therefore, death provides a kind of existential "North Pole" around which other ontological issues orient. *Existence*, the centerpiece of existentialist philosophy, can be defined as the opposite of death. *Anxiety,* when understood in the sense of the original German *(angst)*, is anguish about "losing being." Existentialists vary widely in how they regard death (e.g., Heidegger regards death as the most authentic touchstone of reality, while Sartre sees it as the ultimate *absurdity*), but none fails to make death a central concern.

The existentialists' insistence on including the dark side of life in their analyses brings to mind a comment made by writer and Nobel Laureate, Isaac Bashevis Singer. When asked if he believed in God, Singer replied, "I'm not sure about God but I know there is a Devil" (cited in Kendler, 2000, p. 23).

The human curse: ever-present awareness. For existentialists, death—like its life-sustaining opposite, oxygen—is ever present. Death is the 900-pound gorilla that lurks in the darkness just beyond the warmth of our existential campfires. Death is the pale horse that gallops through the night not to warn us that "The British are coming!" but to remind us that our final hour inexorably approaches. Death is our uniquely human existential curse. Although we share our dust-to-dust destiny with frogs, grasshoppers, canaries, and all manner of living creatures, only we humans are doomed to incessantly ponder our plight, while they hop and flit about as if there were always a tomorrow.

Even our sex-and-violence "entertainment" appears as an attempt to grapple with our inexorable demise by allowing us to view death while simultaneously pumping up our vitality. Television viewers alternate between *Sex in the City* and *Crime Scene Investigation*, while moviegoers choose between "chick flicks" and "action films." Readers ply their fantasies with steamy scenes from Danielle Steele or heroic images from *The Hunt for Red October*. Even as we instruct our friends or ourselves, "Slow down, it's not a matter of life and death!" we are aware that ultimately everything *really is* a matter of life and death.

Becker faces off with death. In his Pulitzer Prize-winning book, *The Denial of Death* (1973). Ernest Becker shares Samuel Johnson's conviction that thinking about death concentrates the mind:

". . . fear of death is a universal that unites data from several disciplines of the human sciences, and makes wonderfully clear and intelligible human actions. . . . (pp. ix–xi).

The existential (binocular) perspective. If we were to describe the existentialist view of death in one word, it could be *binocular*. Existentialists might agree with Maslow that an awareness of death intensifies one's appreciation of life, but they would insist that while one eye might focus on the love, beauty, and goodness surrounding us, the other must unblinkingly stare evil, ugliness, and death in the face. Only in this way can we attain the depth perception needed to see life in its multidimensionality: good *and* evil, life *and* death.

Lessons from Auschwitz. Viktor Frankl illustrates this binocular perspective in *From Death-Camp to Existentialism* (1959). He tells of arriving in camp and inquiring from other prisoners if anyone knew where he might see one of his friends:

> "You can see him there," I was told.
>
> "Where?" A hand pointed to the chimney a few hundred yards off, which was sending a column of flame up into the grey sky of Poland. It dissolved into a sinister cloud of smoke.
>
> "That's where your friend is, floating up to Heaven," was the answer. (p. 11)

However, even in such savage circumstances Frankl managed to extract existential meaning by thinking of love during one of the enforced marches (recounted earlier in the *Personal Perspective* narrative).

TABLE 12.2

Becker at a Glance

MODEL OF PERSONALITY	DESCRIPTION	DYNAMICS
What Are the Parts?	***Whole person:*** for Existentialists the whole person is the only meaningful "part."	In place *of libido,* Becker believes *that fear of death* permeates each person's personality. Since *terror of death* influences all aspects of the personality, only a holistic analysis makes any sense.
What Makes a Person Go?	***Terror (of death):*** Becker sees *terror,* not *libido,* as the master motive.	*Terror of death* is rendered doubly poignant by its *certainty* and by our *awareness.*
What Makes a Person Grow?	***Anal stage:*** Becker reinterprets Freud's developmental stages in existential terms. For example, *anality* isn't primarily about toilet training; rather, feces provide a metaphor of our own *physicalness, decay,* and *waste.* Toilet training represents a triumph over our physicalness—existentially a symbol of life conquering death.	Becker sees developmental "stages" as symbols of much larger existential issues. Thus, *anality* is about overcoming the limitations of our physicality; *repression* is the attempt to *partialize* the world into bite-sized, manageable portions; and *transference* is an attempt to deal with the fear of death.
What Makes a Person Unique?	Humans are uniquely *aware* of their inescapable mortality. This colors every aspect of personality functioning.	Humans are unique among all living things regarding their *awareness* and *terror of death.*

What Are the Parts?

Existentially expanding psychoanalysis. Since Becker was influenced by Rank, who in turn was influenced by Freud, we encounter many apparently familiar psycho-analytic constructs. However, Becker refurbishes these terms with new, existentially expanded meanings. And, like other existentialists Becker avoids dissecting personality into clearly-defined "parts."

What Makes a Person Go?—Terror!

Terror of death. Since Becker existentially focuses on the whole person rather than on personality "parts," we shouldn't be surprised to find that he doesn't dice up motivational theory into bite-sized reinforcers or pocket-sized punishers. Nor does he divide libido into packages of cathected sexual energy as did Freud. On the contrary, *all* motives, *all* drives, *all* goals are seen to issue from one mighty, overarching, master motive—the *terror of death*. Becker acknowledges this at the outset: "this whole book [*The Denial of Death*] is a network of arguments based on the universality of the fear of death, or 'terror' as I prefer to call it . . ." (1973, p. 15).

Certainty of death. The terror of death is intensified by its certainty. Centuries ago, Solomon (thought by many to be the wisest of all philosophers) asserted that humans have no advantage over animals: "Man's fate is like that of the animals; the same fate awaits them both: As one dies so does the other. All have the same breath; man has no advantage over the animal. . . . All go to the same place; all come from dust, and to dust all return" (Ecclesiastes 3: 19–20, New International Version).

Awareness—the skull grinning in at the banquet. Becker eloquently echoes Solomon's sentiments—rendering them even more terrifying by focusing on the excruciating anguish that *awareness* brings:

> Man is literally split in two: he has an awareness of his own splendid uniqueness in that he sticks out of nature with a towering majesty, and yet he goes back into the ground a few feet in order blindly and dumbly to rot and disappear forever. It is a terrifying dilemma to be in and to have to live with. The lower animals are, or course, spared this painful contradiction. (Becker, 1973, p. 26)

Over a century ago, William James (1902/1958, p. 121) referred to death as "the worm at the core" of humankind's happiness. Although people might party and celebrate in a desperate attempt to forget their mortality, James insisted that they could never escape the ominous awareness of death: "even living in the moment, ignoring and forgetting, still the evil background is really there to be thought of, and the skull will grin in at the banquet" (James, 1902/1958, p. 281).

Becker insists that the great driving force behind our lived existential experience is *not* libido—sex is only a temporary diversion—the master motive, the ultimate paradox, the great terror is that we are dying. Right now. You and I. And worst of all, we *know* it! This terrifying awareness renders Freud's observations not so much obsolete as in need of expansion. Becker invites us to examine death—the "worm at the core"—under the microscope, to invite the "grinning skull" inside. Only by consciously co-mingling the terrifying awareness of our inevitable death with the jubilation of our aliveness can we achieve a balanced existential experience. Solomon would have agreed: "It is better to go to a house of mourning than to go to a house of feasting," he wrote, "for death is the destiny of every man; the living should take this to heart. Sorrow is better than laughter, because a sad face is good for the heart" (Ecclesiastes 7:2–3).

Personal terrorism. Since 9/11, *terrorism* has taken on new meaning; it has become part of our collective consciousness. It has international dimensions, taking us via the nightly news to faraway places we might never have thought about before—Afghanistan, Iraq, Nasiriyah, Musayyib. For some, terrorism intruded into their lives with the loss of loved ones either during the attack on the Trade Towers or in subsequent military conflicts. However, for most of us the terrorism of 9/11 remained distant and vicarious. It was someone else sobbing with grief over the firefighter who would never return, it was another family that lost their mother at the Trade Center that tragic morning.

However, Becker reminds us, that the terror of death skips no one. It is both international and personal. It's not only about vicariously grieving with someone on the evening news, it's about wondering, When my time comes, how will I go—heart attack? cancer? Alzheimer's? And where will I go *to*? Is my destination dust, or do I get to go around again? Will there be another cycle? If so, *where*? These and countless other questions existentially terrify us in the most personal, inescapable ways.

What Makes a Person Grow?

Reinterpreting Freud's developmental stages. We've seen how existentialists expand motivational theories, and we find a similar kind of redefining of developmental stages. Becker believes that our ever present awareness that we will become food for worms shapes our personality far more profoundly than does past conditioning or potty training. He views development as an unfolding struggle to deal with the terrorizing awareness of our inevitable destination.

The existential meaning of the anal stage of development. Becker existentially expands Freud's anal stage to include much more than toilet training. He offers the following existential explanation of **anality:** *"The anus and its incomprehensible, repulsive product represents . . . the fate . . . of all that is physical: decay and death"* (Becker, 1973, p. 31, emphasis added). He agrees with psychoanalysts and others who see the anal personality style as an over-controlling *modus operandi* whereby an individual attempts to avoid risk, accidents, or death, by the obsessive use of rituals and routines. However, Becker sees *existential angst* about dying as the real core of anality. He cites anthropological evidence for the universality of anal angst, referring to the men of the Chagga tribe, who "wear an anal plug all their lives, pretending to have sealed up the anus and not to need to defecate. An obvious triumph over mere physicalness" (1973, p. 32).

This existential split between our splendid humanity and our decaying bodies was famously captured by Swift in one of his poems where a young man experiences the gross contradiction of anality in his lover:

Nor wonder how I lost my Wits;
Oh! Caelia, Caelia, Caelia shits! (quoted in Brown, 1959, p. 189)

Reinterpreting repression as partialization. Another example of existentially expanding psychoanalytic terms is **partialization,** *the process by which ordinary people divide up reality into manageable portions.* As Becker picturesquely puts it:

> the "normal" man bites off what he can chew and digest of life, and no more. In other words, men aren't built to be gods, to take in the whole world; they are built like other creatures, to take in the piece of ground in front of their noses. Gods can take in the whole of creation because they alone can make sense of it. . . . But as soon as a man lifts his nose from the ground and starts sniffing at eternal problems like life and death, the meaning of a rose or a star cluster—then he is in trouble. (Becker, 1973, p. 178)

Serving-sized portions of pie. *Partialization* can be thought of as carving up the apple pie of experience into serving-sized portions which are additionally *partialized* with one's knife and fork, and still further *partialized* by chewing and swallowing. Served-up pie provides a more existential metaphor of repression than Freud's famous "iceberg" analogy, because it suggests that *all* experience is partialized—not just the unacceptable urges or fantasies contained in the vast volume of "ice" beneath the surface of awareness.

Contemporary brain scientists have demonstrated that we *partialize* most of our experience in order to focus on the task at hand. The driver of a car is "unconscious" of depressing the clutch and grasping the gear shift, not because pumping the clutch symbolizes intercourse, nor because grasping the shift knob is reminiscent of masturbation, but because it is necessary to *focus* on traffic without distractions. Repression isn't primarily about keeping *censored* or *objectionable* mental contents out of awareness, it serves to *partialize* life into more manageable portions. As Becker sees it:

> The great boon of repression is that it makes it possible to live decisively in an overwhelmingly miraculous and incomprehensible world, a world so full of beauty, majesty, and terror that if animals perceived it all they would be paralyzed to act. . . . It is appalling, the burden that man bears, the *experiential* burden. (Becker, 1973, pp. 50–51)

Transference as fear of death. In Becker's view, *transference* becomes an existential crucible containing mankind's molten terror of nothingness. As the growing child becomes increasingly aware of her true existential condition—*vulnerable and dying*—she correspondingly seeks security in the form of powerful transference objects, existentially reverberating with Gorki's famous statement regarding Tolstoi: "I am not bereft on this earth, so long as this old man is living on it" (Becker, 1968, p. 192). It is this sort of safety-by-association that leads us to *transfer* power and omnipotence onto others so that it might "rub off" on us. Rank quotes Harrington as saying: "I am making a deeper impression on the cosmos because I know this famous person. When the ark sails I will be on it" (Rank, 1968a, p. 407).

Animal or angel?—Rank's dialectic. Rank's theories included the notion of God, not as a neurotic defense or a simple reflex born of superstition or insecurity, but as an object of a genuine life-longing. In this way Rank transcended Freud's jaundiced view of faith as immature dependency; instead, he echoed Kierkegaard's conception of spirituality as the dialectical antithesis to our existential angst regarding our date with death:

> If man were a beast or an angel, he would not be able to be in dread. Since he is a synthesis he can be in dread. . . . The spirit cannot do away with itself. . . . Neither can man sink down into vegetative life. . . . He cannot flee from dread. (Kierkegaard, 1844, pp. 139–140)

As Becker put it, "Man's anxiety is a function of his sheer ambiguity and of his complete powerlessness to overcome that ambiguity, to be straightforwardly an animal or an angel" (1973, p. 69). In this way Becker views the Freudian urge to merge with Mommy or to identify with Daddy as arising not from childhood cowardice or castration anxieties, but from the earliest existential consciousness that we are both living *and* dying. Becker dredges up terror from the deepest unconscious layers of personality, while pulling down angst from the stratosphere of existential philosophy, to locate both the dread of dying and the zest for living within the same personality.

What Makes a Person Unique?

We have already noted that the uniqueness of each person's experience is intrinsic to existential thought; but such singularity is not the warm, glowing, one-of-a-kind distinctiveness that humanists like to portray. According to existentialists, each person must courageously create his own peculiar identity even while living in a vast and "uncaring" universe filled with stardust and galaxies of unfathomable dimensions. Among all the living flora and fauna of our planet, we humans are *uniquely aware* that we will die. That is the burden that all existentialists—poets, psychologists, psychoanalysts, theologians, and writers alike—grapple with. We conclude our discussion of Becker with his portrait of the artist as a model of heroic synthesis.

SUMMARY OF HEROIC SYNTHESIS

Becker (and Rank) viewed the neurotic as someone who rigidly or excessively partialized experience. This is a person who becomes too narrowly focused on self or upon a particular aspect of a problem, failing to see the "big picture." In this way she fails to synthesize existence and nothingness by leaving behind a lasting gift.

Rank's synthesis—cosmic heroism. In *Art and Artist* (1968a), Rank wrote that art was the ultimate synthesis to humankind's inescapable duality. In the concrete creation of a work of art, the artist merges her mortality with her creation while at the same time expansively extending herself in the direction of immortality. Becker agreed: "In the creative genius we see the need to combine the most intensive Eros of self-expression with the most complete Agape of self-surrender. (Becker, 1973, p. 173).

Giving your gift. The artist becomes the prototype for all humankind, with the psychologically well adjusted functioning as successful "artists"—living fully and sensually *in* the world, while creatively shaping their existence into a unique "gift" to the powers beyond. Becker summarized it well:

> The whole thing boils down to this paradox: if you are going to be a hero then you must give a gift. . . . If you are an artist you fashion a peculiarly personal gift. . . . The great scientific world-shaker Newton was the same man who always carried the Bible under his arm. (1973, p. 173)

Here Becker emphasizes that one should not circumscribe one's life with the small "beyonds" that are near at hand—tranquillizing oneself with the trivia of the ordinary—but should reach for the highest "beyonds of spirituality. Only by surrendering to nature on the highest level can human beings conquer death. Thus, *heroic synthesis* reaches beyond sex, beyond relating to a "significant other," beyond the bounds of organized religions, to a transcendent Higher Power. In the end, "giving one's gift" becomes the synthesis of one's life.

My gift. To put it more personally, this text is my gift—my attempt to "make a difference." For much of my professional life I've swum in the stream of ambiguity known as "clinical practice." I think I've learned a few things along the way, but so what? At this point in my career, I'm more than half way "there" and what do I have to show for it? Some diplomas and licenses on the walls of my office? An impressive bibliography of articles published and papers presented? In the end, it's the love of my wife and family that matters most—but even that is a bit narrow. So I offer my gift, hoping through these black squiggles on white paper to touch your life with mine— and with the lives of family, friends, students, and clients who have touched me with their trust. To the extent that we achieve a measure of interconnectedness, my life— and yours too!—will differ from that of the grasshoppers.

FACING THE TOUGH TWINS

Is It Testable?

Science as partialization. Becker is not antiscience; rather, he sees science as the *partialization* of a much larger whole: "The urge to cosmic heroism, then, is sacred and mysterious and not to be neatly ordered and rationalized by science and secularism" (1973, p. 284).

Like May, he sees science as a vital—but incomplete—story of life. An entire discipline (*thanatology*) now seeks to scientifically understand issues surrounding death and dying, and Becker and Rank would have no quarrel with such a focus. Becker cites a wide range of anthropological and psychological data in support of his ideas, and what we encounter in his work is a sense of awe and reverence for life *and* death, not an antiscience attitude.

Becker's closing sentence illustrates why his most central dialectic (giving your "gift") is difficult to scientifically investigate: "The most that any one of us can seem to do is to fashion something—an object or ourselves—and drop it into the confusion, make an offering of it, so to speak, to the life force" (1973, p. 285). Nonetheless, as the following research illustrates, even existential constructs such as "nothingness" can be approached scientifically.

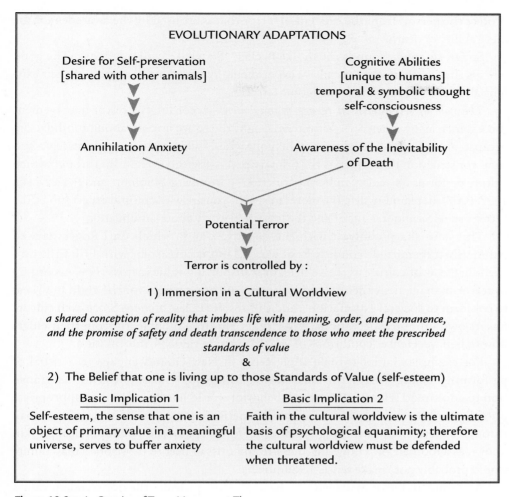

Figure 12.3 ■ *An Overview of Terror Management Theory*

Terror management research. The work of Greenberg, Solomon, and Pyszczynski (1997) on terror management illustrates how even such existentially esoteric constructs as "nothingness" can be investigated in the laboratory. See Figure 12.3 for an overview. We will briefly consider only a few studies to illustrate how psychologists have managed to operationally define and study *terror*. Sounding much like Becker, they see self-consciousness as both a blessing and a terror:

> Self-consciousness also engenders a vast potential for both awe and terror; awe, because knowing that one is alive . . . make[s] one aware of the grandness and complexity of the universe . . . terror, because knowing that one is alive necessitates the horrifying recognition of one's vulnerabilities and inevitable death . . . (Greenberg, Solomon, and Pyszczynski, 1997, p. 65)

According to terror-management theory, humans create *culture* to provide a world of meaning that supersedes the natural world and elevates persons above other animals and life forms. Their theory posits that *self-esteem* and *culture* collaborate to protect the person from the existential terror that is aroused by the awareness of the inevitability of death.

So far, so good—sounds much like Becker. "So what?" you might ask. The good news is that these investigators have experimentally tested many aspects of their existential theory. Let's look at some recent research.

The role of self-esteem in terror management. According to terror-management theory, increasing a person's self-esteem ought to reduce anxiety about annihilation, because, according to Greenberg and his colleagues, "self-esteem is . . . ultimately a cultural construction that serves as the primary psychological mechanism through which culture performs its anxiety-buffering function" (Greenberg, Solomon, and Pyszczynski, 1997, p. 67). In plain English, the more "in synch" you are with cultural expectations, the better you'll feel about yourself and the less you'll worry about annihilation.

This is in sharp contrast with the negative way in which Carl Rogers viewed parentally transmitted "conditions of worth," but is consistent with Erik Erikson's friendlier view of culture as the vehicle for transporting values across time. According to terror-management theory (and Erikson), culture outlines for the child how best to conform to societal expectations, and this results in less anxiety. Since each culture has its own unique expectations, and rituals, children must learn from their elders how to behave. Hence "conditions of worth" provide valuable information.

For example, Sambian male adolescents in New Guinea engage in a ritual of performing fellatio with all the male elders of the group as part of the normal transition to adulthood (Herdt, 1982). Such behavior would hardly be deemed appropriate outside Sambian culture. Similarly, such American rituals as shooting a basketball through a metal hoop, attacking one another for the possession of a spherical pigskin known as a football, or "chugging" massive amounts of beer to prove one's masculinity would probably not "make sense" to Sambians.

According to terror-management theory, culture provides the transcendent values that enable one to face annihilation with composure. Since self-esteem is a measure of cultural conformity, it follows that high self-esteem (cultural conformity) ought to be associated with lower anxiety. Research findings support this view. When self-esteem was increased in experimental subjects by means of bogus feedback on intelligence or personality tests, they showed less anxiety later when viewing graphic death-related videos. They also showed less physiological arousal in response to the threat of electric shock (Greenberg, Solomon, Pyszczynski, Rosenblatt, Burling, Lyon, and Simon, 1992).

Prostitutes and prejudice. Looking at the other side of the equation, numerous studies have demonstrated that increasing a person's awareness about death *(mortality salience studies)* increases one's terror of dying. Subjects in mortality-salience conditions are typically asked to write a few sentences about what they think will happen when they physically die, including describing their emotions about dying. In the control group, participants are asked to write about such things as watching television or experiencing dental pain. Subsequently, all subjects are asked to make judgments about persons who either conform with or threaten their cultural worldview.

In one such mortality-salience study (Rosenblatt, Greenberg, Solomon, Pyszczynski, & Lyon, 1989), municipal court judges in mortality-salience conditions were compared with those in control conditions to see if they viewed "moral transgressors" as more threatening to their worldview, and thus more anxiety-arousing. As predicted, judges in the mortality-salience condition set higher bonds for alleged prostitutes than did judges in the control condition (average bonds of $455 versus $50, respectively).

Similarly, white Americans' attitudes toward black Americans can be shown to vary as a joint function of mortality-salience conditions and the extent to which blacks are seen as either conforming to or threatening white Americans' cultural worldview. In a recent study (Simon, Waxmonsky, Greenberg, Pyszczynski, & Solomon, 1996), after a mortality-salience manipulation, white subjects read an essay supposedly written by a black person who portrayed himself as either culturally stereotypic or nonstereotypic. The stereotypic confederate dressed like a rap star from MTV and wrote about spending summers drinking beer and cruisin' for honeys with the homeboys. The counterstereotypic confederate dressed like an engineering student and wrote about playing chess and attending summer school. As seen in Table 12.2, in the absence of mortality salience, the counterstereotypic black was liked better; however, under conditions of mortality salience, the stereotypic black was preferred.

Apparently, stereotypes serve to maintain the stability of one's cultural worldviews and thus soothe one's anxieties about death. Similar findings were obtained when studying Christians and Jews (Greenberg, Pyszczynski, Solomon, Rosenblatt, Veeder, Kirkland, & Lyon, 1990). Christians viewed other Christians more positively and Jews more negatively when mortality salience was increased. Similarly, Oschmann and Mathy (1994) found that among German university students, mortality salience led German students to sit closer to a German confederate and father away from a Turkish confederate. Notice that in this latter study, the dependent variable was actual behavior (sitting closer or farther), not just a self-reported attitude.

Aggression and hot sauce. Terror management theory predicts that aggression toward "outsiders" will be increased by mortality salience. Accordingly, after a mortality salience induction, conservative and liberal participants were each given the opportunity to dispense varying amounts of hot sauce to another participant in the study who strongly criticized the liberal or conservative position and who claimed to dislike spicy foods (McGregor, Lieberman, Greenberg, Solomon, Arndt, & Simon, 1996). A computer search of newspaper accounts yielded over twenty-five instances of the use of hot sauce as a means of assault or abuse, so this was deemed an appropriate behavioral measure of aggression. As predicted, mortality-salient subjects administered substantially greater amounts of hot sauce to be consumed if the target subject had criticized their preferred political positions.

TABLE 12.3

Mortality Salience, Racial Stereotypes, and Terror Management

CELL MEANS FOR LIKING[a]

CONFEDERATE	MORTALITY SALIENT	TV CONTROL
Stereotype consistent	7.86$_a$	2.69$_b$
Neutral	5.81$_c$	5.20$_c$
Stereotype inconsistent	4.36$_c$	7.15$_a$

Adapted from Greenberg, Solomon, and Pyszczynski, 1997

[a] Scores could range from 1 = negatively valenced response to 9 = positively valenced response. Means that do not share a common subscript differ at $p < .05$.

Funeral homes and mirrors. Finally, as Freud would undoubtedly have predicted, terror management is not necessarily a conscious process. Pyszczynski, Schimel, Greenberg, & Solomon (1996) interviewed subjects about the social value of various charities in the city. The interviews were carried out either directly in front of a funeral home (mortality-salience condition) or 100 yards away (control condition). Mortality-salience conditions led to increased ratings of the value of charities.

Investigating the relationship of self-awareness to mortality awareness, Arndt, Greenberg, Pyszczynski, Simon, & Solomon (1996) randomly assigned subjects to write either about their own death (mortality-salience condition) or about an important exam (control condition) in a cubicle that either did or did not contain a large mirror (a standard procedure to induce self-focused attention; cf. Duval & Wicklund, 1972). As predicted, the mirror caused participants writing about death to spend less time in the cubicle, but had no effect on the amount of time spent by control subjects.

Summary of terror management research. This brief review of terror management research serves to support Becker's hypothesis that *fear of dying* is a potent motivator of human behavior. Even more importantly, we've seen how personality psychologists can operationalize and test even such existential constructs as "nothingness." Although such constructs are usually framed at levels of analysis significantly above the *Physiological* and *Situational Zones,* these terror management studies demonstrate how creativity and ingenuity can overcome obstacles to investigating existential constructs.

Hardiness—a contemporary analysis of existential courage. As we learned in this chapter, one of the defining characteristics of existentialists is their insistence that we face evil directly, look death in the face, stand bravely at the edge of the abyss. In our modern world *stress* has become a bad word—something we think we ought to avoid if at all possible. Echoing such existentialists as Sartre, Salvatore Maddi contends that life without stress would be boring and inauthentic. Those who seek to avoid stress risk living a "vegetative" lifestyle. Maddi (1985, 2003) has operationalized "existential courage," calling it **hardiness,** *embracing instead of avoiding stressful and challenging experiences.* This is yet another example of how personality psychologists can experimentally examine existential concepts.

Is It Useful?

Splendidly so! Becker eloquently resuscitates Rank, adding breathtaking insights of his own. He convincingly argues that the *terror of death*—not libido—is the force motivating most human activity. With the possible exception of adolescents (whose libidos are at zenith levels and who maintain the temporary illusion that they will live forever), Becker's work is relevant to all. There is no way to cancel our trip with the gazelles and grasshoppers to oblivion, but Becker's courageous confrontation with death, both in his writing and in his own battle with cancer, is truly his *gift* to the rest of us. His brilliant analysis of the ultimate existential dialectic—*life versus death*—is surpassed by few, Solomon, perhaps, being the most notable exception.

Chapter Summary

In this chapter we have seen how existentialists have sought to bring some balance into the warmly optimistic portrait of human nature painted by the humanists. Tragedy, death, and evil are faced head-on by existentialists, who urge us to live courageously and responsibly as we seek to extract existential meaning from our experiences. Existential meaning helped Viktor Frankl survive the sinister shadows of Auschwitz, and while fighting tuberculosis, Rollo May found meaning in the apparent contradictions of life by *synthesizing dialectical* opposites into higher-order wholes.

While he was dying of cancer, Ernest Becker formulated an impressive existential analysis of how the fear of dying colors much of what humans do. Data from terror-management research appears consistent with Becker's formulations. One of the most impressive things about this research is that it illustrates that even highly abstract, existential concepts can be experimentally investigated.

Points to Remember

1. Existentialists balance the warmth and optimism of humanism by including evil, tragedy, and death in their analyses. They address issues from the broadest perspective possible—the *ontological perspective. Ontology* is the study of *ultimate concerns.*

2. Some existentialists (e.g., Sartre, Camus, Neitzsche) pessimistically conclude that existence is *absurd;* others (e.g., Kierkegaard, Tillich, May) resolve and integrate absurdity and evil with the *positives* of goodness, truth, love, and a Higher Power. They call others to transcend tragedy with courage, to fight evil with love, and to live creatively in the shadow of one's inevitable mortality without being depressed or dominated by it.

3. Existentialists analyze existence at three different levels: *The Physiological Zone* surrounds our biological existence as mammals; *the Insight Zone* encompasses our subjective, introspective world; and *the Social* and *Transpersonal Zones* consists of our psychological relationships with others and our transpersonal relationships with God/gods.

4. Rollo May resolved opposites using *Hegelian dialectics* (*thesis versus antithesis* leads to *synthesis* at a higher level). For example, the antithetical notions of *love versus sex* can be synthesized at a higher level of *intimate relationship.*

5. Much of May's thinking revolved around *six ontological principles: (1) awareness, (2) centeredness, (3) consciousness, (4) courage for self-affirmation, (5) participation with others, and (6) anxiety about nothingness.*

6. *Death* is a defining issue among philosophers and psychologists—separating the existentialists' angst and absurdity about "nothingness" from the homogenous happiness of the humanists. Existentialists view human experience *binocularly,* insisting that while one eye might focus with the humanists on love, beauty, and goodness, the other must unblinkingly stare evil, ugliness, and death in the face.

7. Ernest Becker directly confronted *anxiety about nothingness*, arguing that the *terror of death*—not *sexual libido*—is the compelling force behind all human experience. Becker synthesizes existential philosophy and Otto Rank's psychoanalysis, reinterpreting such Freudian concepts as *repression* and *transference* from a *terror-of-death* point of view. Becker's synthesis is as breathtaking in scope and clarity as it is convincing in its logic.

8. The terror of death is made the more frightening by its inevitability—no one escapes. As Becker so vividly puts it, we all "go the way of the grasshopper, even though it takes longer."

9. Using Rank's work as his platform, Becker concludes that by losing oneself in a work of art, the artist achieves the ultimate synthesis of living life fully—at the edge—and at the same time triumphing over death.

10. For Becker and Rank, the *successful artist* is the *quintessential model of "good mental health,"* while the *neurotic* is seen as a *failed artist*.

Key Terms

Agoraphobia (465)	Existentialism (450)
Alienation (461)	Hardiness (478)
Anality (471)	Intentionality (458)
Antithesis (455)	Mitwelt (456)
Consciousness of Self (455)	Ontology (448)
Creative Self-Consciousness (462)	Partialization (472)
Da (456)	Sien (456)
Dasien (456)	Social Phobia (465)
Destiny (456)	Synthesis (455)
Dialectic (455)	Thesis (455)
Eigenwelt (456)	Umwelt (456)
Existential Angst (448)	Will (456)
Existential Crisis (448)	

Web Sites

Rollo May

http://counsellingresource.com/types/existential/index.html. Counselling Resource. This Web site introduces, along with many others, the existential method of counselling. Readers interested in finding a therapist from a particular perspective may be able to locate one by using this site.

www.tameri.com/csw/exist/. The Existentialist Primer. This Web site gives an in-depth discussion of existentialism, its history, philosophers, and fields of influence, including the existential psychology of Rollo May.

Ernest Becker

http://faculty.washington.edu/nelgee/. The Ernest Becker Foundation. This organization is dedicated to reducing human violence. Read about their conference, lectures, and more!

Learning on the Lighter Side

The movie *Schindler's List* (1993) captures the existential polarities of life and death in the horrors endured by the Jews in Poland during the war, as well as the synthesizing courage of Oskar Schindler in saving many.

The movie *Ordinary People* (1980) portrays existential themes of alienation and the search for meaning in the midst of sorrow and loss.

Looking Ahead

In our next chapter, studying the work of Carl Jung, we will come to our broadest level of analysis, the *Transpersonal/Spiritual Zone*. Transpersonal psychologists address such ultimate issues as the meaning of our existence in much the same way as we have just seen with May, Becker, and others. Beyond that, however, they also probe the nature of the universe, our relationship to God (or gods), the evidence for an afterlife, and other such dimensions commonly known as *spirituality*. Questions include: "Is there a God?" or "Will I live again (somewhere, somehow, sometime) after my earthly existence ends?" Although such questions have traditionally been left to philosophers and theologians, there has been a steady increase in the number of psychologists willing/wanting to explore these issues from the perspective of personality or social psychology.

Carl Jung began his career sharing much in common with Freud, but they soon parted company because Jung sought to use the construct of a *collective unconscious* to connect our individual personalities with our ancestral past. We will discuss this in greater detail in the next chapter, but here we need only note that such broad constructs quickly take us beyond the realms of traditional science. Indeed, *transpersonal* psychology might be called *transscientific* psychology, because it attempts to explore territories that remain beyond the reach of laboratory science.

The important thing to remember as we move through the final chapters of our text is that broader is not necessarily *better*—it's just *different*. To many scientifically oriented psychologists, transpersonal theories appear to exist on the "fringes" of respectable science. And indeed, transpersonal psychologists might reply, "Guilty as charged!"—quickly adding that science was not designed to evaluate faith or spirituality even though such concerns are important to billions around the globe. We will find that transpersonal psychologists seek to include spirituality within personality, even while many spiritual constructs prove difficult or impossible to research.

chapter 13

Transpersonal Theories of Personality

William James and Carl Jung

IN THIS CHAPTER YOU CAN

1. Learn how *transpersonal psychology* expands traditional notions of the *self* beyond one's skin and beyond present time.

2. Discover that William James, the "father" of American psychology, had a deep interest in higher (transpersonal) levels of consciousness.

3. Find out that Jung agreed with Freud that personality is based on a "deep" *personal unconscious;* however, he went even deeper and wider by adding a *collective unconscious,* which he believed connects us with our ancestral past.

4. Learn that even as a young child Jung experienced *intense dreams* and *visions,* which continued throughout his adulthood as well. At times, his visions appeared almost psychotic; however, he ultimately translated his inner turmoil into a theory of personality that balances internal experiences with external realities.

5. Learn how, early in his career, Jung conducted research utilizing a *word-association test* to study unconscious processes, initially winning Freud's admiration. However, Jung *ultimately disagreed with the importance Freud placed on sexuality as a master motive* and they parted ways—bitterly.

6. Understand that Jung's *psyche* is a "big tent" of personality that includes the *ego, personal unconscious,* and *collective unconscious.* Additionally, Jung included within personality the *soul,* which makes possible a transcendent connection with higher power(s).

7. Appreciate how *individuation* is a lifelong developmental process by which opposing elements of the psyche are *balanced within the personality.* The *second half of life* is a time of continuing growth—especially in the *spiritual realm,* in which prior experience plays a vital role.

A PERSONAL PERSPECTIVE

"Good Luck Mr. Gorski!"

"Good luck Mr. Gorski!" Grof (1998, pp. 94–95) illustrates Jung's concept of *transpersonal synchronicity* with an anecdote about American astronaut Neil Armstrong, who uttered the famous words: "One small step for man; one giant leap for mankind." Less well known are the words he muttered while climbing back into the lunar module: "Good luck Mr. Gorski!" Curious reporters tried to get Armstrong to explain what he meant by that statement, thinking perhaps it was a dig at one of the Soviet cosmonauts, but he refused to elaborate. Since there were no cosmonauts by the name of Gorski, the frustrated journalists remained baffled and the matter was finally forgotten.

Some years later, when the Gorskis were deceased, Armstrong felt free to disclose that Mr. Gorski and his wife had lived nextdoor to the Armstrongs when Neil was a boy. One day, when Neil and his friends were playing ball in his backyard, the ball landed in the garden just below the Gorskis' open bedroom window. Neil was appointed to retrieve the errant ball, and as he sneaked into the neighbors' garden on his appointed mission, he overheard the Gorskis in the middle of a heated argument. "Oral sex? You want oral sex?" screamed Mrs. Gorski. "You'll get oral sex the day the kid next door walks on the moon!"

Commentary

Jung coined the term **synchronicity** to mean *"coincidence in time of two or more causally un-related events which have the same or a similar meaning"* (1960, p. 441). Numerous books have been written (Halberstam & Leventhal, 1997, 1998) documenting extraordinary "coincidences," explained not only in terms of Jung's *synchronicity,* but also as *providential interventions* of Spirit. In one such story, a person took a wrong bus and sub-sequently ended up deciding to visit a friend who lived in that distant part of the city where he seldom traveled:

> Johnson impulsively decided to get off the bus and visit her, since he was in the area. He made his way to her apartment and knocked. There was no answer. Then he smelled gas. He knocked again and shouted. Still no answer. Johnson broke down the door and discovered the woman lying unconscious, her head in the oven, a suicide attempt. Fortunately, Johnson was just in time to save her life. (Halberstam & Leventhal, 1998, p. 89)

In another example of a "small miracle," two college students planned to spend the day picnicking at a lake, but because of multiple problems with their car (e.g., broken fan belt, dead battery, etc.) they arrived late in the day to find the lake deserted:

> "I just can't believe our day," Chris grumbled to Steve. "We came all this way for nothing!"
> *"Help!"* they suddenly heard a young voice shout.
> *"Help us, please!"* a second voice cried.
> For a frozen moment, Chris and Steve were motionless, their gaze riveted on the sight of two little boys flailing in the lake. Then the two—certified life-guards both—raced to the water's edge and dove in. They pulled out the kids, administered CPR, and saved their lives. (Halberstam & Leventhal, 1998, p. 106)

Some of life's most meaningful experiences cannot be reduced to dependent and independent variables, cannot be understood from a statistical perspective. In this chapter, we will include a discussion of how transpersonal psychologists account for life events that take place outside the reach of empirical research technologies.

TRANSPERSONAL PSYCHOLOGY—THE BROADEST OF "BIG TENTS"

Defining transpersonal psychology. Let's begin by defining some key terms. **Transpersonal psychology** is *the broadest possible psychology, with a scope that includes transcendent experiences that are beyond the reach of empirically based scientific inquiry.* Not only does transpersonal "go beyond" the person, it frequently goes beyond scientific methodologies as well, seeking to understand our universe in more expansive ways.

If we compare our journey so far to climbing a series of stairs to higher and broader levels of analysis, entering the *Transpersonal Zone* is a bit like stepping out onto the roof and viewing the galaxies of the night sky.

Transcendent. In our usage, *transcendent* will remain neutral with respect to secular versus spiritual dimensions. **Transcendent experience** means that *a person has encountered something beyond and above ordinary, consensually shared experience—often in an inspiring or uplifting way.* Although the hallucinations of a person suffering from schizophrenia might be "beyond" ordinary experience, we wouldn't consider them transcendent. The psychotic experience that "My intestines are rotting and I'm giving off foul odors" would hardly be inspiring or uplifting. However, highly developed delusions of visiting other planets (e.g., the case study "Jet-propelled couch" reported by Lidner, 1982) might be experienced as *transcendent.* More commonly, listening to "uplifting" music or gazing at the night sky through a telescope might become a *transcendent* experience. Watching logs crackle in a fireplace might be relaxing, but not necessarily transcendent.

Spiritual/Religious. Some people use the term *spiritual* as a synonym for *religious;* but most personality psychologists (e.g., Piedmont, 1999; Rayburn & Richmond, 2002; Zinnbauer, Pargament & Scott, 1999) use the term *spiritual* to include *transcendent, nonreligious* experiences as well. We will use the terms **religious** or **spiritual** when describing *transpersonal experiences that include a "Higher Power."* Thus, if a choir and orchestra were performing Handel's *Messiah* and a listener or musician were "drawn upward toward God" in the majesty of the *Hallelujah Chorus,* this could be considered a *religious* or *spiritual* transcendent experience. On the other hand, one might transcendently be "caught up" in the music and enthusiasm of a live Elton John concert without feeling closer to a "higher power."

Secular and spiritual varieties of transpersonal psychology. In the previous chapter, we encountered both secular and spiritual versions of *existentialism* ranging from Sartre's pessimism to Kierkegaard's leap of faith toward God. Similarly, in the present chapter we will find both secular and spiritual versions of *transpersonal* psychology. For some theorists, *transpersonal* might mean movement toward a Higher Power, whereas for others it simply implies expansiveness—even transcendence—but not in pursuit of a divine "Spirit" or "Center" of the cosmos.

A wide array of definitions for transpersonal psychology. We are about to discover that transpersonal psychology—like existentialism—has many faces. This shouldn't surprise us. We already know that religions flourish on our planet in almost endless varieties, and since transpersonal psychologists frequently incorporate spiritual elements into their theories, the possible number of transpersonal–spiritual combinations is nearly limitless. Still, not all transpersonal psychologists have in mind making a spiritual "leap to God" as did Kierkegaard, or being in touch with the *imago Dei* (image of God) within us, as described by Jung. We will discover that what all transpersonal psychologists *do* have in common is a willingness to explore events that transcend laboratory science. They are willing to explore what they see as "higher levels of consciousness"—experiences that are difficult to measure or quantify.

Early definitions of transpersonal psychology. In the first issue of the *Journal of Transpersonal Psychology,* Sutich offered a definition of transpersonal psychology that emphasized the transcendent capacities of people:

Transpersonal (or "fourth force") Psychology is the title given to an emerging force in the psychology field by a group of psychologists and professional men and women from other fields who are interested in those *ultimate* human capacities and potentialities that have no systematic place in positivistic or behavioristic theory ("first force"), classical psychoanalytic theory ("second force"), or humanistic psychology ("third force"). (1969, p. 15)

Recent definitions of transpersonal psychology. More recently, Lajoie & Shapiro surveyed some forty definitions that appeared in the subsequent quarter century and concluded that "Transpersonal psychology is concerned with the study of humanity's highest potential and with the recognition, understanding, and realization of unitive, spiritual, and transcendent experiences" (1992, pp. 79–98).

In much the same vein, Walsh & Vaughan described transpersonal experiences as: ". . . experiences in which the sense of identity extends beyond *(trans)* the individual or personal to encompass wider aspects of humankind, life, *psyche,* and cosmos" (1993, p. 3).

Transpersonal traffic travels mostly east. Most transpersonalists tilt eastward. They appear to embrace the Buddha's enlightened view that relief of suffering comes from *detachment.* Whereas a Western therapist might focus on problem solving, behavior change, or insight, the transpersonal therapist, like the Eastern guru, would more likely encourage detachment and disidentification.

Once we move beyond empirically based definitions of science and traditional "skin-as-boundary" definitions of *persons,* our level of analysis broadens markedly. When we enter the *Transpersonal Zone* (e.g., connecting with Jungian archetypes residing in the collective unconscious, encountering selves from previous incarnations, discovering God within, or aspiring to merge with Brahman), we embark on a journey with few road signs and meager maps. Postmodern "travel agents," with their preference for "story" in place of science, reassure us that although maps of our destination are hard to come by, shamans and gurus abound. Transpersonalists tend to travel light, leaving behind the usual scientific "suitcases" stuffed with statistical techniques and experimental methodologies.

Transpersonal psychologists appear to privilege Eastern religions more than Western faiths. For example, in a recent personality text authored by two leading transpersonal psychologists (Fadiman & Frager, 2002), three entire chapters are devoted to the mystical traditions of Yoga, Zen, and Sufism, while the text largely ignores the *monotheistic (one-god)* traditions of Judaism, Christianity, or Islam. Next, we consider the work of two pioneer transpersonal psychologists: William James and Carl Jung.

THE TRANSPERSONAL PSYCHOLOGY OF WILLIAM JAMES (1842–1910)

William James, considered by many to be the "father" of American psychology, was born in 1842, some thirty years before Carl Jung. Twice elected president of the American Psychological Association, James profoundly influenced American psychology throughout the nineteenth and twentieth centuries. He explored the full range of human consciousness from brainstem functioning to religious ecstasies. Here we will briefly focus on his view of the developing *self* (evolving from *biological,* to *material,* to *social,* to *spiritual*).

Levels of consciousness in the psychology of William James. James described the *biological self* as comprised of our physical features, genetic makeup, and physiological processes. At a broader level, James included in the *material self* the complete inventory of a person's possessions: ". . . not only his body and his psychic powers, but his clothes and his house, his wife and children, his ancestors and friends, his reputation and works, his lands and horses, and yacht and bank-account." (James, 1890, vol. 1, pp. 291–292)

To these biological and material aspects of self James added an *interpersonal* level which he termed the *social self:* "A man's social self is the recognition which he gets from his mates" (James, 1890, vol. 1, p. 293). Finally, in keeping with our current discussion, James described the *spiritual self* as "the most enduring and intimate part of the self" (1890, vol. 1, p. 296). He wrote an entire volume on spirituality (*Varieties of Religious Experience,* 1902/1958) that is still considered one of the greatest works of its kind.

Consciousness-expanding substances. William James was keenly interested in the influence of various plant substances on consciousness, and he experimented with several mind-altering chemicals as early as the age of twelve. Like other physicians of that era (recall Freud's fascination with cocaine), James personally experimented with mind-altering substances such as nitrous oxide (laughing gas), chloroform, and chloral hydrate. He also ate peyote buttons when investigating the mind-altering properties of this cactus (Fadiman & Frager, 2002, p. 292).

Half a century later, in April 1943, Swiss chemist Albert Hoffmann serendipitously discovered the potent psychoactive properties of lysergic acid diethylamide, commonly known as LSD. While synthesizing a sample of LSD, Hoffmann accidentally intoxicated himself with the condensation products during the purification procedure. He experienced dramatic psychological changes, which he suspected were due to the drug, so he later ingested 250 micrograms of LSD to test his suspicions. His reactions to the drug were dramatic. He experienced a fantastic world of brilliant colors, intense emotions, and undulating forms. He reported his experience to a colleague, who became sufficiently interested to conduct the first scientific study of LSD (Stoll, 1947).

By the mid-1960s LSD had become widely available on the black market, and "acid," as it came to be known, was used by masses of young people. This polarized Americans into the mostly youthful LSD proselytes who saw it as a panacea for a "sick" materialistic society, and the general public who were frightened by daily reports of disastrous results from the recreational use of LSD. Stories (mostly untrue) abounded of LSD users who were blinded by staring into the sun for hours or killed by walking out the window of high-rise apartments.

Some transpersonal psychologists (e.g., Grof, 1998) have conducted extensive research on the role of LSD and other mind-altering substances in expanding consciousness. However, it's probably safe to say that most contemporary transpersonal psychologists do not see psychedelic experiences as the royal road to expanded consciousness, preferring instead to use meditation, yoga, and other such approaches in their search for heightened consciousness.

Summarizing the work of William James and other early pioneers, we can say that they were not locked into narrow definitions of personality or of science. Nor were they convinced, as subsequent generations of behaviorists would be, that all transpersonal experiences are delusional fantasies. Near the end of his life, even Freud, who had viewed all forms of religion as a neurotic longing for an exalted father figure, stated that he would not characterize the study of "so-called occult psychic phenomena as unscientific, discreditable or even as dangerous" (Freud, 1960, p. 334). Apparently, even the father of psychoanalysis had some transpersonal leanings.

THE TRANSPERSONAL PSYCHOLOGY OF CARL GUSTAV JUNG (1875–1961)

Carl Jung (pronounced YOOng) was Freud's early ally and, for a short while, his hand-picked successor. In Jung's work we find much that reminds us of Freud (e.g., unconscious motivation, conflict, defense), but we will also discover profound differences that lead us to locate Jung in the *Transpersonal Zone*. The most obvious difference between Jung and Freud was Jung's formulation of a *collective unconscious,* which *transpersonally* expanded the boundaries of Freud's *personal* unconscious by including ancestral forces and spiritual imagoes alongside Freud's biologically based instincts.

Jung challenged the cause-to-effect reasoning of Freud and classical physics by emphasizing the importance of **teleology,** *the idea that behavior is "pulled" by future goals more than "pushed" by past conditioning or current situational stimuli.* Additionally, as we learned earlier, Jung introduced his controversial notion of *synchronicity* to account for "coincidences." It is because of such vast, overarching, *beyond-the-person* concepts that one contemporary writer correctly described Jung as "the first clinical transpersonal psychiatrist," adding that "Jung's work in the transpersonal realm prefigured much of what is current in the field" (Scotton, 1996, p. 39).

Jung's transpersonal psychology. Writing in his autobiography shortly before his death, Jung described his version of "depth psychology" in the following way:

Life has always seemed to me like a plant that lives on its rhizome [the root-like structure below the soil]. Its true life is invisible, hidden in the rhizome. The part that appears above the ground lasts only a single summer. Then it withers away—an ephemeral apparition. . . . Yet I have never lost a sense of something that lives and endures underneath the eternal flux. What we see is the blossom, which passes. The rhizome remains. (1961a, pp. 3–4)

For Jung, the "rhizome" of personality was the *collective unconscious*—a vast subterranean network that not only connects us, with others in our present lives, but also taps into an ancestral network reaching back through eons of time.

Visions of eternity—Jung's transcendent psychology. The "rhizome" metaphor vividly depicts Jung's transpersonal "roots" in the vast underground of collective unconscious life. On the same pages that Jung uses the "rhizome" metaphor, he also unfurls his *transcendent* colors, confessing that he views the inner life as an avenue to the *eternal*. Whereas Freud saw dreams as the royal road to the unconscious, Jung viewed dreams as pathways to eternity: "That is why I speak chiefly of inner experiences, amongst which I include my dreams and visions. . . . All other memories of travels, people and my surroundings have paled beside these inner happenings" (1961a, pp. 4–5).

Background Check

Childhood and youth. Born July 26, 1875, in the Swiss village of Kesswyl, Carl Jung grew up in the university town of Basel, where his father was a pastor in the Swiss Reformed Church and his mother was the daughter of a theologian. Two themes stand out in his childhood: (1) the conviction that he was two persons, and (2) the belief that he was entrusted with "secret" revelations in the form of visions and dreams.

Two persons residing in one body. Jung's mother exerted a profound influence on her young son, behaving in such contradictory ways that young Carl suspected his mother was really two persons in one body. Sometimes she was extremely kind, with a great sense of humor; at other times she was authoritarian and ruthless. Today, she might be diagnosed as having a borderline personality disorder or suffering from a bipolar condition. Describing how he responded to the negative side of his mother, Jung remembered being "struck to the core of my being, so that I was stunned into silence" (1961a, p. 49).

Jung subsequently incorporated the concept of dual personalities into his own life, believing that—like his mother—he also was two different people living in one body. One of these personalities (a schoolboy) he labeled number one, the other (a wise old man) he labeled number two. It is hardly surprising that in Jung's mature theory, personality is comprised of two opposing components: the *ego complex* residing in the conscious mind and the *shadow complex* residing in the collective unconscious. We will discuss this in more detail shortly, but here we simply note how Jung's mother shaped her son's psyche and influenced his theory of personality.

Early dreams and visions. Perhaps the constant bickering of Jung's parents combined with his dislike

"I feel like there are two people in this body!"

of school to increase Carl's sense of isolation, but whatever the reason, Jung spent much of his childhood disengaged from family and friends, living in a world of visions and dreams. Jung's earliest terrifying dream occurred between the ages of three and four, and it haunted him for the remainder of his life. In the dream he was standing in front of a golden throne:

> Something was standing on it [the throne] which I thought at first was a tree trunk twelve to fifteen feet high and about one and a half to two feet thick. It was a huge thing, reaching almost to the ceiling. But it was of curious composition: it was made of skin and naked flesh, and on top there was something like a rounded head with no face and no hair. On the very top of the head was a single eye, gazing motionlessly upward. (Jung, 1961a, p. 12)

Terrified at the sight of this huge column of flesh, little Carl feared that at any moment it would crawl off the throne and devour him. Jung confessed that this dream haunted him for years, keeping him awake with worry and causing him nightmares when he slept. Ironically, this "phallic" dream appears to illustrate the very phenomenon Jung later rejected about Freud's theory—childhood sexuality. Such a nightmare could have been the result of sexual molestation, or it may have arisen spontaneously. We shall never know. Whatever the source(s), Jung's dreams and visions remained a closely guarded secret.

Keeping it all inside. He confessed that although he had the urge to disclose his dreams, he carried them as secrets until late in his adult life.

> As a matter of fact I did not say anything about the phallus dream until I was sixty-five. . . . a strict taboo hung over all these matters, inherited from my childhood. I could never have talked about them with friends.
>
> My entire youth can be understood in terms of this secret. It induced in me an almost unendurable loneliness. My one great achievement during those years was that I resisted the temptation to talk about it to anyone. (1961a, p. 41)

Adult life. Many of the elements of Jung's early life (e.g., a fantasy friend, special language, fantastic dreams, and grandiose daydreams) might be considered part of the normal fantasy life of a child. However, his carefully guarded dreams and secrets increased rather than diminished as he became an adult, and even in his eighties, shortly before his death, he continued to experience a powerful, secret inner life:

> Thus the pattern of my relationship to the world was already prefigured [in childhood]: today as then I am a solitary, because I know things and must hint at things which other people do not know, and usually do not even want to know. (Jung, 1961a, pp. 41–42)

Freud's heir apparent. Jung's life intersected with Freud's at a time when the founder of psychoanalysis was about to turn fifty. Freud saw in Jung the prospect of a fair-haired, non-Jewish protagonist for his beloved psychoanalysis. Freud and

Jung's first face-to-face meeting took place in Freud's home during February 1907. It was a thirteen-hour marathon that so favorably impressed Freud that he decided Jung would become his successor—the torchbearer for psychoanalysis. However, Freud and Jung's enthusiastic father–son, founder–successor relationship was doomed from the beginning by their fundamental differences regarding the role of sexuality as the master motive. Jung attempted to widen the meaning of libido to include not only sexual energy, but general mental energy as well. Their relationship steadily deteriorated, and by December of 1912, Freud could no longer tolerate their differences, describing Jung as "all out of his wits, he is behaving quite crazy" (quoted in Gay, 1988, p. 235). In April of 1914, Jung resigned as president of the International Psychoanalytic Society and his relationship with Freud ended, buried by the usual layers of bitterness and suspicion that Freud invariably heaped on those who dared to disagree with him.

War without, war within. Jung's breakup with Freud coincided with the outbreak of World War I. For emotionally upset persons, reality boundaries sometimes become blurred, allowing external events to ooze into the inner world where they become loaded with the freight of personal meanings. Such appeared to be the case with Jung:

> Now my task was clear: I had to try to understand what had happened [with Freud]. . . . I was afraid of losing command of myself and becoming a prey to the fantasies. . . . the same psychic material which is the stuff of psychosis and is found in the insane. . . . It was only toward the end of the First World War that I gradually began to emerge from the darkness. (Jung, 1961, pp. 176–178, 188, 195)

Zeitgeist

Early scientist-practitioner. It is remarkable that Jung, whose early life was so permeated with dreams, visions, and fantasies, made his professional debut as a *researcher;* however, this illustrates the power of the *Zeitgeist.* After completing his medical training, Jung worked at the psychiatric clinic for the University of Zurich under the direction of Eugen Bleuler, who was a towering figure among the psychiatrists of his day (he first coined the terms *schizophrenia* and *autism*). Bleuler was a brilliant and innovative researcher who hoped, by research, not only to obtain a better understanding of individual patients, but also to advance science. Jung apparently caught this spirit of scientific inquiry from Bleuler and began pursuing his own studies of word associations, viewing his word-association test as somewhat similar to Freud's free association method—a window to the unconscious mind:

> The experiment is made. . . . with a list of say a hundred words. You instruct the test person to react with the first word that comes into his mind as quickly as possible after having heard and understood the stimulus word. . . . You ask a simple word that a child can answer, and a highly intelligent person cannot reply. Why? That word has hit upon what I call a **complex,** *a conglomeration of psychic contents characterized by a peculiar or perhaps painful feeling-tone, something that*

is usually hidden from sight. It is as though a projectile struck through the thick layer of the *persona* [public face or mask of personality] into the dark layer. (Jung, 1968, p. 53, bolding and emphasis added)

ASKING THE BIG FOUR QUESTIONS

Ellenberger (1970), an eminent historian of psychoanalysis, contends that many a personality theorist (artist, musician, composer, or writer) has experienced a **creative illness,** *or an intense emotional struggle during which the person experiences depression, neurosis, or even psychosis—but never loses his or her preoccupation with a particular idea or gives up searching for a certain truth.* Out of such "creative illnesses" symphonies are composed, pictures are painted, novels are written, and personality theories created.

Prophet or psychotic? Perhaps more than most, Jung's theory of personality not only embodies his clinical and scientific insights, but also includes his personal struggles to make sense of life. Jung's biographers are divided on whether his dreams and visions were evidence—as he himself believed—of a special perceptiveness in transpersonal and transcendent realms, or whether they were the hallucinations of a troubled psychotic. Van der Post (1975) sees Jung's life as a voluntary voyage of self-discovery, whereas Stern (1976) says that Jung experienced a series of full-blown psychotic episodes. Recall that even as a three- or four-year-old, Jung was overwhelmed by a "vision" containing overpowering phallic and religious motifs. This foreshadowed his lifelong balancing act between inner life and external realities:

> After the parting of the ways with Freud, a period of inner uncertainty began for me. It would be no exaggeration to call it a state of disorientation. I felt totally suspended in mid-air, for I had not yet found my own footing. . . . I lived as if under constant inner pressure. At times this became so strong that I suspected there was some psychic disturbance in myself. (Jung, 1961a, pp. 170, 173)

So, was Jung a psychotic or a prophet? Probably a bit of both. At times he appeared overwhelmed by powerful psychotic-like visions and forces, but he was able to creatively transform (sublimate) these into a theory of personality that balanced inner life with situational realities.

The Salvador Dali of personality theorists. The famous artist Salvador Dali (1904–1989) described his paintings as "hand-painted dream photographs." His work includes violent and sexual content as well as images of the stark, desolate landscapes of the Catalonia region of Spain where he was born. Additionally his work frequently contains complicated and puzzling symbols. Similarly, we might describe Jung's archetypes as "hand-painted dream photographs." His *collective unconscious* contained dreams, visions, and symbols that appeared to emerge from deep within himself, and that apparently carried him beyond the range of normal or neurotic experiences into a harrowing world of inner turmoil where fantasy and reality coexisted as equal players.

Thus, Jung's transpersonal theory emerged from a mind fermenting with fantasies and permeated with archetypes and nightmarish images; yet it appears remarkably

TABLE 13.1

Jung at a Glance

MODEL OF PERSONALITY	DESCRIPTION	DYNAMICS
What Are the Parts?	*Psyche* includes *ego* (everything of which we are conscious), *personal unconscious* (contains *complexes:* thoughts, feelings, or memories that cluster around a shared theme), and **collective unconscious** (contains images and archetypes that we share in common with all humankind from the beginning of time). *Self* is the broadest archetype in the collective unconscious, integrating the entire psyche. *Soul* is that part of the psyche that establishes a connection with God (gods).	Near the surface, the psyche contains a *personal unconscious,* but at the deepest levels it consists of the *collective unconscious,* which includes *symbols, mytns,* and *archetypes* connecting us to the ancestral past of all humankind.
What Makes a Person Go?	Three levels of motivation include: *Causality:* a low-level, behavioristic kind of motivation based on past experiences. *Teleology:* goal-directed, future-oriented functioning for a purpose. *Synchronicity:* "meaningful coincidences" that are "lucky," "miraculous," "providential," or otherwise beyond understanding.	*Opposition* is the heart of Jung's motivational system. Every component of the pyche has its opposite (e.g., masculine versus feminine; introversion versus extraversion, etc). Jung adapts a number of laws of physics (such as "for every action, there is an equal and opposite reaction") and uses them as metaphors in his theory of motivation.
What Makes a Person Grow?	Jung presents loosely defined stages: *Childhood:* a time of learning to walk, talk, and develop survival skills *Adolescence:* a time when that *true psychic birth* takes place *Youth (20–35):* a time of completing separation from family of origin *Middle life and old age (40–later years):* the second half of life, a period of continued growth, especially in the search for existential and spiritual meaning	*Individuation:* a lifelong tendency toward self-realization (similar to what humanists refer to as self-actualization) *Transcendence:* the transpersonal harmony that reaches *beyond* the self to transpersonally encounter all of humankind—past, present, and future
What Makes a Person Unique?	Uniqueness emerges from each person's distinctive combination of *attitudes (introversion versus extraversion)*, *endopsychic functions (internal relationships within the psyche)*, and *ectopsychic functions (sensation, thinking, feeling, and intuition)*.	In addition to the many possible combinations of attitudes and functions, each person has a unique combination of past history, favorite myths, admired archetypes, and transcendent experiences.

balanced. This balanced synthesis (among thinking, feeling, sensation, and intuition) comprises the core of what Jung considered to be optimal functioning.

What Are the Parts?

Jung used the term *psyche* in place of *mind* because he wanted to avoid the implication that the psyche is primarily conscious. Instead, he wanted to emphasize that the *psyche* was comprised of both conscious and unconscious processes, and that the *unconscious* included both a *personal unconscious* (similar to the one in Freud's model) and a *collective unconscious* (unique to Jung's theory).

Psyche—a "big tent" with porous boundaries. For Jung, **psyche** *includes the entire personality.* Since the *collective unconscious* is comprised of *shared* human experiences that have occurred over the course of billions of years of evolutionary development, the *psyche* cannot be understood as a closed system (like Freud's hydraulic model); it is, instead, a *transpersonal meeting place* where past, present, and future come together under one roof. Rychlak described the Jungian *psyche* as "a *region*, a kind of multidirectional and multitemporal housing within which identities of the personality like the ego can move about . . ." (1981, p. 181, emphasis in original).

Ego. Jung's **ego** *includes everything of which we are conscious.* It includes *all* that we perceive, remember, think about, or emotionally experience. Our *ego* contains our unique identity and gives us a sense of continuity over time. It is through our ego functions that we establish stable relationships with others and perceive ourselves as the same person in various situations. For Jung, ego is the center of consciousness, but *not* the center of personality—that is the function of the *self* (which we will discuss shortly).

Personal unconscious. The **personal unconscious** *includes material that was once conscious but is now temporarily "out of mind," forgotten, or permanently repressed.* Thus, Jung's *personal unconscious* includes Freud's *preconscious* (momentarily out-of-focus but easily recalled thoughts or feelings), as well the *unconscious* (deeply repressed) elements.

Complexes of the personal unconscious. Jung said that "The contents of the personal unconscious are chiefly the *feeling-toned complexes* . . ." (1959, p. 4). **Complexes** *include thoughts, feelings, and memories that cluster around a shared emotional core.* A *complex* acts as a "magnet" pulling together thoughts, feelings, and behaviors, much as a baseball fan might collect caps, T-shirts, pennants, and various memorabilia related to a favorite team. There is a "snowball effect" in complex formation, because as more elements are added, the larger and more powerful the complex grows. For this reason, Jung's theory is sometimes described as an "adhesive model" (Rychlak, 1981, p. 185). Others have described Jungian complexes as having "constellating power" (Engler, 1999, p. 75).

Transpersonal (collective) unconscious. Jung's most creative and controversial construct, the **collective unconscious,** *contains the primordial images and ideas common to all humans from the beginning of time.* It is this construct of the *collective unconscious* that established Jung as the first *transpersonal* psychologist. The collective unconscious is more than the product of an *individual's* history or biology; it is the gateway to the history of the *entire human race*. Jung describes the collective unconscious as a "deposit of ancestral experience from untold millions of years, the echo of prehistoric world events to which each century adds an infinitesimally small amount of variation and differentiation" (1928, p. 162). He states that he chose the term "collective" because "this part of the unconscious is not individual but universal . . . it has contents and modes of behaviour that are more or less the same everywhere in all individuals . . . and constitutes a common psychic substrate . . . which is present in every one of us. (Jung, 1959, pp. 3–4)

Symbols—the language of the collective unconscious. For Jung, *symbols* are far more than verbal or pictorial representations; **symbols** *present the nature of our universe in the language of the collective unconscious.* Unlike metaphors or allegories, by which we communicate conscious contents, Jung regarded *symbols* as the language of the *unconscious:* ". . . the best possible expression for an unconscious content whose nature can only be guessed, because it is still unknown" (Jung, 1959, p. 6). He recognized a wide array of symbols, ranging from the broad and universal symbols at the "bottom" of the collective unconscious to the more personal symbols existing closer to conscious awareness.

Synthesizing power of symbols and myths. Jung's love for symbols shines through in almost every process that he seeks to explain. Whereas existential psychologists such as Rollo May resolved opposites by analysis or synthesis, Jung used symbols and myths to synthesize opposites.

Jung saw *myths* not as the products of our conscious minds but as arising from the *collective unconscious.* In his travels and studies of primitive cultures in Africa, America, and other places, Jung found general story lines that were consistent across cultures. Mythical accounts involving a masculine hero-figure who saved a civilization during time of drought, war, or moral decay appeared similar even in cultures that had no contact with one another. Based on these common themes, Jung used the term *archetype* to describe such primordial "heroes." We will discuss this in more detail shortly, but here we note that the symbolic, mythical nature of an archetype lends itself well to assimilating and synthesizing opposites. Thus Jung's *Mother* archetype symbolizes both the loving, nurturing Earth Mother *and* the manipulative, cruel Witch (much as Jung's own mother alternated between states of being nurturing and witchy).

A contemporary perspective on myths and symbols. During the late 1980s journalist Bill Moyers interviewed anthropologist Joseph Campbell regarding "the power of myth." This resulted in a six-hour PBS series, as well as a book by the same title (Campbell, 1988). Although one searches in vain for references to Jung in this book, Campbell understands myth in much the same way as did Jung. Although there is no reference to the *collective unconscious* or other Jungian terms, Campbell's explanation of myths would likely have brought a smile to Jung's face:

> Myth opens the world to the dimension of mystery. To the realization of the mystery that underlies all forms. If you lose that, you don't have a mythology. If mystery is manifest through all things, the universe becomes, as it were, a holy picture. (Campbell, 1988, p. 31)

Campbell went on to discuss the cosmological, sociological, and pedagogical functions of myths, suggesting—as Jung did earlier—that "The stages of human development are the same today as they were in ancient times. . . . I would say that is the basic theme of all mythology—that there is an invisible plane supporting the visible one" (Campbell, 1988, pp. 70, 71).

Archetypes—"suitcases" of the collective unconscious. Jung referred to the contents of the collective unconscious as *archetypes*. The **archetype** *is a universal predisposition to act or respond in a certain manner.* Since *archetypes* are presumed to arise from the deepest regions of the collective unconscious, Jung also referred to them as *primordial images*. We might think of *archetypes* as the "suitcases" of the collective unconscious. Each piece is designed to carry certain items (e.g., clothing, hats, jewelry and personal items, shaving supplies, sports equipment, musical instruments, etc.). However, since no two persons pack alike, specific contents vary from person to person. According to Jung, our *archetypes*, like our luggage, are *generic* until they become filled with personal items. Thus my "sports bag" might contain ice skates, swimming goggles, or a tennis racket; yours might be carrying scuba fins, a volleyball, and golf clubs.

Even moms—who rank at the top of most psychologists' list of primary influences—are seen by Jung as personalized variants of a larger, more universal *mother archetype:*

> I attribute to the personal mother only a limited significance. . . . all those influences which the literature describes as being exerted on children do not come from the mother herself, but rather from the archetype projected upon her, which gives her a mythological background and invests her with authority. . . . (Jung, 1959, p. 82)

Jung described *archetypes* as "among the inalienable assets of every psyche" (1959, p. 84), and stated that "archetypes are not predetermined as regards their content, but only as regards their form. . . . The archetype in itself is empty . . . a possibility of representation. . . ." (1959, p. 79)

As real as kidneys. The archetype contains patterns and predispositions that humankind has encountered throughout evolutionary history: falling in love with a "perfect" other, dancing, making love, making music, watching the waves of the ocean, observing the sun rise or set, and other such experiences. Since *archetypes* are never fully conscious, they appear in the form of dreams, myths, symbols, art, rituals, and symptoms. Understanding archetypes is essential to comprehending Jung, because the archetype is the heart of his theory. It is clear that he considers archetypes to be more than metaphors, more than fantasies: "There is no 'rational' substitute for archetypes any more than there is for the cerebellum or the kidneys" (Jung, 1959, p. 161).

Next, we'll discuss a few of Jung's archetypes (see Table 13.1), keeping in mind that each particular archetype—like the *Mother archetype*—is a generic, universal *form* that becomes filled with our own unique experiences. Speaking of the *Mother archetype,* Jung said: "The structure is something given, the precondition that is formed in every case. And this is the *mother,* the matrix—the form into which all experience is poured (Jung, 1959, pp. 101–102).

TABLE 13.2

A Partial Listing of Jungian Archetypes

Anima includes Goddess, Witch, Soul—feminine side of the male psyche
Animal such as Horse, Snake, etc.
Animus masculine side of the female psyche
God
Hermaphrodite
Hero the conqueror of enemies and evil forces, including Redeemer, Figure, Mana Personality
Maiden
Great Mother the ultimate good and bad mother, including Earth Mother, Primordial Mother
Original Man
Self including Christ, Circle, Quaternity, Unity—the ultimate unity of personality
Shadow
Soul
Trickster/Clown animalistic prankster
Wise Old Man spiritual father, including Lucifer

Jung believed there are innumerable archetypes and that listing them is not of much value: "It is no use at all to learn a list of archetypes by heart. Archetypes are complexes of experience that come upon us like fate, and their effects are felt in our most personal life" (Jung, 1959a, p. 30).

Personifying versus transforming archetypes. Jung described two major kinds of archetypes. **Personifying archetypes** *have humanlike identities (e.g., Earth Mother, Wise Old Man, and Clown).* **Transforming archetypes** *do not necessarily display human personalities, but may include geometric figures, situations, places, and things that allow elements of the collective unconscious to express themselves in ways that transform or reconfigure the personality.* Examples of transforming archetypes include circles, quaternity (a set of four), the Shadow, and—most important of all—the *Self.*

Archetypes resolve opposites. Archetypes are bipolar—embodying (and thereby synthesizing) opposites. Frequently they appear as mixed combinations. For example, Jung describes the *Mother archetype* as:

> . . . associated with things and places standing for fertility and fruitfulness: the cornucopia, a ploughed field, a garden. . . . Hollow objects such as ovens and cooking vessels are associated with the mother archetype. . . . Added to this list there are many animals, such as the cow, hare, and helpful animals in general . . . All these symbols can have a positive favourable meaning. . . . On the negative side the mother archetype may connote anything secret, hidden, dark; the abyss, the world of the dead, anything that devours, seduces and poisons, that is terrifying and inescapable like fate. (1959, p. 81)

Archetypes link us with our ancestral past. Jung turns personality theory upside down with his emphasis on the collective unconscious and its archetypes. In Jung's world we do not ascend Maslow's hierarchy to actualize ourselves in the mountaintop atmosphere of "peak" experiences. Instead, Jung has us descend deeply into the cellars of our psyches to encounter archetypal gods and demons. For Jung, archetypes (and self-knowledge) ooze upward from the primordial soup of our evolutionary origins more than from our families of origin. Our *actual* mothers are mere reflections of the *transcendent archetypal mother.* Consciousness appears as surface ripples on the vast ocean of the collective unconscious.

Four typical archetypes. In concluding our "parts" section, we will briefly examine four of Jung's most commonly discussed archetypes. This is somewhat like discussing only four letters of the alphabet, but space does not allow us to examine the rich complexity of Jung's entire array of archetypes, so we will discuss four of the most important.

(1) Persona. In Latin, *persona* referred to the masks worn by actors in ancient Roman and Greek dramas, and Jung used **persona** to mean *the social role one plays in society—the "public" personality.* Like other archetypes, the *persona* synthesizes polarities, in this case the polarity between the *real self* and *social expectations.* The *persona* strikes a compromise between a person's true identity and social identity:

> Every calling or profession, for example, has its own persona. . . . A certain kind of behavior is forced on them by the world, and professional people endeavor to come up to these expectations. Only, the danger is that they become identical with their personas—the professor with his text-book, the tenor with his voice. Then the damage is done; henceforth he lives exclusively against the background of his own biography. (Jung 1959, p. 123)

The *persona,* as described above, seems like a conscious attempt at presenting oneself in the most favorable light—don't we all do that? However, Jung's *persona* includes a more *transpersonal, universal* quality that wells up from the collective unconscious to facilitate one's survival as a member of the "herd." Primates and other higher mammals typically operate within structured social systems, and a failure to understand or comply with such social expectations would lessen one's chances for survival.

(2) Shadow. Far broader than Freud's personal unconscious, Jung's **Shadow** *includes all repressed and unacceptable motives, desires, and tendencies existing in both the personal and transpersonal realms of the psyche.* Feelings and ideas that are rejected by the ego as intolerable and inadmissible, coalesce to form an alternate "splinter personality" that balances and compensates the conscious personality. Jung described the *Shadow* as "the negative side of the personality, the sum of all those unpleasant qualities we like to hide, together with the insufficiently developed functions and the contents of the personal unconscious" (1953, p. 65).

The *Shadow* contains the negative underside of personality reflected in symbols that include the devil, demons, evil spirits, and the like. However, Jung deliberately chose the term *shadow* to emphasize that it contains *necessary* and *unavoidable* aspects of our psyche. Just as there can be no sun without creating shadows, the balanced psyche must include both light and darkness. Just as psychoanalysts believe we can only ignore our unconscious at the peril of being blindly driven by it, Jungians believe that an attempt to deny the shadow leads to a life of hypocrisy and superficiality:

> The shadow is a living part of the personality and therefore wants to live with it in some form. . . . The darkness which clings to every personality is the door into the unconscious and the gateway of dreams, from which those two twilight figures, the shadow and the anima, step into our nightly visions or, remaining invisible, take possession of our ego-consciousness. (Jung 1959, pp. 20, 123)

(3) Anima and animus—Jung's androgynous view of gender. The word **androgyny,** *meaning coexistence of stereotypical female and male characteristics in the same person,* comes from two Greek roots: *andro,* meaning male, and *gyn,* meaning female. In traditional thinking, sex roles have been somewhat stereotypically defined and rigidly enforced—moms stayed at home and raised kids, dads went to work at the factory or the office. Freud's male-centered psychoanalysis reinforced such clearly defined roles. Modern and postmodern thinkers (including, but not restricted to, feminists) have rejected such rigidities, asserting that "real men" *can* eat quiche, change diapers, shed tears, and even become stay-at-home dads without losing their testicles in the process.

On the issue of androgyny, Jung was well ahead of Freud and other contemporaries, insisting that none of us is purely male or female. As Jung put it: "No man is so entirely masculine that he has nothing feminine in him" (1966, p. 189). Jung realized that the more traditional "feminine" traits such as intuition, tenderness, gregariousness, and sentimentality brought a balance to the whole personality that was lacking in the "macho" male.

Anima—the lady living inside. Not surprisingly, Jung dealt with gender roles by means of archetypes from the collective unconscious. The **anima** *is the archetypal feminine side of the male psyche.* In Jung's theory men's collective experiences with women have included interactions with females as mothers, daughters, sisters, friends—perhaps even heavenly goddesses. All of these ancestral experiences are carried in the *anima archetype,* allowing a man who is in touch with his *anima* to be a tender, loving, effective parent, spouse, or friend with women. The androgynous male is less likely to be homophobic, less likely to insist on rigid cultural definitions of what it means to "be a man."

Still, although Jung has been considered much friendlier to women than Freud, his writings have been criticized for including stereotypes of women as well as potentially racist ideas about other groups such as blacks and primitive people. He strongly insisted that the psyches of men and women differ significantly from one another and that the man or woman who oversteps the boundaries of assigned gender roles risks losing his or her identity.

Animus—masculine strength for the twenty-first century woman. Just as the anima archetype infuses the male with an unconscious dose of femininity, the **animus** *is the masculine side of the female psyche,* furnishing the balanced woman a healthy measure of competitiveness, independence, aggression, adventurousness, and other such "traditionally masculine" traits. As with the anima, the animus also brings into the female personality the collective wisdom of eons of interactions with fathers, sons, brothers, loved ones, and male hunters and warriors—perhaps even gods. The *animus* provides females with added toughness, as well as insight regarding how males view the world. This facilitates more optimal relationships with the opposite gender.

A gender balancing act. As we noted earlier, Jung was concerned that masculinity and femininity not become homogenized. He believed that *anima* and *animus* functioned best as counterbalances in each gender—not as homogenizers—and he urged people not to go overboard in developing their complementary traits: "A woman possessed by the animus is always in danger of losing her femininity, her adapted feminine persona, just as a man in like circumstances runs the risk of effeminacy" (1966, p. 209). He wasn't very precise on how one might maintain an appropriate gender-role balance, or how one might assess having gone "too far." Nevertheless, as elsewhere in his theory, Jung was advocating for *balance*—a broad balance that synthesized opposites (in this case male and female) into complementary wholes.

P.S.: If you have trouble remembering anima versus animus—which one is feminine and which is masculine—just think of your "Ma" in ani*ma* and your Dad's *muscles* in ani*mus*.

(4) Self—the great synthesizing archetype. Jung regarded the *psyche* (personality) as a vast ocean of opposites (e.g., ego versus shadow, personal unconscious versus collective unconscious). *Opposition* is the cornerstone of Jung's entire theory: "there can be no reality without polarity" (1959, p. 267). He conceptualized the *self* as the great synthesizer of opposites. The **self** *synthesizes and integrates the entire psyche. It is the broadest archetype—containing the totality of opposites—striving to harmonize both the corruption and the perfection that are humankind's ancestral heritage.* Whereas most archetypes are considered "built-in" equipment, the *self* is a *potential* archetype that exists both as a component and as a *goal*: ". . . the self is our life's goal, for it is the completest expression of that fateful combination we call individuality" (Jung, 1953a, p. 238).

The self is so broad that even if it becomes fully developed, the person can never be entirely in touch with it: "There is little hope of our ever being able to reach even approximate consciousness of the self, since however much we may make conscious there will always exist an indeterminate and indeterminable amount of unconscious material which belongs to the totality of the self" (Jung, 1953a, p. 175).

When the *self* does develop, it usually occurs as a middle- or late-life achievement that capitalizes on all the wisdom the person has accumulated. Jung described the all-encompassing nature of the *self* in the following way: "The self is not only the centre but also the whole circumference which embraces both conscious and unconscious; it is the centre of this totality, just as the ego is the centre of the unconscious mind" (1953b, p. 41).

Jung viewed the formation of a *self* as the ultimate accomplishment of personality development—an achievement that not everyone attained. The *self archetype,* unlike other archetypes that emerge from the murky depths of the collective unconscious, exists primarily as a *potential for unity.* When this unity is realized, the contents of the shadow, persona, and ego are acknowledged and synthesized by the *self.*

In the psychologically mature person (corresponding to Maslow and Rogers's *self-actualized* individual) the *self* synthesizes and balances the many opposites of the

Figure 13.1 ■ *Self*

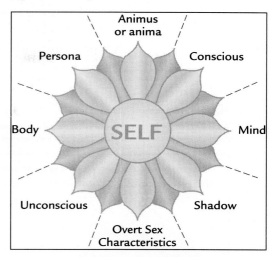

The Archetype that Synthesizes Opposites into Unity.

psyche. Such a person accepts that he or she is both loving and hateful, generous and selfish, lively and lazy, virtuous and evil. In such persons the *self* is broad enough to incorporate all the opposites of the psyche as well as the intrinsic polarities of the archetypes. This is why Jung used terms like *wholeness, center of personality,* and *totality* to describe the *self.*

Figure 13.2 ■ *Jungian Archetypes*

According to Jung, archetypes are comprised of *opposites* that are in dynamic balance. Archetypes consist of two kinds—*transforming* and *personifying*—but whatever kind they are, all archetypes function to balance personality by including and integrating opposites.

Transforming Archetypes include geometric figures and other depictions that assist elements of the collective unconscious in synthesizing opposites in the personality. The following are an illustrative sampling:

Mandalas *Yin & Yang* *Crosses*

Snowflakes *Other Geometric Figures*

Personifying Archetypes also assist the collective unconscious in balancing the conscious personality; however, these portrayals include humanlike identities.

Mask *Shadow* *Hero* *Villain*

Mandala—symbol of balance. The **mandala** *is a concentrically balanced geometric figure, such as a circle enclosing a square, that in Hindu or Buddhist traditions symbolizes the universe.* This is what we earlier referred to as a *transforming archetype* instead of a *personifying archetype.* Obviously a square inside a circle doesn't resemble a human personality—even though you might think your parents are "squares"! Jung believed the *mandala* symbolizes the mature self's synthesis of the entire psyche.

> Mandala means a circle, more especially a magic circle, and this form of symbol is not only to be found all through the East, but also among us. . . . For the most part, the mandala form is that of a flower, cross, or wheel, with a distinct tendency toward four as the basis of the structure. (Jung, 1945, p. 96)

Mandala—symbol of the transpersonal self. For Jung the *mandala* takes on a life of its own with power to superimpose order on psychic chaos:

> Mandalas . . . usually appear in situations of psychic confusion and disorientation. The archetype . . . represents a pattern of order which, like a psychological "view-finder" marked with a cross or circle divided into four, is superimposed on the psychic chaos so that each content falls into place and the weltering confusion is held together by a protective circle. . . . (1964, vol. 10, p. 397)

Precisely how this occurs is left unexplained.

Soul. Above and beyond the *self,* Jung postulates a **soul,** *which is that aspect of the psyche that enables one to establish a transcendent connection with God.* It is through the *soul* that Jung believes humans relate to God: ". . . the soul must contain in itself the faculty of relation to God . . . otherwise a connection could never come about" (1953, vol. 12, p. 12). Writing of the *soul,* Jung said, "If the human [soul] is anything, it must be of unimaginable complexity and diversity, so that it cannot possibly be approached through a mere psychology of instinct" (1961, vol 4, p. 331).

Jung compares the *soul* to the galaxies of the night sky: "Beside this picture [of the soul] I would like to place the spectacle of the starry heavens at night, for the only equivalent of the universe within is the universe without . . ." (1961, vol. 4, p. 331).

What Makes a Person Go?

Historical determinism versus goal-oriented teleology. In the *Physiological* and *Behavioral Zones,* Jung employs *compositional* and *situational causes* to explain how prior experiences shape the adult personality. In this he agrees with Freud as well as with the behaviorists in asserting that past events shape present behaviors. However, like Adler, Jung regards most behavior as **teleological:** *goal-directed, future-oriented, "for-the-sake-of-which" functioning that arises from within the person and fulfills a specific purpose.*

Transpersonal causality. In the *Transpersonal Zone,* Jung introduces one of his most controversial concepts, **synchronicity**—*"meaningful coincidences"—events that* appear *related in ways that cannot be explained in ordinary terms; sometimes referred to as "lucky," "miraculous," "providential," or otherwise beyond our usual understandings.* As we are about to discover, *teleology* and *synchronicity* are Jung's favorite causal explanations. Jung uses *teleology*—the psyche's forward-leaning tilt into the future—to synthesize the countless opposites within the personality, and he uses *synchronicity* to explain "coincidental" happenings in the transcendent realm.

Opposition—the heart of Jung's motivational system. Freud was attracted by opposites, Kelly built opposites into his bipolar personal constructs, and May sought to synthesize the great dialectical opposites of existence. Jung, however, even more than other personality psychologists, made opposition the cornerstone of his theory. Every component of the Jungian psyche has its *opposite*: conscious versus unconscious, feminine versus masculine, introversion versus extraversion, progression versus regression—the list goes on. *Opposition* is built into the architecture of the psyche at all levels. In our current discussion we will see how Jung uses polarities to prime the motivational pump that energizes the entire personality. His core motivational construct is the **principle of opposites:** *for any tendency in one direction there is an opposite tendency* (1954, p. 77).

Misleading metaphors. All of this talk about forces, energy, and opposites can be quite confusing, because by using physics terminology Jung appears to be describing mental life in terms of billiard-ball, physics-based notions of causality. Nothing could be further from the truth. These various "laws" borrowed from physics are merely *metaphors* for Jung's psychological system of opposites.

This is why we have located Jung in the *Transpersonal Zone* of our grid. Although he uses "physics-sounding" vocabulary, his entire theory is permeated with transpersonal, transcendent, symbolic concepts that can only be rightly understood at the broadest levels of analysis. Thus, if we take Jung's principles of *opposition* or *entropy* literally, he sounds more like a physicist than a psychiatrist. However, his use of *opposition* has more in common with Hegel's philosophical notion that "everything carries within itself its own negation" than with any laws of physics. We can only understand Jung when we realize that most of his theoretical constructs are philosophical rather than physical in nature.

Biological instincts versus "spiritual" instincts. Consequently, we aren't surprised to find Jung using terms like *psychic energy* or *instinct* in a metaphoric rather than mechanical sense. Unlike Newton or Freud, who used terms like *energy* or *instinct* in mechanical or biological ways, Jung—like Adler—stated that "Life is teleology *par excellence;* it is the intrinsic striving towards a goal, and the living organism is a system of directed aims which seek to fulfill themselves" (1960, pp. 406–406).

Bridging the opposites of psyche and soma. Recall that Freud used *instinct* to bridge the gap between the mind and the body. Jung, however, used the term *instinct* much more holistically than did Freud. Blending structure and function, Jung insisted that although the psyche's existence depends on the physiological functioning of the brain, one cannot explain the psyche in biological terms, any more than one can explain dancing in terms of the anatomy and physiology of the legs.

Past versus present—Jurassic Park. The greatest opposites in Jung's system are *past versus present.* According to Jung, while our physical bodies were evolving throughout evolutionary time, a parallel evolution was taking place in our minds. Accordingly, Jung viewed the mind as a menagerie of archetypes that emerged from the primordial past to stream into the contemporary conscious experiences of the psyche. We might think of Jung's *psyche* as a "psychological Jurassic Park," where highly evolved animals utilizing complex apparatuses (e.g., human scientists in SUVs) co-mingle with archetypal dinosaurs. From what Jung disclosed in his autobiography, this chaotic fusion of past archetypal images—with present sensations and experiences—probably reflected not only his creative genius, but also his personal emotional struggles.

"Magnetic" constellating forces in the psyche—from data to "spirits." Early in his career, Jung became famous for his experiments utilizing the **word-association test:** *a list of one* hundred *stimulus words (e.g., water, to cook, flower, child, to dance, frog, woman, money, to kiss, etc.) to which subjects are asked to respond as quickly as possible with the first word that comes to mind.* Using a stopwatch, Jung discovered that reaction times varied greatly, and he came to believe that hesitations or prolonged reaction times were indications of underlying emotional difficulties. He asserted that these *collections* of thoughts or ideas were held together by shared emotions and he called these collections *complexes.*

Based on this research, Jung formulated what he termed a **complex:** *a cluster of emotionally loaded thoughts or ideas.* For Jung it was then a small step to move from his experimentally based finding that words and meanings cluster around emotions, to endow such *complexes* with a life of their own. He described them as

> psychic fragments . . . [that] appear and disappear according to their own laws. . . .
> In a word, complexes behave like independent beings. . . . In the voices heard by the insane they even take on a personal ego-character like that of the spirits who manifest themselves through automatic writing and similar techniques" (1960, p. 121).

This is typical Jungian theorizing. Beginning with scientific methodology and data-based observations, he formulates new constructs that have motivational lives of their own, operating autonomously within the "big tent" of the psyche in ways that are difficult to describe and impossible to prove.

Summary of Jung's motivational theory. In the end, Jung formulated a theory of motivation in which the vitality and spirits from our primordial past flow into the present and shape the future. One might compare Freud's psychoanalysis to an aquarium, and Jung's transpersonal theory to a pond in the woods, respectively. Whereas Freud's "aquarium" of psychoanalysis is relatively clean and well kept (a few carefully chosen fish and some selected coral), Jung's "pond in the woods" *psyche* is much more messy—exploding with life—as portrayed in those pictures in high school biology texts where one sees a cross section of a pond brimming with fish, ferns, crabs, slugs, seaweed, snakes, worms, dragonflies, water bugs, frogs, tadpoles, and minnows—to name only a few.

Jung founded his entire theory on a "pond-in-the-woods" *collective unconscious* that contains countless archetypes in various stages of tadpole-to-toad evolutionary development. Through dreams, visions, and fantasies, such archetypes come to life in various regions of the psyche. Since each archetype has a life of its own, the influence of archetypes on personal experience is often more chaotic than orderly. Yet Jung conceives that over a lifetime of struggle and evolving (*individuating*), some persons develop a *self* that brings balance and order to the psyche in the midst of this chaotic carnival of ancestral archetypes.

What Makes a Person Grow?

Individuation—the fulfillment of self. We have discovered that the *collective unconscious* is Jung's structural foundation for personality, and *balancing of opposites* is the motivational center. Next, we are about to learn how *individuation* provides developmental direction. **Individuation** *is a lifelong tendency toward self-realization during which an increasingly larger number of components of the psyche are recognized and allowed expression. Individuation* is a process wherein the *self* balances opposites within the conscious sphere as well as reconciling opposites between the conscious and unconscious.

Transcendence. Although *individuation* and *transcendence* might appear as two sides of the same coin, there is a difference in focus. Whereas *individuation* develops and balances the polarities within the individual *self*, **transcendence** *synthesizes the many contradictory and conflicting systems of the self into an integrated whole that resonates with all of humankind. Individuation* is personal process; *transcendence* is transpersonal, reaching *beyond* to facilitate harmonious interactions with all of humankind—ancestral, contemporary, and future.

Developmental Stages. Jung described development in broad, loosely defined stages. He was critical of Freud's attempts to explain current behavior by tracing it to various fixation points during earlier years. In contrast to Freud, who emphasized the first five or six years of life as the most crucial, Jung (like Erikson) asserted that important developmental changes occur well beyond childhood and adolescence. Half a century ahead of the current trend in lifespan courses, Jung insisted that growth continues into middle and late life.

Childhood (birth to adolescence). During this era, the child expends energy on learning to talk, walk, and develop other skills necessary for survival. Following the fifth year, more energy is directed toward sexual activities which reach a peak during adolescence. However, Jung could never agree with Freud regarding the incestuous desires of children. Although he acknowledged that some parents involve their children in incestuous activities, Jung always viewed such relationships as abnormal, not a universal foundation for psychological growth, as Freud postulated the oedipal triangle to be.

Adolescence. With the onset of puberty between ages ten and thirteen, the person enters an extremely important stage of life. According to Jung, it is during adolescence that "true psychic birth" takes place (1960, vol. 8, p. 391). Again we see Jung emphasizing the importance of later stages; he felt that females leave adolescence around age nineteen, and males continue on to twenty-five before becoming adults (1954, vol. 17, p. 52). During this era the urge for sexual gratification is intense, but there is also the challenge (as emphasized by Erikson as well) of deciding on a satisfying work career. From Jung's perspective, one of the major problems of this stage is the threat of identifying with one's *persona* or public personality instead of being fully engaged with one's entire psyche. For the first time, the person is seriously threatened by one-sided development (1960, vol. 8, p. 391).

Youth (20–35). For most people the years from about twenty to thirty-five are a time of completing the separation from family dependency. Marriage, rearing children, purchasing a home, and striving for success in one's career are some of the challenges that young adults must meet.

Middle life and old age (forty to the later years of life). Since it is during middle age that a person begins to individuate and determine the meaning of life, this stage is seen by Jung as the most important. The psychic challenge facing the person during the second half of life is that of developing *balance*. Based on the fact of having lived this long, the person begins to realize that the meaning of life is not found *only in the conscious*. Jung believed that the first half of life is spent in enlarging consciousness by learning, acquiring possessions, and investigating the external world (neglecting the *unconscious* in the process). During the second half of life, the activities and growth of the first half begin to bear fruit; children mature and leave home, careers experience fulfillment, and more time becomes available for psychological growth and spiritual development. Jung believed that the older person must "look inward," rather than look backward:

> Our life is like the course of the sun. In the morning it gains continually in strength until it reaches the zenith-heat of high noon. . . . But it is a great mistake to suppose that the meaning of life is exhausted with the period of youth and expansion. . . . The afternoon of life is just as full of meaning as the morning. . . . (1953a, pp. 74–75)

Balancing act. Such looking inward after forty is but one of the many ways in which Jung believed successful people bring their lives into balance. As he put it, "man's values, and even his body, do tend to change into their opposites" (1960, vol. 8, p. 398). Physiologically, males become more feminine and females become more masculine.

The search for existential meaning. Jung observed that "About a third of my cases are not suffering from any clinically definable neurosis, but from the senselessness and aimlessness of their lives; I should not object if this were called the general neurosis of our age. Fully two-thirds of my patients are in the second half of life" (1954, vol. 16, p. 41). This is in contrast to Freud's patients, who were considerably younger, so far as we can tell.

During the second half of life, the great existential "balancing act"—life versus death—must be confronted, and Jung felt spirituality was an important aspect of this process. Rather than viewing religious expressions from a Freudian perspective as sublimated expressions of childhood dependencies, Jung considered them extremely important manifestations of the transpersonal unconscious in creating unbroken teleology from the primordial past into an eternal afterlife.

Spirituality during the second half of life. Jung might say to a depressed older patient: "Your picture of God or your idea of immortality is wasted away, consequently your psychic metabolism is out of gear" (1960, vol. 8, p. 403). Since it is during this era that people grapple with the meaning of life, spirituality becomes an important aspect of individuation and transcendence: "Of all my patients past middle life, that is, past thirty-five, there is not one whose ultimate problem is not one of religious attitude. . . . and none is really cured who has not regained his religious attitude, which naturally has nothing to do with creeds or belonging to a church" (quoted in Wehr, 1987, p. 292).

Summary of Jung's developmental theories. As we have learned so far, in the world of Jungian personality theory there is much ebb and flow among the various components of the psyche. Parts, motives, and development mingle and merge in loosely connected, vaguely explained ways. As we conclude with the final question of our "Big Four," we will find Jung's consideration of *attitudes* and *functions* refreshingly scientific. In place of ancestral archetypes that emerge out of the darkness of the collective unconscious to shape current behaviors in vague and unexplained ways, we will learn how Jung blends two basic attitudes and four functions into eight personality styles.

What Makes a Person Unique?

Uniqueness abounds in Jung's theory because even though he links us to a common ancestral past by means of the collective (transpersonal) unconscious, there remains much room for variation. For example, the *archetypes* that emerge from the primordial past that we share with all animals become infused with meanings that are uniquely our own. In what follows, we will learn that, although everyone has varying proportions of two basic attitudes and four main psychological functions, there is much room for variation and uniqueness within each of these eight personality styles.

Two basic attitudes—introversion and extraversion. Remember when your mother told you "Change your attitude!—or there will be no trip to the zoo"? Most of us grew up thinking of *attitudes* as something we could put on or take off—like the shirts or blouses hanging in our closets. For Jung, however, **attitude** *is a general orientation of the psyche in relationship to the world.* In other words, it's the direction—inward or outward—that your personality is tilted. And, consistent with his love for opposites, Jung sees two major possibilities: *introversion* and *extraversion.* However, we should be aware that Jung regards these as the extreme poles, and that most people range somewhere in between.

Introversion and extraversion. The terms *introversion* and *extraversion* have become so commonplace in our world that even your taxicab driver knows that **introverts** *prefer to be in tune with their own inner world of ideas, thoughts, and fantasies,* whereas **extraverts** are *oriented to the outside world, and seem to be bubbling with enthusiasm for people, parties, and fun.* This is one of the most popular personality dimensions along which we classify ourselves and others: *"She's really outgoing!" "He's kind of quiet."*

According to Jung, *attitude* refers to a person's habitual state of *consciousness,* which is always counterbalanced by the opposite attitude in the *unconscious.* Thus the consciously *introverted* person has an unconscious *extravert* buried underneath. We see this in the case of the shy, timid CPA who sings wildly on karaoke night, or who performs in a local drama group.

Four ectopsychic functions—sensation, thinking, feeling, and intuiting. We have already discussed most of Jung's *endopsychic* processes or functions (e.g., the *ego,* the *complexes* of the personal unconscious, *archetypes* of the collective unconscious, the *self,* and the *soul*). Jung theorized that the mind is also equipped with four **ectopsychic functions** *for dealing with the outside world.*

Sensation. The first ectopsychic function is **sensation,** *the sum total of external facts provided by the senses.* Sensations provide the raw materials for relating to the world, but not the details: "Sensation tells me that something *is;* it does not tell me *what* it is" (Jung, 1968, p. 11).

Thinking. The second ectopsychic function, **thinking,** *refines and makes sense of these raw sensations.* If one wants to know what thinking is, one should never ask a philosopher, advised Jung, "because he is the only man who does not know what thinking is. Everybody else knows what thinking is. . . . Thinking in its simplest form tells you *what* a thing is. It gives a name to the thing. It adds a concept because thinking is perception and judgement" (1968, p. 11).

Feeling. According to Jung, **feeling** *gives value to things.* As he put it, "Feeling informs you through its feeling-tones of the values of things. Feeling tells you for instance whether a thing is acceptable or agreeable or not. It tells you what a thing is *worth* to you" (1968, p. 12). Jung went on to explain that *thinking* and *feeling* are difficult to do at the same time: "they hinder each other. Therefore when you want to think in a dispassionate way, really scientifically or philosophically, you must get away from all feeling-values" (1968, p. 12).

This notion that sound decisions come from a "cool head" is not original with Jung, but hearkens back to Descartes's dualistic splitting of the person into a thinking mind and a feeling body. Modern researchers disagree. Antonia Damasio, for example, insists that

> The human brain and the rest of the body constitute an indissociable organism.
> . . . The organism interacts with the environment as an ensemble: the interaction
> is neither of the body alone nor of the brain alone. . . . mental activity, from
> its simplest aspects to its most sublime, requires both brain and body proper.
> (1994, pp. xvi–xvii)

When *feelings* are absent or muted because of neurological damage or disease, Damasio observes that *thinking* is seriously impaired. Since the organism is an *ensemble* of integrated biochemical and neural circuits between every part of the body and the brain, an impairment of *feelings* seriously distorts *thinking.* At the very least, when we view Jung's four functions in the light of modern neuroscience, any sharp boundaries among them begin to blur, and they appear more as an *ensemble* of interconnected functions at many levels of analysis.

Intuition. Jung's fourth ectopsychic function is **intuition,** *an amorphous, indistinct, somewhat mystical process (we sometimes describe as "having a hunch") by which we negotiate the unknown.* Not surprisingly, Jung appears to like this function best, as it goes beyond the ordinary: "Sensation tells us that a thing *is.* Thinking tells us *what* that thing is, feeling tells us what it is *worth* to us. Now what else could there be . . ." (Jung, 1968, p. 12). Jung answers his rhetorical question by defining *intuition* as

> . . . a sort of miraculous faculty. . . . I am "very mystical," as people say. This is
> one of my pieces of mysticism! Intuition is a function by which you see around
> corners, which you really cannot do; but if you are on the Stock Exchange or in
> Central Africa, you will use your hunches like anything. (1968, pp. 13–14)

Jung describes *intuition* as a function that helps one to negotiate unknown *times* and unknown *situations.* In terms of *time,* intuition allows one to intuitively peer into the future: "You cannot, for instance, calculate whether when you turn round a corner in the bush you will meet a rhinoceros or a tiger—but you get a hunch, and it will perhaps save your life" (1968, p. 14). Clearly, Jung sees *intuition* as a valuable tool for people living creative, risk-taking lives: "Inventors will use it and judges will use it. Whenever you have to deal with strange conditions where you have no established values or established concepts, you will depend upon the faculty of intuition" (1968, p. 14). Jung summarizes by stating that "intuition is a sort of perception which does not go exactly by the senses, but it goes via the unconscious, and at that I leave it and say 'I don't know how it works . . .'" (1968, pp. 14–15). Jung adds that "we must be very grateful that we have such a function which gives us a certain light on those things which are round the corners" (1968, pp. 14–15).

It might appear that Jung employs the construct of *intuition* in a subjective, mystical sense; but keep in mind that *intuition* is utilized in the service of dealing with what is around the next corner—*actually out there*. Whether one is negotiating unknowns in the jungles of Africa or in corporate America, *intuition* utilizes the wisdom of the unconscious to help the person anticipate and master new challenges.

Figure 13.3 ■ *Functions of the Psyche*

Eight Personality Types (styles)

Jung employs the two attitudes and four functions to outline eight psychological styles. He cautions us that there is wide variation within each type, and that as the elements of the personal and transpersonal unconscious shift and change, the entire psyche changes. Finally, we do well to keep in mind that no single type is considered superior to others—each has its own particular strengths and weaknesses.

We have briefly summarized each style in Table 13.3, where you will notice the extraverted styles are on the left and the introverted on the right. Also, note that they

TABLE 13.3

Eight Jungian Psychological Styles

EXTRAVERTED STYLE	INTROVERTED STYLE
Thinking Extraverts: These individuals value *facts* above all. Since they subjugate emotions, feelings, and intuitions to logic, they frequently appear *rigid, cold,* or *inflexible*. Their moral code is similarly intolerant of exceptions, and they appear dogmatic. This style is also known as "obsessive-compulsive."	**Thinking Introverts:** These people are practical and fact-oriented, but so turned inward that they fit the stereotype of the typical "egghead" or "computer nerd." They tend to ignore the practical issues of everyday life in the style of the "absent-minded professor." With mostly intellectual and abstract interests and a strong need for privacy, they sometimes have difficulties in social relationships.
Feeling Extraverts: These persons desire to be in harmony with the external world, but trust their *feelings* more than *facts*. Often described as *intense, effervescent,* and *gregarious*, they are frequently given to loud, gushing talk and intense emotional displays. They seek social situations, maximize emotions, and repress thinking.	**Feeling Introverts:** These persons are highly conscious of their inner feelings, but because they are turned inward, they frequently appear indifferent or cold toward others—sometimes seeming to assume an air of superiority. Their apparent lack of empathy for others, combined with their excessive focus on self, is sometimes described as *narcissistic*.
Intuitive Extraverts: They tend to be creative and find new ideas appealing, but they sometimes find it difficult to stick with something until completion. Decisions are based on "hunches" or "whims" rather than on facts. They are described as *visionary, creative,* and *changeable*. They are in touch with their unconscious wisdom and tend to repress sensing in favor of intuitions.	**Intuitive Introverts:** With intuition as king and a focus on inner experience, these individuals tend to be seen as *mystics, dreamers,* or just *"different."* They fit the stereotype of the "peculiar artist" or "mad scientist" who sometimes turns out strange but beautiful creations. They sometimes become so shaped by their inner lives that they appear as "oddballs." Following his break with Freud, Jung apparently functioned in this mode.

(continued)

TABLE 13.3 *(continued)*

Eight Jungian Psychological Styles

EXTRAVERTED STYLE	INTROVERTED STYLE
Sensing Extraverts: Always searching for new sensory experiences, such people may become connoisseurs of fine food and wines, or discriminating art critics. Since they tend to be gregarious and nonintrospective, they are usually good company, paying attention to others and to external details. They tend to repress intuition.	**Sensing Introverts:** Such persons focus on objective sensory events and are described as *calm, passive,* and *artistic.* They tend to experience sensory events in very clear-cut categories as either good or evil—as judged by themselves. They remain calmly unperturbed if others disagree with them.

are arranged hierarchally with the most irrational function (sensing) at the bottom and the most rational (thinking) on the top. That should help you to understand and remember them because that's how functions "stack up" for most of us. We experience *sensations* as "gut-level" emotions in our groins and viscera, we perceive *intuition* as a more generalized "feeling in our bones," we *feel* (place value upon) things with our heart, and we are "thinking over" things with our heads. As you study the table, think about which combinations most closely describe your own style.

More recently (Myers, 1962), Katherine Briggs, and her daughter Isabel Briggs Myers, have developed the **Myers–Briggs Type Indicator (MBTI):** a *personality test that classifies people along four personality dimensions: Extraversion-Introversion (E-I), Sensing-Intuition (SN), Thinking-Feeling (TF), and Judgement-Perception (JP).* This appears generally consistent with Jung's ectopsychic functions. With these four dichotomies, sixteen different four-letter combinations are possible. Using this sort of classification, an ESFJ would be an extraverted person who senses, feels, and judges. That kind of person would be quite different from an ISTP, a person with an introverted personality style who senses, thinks, and perceives.

The MBTI has proved enormously popular—approximately two million people take this personality test each year (Burger, 2000, p. 137). Respondents answer 166 questions designed to tap into the various dimensions such as introversion, extraversion, sensing, intuiting, etc.:

Given a free evening, I would prefer to
a. stay home by myself.
b. go out with other people.

In making a decision, it is more important to me to
a. come up with a correct answer.
b. consider the impact of the solution. (Myers, 1962)

Based on such self-reports persons can be classified as a blend or mixture of these 16 different typological categories. Typologies have had a long history in clinical work, but the MBTI adds a significant bank of research data to undergird the more speculative aspects of theory. For example, Macdaid, McCaulley, and Kainz (1986) published an *Atlas of Type Tables* in which they reported data from over 200,000 subjects ranging from high school dropouts to law school graduates.

We will present only a small sampling of their data to give you a feel for how Jung's ideas might be applied today. It's no surprise that the data indicates that writers, artists, and entertainers tend to be *intuitive* extraverts or *intuitive* introverts. Certified public accountants, low-level managers, and retail store managers tend to be *thinking* introverts or extraverts, whereas CEOs and high-level managers show a balance of the *intuitive* and *thinking* styles. You probably would expect psychologists, counselors, and social workers to be high on *intuitive* dimensions, but it might surprise you to find that computer specialists, engineers, chemists, and biologists are well represented in the *intuitive* domain as well as in the *thinking* categories. This appears to support Jung's notion that *balance* is a crucial ingredient for success even in the "hard" sciences.

Although a complete discussion of the MBTI is beyond the scope of our text, an easy-to-read paperback, *Essentials of Myers-Briggs Type Indicator Assessment* (Quenk, 2000), provides a good overview of how the MBTI is used in the real world.

FACING THE TOUGH TWINS

One might guess that Jung's theory would do poorly confronting our "Tough Twins." Nonetheless, out of Jung's troubled, inner-oriented, symbolically dominated mind there emerged a theory that apparently brought balance to his inner turmoil and simultaneously brought theoretical balance to the biological determinism of Freud and the behavioral determinism of Watson and Skinner. Out of the dark, primordial worlds of archetypes and symbols, Jung formulated a theory of surprising balance.

Is It Testable? At the broadest levels—in the *Transpersonal Zone*—Jung's theory is difficult to test. Many of his "big potatoes" constructs function as heuristic *metaphors,* or creative expressions of existential truths; however, there is simply no way to visit our ancestral past, and it is impossible to measure the collective unconscious. Science offers no tools that allow us to empirically evaluate *archetypes, synchronicity,* and a host of other Jungian constructs. In this sense, Jungian theory appears even more difficult to falsify than Freud's. Psychoanalysis postulates a *personal* unconscious that is not an ancestrally based collective unconscious permeated with archetypes and mythical symbols. Jung's ideas have, however, heuristically stimulated a number of writers, comparative mythologists, and other scholars to seriously consider how our shared heritage *(culture)* influences our lives. What Jung called the *collective unconscious* appears to share much in common with what anthropologists and other behavioral scientists call *culture.*

The good news is that what Jung probably considered to be the more "shallow" and mundane aspects of his theory have stood the test of time and are widely respected today. Nearly a century ago, Jung reported his research findings (*Studies in Word Association,* 1918). Others have also studied word-associations (e.g., Cramer, 1968; Levy, 1956; Rabin & Haworth, 1960; Woodworth & Schlosberg, 1954); however, Jung's unique contribution was his belief that word-associations provided access to *unconscious processes.* This is what first brought him into favor with Freud. Although interest in this area was somewhat flat for a number of years, a renewed enthusiasm for cognitive psychology has revitalized interest in word associations as clinical assessment tools in the form of the *Word Association Test* (Cramer, 1968), as well as the study of associative learning and memory in the laboratory (Anderson & Bower, 1974). Both the Swiss psychiatrist, Hermann Rorschach, who is famous for his "Inkblot Test," as well as Henry Murray, author of the Thematic Apperception Test (TAT), were strongly influenced by Jung.

However, in the area of personality assessment, Jung's most important legacy may be that his ideas may have inspired the development of the Myers–Briggs Type Indicator (MBTI). As we just learned, this test has been widely used in organizational consulting, career counseling, job selection, and numerous other nonpsychiatric applications. It has generated considerable research (Myers and McCaulley, 1985), and has been used in relating personality types to various challenges in such areas as risk tolerance, problem solving, and conflict management (Gardner & Martinko, 1996). Suggested applications have ranged from such private enterprises as parenting, to such broad areas as church growth or the delivery of health care. For example, Neff (1988) offers parents homey advice on how to use the MBTI to better understand themselves and their children, and Edwards (1993) sees the MBTI as essential to understanding church congregational dynamics.

Allen and Brock (2000) suggest using the MBTI in health care settings to enhance communications between patients and health care professionals. For example, in breaking bad news to patients, the MBTI perspective would suggest that *sensing thinking (ST)* patients like to hear the "straight facts" presented with clarity, honesty, and (to some extent) sympathy; whereas the *sensing feeling (SF)* types would prefer to be told the truth in a kindly way with empathy, caring, and personal attention. Difficulties can arise when, for example, a nurse with a preference for *feeling* experience interacts with a patient who prefers a *thinking* mode. However, with an enhanced understanding of types, and a respect for individual differences, such communication barriers can be more easily negotiated. They cite the example of Sally (a nurse who was a *feeling* type) visiting a patient (who was a *thinking* type) at home to give him a treatment:

> He did not talk about his cancer or his personal reflections on his imminent death. Afterwards they walked down the garden, which was a huge effort for him. Sally said to him, "Fred you have had a wonderful life" and he said, "I know." Sally had been able to honor Fred's needs, even though they were different from her own. (Allen and Brock, 2000, p. 98)

Had Sally been treating a patient who was also a *feeling* type, one might imagine a long discussion during which the patient would have "gotten his feelings out," instead of merely replying "I know." But understanding that various personality types are not good or bad, better or worse, but merely different, Sally was able to respect Fred's mode of dealing with dying without imposing her own wishes.

Is It Useful?

Like Adler, whose ideas (e.g., birth order, inferiority complexes, compensation, etc.) became so much a part of mainstream culture that he is frequently not credited with having formulated them, Jung's influence frequently remains submerged below the level of cultural awareness. However, even with minimal probing, we find Jung's influence in such diverse areas as sexuality, development, cultural awareness, spirituality, and psychotherapy.

Sexuality, development, and cultural awareness. Jung's account of the dual nature of sexuality (first published in the mid-1940s) provided the conceptual basis for *androgyny,* a topic in which interest revived in the early 1970s, when Anne Constantinople questioned the assumption that masculinity was the opposite of femininity (1973) and Sandra Bem developed a gender-identity measure (1974). Interest in *androgyny* remained high (e.g., Kaplan, 1979; Kaplan & Sedney, 1980), spawning multiple studies. Some studies (e.g., Bem, 1975; Bem & Lenney, 1976; Bem, Martyna, & Watson, 1976) found that androgynous people, regardless of gender, responded more flexibly in a variety of situations—behaving more nurturantly when dealing with people in need, but becoming assertive when their rights were in danger of being violated. There is evidence that androgynous females have fewer psychological problems than masculine- or feminine-stereotyped persons (Burchardt and Serbin, 1982), and another study found that androgynous college assistant professors experienced greater personal satisfaction, but also an increased amount of work stress than their more stereotypic counterparts (Rotherman and Weiner, 1983).

However, other studies (e.g., Bassoff and Glass, 1982; Taylor and Hall, 1982) seem to indicate that the presence of *masculine* personality characteristics, rather than the synthesis of both masculinity and femininity, appears to correlate better with various measures of mental health. Confusing the issue even further, Dorgan, Goebel, and House (1983) found that depending on how one measures self-esteem, different results may be obtained in studies of androgyny. Whatever the final conclusions may turn out to be, Jung's theories have catalyzed many interesting questions regarding gender.

Jung's attention to the second half of life has served to pry clinicians loose from Freud's focus on the first five years, providing (along with Erikson and others) a theoretical framework within which we can better understand older persons as they cope with the passages of late life—including death (Moraglia, 1994; Mogenson, 1990). In our postmodern, culturally diverse world, Jung's ideas of how the *self* evolves and achieves balance in different cultural settings can sensitize us to issues that are frequently overlooked (Hauke, 2000; Sliker, 1992; Thrasher, 1991).

Synthesizing spirituality and psychology. Earlier we noted how expansively Jung's ideas about symbols, archetypes, and spirituality could range. However, his feet did occasionally touch the ground, and nowhere is this more evident than in his influence on "Bill W.," one of the founders of Alcoholics Anonymous. Bill credits Jung with helping him to understand the importance of spirituality in recovery from addiction (W., 1988). In a letter to Bill W., Jung expressed concern for "Ronald H." in the following words:

> His craving for alcohol was the equivalent, on a low level, of the spiritual thirst of our being for wholeness, expressed in medieval language: the union with God. . . . You see, "alcohol" in Latin is *spiritus* and you use the same word for the highest religious experience as well as for the most depraving poison. (1984, pp. 197–198)

Jung's synthesis of psychology and spirituality has influenced a number of contemporary writers (e.g.. Kelsey, 1974, 1982; Sanford, 1968, 1981). Caprio and Hedberg's *Coming Home: A Handbook of Exploring the Sanctuary Within* (1986) offers a practical guide for synthesizing Jungian psychological concepts with Christian spirituality. Spiegelman and Miyuki (1985) offer a synthesis of Jungian psychology and Buddhism, and Spiegelman (1982) has discussed the relationships between Jungian theory and Jewish mysticism (1982), as well as how Jung's ideas pertain to Hinduism (Spiegelman & Vasavada, 1987). And, as we pointed out earlier, the Myers–Briggs Type Indicator has been of particular significance to pastors and counselors concerned with church growth.

Jungian psychotherapy. Jung believed people become maladjusted when they have no proper *symbols* through which *archetypes* can express themselves, and thereby fail to achieve a balancing of the personality.

According to Jung, act as bridges between the unconscious and conscious portions of the psyche. Jungian therapists use **symbols of transformation** to *transform libido from an unexpressed potential into an actual expression.* For example, if a patient complains that she "has no reason for living," the Jungian therapist might help her to discover the appropriate archetype (e.g., Hero, Goddess, Earth Mother, etc.) that might serve to transform the stored up libido from repressed archetypes into meaningful, conscious expression. In this way the therapist assists the client in overcoming the *one-sidedness* of a psyche filled with repressed complexes. Jung believed that having a ready repertoire of symbols was as important as having food to eat or liquid to drink.

Balance, growth, and the assimilation of opposites. Since, according to Jung, life turns on *polarities,* many of the major problems of life involve choosing among alternatives. Resolving such conflicts gives life zest and meaning; it is only when polarization becomes rigid that mental illness ensues. Thus, Jungian therapists seek to bring the two halves of their clients' psyches back in balance. This is not always easy, however, because the *conscious* and *unconscious* do not easily communicate with each other. Like Freudian psychoanalysts who seek to "make the unconscious conscious," Jungian therapists facilitate *confrontation with the unconscious,* thereby permitting the person to communicate with previously repressed aspects of the psyche. Through such *assimilation of the shadow half* of personality, *wholeness* can be achieved and balance restored.

Four stages of therapy: confession, elucidation, education, and individuation. During the early stages of therapy, *confession* results in emotional *catharsis.* Like Freud and Breuer, Jung believed that for healing to take place such confessions must be more than intellectual statements or explanations; they must involve *emotions.* As therapy progresses, clients naturally move from confession to an exploration of their past lives, and here the therapist assists by *elucidating* and clarifying issues. During the *educative* phase of treatment, the therapist helps the client to change behaviors or thinking and to fill deficiencies in relating to others or in understanding oneself. For many clients these three phases are sufficient to achieve balance.

For some extraordinary clients who have potentials beyond the average (Maslow might refer to them as "Peak Experiencers"), Jung sought to bring about a balancing of the psyche and enhancement of selfhood in a process he called *individuation.* Jung might ask a patient to take some aspect of a dream, fantasy image, or fleeting archetype and to spontaneously elaborate and develop it (similar to how Freud might have a patient free-associate). However, instead of functioning as an analytic "blank screen," Jung actively assisted clients in developing and elaborating such images: "This, according to individual taste and talent, could be done in any number of ways, dramatic, dialectic, visual, acoustic, or in the form of dancing, painting, drawing, or modelling" (Jung, 1960, p. 202). Thus, a patient who kept experiencing the image of a tree in his dreams might paint it, write about it, sculpt it, dance around it, or in various other ways spontaneously try to bring it meaning. In this way the tree becomes consciously integrated into the psyche, bringing it more into balance.

SUMMARY OF JUNG'S TRANSPERSONAL THEORY

Jung viewed the *collective unconscious* as the source of all psychic contents that do not arise directly from experience. Extending across all time and all cultures the *collective unconscious* encompass all of evolutionary history in the form of *archetypal* propensities to behave in certain ways. Archetypes act both as psychological "magnets" (attracting certain kinds of experiences while repelling others) as well as "suitcases" (for transporting ancient ancestral experiences into the contemporary psychic landscape). Jung's collective unconscious irretrievably places the psyche *outside* the skin of the person into the middle of an evolutionary stream where everything is interconnected. It doesn't get more *transpersonal* than that!

The *collective unconscious* is the transpersonal bridge by which Jung connects contemporary experience to past ancestors and to future generations. It allows one to transcend Freud's deterministic libido forces and family-of-origin dynamics, and provides an alternative to the learning-and-conditioning theories of Watson and Skinner. Jung even transcends the humanistic theories of Rogers and Maslow, which provide no mechanism for reaching back to ancestral times or forward to the next life. Thus, Jung emerges as *the* pioneer transpersonal psychologist, and once the "toothpaste" of transpersonalism was outside the "tube" of psychoanalysis, behaviorism, and humanism, things could never be the same again. Whatever your opinion of transpersonal psychology—from plausible to preposterous—it is here to stay.

A SAMPLING OF OTHER FACETS OF TRANSPERSONAL PSYCHOLOGY

Naturalistic transpersonalism. Maslow said that he considered "Third Force" humanistic psychology a transitional preparation for an even "higher" Fourth Psychology that was "transpersonal, transhuman, centered in the cosmos rather than in human needs and interest, going beyond humanness, identity, self-actualization, and the like . . ." (Maslow, 1968, pp. iii–iv). However, Maslow's transpersonalism was not *spiritual* in a theological sense. While acknowledging the need for something "bigger than we are," he did not envision transpersonal psychology as necessarily a leap toward God, but rather a "new, naturalistic, empirical, non-churchly" commitment (Maslow, 1968, pp. iii–iv).

Spiritual transpersonalism. Scotton (1996a) sees transpersonal experiences as occurring at the highest levels of human consciousness along a spectrum ranging from ". . . the *prepersonal* (before the formation of a separate ego), to the *personal* (with a functioning ego), to the transpersonal (in which the ego remains available but is superseded by more inclusive frames of reference)" (1996, p. 4). Scotton specifically includes *spiritual* as part of his transpersonalism, distinguishing it from *religious:*

> *Religious* refers to the belief system of a specific group. . . . *Spiritual* refers to the realm of the human spirit, that part of humanity that is not limited to bodily experience. *Transpersonal experience,* in addressing all human experience beyond the ego level, includes spiritual experience but also includes embodied human experience of higher levels. (Scotton, 1966, p. 4)

Scotton offers an example of transpersonal functioning that transcends the ego level while remaining embodied within persons. He cites as examples Martin Luther King's civil rights workers, who were willing to nonviolently risk their lives for higher values.

Synthesizing science and spirituality—Fadiman's transpersonal psychology. James Fadiman insists that scientific methodologies ought to be used to study a broad range of spiritual traditions within transpersonal psychology:

> Transpersonal psychology is bringing together the insights of the individualistic psychologies of the West with the spiritual psychologies of the East and Middle East. The realization that our own training has been limited and that Western ideas are not the center of the psychological universe is disturbing at first. The feeling passes when one becomes aware of the amazing amount of work that has already been accomplished, but which awaits validation with the scientific and experimental tools of Western psychology. . . . (Fadiman, 1980, p. 181)

As we emphasized earlier in our text, each *zone* has its own special contribution to make. Reality includes both genes and galaxies, and although transpersonal psychology is the broadest of the "big tents" of personality paradigms, it does not necessarily contain more "truth" than the other *zones* of our grid. Transpersonal theories merely provide a *different* perspective on "truth" from that found in the more reductionistic theories we encountered in the compositional or behavioral zones.

Transpersonal psychology co-mingles science and spirituality. We have already discovered that most theories of personality have been tinted by the spiritual experiences of their founders and colored by the spiritual zeitgeists of their particular eras. However, spirituality has seldom been incorporated as a core component of the final theory. For example, although Freud's work was undoubtedly influenced by his Jewishness, psychoanalysis can be practiced by Presbyterians and Pentecostals as well. Similarly, although Carl Rogers's early ministerial training may have colored his view of human nature, his client-centered theory can be utilized by Methodists, Muslims, or Mormons alike. In this chapter we will learn how transpersonal psychologists integrate spirituality into their theories of personality.

Equal time for spirituality. Transpersonal psychologists blend spiritual and psychological constructs in such a seamless way that it becomes difficult to disentangle them. Jim Fadiman, a leading transpersonal psychologist, described this co-mingling of *psychological theory* and *spiritual traditions:* "Transpersonal psychologists draw heavily on the accumulated psychological literature outside the American mainstream. Examples of the ideas influencing current transpersonal therapists can be drawn from Buddhism, Sufism, and Yoga . . ." (1980, p. 176).

Since transpersonal *theories* co-mingle psychology and spirituality, we are not surprised to find that transpersonal *therapies* also blend

> . . . both Eastern and Western methods for working with consciousness. Various forms of meditation and Yoga may be added to more conventional techniques. . . . the transpersonal concept of health goes beyond belief in ego development as the summit of mental health. Ultimately, the disidentification from ego and the discovery of one's own true nature may be considered tantamount to liberation or awakening. (Walsh & Vaughan, 1980, pp. 165, 169)

Along this same line, another transpersonalist wrote: "When does the attraction of the pleasures of the senses die away? When one realizes the consummation of all happiness and all pleasure in God—the indivisible, eternal ocean of bliss." (Ramakrishna, 1965, p. 93)

Bugental (1980) aptly illustrates this Eastern emphasis:

> Presence, being here, centeredness, and immediacy—all are terms to point to a fundamental reality. Only in this moment am I alive. All else is to some measure speculative. . . . *Most of us are truly present in the moment but rarely.* . . . The heart of the matter is simple, fundamental, and often totally overlooked—*the true home of each of us is in inner experiencing.* . . . (1980, pp. 193–195)

FACING THE TOUGH TWINS

Is It Testable?

As we consider Yoga, Zen, Sufism, and other transpersonal theories, we do well to imbibe their enthusiasm and expansiveness while retaining some scientific skepticism. Although we cannot refute transpersonal theories by the same rigorous criteria we might apply to more behavioral or cognitive theories (e.g., falsifiability, replicability, double-blind procedures, etc.), we can still insist on *conceptual rigor* and *theoretical logic.* Thus, as we consider Grof's (1998) enthusiastic endorsement of LSD as a mind-opening path to enlightenment, we do well to remember that a drug-facilitated mind-expanding *experience* does not necessarily provide an accurate map of reality. Grof conducted over Four thousand psychedelic sessions over forty years, and he presents these mind-altering *experiences* as *evidence* for such spiritual phenomena as reincarnation:

> . . . it is not only possible but very common to experience episodes from the lives of people in various historical periods and different countries of the world. . . . For example, we can experience a situation in which we were killed by a tiger or trampled to death by an elephant. Over the years I have also witnessed some past life experiences . . . where the experiencer died in an avalanche or was crushed by a falling tree. . . . The existence of past life experiences with all their remarkable characteristics is an unquestionable fact that can be verified by any serious researcher who is sufficiently open-minded and interested to check the evidence. (Grof, 1998, pp. 177–178)

A more careful scientist might acknowledge that whatever a person *experiences* in a psychedelic session (or in four thousand, for that matter!) offers no "hard" data regarding whether that person existed in a former life.

Another transpersonal theorist relies on metaphors instead of data, attempting to prove his points with poetry in place of research:

> You're on a nice nature walk, relaxed and expansive in your awareness, and you look at a beautiful mountain, and wham!—suddenly there is no looker, just the mountain—and you are the mountain. . . . You don't look at the sky, you are the sky. You can taste the sky. It's not out-there. As Zen would say, you can drink the Pacific Ocean in a single gulp, you can swallow the Kosmos whole. . . . (Wilber, 2000, pp. 184–185, 206)

Obviously, no researcher is going to experimentally verify that someone has swallowed the Pacific Ocean in a single gulp. Here, falsifiability in the usual sense is not possible. Does this mean we should reject all of Wilber's theorizing (throw out the baby with the . . . "Pacific Ocean")? Hardly. But we must evaluate transpersonal and spiritual theories by employing scholarly criteria such as plausibility, persuasiveness, cogency, coherence, and logic. Because a theory is not *empirically* accessible does not prevent us from carefully evaluating its validity claims.

Is It Useful? Apparently so. The Institute of Transpersonal Psychology in Palo Alto, California, appears to be thriving, and there seems to be no lack of students interested in exploring what Maslow termed the "farther reaches of human nature." And, if the bookshelves of your local bookseller are any indication, transpersonal theories are here to stay. Trendy transpersonal books (e.g., Shirley MacLaine's *Dancing in the Light;* Marilyn Ferguson's *The Aquarian Conspiracy;* and James Redfield's *The Celestine Prophecy*) share space on the best-seller shelves with more serious presentations (e.g., James Austin's *Zen and the Brain;* Fritjof Capra's *Web of Life;* John Mack's *Abduction: Human Encounters with Aliens;* and Zohar and Marshall's *The Quantum Society: Mind, Physics, and a New Social Vision*). Moviegoers line up to see the latest installment of *The Matrix* trilogy, much as they did for the earlier *Star Wars* series.

In a world threatened by terrorism, tsunamis, and tribal hatreds, human beings seek to meet some of their higher "meta-needs" for peace, intimacy, and beauty. They look beyond immediate circumstances to worlds beyond the palpable—to God or gods that promise meaning and even immortality.

Chapter Summary

Transpersonal psychologists are in sharp contrast to Freud and Marx, who saw religion as infantile dependency. Transpersonal psychologists of all stripes—like their theological counterparts—embrace the spiritual journey. They see searching "beyond" the person as positive growth.

Today we find many traditional disciplines, from physics to medicine, showing a renewed interest in incorporating spirituality. Some of the hottest research topics in psychology include the study of forgiveness, repentance, and other traditionally theological topics (e.g., Worthington, 1998; McCullough, Pargament, & Thoresen,

2000; Berecz, 2001). Meanwhile, medical researchers probe the effects of prayer on recovery, or seek to understand if meditation increases longevity.

In this chapter we have studied transpersonal and spiritual theories of personality, stretching our thinking beyond the usual empirical boundaries of science—even suggesting that theology can be understood as personality theories about God(s). Transpersonal psychologists believe that personality theories that fail to include spirituality offer an incomplete account of human functioning. Existential theologian Paul Tillich observed that humans have a "passion for the infinite" (1957, p. 8); and he suggested that religion, in the broadest sense, always includes *ultimate concerns*. Likewise, transpersonal psychologists insist that personality theories ought to include *ultimate concerns* because faith remains an integral part of psychological functioning for billions around the globe. We have included spiritual and transpersonal theories in our text because to do otherwise would have been (to borrow Emmon's apt phrase) "the equivalent of committing academic malpractice" (1999, p. 7).

Points to Remember

1. *Transpersonal psychology* transcends within-the-skin personality, allowing the self to expand beyond epidermal boundaries and temporal constraints. The contemporary forces of *postmodernism* in literature and philosophy and *relativity theory* in physics have fanned the glowing embers of Jung's *collective unconscious* into a bonfire of transpersonal psychology in which the self is simultaneously more expansive but also less precisely defined.

2. Sometimes called the "Fourth Force," transpersonal psychology moves beyond humanistic concerns with self-actualization and existential considerations of meaning to seek *spiritual transcendence*. Such transcendence may be either religious or secular in tone—when *secular,* it includes *a personal-plus* dimension that may include other times, places, or people; when *religious,* it involves relating to a *Higher Power.*

3. Whether religious or secular, transpersonal psychology typically involves a *dialectical synthesis* of past, present, and future (as in Jung's collective unconscious), Eastern versus Western philosophies, self versus others, good versus evil, etc.

4. William James, the "father" of American psychology, had a deep interest in "higher" states of consciousness, which included spiritual experiences. His book *Varieties of Religious Experience* is still considered an important classic.

5. Jung agreed with Freud that personality is based on a "deep" *unconscious* infrastructure; however, he went even deeper and wider by adding a *collective unconscious,* which included experiences from ancient eons as well as contemporary and future elements. Jung agreed with Adler's emphasis on the importance of *future goals,* and he was also averse to explaining all behaviors as ultimately deriving from a sexual drive.

6. Like Freud, whose theories were profoundly influenced by his relationship with his mother, Jung became convinced that—like his mother—all people were comprised of two contrasting personalities living within one body. As a child he

labeled one of his personalities the "schoolboy," and the contrasting one "wise old man." He spent his entire adult life struggling with the polarities within himself and finding a balance between his inner life and external realities. The major polarity in his theory occurs between the *ego complex* in the *conscious mind* and the *shadow complex* in the *collective unconscious*.

7. As a young child Jung experienced *intense dreams and visions,* which continued in his adult years as well. Ultimately, he translated his inner turmoil into a theory of personality that relies heavily on inner experiences, but balances these with appropriate external checkpoints.

8. Early in his professional career Jung became famous for his research utilizing the *word-association test* to study unconscious processes. This won him Freud's admiration and led Freud to later designate Jung the heir apparent to psychoanalysis. However, they *ultimately disagreed about the importance of sexuality as a master motive,* so their friendship ended in bitterness. Jung went on to found his own *transpersonal variation of depth psychology,* which he called *analytic psychology.*

9. Following his bitter parting with Freud, Jung struggled with inner demons of psychotic proportions. Out of his *creative illness* Jung formulated a theory of personality that achieves a remarkable balance between the chaotic dreams, visions, and fantasies of inner life, and the facts and figures of external reality.

10. Jung's *psyche* is the "big tent" of personality, with the *ego, personal unconscious,* and *collective unconscious* as major players. Additionally, Jung includes the *soul* as that part of personality that enables us to establish a transcendent connection with a higher power. Jung's *collective unconscious* includes *archetypes* that allegedly gain us access to our ancestral past. Four of the principal archetypes include *persona,* or the public side of personality; the *shadow,* or the repressed side of personality; the *anima* and *animus,* the androgynous sides of personality; and *self,* the great synthesizer of personality.

11. Jung goes beyond the material and efficient causalities of biology and behaviorism to emphasize—as did Adler—the *teleological importance of goals.* Additionally he introduced the controversial notion of *synchronicity* to explain *miraculous, lucky,* or otherwise *meaningful coincidences.*

12. *Opposition (for any tendency in one direction there is an opposite tendency)* is at the heart of Jung's motivational system. The *constellating power* of a complex enables it to *attract clusters of emotionally charged elements, "snowballing" them into larger and larger complexes.*

13. *Individuation* is the lifelong developmental process by which the components of the psyche are *organized into a balanced personality. Transcendence* refers to an even broader integration of the self with all of humankind. Unlike Freud, who emphasized the first five years as the most crucial for development, Jung saw the *second half of life* as a time of continuing growth—especially in the *spiritual realm,* where the wisdom of prior experience plays a crucial role.

14. Jung blends *two basic attitudes* (introversion and extraversion) and *four psychological functions* (sensation, thinking, feeling, and intuition) to formulate *eight personality styles* to describe individual uniqueness.

15. Jungian therapists assist clients in *creating symbols of transformation* to *balance their personalities* by *assimilating opposites.* Most clients find the first three stages of therapy *(confession, elucidation, and education)* sufficient to achieve balance. A few exceptionally creative people go on to the fourth stage *(individuation)* to experience a more complete balancing of the psyche.

16. Many of Jung's basic constructs (e.g., the collective unconscious, synchronicity, etc.) are not falsifiable; however, his theory has heuristically spawned the widely used Myers–Briggs Type Indicator and has profoundly influenced our views of sexuality, adult development, and cultural awareness. Jung uses the *symbols* and *archetypes* of the *collective unconscious* to link us with our ancestral past, and he employs the process of *transcendence* to transport us into the future. By thus moving outside the skin of the body and beyond the temporality of the present, Jung earns the distinction of being the first *transpersonal psychologist.*

Key Terms

Androgyny (498)

Anima (498)

Animus (498)

Archetype (495)

Attitude (506)

Collective Unconscious (493)

Complex (490, 493, 503)

Creative Illness (491)

Ectopsychic Functions (506)

Ego (493)

Extraverts (506)

Feeling (507)

Individuation (504)

Introverts (506)

Intuition (507)

Mandala (501)

Myers–Briggs Type Indicator (MBTI) (510)

Persona (497)

Personal Unconscious (493)

Personifying Archetypes (496)

Principle of Opposites (502)

Psyche (493)

Religious/Spiritual (484)

Self (499)

Sensation (506)

Shadow (497)

Soul (501)

Symbols (494)

Symbols of Transformation (514)

Synchronicity (483, 501)

Teleological (501)

Teleology (487)

Thinking (506)

Transcendence (504)

Transcendent Experience (484)

Transforming Archetypes (496)

Transpersonal Psychology (483)

Word-Association Test (503)

Web Sites

William James

http://williamjamesstudies.press.uiuc.edu/mission.html. William James Studies. This peer-reviewed journal, published by the University of Illinois, can be accessed by students and scholars. Download their publications for free.

Carl Jung

www.dreamstell.net/. Dreams Tell. If you'r looking for an extensive guide to dream interpretation, you've hit the jackpot! This Web site offers free dream interpretation and a dictionary for dream symbols.

http://thelifeboatforum.com. The Lifeboat. An active open forum where you can discuss Jungian psychology, dreams, and more!

http://en.wikipedia.org/wiki/Carl_Jung. Wikipedia. This page on Carl Jung is extensive, with references to dozens of related books, movies, music, and links to Web sites.

Learning on the Lighter Side

The Lord of the Rings films are filled with Jungian archetypes. Gandalf is the *wise old man* and Frodo is the youthful *hero* on an archetypal quest. Gollum plays the *shadow,* and women like Galadriel are powerful *anima* figures. Similarly, in the *Star Wars* trilogy Luke Skywaker is the youthful *hero,* Darth Vader is the *shadow,* and Obi-Wan Kenobi the *wise old man.*

Jurassic Park, the 1993 science fiction movie in which dinosaurs are cloned from prehistoric mosquitos, provides the viewer an emotional experience that might not be unlike what Jung himself experienced as he did battle with archetypes from the past that oozed into the present.

Finally, in the 1989 Disney movie *Honey I Shrunk the Kids,* an inventor designs a machine that shrinks objects to a small fraction of their original size. The movie derives its comedic plot from what follows after a family's two children accidentally become "shrunken." Similarly, transpersonal psychologists maintain that traditional theories of personality shrink us by their failure to address issues of spirituality. They promise to swell and stretch—rather than shrink—our concepts of ourselves and our God/gods.

Looking Ahead

As we near the end of our journey and "look ahead" one last time, I suspect we all might be secretly breathing a small sigh of relief—you, because you've finished reading; and I, because I've finished writing. I hope that your sigh of relief—like mine—might be accompanied by a sense of accomplishment. It's been a great ride, and as we head down the "home stretch," we will briefly look over our shoulders, reminding ourselves of where we've been and what we've learned, and we'll look ahead to anticipate the future as well.

As we look back, we will recognize that most personality theories reflect something of the experiences of their founders. We'll also notice that they tilt toward healing and are not so much "right" or "wrong" as more or less *useful.* Consistent with what we have just studied, we'll notice that most people do not live by science alone, but also seek some sort of transpersonal/spiritual experiences as well.

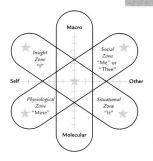

Putting Personality All Together

or at least synthesizing *some* of it!

chapter 14

IN THIS CHAPTER YOU CAN

1. Discover that personality theories share much in common with each other and with other scientific theories.

2. Note how personality theories frequently reflect the experiences of their founders.

3. Appreciate that personality theories tilt toward *healing*.

4. Recall how theories vary significantly in how they assign personal agency.

5. Emphasize that personality operates in different zones.

6. Know that personality theories are not so much "right" or "wrong" as they are more or less *useful*.

7. Discover that *people do not live by science alone*.

8. Predict that the future is bright for personality psychology.

A PERSONAL PERSPECTIVE

"Alice in Wonderland"

Whatever your preferred zone of analysis, at various times during our journey through our text you might have felt like Alice in Wonderland as she explored the large rabbit hole under the hedge. Alice, you may recall, changed sizes a number of times, first becoming only ten inches high as a result of drinking a small bottle of potion, then, after eating a small currant cake, suddenly growing so tall that "when she looked down at her feet, they seemed to be almost out of sight, they were getting so far off" (Carroll, 1982, pp. 8–10).

Such size transitions were not easy for Alice—changing the level of analysis is never easy for anyone—so, here at the conclusion of our journey, you may feel a bit like Alice when she had the following conversation with the Caterpillar:

> "I think I must have been changed several times. . . . and being so many different sizes in a day is very confusing."
>
> "It isn't," said the Caterpillar.
>
> "Well perhaps *your* feelings may be different," said Alice: "all I know is, it would feel very queer to *me*." . . . . there was silence for some minutes.
>
> The Caterpillar was the first to speak.
>
> "What size do you want to be?" it asked.

"Oh, I'm not particular as to size," Alice hastily replied; "only one doesn't like changing so often you know."

"I *don't* know," said the Caterpillar. . . .

"Well, I should like to be a *little* larger, Sir, if you wouldn't mind," said Alice: "three inches is such a wretched height to be."

"It is a very good height indeed!" said the Caterpillar angrily, rearing itself upright as it spoke (it was exactly three inches high). (Carroll, 1982, pp. 28–29, 32)

Commentary

Our study of personality at various levels of analysis has required us to "change sizes" numerous times. We may have felt "only three inches tall" in the *Physiological Zone,* where personality is measured in molecules and chromosomes. In the *Transpersonal Zone,* confronted with questions of cosmic proportions, we may have sometimes felt as Alice did, that our feet were "almost out of sight." However, as we explore the experiential world of transpersonal and spiritual thinkers to "walk a mile in their moccasins," we may find some of their theories to be logically compelling, even if lacking in laboratory-based "proofs." Viewed from inside, spirituality might not be so alien as we first thought. Most people experience their own faiths as comfortably familiar—just as "wetness" does not feel strange to a fish, or being "only three inches tall" doesn't feel odd to caterpillars.

Here, in our last chapter, we'll not be satisfied with staying in our familiar-sized comfort zones, merely peering into the "rabbit holes" of reductionism or the "black holes" of transpersonal spirituality from a safe, cynical distance. Instead, like Alice, we will explore the crooks and crannies of both scientific empiricism and transpersonal spirituality one last time—from the inside out. We will respect those who seek truth by peering into microscopes as well as those who search for it through meditation.

Completing our "final ascent," we will seek to synthesize all levels of analysis into a holistic portrait of personality that is based primarily on an empirical scientific foundation, but that also allows for spirituality and other transpersonal experiences. We will encounter a number of difficult-to-falsify but logically possible views of the universe that may require mental "size changes" of cosmic proportions. We may discover—as countless others have—that a life of faith in someone or something greater than ourselves offers opportunities for solving the great dialectical dilemmas of existence: e.g., being versus nonbeing, good versus evil, life versus death. Compositionists and behaviorists insist that the "inner life" is irrelevant, while humanists, existentialists, and transpersonalists contend that a complete accounting of personality must include spirituality as well. So, we're off to explore both "rabbit holes" and cosmic "black holes"—size be damned!

The disparity between the title and subtitle of this chapter captures something of the dilemma experienced by personality psychologists from Freud to Funder. We want to understand how inner thoughts, feelings, and impulses influence how a person perceives, construes, and reacts to the surrounding environment. Personality psychologists seek to understand the *whole* person in a *real-life* situation—not just motives, feelings, or cognitions in isolation.

Mission impossible? However, even as we dream of *holistically* understanding a breathing, walking, thinking, laughing, crying, humming human being—living life outside the laboratory—we suspect it can't be done. As Funder puts it:

> There is only one problem with this mission. It is impossible. . . . If you try to understand everything about a person all at once, you will immediately find yourself completely overwhelmed. Your mind, instead of attaining a broad understanding, may go blank. This is the problem with trying to see everything at the same time. (Funder, 2004, p. 5)

Still, in spite of the difficulties, we like to think big. Like sunflowers whose heliotropism causes them to continually turn toward light, personality psychologists appear to have a "*holo*tropism" that causes them to continually turn toward studying individuals *holistically*. Even a theorist like Eysenck—renowned for his insistence on empiricism—tried to relate molecular measures of physiological functioning (e.g., eyeblink and GSR conditioning, 1965b; cortical arousal, 1967; testosterone and monoamine oxidase levels, 1990b) to such sweeping macro constructs as introversion and extraversion.

From primates to peace. Abraham Maslow who earned his doctorate studying primates in the laboratory, ultimately wanted to work for world peace. He recalled that one day, following Pearl Harbor, he was driving home when his car was stopped by a "poor, pathetic parade." He noticed "Boy Scouts and fat people and old uniforms and a flag and someone playing a flute off-key":

> As I watched, tears began to run down my face. I felt we didn't understand any of them. I felt that if we could understand, then we could make progress. I had a vision of a peace table, with people sitting around it, talking about human nature and hatred and war and peace and brotherhood. . . . That moment changed my whole life and determined what I have done since. . . . I wanted to prove that human beings are capable of something grander than war and prejudice and hatred. I wanted to make science consider all the problems that nonscientists have been handling—religion, poetry, values, philosophy, art. (Maslow, quoted in Hall, 1968, pp. 54–55)

Still, Maslow remained conflicted his entire life between his University of Wisconsin–induced commitment to scientific rigor and his wish to study "the farther reaches of human nature" (1971). He remained defensive about his "soft," third-force theories. Near the end of his life he confessed that he had "been tense for weeks & weeks—bad sleep, fatigue, preoccupation, etc. Partly due, according to dreams, to getting all wound up & a little awed & scared by tremendous implications of work I'm doing contrasted with very shaky foundations it's all based on. So get scary dreams . . ." (Lowry, 1982, p. 79).

From schedules of reinforcement to Walden II. B. F. Skinner, the most renowned behaviorist of the twentieth century, couldn't remain content with the laboratory science he outlined in *The Behavior of Organisms: An Experimental Analysis* (1938) and *Schedules of Reinforcement* (Skinner & Ferster, 1957). So, sandwiched between these two scientific treatises—with a decade on each side—was his utopian fantasy *Walden II* (1948) in which he proposed (literally) to change the world:

> Not only can we not face the rest of the world while consuming and polluting as we do, we cannot for long face ourselves while acknowledging the violence and chaos in which we live. The choice is clear: either we do nothing and allow a miserable and probably catastrophic future to overtake us, or we use our knowledge about human behavior to create a social environment in which we shall live productive and creative lives and do so without jeopardizing the chances that those who follow us will be able to do the same. Something like a Walden Two would not be a bad start. (Skinner, 1976)

Personality psychologists appear to revel in the meaning and personal relevance of the sweeping constructs that personality theory provides, yet they struggle to maintain their scientific integrity while investigating such whole-person concepts. Unlike philosophers, theologians, and mystics, who feel free to seek truth through logic, faith, or meditation, personality psychologists remain committed to the methods of scientific inquiry. No matter how much they stand on their tiptoes—stretching to deploy their constructs at ever-higher levels of application—they never quite leave their scientific moorings. Even a contemporary transpersonal psychologist suggests that the spiritual psychologies of the East and Middle East ought to be subject to "validation with the scientific and experimental tools of Western psychology . . ." (Fadiman, 1980, p. 181).

Do personality theories share anything in common? So, at the end of thirteen chapters of study, can we find commonalities among the many theories of personality that we have encountered? I think we can. For the most part, personality researchers are "big-picture" scientists who seek to provide us "whole-person" profiles of personality. Some believe this is best achieved "bottom-up" by first building a biochemical foundation; others believe a "top-down" approach helps to sharpen our focus on the core issues that deserve further investigation. As a result of encountering theories of personality in different *zones,* we are now in a position to synthesize the follwing:

(1) Personality theories share much in common with each other and with other scientific theories, (2) they frequently reflect the life experiences of their founders, (3) they tilt toward healing, (4) they vary in assigning personal agency, (5) they operate at different levels of analysis, (6) they are not so much "right" or "wrong" as they differ in usefulness, and (7) people—including Freud—do not live by science alone. Let's look at each of these in more detail.

(1) PERSONALITY THEORIES SHARE MUCH IN COMMON WITH ONE ANOTHER, BUT COMPARISONS HAVE NOT ALWAYS BEEN EASY

If there's one primary lesson from the past thirteen chapters, it is that *theory building is what science is all about.* Whether we are formulating a theory of personality or a theory of microbiology, whether we are studying people, petunias, or paramecia, we find ourselves asking "Big Four" kinds of questions regarding parts, motives, development, and uniqueness. Such questions haunt us in every nook and cranny of the known universe. Our answers vary, of course, depending upon our zones of investigation, but the questions remain similar.

The "Big Four"—all over the place. Scientists who study living systems seek to specify the components of such systems and understand what energizes them. Whether we are psychologists or zoologists, we try to discern how the various parts of living systems manage to maintain their unique identities while still growing and changing. We wonder, for example, how mammalian hearts manage to pump enough blood—around the clock, day or night, 24-7, including holidays!—to keep their owners alive, while still managing to grow, change, and perform necessary self-repair. What keeps hearts from changing into lungs—which do equally astonishing things with oxygen? In nonliving systems, similar questions are posed in slightly modified ways: What are the parts of a black hole? What makes it go? What makes it grow? What makes it unique?

Consequently, near the end of our intellectual journey, we have not merely read an "encyclopedia" of ideas about human personality, we have become theory builders: scientists who are prepared to ask questions in operationally definable ways; scholars who are motivated to find data-based answers; thinkers who insist on reasonableness of the untestable. We have learned how science works and we can now ask our "Big Four" questions about almost any theory from micro-theories about enzymes and neurotransmitters to macro-theories about economics in a free market. From theories about subatomic quarks to cosmological theories about the Big Bang, we expect to find reasoned constructs.

Personality theories have the potential to integrate other areas of psychology. Personality theories tend to occupy mid-level zones on the vertical (molecular–macro) continuum, as well as centrist locations on the horizontal (self–other) axis. They are ideally located for *synthesizing* and *integrating* other subfields of psychology. With a wide array of investigative techniques and theoretical constructs at their disposal, personality psychologists are uniquely equipped to investigate emotions, cognition, motives, social skills, temperament—and all the other topics encountered in Psych 101 courses—and to seamlessly co-mingle these in seeking to understand the experience of living, breathing, whole persons.

Sadly, this opportunity has seldom been capitalized upon because of the way personality psychology has traditionally been taught. Following Hall and Lindzey's (1957) classic approach, most personality textbooks have followed a historical, encyclopedic, theory-by-theory approach, broadly grouping psychoanalytic, behavioristic, or humanistic theories under separate "umbrellas." There has been little integration and no way for students to compare constructs across theories—no way to compare "apples with apples."

A new *Zeitgeist*. Today, there exists a *Zeitgeist* for integration among personality psychologists. Since I first began work on this text in early 2000, number of personality textbooks (e.g., Mischel, Shoda, & Smith, 2003; Pervin, 2003; Mayer, 2005) have also taken a more integrative approach. However, many of these texts have included intimidating amounts of research findings—challenging for undergraduate minds to absorb even when systematically organized.

Our text has included current research in the context of the lives and theories of the "grand masters"—Freud, Kelly, Rogers, and others—because my experience is that students love a story. And if you can capture the *person* of Skinner or Maslow, their theories of *personality* become easier to understand and remember. Picturing Freud, the favorite son, smoking his ever present cigar, carefully indoctrinating his daughter Anna, and caustically dismissing those who dared to differ with him, you can better appreciate how Freud viewed personality as a closed system permeated with intrapsychic conflict. In many ways we can see psychoanalysis as a metaphor of the mind of Freud.

When these classic theories are mapped into their appropriate *zones*, their relationships to one another and to more contemporary, research-based "mini-theories" become more clear. Hopefully, you have experienced the best of both worlds—classic theories and contemporary research—seamlessly co-mingling with your own experiences in living. Next, we will briefly recap how the private lives of personality psychologists have influenced their work.

(2) PERSONALITY THEORIES FREQUENTLY REFLECT THE LIFE EXPERIENCES OF THEIR FOUNDERS

The eminent historian of psychoanalysis, Ellenberger (1970), concluded that personality formulations are the means by which theorists solve their personal crises. Another scholar suggested that the typical personality theorist is ". . . someone who feels insecure, sometimes to the point of inferiority. Frequently, but not universally, the personality theorist-to-be felt unwanted by one or both parents" (Monte, 1999, p. 938).

The apple (of theory) doesn't fall far from the tree. This is consistent with what we have learned in our Background Checks. At least in the case of the "grand" theories, there frequently appears to be a relationship between family-of-origin dynamics and theoretical constructs. For example, Freud's fondness for his mother appears reflected in the centerpiece of psychoanalysis—the Oedipus complex.

Melanie Klein, the youngest of four children, was not breast-fed by her mother as were her siblings. As a five-year-old, she lost her beloved older sister to death; as a teen, she lost her older brother; and as an adult, she lost her husband, psychoanalyst, and even her own son. It is hardly surprising that her theory of personality viewed weaning as a major interpersonal crisis and death as a primary drive. Practicing during wartime, she believed the inner world of infants and children was filled with terrifying images of death and mayhem.

By contrast, Donald Winnicott was surrounded by numerous nurturing "mothers," and he came to view psychological development as a series of positive experiences with "good enough" mothers. Karen Horney's resentment of her father's preference for her brother evolved into a feminist theory that was among the first to challenge "father" Freud's male-centered psychoanalysis. Erik Erikson's early experiences of identity confusion (as a blond stepson in a Jewish household) undoubtedly contributed to his theoretical emphasis on the importance of ego identity. Alfred Adler's childhood illnesses and near-death experiences likely formed the foundation for his most basic construct: organ inferiority and compensation. His perpetual losing out to his more athletic older brother no doubt magnified the importance of birth order in his theory.

One of the clearest connections between early family experiences and later theorizing is found not in Freud's fondness for his mother, but in Maslow's loathing for his. Maslow's mom was so malignant (remember? she smashed the kittens' heads against the basement wall) that near the end of his life Maslow wrote: ". . . the whole thrust of my life-philosophy and all my research and theorizing also has its roots in a hatred for and revulsion against everything she stood for" (Lowry, 1979, p. 958).

In the case of the classic big-picture theories, the ties between childhood experiences and later theoretical formulations are easily traced. In the case of contemporary "mini-theories," we find less autobiographical and historical context; nonetheless, it does not seem too much of a stretch to surmise that if a personality researcher chooses to study the sleeping patterns of "night owls" versus "morning larks" (e.g., Horne & Ostberg, 1976; Revelle, Humphreys, Simon, & Gilliland, 1980; Watts, 1982) she might have experienced difficulties waking up in the morning, getting to bed on time, or adjusting to the sleep cycles of other family members.

Healing oneself and others. Much of what remains significant for us as adults can frequently be traced to sensitizing experiences during development. The rape counselor likely experienced sexual abuse or was close to someone who did. The family therapist probably grew up in a home where conflict and chaos were present. The addiction specialist doubtless struggled with addictions himself or came from a family where someone did. Does this mean that the urge for self-healing invalidates the theories motivated by such strivings? Not necessarily.

A person who has experienced certain calamities and crises may be more attuned to the relevant variables; but, conversely, he might also be desensitized to other important factors. That's why personality psychologists ultimately turn to experimentation and data for their answers. Experiential learning and scientific validation are two very different processes, and although researchers may be inspired by—even driven by—their own personal experiences, at the end of the day, it is experimental *validation* that should shape science.

(3) PERSONALITY THEORIES TILT TOWARD HEALING

We have suggested that personality theories frequently grow from the soil of childhood frustrations and family conflict, perhaps functioning as a form of self-healing. It should not surprise us, then, to discover that seeking internal harmony has been one of the primary goals of personality theorists from earliest times. Whether it was the ancient Egyptians employing aromatic fumigations to woo the "wandering uterus" back to its proper location, or the Greeks attempting to balance body humors through bloodletting, personality specialists have tried to use their knowledge to heal themselves and others.

Personality theories promote harmony. In more modern times, Freud's psychoanalysis was primarily a program for healing. Freud earned his daily bread by helping others to reduce conflict. The entire thrust of psychoanalysis—"where id was there ego shall be"—was to reduce unconscious conflict through conscious awareness. This healing trend was also obvious in the work of Erik Erikson who, like Freud, saw the individual self (ego) "sandwiched" between biological impulses arising from within and societal expectations "out there." According to Erikson, the balancing of polarities takes place in a series of psychological tugs-of-war that he termed psychosocial stages of development.

Karen Horney's theory of personality was designed to heal what she considered the core neurotic conflict: alienation between the real self and the idealized self. Her remedy was much like the self-actualizing solutions later proposed by the humanists: "You need not, in fact cannot, teach an acorn to grow into an oak tree, but when given a chance, its intrinsic potentialities will develop" (Horney, 1950, p. 17). Carl Rogers's notion of incongruence between self and experience echoes Horney's core conflict. According to Rogers, such incongruence is healed by empathy and by unconditional positive regard.

From laboratory experimenters to social healers. We shouldn't be astonished to discover that personality theories formulated by practicing clinicians are permeated with healing ingredients. However, we might be surprised to learn how many psychologists trained as laboratory researchers evolved into healers. We discovered earlier that Abe Maslow was mentored by psychology's preeminent primatologist, Harry Harlow. Maslow, the humanist-to-be, not only studied monkeys, he became fond of them: "I was fascinated with them. I became fond of my individual monkeys in a way that was not possible with my rats" (Maslow, cited in Hoffman, 1988, p. 49). Apparently, for Maslow, the objects of his experimental scrutiny became his "friends," and Skinner, the most famous of all behaviorists, reported that he felt more affirmed by his rodents and feathered friends than by people:

> . . . my effects on other people have been far less important than my effects on rats and pigeons—or on people as experimental subjects. That is why I was able to work for almost twenty years with practically no professional recognition. People supported me, but not my line of work; only my rats and pigeons supported *that* . . . (Skinner, 1967, p. 408).

Since Maslow became fond of his primate pals and Skinner felt affirmed by his rats and pigeons, it doesn't surprise us that they subsequently tried to help people live more fulfilling lives. But, what about a psychologist like Martin Seligman, who shocked laboratory dogs (much to the horror of animal-rights activists) into whining helplessness (Seligman & Maier, 1967)?

Seligman discovered that when dogs are placed in a situation where they cannot avoid shocks, they quickly give up trying to escape and, after the first few shocks, simply lie in a corner and whine—a phenomenon Seligman described as "learned helplessness." This research provided the foundation for a "learned-helplessness" theory of human depression (Seligman, 1974; Seligman, Abramson, Semmel, & Von Beyer, 1979; Seligman, Castellon, Cacciola, Schulman, Luborsky, Ollove, & Downing, 1988).

Whining dogs and a whining daughter. Would you predict that Seligman would become a leader in the positive psychology movement? You might wrap your mind around Skinner's or Maslow's "fondness" for their lab animals morphing into helping people, but what about a guy who shocks dogs? You might consider it quite a leap—from whining dogs to depressed people—but it gets even better. Seligman's real epiphany regarding what's important in psychology didn't originate with whining dogs, it began with a whining daughter. You'll probably recall how Seligman (Chapter 11) was working in the garden with his five-year-old daughter when he scolded her for dancing around and singing instead of pulling weeds. She responded:

> Daddy, do you remember my fifth birthday? From the time I was three to the time I was five, I was a whiner. I whined every day. When I turned five, I decided not to whine anymore. That was the hardest thing I've ever done. And if I can stop whining, you can stop being such a grouch. (Seligman & Csikszentmihalyi, 2000, pp. 5–6)

Seligman remembers this incident as an epiphany—when he first realized that rearing children involved much more than eliminating whining; it was about "identifying and nurturing their strongest qualities, what they own and are best at, and helping them find niches in which they can best live out these strengths" (2000, p. 6). And from there it was a small step to suggest that "psychology is not just the study of pathology, weakness, and damage; it is also the study of strength and virtue. Treatment is not just fixing what is broken; it is nurturing what is best" (2000, p. 7).

(4) PERSONALITY THEORIES VARY IN ASSIGNING PERSONAL AGENCY

Perhaps personality psychology's most enduring theoretical chasm has been the person-versus-situation assignment of agency. Compositionists, behaviorists, and trait theorists have traditionally argued that circumstances or chromosomes determine behavior; whereas ego analysts, humanists, and existentialists have insisted that personality is powered by an inner, *agentic self.* In our text we have mapped this debate as the *horizontal axis* of our grid. At the most personal level, how you view this topic strongly colors whether you perceive yourself to be a product of your surroundings or the pilot of your own destiny.

A centuries-old philosophical squabble has been declared a "draw." Although this philosophical "Continental Divide" has separated scholars for centuries, it was recently declared a "draw" by personality psychologists who devised an *interactional* solution: behavior is a function of *both* the person and the situation.

Such an interactional settlement is consistent with the zonal perspective of our text. By locating various personality theories at specific intersections of the vertical and horizontal axes, we can more easily see how theories differ in the emphasis they place upon either the *person* or the *situation.* It also becomes more clear that at any location—in any zone—a personality theory must account for *both* personal and circumstantial variables, and explain how they *interact* to produce observable behaviors.

(5) MOST PERSONALITY THEORIES HAVE A "CENTER OF GRAVITY" LOCATED IN ONE PARTICULAR *ZONE*

We have discovered that although some theories extend over several levels of the vertical axis or span more than one location on the horizontal axis, most have a "center of gravity" that tends to settle in a particular zone. Zones serve as "launch pads" from which we may move in various directions: back and forth horizontally, up or down vertically, or diagonally. Some psychologists are reluctant to admit that their particular theory does not apply across *all* zones of analysis. To acknowledge such limitations apparently wars with their expansive *holism*. However, since our vertical hierarchy is inherently *holistic* (e.g., ranging from peptides to people or from quarks to supernovas), and our horizontal axis represents a dynamic *interaction* of persons and situations, mapping a theory into its appropriate zone will not limit our ability to study issues either more microscopically or more abstractly.

Part–whole relationships. Our vertical axis is a visual metaphor of the part–whole relationships that exist within any system (e.g., cells, tissues, organs, and systems in the human body). However, whether we are working *within* a particular theory or *between* theories, intellectual traffic ought to move freely in both directions—from parts to wholes, and from wholes to parts. Thus a physician might choose to specialize in treating a single part (e.g., nephrologist, cardiologist, ophthalmologist) or prefer to work on the whole system (family practice). Similarly a personality psychologist might find herself working in a particular zone (e.g., as an eating-disorder specialist, or as a behaviorist primarily interested in the functional analysis of behavior), or she may be eclectically employing a variety of perspectives (e.g., behavioral, psychoanalytic, and transpersonal).

To recognize that a particular personality theory functions most efficiently in a particular zone need not be limiting. Understanding that part–whole relationships exist both within theories and between theories encourages information exchange across different levels of analysis. Although scientists frequently speak different languages, they usually share a common interest in the "Big Four" questions—at whatever level of analysis they conduct their investigations.

(6) PERSONALITY THEORIES ARE NOT "RIGHT" OR "WRONG" SO MUCH AS THEY ARE MORE OR LESS *USEFUL*

Jules Henri Poincare (1854–1912) was a brilliant French mathematician who lived during a time of great scientific upheaval—just prior to Einstein's proposal of the theory of relativity. For centuries, mathematical "truth" had been considered infallible—beyond doubt—but a fissure developed that threatened to become a chasm. Euclidian geometry had always been considered true beyond question—unshakable. That is, until a German by the name of Riemann came along and formulated another equally "true" geometry. During Pioncare's day, this seismic shift was changing the mathem geometry was "true."

Poincare concluded that one geometry cannot be more true than another—only more *convenient*. He understood that mathematicians—like other scientists—focused on some "facts" and ignored others. And, since there is a near-infinity of "facts" from which to choose, the mathematician must *select* which facts she will attend to. Here is where theory plays such a crucial role. Theory provides us the spectacles (or "blinders") through which we see our "facts." And once we put on our theoretical glasses, our vision becomes more focused and more limited in range. Yet focus we must; because, as one writer put it: "There is no more chance that an unselective observation of facts will produce science than there is that a monkey at a typewriter will produce the Lord's Prayer" (Pirsig, 1974, p. 264).

All theory builders, in all disciplines, try to select and interpret facts in ways that make sense of the surrounding world. Poincare believed that mathematical solutions were subliminally selected on the basis of the *harmony* that they brought to numbers—on the basis of geometric elegance. Such anecdotes from the history of science remind us that personality theories—like geometry—cannot be true or false, only more or less *convenient*, more or less *clarifying*. Just as mathematicians seek to devise solutions that create *harmony* among numbers, personality psychologists seek to formulate theories that promote harmony among psychological forces within the person, and harmony between the person and his or her circumstances.

(7) PEOPLE—INCLUDING FREUD—DO NOT LIVE BY SCIENCE ALONE

Although we concluded earlier that *validation* must shape our science, empiricism is hardly adequate for shaping our lives. The really big questions—the ones that guide our personal lives—seek answers that can never be found empirically: "Who am I?" "Why am I here?" "Is there life after death?" "Does God exist?" These are not the kinds of questions laboratory procedures can answer. In such quests *validation* has limits.

Here we do well to maintain a distinction between validating a theory and attempting to live a meaningful life. Science ought to trump faith, hope, or love when it comes to deciding which theories of personality best describe human functioning; but when it comes to figuring out "what it all means," empirical methodologies fail to satisfy. Learning how to live a "loving" life (defined in your own spiritual way) seems at least as important as discovering the right answers to empirical questions.

The study of human personality is incomplete if we exclude faith and spirituality. A *holistic* analysis attempts to address the entire array of human concerns—spirituality included. If we fail to include spirituality in our zones of analyses, we imply that the blood-and-guts paradigms of the lower levels are somehow more "real" than the existential, spiritual concerns of higher levels.

With 1.3 billion Muslims, 2.2 billion Christians, and 800 million Hindus believing in a higher power (to name but three of the most prominent world religions), we can safely estimate that at least two-thirds of the six billion people sharing our planet believe in some sort of divine presence. To ignore this reality while we claim to study human personality seems puzzlingly paradoxical—unless, of course, we take into account Feud's tremendous influence.

Religion as neurosis. Freud described himself as "profoundly irreligious" (Hale, 1971, pp. 105, 195). He was not merely indifferent to religion, he actively hated it—at least in the case of Roman Catholicism. When urged to flee the Nazis, Freud is said to have retorted that his "true enemy" was not the Nazis but "the Roman Catholic Church" (Laforgue, 1956, p. 344). Freud believed that "A personal God is, psychologically, nothing other than an exalted father" (1910, p. 123), adding that this "longing for the father constitutes the root of every form of religion" (1913, p. 148). In *The Future of an Illusion* (1927) Freud raises the question of whether humankind might someday be psychologically strong enough to get by without the comforting "illusions" of religious belief.

The roots of Freud's hostility to Christian religions were multiple and interwoven. His early negative experiences with his Catholic nanny probably formed the basis of his hatred toward Roman Catholicism. She taught him about her religion, including vivid accounts of souls in hell (Freud, 1954, p. 220). The anti-Semitism of 19th-century Vienna likely contributed to his contempt for "the Christian Aryan variety" of religion. However, his hatred of religious rituals included his own Jewish traditions—he witnessed the Jewish wedding of a friend with "fascinated horror" (Jones, 1953, p. 140). In the end, however, even Freud admitted that his own variety of religion (psychoanalysis) was not the entire picture. In a letter written July 24, 1921, he had this to say:

> I am not one of those who dismiss *a priori* the study of so-called occult psychic phenomena as unscientific, discreditable or even as dangerous. If I were at the beginning rather then at the end of a scientific career, as I am today, I might possibly choose just this field of research, in spite of all difficulties. (Freud, 1960, p. 334)
>
> Freud admits, however, that he would bring a lot of cynicism to such a study:
>
> . . . because I cannot rid myself of certain skeptical materialistic prejudices. . . . Thus I am utterly incapable of considering the "survival of the personality" after death even as a scientific possibility. . . . In consequence I believe it is better if I continue to confine myself to psychoanalysis. (Freud, 1960, p. 334)

Spirituality is part of a holistic portrait of personality. All the world's great religions insist upon *holistically* attending to the entire range of human functioning. In the Judeo–Christian tradition the apostle Paul put it this way:

> Now the body is not made up of one part but of many. If the foot should say "Because I am not a hand I do not belong to the body," it would not for that reason cease to be part of the body. And if the ear should say "Because I am not an eye, I do not belong to the body," it would not for that reason cease to be part of the body. . . . But in fact God has arranged the parts in the body, every one of them, just as he wanted them to be. (I Corinthians 12:14–18)

The Qur'an denounces those who fail to develop spiritual sensitivities along with their intellectual abilities:

> Although they have minds, yet they do not understand the true meaning of life. They have eyes but refuse to see Allah's power of creation and how the whole universe is given cohesion by all its interdependent parts. They have ears but do not listen attentively to His Message nor the sermons of the Prophet calling them to Allah. (Q 7:179)

And, if Freud was cynical about religion, the most literary of personality theorists, William Shakespeare, was not: "God shall be my hope, my stay, my guide, and lantern to my feet" (quoted in Toropov and Buckles, 1997, p. 239).

Our particular spiritual preferences are probably not as important as how we live our lives. Mahatma Gandhi said, "I consider myself a Hindu, Christian, Moslem, Jew, Buddhist, and Confucian" (quoted in Toropov and Buckles, 1997, p. 239).

Next, we will briefly look at some of the world's great spiritual traditions, to learn how they might be synthesized with theories of personality to achieve a more holistic portrait of the person. In the future, we might hope to see more interdisciplinary teams comprised of personality psychologists, cultural psychologists, comparative religion scholars, and anthropologists seriously seeking to understand the role of spirituality in the formation of personality. The following survey is intended as a catalyst to such efforts.

A BRIEF SURVEY OF THE WORLD'S GREAT RELIGIONS

As we noted, Freud's attitude, that faith (in anything other than psychoanalysis) was an infantile regression or a neurotic dependency, permeated personality theory for decades. However, sixty years ago, Gardner Murphy predicted: "In a future psychology of personality there will surely be a place for directly grappling with the questions of man's response to the cosmos. . . . of which he is a reflection" (1947, p. 919).

This "future" has arrived. Although previous generations of Freudians, behaviorists, and cognitive psychologists showed little interest in spirituality as it relates to personality, this is now changing—not only in psychology but in other disciplines as well. For example, medical professionals have become increasingly interested in the relationship of spirituality to healing and to health maintenance. Personality psychologists are beginning to seriously examine the role of spirituality in psychological experience. In his book titled *The Psychology of Ultimate Concerns: Motivation and Spirituality in Personality* (1999), personality psychologist Robert Emmons states that his research into the relationships among spirituality, personal goals, well-being, and human potential led him to conclude that he could no longer ignore spirituality:

> To do so, I believe, would have been the equivalent of committing academic malpractice. As a personality psychologist who professed a desire to understand the person in his or her entirety, I was guilty of ignoring what for many people is precisely what makes their life meaningful, valuable, and purposeful. (Emmons, 1999, p. 6)

As we explore some of the world's great spiritual traditions, we will discover that theology and personality psychology share much in common.

Theology as personality theories about God/gods

We suggested earlier that all practicing psychologists are personality theorists who ask questions about why people behave as they do. Now we widen the circle to include theologians as well, because they ask the Big Four questions about divinity: What are God's parts? What makes God go? How does God change? What makes God unique? Much as theologians might wish to privilege their discipline as "holy," theology is the very human enterprise of formulating (personality) theories about God/gods.

Perhaps much of the historical antipathy between theology and psychology derives not so much from Marx's and Freud's attempts to characterize religion as a form of neurotic dependency, but rather from the fact that psychologists and theologians share a similar quest: formulating personality theories to assist us in better understanding ourselves and others (including God/gods).

Transpersonal psychologists as theologians. As we learned in the previous chapter, transpersonal psychologists frequently "moonlight" as theologians, seeking to understand not only *human* nature, but *divine* nature as well. We typically find transpersonal psychologists pushing the quest for understanding to the edge of the envelope—seeking to include spirituality in their formulations. In the *Transpersonal Zone,* at the most expansive levels of analysis, the theoretical tunes are frequently *duets* of psychology and theology.

Which direction to God/gods?—mapping our quest for Higher Power(s). Figure 14.1 will assist us in navigating the *Transpersonal Zone.* As we examine the transpersonal and spiritual traditions of East and West, we will employ a map that is somewhat similar to the one we used for mapping theories of personality.

Figure 14.1 ■ *Mapping the Personality of God in the Transpersonal/Spiritual Zone*

Lower left quadrant: *Micro-merging Zone.* In the lower left quadrant, we encounter Buddhism, Neo-paganism, New Age syntheses, and the new physics, all of which share in common the view that divinity is found *everywhere*. As Pirsig put it: "The Buddha, the Godhead, resides quite as comfortably in the circuits of a digital computer or the gears of a cycle transmission as he does at the top of a mountain or in the petals of a flower" (1974, p. 26). In this zone, the faithful seek to recognize God/gods in *everything*. The urge to merge coincides with the realization that if God can reside in the gears of my bicycle, He or she can reside within me as well. If each spoke of my bike rim contains God/gods, then surely my head and my heart can also be permeated with Spirit.

Lower right quadrant: *Pantheistic Worship Zone.* In the lower right quadrant we find the nature-worship traditions, of which Shinto—the former state religion of Japan—is a prime example. Here we find a practical emphasis on cleanliness and purity alongside a reverence for nature. For example, there is actual worship of the sun goddess *Amaterusa*. Some New Age syntheses tilt toward worship of nature, while others take a more web-of-life, we-are-part-of-everything approach—straddling both bottom quadrants.

Upper right quadrant: *Monotheistic Worship Zone.* Here we find the transcendent, monotheistic one-God-above-all formulations of Judaism and Christianity. God is held in highest reverence and worshiped as the *Divine One* who created and sustains the universe. Other variants of this include the *Higher Power* of Alcoholics Anonymous' and African and Native American versions of the *Great Spirit*. What characterizes these theologies is their emphasis on a God who is "out there," "above all," and toward whom our appropriate response is *worship*.

Upper left quadrant: *Macro-merging Zone.* In this quadrant we encounter Islam's version of monotheism ("There is no God but Allah"), which holds *Allah* in highest reverence while at the same time encouraging the faithful to seek unity with Allah ("I am nothing separate from or other than the Absolute"). Sufism has been referred to as the "mystical core" of Islam, and Sufis not only *worship*, but seek to lose their personal identities in *merging* with *Allah*:

> Thou didst contrive this "I" and "we" in order that
> Thou mightest play the game of worship with Thyself,
> That all "I's" and "thous" should become one soul
> and at last be submerged in the Beloved. (Arasteh, 1972, p. 146)

Hindus also share a similar "worship-and-merge" orientation in which believers are taught that clinging to one's own self-identity is like assuming an alias that makes union with *Brahman* (the single transcendent reality) impossible. Hindus are *both* monotheistic *and* polytheistic, worshiping a "trinity" of Gods (Brahma, Vishnu, and Shiva) as well as a profusion of lesser gods who are viewed as user-friendly manifestations of the *Ultimate God*. In this way, Hindus blend Western monotheism with Eastern mystical merging. In the words of Ramana Maharishi: "Guru, God, and Self are one" (Toropov and Buckles, 1997, p. 238).

In short, although it is far beyond the scope of our text to examine each of these spiritual traditions in depth, it appears that theology—like personality psychology—involves theory building. Since people seek God/gods in terms of their own psychological understandings, it should not surprise us to find parallels between personality theories and theology paradigms. Next, we will examine each *Zone* more closely.

Seeking Spirituality in the *Micro-merging* and *Pantheistic Zones*

For purposes of our current discussion, we will consider the two bottom quadrants together, referring to them as the *Micro-merging* and *Pantheistic Worship Zones*.

Physicists—the new high priests of the nature gods. The mythic gods and goddesses of the ancient Greeks were gradually replaced by observation-based science. Supernatural explanations were deposed by scientific theories that focused on the role of bacteria and germs, in place of gods or demons, in causing illness. However, the gains in scientific precision were frequently accompanied by losses in spiritual meaning. Whereas the ancient Greeks traveled in the company of their gods as they sailed the oceans, tilled the soil, danced, or made love, the postmodern person frequently feels as if she is traveling alone in a world that is scientifically sensible but spiritually sterile.

Although empiricism has proven a worthy ally in the laboratory, it has been a poor traveling companion for those seeking existential meaning or spiritual significance. The recent resuscitation of nature gods might be fueled by an existential emptiness that science fails to fill. At a time when respect for organized religion is waning, the new "high priests" of physics use metaphors that promise seekers both scientific respectability and spiritual companionship. Likewise, transpersonal theories of psychology appear to have flourished in the aftermath of the Freudian and Skinnerian storms that obliterated any traces of spirituality on the beaches of American psychology.

Gaia—the living Earth. The idea of a living Earth is an ancient allegory; however, the term "Mother" Earth took on new meaning when NASA scientists made it possible for us to view our "Mother" from outer space, perceiving her as the swirling blue-and-white beauty that she is.

When NASA scientists hired British biochemist and inventor James Lovelock to assist in designing measures to detect life, Lovelock and his colleagues proposed the **Gaia** (GAY uh) **hypothesis:** *the view that earth functions as a "living organism" that self-regulates conditions of land, water, and atmosphere in order to maintain an environment favorable to life.* Gaia theory, named after the ancient Greek goddess of the Earth, provides an alternative to the classical view that Earth is a dead planet made up of inanimate rocks, oceans, and an atmosphere. Instead, Earth is seen as "a real system, comprising all of life and all of its environment tightly coupled so as to form a self-regulating entity" (Lovelock, 1991, p. 12).

"Now you see them, now you don't"—fleeting gods of the Gaia. It is but a small step from perceiving a "living" Earth to worshiping a panoply of nature-based gods. However, these gods of the Gaia differ substantially from Allah or Yahweh—the mighty monotheistic God whose portrait emerges from the pages of the Qur'an or the Torah. In sharp contrast to the eternal, unchanging God of the great monotheistic religions, the new physics-based gods can be glimpsed only briefly as they manifest themselves in a "cosmic dance of temporary realities." These gods appear ephemeral and evanescent, existing for nanoseconds in forms that are difficult to measure. Nevertheless, Zohar and Marshall insist that the "particles and waves that are manifest, though impermanent, are not 'illusions' as in Hindu philosophy. In quantum physics, the emphasis is on temporary and shifting reality rather than on unreality" (Zohar & Marshall, 1994, p. 237).

In contrast to the omnipotent God/gods of the world's great religions, the new gods of quantum physics are so much a part of *Gaia*—as are we—that God appears to partially depend on us in order to reach his or her fullest development. In Zohar and Marshall's words: "We are the instruments of His own unfolding potential" (1994, p. 241).

Nature gods. The gods of nature emerge in an infinite variety of shapes and sizes, ranging from subatomic quarks and invisible benzene rings to poppy seeds, petunia blossoms, and Milky Way–sized galaxies. Among traditional religions, **Shinto,** *a nature-focused indigenous religion of Japan,* provides a clear illustration of nature-based faith. Shinto emphasizes the harmony of natural beauty with a variety of rituals celebrating purity, clarity, and contact with nature. Contemporary Shinto practice continues to emphasize traditions and rituals of the natural world in place of theological doctrines.

Reverence for nature's cycles and the celebration of seasonal changes also characterize **Neo-paganism,** *which holds all nature in reverence, and honors earth as "Mother."* Seasonal and nature observances have traditionally been an important part of nature worship, and contemporary Neo-Pagan groups continue to celebrate such natural events as the *winter solstice* (shortest day), *spring equinox* (when day and night are of equal length), *summer solstice* (longest day), *fall equinox* (the second calender-point of equality between day and night), as well as various other nature-based events.

Summary of the nature gods. The recent flourishing of *Gaia* gods and web-of-life divinities shares much in common with the traditional nature-based rituals of Shinto and the seasonal celebrations of Neo-Paganism. These recent *Gaia* portraits are being painted with the brush of quantum physics, thus endowing *Gaia* with a level of scientific respectability not apparent in Shinto or Neo-Pagan formulations.

Seeking Spirituality in the *Monotheistic Worship Zone*

Next, we will consider what kind of God or gods appear most consistent with the worship traditions of the upper right quadrant. We discover that Moses and Muhammad are the Watsons and Skinners of Jewish and Islamic theology. Within these great monotheistic religious traditions, *behavior* matters most.

Yahweh—behavioristic God of the Torah. Three of the five books of the Torah (Leviticus, Numbers, and Deuteronomy) could be described as "behavior-mod" manuals, providing detailed *behavioral contingencies* for relating to Yahweh. Nothing is left to chance. It doesn't matter how you *feel,* or what your *motives* might be—this is biblical behaviorism at its best. In the concluding chapters of Deuteronomy, we find Moses, the aged leader of Israel, listing the blessings for obedience and the curses

"It's called monotheism, but it looks like downsizing to me."

"Are you sure you don't want to add something about smoking?"

for disobedience, much as a contemporary behaviorist might list the reinforcing or punishing contingencies of a token economy. And, like all good behaviorists, Moses tells the people, "It's up to you":

> See, I set before you today life and prosperity, death and destruction. For I command you today to love the Lord your God, to walk in his ways, and to keep his commands, decrees and laws; then you will live and increase, and the Lord your God will bless you . . . . But if your heart turns away and you are not obedient, and if you are drawn away to bow down to other gods and worship them, I declare to you this day that you will certainly be destroyed. . . . Now choose life, so that you and your children may live and that you may love the Lord your God, listen to his voice, and hold fast to him. (Deuteronomy 30: 15–17, 19, 20)

Jesus Christ—psychoanalyst/humanist/existentialist. In the narratives of the life of Jesus Christ, as recorded in the first four books of the Christian New Testament (known as the **Gospels**—*literally translated, "good news"*), we find a shift from the *behaviorism* of the Torah and the Qur'an toward the *inner life*. Behavior is no longer the end-all of spiritual experience—*motives* now trump behavior. Jesus shifts attention to the inner life much as Freud focused on motives lurking below the surface of consciousness. Appearing as a humanist or existentialist, Jesus emphasizes *meaningful living* over mere behavioristic traditions. In one of the clearest illustrations regarding primacy of the inner life, Luke relates the following story:

> As he looked up, Jesus saw the rich putting their gifts into the temple treasury. He also saw a poor widow put in two very small copper coins. "I tell you the truth," he said, "this poor widow has put in more than all the others. All these people gave their gifts out of their wealth; but she out of her poverty put in all she had to live on." (Luke 21:1–4, NIV)

Here we find Jesus analyzing the motives beneath the behavioral surface, much as Freud and his followers subsequently did. Jesus appeared to function more as a psychoanalyst than as a behaviorist. His consistent emphasis was on inner dynamics.

We can see in Figure 14.1 that as we move from Yahweh and Allah toward Jesus, and from there to the Holy Spirit, there occurs a progressive shift to the left (merging-with-God) side of our map. Shifting from the behavioral emphasis of Torah-based Judaic traditions to the more mystical religions, we find ourselves placing more emphasis on subjective experience. This is where Eastern and Western spiritual paradigms differ most profoundly. The great meditative traditions of the East (e.g., Hinduism, Buddhism, and Sufism) seek to *merge* with God, while the monotheistic Judeo–Christian traditions *worship* a God *out there*.

This boundary between persons and God remains distinct within Islamic and Judaic theology. Allah and Yahweh are clearly "out there," and believers follow carefully delineated *behavioral* pathways of obedience and submission (e.g., the word *Islam* translates as "submission" to God).

Holy Spirit—Christian Mysticism. Next, moving even closer to the center of our map, we consider the most mystical member of the Christian trinity—the *Holy Spirit*. Christian theology portrays a *family* of God operating at three different levels: Yahweh appears as a behaviorist, Jesus reminds us of psychoanalysis, and the Holy Spirit appears much more mystical.

Pentecostal hurricane blows into town. The Christian church of the New Testament emerged in the aftermath of a massive mystical experience:

When the day of Pentecost came, they were all together in one place. Suddenly a sound like the blowing of a violent wind came from heaven and filled the whole house where they were sitting. They saw what seemed to be tongues of fire that separated and came to rest on each of them. All of them were filled with the Holy Spirit. (Acts 2:1–4)

Turning inward. After the Holy Spirit infused the believers with his/her presence on the day of Pentecost, Christian history took a sharp left turn—inward—focusing on subjective spiritual experience. Never before had God been housed in imperfect human bodies. Jesus—believed by Christians to be the Incarnation of God—was believed never to have sinned; by contrast, at Pentecost the Holy Spirit merged with less-than-perfect human beings. This unprecedented event was apparently verified by "tongues of fire" (Acts 2:3) that hovered, halo-like, over their heads.

Still, even amid such mass mysticism, we notice that the *direction of infusion* is from *outside*. For the first time in Judeo-Christian history, the "out-there/up-there" God descends to infuse the believers with his/her Holy Spirit. Here is incarnation—not in the single person of Jesus Christ, but on an unprecedented mass scale. Nevertheless, the *Divine Source* is still *out there!*

This is probably the single most important psychological distinction between Judeo-Christian styles of worship and Eastern mystical religions. Jews and Christians worship a *transcendent* God who resides "out there" or "up there"—never originating from within. God is always "out there." This contrasts with Eastern mystics who frequently search for God *within*. Next, we will analyze several Eastern mystical traditions, and conclude by offering an overview of transpersonal theories of psychology, analyzing how they relate to the various faiths we have explored.

Seeking Spirituality in the *Macro-merging Zone*

Looking to the left, in the *Macro-merging Zone,* we find much in the Islamic faith that is in fundamental agreement with the Judeo-Christian view of God. This is hardly surprising, since Muslims, Jews, and Christians all consider themselves descended from Abraham, "Father of the Faithful." Both Muslim and Jewish traditions emphasize *One God,* who requires moral *behavior,* not merely worship or devotion. The term **Muslim** means *one who submits,* and the Islamic faith teaches specific behavioral and social codes of conduct. Like Jewish rituals, Muslim worship emphasizes *behavior*. Prayer, for example, is not merely a meditative, subjective experience; it involves carefully prescribed *behaviors*. Muslims pray five times a day—at dawn, noon, afternoon, evening, and nightfall—and they ceremonially wash their faces, hands, and feet before praying. Prayers include the reciting of phrases of praise as well as passages from the Qur'an. Worship requires specific behaviors such as bowing from the hips and kneeling with one's face to the ground. For both Jews and Muslims, worship is behaviorally based, with less emphasis on the contemplative or meditative aspects. Like the God they worship, the rituals and ceremonies are "out there." How you "feel" inside is not of primary importance, *behavior* is the bottom line.

In summary, it doesn't seem like an exaggeration to say that both the Torah and Qur'an function somewhat as religious behavior-mod manuals. Both endorse the idea that God grants worldly success to faithful worshipers. However, a major difference is that Muslims seek to *merge* with Allah as the ultimate goal of their worship.

Taoism: Seeking existential simplicity and immortality. Taoism, literally, means *the effortless path*. Taoism is native to China, where it gained in popularity around 500 B.C.E., partly as a reaction against Confucianism's emphasis on correct relationships within social hierarchies. By contrast, Taoism emphasized a *meditative life in harmony with the patterns of nature*. It wasn't until the 100s B.C.E. that Taoism began to develop as an organized religion.

Taoism spans nearly all the zones of our grid from physics to existentialism. Taoists first seek harmony with nature rather than through social relations. This contrasts sharply with Confucianism, which seeks to create an ideal society through ceremony, duty, public service, and other social relationships. Like the constructivists, humanists, and existentialists of the *Insight Zone,* Taoists focus more on individual development than on group relations. The Taoist sensitivity to nature has had a great influence on Chinese art and literature. Like the existentialists, Taoists have addressed problems of meaning, suffering, evil, and death—issues largely ignored by Confucianism.

Tao includes a concise scripture that plants both feet on the ground. The farmer is the quintessential Taoist, seeking to live in harmony with the seasonal patterns of nature in order to experience the power of the *Tao*. Taoist practice is derived from the **Tao Te Ching** *(literally: Ching = text, Te = power/integrity, Tao = path)*, one of the world's shortest but most influential religious texts. In less than five thousand words, this handbook of *power for the pathway* outlines the principles of life with brevity:

> As to dwelling, live near the ground.
> As to thinking, hold to that which is simple.
> As to conflict, pursue fairness and generosity.
> As to governance, do not attempt control.
> As to work, do that which you like doing.
> As to family life, be fully present.
> (from the *Tao Te Ching,* quoted in Toropov and Buckles, 1997, p. 177)

Summary of Taoism. Taoism is both a philosophy and a religion. As a *philosophy,* Taoism pursues personal happiness and fulfillment, much as humanists and existentialists seek self-actualization and meaning. As a *religion,* Taoism promises immortality to those who align themselves with the power of the Tao. Taoism is a religion rich in ceremonies, rituals, and practices designed to facilitate happiness and to acquire immortality. In addition to connecting with a multiplicity of gods, ancestors, and spirits, Taoists utilize magic, meditation, breath control, special diets, astrology, and even witchcraft as they seek serenity and joy in the present and for eternity. Taoists view life as an evolving spiritual journey in which, as one becomes increasingly in synch with the rhythms of the universe, the power of *te* flows freely into one's life, permitting unity with the mystical. Then, like a river flowing to the sea, one's life follows certain ordained routes while gradually accessing the power of *te* to carve out new channels as well.

So far, we have discovered that Jews, Christians, and Muslims worship *One God* out there; Confucianists seek *harmony in personal relationships;* and Taoists seek to *dance to the rhythm of the universe.* By contrast we will now find that Hindus and Buddhists seek God/gods *within.*

Hinduism and Buddhism—something for everyone. Hinduism is a philosophical and religious system so vast and all-encompassing that most Western scholars—typically rigorous and reductionist—have a difficult time wrapping their minds around it. **Hindu** *means Indian, and encompasses most (but not all) of the diverse religious traditions and practices of India.* Hinduism cannot be traced to a single person or god, so believers regard it as having existed forever. We might wonder how a religion without a charismatic founder or distinctly defined doctrines could attract some 800 million followers. Perhaps the answer lies in recognizing that Hinduism utilizes Piaget's twin developmental processes *(assimilation* and *accommodation)* on a massive scale. The earliest records of Hinduism indicate that it followed an "inclusive" approach, assimilating and accommodating competing cultural practices and religious creeds. Today, Hinduism still endeavors to reconcile tensions and differences among the countless sects that comprise its soul.

Mysticism—the epoxy of Hinduism. *Personal mysticism* is the epoxy that allows Hinduism to accommodate so many different sects without exploding in all directions. Hindus value personal experience over corporate cohesiveness, and believers seek to *experience* the Transcendent Absolute in an *Eastern, mystical* manner. Hinduism has somehow managed to synthesize loosely connected religious beliefs with pragmatic practices like yoga, meditation, and chanting to facilitate *personal* spiritual growth. Though surrounded by a glut of gods, each Hindu worshiper seeks union with the Ultimate in his or her own unique way, utilizing whichever gods or techniques prove personally useful. Hinduism does not yield to the sort of straightforward analyses we have come to expect from psychologists and other scientists. Instead, we might imagine the following dialog:

Westerner Spiritual Seeker: "So, do you worship One God or a whole bunch of gods?"

Hindu: "That's correct!"

Westerner: "Look, this is important—please don't play mind games with me! How many gods do you worship, One or many?"

Hindu: "How many do you want?"

Westerner: "It sounds to me like you're straddling the fence!"

Hindu: "And it sounds to me like you're trying to define the Brahman, the Ultimate, the Eternal in your own terms."

Westerner: "How can you worship something or someone you can't define?"

Hindu: "How can *you* worship Someone you *can* describe?"

Westerner: "This is going nowhere."

Hindu: "And everywhere."

Westerner: (frustrated) "I give up!"

Hindu: "Now, my friend, you've taken the first step. No *description* of Brahman is possible, but *direct experience* is."

Westerner: "Where do I go from here?"

Hindu: "Where do you want to go?"

■ ■ ■

One self or many? Since the question regarding "One God or many?" remained unresolved by our imaginary dialogue, we might be surprised to find that with respect to humans, the issue of "one self or many selves" is clearly decided. In Hindu thought, there exists *no separate personal self.* The (Western) perception of oneself as an independent or separate self is seen as a serious spiritual delusion, making unity with *Atman* (the ultimate, universal Self) much more difficult, if not impossible. Their sacred writings remind Hindu believers that clinging to one's own separate identity makes recognition of the true Self impossible. Carl Jung, Harry Stack Sullivan, and contemporary transpersonal psychologists also view the self in a broad, beyond-the-skin, way. More about this shortly.

Reincarnation and karma. Understanding **reincarnation,** *or the coming back into the flesh,* is basic to understanding Hinduism, Buddhism, and other religions originating in India. According to these faiths, life is a continuous cycle of death and rebirth *(reincarnation).* Such life–death–rebirth cycles follow the behavioristic **law of karma:** *a person's situation in life results from his or her karma (deeds) in previous lives.* The ultimate goal—after a series of higher and higher reincarnations—is to completely escape the cycle of death and reincarnation, and to *merge* with the Ultimate Self of the universe.

God everywhere and in everything. Hindus believe that *Brahman* is present everywhere. The ultimate goal for a Hindu is to escape the cycle of death and reincarnation and to merge with the Absolute. In the meantime, however, *everything* encountered along the way is seen as sacred. This might easily be misunderstood by a Westerner watching a Hindu chanting in front of a statue or offering incense or flowers to this figure. For the devoted Hindu, however, this would not be "idolatry," rather it would be a way of honoring a particular manifestation of the Absolute One.

In summary, although Hinduism provides believers a "Big Three" of deities somewhat similar to the Trinity worshiped by Christians, this is supplemented by a profusion of lesser deities, providing a variety of entry points into the faith, allowing each person to find his or her own way to ultimate union with Brahman.

Hinduism's cornucopia of gods, gurus, ceremonies, and celebrations insures that believers will encounter no shortage of spiritual supplies on their journey toward

Brahman. Even at the "yoga bar," the faithful are allowed to choose the flavors best suited to speed spiritual growth. Unlike Westerners, who study yoga mostly for health reasons, Hindus practice **yoga** *(discipline)* to facilitate spiritual growth. Under the guidance of a **guru** *(teacher)*, **students** *(yogis or yogins)* are taught that the soul is completely separate from the rest of the person. It is believed that this understanding will enable the person's soul to gain release *(moksha)* from the cycle of death and reincarnation.

Summary of Hinduism. A spiritual Baskin Robbins. Hinduism greets the Western spiritual seeker with a dizzying array of deities and offers countless ways to worship. For Western minds accustomed to monotheistic or trinitarian theologies, Hinduism appears "over-the-top" polytheistic. Yet, in fairness, it must be emphasized that the Hindu panoply of lesser gods is viewed by devout Hindus as the many-faceted face of the *One Absolute Brahman.* Like a large, glittering diamond, each facet reflects a unique portion of the light spectrum while still remaining part of the whole jewel.

I am reminded of the first time I encountered a Baskin Robbins ice cream shop. Having previously tasted ice cream only as vanilla, chocolate, strawberry, or butter pecan, I wasn't certain what to make of "moosetracks," "cookie dough," "bubble gum," or "kiwi." Eventually, however, I came to realize that it's all just ice cream. Sure, the flavors ranged from delicious or delightful to insipid or yucky, but in the end it was all ice cream. Similarly, to Westerners who are accustomed to the vanilla–chocolate–strawberry stability of the Trinity, or the butter–pecan reliability of Yahweh or Allah, the spiritual choices of Hinduism appear overwhelming—until, that is, one realizes it's all *Brahman.*

A final word. We will conclude by returning to our earlier "dialogue" regarding Hindu worship:

Western seeker: "Hey! I've got a plane to catch—no more time for mind games. So, just give it to me straight, do you guys worship *One* God or *many*?"

Hindu: "You are right!"

Westerner: (barely audibly—as a frustrated whisper) "It's no use! I'll never figure this out."

Hindu: "Ah, finally, he's getting it."

▦ ▦ ▦

Buddhism—a peace-loving cousin. Among world religions, Buddhism is unique in having successfully translated its teaching of love and transcendent purpose into a large-scale system of pacifism and nonviolence. Acts of hatred and bloodshed between Muslims and Hindus have troubled India for centuries, and the historical face of Christianity is blemished with the pockmarks of crusades, inquisitions, and burnings at the stake. Indeed, in our present time, religion has frequently been associated with suicidal martyrs in the Middle East or car bombs in Northern Ireland rather than with loving kindness peacefully practiced. There has never been a war or military campaign launched in the name of Buddha, and there likely never will be.

We will briefly survey the ingredients of this gentle system. Like Hinduism, the Buddhist religion includes a wide assortment of techniques and beliefs; however, all

Buddhists share a common faith in what has been described as the **three jewels:** *faith in (1) Buddha; (2) dharma—the teachings of the Buddha; and (3) sangha—the religious community he founded.*

The four noble truths and the eightfold pathway. The primary spiritual motive in Buddhism—as in Hinduism—is to escape the painful cycle of death and reincarnation. In order to assist his followers in making their "escape," the Buddha taught the **Four Noble Truths:** *(1) life is suffering; (2) suffering is caused by craving and attachment; (3) craving and attachment can be overcome; (4) the route to transcendence follows an eight-lane highway.* This is called the **Eightfold Pathway:** *(1) gaining knowledge of the truth; (2) resisting evil; (3) saying nothing to hurt others; (4) respecting life and property; (5) working at a job that does not injure others; (6) striving to keep one's mind free of evil; (7) controlling one's feelings; and (8) practicing proper concentration.*

Seeking Nirvana (not the rock band!). Just as Hindus seek union with Brahman, Buddhists seek **Nirvana,** *a state of perfect peace and blessedness that enables the believer to escape the painful cycles of death and rebirth.* By discovering a middle pathway between self-denial and self-indulgence, the Buddha, himself, entered *Nirvana,* and subsequently devoted his life to assisting others in achieving this balanced enlightenment.

Beyond the self. In much the same way that Hindus view the *independent self* as a fiction of Western imagination, Buddhists insist that the *abiding self* is a delusion. Not only is this true of the *self,* it extends to all reality. The Buddha taught that *any* conception that divides one phenomenon from another—e.g., a blade of grass from a meditating woman—is an illusion. Nothing exists independently or permanently. According to the Buddha, when we deeply understand a blade of grass (or a snowflake), we come to realize that it is merely a transitory process of nature, as is the meditating woman. Drawing distinctions based on imagined separateness is, according to Buddhists, a form of hallucination.

Divinity and self become indistinguishable. If one accepts the Buddha's "no-distinctions-possible" view of reality, it follows with hardly a spiritual hiccup that distinctions between one's own *self* (an illusory entity) and *Brahman* (undefinable in any religious tradition) melt into oceanic oneness. The Buddha described *Nirvana* as a place where "one no longer cherishes the dualisms of discrimination; where there is no more thirst nor grasping; where there is no more attachment to external things" (quoted in Toropov & Buckles, 1997, p. 142).

This is Eastern mysticism of a potent variety. The transcendent *Absolute* and the illusory *self* merge in a mystical amalgam that dissolves even Creator–creature dualisms. With divine–human distinctions no longer discernable, "worship" of the Judeo–Christian variety appears obsolete. A number of contemporary transpersonalists share a similar "mystical oneness" perspective in common with ancient Eastern mystics. With divine–human boundaries thus dissolved, there remains only a mystical ocean in which humans and God/gods relate as coevolutionary partners: "The human species has a special coevolutionary capacity and responsibility," contends Falk (1992, p. 36). This leads Zohar and Marshall to muse that "Perhaps the 'Second Coming' for which so many people have waited is nothing else but this—the realization that *we* are that 'coming.' *We* are the messiah. The job of transforming and saving the world is down to us" (1994, p. 243).

Do such statements reflect devotion or blasphemy? Are they worshipful or sacreligious? Much depends on perspective (Eastern or Western), but they are logically consonant with the mystical dissolving of divine–human boundaries. The common denominator in both Eastern and Western religions appears to be a longing, on the part of the devout believer, to escape mortality by participating in something larger than oneself. "Merging" with divinity functions to reassure the faithful that this life isn't the end of one's *self.*

Summary of Buddhism. Earlier, we compared Hinduism to a spiritual Baskin Robbins—rich in a diversity of "flavors." Buddhism's bounty is manifested more in its diverse array of techniques than in its assembly of gods. Although Buddhists recognize many of the Hindu gods, the Buddha taught that these gods did not have authority over daily human life, but were subject to the same universal laws that govern human beings. Therefore, one should not seek divine intervention, but focus, instead, on the singleminded pursuit of individual spirituality. Thus, the main thrust of Buddhism over the centuries has not been the elaboration of new deities, but the development and refinement of *techniques* such as meditation, and *moral precepts* such as the Four Noble Truths or the Eightfold Pathway. This has given followers many choices and options—but primarily in the arena of spiritual self-improvement rather than in finding new gods.

SYNTHESIZING PERSONALITY PSYCHOLOGY AND SPIRITUALITY

In previous chapters we studied most of the major theories of personality, and now we have "surfed" most of the world's great religions as well. We are now in a position to understand how transpersonal psychologists integrate personality psychology and spirituality. Since this area is so broad, we will mainly *illustrate* the process of integration, rather than examine the various syntheses in detail.

What Are the Parts?

As we learned in the previous chapter, Jung's *collective unconscious* is a *transpersonal* cornucopia, containing the heritage of humankind's biological, psychological, and spiritual evolution. It is but a small step from Jung's transpersonal psycho-spirituality to Eastern mysticism. Carl Jung first formulated a *self* that appeared Freud-friendly, within-the-skin, and "Western." However, by making the *collective unconsciousness* (which spanned the past, present, and future) the cornerstone of his theory, Jung veered sharply toward the East, leaving empiricism to ride off into the (Western) sunset. The Jungian *self* no longer functioned in a Western way—as a psychological "gyroscope"—stabilizing the personality from a central core.

Jung shaped the *self* into an Eastern entity that appeared more like Brahman or the Void than a personality construct. He even came to spell *Self* with an upper-case "S," in much the same way that monotheists show reverence by using the upper-case "G" when referring to God. Jung believed that if he were at one with the Self, he could have a knowledge of everything; including events of pre-history as well as life on other planets. He believed this oneness with the Self would enable him to speak sanskrit or read cuneiform.

Eastern versus Western views of the self. We have learned that most Eastern thinkers and many transpersonal psychologists see the self *not* as a central, anchoring construct, but as a spiritual entity that seeks to merge with Spirit. Such a *Self*—the kind described by Jung—is thought to possess godlike qualities of transcendence: "The knowing Self is not born; It does not die. It has not sprung from anything; nothing has sprung from It. Birthless, eternal, everlasting, and ancient, It is not killed when the body is killed" [(*Katha Upanishad*, I:ii, 18) quoted in Fadiman & Frager, 2002, p. 488].

By contrast, most Western psychologists see *self* as the center of the person. *Self* is the central construct in *self-actualizing* theories such as those of Rogers and Maslow, but it is also an indispensable core in most other Western theories of personality. Trait theories and psychoanalysis are inconceivable without some sort of psychological center in the form of a self or an ego.

For the most part, transpersonal psychologists tend not to wrangle about which view of the self is right and which is wrong. Instead, in the Eastern style of the great Zen masters, they stimulate their students to find their own unique pathways. Attempting to persuade through personal experiences, poetry, metaphor, and a wide variety of non-empirically validated anecdotes, they tend to be welcoming more than discriminating in their approach to knowing.

What Makes a Transpersonal Person Go? What Makes a Transpersonal Person Grow?

In transpersonal theories of personality, Eastern philosophies and religions blend with Western thought in such seamless ways that it is difficult to separate motivational and maturational constructs. However, since *yoga* and *Zen* are frequently seen by Westerners as the superhighways to transcendental growth, we will briefly consider them both, especially noting the differences between these formulations and Western motivational constructs such as instincts, drives, reinforcers, or punishers. Nonetheless, in spite of vast differences, we will also notice some similarities to Western constructs—especially in the higher-level humanistic constructs such as self-actualization and peak experiences.

Yoga—turning inward for enlightenment. The word **yoga** means *to join* or *to unite*. Self-realization, the ultimate goal of all yoga practice, is achieved by turning consciousness inward, where it can be united with its source, the Self. Instead of frantically seeking pleasure in external entertainments, outward accomplishments, or sensual experiences, the ideal of yoga is to discover joy at its source—the Self within. Yoga assists the practitioner in developing a **pure mind**—*a mind without attachments, a mind unencumbered by sensual pursuits or distracted by the "noise" of intellectual games.* yoga techniques are designed to still the mind and calm the body so that awareness of Self becomes possible.

A parable illustrates this with the experience of a musk deer, whose musk glands become active during mating season. A young deer becomes bewitched by the tantalizing scent of musk, and frantically runs through the forest, becoming entangled in underbrush or even plunging over a cliff in search of the source—failing to realize it is within itself.

Numerous schools of Yoga. Given the diversity of Hindu religious beliefs, it is hardly surprising that several major schools of yoga emerged in India. *Janana-yoga* summons the powers of the mind through meditation, *bhakti-yoga* encourages love toward God, *karma-yoga* emphasizes service to others, and *raja-yoga* combines all three into a single discipline assisting the practitioner to develop control over the body. Some *yogis* are able to develop exceptional control over such functions as metabolism and blood flow through *hatha-yoga,* which has become popular in the West.

A *guru* guides the student through eight stages on the journey toward spiritual liberation: (1) disciplined behavior, (2) positive values, (3) body postures, (4) breath control, (5) control of the senses, (6) focusing of the mind on a chosen object, (7) meditation, and (8) *samadhi,* which is a stage of mental concentration enabling the yogi to understand that his or her soul is pure, free, and empty of all content. Having completed all eight stages, the student achieves **kaivalya,** *a condition in which the soul is totally isolated from the body and from all other souls.*

Two major schools of Zen—sitting or focusing. Zen *is an East Asian form of Buddhism practiced primarily in Japan, which has also become popular in the United States. Zen* comes from the Sanskrit word meaning "meditation," and there are two major styles of Zen: simply sitting with concentrated awareness, or focusing on a **koan,** *a baffling riddle or question that cannot be solved by mere logic or thinking.*

Meditation on a koan. The *koan* is designed to make the Zen student realize the limitations of logic and linear thinking. Zen masters are convinced that words can never express ultimate reality, so *koans* are designed to stop the thought process and prepare the student for a mystical, nonverbal *satori* experience of enlightenment. One of the most famous *koans* ("You can make the sound of two hands clapping. Now what is the sound of one hand?") illustrates how a *koan* confronts the Zen student with the limitations of language, logic, and linear thinking. The goal of Zen is *enlightenment.* However, this is not the *intellectual* understanding familiar to Western minds who are more interested in logical comprehension, but the experience of **satori,** *a state of spiritual enlightenment. Satori* enlightenment is not some mystical, other-worldly transcendence but a clearer vision of one's own situation and inner reality. Thus, when Zen master Po-chang was asked to define Zen, he said: "When hungry eat, when tired sleep" (quoted in Capra, 1991, p. 124).

> Similarly, when a monk told Joshu: "I have just entered the monastery. Please teach me."
> Joshu asked: "Have you eaten your rice porridge?"
> The monk replied: "I have eaten."
> Joshu said: "Then you had better wash your bowl." (Reps, 1989, p. 96)

"Just sitting." Alternatively, in place of focusing on a *koan,* the meditator seeks to achieve a state of concentrated awareness that is neither relaxed nor tense but totally alert. The meditator observes thoughts without getting entangled in them, much as one might watch traffic passing by on the street. Still, meditation and mindfulness go together, and Zen students are instructed to remain in the moment:

> You've got to practice meditation when you walk, stand, lie down, sit, and work, while washing your hands, washing the dishes, sweeping the floor, drinking tea, talking to friends, or whatever you are doing. . . . When you are washing the dishes, washing dishes must be the most important thing in your life. (Hanh, 1976, pp. 3–4)

This attitude of alert awareness and sensitivity to one's inner life, combined with less reliance on logic and linear reasoning, provide the conditions for *satori.* This leads quite naturally to questions regarding unique identity. If one achieves a state of *satori*, does self become merged with the oceanic cosmos, or am I still me?

What Makes a Transpersonal Person Unique?

Uniqueness in transpersonal theories invariably involves the *self*. The wide array of formulations is impossible to discuss thoroughly, so we will illustrate with a brief discussion of the Sufi teachings on the topic.

Self in Sufi teachings. **Sufism** *has been described as the mystical core of Islam, emphasizing self-knowledge as the pathway to knowledge of God.* In Sufi teachings there are two selves: self within society and the true self. The goal of Sufi experience is to shift people's identity from the social self to the true self, to help people accept themselves as they are (how they speak, how they walk, how they eat, and so forth). Thus, in the Sufi tradition, uniqueness would be highly valued if it evolved from the *true self* within and not primarily from external social forces. This reminds us of Rogers's emphasis on *congruence* with one's organismic valuing process instead of compliance with external *conditions of worth*.

Summary of Transpersonal/Spiritual Theories

The eminent Bible translator, J. B. Phillips, wrote a book entitled *Your God is Too Small* (1961), in which he sketched a number of portraits of God ranging from Pale Galilean or Parental Hangover to Resident Policeman or Grand Old Man. He stated that "It is obviously impossible for an adult to worship the conception of God that exists in the mind of a child of Sunday-school," and concluded that we have "only just begun to comprehend the incredibly complex Being who is behind what we call 'life'" (pp. 7–8).

We have just surveyed—albeit only "scratching the surface"—most of the world's prominent religions. Billions of people around the globe seek to transcend their daily experiences by *transpersonally* and *spiritually* connecting with something or someone beyond themselves. Personality psychologists have sometimes been guilty of "shrinking" spiritual quests by defining them as infantile dependency needs or narcissistic yearnings for immortality. Such cynical "shrinking" diminishes both psychology and theology. Transpersonal psychology cannot pass as "hard science"—lacking, as it does, the empirical moorings of behavioristic, cognitive, or trait theories. Nonetheless, in concluding our journey, we have attempted to offer a fuller accounting of personality by incorporating rather than deriding transpersonal/spiritual theories.

CONCLUSION: THE FUTURE LOOKS BRIGHT FOR PERSONALITY PSYCHOLOGY

In an era when multidisciplinary research teams are the rule, the ability to communicate with other scientists is crucial. Being somewhat centrally located (both hierarchically and horizontally) with respect to other disciplines, personality psychologists are in a unique position to facilitate cross-disciplinary communication. The study of personality theories can also lead to a more integrated understanding of the numerous subfields within psychology itself. Much depends on how effectively personality psychologists will be able to get their own house in order by creating coherent portraits of real, live, breathing persons functioning as whole persons in the real world. This appears to be occurring as theory-by-theory texts are being replaced by those that attempt to integrate and systematize the study of personality. However, many of these more integrated texts have deemphasized the "grand" theories, replacing them with research-grounded mini-theories. Although such texts furnish encyclopedic coverage of numerous experiments and findings, they sometimes provide little in the way of overarching theories that put findings in a larger context and assist students in remembering the multitude of terms and definitions.

In our text, I have tried to keep most of the major theories intact, even providing information about the *persons* behind the theories. Hopefully, our grid has enabled you to place each major theory in its own particular zone(s). Now, with the major theories located in their appropriate zones, you will be able to compare theories—apples with apples—as well as consider how and where new findings fit into the grand scheme of things. Most important, as you try to locate the personality theory best suited to help you cope with an annoyance or solve a predicament, you will always have a "map" to guide you to the best ideas and the most relevant questions. As new findings emerge and coalesce into fresh mini-theories, you will have a familiar map to consult. We've reached the end of our journey together, and this is hardly the place to undertake further analyses or attempt more summarizing, so I leave you with three wishes.

Three wishes. When working with children in a clinical setting, I frequently ask them to make "three wishes" as a way of assessing what things are important to them. I would like to close by sharing my three wishes for you: (1) I hope these chapters have equipped you to understand yourself and others better and that you will feel more congruent as a result. (2) I hope you have caught my love for theories of personality—this *is* the most exciting stuff in the world to study! (3) Finally, I hope you will respect your inner voices if they nudge you toward "something more" in seeking a Higher Power or a Divine One(s) in your life.

Points to Remember

1. Personality psychologists try to study the "whole person" embedded in her biological, social, and spiritual context. This is less the case in contemporary "mini-theories" (where investigators focus more precisely on specific aspects of functioning) than it was in the "grand" theories of psychoanalysis, behaviorism, or humanism. Still, personality psychologists strive to understand the whole person functioning as a biological creature in a social context.

2. Personality theories share much in common with each other and with other scientific theories. It is the *method* of inquiry and the *precision* with which investigators ask questions—*not* the object of study—that determines if one is a scientist. The "Big Four" questions, whether asked about people, beetles, or black holes, lead us in the direction of all scientific inquiry.

3. Theories of personality frequently reflect the experiences of their founders. This is especially the case with the classic "grand" theories. However, since most career decisions are influenced by early childhood experiences, we might expect personality researchers to be interested in things that are personally relevant.

4. Personality theories tilt toward healing. Since it appears that many traditional personality theorists were seeking to work out their own emotional problems, it doesn't surprise us to find their theories permeated with healing ideas. This tilt toward healing has persisted in a trend that might be seen as a revitalized twenty-first-century version of *humanism—positive psychology.*

5. Theories vary significantly on how they assign personal agency. Behaviorists still insist that situational variables are primary, and existentialists continue to assign personal responsibility to the person; but there is widespread recognition that persons and situations *interact* and *interpenetrate* in ways that cannot easily be disentangled. Thus, *cognitive behaviorism* is an interactional recognition of such interfacing.

6. Theories are not so much "right" or "wrong" as they are more or less *useful.* Theories are intellectual "lenses"—focusing and clarifying, but also *narrowing* our vision. Each level of theorizing has its own preferred focus. If you're headed for the beach to watch the sun set or the moon rise, a blanket will probably do, but if you're going on a whale watch, you might want to take along your binoculars. And if you work in a medical lab where people count white blood cells or look for hairline bone fractures, you'll likely be peering into a microscope or reading X-ray images.

7. Theories of personality operate in different *zones.* This remains, perhaps, the single most important concept of our text: replacing an "either–or/true–or–false" attitude with a "grid" that includes a *vertical hierarchy of part–whole relationships and a horizontal self–other axis.*

8. People—including Freud—do not live by science alone. Most of the world's population puts stock in faith of one sort or another. Following Freud's lead, many personality psychologists have displayed "spiritualphobia" to some degree or another, viewing religion as some sort of inherent weakness or neurotic search for a lost father figure. Even Freud, however, acknowledged that psychoanalysis did not address all the big questions, and late in life he showed some interest in the occult.

9. Theology can be seen as personality theory about God/gods. Parallels can be seen between how people relate to one another and how they relate to Higher Power(s).

10. In the *Micro-merging* and *Pantheistic Zones,* we find the *nature gods.* From this perspective, Earth is a living organism and every manifestation of life—from the smallest rivulet to the most expansive ocean—is seen as an expression of the gods of the *Gaia* (the living Earth). Shinto (Japan's nature-oriented religion), neo-paganism and deep-ecology religions all hold nature in reverence and honor Earth as "Mother."

11. In the *Monotheistic Worship Zone,* followers of Christianity, Judaism, and Islam worship Yahweh or Allah. The religious requirements and rituals of these great monotheistic faiths are awash with *behavioral* specifics—in the style of a religious "token economy." In contrast to the God-within emphasis of Eastern religions, the monotheists worship a God who is "out there" and "above."

12. Jesus Christ appeared as a humanistic, existential psychoanalyst. The Gospel narratives (first four books of the Christian New Testament) relate numerous

incidents in which Jesus analyzed *motives* underlying behaviors in much the manner of a psychoanalyst. Jesus rejected the behaviorist religion of his day, promoting a more dynamic motive-based understanding.

13. The fifth book of the Christian New Testament (Acts of the Apostles) introduces a *mystical God* known to Christians as the *Holy Spirit.* However, Christian mysticism differs directionally from Eastern religions because although the *Holy Spirit* is thought to work mystically and transcendentally, it comes from "above," not from within.

14. Taoism emphasizes the importance of *emptiness* (which humanists, existentialists, or Five-Factor trait theorists might term *openness*). At the same time, Taoism stresses a connection to nature as well.

15. The mystical/meditation traditions of Hinduism and Buddhism offer believers "one-stop shopping," providing a profusion of religious beliefs, techniques, and rituals—all available under the same roof.

16. *Transpersonal ("Fourth Force")* psychology offers a "big tent" of ideas where all seekers are welcome. Although some transpersonal psychologists (e.g., Fadiman, 1980) suggest that the spiritual psychologies of the East and Middle East should be subject to scientific and experimental validation, other transpersonal psychologists are willing to incorporate transcendent and spiritual dimensions of personality that are clearly beyond the reach of laboratory methods.

17. Whereas Western psychologists see the *self* as the center of the person, most Easterners—along with many transpersonalists—seek to *escape* the nature-based (Western) self and merge with the universal (Eastern) Self, which is seen as ancient, eternal, birthless, and everlasting.

18. Yoga and Zen are Eastern methods for turning inward to find "enlightenment."

19. Although transpersonal and spiritual theories are breathtaking in scope—easily skipping from molecules and mitochondria to the Milky Way galaxy—there remains a scientifically unsettling lack of testability to many of the central constructs. Nonetheless, widely accepted scholarly criteria (e.g., plausibility, persuasiveness, cogency, coherence, and logic) ought to be applied to transpersonal and spiritual theories if they are to earn our respect and prove worthy of our time. Everything of importance in our lives is not *empirically* verifiable, but clear thinking—inside or outside the laboratory—must always be prized by psychologists of all persuasions.

Key Terms

Eightfold Pathway (546)
Four Noble Truths (546)
Gaia Hypothesis (538)
Gospels (540)
Guru (544)
Hindu (543)

Kaivalya (549)
Koan (549)
Law of Karma (544)
Muslim (542)
Neo-Paganism (539)
Nirvana (546)

Web Sites

www.bbc.co.uk/religion/religions. The BBC. Interested in more religions? Visit this Web site to read brief overviews of many of the world's religions and their history, beliefs, customs, holy days, worship practices, and much more.

http://en.wikipedia.org/wiki/Portal:Psychology. Wikipedia. This well-known online encyclopedia now has a Psychology Portal where you can browse literally hundreds of topics in psychology categorized into a manageable format.

www.pbs.org/wgbh/aso/mytheory/freud./ PBS.org. See if you can remember all that you've learned. Play this fun game and try to guess who the theorists are.

Learning on the Lighter Side

Over the next year, find four friends of diverse faiths and attend a spiritual service with each. Pay special attention to the differences and similarities of worship, meditation, or yoga activities as you attend synagogues, Zen temples, Yoga ashrams, cathedrals, mosques, Sufi centers, or Christian chapels or churches. Try to emotionally 'get into' the experience as best you can.

Adams, F. (1939). *The genuine works of Hippocrates: Translated from the Greek.*

Adams, G. R., & Fitch, S. A. (1982). Ego stage and identity status development: A cross-sequential analysis. *Journal of Personality and Social Psychology, 43,* 547–583.

Adler, A. (1907). The study of organ inferiority and its psychical compensation. In H. L. Ansbacher & R. R. Ansbacher (eds.), *The individual psychology of Alfred Adler.* New York: Harper, 1956.

Adler, A. (1908). The aggression drive in life and neurosis. In H. L. Ansbacher & R. R. Ansbacher (eds.), *The individual psychology of Alfred Adler.* New York: Harper, 1956.

Adler, A. (1927). *Understanding human nature.* Greenwich, CT: Fawcett.

Adler, A. (1929). *The science of living.* New York: Greenberg Publishers.

Adler, A. (1931). *What life should mean to you.* New York: Putnam.

Adler, A. (1936/1964). *Social interest: A challenge to mankind,* pp. 262–289. New York: Putnam, 1975.

Adler, A. (1954). *Understanding human nature.* New York: Fawcett World Library.

Adler, A. (1958). *What life should mean to you.* New York: Capricorn Books.

Adler, A. (1964a). *Problems of neurosis.* New York: Capricorn Books.

Adler, A. (1964b). *Social interest: A challenge to mankind.* New York: Capricorn Books.

Adler, A. (1968). *The practice and theory of individual psychology.* Totowa, NJ: Littlefield, Adams, & Co.

Adler, A. (1983). The problem of distance. In A. Adler (1983), *The practice and theory of individual psychology* (pp. 100–108). Totowa, NJ: Littlefield, Adams. (Original work published 1914).

Adorno, T. W., Frenkel-Brunswik, E., Levinson, D. J., & Sanford, R. N. (1950). *The authoritarian personality.* New York: Harper & Brothers.

Alcock, J. (2001). *The triumph of sociobiology.* New York: Oxford University Press.

Alexander, F. (1950). *Psychosomatic medicine: Its principles and applications.* New York: Norton.

Allen, J., & Brock, S. A. (2000). *Health care communication using personality type: Patients are different!* Philadelphia, PA: Routledge.

Allport, G. W. (1937). *Personality: A psychological interpretation.* New York: Holt, Rinehart & Winston.

Allport, G. W. (1950). *The individual and his religion.* New York: Macmillan.

Allport, G. W. (1955). *Becoming: Basic considerations for a psychology of personality.* New Haven, CT: Yale University Press.

Allport, G. W. (1961). *Pattern and growth in personality.* New York: Holt, Rinehart and Winston.

Allport, G. W. (1965). *Letters from Jenny.* New York: Harcourt Brace Jovanovich.

Allport, G. W. (1966). [Autobiography] In E. G. Boring & G. Lindzey (eds.), *A history of psychology in autobiography* (Vol. V). New York: Appleton-Century-Crofts.

Allport, G. W., & Odbert, H. S. (1936). Trait-names: A psycholexical study. *Psychological Monographs, 47,* 171.

Allport, G. W., & Postman, L. (1947). *The psychology of rumor.* New York: Henry Holt.

Allport, G. W., & Ross, J. M. (1967). Personal religious orientation and prejudice. *Journal of Personality and Social Psychology, 5,* 432–443.

American Psychiatric Association (1994). *Diagnostic and statistical manual of mental disorders* (4th ed.). Washington, DC.

Anastasi, A. (1988). *Psychological testing* (6th ed.). New York: Macmillan.

Andersen, S. M., & Berk, M. S. (2005). The social-cognitive model of transference: Experiencing past relationships in the present. In C. C. Morf & O. Ayduk (eds.), *Current directions in personality psychology* (pp. 125–136). Upper Saddle River, NJ: Pearson Education, Inc.

Andersen, S. M., Reznik, I., & Chen, S. (1997). The self and others: Cognitive and motivational underpinnings. In J. G. Snodgrass & R. L. Thompson (eds.), *The self across psychology: Self-recognition, self-awareness, and the self-concept* (pp. 233–275). New York: New York Academy of Science.

Anderson, J. R., & Bower, G. H. (1974). *Human associative memory*. New York: John Wiley & Sons.

Ansbacher, H. L., & Ansbacher, R. R. (eds). (1956). *The individual psychology of Alfred Adler*. New York: Basic Books, Inc.

Ansbacher, H. L., & Ansbacher, R. R. (eds.). (1964). *Superiority and social interest*. Evanston, IL: Northwestern University Press.

Ansbacher, H. L., & Ansbacher, R. R. (eds.). (1973). *Superiority and social interest: A collection of later writings*. New York: Viking Compass.

Arasteh, A. R. (1972). *Rumi the Persian: Rebirth in creativity and love*. Tucson, AZ: Omen Press.

Ardrey, R. (1970). *The social contract*. New York: Atheneum.

Aries, E., & Moorhead, K. (1989). The importance of ethnicity in the development of identity of Black adolescents. *Psychological Reports, 65 (1)*, 75–82.

Arndt, J., Greenberg, J., Pyszczynski, T., Simon, L., & Solomon, S. (1996). *Terror management and self-awareness: Evidence that mortality salience provokes avoidance of the self-focused state*. Unpublished manuscript, University of Arizona: Tucson, AZ.

Asch, S. E. (1956). Studies of independence and conformity: A minority of one against a unanimous majority. *Psychological Monographs, 70* (9, Whole No. 416).

Aspy, D., & Roebuck, F. (1974). From human ideas to humane technology and back again, many times. *Education, 95*, 163–171.

Austin, J. H. (1999). *Zen and the brain: Toward an understanding of meditation and consciousness*. Boston: MIT Press.

Azar, B. (2002). Pigeons as baggage screeners, rats as rescuers. *Monitor on Psychology, 33, # 9*, p. 42.

Baillargeon, R., & DeVos, J. (1991). Object permanence in young infants: Further evidence. *Child Development, 62*, 1227–1246.

Balay, J., & Shevrin, H. (1988). The subliminal psychodynamic activation method. *American Psychologist, 43* (3), 161–174.

Bandura, A. (1965). Influence of models' reinforcement contingencies on the acquisitions of imitative responses. *Journal of Personality and Social Psychology, 1*, 589–595.

Bandura, A. (1977). *A social learning theory*. Englewood Cliffs, NJ: Prentice-Hall.

Bandura, A. (1986). *Social foundations of thought and action: A social cognitive theory*. Englewood Cliffs, NJ: Prentice Hall.

Bandura, A., Adams, N. E., & Beyer, J. (1977). Cognitive processes mediating behavioral change. *Journal of Personality and Social Psychology, 35*, 125–139.

Bannister, D., & Fransella, F. (1971). *Inquiring man: The theory of personal constructs*. New York: Penguin.

Barash, D. P. (1979). *The whisperings within: Evolution and the origin of human nature*. New York: Penguin.

Barash, D. P. (1986). *The hare and the tortoise: Culture, biology, and human nature*. New York: Penguin.

Baron, R. A. (1978). The influence of hostile and non-hostile humor upon physical aggression. *Personality and Social Psychology Bulletin, 4*, 77–80.

Barrett, P., & Eysenck, S. (1994). The assessment of personality factors across 25 countries. *Personality and Individual Differences, 5*, 615–632.

Bassoff, E. S., & Glass, G. V. (1982). The relationship between sex roles and mental helath: A meta-analysis of twenty-six studies. *Counseling Psychologist, 10*, 105–112.

Bateson, G. (1971). *Steps toward an ecology of mind*. New York: Ballantine.

Beck, A. T. (1967). *Depression: Clinical, experimental and theoretical aspects*. New York: Harper & Row.

Beck, A. T. (1976). *Cognitive therapy and the emotional disorders*. New York: International University Press.

Becker, E. (1968). *The structure of evil: An essay on the unification of the science of man*. New York: Braziller.

Becker, E. (1973). *The denial of death*. New York: The Free Press.

Beebe, B., & Stern, D. (1977). Engagement-disengagement and early object experiences. In M. Freedman & S. Grand, eds., *Communicative structures and psychic structures*. New York: Plenum Press.

Bem, S. L. (1974). The measurement of psychological androgyny. *Journal of Consulting and Clinical Psychology, 42*, 155–162.

Bem, S. L. (1975). Sex-role adaptability: One consequence of psychological androgyny. *Journal of Personality and Social Psychology, 31*, 634–643.

Bem, S. L., & Lenney, E. (1976). Sex typing and avoidance of cross-sex behavior. *Journal of Personality and Social Psychology, 3*, 48–54.

Bem, S. L., Martyna, W., & Watson, C. (1976). Sex typing and androgyny: Further exploration of the expressive domain. *Journal of Personality and Social Psychology, 34*, 1016–1023.

Benjamin, L. T. (2001). American psychology's struggle with its curriculum: Should a thousand flowers bloom? *American Psychology, 56*, 735–742.

Berecz, J. M. (1968). Phobias of childhood: Etiology and treatment. *Psychological Bulletin, 70,* 694–720.

Berecz, J. M. (1972). Modification of smoking behavior through self-administered punishment of imagined behavior: A new approach to aversion therapy. *Journal of Consulting & Clinical Psychology, 38* (2), 244–250.

Berecz, J. M. (1973). The treatment of stuttering through precision punishment and cognitive arousal. *Journal of Speech and Hearing Disorders, 38* (2), 256–257.

Berecz, J. M. (1976). Cognitive conditioning therapy in the treatment of stuttering. *Journal of Communication Disorder, 9,* 301–317.

Berecz, J. M. (1979). Maintenance of nonsmoking behavior through self-administered wrist-band aversion therapy. *Behavior Therapy, 10,* 669–675.

Berecz, J. M. (1992). *Understanding Tourette syndrome, obsessive compulsive disorder, and related problems: A developmental and catastrophe theory perspective.* New York: Springer Publishing Company.

Berecz, J. M. (1998). *Sexual styles: A psychologist's guide to understanding your lover's personality.* Atlanta, GA: Humanics.

Berecz, J. M. (1999) *All the presidents' women: An examination of sexual styles from presidents Truman to Clinton.* Lake Worth, FL: Humanics.

Berecz, J. M. (2001). All that glitters is not gold: Bad forgiveness in counseling and preaching. *Pastoral Psychology, 49,* 253–276.

Bernal, M. E., Knight, G. P., Garza, C. A., Ocampo, K. A., et al. (1990). The development of ethnic identity in Mexican-American children. *Hispanic Journal of Behavioral Sciences, 12* (1), 3–24.

Bernard, M. E. (1986). *Staying alive in an irrational world: The psychology of Albert Ellis.* Melbourne, Australia: Carlton & Macmillan.

Berne, E. (1961). *Transactional analysis in psychotherapy.* New York: Grove Press.

Berne, E. (1964). *Games people play: The psychology of human relationships.* New York: Grove Press.

Berne, E. (1966). *Principles of group treatment.* New York: Oxford University Press.

Berne, E. (1967). Transactional Analysis. In H. Greenwald, ed., *Active psychotherapy.* New York: Atherton Press.

Berne, E. (1973). *Transactional analysis in psychotherapy.* New York: Ballantine Books.

Berne, E. (1977). *Intuitions and ego states: The origins of transactional analysis, A series of papers by Eric Berne, M. D.* New York: Harper & Row.

Berne, E. (1978). *What do you say after you say hello?* New York: Grove Press, Inc.

Bieri, J. (1955). Cognitive complexity-simplicity and predictive behavior. *Journal of Abnormal and Social Psychology, 51,* 61–66.

Bisson, T. (1991). They're made out of meat. From a series of stories entitled "Alien/Nation." *Omni,* April. Quoted in Pinker, 1997, p. 96.

Block, J. (1961). *The Q-Sort method in personality assessment and psychiatric research.* Springfield, IL: Charles C. Thomas.

Bodden, J. C. (1970). Cognitive complexity as a factor in appropriate vocational choice. *Journal of Counseling Psychology, 17,* 364–368.

Bolles, R. C. (1970). Species-specific defensive reactions and avoidance learning. *Psychological Review, 77,* 32–48.

Boring, E. G. (1957). *A history of experimental psychology* (2nd ed.). New York: Appleton-Century-Crofts.

Boss, M. (1963). *Psychoanalysis and daseinsanalysis.* New York: Philosophical Library.

Bottome, P. (1957). *Alfred Adler: A portrait from life.* New York: Vanguard.

Bourne, E. (1978). The state of research on ego identity: A review and appraisal: I. *Journal of Youth and Adolescence, 7,* 223–251.

Bourne, P. G. (1997). *Jimmy Carter: A comprehensive biography from Plains to postpresidency.* New York: Scribner.

Bousfield, W. A. (1953). The occurrence of clustering in the recall of randomly arranged associates. *Journal of General Psychology, 49,* 229–240.

Bowen, M. (1961). Family psychotherapy. *American Journal of Orthopsychiatry, 31,* 40–60.

Bowen, M. (1976). Principles and techniques of multiple family therapy. In P. J. Guerin (ed.), *Family therapy: Theory and practice.* New York: Gardner Press.

Bowen, M. (1978). *Family therapy in clinical practice.* New York: Jason Aronson.

Bowers, B. J., McClure-Begley, T. D., Keller, J. J., Paylor, R., Collins, A. C., & Wehner, J. M. (2005). Deletion of the α7 nicotinic receptor subunit gene results in increased sensitivity to severe behavioral effects produced by alcohol. *Alcoholism: Clinical and experimental research, 29,* 295–302.

Bowlby, J. (1969). *Attachment and loss. Vol. 1: Attachment.* New York: Basic Books.

Braaten, L. J. (1961). The main theories of "existentialism" from the viewpoint of a psychotherapist. *Mental Hygiene, 45,* 10–17.

Bradbury, T. N., Rogge, R., & Lawrence, E. (2001). Reconsidering the role of conflict in marriage. In A. Booth, A. C. Crouter, & M. Clements (eds.), *Couples in conflict,* pp. 59–81. Mahwah, NJ: Erlbaum.

Brady, J. P., & Lind, D. L. (1961). Experimental analysis of hysterical blindness: Operant conditioning techniques. *Archives of general psychiatry, 4,* 331–339.

Brazelton, T. B., & Als, H. (1979). Four early stages in the development of mother–infant interaction. *The Psychoanalytic Study of the Child, 34:* 349–371.

Bregman, E. O. (1934). An attempt to modify the emotional attitudes of infants by the conditioned response technique. *Journal of Genetic Psychology, 45,* 169–198.

Breland, K., & Breland, M. (1961). The misbehavior of organisms. *American Psychologist, 16,* 681–684.

Breuer, J., & Freud, S. (1893-1895). *Studies on hysteria.* Vol. II of *The standard edition of the complete psychological works of Sigmund Freud.* London: Hogarth Press, 1955.

Briggs, J., & Peat, F. D. (1989). *Turbulent mirror: An illustrated guide to chaos theory and the science of wholeness.* New York: Harper & Row.

Briggs, S. R. (1989). The optimal level of measurement of personality constructs. In D. M. Buss & N. Cantor (eds.), *Personality psychology: Recent trends and emerging directions*, pp. 246–260. New York: Springer-Verlag.

Brodie, F. M. (1981). *Richard Nixon: The shaping of his character.* New York: Charles Scribner's Sons.

Brody, G. H. (2005). Siblings' direct and indirect contributions to child development. In C. C. Morf & O. Ayduk (eds.), *Current directions in personality psychology*, pp. 143–148. Upper Saddle River, NJ: Pearson Education, Inc.

Brody, G. H., Kim, S., Murry, V. M., & Brown, A. C. (2003). Longitudinal direct and indirect pathways linking older sibling competence to the development of younger sibling competence. *Developmental Psychology, 39,* 618–628.

Brown, N. O. (1959). *Life against death: The psychoanalytic meaning of history.* New York: Viking Books.

Browning, D. S. (1973). *Generative man: Psychoanalytic perspectives.* Philadelphia, PA: The Westminster Press.

Bruner, J. S. (1957). Going beyond the information given. In H. E. Gruber, K. R. Hammond, & R. Jessor (eds.), *Contemporary approaches to cognition*, pp. 41–60. Cambridge, MA: Harvard University Press.

Bruner, J. S., Goodnow, J. J., & Austin, G. A. (1956). *A study of thinking.* New York: Wiley.

Brussell, E. E. (1988). (ed.) *Webster's new world dictionary of quotable definitions: Second edition.* Englewood Cliffs, NJ: Prentice Hall.

Bryant, B. L. (1987, March). Birth order as a factor in the development of vocational preferences. *Individual Psychology: Journal of Adlerian Theory, Research,* and *Practice, 43 (1)*, 36–41.

Bryant, R. A., & McConkey, R. M. (1989). Visual conversion disorder: A case analysis of the influences of visual information. *Journal of abnormal psychology, 98,* 326–329.

Buber, M. (1955). *Between man and man.* Boston: Beacon

Bugental, J. (1980). Being levels of therapeutic growth. In R. Walsh & F. Vaughan (eds.), *Beyond ego*, pp. 175–181. Los Angeles: Tarcher.

Bugental, J. F. T. (1964). The third force in psychology. *Journal of* Humanistic *Psychology, 4,* 19–25.

Burchardt, C. J., & Serbin, L. A. (1982). Psychological androgyny and personality adjustment in college and psychiatric populations. *Sex Roles, 8,* 835–851.

Burger, J. M. (2000) *Personality* (5th ed.). Stamford, CT: Wadsworth/Thompson Learning.

Burris, C. T., & Jackson, L. M. (1999). Hate the sin/love the sinner, or love the hater? Intrinsic religion and responses to partner abuse. *Journal for the Scientific Study of Religion, 38,* 160–174.

Buss, D. M. (1987). Sex differences in mate selection criteria: An evolutionary perspective. In C. Crawford, M. Smith, & D. Krebs (eds.), *Sociobiology and psychology: Ideas, issues, and applications*, pp. 335–351. Hillsdale, NJ: Lawrence Earlbaum Associates.

Buss, D. M. (1989). Conflict between the sexes: strategic interference and the evocation of anger and upset. *Journal of Personal and Social Psychology, 56,* 735–747.

Buss, D. M. (1991). Evolutionary personality psychology. *Annual Review of Psychology, 42,* 459–491.

Buss, D. M. (1994). *The evolution of desire.* New York: Basic Books.

Buss, D. M., Block, J. H., & Block, J. (1980). Preschool activity level: Personality correlates and developmental implications. *Child Development, 51,* 401–408.

Butz, M. (1992). The fractal nature of the development of the self. *Psychological Reports, 71,* 1043–1063.

Cacioppo, J. T., Petty, R. E., Losch, M. E., & Kim, H. S. (1986). Electromyographic activity over facial muscle regions can differentiate the valence and intensity of affective reactions. *Journal of Personality and Social Psychology, 50,* 260–268.

Calhoun, J. B. (1956). A comparative study of the social behavior of two inbred strains of house mice. *Ecol. Monogr., 26,* 81–103.

Campbell, J. (1988). *The power of myth.* New York: Doubleday.

Campbell, J. B., & Hawley, C. W. (1982). Study habits and Eysenck's theory of introversion-extraversion. *Journal of Research in Personality, 16,* 139–146.

Canlin, T., Zuo, Z., Kang, E., Gross, J., Desmond, J. E., & Gabrielil, J. D. (2001). An fMRI study of personality influences on brain reactivity to emotional stimuli. *Behavioral Neuroscience, 115,* 33–42.

Cannon, L. (1991). *President Reagan: The role of a lifetime,* p. 57. New York: Simon & Schuster.

Cannon, T. D., Kapiro, J., Lonnqvist, J., Huttunen, M., & Koskenvuo, M. (1998). The genetic epidemiology of schizophrenia in a Finnish twin cohort. *Archives of General Psychiatry, 55,* 67–74.

Caparulo, B. K., Cohen, D. J., Rothman, S. L., Young, J. G., Katz, J. D., Shaywitz, S. E., & Shaywitz, B. A. (1981). Computed tomograpohic brain scanning in children with developmental neuropsychiatric disorders. *Journal of the American Academy of Child & Adolescent Psychiatry, 20,* 338–357.

Caplan, P. J. (1979). Erikson's concept of inner-space: A data-based reevaluation. *American Journal of Orthopsychiatry, 49,* 100–108.

Capra, F. (1991). *The tao of physics* (3rd ed.). Boston: Shambala. 3rd updated ed., 1991.

Caprio, B., & Hedberg, T. (1986). *Coming home: A handbook for exploring the sanctuary within.* New York: Paulist Press.

Carlsson, K., Petersson, K. M., Lundquist, D., Karlsson, A., Ingvar, M., & Ohman, A. (2004). Fear and the amygdala: Manipulation of awareness generates differential cerebral responses to phobic and fear-relevant (but nonfeared) stimuli. *Emotion, 4,* 340–353.

Carment, D. W., Miles, G. D., & Cervin, V. B. (1965). Persuasiveness and persuadability as related to intelligence and extraversion. *British Journal of Social and Clinical Psychology, 4,* 1–7.

Caro, R. A. (1983). *The years of Lyndon Johnson: The path to power.* New York: Knopf.

Caro, R. A. (1990). *The years of Lyndon Johnson: Means of ascent.* New York: Knopf.

Carpenter, G. (1974). Mother's face and the newborn. *New Scientist, 61:* 742.

Carr, E. G., & Durand, V. M. (1985). Reducing behavior problems through functional communication training. *Journal of Applied Behavior Analysis, 18,* 111–126.

Carr, J. E., Coriaty, S., & Dozier, C. L. (2000). Current issues in the function-based treatment of aberrant behavior in individuals with developmental disabilities. In J. Austin & J. E. Carr (eds.), *Handbook of applied behavior analysis,* pp. 91–112. Reno, NV: Context Press.

Carroll, L. (1982). *The complete illustrated works of Lewis Carroll.* New York: Avenel Books.

Carruth, H. (1994). Quoted in Sartre, J. P., *Nausea.* New York: New Directions Publishing Corporation.

Carter, J. (1975). *Why not the best?* Nashville, TN: Broadman Press.

Caspi, A., Elder, G. H., & Bem, D. J. (1987). Moving against the world: Life-course patterns of explosive children. *Developmental Psychology, 23,* 308–313.

Cattell, R. B. (1943). The description of personality: Basic traits resolved into clusters. *Journal of Abnormal and Social Psychology, 38,* 476–506.

Cattell, R. B. (1946). *The description and measurement of personality.* Yonkers, NY: World Book Co.

Cattell, R. B. (1948). Concepts and methods in the measurement of group syntality. *Psychological Review, 55,* 48–63.

Cattell, R. B. (1950). *Personality: A systematic, theoretical, and factual study.* New York: McGraw-Hill.

Cattell, R. B. (1957). *Personality and motivation: Structure and measurement.* Yonkers, New York: World Book.

Cattell, R. B. (1990). Advances in Cattellian personality theory. In L. A. Pervin (ed.), *Handbook of personality theory and research.* New York: Guilford.

Chang, R., & Page, R. C. (1991). Characteristics of the self-actualized person: Visions from East and West. *Counseling & Values, 36 (1),* 2–10.

Chapman, A. H. (1976). *Harry Stack Sullivan: His life and his work.* New York: G. P. Putnam's Sons.

Chodorow, N. J. (1978). *The reproduction of mothering.* Berkeley: University of California Press.

Chodorow, N. J. (1989). *Feminism and psychoanalytic theory.* New Haven, CT: Yale University Press.

Chodorow, N. J. (1994). *Femininities masculinities, sexualities: Freud and beyond.* Lexington, KY: University Press of Kentucky.

Chodorow, N. J. (1995). Gender as personal and cultural construction. *Signs, 20,* 516–544.

Chodorow, N. J. (1999). *The power of feelings.* New Haven: Yale University Press.

Chomsky, N. (1957). *Syntactic structures.* The Hague: Mouton.

Chomsky, N. (1959). Review of *Verbal behavior,* by B. F. Skinner. *Language, 35,* January–March, 30, 38.

Chomsky, N. (1987). *Knowledge of language: Its nature, origin, and use.* New York: Praeger.

Chomsky, N. (1988). *Language and problems of knowledge.* Cambridge, MA: MIT Press.

Choron, J. (1963). *Death and Western thought.* New York: Collier Books.

Church, A. T., & Burke, P. J. (1994). Exploratory and confirmatory tests of the Big Five and Tellegen's three- and four-dimensional models. *Journal of Personality and Social Psychology, 66,* 93–114.

Churchland, P., & Churchland, P. S. (1994). Could a machine think? Quoted in E. Dietrich (ed.), *Thinking computers and virtual persons: Essays on the intentionality of machines.* Boston: Academic Press.

Ciaccio, N. (1971). A test of Erikson's theory of ego epigenesis. *Developmental Psychology, 4,* 306–311.

Clark, A. (1997). *Being there: Putting brain, body, and world together again.* Cambridge, MA: The MIT Press.

Cloninger, C. R. (1986). A unified biosocial theory of personality and its role in the development of anxiety states. *Psychiatric Developments, 3,* 167–226.

Cloninger, C. R. (1987). A systematic method for clinical description and classification of personality variants: A proposal. *Archives of General Psychiatry, 44,* 573–588.

Cloninger, C. R. (1991). Brain networks underlying personality development. In B. J. Carroll and J. E. Barrett (eds.), *Psychopathology and the brain,* pp. 183–208. New York: Raven Press.

Cloninger, C. R. (1999). *Personality and psychopathology.* Washington, DC: American Psychiatric Press.

Cloninger, C. R., Sigvardsson, S., & Bohman, M. (1988). Childhood personality predicts alcohol abuse in young adults. *Alcoholism Clinical and Experimental Research, 12,* 494–505.

Cloninger, C. R., Svrakic, D. M., & Przbeck, T. R. (1993). A psychobiological model of temperament and character. *Archives of General* Psychiatry, *50,* 975–990.

Cohen, D. (1979). *J. B. Watson: The founder of behaviourism.* London: Routledge and Kegan Paul.

Cohen, J., & Stewart, I. (1994). *The collapse of chaos.* New York: Viking.

Colby, K. M. (1981). Modeling a paranoid mind. *Behavioral and Brain* Sciences, *4,* 515–560.

Condon, W. S., & Sander, L. (1974). Neonate movement is synchronized with adult speech. *Science, 183,* 99–101.

Constantinople, A. (1973). Masculinity-femininity: An exception to a famous dictum? *Psychological Bulletin, 80,* 389–407.

Costa, P., & McCrae, R. (1992). Revised NEO Personality Inventory: NEO PI and NEO Five-Factor Inventory (NEO FFI) professional manual. Odessa, FL: Psychological Assessment Resources.

Costa, P. T., Jr., and McCrae, R. (1985). *The NEO personality inventory manual.* Odessa, FL: Psychological Assessment Resources.

Council, J. R. (1993). Context effects in personality research. *Current Directions in Psychological Science, 2,* 31–34.

Cramer, P. (1965). Recovery of a discrete memory. *Journal of Personality and Social Psychology, 1,* 326–332.

Cramer, P. (1968). *Word association.* New York: Academic Press, Inc.

Cramer, P. (1991). *The development of defense mechanisms: Theory, research and assessment.* New York: Springer-Verlag.

Cramer, P. (1997). Evidence for change in children's use of defense mechanisms. *Journal of Personality, 65,* 233–247.

Cramer, P. (1998). Coping and defense mechanisms: What's the difference? *Journal of Personality, 66,* 919–946.

Cramer, P. (2000). Defense mechanisms in psychology today: Further processes for adaptation. *American Psychologist, 55,* 637–646.

Cramer, P., & Block, J. (1998). Preschool antecedents of defense mechanism use in young adults. *Journal of Personality and Social Psychology, 74,* 159–169.

Crawford, C., Smith, M., & Krebs, D. (eds.) (1987). *Sociobiology and psychology: Ideas, issues, and applications.* Hillsdale, NJ: Lawrence Earlbaum Associates.

Cross, W. (1971). The Negroe-to-Black conversion experience. *Black World,* 13–27.

Cross, W. E., Jr. (1991). *Shades of black: Diversity in African-American identity.* Philadelphia: Temple University Press.

Csikszentmihalyi, M. (1990). *Flow: The psychology of optimal experience.* New York: HarperCollins.

Cuvo, A. J., & Davis, P. K. (2000). Behavioral acquisition by persons with developmental disabililties. In J. Austin & J. E. Carr (eds.), *Handbook of applied behavior analysis,* 39–60. Reno, NV: Context Press.

Dallek, R. (1991). *Lone star rising: Lyndon Johnson and his times 1908–1960.* New York: Oxford University Press.

Daly, M., & Wilson, M. (1988). *Homicide.* New York: Aldine deGruyter.

Damasio, A. R. (1994). Descartes' error: Emotion, reason, and the human brain. New York: Putnam.

Daudet, L. (1915). *Souvenirs des milieux literaires, politiques, artistiques et medicaux de 1885 a 1905.* 2nd series: *Devant la douleur* (Paris: Nouvelle Librairie Nationale).

Davis, R., & Millon, T. (1999). Models of personality and its disorders. In T. Millon, P. H. Blaney, & R. D. Davis (eds.),

Oxford textbook of psychopathology, pp. 485–522. New York: Oxford University Press.

Dawkins, R. (1989). *The selfish gene.* (first published 1976) London: Oxford University Press.

Dawson, M. R. W. (1998). *Understanding cognitive science.* Malden, MA: Blackwell Publishers Inc.

DeCarvalho, R. J. (1991). *The founders of humanistic psychology.* New York: Praeger.

Digman, J., & Takemoto-Chock, N. (1981). Factors in the natural language of personality: Reanalysis, comparison, and interpretation of six major studies. *Multivariate Behavioral Research, 16,* 149–170.

Digman, J. M. (1994). Historical antecedents of the five-factor model. In P. T. Costa, Jr., and T. A. Widiger, eds., *Personality disorders and the five-factor model of personality.* Washington, DC: American Psychological Association.

Dinkmeyer, D. (1989). Adlerian psychology: *A Journal of Human Behavior, 26,* 1.

Dinkmeyer, D., & McKay, G. (1976). *Systematic training for effective parenting.* Circle Pines, MN: American Guidance Service.

DiPietro, J. A. (2005). The role of prenatal maternal stress in child development. In C. C. Morf & O. Ayduk (eds.), *Current directions in personality psychology,* pp. 33–39. Upper Saddle River, NJ: Pearson Education, Inc.

Dollard, J., Doob, L. W., Miller, N. W., Mowrer, O. H., & Sears, R. R. (1939). *Frustration and aggression.* New Haven, CT: Yale University Press.

Dollard, J., and Miller, N. E. (1950). *Personality and psychotherapy: An analysis in terms of learning, thinking, and culture.* New York: McGraw-Hill Book Co.

Donahue, M. J. (1985). Intrinsic and extrinsic religiousness: Review and meta-analyses. *Journal of Personality and Social Psychology, 48,* 400–419.

Dorgan, M., Goebel, B. L., & House, A. E. (1983). Generalizing about sex role and self-esteem: Results or effects? *Sex Roles, 9,* 719–724.

Downey, D. B. (2001). Number of siblings and intellectual development: The resource dilution explanation. *American Psychologist, 56,* 497–504.

Dreyfus, H. L. (2001). *Existentialism.* Microsoft, Encarta, Online Encyclopedia, http://encarta.msn.com.

Dugger, R. (1982). *The politician: The life and times of Lyndon Johnson: The drive for power from the frontier to master of the Senate.* New York: W. W. Norton.

Duval, S., & Wickland, R. A. (1972). *A theory of objective self-awareness.* New York: Academic Press.

Easterby-Smith, M. (1980). How to use repertory grids in human resource development. *Journal of European Industrial Training, 4* (1, Whole No. 2).

Eaves, L. J., Silberg, J. L., Meyer, J. M., Maes, H. H., Simonoff, E., Pickles, A., Rutter, M., Neale, M. C., Reynolds, C. A., Erikson, M. T., Heath, A. C., Loeber, R., Truett, K. R., & Hewitt, J. K. (1997). Genetics and developmental psychopathology: 2. The main effects of genes and environment on behavior problems in the Virginia Twin Study of Adolescent Behavioral Development. *Journal of Child Psychology & Psychiatry, 38,* 965–980.

Edelman, G. M. (1987). *Neural Darwinism: the theory of neuronal group selection.* New York: Basic Books.

Edelman, G. M. (1992). *Bright air, brilliant fire: On the matter of the mind.* New York: Basic Books.

Eden, C., & Sims, D. (1981). Computerised vicarious experience: The future of management induction? *Personnel Review, 10,* 22–25.

Edwards, L. (1993). *How we belong, fight, and pray: The MBTI as a key to congregational dynamics.* New York: The Alban Institute.

Efran, J. S., & Fauber, R. L. (1999). Radical constructivism: Questions and answers. In R. A. Neimeyer and M. J. Mahoney (eds.), *Constructivism in psychotherapy,* pp. 275–304. Washington, DC: American Psychological Association.

Elkind, D. (1994). *A sympathetic understanding of the child: Birth to sixteen* (3rd ed.) Boston: Allyn & Bacon.

Elkind, D., & Bowen, R. (1979). Imaginary audience behavior in children and adolescents. *Developmental Psychology, 15,* 33–44.

Ellenberger, H. (1972). The story of "Anna O.": A critical review with new data. *Journal of History of the Behavioral Sciences, VIII,* 267–279.

Ellenberger, H. F. (1970). *The discovery of the unconscious: The history and evolution of dynamic psychiatry.* New York: Basic Books.

Elliot, B. A. (1992). Birth order and health: Major issues. *Social Science & Medicine, 35 (4),* 443–452.

Ellis, A. (1955). New approaches to psychotherapy techniques. *Journal of Clinical Psychology Monograph Supplement,* Brandon, VT.

Ellis, A. (1957). *How to live with a neurotic.* New York: Crown.

Ellis, A. (1958). Rational psychotherapy. *Journal of General Psychology, 59,* 35–49.

Ellis, A. (1960). The art and science of love. New York: L. Stuart.

Ellis, A. (1962). *Reason and emotion in psychotherapy.* Secaucus, NJ: Lyle Stuart, Inc.

Ellis, A. (1970). Tribute to Alfred Adler. *Journal of Individual Psychology, 26,* 11–12.

Ellis, A. (1978). Toward a theory of personality. In R. J. Corsini (ed.), *Readings in current personality theories.* Itasca, IL: Peacock.

Ellis, A. (1986). *The handbook of rational-emotive therapy.* New York: Springer.

Ellis, A. (1988). *How to refuse to make yourself miserable about anything–yes anything.* New York: Lyle Stuart.

Ellis, A. (1991). My life in clinical psychology. In C. E. Walker (ed.), *The history of clinical psychology in autobiography,* Vol. 1, pp. 1–37. Pacific Grove, CA: Brooks/Cole.

Ellis, A. (1994). *Reason and emotion in psychotherapy, revised and updated.* New York: Carol Publishing.

Ellis, A. (1996). Responses to criticisms of Rational Emotive Behavior Therapy. *Journal of Rational Emotive and Cognitive Therapy, 14,* 97–121.

Ellis, A., & Becker, I. (1982). *A guide to personal happiness.* North Hollywood, CA: Wilshire.

Ellis, A., & Dryden, W. (1987). *The practice of rational emotive therapy.* New York: Springer.

Ellis, A., & Greiger, R. (1977). *Handbook of rational emotive therapy.* New York: Julian Press.

Ellis, A., & Harper, R. A. (1975). *A new guide to rational living.* North Hollywood, CA: Wilshire Books.

Ellsworth, P. C., & Smith, C. A. (1988). From appraisal to emotion: Differences among unpleasant feelings. *Motivation and Emotion, 12,* 271–302.

Emmons, R. A. (1999). *The psychology of ultimate concerns.* New York: The Guilford Press.

Engler, B. (1999). *Personality theories: An introduction.* Boston: Houghton Mifflin.

Epstein, S. (1967). Toward a unified theory of anxiety. In B. A. Maher (ed.), *Progress in Experimental Personality Research.* New York: Academic Press.

Ericksen, S. C. (1958). The core curriculum is a dependent variable. *American Psychologist, 13,* 56–58.

Erikson, E. H. (1963). *Childhood and society.* Second Edition. New York: Norton.

Erikson, E. H. (1958). *Young man Luther: A study in psychoanalysis and history.* New York: Norton.

Erikson, E. H. (1959a). *Gandhi's truth: On the origins of militant nonviolence.* New York: Norton.

Erikson, E. H. (1959b). *Identity and the life cycle: Selected papers,* Psychological Issues Monographs, Vol. I, No. International University Press.

Erikson, E. H. (1964). *Insight and responsibility: Lectures on the ethical implications of psychoanalytic insight.* New York: Norton.

Erikson, E. H. (1970). Autobiographic notes on the identity crisis. *Daedalus,* Vol. 99, No. 4.

Erikson, E. H. (1977). *Toys and reasons: Stages in the ritualization of experience.* New York: Norton.

Erikson, E. H. (1982). *The life cycle completed.* New York: Norton.

Erikson, J. M. (1997). *The life cycle completed: Extended version.* New York: W. W. Norton.

Ernst, C., & Angst, J. (1983). *Birth order: Its influence on personality.* New York: Springer-Verlag.

Evans, R. I. (1964). *Dialogue with Erik Erikson.* New York: Praeger Publishers, 1981.

Evans, R. I. (1973). *Jean Piaget: The man and his ideas.* New York: E. P. Dutton & Co., Inc.

Evans, R. I. (1975). *Carl Rogers: The man and his ideas.* New York: E. P. Dutton & Co., Inc.

Eysenck, H. J. (1957). *The dynamics of anxiety and hysteria.* London: Routledge & Kegan Paul Limited.

Eysenck, H. J. (1960). *The structure of human personality.* London: Methuen.

Eysenck, H. J. (1964). Principles and methods of personality description, classification and diagnosis. *British journal of psychology, 55,* 284–294.

Eysenck, H. J. (1965a). *Smoking, health, and personality.* New York: Basic Books.

Eysenck, H. J. (1965b). Extraversion and the acquisition of eyeblink and GSR conditioned responses. *Psychological Bulletin, 63,* 258–279.

Eysenck, H. J. (1967). *The biological basis of personality.* Springfield, IL: Charles Thomas, Publisher.

Eysenck, H. J. (1973). *Eysenck on extraversion.* New York: John Wiley & Sons.

Eysenck, H. J. (1977). Personality and the clarification of adult offenders. *British Journal of Criminology, 17,* 169–179.

Eysenck, H. J. (1980). Hans Jurgen Eysenck: Autobiographical essay. In G. Lindzey (ed.), *A history of psychology in autobiography,* Vol. VII. New York: W. H. Freeman.

Eysenck, H. J. (1990a). *Rebel with a cause: The autobiography of Hans Eysenck.* London: W. H. Allen.

Eysenck, H. J. (1990b). Biological dimensions of personality. In L. A. Pervin (ed.), *Handbook of personality: Theory and research.* New York: Guilford Press.

Eysenck, S. B. J., Eysenck, H. J., & Barrett, P. (1985). A revised version of the psychoticism scale. *Personality and Individual Differences, 6,* 21–29.

Eysenck, H. J., & Eysenck, S. B. G. (1976). *Psychoticism as a dimension of personality.* New York: Crane, Russak.

Eysenck, H. J., & Wilson, G. D. (1973). *The experimental study of Freudian theories.* London: Methuen (American edition: Harper & Row).

Fadiman, J. (1980). The transpersonal stance. In R. Walsh & F. Vaughan (eds.), *Beyond ego,* pp. 175–181. Los Angeles: Tarcher.

Fadiman, J., & Frager, R. (2002). *Personality & Personal Growth* (5th ed.). Upper Saddle River, NJ: Prentice Hall.

Fahrmeier, E. D. (1978). The development of concrete operations among the Hausa. *Journal of Cross-Cultural Psychology, 9,* 23–44.

Falk, R. (1992). *Explorations on the edge of time.* Philadelphia: Temple University Press.

Fancher, R. E. (1990). *Pioneers of psychology* (2nd ed.). New York: W. W. Norton & Company.

Farley, F. (2000). Obituary: Hans J. Eysenck (1916–1997), *American Psychologist, 55,* 674–675.

Farone, S. V., & Tsuang, M. T. (1990). Genetic transmission of major affective disorders: Quantitative models and linkage analyses. *Psychological Bulletin, 108,* 109–127.

Ferster, C. B., & Skinner, B. F. (1957). Schedules of reinforcement. Englewood Cliffs, NJ: Prentice Hall.

Fincham, F. D. (2005). Marital conflict: Correlates structure, and context. In C. C. Morf & O. Ayduk (eds.), *Current directions in personality psychology,* pp. 149–156. Upper Saddle River, NJ: Pearson Education, Inc.

Fisher, A. (1991). A new synthesis comes of age. *Mosaic (NSF), 22,* 1–17.

Fisher, S., & Greenberg, R. P. (1977). *The scientific credibility of Freud's theories and therapy.* New York: Basic Books.

Fisher, S., & Greenberg, R. P. (1985). *The scientific credibility of Freud's theories and therapy.* New York: Columbia University Press.

Fisher, S., & Greenberg, R. P. (1996). *Freud scientifically reappraised: Testing the theories and therapy.* New York: John Wiley & Sons, Inc.

Fleeson, W. (2001). Towards a structure and process-integrated view of personality: Traits as density distributions of states. *Journal of Personality and Social Psychology, 80,* p. 1015.

Fleeson, W. (2005). Moving personality beyond the person–situation debate. In C. C. Morf & O. Ayduk (eds.), *Current directions in personality psychology,* pp. 15–24. Upper Saddle River, NJ: Pearson Education, Inc.

Ford, G. R. (1979). *A time to heal.* New York: Harper & Row and The Reader's Digest Association, Inc.

Forel, S. (1935). *Ruckblick auf mein Leben.* Zurich: Europa-Verlag, p. 64.

Frankl, V. E. (1959). *From death-camp to existentialism: A psychiatrist's path to a new therapy.* Boston: Beacon Press.

Frankl, V. E. (1960). *The doctor and the soul, an introduction to logotherapy.* New York: Knopf.

Freedman, M. B., Leary, T. F., Ossorio, A. G., & Coffey, H. S. (1951). The interpersonal dimension of personality. *Journal of Personality, 20,* 143–161.

Freeman, L. (1972). *The story of Anna O.* New York: Walker & Co.

Freud, A. (1926, 1927). *The psychoanalytic treatment of children.* New York: Schocken Books, 1964.

Freud, A. (1946). *The ego and the mechanisms of defense.* New York: International Universities Press.

Freud, A. (1965). *Normality and pathology in childhood.* In Vol. 6 of *The Writings of Anna Freud.* New York: International Universities Press.

Freud, E. L. (1960). *Letters of Sigmund Freud.* New York: Basic Books.

Freud, S. (1895). Project for a scientific psychology. *Standard edition,* Vol. 1. London: Hogarth Press, 1966.

Freud, S. (1900). The interpretation of dreams I. *Standard edition,* Vol. 4. London: Hogarth Press, 1953.

Freud, S. (1900–1901). The interpretation of dreams II. *Standard edition,* Vol. 5. London: Hogarth Press, 1953.

Freud, S. (1901). The psychopathology of everyday life. *Standard edition,* Vol. 6. London: Hogarth, 1960.

Freud, S. (1905a). Three essays on the theory of sexuality. *Standard edition,* Vol. 7. London: Hogarth, 1953.

Freud, S. (1905b). Jokes and their relation to the unconscious. *Standard edition,* Vol. 8. London: Hogarth, 1960.

Freud, S. (1910). Five lectures on psychoanalysis, Leonardo da Vinci, and other works. Vol. 11. London: Hogarth, 1957.

Freud, S. (1911–1913). The case of Schreger, papers on technique, and other works. *Standard edition,* Vol. 12. London: Hogarth, 1958.

Freud, S. (1912). The dynamics of transference. *Collected papers,* Vol. 2. New York: Basic Books, Inc.

Freud, S. (1913–1914). Totem and taboo, and other works. *Standard edition,* Vol. 13.

Freud, S. (1915). Instincts and their vicissitudes. *Colleted Papers,* Vol. 4. New York: Basic Books.

Freud, S. (1915–1916). Introductory lectures on psycho-analysis (parts I & II). *Standard edition.* Volume 15. 1961.

Freud, S. (1916). *Leonardo da Vinci: A study in psychosexuality.* New York: Vintage Books.

Freud, S. (1916–1917). Introductory lectures on psycho-analysis (part III). *Standard edition,* Vol. 16. London: Hogarth, 1963.

Freud, S. (1920). Beyond the pleasure principle, group psychology and other works. *Standard edition,* Vol. 18. London: Hogarth, 1955.

Freud, S. (1921). Group psychology and the analysis of the ego. *Standard edition,* Vol. 18. London: Hogarth, 1955.

Freud, S. (1923). The ego and the id. *Standard edition,* Vol. 19. London: Hogarth, 1959.

Freud, S. (1925). An autobiographical study. *Standard edition,* Vol. 20. London: Hogarth, 1961.

Freud, S. (1926). The question of lay analysis. *Standard edition,* Vol. 20. London: Hogarth, 1959.

Freud, S. (1927–31). *The future of an illusion, civilization and its discontents, and other works. Standard edition,* Vol. 21. London: Hogarth, 1961.

Freud, S. (1933). New introductory lectures on psycho-analysis, trans. and ed. James Strachey. New York: W. W. Norton, 1965.

Freud, S. (1935). An autobiographical study, trans. James Strachey. New York: W. W. Norton, 1952.

Freud, S. (1937–1939). Moses and monotheism, An outline of psychoanalysis, and other works. *Standard edition,* Vol. 23. London: Hogarth, 1964.

Freud, S. (1938). *General introduction to psychoanalysis,* trans. J. Riviera. New York: Garden City Publishing Company.

Freud, S. (1940). *The standard edition of the complete psycho-logical works of Sigmund Freud.* London: Hogarth Press: Vol. 23, *Moses and monotheism, an outline of psychoanalysis, and other works.* London: Hogarth, 1964.

Freud, S. (1940–52). *Gesammelte Werke.* 18 Vols. London: Imago.

Freud, S. (1949). *An outline of psychoanalysis.* New York: Norton.

Freud, S. (1954). *The origin of psychoanalysis: Letters to Wilhelm Fliess, drafts and notes, 1897–1902.* Marie Bonaparte, anm Freud, & Ernst Kris (eds.) New York: Basic Books.

Freud, S., & Jung, C. G. (1974). *The Freud/Jung letters.* William McGuire (ed.) Princeton, NJ: Princeton University Press.

Freud-Bernays, A. (1940). My brother, Sigmund. *American Mercury,* 335–342.

Friedan, B. (1977). *The feminine mystique.* New York: Dell.

Fromm, E. (1941). *Escape from freedom.* New York: Farrar & Rinehart.

Fromm, E. (1955). *The sane society.* New York: Rinehart.

Fromm, E. (1956). *The art of loving.* New York: Bantam Books (also published by Harper).

Fromm, E. (1959). *Sigmund Freud's mission: An analysis of his personality and his influence.* New York: Harper & Brothers Publishers.

Fromm, E. (1962). *Beyond the Chains of Illusion: My encounter with Marx and Freud.* New York: Simon & Schuster.

Fromm, E. (1964). *The heart of man.* New York: Harper & Row.

Fromm, E. (1973). *The anatomy of human destructiveness.* New York: Rinehart.

Fromm, E. (1976). *To have or to be?* New York: Harper & Row.

Fromm, E., & Maccoby, (1970). *Social character in a Mexican village.* Englewood Cliffs, NJ: Prentice-Hall.

Frost, R. (1915). *The Road Not Taken.* Quoted in N. Foerster (ed.), *American poetry and prose.* Boston: Houghton Mifflin.

Fujioka, T., Fujioka, A., Tan, N., Chowdhury, G., Mouri, H., Sakata, Y., & Nakamura, S. (2001). Mild prenatal stress enhances learning performance in non-adapted rat offspring. *Neuroscience, 103,* 301.

Fuller, A. (1994). *Psychology and religion.* Lanham, MD: Littlefield Adams.

Fullerton, C. S., Ursana, R. J., Harry, P., Wetzler, H. P., & Slusarcick, A. (1989). Birth order, psychological well-being, and social support in young adults. *Journal of Nervous & Mental Disease, 177* (9), 556–559.

Funder, D. C. (2004). *The personality puzzle.* New York: Norton.

Furman, M. E., & Gallo, F. P. (2000). *The neurophysics of human behvior: Explorations at the interface of brain, mind, behavior, and information.* Boca Raton, FL: CRC Press.

Gallistel, C. R. (1998). Symbolic processes in the brain: The case of insect navigation. In D. Scarborough and S. Sternberg (eds.), *Methods, models, and conceptual issues: An invitation to cognitive science, Volume 4.* Cambridge, MA: MIT Press.

Gardner, H. (1983). *Frames of mind: The theory of multiple intelligences.* New York: Basic Books.

Gardner, H. (1984). *The mind's new science.* New York: Basic Books.

Gay, P. (1988). *Freud: A life for our time.* New York: Norton.

Gedo, J. E. (1991). *The biology of clinical encounters: Psycho-analysis as a science of mind.* Hillsdale, NJ: The Analytic Press.

Gendlin E. T. (1981). *Focusing* (2nd ed.). New York: Bantam Books.

Gendlin, E. T. (1988). Carl Rogers (1902–1987). *American Psychologist, 43,* 127–128.

Gergen, K. (1985). The social constructionist movement in modern psychology. *American Psychologist, 40,* 266–275.

Gergen, K. (1991a). *The saturated self.* New York: Basic Books.

Gergen, K. (1991b). The saturated family. *Family Therapy Networker, 15,* 26–35.

Giese, H., & Schmidt, S. (1968). *Student sexualitat.* Hamburg: Rowohlt.

Gleick, J. (1987). *Chaos: Making a new science.* New York: Penguin Books.

Goldberg, A. (1990). *The prisonhouse of psychoanalysis.* Hillsdale, NJ: The Analytic Press.

Goldberg, L. R. (1981). Language and individual differences: The search for universals in personality lexicons. In L. Wheeler (ed.), *Review of Personality* and *Social Psychology,* pp. 141–165. Beverly Hills, CA: Sage.

Golding, W. (1962). *Lord of the flies.* New York: Coward-McCann.

Goldstein, K. (1939). *The organism.* New York: American Book.

Gossette, R. L., & O'Brien, R. M. (1992). The efficacy of rational–emotive therapy in adults: Clinical fact or psychometric artifact? *Journal of Behavior Therapy and Experimental Psychiatry, 23,* 9–24.

Gottesman, I. I. (1991). *Schizophrenia genesis: The origins of madness.* New York: W. H. Freeman.

Goubet, N., & Clifton, R. K. (1998). Object and event representation in 6½-month-old infants. *Developmental Psychology, 34,* 63–76.

Gould, S. J. (1978). Sociobiology: The art of story telling. *New Scientist, 80,* 530–533.

Gould, S. J., & Lewontin, R. C. (1979). The spandrels of San Marco and the Panglossian paradigm: A critique of the adaptionist programme. *Proceedings of the Royal Society of London, 205,* 581–598.

Gray, J. (1990). Brain systems that mediate both emotion and cognition. *Motivation and Emotion, 4,* 269–288.

Gray, J. A. (1964). *Pavlov's typology.* New York: Macmillan.

Gray, J. A. (1972). *The psychology of fear and stress.* New York: McGraw-Hill.

Gray, S. W. (1986). The relationship between self-actualization and leisure satisfaction. *Psychology, 23,* 6–12.

Graziano, W. G., & Eisenberg, N. (1997). Agreeableness: A dimension of personality. In R. Hogan, J. A. Johnson, and S. Briggs (eds.), *Handbook of personality psychology,* pp. 795–824. New York: Academic Press.

Greenberg, J., Pyszczynski, T., Solomon, S., Rosenblatt, A., Veeder, M., Kirkland, S., & Lyon, D. (1990). Evidence for terror management theory II: The effects of mortality salience reactions to those who threaten or bolster the cultural worldview. *Journal of Personality and Social Psychology, 58,* 308–318.

Greenberg, J., Solomon, S., Pyszczynski, T. (1997). Terror management theory of self-esteem and cultural worldviews: Empirical assessments and conceptual refinements. In M. P. Zanna (ed.), *Advances in experimental social psychology,* pp. 61–139. New York: Academic Press.

Greenberg, J., Solomon, S., Pyszczynski, T., Rosenblatt, A., Burling, J., Lyon, D., & Simon, L. (1992). Assessing the terror management of self-esteem: Converging evidence of an anxiety-buffering function. *Journal of Personality and Social Psychology, 63,* 913–922.

Greenberg, L., & Pascual-Leone, J. (1999) A dialectical constructivist approach to experiential change. In R. A. Neimeyer & M. J. Mahoney (eds.), *Constructivism in psychotherapy,* pp. 195–231. Washington, DC: American Psychological Association.

Greening, T. (2001). Five basic postulates of humanistic psychology. *Journal of Humanistic Psychology, 41,* 3.

Greenwald, A. G. (1992). Unconscious cognition reclaimed. *American Psychologist, 47,* 766–799.

Grof, S. (1998). *The cosmic game: Explorations of the frontiers of human consciousness.* Albany, NY: State University of New York Press.

Grosskurth, P. (1986). *Melanie Klein: Her world and her work.* Cambridge, MA: Harvard University Press.

Grossman, Lev. (2003). "Can Freud Get His Job Back? *Time, 161, No. 3,* pp. 76–82.

Gruenfeld, D. H. (1995). Status, ideology, and integrative complexity on the U.S. Supreme Court: Rethinking the politics of political decision making. *Journal of Personality and Social Psychology, 68,* 5–20.

Guest, W. (1985). *Societal changes: Implications for education.* Unpublished report to Superintendent of Schools, Rio Linda Unified School District, Rio Linda, CA.

Guntrip, H. (1971). *Psychoanalytic theory, therapy, and the self.* New York: Basic Books.

Gurman, A. S. (1977). The patient's perception of therapeutic relationships. In A. S. Gurman &

A. M. Razin (eds.), *Effective psychotherapy: A handbook of research.* Oxford: Pergamon Press.

Guthrie, E. R. (1952). *The psychology of learning* (revised edition). New York: Harper & Row.

Guthrie, E. R. (1959). Association by contiguity. In S. Koch (ed.), *Psychology: A study of a science* (Vol. 2). New York: McGraw-Hill.

Hair, J. F., Anderson, R. E., Tatham, R. L., & Black, W. C. (1998). *Multivariate data analysis* (fifth edition). Upper Saddle River, NJ: Prentice Hall.

Hale, N. G., Jr. (ed.) (1971). *James Jackson Putnam and psychoanalysis.* Cambridge, MA: Harvard University Press.

Hall, C. S., & Lindzey, G. (1957) *Theories of personality.* New York: Wiley.

Hall, C. S., & Lindzey, G. (1978) *Theories of personality* (3rd ed.). New York: Wiley.

Hall, M. H. (1968, July). A conversation with Abraham H. Maslow. *Psychology Today,* pp. 35–37, 54–57.

Halverson, C. F., Kohnstamm, G. A., and Martin, R. P. (eds.). (1994). *The developing structure of temperament and personality from infancy to adulthood.* Hillsdale, NJ: Erlbaum.

Hamilton, E. (1969). *Mythology: Timeless tales of gods and heroes.* New York: Mentor Books.

Hamilton, W. D. (1964). The genetical evolution of social behavior I & II. *Journal of Theoretical Biology, 7,* 1–52.

Hammond, D. C. (ed.), (1990). *Handbook of hypnotic suggestions and metaphors.* New York: Norton.

Hampden-Turner, C. (1981). *Maps of the mind.* New York: Macmillan.

Hanh, T. N. (1976). *The miracle of mindfulness.* Boston: Beacon Press.

Hannush, M. J. (1987). "John B. Watson remembered: An interview with James B. Watson," *Journal of the History of the Behavioral Sciences, 23,* 137.

Harlow, H. F. (1953). Mice, monkeys, men, and motives. *Psychological Review, 60,* 23–32.

Harlow, H. F. (1958). The nature of love. *American Psychologist, 13,* 673–685.

Harlow, H. F. (1973). *Learning to love.* New York: Ballantine Books, Inc.

Harris, J. R. (1995). Where is the child's environment? A group socialization theory of development. *Psychological Review, 102,* 458–489.

Hartmann, H. (1939). *Ego psychology and the problem of adaptation.* New York: International Universities Press.

Hassan, I. (1987). *The postmodern turn.* Columbus: Ohio State University Press.

Hatfield, J. H. (2000). *Fortunate son: George W. Bush and the making of an American president.* New York: St. Martin's Press.

Hauke, C. (2000). *Jung and the postmodern.* New York: Routledge.

Hauser, M. D., Chomsky, N., & Fitch, W. T. (2002). The faculty of language: What is it, who has it, and how did it evolve? *Science, 298,* 1569–1579.

Hebb, D. O. (1949). *The organization of behavior.* New York: Wiley.

Hebb, D. O. (1959). A neuropsychological theory. In S. Koch (ed.), *Psychology: A study of a science: Volume 1. Sensory, perceptual, and physiological formulations.* New York: McGraw-Hill.

Heimberg, R. G., Liebowitz, M. R., Hope, D. A., Schneier, F. R., Holt, C. S., Welkowitz, L. A., Juster, H. R., Campeas, R., Bruch, M. A., Cloitre, M., Fallon, B., Klein, D. F. (1998). Cognitive behavioral group therapy vs. phenelzine therapy for social phobia: 12-week outcome. *Archives of General Psychiatry, 55,* (12), pp. 1133–1141.

Herdt, G. (1982). *Rituals of manhood.* Berkeley: University of California Press.

Herek, G. M. (1987). Religious orientation and prejudice: A comparison of racial and sexual attitudes. *Personality and Social Psychology Bulletin, 13,* 34–44.

Higgins, E. T. (1987). Self-Discrepancy: A theory relating self and affect. *Psychological Review, 94,* 319–340.

Hiroto, D. S., & Seligman, M. E. P. (1975). Generality of learned helplessness in man. *Journal of Personality and Social Psychology, 31,* 311–327.

Hoffman, E. (1988). *The right to be human: A biography of Abraham Maslow.* Los Angeles: Jeremy P. Tarcher.

Hoffman, H. G., Garcia-Palacios, A., Carlin, A., Furness, T. A. III, Botella-Arbona, C. (2003). Interfaces that heal: Coupling real and virtual objects to treat spider phobia. *International Journal of Human–Computer Interaction 16,* (2), 283–300.

Hogan, R. (1983). A socioanalytic theory of personality. *Nebraska symposium on motivation, 1982: Personality–Current Theory and Research,* ed. M. M. Page. Lincoln: University of Nebraska Press.

Hogan, R. (1996). A socioanalytic perspective on the five-factor model. In J. S. Wiggins (ed.), *The five-factor model of personality: Theoretical perspectives,* pp. 163–179. New York: Guilford Press.

Holland, J. G., & Skinner, B. F. (1961). *The analysis of behavior.* New York: McGraw-Hill.

Holmes, D. S. (1968). Dimensions of projection. *Psychological Bulletin, 69,* 248–268.

Holmes, D. S. (1978). Projection as a defense mechanism. *Psychological Bulletin, 85,* 677–688.

Holt, R. R. (1973). *Abstracts of the standard edition of the complete psychological works of Sigmund Freud with an introduction on reading Freud.* New York: Jason Aronson.

Hormuth, S. E. (1986). The sampling of experiences in situ. *Journal of Personality, 54,* 262–293.

Horne, J. A., & Ostberg, O. (1976). A self-assessment questionnaire to determine morningness–eveningness in human circadian rhythms. *International Journal of Chronobiology, 4,* 97–110.

Horney, K. (1937). *The neurotic personality of our time.* New York: Norton.

Horney, K. (1939). *New way in psychoanalysis.* New York: Norton.

Horney, K. (1942). *Self-analysis.* New York: Norton.

Horney, K. (1945). *Our inner conflicts.* New York: Norton.

Horney, K. (1946). *Are you considering psychoanalysis?* New York: Norton.

Horney, K. (1950). *Neurosis and human growth.* New York: Norton.

Horney, K. (1967). *Feminine psychology.* New York: Norton.

Horney, K. (1980). *The adolescent diaries of Karen Horney.* New York: Basic Books.

Hovland, C. I. (1952). A "Communication Analysis" of concept learning. *Psychological Review, 59,* 461–472.

Howard, J. W., & Dawes, R. M. (1976). Linear prediction of marital happiness. *Personal and Social Psychology Bulletin, 2,* 478–480.

Hubel, D. H., & Wiesel, T. N. (1959). Receptive fields of single neurons in the cat's striate cortex. *Journal of Physiology, 148,* 574–591.

Hubel, D. H., & Wiesel, T. N. (1962). Receptive fields, binocular interaction, and functional architecture in the cat's visual cortex. *Journal of Physiology, 160,* 106–154.

Hull, C. L. (1943). *Principles of behavior.* Englewood Cliffs, NJ: Prentice-Hall.

Ingersoll, E. W., & Thoman, E. B. (1994). The breathing bear: Effects on respiration in premature infants. *Physiology & Behavior, 56,* 855–860.

International Study Project. (1972). *Abraham H. Maslow: A memorial volume.* Monterey, CA: Brooks/Cole.

Ishiyama, F. I., Munson, P. A., & Chabassol, D. J. (1990). Birth order and fear of success among midadolescents. *Psychological Reports, 66* (1), 17–18.

Jacobson, E. (1938). *Progressive relaxation.* Chicago: University of Chicago Press.

Jacoby, L. L. (1991). A process dissociation framework: Separating automatic from intentional uses of memory. *Journal of Memory and Language, 30,* 513–541.

James, M., & Jongeward, D. (1971). *Born to win: Transactional analysis with Gestalt experiments.* Reading, MA: Addison-Wesley Publishing Co. Inc.

James, W. (1890). *Principles of psychology* (2 vols.). New York: Henry Holt. Unaltered republication, New York: Dover, 1950.

James, W. (1902/1958). *The varieties of religious experience.* New York: New American Library of World Literature.

Jankowicz, A. D., & Hisrich, R. (1987). Intuition in small-business lending decisions. *Journal of Small Business Management, 25,* 45–52.

Joe, V. C., McGee, S. J., & Dazey, D. (1977). Religiousness and devaluation of a rape victim. *Journal of Clinical Psychology, 33,* 64.

Johnson-Laird, P. N. (1988). *The computer and the mind: An introduction to cognitive science.* Cambridge, MA: Harvard University Press.

Jones, E. (1953). *The life and work of Sigmund Freud Vol 1.* New York: Basic Books.

Jones, E. E., & Davis, K. E. (1965). From acts to dispositions: The attribution process in person perception. In L. Berkowitz (ed.), *Advances in experimental social psychology* (Vol. 2, pp. 220–266). New York: Academic Press.

Jones, M. C. (1924). A laboratory study of fear: The case of Peter. *Journal of Genetic Psychology, 31,* 308–315.

Jung, C. G. *The collected works of C. G. Jung,* ed. H. Read, M. Fordham, and G. Adler. Bollingen Series. New York: Pantheon Books, and London: Routledge & Kegan Paul.

Vol. 1. (1957). *Psychiatric studies.*

Vol. 3. (1960). *The psychogenesis of mental disease.*

Vol. 4. (1961b). *Freud and psychoanalysis.*

Vol. 5. (1956). *Symbols of transformation.*

Vol. 6. (1971). *Psychological types.*

Vol. 7. (1953a). *Two essays on analytical psychology.*

Vol. 8. (1960). *The structure and dynamics of the psyche.*

Vol. 9i. (1959a). *The archetypes and the collective unconscious.*

Vol 9i. (1959b). *Aion.*

Vol. 10. (1964). *Civilization in transition.*

Vol. 11. (1958). *Psychology and religion: West and east.*

Vol. 12. (1953b). *Psychology and alchemy.*

Vol. 13. (1963). *Alchemical studies.*

Vol. 14. (1963). *Mysterium coniunctionis.*

Vol. 15. (1966). *The spirit in man, art, and literature.*

Vol. 16. (1954). *The practice of psychotherapy.*

Vol. 17. (1954). *The development of personality.*

Jung, C. G. (1961a). *Memories, dreams, reflections*, ed. A. Jaffe. New York: Pantheon.

Jung, C. G. (1968). *Analytic psychology: Its theory and practice* (The Tavistock Lectures.) New York: Pantheon.

Jung, C. G. (1984). *Selected letters of C. J. Jung, 1909–1961.* (G. Adler, ed.). Princeton, NJ: Princeton University Press.

Jung, C. J. (1918). *Studies in word-association: Experiments in the diagnosis of psychopathological conditions carried out at the psychiatric clinic of the University of Zurich.* New York: Russell & Russell. (Reissued, 1969).

Jung, C. J. (1928). *Contributions to analytic psychology.* New York: Harcourt Brace Jovanovich.

Jung, C. J. (1945). *The secret of the golden flower.*

Kaczor, L. M., Ryckman, R. M., Thornton, B., & Kuelnel, R. H. (1991). Observer hyper-competitiveness and victim precipitation of rape. *Journal of Social Psychology, 131,* 131–134.

Kahn, S., Zimmerman, G., Csikszentmihalyi, M., & Getzels, J. W. (1985). Relations between identity in young adulthood and intimacy at midlife. *Journal of Personality and Social Psychology, 49,* 1316–1322.

Kahr, B. (1996). *D. W. Winnicott: A biographical portrait.* New York: International Universities Press.

Kamphuis, J. H., Emmelkamp, P. M. G., & Krijn, M. U. (2002). Specific phobia. In M. Hersen (ed.) *Clinical behavior therapy: Adults and children,* pp. 75–89. New York: Wiley.

Kandel, E. R., Schwartz, J. H., and Jessell, T. M. eds. (1991). *Principles of neural science, third edition.* New York: Elsevier.

Kant, I. (1965). *Critique of pure reason* trans. N. Kemp Smith. New York: Macmillan.

Kantrowitz, R. E., & Ballou, M.A. (1992). A feminist critique of cognitive–behavioral therapy. In L. S. Brown & M. Ballou (eds.), *Personality and psychopathology: Feminist reappraisals,* pp. 70–87. New York: Guilford Press.

Kaplan, A. (1979). Clarifying the concept of androgyny: Implications for therapy. *Psychology of Women Quarterly 3,* 223–230.

Kaplan, A., & Sedney, M. A. (1980). *Psychology and sex roles: An androgynous perspective.* Boston: Little, Brown.

Karier, C. J. (1986). *Scientists of the mind: Intellectual founders of modern psychology.* Chicago: University of Illinois Press.

Kegan, R. (1982). *The evolving self.* Cambridge, MA: Harvard University Press.

Keller, F. S. (1968). Good-bye teacher. *Journal of applied behavior analysis, 1,* 69–89.

Kelly, G. A. (1955). *The psychology of personal constructs.* (2 vols.). New York: W. W. Norton & Co., Inc.

Kelly, G. A. (1958). Man's construction of his alternatives. In G. Lindzay (ed.), *Assessment of human motives.* New York: Holt, Rinehart & Winston.

Kelly, G. A. (1969). The autobiography of a theory. In B. Maher (ed.), *Clinical psychology and personality: Selected papers of George Kelly,* pp. 40–65. New York: Wiley.

Kelly, G. A. (1970). A summary statement of a cognitively-oriented comprehensive theory of behavior. In J. C. Mancuso (ed.), *Readings for a cognitive theory of personality,* pp. 27–58. New York: Holt, Rinehart and Winston, Inc.

Kelly, G. A. (1977). The psychology of the unknown. In D. Bannister (ed.), *New perspectives in personal construct theory,* pp. 1–19. London: Academic Press.

Kelly, H. H. (1967). Attribution theory in social psychology. In D. Levine (ed.), *Nebraska symposium on motivation* (Vol. 15, pp. 192–238). Lincoln: University of Nebraska Press.

Kelsey, M. (1974). *God, dreams, and revelation: A Christian interpretation of dreams.* Minneapolis: Augsburg.

Kelsey, M. (1982). *Christo-psychology.* New York: Crossroad.

Kendler, H. H. (2000). *Amoral thoughts about morality: The intersection of science, psychology, and ethics.* Springfield, IL: Charles C. Thomas.

Kidwell, J. (1982). The neglected birth order: Middleborns. *Journal of Marriage and the Family, 44,* 225–235.

Kierkegaard, S. (1844). *The concept of dread,* trans. Walter Lowrie. Princeton, NJ: Princeton University Press edition, 1957.

Kierkegaard, S. (1944). *Either/Or: A fragment of life.* Vol. II trans. Walter Lowrie. Princeton, NJ: Princeton University Press.

Kiesler, D. J. (1982). Interpersonal theory for personality and psychotherapy. In J. C. Anchin & D. J. Kiesler (eds.), *Handbook of interpersonal psychotherapy,* pp. 3–24. Elmsford, NY: Pergamon.

Kiesler, D. J. (1983). The 1982 interpersonal circle: A taxonomy for complementarity in human transactions. *Psychological Review, 90,* 185–214.

Kiesler, D. J. (1985). *The 1982 interpersonal circle: Acts version.* Unpublished manuscript, Virginia Commonwealth University, Richmond.

Kiesler, D. J. (1996). *Contemporary interpersonal theory and research: Personality, psychopathology, and psychotherapy.* New York: John Wiley.

Kihlstrom, J. F. (1987). The cognitive unconscious. *Science, 237,* 1445–1452.

Kirschenbaum, H. (1979). *On becoming Carl Rogers.* New York: Delacorte Press.

Kirschenbaum, H., & Henderson, V. (eds.). (1989). *Carl Rogers: Dialogues.* Boston: Houghton Mifflin.

Kirsner, D. (2000). *Unfree associations: Inside analytic institutes.*

Kitayama, S., & Markus, H. R. (1992, May). *Construal of self as cultural frame: Implications for internationalizing psychology.* Paper presented to symposium on Internationalization and Higher Education, Ann Arbor, MI.

Klein, M. (1923a). Early analysis. In *Love, Guilt and Reparation and Other Works 1921–1945,* pp. 77–105. London: Hogarth Press, 1975.

Klein, M. (1927). Notes on "A dream of forensic interest" by Douglas Bryan. *International Journal of Psycho-Analysis, 9,* 255–258.

Klein, M. (1928). Early stages of the Oedipus complex. In *Love, guilt, and reparation and other works 1921–1945,* pp. 139–169. London: Hogarth Press, 1975.

Klein, M. (1932). *The psycho-analysis of children.* London: Hogarth, 1975.

Klein, M. (1935). A contribution to the psychogenesis of manic–depressive states. In *Love, guilt and reparation and other works 1921–1945.* London: Hogarth Press.

Klein, M. (1936). Weaning. In *Love, guilt and reparation and other works 1921–1945,* pp. 262–289. London: Hogarth Press, 1975.

Klein, M. (1955). The psycho-analytic play technique: Its history and significance. In *Envy and Gratitude and Other Works 1946–1963,* pp. 122–140. London: Hogarth Press, 1975.

Klein, M. (1961). *Narrative of a child analysis.* London: Hogarth Press.

Kline, P. (1972). *Fact and fantasy in Freudian theory.* London: Methuen. (American edition published by Harper & Row).

Kohlberg, L., Levine, C., & Hewer, A. (1983). *Moral stages: A current formulation and a response to critics.* Basel, Switzerland: Karger.

Kohut, H. (1977). *The restoration of the self.* New York: International Universities Press.

Kohut, H., & Wolff, E. (1978). The disorders of the self and their treatment: An outline. *The International Journal of Psychoanalysis, 59,* 413–425.

Kolb, B., & Whishaw, I. Q. (1990). *Fundamentals of human neuropsychology,* 3rd edn. New York: W. H. Freeman & Co.

Korzybski, A. (1958). *Science and sanity: An introduction to non-Aristotelian system and general semantics* (4th ed.). Lake Shore, CT: Institute of General Semantics.

Kosslyn, S. M. (1991). A cognitive neuroscience of visual cognition: Further developments. In R. H. Logie & P. A. Vroon (eds.), *Mental images in human cognition,* pp. 351–381. Amsterdam: North-Holland.

Krippner, S. (ed.). (1972). The plateau experience: A. H. Maslow and others. *Journal of Transpersonal Psychology, 4,* 107–120.

Kuhn, M., & McPartland, T. S. (1954). An empirical investigation of self-attitudes. *American Sociological Review, 19,* 69–76.

Kunc, N. (1992). The need to belong. In R. Villa, J. Thousand, W. Stainback, & S. Stainback (eds.), *Restructuring for caring and effective education.* Baltimore: Paul H. Brookes.

Kung, H. (1979). *Freud and the problem of God.* New Haven, CT: Yale University Press.

Laan, E., Everaerd, W., van Bellen, G., & Hanewald, G. J. F. P. (1994). Women's sexual and emotional responses to male- and female-produced erotica. *Archives of Sexual Behavior, 23 (2),* 153–169.

Lachman, R., Lachman, J., & Butterfield, E. C. (1979). *Cognitive psychology and information processing: An introduction.* Hillsdale, NJ: Lawrence Earlbaum Associates.

Laforgue, R. (1956). Personal memories of Freud. In H. M. Ruitenbeek, *Freud as we knew him,* 1973, pp. 341–349. Detroit, MI: Wayne State University Press.

Laing, R. D., Phillipson, H., & Lee, A. R. (1966). *Interpersonal perception: A theory and a method of research.* New York: Springer.

Lajoie, D., & Shapiro, S. (1992). Definitions of transpersonal psychology: The first twenty-three years. *Journal of Transpersonal Psychology 24,* 79–98.

Lamielle, J. T. (1981). Toward an idiothetic psychology of personality. *American Psychologist, 36,* 276–289.

Langer, W. (1972). *The mind of Adolf Hitler: The secret wartime report.* New York: Basic Books.

Larsen, R. J. (1989). A process approach to personality: Utilizing time as a facet of data. In D. Buss &

N. Cantor (eds.), *Personality psychology: Recent trends and emerging directions*, pp. 177–193. New York: Springer-Verlag.

Larsen, R. J., & Buss, D. M. (2002). *Personality psychology: Domains of knowledge about human nature.* New York: McGraw-Hill.

Larsen, R. J., & Kasimatis, M. (1990). Individual differences in entrainment of mood to the weekly calender. *Journal of Personality and Social Psychology, 58,* 164–171.

Latane, B. (1981). The psychology of social impact. *American Psychologist, 36,* 343–356.

Lather, P. (1992). Postmodernism and the human sciences. In S. Kvale (ed.), *Psychology and postmodernism,* pp. 88–109. Newbury Park, CA: Sage.

Lavine, T. Z. (1984). *From Socrates to Sartre: The philosophical quest.* New York: Bantam Books.

Leahey, T. H. (1987). *A history of psychology* (2nd ed.) Englewood Cliffs, NJ: Prentice-Hall.

Leak, G. K. (1974). Effects of hostility arousal and aggressive humor on catharsis and humor preference. *Journal of Personality and Social Psychology, 30,* 736–740.

Leary, M. R. (1999). The social and psychological importance of self-esteem. In R. M. Kowalski & M. R. Leary (eds.), *The social psychology of emotional and behavioral problems: Interface of social and clinical psychology,* pp. 197–221. Washington, DC: American Psychological Association.

Leary, M. R. (2005). Making sense of self-esteem. In C. C. Morf & O. Ayduk (eds.), *Current directions in personality psychology,* pp. 137–142. Upper Saddle River, NJ: Pearson Education, Inc.

Leary, M. R., & Downs, D. L. (1995). Interpersonal functions of the self-esteem motive: The self-esteem system as a sociometer. In M. H. Kernis (ed.), *Efficacy, agency, and self-esteem,* pp. 123–144. New York: Plenum Press.

Leary, T. (1957). *Interpersonal diagnosis of personality: A functional theory and methodology for personality evaluation.* New York: The Ronald Press.

Leary, T. F., & Coffey, H. S. (1955). Interpersonal diagnosis: Some problems of methodology and validation. *Journal of Abnormal and Social Psychology, 50,* 110–124.

Leith, G. (1974). Individual differences in learning: Interaction of personality and teaching methods. In *Personality and academic process,* pp. 14–25.

Leonard, G. (1983, December). Abraham Maslow and the new self. *Esquire Magazine,* pp. 326–336.

Lerman, H. (1992). The limits of phenomenology: A feminist critique of the humanistic personality theories.

In L. S. Brown & M. Ballou (eds.), *Personality and psychopathology.* New York and London: Guilford Press.

Levant, R. F., & Schlien, J. M. (eds.) (1984). *Client-centered therapy and the person-centered approach: New directions in theory, research, and practice.* New York: Praeger.

Levin, R. (1991). *Mapping the mind.* Hillsdale, NJ: The Analytic Press.

Levy, S. (1956). Sentence completion and word association tests. In D. Brower & L. E. Abt (eds.), *Progress in clinical psychology.* Vol. 2. New York: Grune & Stratton.

Lewicki, P., Hill, T., & Czyzewska, M. (1992). Nonconscious acquisition of information. *American Psychologist, 47,* 796–801.

Lewis, C. S. (1970). *The grand miracle.* New York: Ballantine.

Lewis, C. S. (1995). *Surprised by joy* (revised edition). New York: Harcourt.

Lewis, T., Amini, F., & Lannon, R. (2000). *A general theory of love.* New York: Random House.

Lewontin, R. C. (1998). The evolution of cognition: Questions we will never answer. In D. Scarborough & S. Sternberg (eds.), *Methods, models, and conceptual issues: An invitation to cognitive science.* Volume 4. Cambridge, MA: The MIT Press.

Lewontin, R. C., Rose, S., & Kamin, L. J. (1984). *Not in our genes.* New York: Pantheon.

Lichtenberg, J. (1983). *Psychoanalaysis and infant research.* Hillsdale, NJ: The Analytic Press.

Lidner, R. (1982). *The fifty-minute hour: A collection of true psychoanalytic tales.* New York: Jason Aronson, Inc.

Lieberman, E. J. (1985). *Acts of will: The life and works of Otto Rank.* New York: The Free Press.

Light, P., & Perrett-Clermont, A. N. (1989). Social context effects in learning and testing. In A. Gellatly, D. Rogers, & J. Sloboda (eds.), *Cognitive and social worlds,* pp. 99–112. Oxford: Clarendon Press.

Lorenz, K. (1996). Innate bases of learning. In K. H. Pribram and J. King (eds.), *Learning as self-organization.* Mahwah, NJ: Lawrence Erlbaum Associates.

Lorr, M., & McNair, D. M. (1965). Expansion of the interpersonal behavior circle. *Journal of Personality and Social Psychology, 2,* 823–830.

Lovelock, J. (1991). *Healing Gaia.* New York: Harmony Books.

Lowry, R. J. (ed.). (1979). *The journals of A. H. Maslow* (Vols. I & II). Monterey, CA: Brooks/Cole.

Lowry, R. J. (ed.). (1982) *The journals of Abraham Maslow* (abridged). Lexington, MA: The Lewis Publishing Company.

Ludlum, S. D. W. (1918). Physiological psychiatry. *Medical Clinics of North America, 2,* 895.

Ma, V., & Schoeneman, T. J. (1997). Individualism versus collectivism: A comparison of Kenyan and American self-concepts. *Basic and Applied Social Psychology, 19,* 261–273.

Maccoby, M. (1976). *The gamesman.* New York: Simon & Schuster.

Macdaid, G. P., McCaulley, M. H., & Kainz, R. I. (1986). *Myers–Briggs type indicator atlas of type tables.* Gainesville, FL: Center for Application of Psychological Type.

MacKinnon, D., Jamison, K. R., & DePaulo, J. R. (1997). Genetics of manic depressive illness. *Annual Review of Neuroscience, 20,* 355–373.

Maddi, S. R. (1985). Existential psychotherapy. In S. J. Lynn & J. P. Ganske (eds.), *Contemporary psychotherapies: Models and methods,* pp. 191–219. Columbus, OH: Merrill.

Maddi, S. R. (2003). Hardiness: An operationalization of existential courage. *Journal of Humanistic Psychology* (in press).

Maestripieri, D. (2001). Is there mother–infant bonding in primates? *Developmental Review, 21,* 43–120.

Maestripieri, D., & Zehr, J. L. (1998). Maternal responsiveness increases during pregnancy and after estrogen treatment in macaques. *Hormones and Behavior, 34,* 223–230.

Mahler, M. S. (1968). *On human symbiosis and the vicissitudes of individuation* Vol. I *Infantile psychosis.* New York: International Universities Press.

Mahler, M. S., Pine, F., & Bergman, A. (1975). *The psychological birth of the human infant.* New York: Basic Books.

Mahoney, M. J. (1991). *Human change processes.* New York: Basic Books.

Mandler, G. (1985). *Cognitive psychology: An essay in cognitive science.* Hillsdale, NJ: Lawrence Erlbaum Associates.

Marcel, A. J. (1983). Conscious and unconscious perception: Experiments on visual masking and word recognition. *Cognitive Psychology, 15,* 197–237.

Markstrom-Adams, C. (1992). A consideration of intervening factors in adolescent identity formation. In G. R. Adams, T. P. Gulluotta, & R. Montemayor (eds.), *Adolescent identity formation: Advances in adolescent development. 4,* 173–192. Newbury Park, CA: Sage.

Marrow, A. J. (1969). *The practical theorist: The life and work of Kurt Lewin.* New York: Columbia University Press.

Martin, G., & Pear, J. (2003). *Behavior modification: What it is and how to do it* (7th ed.). Upper Saddle River, NJ: Prentice Hall.

Maslow, A. H. (1943). A theory of human motivation. *Psychological Review, 50,* 370–396.

Maslow, A. H. (1950). Self-actualizing people: A study of psychological health. *Personality symposia:* Symposium # 1 on Values, pp. 11–34. New York: Grune & Stratton, Inc. Reprinted in *Dominance, self-esteem, self-actualization: Germinal papers of A. H. Maslow,* pp. 177–201, R. J. Lowry (ed.). Belmont, CA: Wadsworth Publishing Company.

Maslow, A. H. (1961). "Eupsychia—the good society." *Journal of Humanistic Psychology, 1 (2),* 1–11.

Maslow, A. H. (1964). *Religions, values, and peak-experiences.* New York: Viking.

Maslow, A. H. (1965). *Eupsychian management: A journal.* Homewood, IL: Irwin.

Maslow, A. H. (1966). *The psychology of science: A reconnaissance.* New York: Harper & Row.

Maslow, A. H. (1968). *Toward a psychology of being* (2nd ed.). New York: D. Van Nostrand Co.

Maslow, A. (1970). *Motivation and personality* (rev. ed.). New York: Harper & Row.

Maslow, A. (1971). *The farther reaches of human nature.* New York: Viking, 1971.

Maslow, A. (1987). *Motivation and personality* (3rd ed.). New York: Harper & Row.

Masserman, J. H. (1961). *Principles of dynamic psychiatry* (2nd ed.). Philadelphia: Saunders.

Massey, C. M., & Gelman, R. (1988). Preschoolers' ability to decide whether a photographed unfamiliar object can move itself. *Developmental Psychology, 24,* 307–317.

Masterpasqua, F., & Perna, P. A. (1997). *The psychological meaning of chaos: Translating theory into practice.* Washington, DC: American Psychological Association.

Mathes, E., Zevon, M., Roter, P., & Joerger, S. (1982). Peak experience tendencies. *Journal of Humanistic Psychology, 22,* 92–108.

May, R. (1953). *Man's search for himself.* New York: Norton.

May, R. (1958). Contributions of existential psychotherapy. In R. May, E. Angel, and H. F. Ellenberger (eds.), *Existence: A new dimension in psychiatry and psychology.* New York: Basic Books.

May, R. (1960). Existential bases of psychotherapy. *Journal of OrthoPsychiatry, 1960, 30,* 685–695.

May, R. (1961). *Existence: a new dimension in psychiatry and psychology.* New York: Basic Books, 1958.

May, R. (1969). *Love and will.* New York: Norton (paperback: New York: Delta Books, 1969).

May, R. (1977). Freedom, determinism, and the future. *Psychology, 1,* 6–9.

May, R. (1981). *Freedom and destiny*. New York: Norton.

May, R. (1983). *The discovery of being: Writing in existential psychology*. New York: Norton.

Mayberry, R. I., Lock, E., & Kazmi, H. (2002). Linguistic ability and early language exposure. *Nature, Vol. 417*, 38.

Mayer, J. D. (2005) *Personality psychology: A systems approach* (3rd classroom test ed.). Boston: Pearson, Custom.

Mays, W. (1982). Piaget's sociological theory. In S. Modgil & C. Modgil (eds.), *Jean Piaget: Consensus and controversy*. New York: Praeger Publishers.

McAdams, D. P. (2000). *The person: An integrated introduction to personality psychyology*. Fort Worth, TX: Harcourt College Publishers.

McAdams, D. P., & de St. Aubin, E. (1992). A theory of generativity and its assessment through self-report, behavioral acts, and narrative themes in autobiography. *Journal of Personality and Social Psychology, 62,* 1003–1015.

McAdams, D. P., Diamond, A., de St. Aubin, E., & Mansfield, E. (1997). Stories of commitment: The psychosocial construction of generative lives. *Journal of Personality and Social Psychology, 72,* 678–694.

McAdams, D. P., & Ochberg, R. L. (eds.) (1988). Psychobiography and life narratives. Durham, NC: Duke University Press.

McCarley, R. W., & Hobson, J. A. (1977). The neurobiological origins of psychoanalytic dream theory. *American Journal of Psychiatry, 134,* 1211–1221.

McCrae, R. R., & Costa, P. T., Jr. (1985a). Updating Norman's "adequate taxonomy": Intelligence and personality dimensions in natural languages and in questionnaires. *Journal of Personality and Social Psychology, 49,* 710–721.

McCrae, R. R., & Costa, P. T., Jr. (1985b). Openness to experience. In R. Hogan and W. H. Jones (ed.), *Perspectives in Personality* (Vol. 1, pp. 145–172).

McCrae, R. R., & Costa, P. T., Jr. (1991). Adding *Liebe und Arbeit:* The full five-factor model and well-being. *Personality and Social Psychology Bulletin, 17,* 227–232.

McCrae, R. R., & Costa, P.T., Jr. (1997). Personality trait structure as a human universal. *American Psychologist, 52,* 509–516.

McCrae, R. R., & Costa, P. T., Jr. (2003). *Personality in adulthood: A five-factor theory perspective* (2nd ed.). New York: Guilford.

McCrae, R. R., & Costa, P. T., Jr. (2005). The stability of personality: Observations and evaluations. In C.C. Morf & O. Ayduk (eds.), *Current directions in personality psychology*, pp. 3–8. Upper Saddle River, NJ: Pearson Education.

McCullough, D. (1992). *Truman*. New York: Simon & Schuster.

McCullough, M. E., Pargament, K. I., & Thoresen, C. E. (eds.) (2000). *Forgiveness: Theory, research, and practice*. New York: Guilford Press.

McDougall, W. (1908). *Introduction to social psychology*. London: Methuen.

McDougall, W. (1932). Of the words *character* and *personality*. *Character and Personality, 1,* 3–16.

McGregor, H., Lieberman, J., Greenberg, J., Solomon, S., Arndt, J., & Simon, L. (1996). *Terror management and aggression: Evidence that mortality salience promotes aggression against worldview threatening individuals*. Unpublished manuscript, University of Arizona, Tucson, Arizona.

Mecca, A.M., Smelser, N.J., & Vasconcellos, J. (eds.). (1989). *The social importance of self-esteem*. Berkeley: University of California Press.

Meichenbaum, D. H. (1977). *Cognitive-behavior modification: An integrative approach*. New York: Plenum Press.

Meltzoff, A., & Moore, M. (1977). Imitation of facial and manual gestures by human neonates. *Science, 198:* 75–78.

Meyer, A. (1907). Misconceptions at the bottom of "hopelessness of all psychology." *Psychological Bulletin, 4,* 170–170.

Michael, J. L. (1993). Establishing operations. *The Behavior Analyst, 16,* 191–206.

Michael, R. T., Gagnon, J. H., Laumann, E. O., and Kolata, G. (1994). *Sex in America: A definitive survey*. Boston: Little, Brown, and Company.

Miller, G. A. (1956). The magical number seven, plus or minus two: Some limits on our capacity for processing information. *Psychological Review, 63,* 81–97.

Miller, J. B. (1973). *Psychoanalysis and women*. Baltimore, MD: Penguin Books Inc.

Miller, J. B. (1984). *The development of women's sense of self*. Work in Progress Series. The Stone Center for Developmental Studies, Wellesley College, MA.

Miller, J. B. (1991). The development of women's sense of self. In J. V. Jordan, A. G. Kaplan, J. B. Miller, I. P. Stiver, & J. L. Surrey (eds.), *Women's growth in connection: Writings from the Stone Center,* pp. 11–26. New York: Guilford Press.

Miller, J. B., & Stiver, I. P. (1997). *The healing connection: How women form relationships in therapy and in life*. Boston, MA: Beacon Press.

Minuchin, S. (1974). *Families and family therapy*. Cambridge, MA: Harvard University Press.

Mischel, W. (1968). *Personality and assessment.* New York: Wiley.

Mischel, W. (1971). *Introduction to personality.* New York: Holt, Rinehart and Winston, Inc.

Mischel, W. (1973). Toward a cognitive and social learning reconceptualization of personality. *Psychological Review, 1973, 80,* 252–283.

Mischel, W. (1977). The interaction of person and situation. In D. Magnusson & N. S. Endler (eds.), *Personality at the crossroads: Current issues in interactional psychology.* Hillsdale, NJ: Earlbaum.

Mischel, W. (1979). On the interface of cognition and personality: Beyond the person–situation debate. *American Psychologist, 34,* 740–754.

Mischel, W. (1995). A cognitive–affective system theory of personality: Reconceptualizing situations, dispositions, dynamics and invariance in personality structure. *Psychological Review, 102,* 246–268.

Mischel, W. (1999). Personality coherence and dispositions in a cognitive–affective personality system (CAPS) approach. In D. Cervone and Y. Shoda (eds.), *The coherence of personality: Social–cognitive bases of consistency, variability, and organization,* pp. 61–93. New York: Guilford Press.

Mischel, W., & Baker, N. (1975). Cognitive appraisals and transformations in delay behavior. *Journal of Personality and Social Psychology, 31,* 254–261.

Mischel, W., & Shoda, Y. (1995). A cognitive–affective system theory of personality: Reconceptualizing situations, dispositions, dynamics, and invariance in personality structure. *Psychological Review, 1995, 102,* 246–268.

Mischel, W., & Shoda, Y. (1998). Reconciling processing dynamics and personality dispositions. *Annual Review of Psychology, 49,* 229–258.

Mischel, W., Shoda, Y., & Smith, R. E. (2004). *Introduction to personality.* Hoboken, NJ: Wiley.

Mitchell, A. (1983). *The nine American lifestyles.* New York: Warner Books.

Mitchell, S. (1988). *Relational concepts in psychoanalysis.* Cambridge, MA: Harvard University Press.

Model of personality. Washington, D.C.: American Psychological Association.

Mogenson, G. (1990). The resurrection of the dead: A Jungian approach to the mourning process. *Journal of Analytic Psychology, 35* (3), 317–333.

Monte, C. F. (1999). *Beneath the mask: An introduction to theories of personality.* New York: Harcourt Brace College Publishers.

Moore, B., Mischel, W., & Zeiss, A. (1976). Comparative effects of the reward stimulus and its cognitive representation in voluntary delay. *Journal of Personality and Social Psychology, 34,* 419–424.

Moraglia, G. (1994). C. G. Jung and the psychology of adult development. *Journal of Analytic Psychology, 39,* 55–75.

Morris, D. (1967). *The naked ape.* New York: McGraw-Hill.

Mosak, H. H. (1973). (ed.) *Alfred Adler: His influence on psychology today.* Park Ridge, NJ: Noyes Press.

Murray, H. A. (1938). *Explorations in personality.* New York: Oxford University Press.

Murray, H. A. (1959). Preparations for the scaffold of a comprehensive system. In S. Koch (ed.), *Psychology: A study of a science* (Vol. 3). New York: McGraw-Hill.

Myers, I. B. (1962). *The Myers–Briggs type indicator manual.* Palo Alto, CA: Consulting Psychologists Press.

Myers, I. B., & McCaulley, M. H. (1985). *A guide to the development and use of the Myers–Briggs Type Indicator.* Palo Alto, CA: Consulting Psychologists Press.

Nadder, T. S., Silberg, J. L., Eaves, L. J., Maes, H. H., & Meyer, J. M. (1998). Genetic effects on ADHD symptomatology in 7- to 13-year-old twins: Results from a telephone survey. *Behavior Genetics, 28,* 83–99.

Neimeyer, R. A. (1984). Cognitive complexity and marital satisfaction. *Journal of Social and Clinical Psychology, 2,* 258–263.

Neimeyer, R. A. (1992). Personal constructs in career counseling and development. *Journal of Career Development, 18,* 163–173.

Neimeyer, R. A., & Jackson, T. T. (1997). George A. Kelly and the development of personal construct theory. In W. G. Bringmann, H. E. Luck, R. Miller, & C. E. Early (eds.), *A pictorial history of psychology,* pp. 364–372. Carol Stream, IL: Quintessence.

Neimeyer, R. A., & Mahoney, M. J. (1999). *Constructivism in psychotherapy.* Washington, DC: American Psychological Association.

Nessen, R. (1978). *It sure looks different from the inside.* New York: Simon & Schuster.

Nicholls, J. G., Martin, A. R., & Wallace, B. G. (1992) *From neuron to brain.* 3rd ed. Sunderland, MA: Sinauer Associates.

Nolen-Hoeksema, S., Girgus, J. S., & Seligman, M. E. (1992). Predictors and consequences of childhood depressive symptoms: A 5-year longitudinal study. *Journal of Abnormal Psychology, 101,* 405–422.

Norman, D., Murphy, M., & Gilligan, C. (1982). Sex differences and interpersonal relationships: A cross-sectional sample in the U. S. and India. *International Journal of Aging and Human Development, 14* (4), 291–305.

Norman, W. T. (1963). Toward an adequate taxonomy of personality attributes: Replicated factor structure in peer nomination personality ratings. *Journal of Abnormal and Social Psychology, 66,* 574–583.

Nunberg, H., & Federn, E. ed. & trans. (1974). *Minutes of the Vienna Psychoanalytic Society: Volume III: 1910–1911.* New York: International Universities Press.

Ochsmann, R., & Mathy, M. (1994). *Depreciating of and distancing from foreigners: Effects of mortality salience.* Unpublished manuscript. Universitat Mainz, Mainz, Germany.

Ochsner, K. N., & Lieberman, M. D. (2001). The emergence of social cognitive neuroscience. *American Psychologist, 56,* 717–734.

Offit. A. (1995). *The sexual self: How character shapes sexual experience.* Northvale, NJ: Jason Aronson, Inc.

Orgler, H. (1963). *Alfred Adler: The man and his work.* New York: Capricorn (Putnam).

Ouchi, N. (1981). *Theory Z.* Reading, MA: Addison-Wesley.

Paige, J. M. (1966). Letters from Jenny: An approach to the clinical analysis of personality structure by computer. In P. J. Stone (ed.), *The general inquirer: A computer approach to content analysis.* Cambridge, MA: MIT Press.

Parham, T. A., & Helms, J. E. (1985). Attitudes of racial identity and self-esteem of Black students. *Journal of College Student Personnel, 26 (2),* 194–203.

Parmet, H. S. (1997). *George Bush.* New York: Scribner.

Pavlov, I. P., trans. S. Belsky. (1955). General types of animal and human higher nervous activity. In S. Koshtoyants (ed.), *I. P. Pavlov: Selected works,* pp. 313–343. Moscow: Foreign Languages Publishing House.

Peabody, D. (1985). (ed.) *National characteristics.* New York: Cambridge University Press.

Pelham, B. W. (1993). The idiographic nature of human personality: Examples of the idiographic self-concept. *Journal of Personality and Social Psychology, 64* (4), 665–677.

Penfield, W., & Jasper, H. (1954). *Epilepsy and functional anatomy of the human brain.* Boston: Little, Brown & Company.

Penrose, R., & Gardner, M. (2002). *The emperor's new mind: Concerning computers, minds, and the laws of physics.* New York: Oxford University Press.

Perry, H. S. (1962). *Editorial introduction to Schizophrenia as a human process.* New York: Norton.

Perry, J. "For the Democrats, Pam's is the Place for the Elite to Meet," *The Wall Street Journal,* October 8, 1981.

Pervin, L. A. (2003). *The science of personality.* (2nd ed.) New York: Oxford University Press.

Peterson, C., Maier, S. F., & Seligman, M. E. P. (1993). *Learned helplessness: A theory for the age of personal control.* New York: Oxford University Press.

Phillips, J. B. (1961). *Your God is too small.* New York: Macmillan.

Phinney, J. S. (1992). The multigroup ethnic identity measure. *Journal of Adolescent Research, 7* (2), 156–176.

Piaget, J. (1952a). [Autobiography.] In E. Boring, H. Langfeld, H. Werner, R. Yerkes (eds.), *A history of psychology in autobiography.* Worcester, MA: Clark University Press.

Piaget, J. (1952b). *The origins of intelligence in children.* New York: International Universities Press, Inc.

Piaget, J. (1962). *Play, dreams, and imitation in childhood.* New York: W. W. Norton & Co.

Piaget, J. (1967). *Six psychological studies.* New York: Random House.

Piaget, J. (1970a). *Structuralism.* New York: Random House.

Piaget, J. (1970b). *Genetic epistemology.* New York: W. W. Norton & Co.

Piaget, J., & Inhelder, B. (1969). *The psychology of the child.* New York: Basic Books.

Pickering, A. D., Corr, P. J., & Gray, J. A. (1999). Interactions and reinforcement sensitivity theory: A theoretical analysis of Rusting and Larsen (1997). *Personality and Individual Differences, 26,* 357–365.

Piedmont, R. L. (1999). Does sprituality represent the sixth factor of personality? Spiritual transcendence and the fire-factor model. *Journal of Personality, 67,* 985–1014.

Pinker, S. (1984). *Language, learning, and language development.* Cambridge, MA: Harvard University Press.

Pinker, S. (1997). *How the mind works.* New York: W. W. Norton & Company, Inc.

Pinker, S. (1999). *Words and rules: The ingredients of language.* London: Weidenfeld & Nicholson.

Pirsig, R. M. (1974). *Zen and the art of motorcycle maintenance.* New York: William Morrow & Company.

Plomin, R. (2002). Quoted in "Searching for genes that explain our personalities." *Monitor on Psychology,* Sept. 2002, Vol. 33.

Plomin, R., DeFries, J. C., & McClearn, G. E. (1990). *Behavioral genetics: A primer* (2nd ed.). New York: W. H. Freeman.

Pollock, G. H. (1968). The possible significance of childhood object loss in the Josef Breuer–Bertha

Pappenheim (Anna O.)–Sigmund Freud relationship. *The Journal of the American Psychoanalytic Association, 16,* Oct. 1968.

Popper, K. (1965). *Conjectures and refutations* (revised edition). London: Routledge and Kegan Paul.

Porcerelli, J. H., Thomas, S., Hibbert, S., & Cogan, R. (1998). Defense mechanisms development in children, adolescents and late adolescents. *Journal of Personality Assessment, 71,* 411–420.

Postman, L., Bruner, J. S., & McGinnies, E. (1948). Personal values as selective factors in perception. *Journal of Abnormal and Social Psychology, 43,* 142–154.

Poulin-Dubois, D., & Heroux, G. (1994). Movement and children's attributions of life properties. *International Journal of Behavioral Development, 17,* 329–347.

Pribram, K. H. (1971). *Languages of the brain: experimental paradoxes and principles in neuropsychology.* Englewood Cliffs, NJ: Prentice-Hall, Inc.

Pribram, K. H., and King, J. (eds.) (1996). *Learning as self-organization.* Mahwah, NJ: Lawrence Erlbaum Associates.

Prigogine, I., & Stengers, I. (1984). *Order out of chaos: Man's new dialogue with nature.* New York: Bantam Books.

Pulaski, M. A. S. (1980). *Understanding Piaget: An introduction to Children's Cognitive Development.* New York: Harper & Row.

Pyszcznski, T., Schimel, J., Geenberg, J., & Solomon, S. (1996). *Mortality salience and prosocial activities.* Unpublished manuscript, University of Colorado–Colorado Springs, Colorado Springs, CO.

Quenk, N. L. (2000). *Essentials of Myers–Briggs Type Indicator* assessment. New York: John Wiley & Sons, Inc.

Rabin, A. I., & Haworth, M. R. (1960). (eds.) *Projective techniques with children.* New York: Grune & Stratton, 1960.

Ramakrishna. *Sayings of Sri Ramakrishna.* Madras, India: Sri Ramakrishna Math, 1965.

Rank, O. (1968a). *Art and Artist: Creative urge and personality development.* New York: Agathon Press.

Rayburn, C. A., & Richmond, L. J. (2002). Theobiology: Interfacing theology and science. *American Behavioral Scientist, 45,* 1793–1811.

Reagan, R. (1990). *An American life.* New York: Simon & Schuster.

Rees, L. (1960). Constitutional factors and abnormal behaviour. In H. J. Eysenck (ed.), *Handbook of abnormal psychology.* New York: Basic Books.

Reeves, T. C. (1991). *A question of character: A life of John F. Kennedy.* New York: The Free Press.

Reiter, M., & Sandomir, R. (2007). *The enlightened bracketologist: The final four of everything.* New York: Bloomsbury.

Reps, P. (1989). *Zen flesh, Zen bones.* New York: Anchor Books.

Revelle, W., Humphreys, M. S., Simon, L., & Gilliland, K. (1980). The interactive effect of personality, time of day, and caffeine: A test of the arousal model. *Journal of Experimental Psychology: General, 109,* 1–31.

Rhee, S. H., Waldman, I. D., Hay, D. A., & Levy, F. (1999). Sex differences in genetic and environmental influences in DSM–III–R attention–deficit/hyperactivity disorder. *Journal of Abnormal Psychology, 108,* 24–41.

Rich, G. I. (1928). A biochemical approach to the study of personality. *Journal of Abnormal Social Psychology, 23,* 158–175.

Rieff, P. (1959). *Freud: The mind of the moralist.* Garden City, NY: Doubleday.

Robertson, R., & Combs, A. (eds.). (1995). *Chaos and psychology in the life sciences.* Mahwah, NJ: Erlbaum.

Robinson, M. D., & Clore, G. L. (2002). Belief and feeling: Evidence for an accessibility model of emotional self-report. *Psychological Bulletin, 128,* 934–960.

Robinson, M. D., Solberg, E. C., Vargas, P. T., & Tamir, M. (2003). Trait as default: Extraversion, subjective well-being, and the distinction between neutral and positive events. *Journal of Personality and Social Psychology, 85,* 517–527.

Rock, I. (1957). The role of repetition in associative learning. *American Journal of Psychology, 70,* 186–193.

Rodgers, J. L. (2001). What causes birth order–intelligence patterns? The admixture hypothesis, revisited. *American Psychologist, 56,* 505–510.

Rodgers, J. L., Cleveland, H. H., van den Oord, E., & Rowe, D. C. (2000). Resolving the debate over birth order, family size, and intelligence. *American Psychologist, 55,* 599–612.

Rodgers, J. L., & Rowe, D. C. (1994). Birth order, spacing, and family size. In R. Sternberg (ed.), *Encyclopedia of intelligence,* pp. 204–209. New York: Macmillan.

Roediger, H. L. (1990). Implicit memory: Retention without remembering. *American Psychologist, 45,* 1043–1056.

Roffwarg, H. P., Muzio, J. N., & Dement, W. C. (1966). Ontogenetic development of the human sleep–dream cycle. *Science, 152,* 604–609.

Rogers, C. R. (1942) *Counseling and psychotherapy: New concepts in practice.* Boston: Houghton Mifflin.

Rogers, C. R. (1951). *Client-centered therapy.* Boston: Houghton Mifflin.

Rogers, C. R. (1959). A theory of therapy, personality, and interpersonal relationships, as developed in the client-centered framework. In S. Koch (ed.), *Psychology: A study of a science* (Vol. 3). New York: McGraw-Hill.

Rogers, C. R. (1961). *On becoming a person: A therapist's view of psychotherapy.* Boston: Houghton-Mifflin.

Rogers, C. R. (1963). Actualizing tendency in relation to motives and to consciousness. In M. R. Jones (ed.), *Nebraska Symposium on Motivation.* Lincoln: University of Nebraska Press.

Rogers, C. R. (1966). Client-centered therapy. In S. Arieti (ed.), *American handbook of psychiatry.* New York: Basic Books.

Rogers, C. R. (1967). [Autobiography]. In E. Boring & G. Lindzey (eds.), *A history of psychology in autobiography.* New York: Appleton-Century-Crofts.

Rogers, C. R. (1969). *Freedom to learn.* Columbus, OH: Charles E. Merrill Publishing Co.

Rogers, C. R. (1980). *A way of being.* Boston, MA: Houghton Mifflin.

Rogers, C. R. (1987). The underlying theory: Drawn from experience with individuals and groups. *Counseling and Values, 32,* 38–46.

Rogers, C. R., & Ryback, D. (1984). One alternative to nuclear planetary suicide. In R. F. Levant and J. M. Schlein (eds.), *Client-centered therapy and the person-centered approach: New directions in theory, research, and practice.* New York: Praeger.

Rosenau, P. M. (1992). *Post-modernism and the social sciences: Insights, inroads, and intrusions.* Princeton, NJ: Princeton University Press.

Rosenblatt, A., Greenberg, J., Solomon, S., Pyszczynski, T., & Lyon, D. (1989). Evidence for terror management theory I: The effects of mortality salience on reactions to those who violate or uphold cultural values. *Journal of Personality and Social* Psychology, *57,* 681–690.

Rosenthal, D. A., Gurney, R. M., & Moore, S. M. (1981). From trust to intimacy: A new inventory for examining Erikson's stages of psychosocial development. *Journal of Youth and Adolescence, 10,* 525–537.

Rotherman, M. J., & Weiner, N. (1983). Androgyny, stress and satisfaction. *Sex Roles, 9,* 151–158.

Rotter, J. B. (1990). Internal versus external control of reinforcement: A case history of a variable. *American Psychologist, 45,* 489–493.

Rotter, J. B., & Rafferty, J. E. (1950). *Manual: The Rotter Incomplete Sentences Blank.* San Antonio, TX: Psychological Corporation.

Royce, J. R. (1962). Psychology, existentialism, and religion. *Journal of General Psychology, 66,* 3–16.

Rubins, J. L. (1978). *Karen Horney: Gentle rebel of psychoanalysis.* New York: Dial.

Russell, J. A., Lewicka, M., Niit, T. (1989). A cross-cultural study of a circumplex model of affect. *Journal of Personality and Social Psychology, 57,* 848–856.

Rustay, N., Crabbe, J. C., Wehner, J. (2004). Genetic analysis of rapid tolerance to ethanol's incoordinating effects in mice: Inbred strains and artificial selection. *Behavior Genetics, 34,* 441–451.

Rutter, D. R., Morley, I. E., & Graham, J. C. (1972). Visual interaction in a group of introverts and extraverts. *European Journal of Social Psychology, 2,* 371–384.

Rutter, M., Bolton, P., Harrington, R., & Couteur, A. I. (1990). Genetic factors in child psychiatric disorder: I. A review of research strategies. *Journal of Child Psychology & Psychiatry & Allied Disciplines, 31,* 3–37.

Rychlak, J. F. (1981). *Personality and psychotherapy: A theory-construction approach.* (2nd ed.). Boston: Houghton Mifflin.

Rychlak, J. F. (1990). George Kelly and the concept of construction. *International Journal of Personal Construct Psychology, 3,* 7–19.

Rychlak, J. F. (1994). *Logical learning theory.* Lincoln, NE: University of Nebraska Press.

Rychlak, J. F. (1995). A teleological critique of modern cognitivism. *Theory and Psychology, 5* (4), 511–531.

Rychman, R. M. (1985). Physical self-efficacy and actualization. *Journal of Research in Personality, 19,* 288–298.

Ryckman, R. M., Hammer, M., Kaczor, L. M., & Gold, A. (1990). Construction of a hypercompetitive attitude scale. *Journal of Personality Assessment, 55,* 630–639.

Sampson, E. E. (1989). The deconstruction of the self. In J. Shotter & K. Gergen (eds.), *Texts of identity,* pp. 1–19. Newbury Park, CA: Sage.

Sanford, J. A. (1968). *Dreams: God's forgotten language.* Philadelphia: Lippincott.

Sanford, J. A. (1981). *The man who wrestled with God: Light from the Old Testament on the psychology of individuation.* Ramsey, NY: Paulist Press.

Sartre, J. P. (1957). *Existentialism and human emotion.* New York: Philosophical Library.

Sartre, J. P. (1964). *Nausea,* trans. L. Alexander, New York: New Directions Publishing Corporation. (Original work published 1938).

Sass, L. A. (1992). The epic of disbelief: The postmodern turn in contemporary psychoanalysis. In S. Kvale (ed.),

Psychology and postmodernism, pp. 166–182. Newbury Park, CA: Sage.

Schack, M. L., & Massari, D. J. (1973). Effects of temporal aids on delay of gratification. *Developmental Psychology, 8,* 168–171.

Schiedel, D. G., & Marcia, J. E. (1985). Ego identity, intimacy, sex role orientation, and gender. *Journal of Personality and Social Psychology, 21,* 149–160.

Schulman, B. H. (1973). *Contributions to Individual Psychology.* Chicago: Alfred Adler Institute.

Schwartz, B. (1986). *The battle for human nature: Science, morality, and modern life.* New York: Norton.

Schweder, R. A. (1986). Divergent rationalities. In Donald W. Fiske and Richard A. Schweder (eds.), *Metatheory in Social Science.* Chicago: University of Chicago Press.

Scotton, B. W. (1996). Introduction and definition of transpersonal psychiatry. In B. W. Scotton, A. B. Chinen, & J. R. Battista (eds.), *Textbook of transpersonal psychiatry and psychology.* New York: Basic Books.

Segerstrale, U. (2000). *Defenders of the truth.* New York: Oxford University Press.

Seidenberg, M., & MacDonald, M. (1999). A probabilistic constraints approach to language acquisition and processing. *Cognitive Science, 23,* 569–588.

Seligman, M. E. P. (1974). Depression and learned helplessness. In R. J. Friedman & M. M. Katz (eds.), *The psychology of depression: Contemporary theory and research.* Washington, DC: Winston-Wiley.

Seligman, M. E. P., Abramson, L. V., Semmel, A., & Von Beyer, C. (1979). Depressive attributional style. *Journal of Abnormal Psychology, 88,* 242–247.

Seligman, M. E. P., Castellon, C., Cacciola, J., Schulman, P., Luborsky, L., Ollove, M., & Downing, R. (1988). Explanatory style change during cognitive therapy for unipolar depression. *Journal of Abnormal Psychology, 97,* 13–18.

Seligman, M. E. P., & Csikszentmihalyi, M. (2000). Positive psychology. *American Psychologist, 55* (1), 5–14.

Seligman, M. E. P., & Maier, S. F. (1967). Failure to escape traumatic shock. *Journal of Experimental Psychology, 74,* 1–9.

Sexton, T. L., & Whiston, S. C. (1994). The status of the counseling relationship: An empirical review, theoretical implications, and research directions. *The Counseling Psychologist, 22*(1), 6–78.

Sheldon, W. H. (with the collaboration of C. W. Dupertuis and E. McDermott). (1954). *Atlas of men: A guide for somatotyping the adult male at all ages.* New York: Harper.

Sheldon, W. H. (with the collaboration of S. S. Stevens and W. B. Tucker). (1940). *The varieties of human physique: An introduction to constitutional psychology.* New York: Harper.

Shoda, Y., Mischel, W., & Wright, J. C. (1994). Intra-individual stability in the organization and patterning of behavior: Incorporating psychological situations into the idiographic analysis of personality. *Journal of Personality and Social Psychology, 67,* 674–687.

Shostrom, E. (1963). *Personal orientation inventory.* San Diego, CA: Edits.

Shurcliff, A. (1968). Judged humor, arousal, and the relief theory. *Journal of Personality and Social Psychology, 4,* 360–363.

Siegel, L., & Hodkin, B. (1982). The garden path to the understanding of cognitive development. In S. Modgil & C. Modgil eds., *Jean Piaget: Consensus and controversy.* New York: Praeger Publishers.

Silverman, I. (1987). Race, race differences, and race relations: Perspectives from psychology and sociobiology. In C. Crawford, M. Smith, & D. Krebs (eds.), *Sociobiology and psychology: Ideas, issues, and applications,* pp. 205–221. Hillsdale, NJ: Lawrence Earlbaum Associates.

Silverman, L. H. (1976). Psychoanalytic theory: "The reports of my death are greatly exaggerated." *American Psychologist, 31,* 621–637.

Silverman, L. H. (1983). The subliminal psychodynamic activation method: Overview and comprehensive listing of studies. In J. Masling (ed.), *Empirical studies of psychoanalytic theories,* vol. 1. New York: The Analytic Press (Lawrence Erlbaum).

Silverman, L. H., Lachmann, F. M., & Millich, R. (1982). *The search for oneness.* New York: International Universities Press.

Silverman, L. H., & Weinberger, J. (1985). Mommy and I are one: Implications for psychotherapy. *American Psychologist, 40,* 1296–1308.

Simon, L., Waxmonsky, B., Greenberg, J., Pyszczysnki, T., & Solomon, S. (1996). *Mortality salience and white reactions to stereotypic and non-stereotypic blacks: On the terror management function of stereotypes.* Unpublished manuscript, University of Arizona, Tucson, AZ.

Singer, D. (1968). Aggression arousal, hostile humor, catharsis. *Journal of Personality and Social Psychology Monograph Supplement, 8,* 1–14.

Singer, J. A. (1997). *Message in a bottle: Stories of men and addiction.* New York: Free Press.

Singh, K. (1990). Tough-mindedness in relation to birth order, family size, and sex. *Individual Psychology: Journal of Adlerian Theory, Research & Practice, 46* (1), 82–87.

Skinner, B. F. (1938). *The behavior of organisms: An experimental analysis.* Englewood Cliffs, NJ: Prentice-Hall.

Skinner, B. F. (1948). *Walden II.* New York: The Macmillan Co.

Skinner, B. F. (1950). Are theories of learning necessary? *Psychological* Review, *57,* 193–216.

Skinner, B. F. (1957). *Verbal behavior.* New York: Appleton-Century-Crofts. Reprinted by permission of Prentice Hall, Inc., Englewood Cliffs, NJ.

Skinner, B. F. (1958). Teaching machines. *Science, 128,* 969–977.

Skinner, B. F. (1967). [Autobiography.] In E. G. Boring & G. Lindzey (eds.), *A history of psychology in autobiography* (Vol. 5, pp. 387–413). New York: Appleton-Century-Crofts.

Skinner, B. F. (1971). *Beyond freedom and dignity.* New York: A. Knopf.

Skinner, B. F. (1974). *About behaviorism.* New York: A. Knopf.

Skinner, B. F. (1976). *Walden Two revisited.* New York: Macmillan.

Skinner, B. F. (1987). *Upon further reflection.* Englewood Cliffs, NJ: Prentice-Hall.

Skinner, B. F., and Ferster, C. (1957). *Schedules of reinforcement.* New York: Appleton-Century-Crofts.

Sliker, G. (1992). *Multiple mind: Healing the split in psyche and world.* Boston, MA: Shambala Publications.

Smith, H. S., & Cohen, L. H. (1993). Self-complexity and reactions to a relationship breakup. *Journal of Social and Clinical Psychology, 12,* 367–384.

Solomon (in Ecclesiastes). *The NIV study bible: New international version.* Grand Rapids, MI: Zondervan Bible Publishers.

Spiegelman, J., (1982). *Jungian psychology and the tree of life.* Phoenix, AZ: Falcon Press.

Spiegelman, J., & Miyuki, M. (1985). *Buddhism and Jungian psychology.* Phoenix, AZ: Falcon Press.

Spiegelman, J., & Vasavada, A. (1987). *Hinduism and Jungian psychology.* Phoenix, AZ: Falcon Press.

Spitz, R. (1945). Hospitalism: Genesis of psychiatric conditions in early childhood. *Psychoanalytic study of the child, 1,* 53–74.

Starr, H. E. (1922). The concentration of the mixed saliva considered as an index of fatigue and emotional excitation, and applied to a study of the metabolic etiology of stammering. *American Journal of Psychology, 33,* 394–418.

Steelman L. C. (1985). A tale of two variables: A review of the intellectual consequences of sibship size and birth order. *Review of Educational Research, 55,* 353–386.

Steelman, L. C. (1986). The tale retold: A response to Zajonc. *Review of Educational Research,* 56, 373–377.

Stepansky, P. E. (1983). *In Freud's shadow: Adler in context.* Hillsdale, NJ: The Analytic Press.

Stephenson, W. (1953). *The study of behavior: Q-technique and its methodology.* Chicago: University of Chicago Press.

Stern, P. J. (1976). *C. G. Jung: The haunted prophet.* New York: Dell.

Sternberg, R. J. (1988). *The triangle of love.* New York: Basic Books.

Stevens, B. (1967). Curtain raiser. In C. Rogers & B. Stevens (eds.), *Person to person: The problem of being human: A new trend in psychology.* New York: Pocket Books, 1971.

Stewart, V., & Stewart, A. (1982). *Business applications of repertory grid.* New York: McGraw-Hill.

Stillings, N., Feinstein, M. H., Garfield, J. L., Rissland, E. L., Rosenbaum, D. A., Weisler, S. E., & Baker-Ward, L. (1987). *Cognitive science: An introduction.* Cambridge, MA: MIT Press.

Stolorow, R. D., & Atwood, G. E. (1992). *Contexts of being: The intersubjective foundations of psychological life.* Hillsdale, NJ: The Analytic Press.

Subbotsky, E. V. (1994). Early rationality and magical thinking in preschoolers: Space and time. *British Journal of Developmental Psychology, 12,* 97–108.

Sullivan, H. S. (1940). *Conceptions of modern psychiatry. Collected works of Harry Stack Sullivan, M. D.* (Vol. 1). (Eds. H. S. Perry & M. L. Gawel). New York: W. W. Norton & Co., Inc., 1953.

Sullivan, H. S. (1953). *The interpersonal theory of psychiatry. Collected works of Harry Stack Sullivan, M. D.* (Vol. 1). (Eds. H. S. Perry and M. L. Gawel). New York: W. W. Norton & Co., Inc., 1953.

Sullivan, H. S. (1954). *The psychiatric interview. Collected works of Harry Stack Sullivan, M. D.* (Vol. 1). (Eds. H. S. Perry & M. L. Gawel). New York: W. W. Norton & Co., Inc., 1953.

Sullivan, H. S. (1956). *Clinical studies in psychiatry. Collected works of Harry Stack Sullivan, M. D.* (Vol. 2). (Eds. H. S. Perry, M. L. Gawel, & M. Gibbon). New York: W. W. Norton & Co., Inc., 1956.

Sullivan, H. S. (1962). *Schizophrenia as a human process.* New York: W. W. Norton & Co. Inc., 1956.

Sullivan, H. S. (1964). *The fusion of psychiatry and social science.* New York: W. W. Norton & Co., Inc., 1956.

Sullivan, H. S. (1972). *Personal psychopathology.* New York: W. W. Norton & Co., Inc.

Sulloway, F. J. (1996). *Born to rebel: Birth order, family dynamics, and creative lives.* New York: Pantheon.

Sutich, A. (1969). *Some Considerations regarding transpersonal psychology, 1,* 11–20.

Swann, W. B. (2005). Seeking "truth" finding despair: Some unhappy consequences of negative self-concept. In C. C. Morf & O. Ayduk (eds.), *Current directions in personality psychology,* pp. 100–106. Upper Saddle River, NJ: Pearson Education, Inc.

Swann, W. B., & Hill, C. A. (1982). When our identities are mistaken: Reaffirming self-conceptions through social interactions. *Journal of Personality and Social Psychology, 43,* 59–66.

Sweet, A. A., & Loizeaux, A. (1991). Behavioral and cognitive treatment methods: A critical comparative review. *Journal of Behavior Therapy and Experimental Psychiatry, 22,* 159–185.

Szatmari, P., Jones, M. B., Zwaigenbaum, L., & MacLean, J. E. (1998). Genetics of autism? Overview and new directions. *Journal of Autism & Developmental Disorders, 28,* 351–368.

Taylor, M. C., & Hall, J. A. (1982). Psychological androgyny: Theories, methods and conclusions. *Psychological Bulletin, 92,* 347–366.

Tesch, S. A., & Whitbourne, S. K. (1982). Intimacy status and identity status in young adults. *Journal of Personality and Social Psychology, 43,* 1041–1051.

Thomas, A., Chess, S., Birch, H. G., Hertzig, M. E. and Korn, S. (1964). *Behavioral individuality in early childhood.* London: University of London.

Thornton, B. (1977). Toward a linear prediction of marital happiness. *Personality and Social Psychology Bulletin, 3,* 674–676.

Thrasher, P. (1991). A Jungian view of postmodernism: A response to "Psychology and postmodernity." *Humanistic Psychologist, 19* (2), 242–245.

Thurstone, L. L. (1934). The vectors of mind. *Psychological Review, 41,* 1–32.

Tillich, P. (1952). *The courage to be.* New Haven: Yale University Press.

Tillich, P. (1957). *Dynamics of faith.* New York: Harper & Row.

Tolman, E. C. (1948). Cognitive maps in rats and men. *Psychological Review, 55,* 189–208.

Tolman, E. C. (1952). [Autobiography]. In E. G. Boring, H. Werner, R. M. Yerkes, & H. S. Langfeld (eds.), *A history of psychology in autobiography* (Vol. 4, pp. 323–339). Worcester, MA: Clark University Press.

Tomasello, M. (2000). Do young children have adult syntactic competence? *Cognition, 74,* 209–253.

Toner, I. J., & Smith, R. A. (1977). Age and overt verbalization in delay-maintenance behavior in children. *Journal of Experimental Child Psychology, 24,* 123–128.

Tooby, J., & Cosmides, L. (1994). *Humans that speak, ants that farm.* Quoted in Pinker, *How the Mind Works,* p. 26. New York: Norton, 1997.

Toropov, B., & Buckles, L. (1997). *The Complete Idiot's Guide to the World's Religions.* New York: Alpha Books, a Simon & Schuster Macmillan Company.

"The trouble with Monica." *Time Magazine,* Feb. 9, 1998.

Truax, C. B., & Mitchell, K. M. (1971). Research on certain therapist interpersonal skills in relation to process and outcome. In A. E. Bergin & S. L. Garfield (eds.), *Handbook of psychotherapy and behavior change.* New York: Wiley.

Truman, H. S. (1955). *Memoirs, volume I: Year of decisions.* Garden City, New York: Doubleday.

Tupes, E. C., & Christal, R. E. (1992). Recurrent personality factors based on trait ratings. *Journal of Personality, 60,* 225–251. (Original work published in 1961.)

Ullmann, L., & Krasner, L. (1965). *Case studies in behavior modification.* New York: Holt, Rinehart and Winston, Inc.

Vacc, N. A., & Greenleaf, W. (1975). Sequential development of cognitive complexity. *Perceptual and Motor Skills, 41,* 319–322.

Vaihinger, H. (1911). *The philosophy of 'as if': A system of the theoretical, practical, and religious fictions of mankind.* London: Routledge & Kegan Paul, 1925.

Vaillant, G. E. (1977). *Adaption to life.* Boston: Little, Brown.

Vaillant, G. E. (1992). *Ego mechanisms of defense.* Washington, DC: American Psychiatric Press.

Vaillant, G. E. (1994). Ego mechanisms of defense and personality psychopathology. *Journal of Abnormal Psychology, 103,* 44–50.

Van der Post, L. (1975). *Jung and the story of our time.* New York: Pantheon.

Veith, I. (1977). Four thousand years of hysteria. In M. J. Horowitz (ed.), *Hysterical personality.* New York: Jason Aronson, Inc.

Verhaeghen, P., Cerella, J., & Basak, C. (2004). *Journal of Experimental Psychology: Learning, Memory and Cognition, Vol. 30,* No. 6., 1322–1337.

Vestal, B. (1974). *Jerry Ford up close.* New York: Coward, McCann, & Geoghegan.

Vivekananda, Swami (1978). *Karma-yoga.* Calcutta: Advaita Ashrama.

W., Bill. (1988). *The language of the heart: Bill W's Grapevine writings.* New York: The AA Grapevine, Inc.

Wachtel, P. (1977). *Psychoanalysis and behavior therapy: Toward an integration.* New York: Basic Books.

Waldrop, M. M. (1992). *Complexity: The emerging science at the edge of order and chaos.* New York: Simon & Schuster.

Wallace, R. A. (1979). *The genesis factor.* New York: William Morrow.

Walsh, R., & Vaughan, F. (eds.). (1980). *Beyond ego: Transpersonal dimensions in psychology.* Los Angeles: Tarcher.

Walsh, R., & Vaughan, F. (eds.) (1993). *Truths beyond ego: The transpersonal vision.* Los Angeles: Tarcher.

Waterman, A. S., Geary, P. S., & Waterman, C. K. (1974). Longitudinal study of changes in ego identity status from freshman to the senior year at college. *Developmental Psychology, 10,* 387–392.

Waterman, C. K., Buebel, M. E., & Waterman, A. S. (1970). Relationship between resolution of the identity crisis and outcomes of previous psychosocial crises. *Proceedings of the 78th Annual Convention of the American Psychological Association, 5,* 467–468.

Watson, D. L., & Tharp, R. G. (1993). *Self-directed behavior: Self-modification for personal adjustment.* Pacific Grove, CA: Brooks/Cole.

Watson, J. B. (1913). Psychology as the behaviorist views it. *Psychological Review,* 158–177.

Watson, J. B. (1919). *Psychology from the standpoint of a behaviorist.* Philadelphia, PA: J. B. Lippincott Co.

Watson, J. B. (1926). What the nursery has to say about instincts. In C. Murchison (ed.), *Psychologies of 1925,* pp. 1–34. Worcester, MA: Clark University Press.

Watson, J. B. (1930). *Behaviorism* (rev. ed.). New York: Norton. (Original work published 1925).

Watson, J. B. (1936). *Autobiography.* In C. Murchison (ed.), *A history of psychology in autobiography,* Vol II Worcester, MA: Clark University Press.

Watson, J. B., & McDougall W. (1929). *The battle of behaviorism.* New York: Norton.

Watson, J. B., & Raynor, R. (1920). Conditioned emotional reactions. *Journal of Experimental Psychology, 3,* 1–16.

Watson, J. B., & Raynor, R. (1928). *The psychological care of the infant and child.* New York: Norton.

Watts, A. (1936). *The spirit of Zen.* London: J. Murray.

Watts, B. L. (1982). Individual differences in circadian activity rhythms and their effects on roommate relationships. *Journal of Personality, 50,* 374–384.

Welberg, L., & Seckl, J. (2001). Prenatal stress, glucocorticoids and the programming of the brain. *Journal of Neuroendocrinology, 13,* 113–128.

Wheelis, A. (1973). *How people change.* New York: Harper & Row.

White, R. W. (1960). Competence and the psychosexual stages of development. In S. R. Maddi (ed.), *Perspectives on personality.* Boston: Little Brown, 1971. (Originally published in M. R. Jones (ed.), *Nebraska symposium on motivation.* Lincoln: University of Nebraska Press, 1960).

White, R. W. (1981). Exploring personality the long way. In A. I. Rabin, J. Aronoff, A. M. Barclay, & R. A. Zucker (eds.), *Further exploration in personality,* pp. 3–26. New York: Wiley.

Whiteman, S.D., & Buchanan, C.M. (2002). Mothers' and children's expectations for adolescence: The impact of perceptions of an older sibling's experience. *Journal of Family Psychology, 16,* 157–171.

Widiger, T. A., Trull, T. J., Clarkin, J. F., Sanderson, C., & Costa, P. T., Jr. (1994). A description of the DSM–III–R and DSM–IV personality disorders with the Five-Factor Model of personality. In T. Costa, Jr., & T. A. Widiger (eds.), *Personality disorders and the five-factor model of personality.* Washington, DC: American Psychological Association.

Wiggins, J. S. (1979). A psychological taxonomy of trait-descriptive terms: The interpersonal domain. *Journal of Personality and Social Psychology, 37,* 395–412.

Wiggins, J. S. (1981). *Revised Interpersonal Adjective Scales.* Vancouver, Canada: University of British Columbia.

Wiggins, J. S. (1982). Circumplex models of interpersonal behavior in clinical psychology. In P. C. Kendall & J. N. Butcher (eds.), *Handbook of research methods in clinical psychology.* New York: Wiley, 1982.

Wiggins, J. S., Phillips, N., & Trapnell, P. (1989). Circular reasoning about interpersonal behavior: Evidence concerning some untested assumptions underlying diagnostic classification. *Journal of Personality and Social Psychology, 56,* 296–305.

Wilber, K. (2000). *A brief history of everything.* Boston: Shambhala.

Williams, G. C. (1992). *Natural selection: Domains, levels, and challenges.* New York: Oxford University Press.

Wills, G. (1989). *Reagan's America: Innocents at home.* Garden City, NY: Doubleday.

Wilson, C. (1972). *New pathways in psychology: Maslow and the post-Freudian revolution.* New York: Traplinger Publishing Company.

Wilson, E. O. (1975). *Sociobiology: The new synthesis.* Cambridge, MA: Harvard University Press.

Wilson, E. O. (1978). *On human nature.* New York: Bantam.

Wilson, E. O. (1980). Comparative social theory. *The Tanner lectures on human values.* Presented at the University of Michigan, Ann Arbor, MI.

Wilson, E. O. (1994). *Naturalist.* Washington, DC: Island Press.

Wilson, G. D. (1978). Introversion-extraversion. In H. London and J. E. Exner, Jr. (eds.), *Dimensions of personality*, pp. 217–261. New York: John Wiley & Sons.

Windelband, W. (1894). *History and natural science.* Strassburg, Germany: Heitz.

Winerman, L. (2005). A virtual cure. *Monitor on psychology* 36 (7), 87–89.

Winnicott, C. (1983). Interview with M. Neve. In P. L. Rudnystsky, *The psychoanalytic vocation: Rank, Winnicott and the legacy of Freud,* pp. 181–193. New Haven: Yale University Press, 1991.

Winnicott, D. W. (1945). Primitive emotional development. In *Through paediatrics to psycho-analysis.* New York: Basic Books.

Winnicott, D. W. (1948). Paediatrics and psychiatry. In *Through paediatrics to psycho-analysis.* New York: Basic Books.

Winnicott, D. W. (1951). Transitional objects and transitional phenomena. In *Through paediatrics to psycho-analysis.* New York: Basic Books.

Winnicott, D. W. (1952/1992). *Through paediatrics to psycho-analysis.* New York: Bruner-Mazel.

Winnicott, D. W. (1962). A personal view of the Kleinian contribution. In D. W. Winnicott, *The maturational processes and the facilitating environment. Studies in the theory of emotional development.* New York: International Universities Press.

Winnicott, D. W. (1966). The ordinary devoted mother. In D. W. Winnicott, *Babies and their mothers* (3–14). C. Winnicott, R. Shepherd, & M. Davis (eds.) Reading, MA: Addison-Wesley.

Winnicott, D. W. (1971). *Playing and reality.* Great Britain: Penguin Books.

Winnicott, D. W. (1987). *Babies and their mothers.* C. Winnicott, R. Shepherd, & M. Davis (eds.) Harvard University Press: Cambridge, MA.

Winter, D. G. (1996). *Personality: Analysis and interpretation of lives.* New York: McGraw-Hill.

Wolpe, J. (1958). *Psychotherapy by reciprocal inhibition.* Stanford, CA: Stanford University Press.

Wolpe, J. (1969). *The practice of behavior therapy.* Oxford, England: Pergamon Press.

Woodworth, R. S., & Schlosberg, H. (1954). *Experimental psychology.* New York: Holt.

Worthington, E. L., Jr. (ed.) (1998). *Dimensions of forgiveness.* Philadelphia: Templeton Foundation Press.

Yancy, K. B. (2000). Treatment virtually cures fear of flying. *USA Today Online.* Retrieved November 23, 2003, from http://www.usatoday.com/life/cyber/tech/review/crh424.htm

Zajonc, R. B., & Markus, G. B. (1975). Birth order and intellectual development. *Psychological Review, 82,* 74–88.

Zeigarnik, B. (1927). On finished and unfinished tasks. In W. D. Ellis (ed.), *A source book of Gestalt psychology.* New York: Humanities Press, 1967. (Originally published as "Uber das Behalten von erledigten und unerledigten Handlungen." *Psychologische Forschung,* 1927, *9,* 1–85).

Zinnbauer, B. J., Pargament, K. I., Scott, A. B. (1999). The emerging meaning of religiousness and spirituality: Problems and prospects. *Journal of Personality, 67,* 889–919.

Zohar, D., & Marshall, I. (1994). *The quantum society: Mind, physics, and a new social vision.* New York: Morrow.

Zuckerman, M. (1979). *Sensation seeking: Beyond the optimal level of arousal.* Hillsdale, NJ: Lawrence Erlbaum.

Zuckerman, M. (1984). Sensation seeking: A comparative approach to a human trait. *Behavioral and Brain Sciences, 7,* 413–471.

Zuckerman, M. (1991). *Psychobiology of personality.* Cambridge: Cambridge University Press.

Zuckerman, M. (1994). An alternative five factor model for personality. In C. F. Halverson, G. A. Kohnstamm, and R. P. Martin (eds.), *The developing structure of temperament and personality from infancy to adulthood,* pp. 53–68. Hillsdale, NJ: Erlbaum.

Zuckerman, M. (1995). Good and bad humors: Biochemical bases of personality and its disorders. *Psychological Science, 6,* 325–332.

Zuckerman, M., & Haber, M. M. (1965). Need for stimulation as a source of stress response to perceptual isolation. *Journal of Abnormal Psychology, 70,* 371–377.

Zuckerman, M., Kuhlman, D. M., Joireman, J., Teta, P., & Kraft, M. (1993). A comparison of three structural models for personality: The Big Three, the Big Five, and the alternative five. *Journal of Personality and Social Psychology, 65,* 757–768.

Zukav, G. (1979). *The dancing Wu Li masters: An overview of the new physics.* New York: William Morrow.

Zukav, G. (1989). *The seat of the soul.* New York: Simon & Schuster.

PHOTOS

Page 72: © Omikron/Photo Researchers; Page 74: © Sam Falk/Photo Researchers; Page 168 top: © istockphoto; Page 168 bottom: © Chaim Danzinger/istockphoto; Page 169 top left: © istockphoto; Page 169 top right: © Diane Rutt/istockphoto; Page 169 middle left: © Andreas Reh/istockphoto; Page 169 middle right: © James Cavallini/Photo Researchers; Page 169 bottom: © Andrey Prokhorov/istockphoto; Page 179: © Mary Evans Picture Library/The Image Works; Page 184: © Hulton Archive/Getty Images; Page 262 left: © Rafal Zdeb/istockphoto; Page 262 right: © Thomas Perkins/istockphoto; Page 287 top: © FogStock/IndexOpen; Page 287 bottom: © Chris Lowe/ IndexOpen; Page 390 top: © Image Source/IndexOpen; Page 390 bottom left: © IndexOpen; Page 390 bottom right: © istockphoto; Page 500 top left: © Heidi Priesnitz/istockphoto; Page 500 top center: © alexander briel perez/istockphoto; Page 500 top right: © Claudelle Girard/istockphoto; Page 500 middle left: © Lisa McDonald/istockphoto; Page 500 middle right: © Sergei Popov/istockphoto; Page 500 bottom left: © istockphoto; Page 500 bottom center left: © IndexOpen; Page 500 bottom center right: © George Argyropoulos/ istockphoto; Page 500 bottom right: © istockphoto; Page 508 top: © istockphoto; Page 508 middle left: © Zsolt Biczó/istockphoto; Page 508 middle: © james steidl/istockphoto; Page 508 middle right: © Karen Squires/istockphoto; Page 508 bottom: © Jacob Wackerhausen/istock-photo; Page 536 top left: © IndexOpen; Page 536 top right: © Joshua Blake/istockphoto; Page 536 bottom left: © Anna Ceglinska/istockphoto; Page 536 bottom right: © Mary Gascho/ istockphoto.

FIGURES AND TABLES

Pages 117, 118, 119: Eysenck, Hans (1967). *The Biological Basis of Personality*. Springfield: Courtesy of Charles C. Thomas Publisher, Ltd.; Pages 158, 161: Mischel, Walter & Shoda, Yuichi (1995). *Psychological Review*. Washington, DC: American Psychological Association; Page 324: Reisler, Emil (1983). *Psychological Review*. Washington, DC: American Psychological Association; Page 344: Berne, Eric (1978). *What Do You Say After You Say Hello?* New York: Copyright Grove/Atlantic, Inc.; Page 371: Baillargeon, Renee & DeVos, Julie (1991). Object Permanence in Young Infants: Further Evidence. *Child Development*, 62, page 1230. Oxford: Wiley-Blackwell Ltd.; Page 432: Maslow, Abraham (1971). *The Farther Reaches of Human Nature*. New York: Viking Penguin, a division of Penguin Group (USA) Inc.; Page 455: Sternberg, Robert, & Barnes, Michael (1988). *The Psychology of Love*. New Haven: Copyright Yale University Press; Page 475: Zanna, Mark (1997). *Advances in Experimental Social Psychology* (Vol. 29, 71). Atlanta: Copyright Elsevier.